Foundations of Marketing

www.palgrave.com
Companion Website

www.palgrave.com/foundation

Palgrave Foundations

A series of introductory texts across a wide range of subject areas to meet the needs of today's lecturers and students.

Foundations texts provide complete yet concise coverage of core topics and skills based on detailed research of course requirements suitable for both independent study and class use – *the firm foundations for future study.*

Published
Biology
Chemistry
Contemporary Europe
Economics
Economics for Business
A History of English Literature
Foundations of Marketing
Modern British History
Nineteenth-Century Britain
Physics
Politics

Forthcoming
British Politics
Communication Studies
Global Politics
Modern European History
Philosophy
Sociology

Foundations of Marketing

JONATHAN GROUCUTT

First published 2005 by
PALGRAVE MACMILLAN
Houndmills, Basingstoke, Hampshire RG21 6XS and
175 Fifth Avenue, New York, N.Y. 10010
Companies and representatives throughout the world

PALGRAVE MACMILLAN is the global academic imprint of the Palgrave Macmillan division of St. Martin's Press, LLC and of Palgrave Macmillan Ltd. Macmillan® is a registered trademark in the United States, United Kingdom and other countries. Palgrave is a registered trademark in the European Union and other countries.

ISBN-13: 978-1-4039-0327-1
ISBN-10: 1-4039-0327-1

This book is printed on paper suitable for recycling and made from fully managed and sustained forest sources.

A catalogue record for this book is available from the British Library.

A catalog record for this book is available from the Library of Congress.

Editing and origination by
Curran Publishing Services, Norwich

10   9   8   7   6   5   4   3   2   1
15 14 13 12 11 10 09 08 07 06

Printed and bound in China

The years 2003 and 2004 witnessed the passing of two respected and talented university lecturers whom I had the privilege of knowing. Both Chris and Stuart had the gift of captivating the students' imagination for marketing. They left this world far too early in their lives, and thus we are all the poorer.

This book is dedicated to the memory of
Christopher Berry (London Guildhall University)
and Stuart Rooks (Oxford Brookes University)

The Author

Jonathan Groucutt is a Senior Lecturer in Marketing and Strategy at the Business School, Oxford Brookes University, England. As well as being a writer and academic, Jonathan has considerable business experience including the media industries and over ten years in consultancy.

Jonathan has co-authored books on marketing, e-business, ethics and communication. In addition he has written over 40 business articles. His areas of personal research include complexity theory and its relationship to marketing, the history of marketing thought and the strategic development of the global cruise ship industry.

Jonathan holds Fellowships of the Royal Society of Arts, the Royal Geographical Society and the Academy of Marketing Sciences. In addition he is a member of the American Marketing Association, the Academy of Marketing, the Institute of Direct Marketing, the European Marketing Academy, the European Academy of Management and the Strategic Planning Society. He is also a Network Member of the Centre for Complexity Sciences at the University of Liverpool and an Associate Member of the Institute of Nanotechnology.

Contents

List of figures   *xiii*
List of tables   *xvii*
List of mini cases   *xviii*
Preface   *xxi*
Acknowledgements   *xxvii*

What is the macro environment?   **21**
PESTLE factors   22
Political   22
Economic   28
Societal   31
Legal (regulatory)   34
Environmental–ecological   34
Technology   39
Combinations of events   42
Reversed issues   42
What is the micro environment?   **42**
Micro factors   **42**
Suppliers   43
Employees   43
The local community   44
Local government   44
Intermediaries   44
Customers   44
Competitors and co-operators   45
Retired employees   45
Trade unions   45
Opinion formers   46
Local regulators   46
Control of micro factors   46
Analysing the environment   **46**
The 'What if?' scenario   48
Chapter summary   **48**
Questions for review and reflection   **49**
References   **49**

PART I

The Scope of Marketing

**1 A Brief Introduction to
    Marketing**   **3**
    Learning outcomes   **3**
    What are your favourites?   **3**
    Introduction   **3**
    The origin of marketing   **4**
    An economics approach   5
    A consumer's (or buyer's) approach   6
    The societal approach   6
    The managerial or systems approach   7
    A broader approach   7
    Relationships   9
    Transactions   9
    Time   9
    Dialogue   9
    **The marketer: alchemist, magician,
       sorcerer and medicine man**   **10**
    Marketing as an organisational function   **11**
    Who is engaged in marketing?   **12**
    **Marketing now and tomorrow: current
       and future trends**   **12**
    2004–14?   13
    Chapter summary   **15**
    Questions for review and reflection   **16**
    References   **16**

2 The Marketing Environment   **19**
    Learning outcomes   **19**
    Introduction   **19**
    Market volatilities and chaos theory   **20**
    The marketing environment   **20**

PART 2

Tools and Techniques

**3 Segmentation, Targeting and
    Positioning**   **53**
    Learning outcomes   **53**
    Introduction   **53**
    What is segmentation?   **54**
    B2B segmentation   **55**
    Segmentation characteristics of B2B
       markets   57
    B2C segmentation   **60**

Segmenting by geographic location   60
Segmenting by demographics   60
Segmenting by socio-economic status   60
Segmenting by behaviour   60
Segmenting by lifestyle   61
Formulating a segmentation strategy   **61**
Targeting   61
Positioning   62
Repositioning   63
Perceptual or positioning mapping   63
Chapter summary   **64**
Questions for review and reflection   **65**
References   **65**

4 Marketing Research   66
Learning outcomes   **66**
Introduction   **66**
The role of research in marketing   **66**
Potential benefits   **67**
Understanding the market   67
Forecasting   67
Improving return on investment   67
Exploiting new market opportunities   68
Reducing the level of risk   68
Supporting competitive advantage   68
**A systematic process for marketing
    research**   **68**
Establishing the need for marketing
    research   68
Problem definition   68
Research objective or hypothesis   69
Research brief   69
Identifying the relevant methodology   69
Questionnaire design   69
Data collection   70
Data analysis   70
Research report   70
Marketing research techniques   **70**
Primary research techniques   71
Secondary research techniques   73
Does everyone use marketing research?   **77**
Chapter summary   **77**
Questions for review and reflection   **77**
References   **78**

5 Competitive Intelligence   79
Learning outcomes   **79**
Introduction   **79**
**Defining competitive intelligence:
    what it is and is not**   **80**

Marketing research   80
Competitive intelligence (also known as
    business intelligence)   80
Competitor intelligence   80
Economic intelligence   81
**Why competitive intelligence analysis
    is important to marketers**   **82**
Types of organisational competition   **82**
**The need to understand competitor
    actions and intentions**   **82**
A competitor intelligence system   **86**
Sources of competitor intelligence   **86**
Sales value and volumes   87
Pricing strategies   87
Product ranges and developments   87
Promotional activities and spend   87
Channel management/logistics
    operations   88
Company and management structures   88
Recorded data   88
Observable data   90
Opportunistic data   90
Analysing competitor intelligence   **90**
Industry structure and characteristics   90
Strategic groupings   90
Key competitors   91
Evaluation of the data   91
Potential new competitors   91
Competitor organisations leaving the
    marketplace   91
**Legal and ethical implications of
    competitor intelligence**   **92**
Regulation   92
SCIP Code of Ethics for CI Professionals   95
Chapter summary   **95**
Questions for review and reflection   **95**
References   **96**

6 Strategy in Marketing   97
Learning outcomes   **97**
Introduction   **97**
What is strategy?   **98**
Strategy levels   **99**
Corporate strategy level   99
Business strategy level   99
Functional strategy level   99
The marketing–strategy relationship   **99**
The marketing audit   **100**
Environmental audit   100
Marketing strategy audit   101

Marketing organisation audit 101
Marketing systems audit 101
Marketing productivity audit 101
Marketing function analysis 101
Ansoff's portfolio matrix **102**
The GE matrix **103**
Market attractiveness 103
Business position (also known as
  business strength) 103
SWOT analysis **104**
The five forces model **106**
The threat of new entrants 107
The threat of substitution 108
The power of suppliers 108
The power of buyers 109
Industry competitors (also known as
  intensity of rivalry between current
  competitors) 110
Competitive advantage: generic
  strategies **110**
Competitive scope 110
Competitive advantage 110
Analysis of generic strategies 111
Focus 112
Stuck in the middle 112
Adding value to the product or service **112**
Company infrastructure 112
The human resource management team 112
Technology development 112
Procurement 112
Competitive market positioning
  strategies **113**
Market leader 113
Market challengers 113
Market followers 114
Market nichers 114
Competitive and defensive positions **114**
Position defence 114
Pre-emptive defence 114
Counter-offensive defence 115
Mobile defence 115
Strategic withdrawal 115
Frontal attack 116
Flanking attack 117
Guerrilla attack 117
Chapter summary **117**
Questions for review and reflection **118**
References **118**

7 The Branding of Products and
  Services **119**
Learning outcomes **119**
Introduction **119**
What is branding? **120**
Origins of branding **120**
Consumer and business brands **122**
Why brand? **122**
Protection 122
Values 124
Differentiation 124
Segmentation 126
Selection 126
Awareness 127
Recall 127
Recognition 127
Brands that develop a cult status **127**
Extending the brand (also known as
  brand elasticity) **127**
Valuations and equity 131
Promotion 132
Types of branding **132**
Family brands 133
Individual brands 133
Own-label brands 134
Brand management **134**
The world's most powerful brands **135**
Rebranding **137**
Proactive motivations 137
Reactive motivators 139
Brand longevity — do brands last
  forever? **142**
Reasons for brand longevity 143
The disposal or termination of brands **144**
Risks associated with brand disposal 149
Chapter summary **151**
Questions for review and reflection **151**
References **152**

PART 3

The Marketing Mix

8 The Marketing Mix and
  Relationship Marketing **155**
Learning outcomes **155**
Introduction **155**
The marketing mix debate **155**
The origins of the marketing mix 156

Rationale for extending the marketing
    mix   158
Marketing mix network or architecture   159
Relationship marketing   **160**
What is a relationship?   160
Chapter summary   **164**
Questions for review and reflection   **164**
References   **164**

9 Products   **167**
Learning outcomes   **167**
Introduction   **167**
**What is a product and why are they
    important?**   **167**
Standardisation or adaptation?   **168**
**Reasons for product adaptation –
    international dimension**   **168**
Technical factors   168
Cultural perspectives   169
Legal or regulatory issues   **171**
Safety   171
Market classifications   **171**
Consumer product classifications   171
Industrial and commercial product
    classifications   176
**New product development and service
    innovations**   **178**
The processes involved in determining
    NPD   178
Idea generation (also known as
    exploration)   179
Idea screening (also known as initial
    screening process)   180
Concept testing   183
Business analysis   183
Product development and testing   184
Market testing (also known as test
    launch)   186
Product launch   187
Commercialisation: the diffusion and
    adoption processes   187
Adoption characteristics   190
New product failure   194
The product life cycle concept   **198**
Does the product life cycle concept exist
    in reality?   199
Different shapes and sizes   203
Chapter summary   **205**
Questions for review and reflection   **206**
References   **206**

10 Promotion   **208**
Learning outcomes   **208**
Introduction   **208**
Promotional objectives   **208**
Communication models   **209**
Feedback and noise   213
Promotional strategy and tactics   **215**
Advertising   **215**
Early development phase   215
Modern development phase   217
Challenge and defence phase   218
Types of advertising   220
Types of advertising media   222
Direct marketing   **230**
Direct marketing techniques   231
Kiosks   **232**
Buzz, or word of mouth promotion   **232**
Product placement   **236**
Movie tie-ins   **236**
Merchandising the brand   **237**
Examples of merchandising   237
Celebrity endorsements   **238**
Sponsorship   **239**
Potential benefits of sponsorship   239
Sales promotion   **240**
Types of sales promotion   240
Sales promotions can be too successful   242
Exhibitions, expos and trade fairs   **242**
Public relations   **242**
Scope of public relations   244
Integrated marketing communications   **244**
The future   **246**
Chapter summary   **246**
Questions for review and reflection   **246**
References   **247**

11 Price   **249**
Learning outcomes   **249**
Introduction   **249**
Pricing objectives   **250**
Factors that influence price   **252**
Cost of research and development
    (R&D)   252
Cost of production   252
Additionals: local taxes and surcharges   252
Economic value of the product or
    service   253
Competitive forces   253
Market conditions   253
Geography   254

Pricing tactics 255
Pioneer pricing 255
Price skimming 257
Penetration pricing (predatory pricing) 257
Price matching 257
Variable pricing (flexible pricing) 258
Psychological pricing 258
Prestige pricing 258
Odd-even pricing 259
Single price/double pricing 259
Promotional pricing 259
Trade-in allowances 260
Discount pricing 261
Buy one get one free 261
Book early discount 261
Special event pricing 262
Direct payment mechanisms 262
Professional services pricing 262
Competitive tendering 262
International pricing 263
Ethical and illegal pricing issues 264
Dumping 264
Price fixing – cartel operations 264
Premium pricing issues 266
Bait and switch 266
Chapter summary 266
Questions for review and reflection 266
References 267

12 Place and Placement 268
Learning outcomes 268
Introduction 268
Defining place 268
Place as a physical location 270
Location factors 270
Place as channel management 274
A one-stage channel 274
A two-stage channel 275
Three-stage channels 275
Physical distribution 275
Logistics 276
Porter's supply chain model 277
Retail outlets 280
Markets 280
Vending (automatic retailing) 281
Individual stores 284
Multiples or chain stores 284
Online stores 284
Chapter summary 285
Questions for review and reflection 285

References 285

13 People 287
Learning outcomes 287
Introduction 287
Who is included in 'people'? 288
Right people – right job 290
Building relationships 290
People and not-for-profit organisations 291
What happens when things go wrong? 291
Potential ethical issues 291
Chapter summary 293
Questions for review and reflection 294
References 294

14 Physical Evidence 295
Learning outcomes 295
Introduction 295
Physical evidence and psychology 296
Exteriors 296
The architecture and design of buildings 296
Design of vehicles 297
Landscaping 297
Parking facilities 297
Interiors 298
Ease of access 298
Confines of an environment 298
Product access 298
Foyers, entrance areas and public spaces 299
Signage and corporate identity 300
Space 300
Layout and configurations 301
Seating 302
Security and privacy 303
Cleanliness and hygiene standards 303
Ambience and atmospherics 303
Visual factors 305
Lighting and illumination 305
Colour 305
Uniforms 306
Stationery 306
Presentation 306
Aural factors 307
Music and sounds 307
Olfactory factors 310
Air quality 310
Smells and odours 310
Taste 310
Tactile factors 311
Temperature 311

Touch   311
Chapter summary   311
Questions for review and reflection   311
References   312

15 Processes   **313**
Learning outcomes   313
Introduction   313
Types of processes   314
Technological processes   314
Non-technological processes   319
Combination processes   321
**The need to adapt and change
processes**   321
Process standardisation or adaptation   323
Ethical issues   325
Future issues   325
Chapter summary   326
Questions for review and reflection   326
References   326

16 Psychology   **327**
Learning outcomes   327
Introduction   327
Why psychology?   328
**Key approaches in psychology and
their relationship to marketing**   328
Psychoanalytical aspects   329
Behavioural aspects   331
Humanistic approach   334
The cognitive approach   334
Evolutionary approach   336
Social psychology   336
**The relationship between psychology
and marketing**   337
Categories of buyer behaviour   337
People   337
Culture   339
Lifestyle   339
Financial and economic influences   339
Fear   340
Media   341
Price   342
Necessities   342
Chapter summary   342
Question for review and reflection   342
References   343

17 Performance   **344**
Learning outcomes   344
Introduction   344
What is performance?   344
Measured performance   346
Product or service performance   346
Brand performance   346
Revenue performance and sales
performance   347
Market share   348
Distribution and logistics   349
Marketing plans   349
Experiential performance   349
Quadrant 1: passive participation–
entertainment–absorption   350
Quadrant 2: active participation–
educational–absorption   350
Quadrant 3: active participation–
escapist-immersion   351
Quadrant 4: passive participation–
esthetic (aesthetic)–immersion   353
Experience is a dynamic function   354
Future issues   354
Chapter summary   355
Questions for review and reflection   355
References   356

18 Packages and Packing   **357**
Learning outcomes   357
Introduction   357
What is packaging?   358
Combination or bundling   358
Product or brand packaging   358
Physical packaging   359
Attributes of physical packaging   359
Chapter summary   364
Questions for review and reflection   365
References   365

Notes   *367*
Glossary of marketing terms   *371*
Bibliography   *379*
Index   *389*

Figures

0.1 Timeline development of the marketing mix   xxiii

1.1 A Parisian street with marketing images galore   4
1.2 Stunning architecture such as the Eiffel Tower in Paris acts as a branding not only of Paris but of France   4
1.3 The Taj Mahal at Agra in the Uttar Pradesh region of Northern India   5
1.4 In this weekly Italian market the shoppers have a wide variety of choice of both fresh food and goods including clothing, toys and luggage   5
1.5 Marketing within an organisational context   12
1.6 An example of a B2G product: specially designed fire-fighting flying boats   16
1.7 A familiar sight in most high streets around the world – an eye-catching store window display, an example of B2C marketing   17

2.1 The relationship between macro and micro factors   20
2.2 1.5 litre bottles of Mecca Cola with both English and Arabic text   24
2.3 Passengers on this flight from China to Thailand are requested to wear surgical masks as a safety precaution against SARS   38
2.4 The International Space Station (ISS) is not only an example of how space agencies from different countries can work together for the benefit of human-kind, it is also a laboratory that may help solve some of the world's greatest health dilemmas   41
2.5 The organisation (profit and not for profit)   43

3.1 The STP schematic   54
3.2 A diagrammatic representation of how a mass market can be divided into several sections of segments   55
3.3 A diagrammatic representation of a positioning map for a selection of cruise vacation companies   63
3.4 Two photographs from Hebridean Cruises illustrating the ultra luxury end of the market sector   64

4.1 The indoor market in Barcelona, Spain   67
4.2 The marketing research process   68

5.1 Competitor types   84
5.2 The functions of a competitor intelligence system   87

6.1 The three key levels of strategy in many organisations   98
6.2 Ohmae's strategic triangle   100
6.3 Ansoff's portfolio matrix   102
6.4 The GE matrix or business screen   104
6.5 SWOT analysis incorporating the matching of the organisational analysis with the environmental analysis   106
6.6 The factors that contribute to a SWOT analysis   107
6.7 The five forces model   107
6.8 Porter's value chain concept   113
6.9 Position defence   114
6.10 A pre-emptive defence   114
6.11 Counter-offensive defence   115
6.12 Mobile defence   116
6.13 Strategic withdrawal   116
6.14 Frontal attack   116
6.15 Flanking attack   117
6.16 Guerrilla attacks   117

7.1 The Pan Lounge on board the luxury cruise ship *Hebridean Spirit*   126

8.1 Marketing mix architecture   159
8.2 Customer focus   164

9.1 Consumer product classifications   172
9.2 The *Hebridean Spirit*, an ultra-luxury cruise ship that has 49 bedrooms   175

9.3   Industrial and commercial product
      classifications   176
9.4   The reinforcement process of
      diffusion and adoption   188
9.5   The typical S-shaped diffusion curve   188
9.6   The sequence of adoption   188
9.7   An innovation–decision process   190
9.8   A typical adoption pattern   191
9.9   Desired and typical diffusion patterns   194
9.10 The stereotypical product life cycle   188
9.11 Product life cycle for a fad   205
9.12 Product life cycle for a seasonal
      fashion item   205
9.13 A possible product life cycle for real
      Christmas trees   205
9.14 Life cycle for a product that is
      regularly rejuvenated   205

10.1 EasyJet uses its planes as a
      promotional tool   209
10.2 A simple one-directional
      communication model   210
10.3 The general communications system
      model   210
10.4 Schramm's adaptation of Shannon's
      communication model   211
10.5 An expansion of Schramm's
      communication model   212
10.6 A simplified version of Berlo's model   213
10.7 Sometimes the simplest of tactics help
      a company to break through the
      clutter   214
10.8 The AIDA model   216
10.9 Scott's model   216
10.10 Strong's model   216
10.11 Colley's hierarchy of effects model   218
10.12 Ehrenberg's ATRN model   218
10.13 Vaughn's model   219
10.14 An example of primary advertising   221
10.15 A Parisian news kiosk displaying a
      wide selection of magazines   222
10.16 A poster for Exide batteries at Pune
      railway station, India   223
10.17 Billboards do not have to be
      permanent fixtures   224
10.18 The Government Assembly building
      in Paris adorned with photographic
      mages to advertise a major exhibition   224
10.19 Outdoor advertising does not have to
      be on a large scale to be effective   224
10.20 Some of the merchandising
      undertaken by the Business School at
      Oxford Brookes University   237

10.21 A telecommunications company
      sponsored the sailing regatta on
      Lake Garda, Italy in 2004   239
10.22 The exhibition stand for the
      Australian-based company Muir
      Anchoring Systems at the 2004
      Monte Carlo Boat Show   243

11.1 Yachts, super yachts and mega
      yachts adorning the marina in Monte
      Carlo   250
11.2 The prototype of the Airbus A380 in
      flight   252

12.1 A luxury hotel on the island of
      Cyprus   269
12.2 A TGV prepares for departure from
      Paris's Gare du Nord   272
12.3 Place attachment   274
12.4 A one-stage channel process   275
12.5 The producer sells direct to an
      independent retailer who in turn
      sells the product on to the consumer   275
12.6 The producer sells directly to a
      multiple branch retailer or to a
      wholesale warehouse that in turn
      sells to the multiple-brand retailer.
      The end buyer purchases the
      product from one of the retail
      branches   275
12.7 The producer distributes the product
      to its own franchised retail operation.
      The retailer then sells the product
      on to the end buyer or consumer of
      the product   275
12.8 A two-stage channel in a B2B
      environment. The producer sells to a
      distributor which in turn sells to a
      business user   276
12.9 Here there are two intermediaries
      operating between the producer and
      the end consumer of the product   276
12.10 Bremen Express at sea with her
      cargo of containers   276
12.11 Loose cargoes such as minerals are
      still moved along waterways   278
12.12 A special nuclear flask is loaded
      aboard a ship for transportation   278
12.13 The delicate manoeuvring of a section
      of the Airbus A380 fuselage on a
      multi-wheeled transporter   278
12.14 A freight yard in Washington State,

USA with both open wagons (for carrying minerals) and containers 278

12.15 Packages in a container are loaded on board a Federal Express cargo plane 279

12.16 Michael Porter's supply chain model 279

12.17 A value system 280

12.18 An indoor food market in Barcelona, Spain 281

12.19 Traditional wooden market stalls on the left bank of the River Seine in Paris 281

13.1 The relationship between musicians and an audience 290

13.2 Information and customer care staff are the public face of the organisation 291

14.1 Designed by Norman Foster and Partners the Swiss Re Tower dominates the London Skyline 297

14.2 Examples of landscaping at two luxury hotels 298

14.3 Singapore's Changi International Airport illustrates the use and dimensions of space, the combination of natural and artificial lighting, ease of access and spacious design style 299

14.4 This bookshop at Singapore's Changi International Airport demonstrates both efficiency in terms of the use of shelf space and ease of access 299

14.5 One of the lounges on the Hebridean luxurious cruise ship *Hebridean Spirit* clearly demonstrates space, style and quiet luxury 300

14.6 Clarity of signage is important to the efficient movement of people, especially where there is a risk of congestion, and in a large complex such as an airport 300

14.7 The space between tables on a terrace at a luxury five-star hotel 301

14.8 The relationship between a physical environment and customer behaviour 304

14.9 A luxury five-star hotel bathed in lights at night creates an inviting romantic atmosphere 305

14.10 A small delicatessen in a side street in the old part of Verona in Italy 306

14.11 A perfume shop – a dramatic display which uses a variety of strong warm colours and images to promote upmarket suntan lotions 308

15.1 The relationship between technological and non-technological processes 314

15.2 The linkages between electronic processes 315

15.3 Wincor Nixdorf's compactBank is a self-service system for self-service areas or mini branches 317

15.4 One of the many ATMs that are available in banks, shopping centres, railway stations and petrol service stations 317

15.5 A barcode scanner attached to a Personal Shopping Assistant (PSA) 318

15.6 A miniature RFID chip with antenna is attached to a product 318

15.7 The LG Internet Refrigerator 320

15.8 With intelligent scales the consumer places the product on the scales and the price label is automatically printed out 321

15.9 A personal shopping assistant (PSA) attached to the face of a trolley 322

15.10 A self-check-out system for supermarket shoppers 323

15.11 The spacious arrivals baggage collection area at Singapore's Changi International Airport 324

15.12 The need for rapid transit systems has been an important component of contemporary airport development 325

16.1 Several hundred people enjoy a summer's evening concert at Kenwood, Hampstead in London 328

16.2 People purchase products and services that fulfil their particular lifestyle 339

16.3 A sale at a London men's clothing store 342

17.1 Types of performance 345

17.2 Pine and Gilmore's experience realms 350

17.3 The British Airways London Eye 353

17.4 A pod on the British Airways London Eye which towers over the River Thames near the Houses of Parliament 353

17.5 The stunning snow-capped Atlas Mountains in Morocco 354

17.6 The picturesque town of St Florent
      in Corsica   354
17.7 Adaptation of Pine and Gilmore's
      experience realms   355

18.1 A container is an example of tertiary
      packaging as it contains numerous
      packages in a safe protective
      environment   359

18.2 The main attributes of physical
      packaging   360

18.3 An example of an easy-to-use pour
      device   351
18.4 Tetra-Pak packages   362

Tables

0.1 Marketing and other non-business disciplines xxiv

1.1 Marketing relationships 13
1.2 Groups involved in marketing 14
1.3 Key trends in marketing research according to the MSI 17

2.1 The main global trading groups 23
2.2 Forms of political risk 26
2.3 Business and economic cycles 29
2.4 Cultural orientations and behaviours 31
2.5 Calorie and fat content of McDonald's foods 32
2.6 Demographic factors 33
2.7 Tourist jobs in countries affected by the tsunami 40
2.8 Growth in tourism before the tsunami 40

3.1 The scope and scale of markets 56

4.1 The different research techniques available to marketers 71

5.1 Analysing competitors 85

6.1 Quadrants in Ansoff's portfolio matrix 103
6.2 Market attractiveness factors 105
6.3 Business position factors 106
6.4 Generic strategies 110

7.1 The five Cs of intimacy 124
7.2 Types of extension 129
7.3 Individual brands and their parent companies 133
7.4 The world's top ten brands 136
7.5 Country origins of top 100 brands 136
7.6 The wealth of nations (measured by gross national income) 137
7.7 Brand longevity 146

8.1 Borden's original marketing mix structure 156
8.2 McCarthy's 4Ps 158
8.3 Possible additions to the marketing mix 160

8.4 Booms and Bitner's extensions for the marketing mix 162
8.5 Further extensions to the marketing mix 163

9.1 Product attributes 169
9.2 Lost in translation: examples of product names that did not travel well 171
9.3 Level of hybrid corn seed usage over time 189
9.4 Potential marketing impact on the diffusion process 190
9.5 Colby and Parasuraman's framework for technology readiness 192
9.6 The percentage of the US population that appears to fit certain adoption categories 193
9.7 Strategic and marketing mix issues within the different stages of the product life cycle 200
9.8 Limitations of and objections to the product life cycle concept 204

10.1 Lavidge and Steiner's model 217
10.2 Key forms of ambient media 225
10.3 Types of online advertising 227
10.4 The rationale for merchandising a brand 238
10.5 The value of exhibitions 242
10.6 A selection of key B2B and B2C exhibitions worldwide 243
10.7 The scope of public relations 244

11.1 Tariff and non-tariff barriers 255
11.2 Pricing tactics 256

12.1 Types of shipment 277
12.2 Requirements for service innovation 280

14.1 The cultural meaning of colour 307

16.1 An example of reinforcing behaviour 332
16.2 Types of reinforcement 333
16.3 Schedules of reinforcing behaviour 333
16.4 The relationship between Maslow's hierarchy of needs and marketing 335

Mini cases

2.1 The longshoremen dispute in West Coast USA — 21
2.2 The boycott of US cola drinks — 24
2.3 Political pressure — 25
2.4 War in Iraq — 25
2.5 Political and financial unrest in Venezuela, 2003 — 27
2.6 Nestlé and Ethiopia — 27
2.7 Diageo and national sensitivities — 28
2.8 Obesity — 32
2.9 The cruise industry in US waters: pollution control — 34
2.10 Restrictions on the shipment of wine within the United States in the 21st century — 35
2.11 Storms batter US economy — 36
2.12 The impact of SARS — 38
2.13 A tsunami devastates Southeast Asia — 40
2.14 Studio removes shuttle film trailer — 41
2.15 A restaurant and its suppliers — 43
2.16 The case of the UglyRipe™ tomato — 47

3.1 Segmentation, targeting and positioning within the cruise vacation market — 64

4.1 Module evaluation questionnaires — 73

5.1 The Body Shop — 81
5.2 The political intentions of a government and country — 82
5.3 Crossing the line in the sand — 93
5.4 Konkordski — 94

6.1 European low-cost airlines — 111

7.1 London Hilton, Park Lane, London — 122
7.2 The battle against the movie pirates — 123
7.3 Johnson & Johnson and Tylenol® — 125
7.4 Godzilla® — 128
7.5 Harley-Davidson® — 128
7.6 Kit Kat chocolate bar — 130
7.7 Fashion designers extending their brands — 131
7.8 BIC® — 132
7.9 Premier Foods and Premier Brands — 135
7.10 Lucozade® — 139
7.11 Rebranding the British monarchy — 141
7.12 The transformation of UK holiday 'camps' into holiday centres — 142
7.13 Samaritans — 144
7.14 Rebrandings too far — 145
7.15 Unilever and its strategy for growth — 148
7.16 Sunny Delight — 150

9.1 The Barbie® doll — 170
9.2 Coca-Cola — 170
9.3 Nylon® — 179
9.4 Bisquick™ — 179
9.5 3M and Post-it Notes® — 181
9.6 Viagra® — 184
9.7 The Boeing 777 — 185
9.8 The movies — 187
9.9 The Sinclair C5 — 196
9.10 Crest Whitestrips dental kit — 198
9.11 Rejuvenation of Škoda cars — 199

10.1 Fly posting: an unethical approach to ambient marketing — 226
10.2 Barnardo's — 228
10.3 ipoint: real-time public information system — 233
10.4 When is a national secret not a national secret? When it is a myth, and on the official website — 234
10.5 Eats, Shoots & Leaves — 235
10.6 The rise, rise and further rise of product placement in James Bond movies — 236
10.7 Oxford Brookes University Business School — 237
10.8 Orange™ Prize for Fiction — 240
10.9 Hoover® and the free flights offer — 241

11.1 ESSO® PriceWatch™ Campaign — 257
11.2 London to Oxford coach service — 258
11.3 Tendering: Republic of Botswana — 263
11.4 UK Ministry of Defence and Chinook Helicopters — 263
11.5 International cartel in vitamin supplements — 265

12.1 Holiday Inn Express® — 282

12.2 Food and drink vending machines in
       schools – an ethical issue?   283

13.1 Hotels   289
13.2 British Airways   292
13.3 When is a gift a bribe?   293

14.1 The power of music in Hitchcock's
       Psycho   309

15.1 ATMs   316
15.2 Barcodes and export documentation   317
15.3 Amazon   319
15.4 The intelligent home   320

15.5 METRO Group future store initiative   322
15.6 Credit card applications   323
15.7 Hotel room cleaning   324
15.8 Airport baggage handling   324

16.1 Introducing women to smoking   330
16.2 Dichter and the introduction of the
       Barbie Doll™   331
16.3 The cognitive approach and marketing
       shampoo   336
16.4 Werther's Originals   338

17.1 Science of Sport exhibition   351

Preface

Everyone lives by selling something.
Robert Louis Stevenson (1850–1894)
Scottish novelist
From *Across the Plains* (1892)
'Beggars', Part 3.

■ Welcome to *Foundations of Marketing*

Every aspect of our lives is affected, in one way or another, by the action of marketing, whether we listen to the radio when we wake up, make the coffee, catch the metro, buy birthday cards, listen to our favourite CD or watch a new movie. In all these cases marketing has been used to influence and/or support our purchasing decision. This book seeks to explain how marketing works and how it is influential in most people's lives.

■ Objectives of this book

My overall objectives in writing this text have been to:

◆ Create a text that was relatively easy and direct to read and thus communicate a passion for the subject of marketing. Moreover, I sought to write this text in an 'easy style' language that conveyed the impression of a one-to-one conversation with you, the student. I hope that that has been achieved.

◆ Create an objective view of marketing. Contrary to perhaps 'populist' views, marketing is not a panacea for an inappropriate idea, concept or indeed poor management. Marketing is but one function of an organisation. Therefore marketing must be seen as an integral component within an organisational context.

◆ Provide a contemporary view of marketing. Although there are some historic data

and examples, the main approach is a contemporary one.

◆ Seek possible links between the theoretical aspects of marketing and practical real-world cases or situations. Often marketing is considered in purely theoretical contexts. Although this is valuable for the development and health of the subject, it is important to explore links to the real world. It is only by exploring the links with the real world that we know whether the theory is practical or not. In many cases the theory is transferable; however it is not so in all cases.

◆ Provide an international feel by incorporating a range of examples and mini cases. Generally marketing theory has evolved from American and British universities. In many cases consultants and certain businesses and industries have influenced the development of these theories. However, we should not take for granted that a theory developed within the confines of a Western university should or could work universally. International students, in particular, will be aware of the diverse approaches to marketing products or services within their own countries. In many cases it is unlikely to take a 'standardised' Western approach. With this in mind it is useful for you, the student, to examine this text through two lenses: first as a generally Westernised philosophy, and second considering how this philosophy may be perceived and enacted in different countries, including your own. Explore the international perspectives by discussing them with fellow international students and searching the web. This will help you gain a holistic approach to the subject area.

◆ Provide a platform for the further development of the marketing mix.

◆ Create a platform for debate amongst students. Many of you, I hope, will disagree with some of the content in this book. If so, that's great! Why? Because you are beginning to critically evaluate material and information, seeing whether or not it is applicable to you and/or the country in which you live. Only so much information can be stated in a textbook of this size. It is up to you and your fellow students to take this information, add to it and consider its viability.

Objectivity and critical thinking

This book does not contain everything that there is to know about the subject of marketing. Just imagine the sheer number and weight of volumes to cover such an extensive field of knowledge! It is merely, like every other text-book, a snapshot of ideas, issues, theories, incidents and cases. Moreover, it contains (as do other texts) issues that are debatable and perhaps contentious. If so, the more the better! The rationale, in my view, for any textbook is to encourage you to think critically about the subject area. Indeed every subject you study should be viewed critically.

Glaser (1941, cited in Cottrell 2003), who developed a test for critical thinking, stated:

> Critical thinking calls for a persistent effort to examine any belief or supposed form of knowledge in the light of the evidence that supports it and the further conclusions to which it tends.

As Cottrell (2003) suggests, this is the 'weighing up of the arguments and evidence *for* and *against*' (italics in original). Therefore do not take the subject of marketing at face value: be more analytical in your approach to the subject area.

Increasingly pre-university qualifications in many countries are including critical and analytical thinking on their syllabi. With this approach in mind I have sought to include details within this text that may at first be challenging to the reader. However, my aim is to get you to query and debate issues.

The audience for this book

This book has value for a variety of audiences depending on their individual needs.

♦ Students studying a one-semester module in marketing. Here chapters can be selected to cover the core elements of the one-semester programme. The end-of-chapter questions provide an aid to knowledge and understanding.

♦ Students studying on a pre-university, Foundation or Associate degree (for instance Associate of Business Administration) programme. This includes professional certificate and diploma courses.

♦ Business people who want to refresh or update their knowledge of the subject area. This includes individuals who have never studied marketing before but now require some knowledge as part of their job specification.

♦ Undergraduate students studying on a two to four-year marketing or business degree programme. It will be valuable throughout the length of the programme.

♦ Undergraduate students studying on a modular degree programme where marketing and business modules comprise part of their degree. This is also applicable to students who are majoring in a separate discipline, for instance Psychology, with Business or a related subject as a minor.

♦ Students who have embarked on a postgraduate business-related qualification but have either never studied marketing, or not studied it for a significant period of time. This text will provide a solid foundation on which you can build knowledge and understanding of the subject area.

The structure of the book

This text is divided into three overarching sections:

Part 1 focuses on the definitions and scope of

marketing, and how it relates to both internal and external factors and influences.

Part 2 covers the key tools and techniques that mark the subject's territory. These include segmentation, targeting, positioning and market research. These are the tools that set the basic parameters of marketing. These tools help marketers define the individuals or groups of people they seek to inform and influence through the marketing mix.

In **Part 3** the focus is on the marketing mix. This develops from the original 12 components defined by Borden (1964), through to the 4Ps mnemonic created by McCarthy (1965) and the extended 3Ps from Booms and Bitner's 1981 research. Moreover this text seeks to extend the now generic 7P marketing mix to 10Ps with the inclusion of psychology, performance and packaging (see Figure 0.1). Also considered within this section is the development of the relationship marketing school of thought.

Although the text is divided into sections and chapters, it is vital to consider it as integrated. The various elements, components and techniques that comprise marketing are interrelated and highly dependent on each other. Organisations that do not engage with this connectivity often fail within an increasingly dynamic globalised marketplace. Their rivals, who do see the connectivity, build and support superior forces and thus gain competitive advantage. However, the story does not stop there. This is a continuous process. Gaining competitive advantage is only one move. Maintaining that advantage over the longer term is a much more complex series of moves

and counter moves. All these moves will involve an appreciation of the changing marketing environment.

■ The relationship between marketing and other functional areas of business

Although this book focuses on marketing, the subject should not be viewed in isolation of the other functional areas within the broader subject of business. Marketing is but one, albeit important, function of an organisation. When you study the subject of marketing you should link it to the other functional areas that combine to drive forward an organisation. This is equally applicable to profit-making and not-for-profit organisations (including charities and government agencies).

■ The relationship between marketing and other subject areas

However, it does not stop there. Marketing is one of those subjects that touches, or is touched by, so many other subject areas. As you progress through this text and consider the interrelationships, I hope you will see how and why marketing interfaces with so many other disciplines.

Table 0.1 lists some of the many (direct) non-business disciplines or studies that influence/ impact upon marketing functions and activities. By the end of this text you should be able to make links between the subject of marketing and these disciplines and areas of study. Moreover you should be able to add to the table's contents.

| **Figure 0.1** | Timeline development of the marketing mix |

4Ps	3Ps	3Ps
Product	People	Psychology
Promotion	Physical evidence	Performance
Price	Processes	Packaging
Place		
1960s	1970s	2005

Time line

■ Marketing as an ethical and social responsibility issue

Recently 'marketing' has been criticised for creating, amongst other issues, a global commercialised world, promoting potentially dangerous products (for instance, tobacco) and aiding and abetting a 'greed is good' culture. Marketing has

Table 0.1 Marketing and other non-business disciplines

Mathematics	Psychology	Logistics	Geography	Ecology	Climatology
Sociology	Geology	Art & Design	Communication	Graphics	Ethics
Philosophy	Physics	Geopolitics	Manufacturing	Shipping	Languages
History	Culture	Education	Technology	Computing	Anthropology
Music	Nutrition	Meteorology	Archaeology	Tourism	Hospitality

always been a part of human existence. However, it is not marketing itself that creates the ethical and social dilemmas. It is how individuals and organisations use the tools of marketing that creates such dilemmas. Therefore when studying marketing it is important to bear in mind how it is used to develop and promote a product or service. When considering the tools of marketing view them in terms of individual ethics and organisational social responsibility. Everyone involved in marketing and, indeed business, has an ethical and social responsibility to the rest of society.

The role of the mini cases

Placed throughout this text are over 80 mini cases. The mini cases aim to provide you with:

◆ Snapshots of real practical marketing issues and situations. Many of these are contemporary issues. However, a few historical cases have been used to illustrate certain general situations or particular events.

◆ Links between the practical issues and the theoretical underpinning within each chapter.

◆ A basis upon which to continue research into the subject area. Even contemporary cases date with time. Therefore it will be a useful exercise for you to explore 'What happened next?' The questions at the end of many of the mini cases will help you explore further.

Figures and tables

Throughout the text figures and tables have been used to illustrate specific issues, ideas, concepts and real-world cases. Where appropriate web addresses have been included within the text/note sections to help you discover more on the particular topic areas.

End of chapter questions

Each chapter concludes with a series of questions for review and reflection. Linked to the chapter's Learning Outcomes, they will help you synthesise your subject knowledge. Some questions are designed for self-study while others are linked to sharing knowledge with your fellow students. They can also be used as group work exercises.

Currency of data

Every attempt has been taken to use the most current data and statistics available. Some organisations provide statistics on an annual basis, others every few years. Moreover some statistical data is extremely expensive to acquire. Where this is the case, abstracted data has been used to create an overview of the current situation.

A general health warning

It takes many months to write a work of this length. Because of the length of time between conception and arrival on the bookshelves, situations will have changed. This is especially true where the activities of companies are concerned. What was important or breaking news at the time of writing may not be so now. Micro and macro events may have overtaken those discussed in the book. That does not make them redundant as a learning exercise; far from it. However, it is important to consider many of the issues raised in this book as a snapshot in time. They are something upon which to build your knowledge and understanding, not just of marketing but perhaps the complex world we all inhabit.

■ Marketing mix extension: an introduction to the rationale

As stated earlier, a major section of this text is devoted to the marketing mix. Although there continues to be much debate regarding the empirical basis of the marketing mix, it remains the mainstay of contemporary marketing. Some authors and researchers suggest that relationship marketing is a replacement for the marketing mix. However, I suggest that in many ways the marketing mix and relationship marketing complement each other. Moreover, I further contend that now is the time to extend the marketing mix to encapsulate a further three Ps: Psychology, Performance and Packaging.

Since the establishment of the original 4P framework, numerous authors (see Chapter 8) have suggested extending the mix. In 1981 Booms and Bitner suggested that McCarthy's 4Ps be extended to include Process, Physical Evidence and Participants (People) to support the increasing services component of marketing. Booms and Bitner's additional 3Ps have generally been accepted as a valid addition to the original framework. Thus the literature increasingly discusses the generic 7P marketing mix.

So why incorporate these additional Ps of Psychology, Performance and Packaging? As is suggested in Chapter 8 and elsewhere, psychology has been for centuries the underpinning motivation for why we behave in certain ways. Psychology has provided this underpinning even though as marketers or buyers we might not even have been aware of its influence. In terms of 'modern' Western marketing we only have to read the writings of, for instance, E. St Elmo Lewis in the late 19th and early 20th century, and E.K. Strong Jr. in 1925 to see even then the potency of psychology in product selling. Today psychology is a technique that is used to persuade us to purchase a myriad of products and services.

It has been claimed that accountants and financial directors have always considered marketing as a cost centre rather than a profit centre. Both articles and business books have emphasised that the accounting and finance departments seek to measure every type of performance. The accountants, it has been suggested, are the guardians of performance through due diligence and the balance sheet.

In reality everyone within an organisation is responsible for the performance of the organisation. It cannot rest with one department and one department only. It is a collective operation. Therefore, on this basis, performance should be considered an integral component of the marketing mix. Moreover as you will see in Chapter 17, performance covers a range of issues, from the operational aspects of a product or service to the financial contribution marketing makes to the success or failure of an organisation.

Packaging has often sat uncomfortably between promotions on the one side and product on the other. This may have been satisfactory when packaging was the simple wrapping of a product. Today, packaging is much more than that. Nor is it any longer confined to the physicality of a product. Today services, such as vacations, are packaged. Indeed packaging has a multitude of operational and marketing functions and on that basis needs to be considered as a separate, yet integrated, component of the marketing mix.

■ References

Booms, B. H. and Bitner, M. J. (1981) 'Marketing strategies and organisation structures for service firms', in J. H. Donnely and W. R. George (eds), *Marketing of Services*, Chicago: AMA.

Borden, N. H. (1964) 'The concept of the marketing mix', *Journal of Advertising Research*, June, pp. 2–7.

Cottrell, S. (2003) *The Study Skills Handbook*, 2nd edn, Basingstoke: Palgrave Macmillan.

Glaser, E. (1941) 'An experiment in the development of critical thinking', New York: Teachers' College, Columbia University, cited in S. Cottrell (2003) *The Study Skills Handbook*, 2nd edn, Basingstoke: Palgrave Macmillan.

Lewis, St. Elmo E. (1915) *Getting the Most Out of Business*, New York: Ronald Press.

McCarthy, E. J. (1965) *Basic Marketing*, Homewood, Ill: Irwin.

Strong, E. K. Jr (1925) *The Psychology of Selling and Advertising*, New York: McGraw-Hill.

Acknowledgements

Writing anything, whether it is a concerto or a book, can be a lonely business. You lock yourself away in your study, often buried under papers and notes, and hope to emerge with a comprehensive and coherent piece of work. As the business thinker Tom Peters so aptly stated in his imaginative book *Re-imagine!* 'Writing is a nasty business. One eventually alienates all one's friends'. Hopefully I have not alienated anyone in the process of writing this text!

However, no completed and published book is really the work of one person. Writers are always influenced by experience, by the people around them and other internal and external factors. Moreover, the physical shape of the book is the outcome of many who work behind the scenes. It is they who transfer and shape the work into the book that you hold before you. Therefore a special thank you to the publishing and printing teams involved with this text for all their hard work and patience.

There might be only one name on the front cover of this text, but if it had not been for the support and encouragement of others this book would never have been completed. I particularly want to thank the following individuals for their kindness, continual support and encouragement: Shereen Baig, Ian Bathgate, David Bennett, Chris Blackburn, Peter Boynton, Michael and Elizabeth Brown, Suzanne Burywood, Dr Jack Colford, Professor George Corfield, Brenda and Philip Crook, Glauco de Vita, Christine Ewers, Dr Paul Griseri, Jan Harwell, Geoff Holmberg, Cheryl Hopkins, Colin Horner, Dr John Lang, Elspeth Macfarlane, Ian Marshall, John Muir, Shona Muir, Wendy Muir, Rebecca Peek, Della Rhodes, Judy Slinn, Peter A. Taylor, Sheila Thomson, Simon Williams and Dr Catherine Wang.

I should also like to thank those students who over the years have participated in my marketing and strategy classes. Thank you for your encouragement, constructive criticism and support.

Every effort has been made to contact the copyright holders of material reproduced in this book and to obtain permission for its use. The author and publisher apologise for any instances where permission has not been obtained, and will be happy to rectify this in future editions.

And finally to you, the reader. I hope you find this book an enjoyable and stimulating read that encourages you to explore marketing further.

Jonathan Groucutt
London and Oxford
November 2005

**PART
I**

The Scope of Marketing

A Brief Introduction to Marketing

CHAPTER

I

Contents

Learning outcomes	3
What are your favourites?	3
Introduction	3
The origin of marketing	4
An economics approach	5
A consumer's (or buyer's) approach	6
The societal approach	6
The managerial or systems approach	7
A broader approach	7
Relationships	9
Transactions	9
Time	9
Dialogue	9
The marketer: alchemist, magician, sorcerer and medicine man	10
Marketing as an organisational function	11
Who is engaged in marketing?	12
Marketing now and tomorrow: current and future trends	12
2004–14?	13
Chapter summary	15
Questions for review and reflection	16
References	16

Learning outcomes

After completing this chapter you should be able to:

▶ outline the origins and the different orientations of marketing

▶ debate the role of the marketer within a business environment

▶ evaluate the development of marketing

▶ consider marketing within the 'realistic' real world environment.

■ What are your favourites?

It may seem very strange to start the first chapter of a textbook with a question. However, it is a highly pertinent one. Before reading the Introduction take a few minutes to answer the following brief questions:

◆ What are your three favourite movies? Why are they your favourite movies? What influenced you to go to see them?

◆ What are your three favourite CDs? Why are they your favourite CDs? What influenced you to go to buy them? If you did not buy them, were they a gift to you?

◆ What is your favourite food? Why is it your favourite food? Did anyone or anything influence you to try this food for the first time?

Encapsulated within those brief questions are the basics of marketing. By the time you reach the end of this textbook you will know exactly how pertinent these questions are to you and your understanding of marketing.

Introduction

The aim of this chapter is to 'set the scene', to consider what marketing really is to you and me. It discusses what marketing comprises, its development and how it affects our daily lives. Marketing, as we shall see throughout this text, is composed of many elements from numerous subject areas and disciplines. For instance, economics, sociology, psychology, statistics and mathematics, as well as politics and the law, have all influenced marketing in one form or another.

The actual term 'marketing' may be a creation of recent history, often associated with the dawn of the 20th century. However the actions of marketing date back thousands of years. We know from excavations of caves that early civilizations used 'advertising' to inform other members of the community of events and issues, indeed also to warn them of perils in the area. Equally customers or consumers, as we know them, are far from being a recent phenomenon. Customers are as old as the first transaction between two people.

The social, economic, political and technological changes during the 20th century revolutionised the way we lived and worked. Moreover these 'revolutions' provided the means or the platform for an equally dramatic change in the marketing of products and services linked to dynamic competitive environments. The 21st century obviously remains an unknown quantity. Already in its early years this century has witnessed tremendous growth in certain business sectors, decline in others, increased competition in both home and international markets, societal change and geopolitical turmoil. Where the next 20 or so years will lead us is anyone's guess. However, marketing, in one form

Figure 1.2

© Jonathan Groucutt

Stunning architecture such as the Eiffel Tower in Paris acts as a branding not only of Paris but of France. The same could be said of the Statue of Liberty in New York, the Opera House in Sydney and the Houses of Parliament in London. What other national symbols do you think represent countries? What are the national symbols of your country?

Figure 1.1

© Jonathan Groucutt

Everywhere we go we are being marketed to in one form or another. Marketing is with us each second of our waking lives. This is a Parisian street with marketing images galore. What are the marketing images where you live?

or another, will play an integral role in reacting to change and even shaping change.

■ The origin of marketing

Marketing is something that affects every one of us every waking moment of our lives – even though we may not necessarily be conscious of it. From that very moment we stir out of deep sleep, turn on the radio or television, and walk around the house, we are bombarded by marketing messages. They are not always in the form of advertisements beaming from the radio or television.

Figure 1.3

© Shereen Baig. Reproduced with kind permission.

The Taj Mahal at Agra in the Uttar Pradesh region of Northern India. This imposing extravagant white marble mausoleum has become, in essence, the tourist symbol of traditional India.

Think of the packaging in your kitchen or bathroom. Even on non-commercial radio and television stations there are still marketing messages, in the form of publicity and public relations. Even before we leave the house we have already seen or heard hundreds of marketing messages. Then it just explodes – newspapers, magazines, billboards and posters. There are messages everywhere, invading every aspect of our lives.

All this relates to marketing, but how do we define marketing? This is not as easy as one might think. Indeed as Cooke, Rayburn and Abercrombie (1992) suggested, 'after about 80 years of formal marketing education (thought) there is no consensus on the definition of market'. Has this perspective changed? No. It is perhaps a scary thought that a subject that is a major course at the vast majority of universities has no hard and fast definition. However, being able to debate a definition for marketing allows us to consider the subject as being flexible and dynamic, just like the world we live in.

In the next section we investigate some of the various definitions of marketing, drawing on a range of subject areas. It may well turn out that there is no one definition that fits all aspects of marketing. As marketers we may have to be flexible in our understanding of the subject, and its relationship with us both as individuals and a society, especially within a turbulent macro environment.

An economics approach

With an economics approach the emphasis is on products (usually referred to as goods) and services, sources of supply, the most commonly used channels of distribution and the functions performed during the marketing process (Cooke *et al.* 1992).

Three definitions can be provided on the basis of the economics approach:

> Marketing is the performance of business activities directed toward, and incident to, the flow of goods and services from producer to consumer or user.
> (American Marketing Association (AMA) 1948)

> Marketing embraces all the business activities involved in getting commodities of all kinds, including services, from the hands of producers and manufacturers into the hands of the final consumers. All the business steps through which goods progress on their way to final consumption is the concern of marketing. This is

Figure 1.4

© Jonathan Groucutt

Marketing however is not just about symbols and brands. It is about how we choose the products and services we want to buy. In this weekly Italian market the shoppers have a wide variety of choice of both fresh food and goods including clothing, toys and luggage. They will make decisions based on several factors including quality, price and customer service.

especially true of the points in those stages at which change of ownership takes place.

(McNair et al. 1975)

Marketing is the performance of business activities that direct the flow of goods and services from producer to consumer or user.

(AMA 1960)

As Cooke et al. (1992) state, there are several key words that summarise these definitions:

◆ goods/services

◆ transfer of ownership

◆ storage

◆ flow of goods/services

◆ distribution/transport

◆ functions.

We shall return to these points later.

A consumer's (or buyer's) approach

This perspective arises out of consumers' dissatisfaction with products, services and the organisations that provide them. Linked to this is the subsequent need for governments to protect individual consumer rights through legislation. The dissatisfaction emanated from the following views:

◆ The marketing system was unresponsive to consumer wants.

◆ Marketing practitioners were unscrupulous.

◆ Marketers made claims that were not borne out by the actual performance of the product.

◆ Consumers sought increased product quality.

◆ Increasing concern over hazardous and unsafe products entering the marketplace, especially electrical goods and children's toys.

◆ Concern over misleading advertising, deceptive packaging and labelling.

Three definitions provide an insight into the consumer perspective:

Marketing consists of four general activities: 1. Identifying and selecting the type of customer that the business will cultivate, learning his needs and desires; 2. Designing products or services that the firm can sell at a profit in conformity with customers desires; 3. Persuading customers to buy at the firm's offerings; 4. Storing, moving, and displaying goods after they leave the production site.

(Oxenfeldt 1966)

Note the use of the word 'his'. Perhaps the focus remained male dominated?

That process through which a business enterprise, institution, or organization 1. selects target customers or constituents, 2. assesses the needs or wants of such target customers, and 3. manages its resources to satisfy those customer needs or wants.

(Star et al. 1977)

As Cooke et al. (1992) state, there are several key words that summarise these definitions:

◆ consumer

◆ meet – fulfil – satisfy

◆ product (goods and services)

◆ wants

◆ determine – assess needs

◆ needs

◆ target customers.

We shall return to these points later.

The societal approach

This can be considered as a needs-fulfilling exchange or relationship activity that is present, to a greater or lesser degree, within all cultures. Cooke et al. (1992) suggest that it is the 'process of exchange in society and this process must occur in society so that the consumption of values can occur'. They continue:

The societal view of marketing as exchange relationships begin with the basic idea that most human behaviour is the planned, purposeful quest and search for want satisfaction. Individuals act to satisfy their wants and desires. Goods, services, or ideas are the source of this satisfaction.

Cunningham and Cunningham (1981) suggest that societal marketing performs three essential functions:

1 As an information network – knowing and understanding the consumer's changing needs and wants.

2 Equalising the distribution function – efficiently and effectively managing the supply and demand of products and services.

3 Centralising the exchange function – efficient provision of distribution and payment processing systems.

Two definitions provide an insight into the societal perspective:

Marketing may be thought of as that phase of business activities which human activities are satisfied by the exchange of goods and services, on the one hand, for some valuable consideration – using money or its equivalent – on the other.
(Pyle 1931)

Marketing is the delivery of a standard of living to society.
(Mazur 1947)

As Cooke et al. (1992) state, there are several key words that summarise these definitions:

◆ consumption – relationship
◆ matching
◆ society
◆ exchange
◆ social process
◆ standard of living.

Once again, we shall return to these points later.

The managerial or systems approach

This is the approach of management within individual companies or organisations (including not-for-profit and public sector organisations) to marketing. The emphasis is on how the individual organisation processes marketing and develops the strategic dimensions of marketing activities. Hughes (1978) suggests that marketing managers focus on market analysis and the selection of target market segments, strategy development and the creation of a profit plan. Of course, a profit plan does not exist within a not-for-profit organisation, such as a charity. Nevertheless these organisations need to generate revenues to both develop the organisation and to deliver products/services to its clients: for example, the distribution of food and medical supplies in famine-stricken areas.

The managerial approach can be described as follows:

Marketing is the combination of activities designed to produce profit through ascertaining, creating, stimulating, and satisfying the needs and/or wants of a selected segment of the market.
(Eldridge 1970)

As Cooke et al. (1992) state, there are several key words that summarise this approach:

◆ anticipate (demand)
◆ business – corporation – organisation
◆ goods – services
◆ objectives of organisations
◆ product development – design
◆ stimulate (demand)
◆ assess – determine
◆ create (demand)
◆ meet – fulfil
◆ profit
◆ strategy
◆ target (customers).

A broader approach

While some definitions fit relatively neatly into one of the four categories above, not all definitions do. Perhaps marketing is not as easy to define as we might think?

In the early 1990s Kotler defined marketing as:

A social and managerial process by which individuals and groups get what they need and want through creating and exchanging products of value with others.

(Kotler 1991)

By 2000 he had slightly modified this to:

A societal process by which individuals and groups obtain what they need and want through creating, offering, and freely exchanging products and services of value with others.

(Kotler 2000)

While the differences between the two definitions might appear slight, they are significant. Consider the following:

◆ The second definition has introduced the term 'societal' and removed the managerial element. However, it could be debated that marketing needs management of the process in order for it to be both effective and efficient.

◆ Also in the second definition the word 'freely' is introduced. Marketing involves an exchange of one form or another. This can be an exchange of a product for money. Equally it could be an exchange of an emotional feeling (for instance, a thank you) for a donation to a charity, or a huge hug when we give a gift to a loved one.

◆ In the second definition Kotler has also introduced the word 'service'. While an early focus on marketing was driven by 'products', the last 30 years especially have witnessed a dramatic rise in service-oriented business, covering everything from travel companies to supermarkets. Thus 'service' is a key ingredient in marketing operations, even within a mainly product-based business. This is an element that recurs throughout this text.

Now compare Kotler's views with those of the AMA. In many ways they are similar, only differing in some of the nomenclature and specifics, such as pricing. However, it could be argued that the AMA's definition is more financially focused in terms of transactions.

In the 1960s the AMA defined marketing as:

The process of planning and executing the conception, pricing, promotion and distribution of ideas, goods and services to create exchanges that satisfy individual and organisational goals.

(AMA 1960)

As Cooke et al. (1992) state, definitions of marketing change as a result of environmental changes, or because our knowledge of the subject improves, or indeed through a combination of these two reasons. Marketing as a subject or discipline is therefore evolving. It is important to comprehend marketing as a dynamic and not a static subject. As we shall see as we journey through this textbook, the elements that comprise the marketing discipline are often in a state of flux due to the fluidity of both the micro and macro environments. (See Chapter 2.) It is how the people involved in marketing handle such environments and experiences that often determines whether a product or service is viable or not, and over what time frame.

This is made clear by a new definition issued by the AMA in 2004 (Keefe 2004):

Marketing is an organizational function and set of processes for creating, communicating and delivering value to customers and for managing customer relationships in a way that benefits both the organization and the stakeholder.

While there is still an emphasis on process – that is fundamental to marketing – we now see the use of the words 'value', 'managing customer relationships' and 'stakeholders' being brought to centre stage. These are issues that are reflected throughout this text.

Equally, as Mercer (1997) contends:

Marketing is the *one* (our italics) fundamental activity undertaken by *all* organizations. For most of them it is also the most important contributor to their success or failure.

Mercer (1997) also suggests that marketing is:

Both a relationship with the customer, based upon a series of transactions which, over time, should result in mutual benefit, and a parallel dialogue between you and the customer(s), which communicates the information necessary to define the relationship.

There are several key elements to Mercer's description which define the interaction between customer (buyer) and supplier (seller) as 'complex'. This complexity has often been overlooked.

Relationships

These must be seen as two-directional, not just purely seller to buyer, but also buyer to seller. The seller must understand the needs and wants of the buyer in order to deliver a suitable product and/or service.

Transactions

Traditionally writers have considered transactions purely in terms of the exchange of money for a product. This is a *tangible* transaction: something solid changes hands. Thus there was a view that definitions containing the word 'transaction' were not applicable to not-for-profit organisations, such as charities, as the transactions they dealt in were intangible. However a transaction does not have to include money for a physical product or service: it can equally take place within a charitable environment. For instance, if a person donates 100 euros to a children's charity, three parties benefit from that donation:

◆ the child who receives the direct benefit of the donation

◆ the charity in terms of raising donations and its profile

◆ the individual who donates the 100 euros, whose element of the transaction is the psychological good he or she feels, and the belief that he or she has contributed to helping to provide a child with a better life.

Time

Mercer (1997) refers to 'a series of transactions which, over time, should result in mutual benefit'. The time element could be construed in several ways.

Some transactions take place within a very short time frame. For example, a commuter buying a newspaper from a street corner vendor on his or her way to work is engaged in a quick transaction. Others do not. For example, an individual may want to purchase a product or donate to a charity. He or she is short of funds and unable to do so right away, but intends to do so later, perhaps in a week or a month. One important issue here is the need for the organisation to maintain a dialogue with the prospective customer (see below).

Mercer's statement comes into its own when the buyer and seller develop a relationship. Continual transactions – for example, regular visits to a particular restaurant – can deepen the relationship between the staff/owner and the customer. The mutual benefit derived can be a mixture of:

◆ revenue for the restaurant – not only from the customer but also from the customer's friends (to whom he or she recommends it)

◆ loyalty from the customer in the form of continuing support

◆ the food and ambience that the customer enjoys, and his or her personal feeling of 'reward' for dining at that restaurant.

Dialogue

There must be a dialogue between the buyer and the supplier. This can take two forms.

Supplier to buyer

This is usually in the form of marketing communications such as advertising and public relations. This is where the supplier communicates and promotes the features and benefits of the product or service.

Buyer to supplier

This is where buyers either directly or indirectly state their personal needs and wants. A customer may communicate directly with a company through marketing research, where the company seeks feedback on specific marketing issues. Alternatively, the customer may have an indirect dialogue with the company by switching brands. This indirect dialogue can be seen as informing the company that 'something is wrong with the product'. This 'problem' could be price, quality, accessibility or a combination of factors.

We have looked at a few definitions of marketing, but there are significantly more. McDonald (2002), for example, cites some 30 definitions. Virtually everyone who has written on the subject of marketing has probably put forward his or her own definition in one way or another. So as for many other disciplines, there is no absolute definition. The definitions given vary to a greater or lesser extent, depending on circumstances, attitudes and the time at which they were conceived. At the end of this chapter we briefly consider the future of this discipline called 'marketing'. While it will continue to affect our lives into the distant future, what we call it and how we define it may be different from the terms we use now.

■ The marketer: alchemist, magician, sorcerer and medicine man[1]

As we have seen from the brief examples earlier in this chapter, marketing is universal. However, is it an art or a science? Perhaps marketing is more like sorcery. Think of a sorcerer collecting ingredients from different sources and mixing them into a potion, accompanied with the magical effect of a flash of light and the illusion to follow. To some extent this fits with Culliton's vision of a marketer as a 'mixer of ingredients' (a view we consider fully in a later chapter). Of course sorcerers are more mythical than real, but if we stay with this myth it may help to dispel some of the myths surrounding 'marketing'.

Though mythical, sorcerers were far from perfect. Not all their potions and spells succeeded. When they tried to cure diseases, the patient often died through severe poisoning – and the fate of the sorcerer was anyone's guess. Perhaps the same could be said of alchemists. Alchemy was the medieval dream of using a 'philosopher's stone' to change base metals like iron and lead into gold. It was a combination of chemistry, astrology, philosophy and mysticism, and took hold not only in Europe but in India and China too. No base metal was ever transmuted into gold, but plenty of people spent their lives searching for the formula.

So what has this to do with marketing? In reality a great deal.

Let's consider a Disney movie for a moment. In 1940 the Disney Organization made a movie that has stood the test of time, and remains one of the best-animated movies ever created – *Fantasia*. The movie is a series of vignettes involving animated characters with their actions set to classical music. In one sequence Mickey Mouse™ is a Sorcerer's Apprentice who decides to find another solution to filling the well other than his carrying buckets of water. Through magic he replicates a broom many times over and provides the replicants with arms and hands to carry the buckets. Having given the command to the brooms to fill the well he promptly falls asleep only to be woken by the flow of running water. The well has been filled to overflowing and poor Mickey, now awake, doesn't know how to stop the brooms filling the overflowing well. Panic sets in, but worse is to come as the Sorcerer returns home to see mayhem. With one wave of the hand calm is restored except for a bedraggled apprentice.

In the section heading 'medicine man' was included. There is some link to alchemists here in that many were also considered healers, most notable being Paracelsus.[2] Although medicine men can be associated with native North Americans, the native tribes of South America, Australia's aborigines and African tribes, there is also an association with the charlatans who preached to communities in Victorian England and the emerging townships of 18th and 19th-century North America. These 'medicine men' pronounced that they 'held in their hands a bottle that contained the elixir of life'. At best it was a rough alcohol, at worst it was a poisonous concoction that could lead to an untimely and painful death. Indeed many were simply known as 'snake-oil merchants' doing little to promote the individual seller or merchant in the then 'Wild West'.

So what has any of this got to do with marketing? I can see four separate, but linked, ways in which an analogy can be made.

1   Companies spend billions of dollars on marketing campaigns that either help to sell their goods or services, or do not. The literature is full of companies that have implemented marketing campaigns which for one reason or another have failed. Therefore some of or all of the ingredients in this marketing potion were wrong, or incorrectly mixed.

2   Those with *some* knowledge of marketing do not always have enough knowledge to deal with specific situations and the complications that can ensue. It is sometimes claimed that if you can market cars you can market cosmetics – it's all the same. This is a myth. An understanding of marketing principles is only the start. Then you need to understand the product or service you are marketing, not just in broad terms but in depth. In the movie *Fantasia*, Mickey as the apprentice had a basic understanding of the magician's craft – but not sufficient to achieve what he set out to accomplish, hence the debacle at the end. Marketing comprises a series of techniques or tactics that can be engaged as a part of an overall marketing strategy. This, in turn, feeds into the corporate strategy. For a marketing strategy to be successful the marketer must understand what tactics to use, when and when not to use them, and in what proportion to use them and for how long. It is a skill that is developed over time.

3   Marketers need to have a grip on reality. Research conducted at Cranfield University in the United Kingdom by McDonald (2003) suggests that marketers, consultants and academics have failed to understand the real dynamics of the marketplace. McDonald (2003) found that a significant number of senior marketing practitioners revealed a depressing 'lack of knowledge about the financial impact of marketing expenditure'. He also contends that many companies fail to integrate marketing within corporate strategy decision making, and to measure marketing performance (for example, the link between customer retention and profitability).

4   Marketing is not a cure for all ills. It. For instance, it cannot sell a product or service for which there is no market. It cannot turn around the fortunes of a business that has no markets, no real product or an unsafe product, any more than a government that has continually lied to people can use spin to keep its majority in a democracy. Thus marketers cannot be medicine men who turn a failed product or service into an overwhelming success, no matter how much they believe they can, or how cleverly they manipulate their clients and the public at large. As with the snake oil merchants, the game will unravel, with disastrous consequences for all parties.

Earlier in this chapter a statement was made that marketing is neither a science nor an art. In fact it is a hybrid drawing upon a diverse range of disciplines. Purists would disagree with this view and suggest that it is really a science or an art. However, if you consider the range of disciplines that marketing draws upon, it can really only be classed as a hybrid. Those less disposed to such a description may call marketing a 'thief in the night who steals ideas from other disciplines'. Whichever view you are predisposed to take, remember that it is a 'potion' that cannot cure all ills. Many marketers have believed that they can build a brand in such a way as to gain and sustain competitive advantage, only to see it falter and fail. Equally, organisations have failed to harness the possibilities that marketing may be able to deliver, to in turn falter and fail.

Therefore marketing must be viewed objectively, and a course in marketing does not make a marketer. It is experience, and the knowledge gained from that experience, that makes for a potentially more objective and thus 'successful' marketer.

■ Marketing as an organisational function

While marketing is central to most organisations, it does not stand alone. Figure 1.5 shows a typical arrangement of functional units within an organisation. Each unit has separate functions, procedures and staff, but they are also integrated within the organisation as a whole.

Marketing cannot operate without finance, operations, HRM and other functions within an organisation. Table 1.1 illustrates the linkage between Marketing and other functional units within the organisation.

When marketing works effectively in concert with other functional units, the organisation has an opportunity to create an efficient corporate strategy. Unfortunately, though, many organisations operate in a manner that pays only lip service to functional integration. The organisation might survive in the short term, but its

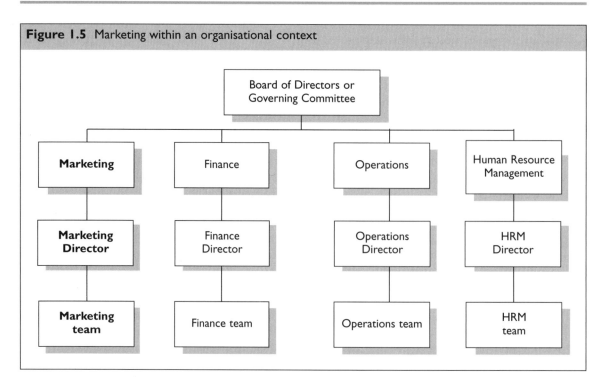

Figure 1.5 Marketing within an organisational context

longer-term future could be in jeopardy, as this is an inefficient use of valuable internal resources. Business history is littered with examples of companies that were once powerful but have since gone bankrupt, or have been acquired and merged into other businesses. In many cases their collapse has been caused by a lack of functional integration and a dynamic and sound corporate strategy.

Who is engaged in marketing?

It would probably be very difficult to find a group or organisation that is not, in some way or another, engaged in marketing. Even tribes within remote jungles often engage in trade through barter. They are 'selling' and exchanging produce to gain a mutual benefit.

Table 1.2 outlines the various groups involved in marketing. The objective here is to consider the vast array of organisations involved in marketing operations, and the groups to which they market. B2C and B2B are widely acknowledged abbreviations, but the other abbreviations given are less well established.

As you can see from the table, every one of us,

in both our working and private lives, has a direct or indirect link to marketing activity. We might take it for granted, but it is with us all our waking lives.

Marketing now and tomorrow: current and future trends

Initially it may seem out of place to comment on future trends towards the end of the first chapter. However, in attempting to understand what marketing is, we need to consider and analyse where marketing is positioned today, and where it may be positioned in the future. While there are numerous industry watchers, in the main the focus of investigation has been the work of the Marketing Science Institute (MSI). In its research it has outlined the key developments and research topics over a ten-year period (see Table 1.3). Many of the issues raised in the MSI research are discussed in this text. However, it is worth briefly considering what might be the 'hot' marketing topics over the next years or so.

Table 1.1 Marketing relationships	
Marketing's relationship with	**Description/comment**
Accounting & Finance	Provides the finance, maintains bank accounts and advises budget preparation. Allocates the funds for marketing activities.
Operations	Marketing works with operations to meet customer needs and wants. The marketing department needs to sell to the quantity of products that can be realistically produced by operations.
Human Resource Management	Develops a Human Resource Strategy for the organisation. Involved in the recruitment of suitable staff (all levels) to work within the marketing department. The instigation of appropriate structures and operational procedures including those legally enforceable such as working hours directives (European Union).
Facilities	This unit provides the resources that enable organisations to function: for example, stationery and other consumables, computers, furniture, telephones and cleaning.

2004–14?

It is easy to speculate; that is part of the fun. So here is some blue-sky thinking for the future:

◆ There will be stronger links between marketing and strategy. It will be the real strategic thinkers who will be able to leverage products or services into the marketplace. Indeed the marketplace may increasingly be looked upon as a battlespace where companies compete for market share.

◆ Competitive sustainability will become increasingly hard to maintain within a global business environment. More of the developing nations will attain developed status, and have the products and services to compete with established companies and brands head to head. The major brands of the future might be not American or European, but Indian, African and Chinese. China-based companies have already created several major brands.

◆ The marketing mix and relationship marketing will combine to form a new approach to how companies and organisations relate to their customers.

◆ Information will be the key to success in the competitive world of the future. Thus compet-

itive intelligence and marketing research will form the platform for the development of new marketing information systems, incorporating real-time analysis.

◆ Computing power will increase, and lead to more embedded systems within the home and office that act on behalf of customers. For instance, remote systems will order products and services automatically. Thus will marketing messages need to be directed to the home computer system rather than the home owner? Will customers use home computers to remove the marketing clutter from their lives?

◆ The World Wide Web and the Internet will grow – but what form will they take, how will we interact with them, and on what scale? Whatever the answers, companies will need to be both proactive and reactive to meet the needs of customers working and living in cyberspace.

◆ Measurement will be critical to truly understanding success or failure. Computer systems will drive the mathematics to interpret real-time movements in products and services.

◆ Customers will seek deliveries at times that suit them. While some companies are already providing such services, not all companies have realised that customers will switch

Table 1.2 Groups involved in marketing

Group	Abbreviation	Description/comment
Business to consumer	B2C	A business (an individual or a multinational company) markets a product or service directly to the consumer – the end user. For example, cruise lines market a Caribbean cruise to potential and current consumers.
Business to business	B2B	Businesses market directly to other businesses. For example, food suppliers market their produce to a cruise line, a hair care company supplies a hairdresser with shampoos and conditioners, or an engine manufacturer supplies a jet engine to a aircraft manufacturer.
Business to employees	B2E	This is also known as internal marketing. Here the organisation is marketing, for example ideas, new practices or a restructuring, to its employees. While not all the elements of the marketing mix (see Chapter 8) are used, key fundamentals such as promotion will be.
Business to government	B2G	This can be approached from two angles. First, a business or an industry could lobby government to adopt or amend a piece of legislation (see Chapter 10 on Promotion). Second, a business can market its products or services directly to government. This covers everything from office furniture to the contract to build the latest nuclear-powered aircraft carrier.
Business to non-governmental organisations	B2NGO	Companies market special facilities and equipment to NGOs, especially for disaster relief: for instance, medicines, rescue equipment (inflatable boats) and transport (heavy lift aircraft that can transport large quantities of relief supplies into terrain-difficult areas).
Government to business	G2B	Governments market their services to businesses and industry. For example, governments may financially support home-country companies or organisations to attend international exhibitions in order to win orders. Such actions can assist in providing a healthy balance of payments (see Chapter 2, The marketing environment). Equally, governments market to companies in other countries. Both the French and Spanish governments marketed their countries to the Disney Organization when Disney considered building a theme park in Europe. In such cases governments offer incentives such as providing infrastructures (road and rail networks), tax incentives and low-cost land.
Government to people	G2P	Democratically elected governments market their policies to the nation. Such governments usually seek to explain why they have increased personal income tax. For example, by stating that it will be allocated to improve health care for everyone. Equally governments market their national identities, not just to their own people but also other nationalities. This is usually achieved through national tourist boards as a means of persuading people in other countries to visit as tourists.
People to government	P2G	The focus here is a particular aspect of public relations, namely lobbying. In this case interested parties or special interest groups (SIGs) market their cause to government. This is usually aimed at persuading the government to introduce, modify or remove a piece of proposed or actual legislation. Lobbyists can either be individuals or more normally groups (of varying sizes). Recent examples in the UK of such P2G activity have been proposals to lower the consenting age for gay relationships and whether or not fox hunting should be banned.

Table 1.2 continued		
Group	**Abbreviation**	**Description/comment**
People to business	P2B	This can be viewed as lobbying and/or boycotting activities. Customers [individuals and groups (free-forming or organised)] may actively lobby/boycott a business in order to force the business to modify its actions or policies. For example, consumers have boycotted companies such as Benetton, Nestlé and Shell over specific practices.
Government to government	G2G	Governments market to other governments, for example, in support of indigenous companies that are pursuing contracts abroad. Equally, one government may use public relations tactics (see Chapter 10) to lobby another government to reduce barriers to market entry (protectionism).
Non-governmental organisations to business	NGO2B	This is marketing activity that supports good works. An example is UNICEF, the United Nations' fund for the care and welfare of children worldwide. Such organisations will actively market to both businesses and organisations that they believe will help fund their welfare programmes in various countries around the world.
Non-government organisations to consumers or non-government organisations to people	NGO2C or NGO2P	Throughout the year but especially at the time of national disasters NGOs market the need for support from individuals, usually in the form of donations. An example is the earthquake that devastated the ancient city of Bam in Iran on Christmas Day 2003 killing an estimated 30,000 people. NGOs, such as the International Red Cross and UNICEF, immediately issued appeals for donations to help the thousands who had been made homeless.

brands based upon delivery slots. This is because people's time is increasingly limited. Companies that cannot adapt their distribution channels to meet customer demands will not survive.

◆ Customers will seek the best deal for them, so brand switching will increase. Companies thus need to position themselves in the group of brands that customers consider. There will no longer be single brands of choice.

◆ Consumers will seek higher ethical standards from companies and organisations. The scandals of the late 1990s and early 21st century have cost stakeholders significantly, for instance, in stock values, life savings and product–service quality. Organisations that fail to meet higher standards will see increasing shareholder power and boycott action.

◆ Clearly these are major issues. However, perhaps the greatest concern facing humankind is the threat of global warming and global dimming (see Chapter 2). Individuals, companies and governments must consider the reality of this environmental threat, and how they tackle this issue might determine the outcomes of many of the trends suggested above.

These are thoughts based upon current trends. However, as we live in an increasingly turbulent world it is really difficult to predict developments over the next few years. Whatever happens it will be a challenge for marketers, no matter what type of organisation they work in.

■ Chapter summary

This chapter has briefly considered some of the developmental aspects of marketing, the organisation of marketing, who is involved in the marketing function, and possible future trends. It has stated that marketing is an amalgamation of various disciplines, so it is dependent on research and development in many disparate subject areas in order for it to evolve further. Equally, marketers must accept

Figure 1.6

© Jonathan Groucutt

An example of a B2G product. These are specially designed fire-fighting flying boats. They collect water in special tanks as they skim across a lake or sea, then fly over a bush or forest fire releasing the water to dampen the flames. These particular aircraft were in action in Corsica. However, they are operated by fire services (usually government agencies) in various countries around the world.

that they too need to explore other disciplines, not only to further the subject but to see how their organisation will compete in the future.

■ Questions for review and reflection

1   Briefly outline the development of marketing as a subject area for study. Why do you think marketing has taken such a route?

2   Do the definitions illustrated in this chapter reflect how you interact with marketing activity?

3   Debate with a group of fellow students the meaning of marketing, and see if you can construct your own definition.

4   'Everyone is engaged in the marketing process.' Discuss this statement.

5   Why do you think that so much emphasis is placed on the study of marketing within business degree programmes?

6   Various suggestions were put forward as to the future development of marketing. Do you agree with these suggestions? What other directions do you think marketing could take in the future?

7   Do you think the term 'marketing' has a future? This may be a question to reflect on after you have considered the contents of this book.

■ References

American Marketing Association (AMA) (1948) 'Report of the definitions committee', *Journal of Marketing* **13** (October), p. 202.

Figure 1.7

© Jonathan Groucutt

This is a familiar sight in most high streets around the world – an eye-catching store window display. It is an example of B2C marketing.

Table 1.3 Key trends in marketing research according to the MSI

1994–6	1996–8	1998–2000	2000–02	2002–04
Successfully introducing new products	Customers and consumers	Marketing metrics and performance measurement	E-business/ e-commerce/impact of the Internet	Assessing marketing productivity (return on marketing) and marketing metrics
Market orientation	Innovation and new products and markets	Understanding the customer experience	Metrics/measuring marketing performance	Brands and branding
Customer relationships	Information technology and new media	Marketing and the Internet	Branding	Managing customers
Information technology and the information highway	Marketing management organisations and processes	Relationship marketing	Managing customer relationships	Growth, innovation and new products
Marketing engineering and empirical generalization	Global marketing	Managing brands: brand equity, product management	Collecting and using marketing knowledge	Understanding customers
Managerial use of information	Management use of information and market research	Marketing innovation: creating customers, creating new products	New product/ innovation	The role of marketing
Brand equity and product management	Brand equity and product and brand management	Marketing knowledge management	Communications	Collecting, interpreting and using information

Source: Lehmann (2002).

AMA (1960) *Marketing Definitions: A glossary of marketing terms*, Chicago: AMA.

Cooke, E. F., Rayburn, J. M. and Abercrombie, C. L. (1992) 'The history of marketing thought as reflected in the definitions of marketing', *Journal of Marketing – Theory and Practice*, Fall, pp. 10–20.

Cunningham, W. H. and Cunningham, I. (1981) *Marketing: A managerial approach*, Illinois: Irwin.

Eldridge, C. E. (1970) *Marketing for Profit*, London: Macmillan.

Hughes, D. G. (1978) *Marketing Management: A planning approach*, Reading, Mass.: Addison-Wesley.

Keefe, L. M. (2004) 'What is the meaning of "marketing"?' *Marketing News*, 15 September, pp. 17–18.

Kotler, P. (1991) *Marketing Management*, New Jersey: Prentice Hall.

Kotler, P. (2000) *Marketing Management*, Millennium edn, Harlow: Prentice Hall.

Lehmann, D. R. (2002) 'What's on marketers' minds?', *Marketing Management* **11**(6) (November/ December), pp. 16–20.

Mazur, P. (1947) 'Does distribution cost enough?', *Fortune* **36** (November), p. 138.

McDonald. M. (2002) *Marketing Plans: How to prepare them; how to use them*, Oxford: Butterworth-Heinemann.

McDonald. M. (2003) 'Marketing died in the last decade', *Interactive Marketing* **5**(2) (October/

December), pp. 144–59.

McNair, M. P., Brown, M. P., Leighton, D. S. R. and England, W. B. (1957) *Problems in Marketing,* 2nd edn, New York: McGraw-Hill.

Mercer, D. (1997) *New Marketing Practice: Rules for success in a changing world*, London: Penguin.

Oxenfeldt, A. R. (1966) *Executive Action in Marketing*, Belmont: Wadsworth.

Pyle, J. F. (1931) *Marketing Principles*, New York: McGraw-Hill.

Star, S. H., Davis, N. J., Lovelock, C. H. and Shapiro, B. P. (1977) *Problems in Marketing*, New York: McGraw-Hill.

Wren, D. (1979) *The Evolution of Management Thought*, 2nd edn, New York: Ronald Press.

The Marketing Environment

CHAPTER 2

● ● ● ●

Contents

Learning outcomes	19
Introduction	19
Market volatilities and	
chaos theory	20
The marketing	
environment	20
What is the macro	
environment?	21
PESTLE factors	22
Political	22
Economic	28
Societal	31
Legal (regulatory)	34
Environmental–	
ecological	34
Technology	39
Combinations of	
events	42
Reversed issues	42
What is the micro	
environment?	42
Micro factors	42
Suppliers	43
Employees	43
The local community	44
Local government	44
Intermediaries	44
Customers	44
Competitors and	
co-operators	45
Retired employees	45
Trade unions	45
Opinion formers	46
Local regulators	46
Control of micro factors	46
Analysing the	
environment	46
The 'What if?' scenario	48
Chapter summary	48
Questions for review	
and reflection	49
References	49

Learning outcomes

After completing this chapter you should be able to:

▶ outline the terminology used to identify micro and macro environments

▶ critically appraise both the micro and macro environments in which organisations must operate

▶ consider how the macro and micro environments affect all aspects of business, in addition to marketing (you may also want to relate this learning outcome to your other studies)

▶ monitor changes that occur within both the macro and micro environments

▶ debate how environmental scanning could help to predict changes within both the micro and macro environments

▶ consider the validity of scenario analysis within a dynamic global business and market environment.

Introduction

This chapter examines the macro and micro environments in which companies and organisations operate. The understanding of these 'environments' is important in the overall appreciation of how marketing operates within our contemporary and often dynamic world. A critical issue to bear in mind is that these environments are not static; they are in a constant state of fluidity. This is an issue that is often overlooked by both writers and students. By the time you read the mini cases within this chapter, the events they depict may have changed manyfold, and probably dramatically. Thus the mini cases are for illustration, and for you to consider how the situations have changed since I wrote them.

The fluidity of these environments illustrates one of the dilemmas facing organisations (both nationally and globally) today. Organisations must both understand and be able to monitor environments in an attempt to be both proactive and reactive to changing conditions. If an organisation fails to successfully read and understand the dynamics, it may face either a reduced market share, or at the worst total extinction. Such marketplace dynamics are not new. For example, the British shipbuilding industry, proud builders of mighty passenger and battleships during the first half of the 20th century, was virtually extinct by the 1970s. It had failed to analyse the changing dynamics of shipbuilding management and the emergence and/or consolidation of highly skilled European and Far Eastern shipyards. While the United Kingdom maintains a pre-eminence in luxury powerboats, it is unlikely to ever see the resurgence of the heavy shipbuilding industry.

Market volatilities and chaos theory

In the introduction I emphasised the need to consider both the micro and macro environments as fluid and dynamic. During the latter half of the 20th century there was an increasing dynamic within the international business environment. This reached beyond the expansion of companies into globalised entities.

Conflicts have become increasingly globalised. The aftermath of 11 September 2001 has placed the world on a terrorist alert. The terrorist attacks in Bali, Kenya, Madrid and London, the actions of the United States in the Gulf, and its stand-off with both North Korea and Iran over their nuclear power programmes, have increased the volatility within the world's economy. With the ever-increased 'connectivity' between nations, no country or region is immune from the political or economic fallout from such volatility.

Chaos theory explores how small events can have large outcomes (and vice versa). It can be applied to business as well as to the natural environment. A changing geopolitical situation in the Middle East can have an impact (to a greater or lesser degree) on a small farming community in Middle America or the highlands of Scotland. Thus when we consider both the micro and macro environments they should not be considered as either separate from each other or separate from events in other parts of the world.

The mini case on the longshoremen's dispute illustrates how an action within one sector of business or the economy can have both a detrimental and positive effect on business. It all depends in which sector of business the company affected operates. As business acts increasingly globally, the complexity of the interactions between environments will increase. An unrelated incident in one part of the world could cause a range of events – some positive, some negative – in other often unconnected business areas in other parts of the world.

The marketing environment

Business and marketing activities are influenced and controlled by a mixture of external and internal factors. These are often referred to as the *macro* and *micro* environments. Figure 2.1 shows the macro environmental factors feeding into the micro environmental factors. As we progress through this chapter you will see the types of influence the macro environment has over the micro environment. However, it is important to note that the micro environment also feeds back into the macro environment. For instance, both employees and major companies have the power (especially through lobbying and the ballot box) of 'influencing' government activities to a greater or lesser extent. However, in other areas such as extreme weather conditions, micro environmental influencers currently have very little or no power to control extreme weather conditions.

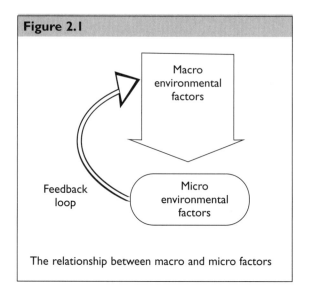

Figure 2.1

Macro environmental factors

Micro environmental factors

Feedback loop

The relationship between macro and micro factors

Mini case 2.1

The longshoremen dispute in West Coast USA

In September 2002 a dispute between management and the longshoremen and women's union over a new contract resulted in a ten-day lockout at 29 international seaports on the West Coast of the United States. In 2002 more than US$300 billion worth of imports and exports flowed through West Coast ports, ranging from industrial machinery and toys to computers, car components, fruit and vegetables. The industrial action resulted in the halting of imports worth approximately US$1 billion per day, and affected a range of manufacturers and consumers in the United States and elsewhere. It risked weakening both US and Asian economies. Although such a lockout would have been disruptive at any time of the year, with the run-up to the November and December Christmas shopping period it was an additional burden on the US economy.

During the lockout inbound ships were forced to anchor off the coast. By the end of the dispute some 200 ships were waiting for off and on-loading.

Since they feared the dispute would continue for some time, Asian car manufacturers with plants in the United States were forced to ship components by air. This added to production costs, as airfreight can cost up to ten times more than shipping. They were also forced to reduce production of some vehicles, and lay off workers over the short term.

The US West coast ports are vital for exports and imports. With many Asian countries only just recovering from recession, the longer the dispute continued, the higher was the risk of their returning to recession. South Korea, for instance, lost an estimated US$354 million worth of trade in the first few days of the lockout.

US trucking companies, many of which were dependent on business from the West Coast ports, were also hit hard by the lockout. Several companies were forced to lay off drivers or give them unpaid leave. This had a direct impact on the drivers' and their families' ability to purchase goods and services, and in turn affected other businesses to a greater or lesser degree.

An upside to this dispute was increased business for Asian airlines. Both Taiwan's China Airlines and South Korea's Asiana increased the number of cargo flights into Los Angeles.

In early October, with the risk of the dispute escalating, the US government announced that President George W. Bush had signed an executive order to create a board of enquiry. Under US law (the 1947 Taft–Hartley Act) this was the first stage in ordering both sides in the dispute back to work. The Act allows for a President with the agreement of a judge to take such action if the dispute presents a threat to the 'national health or safety'.

By mid-October the ports were reopened. However, the build-up of goods on ships in the harbours, in the warehouses and on the docks took weeks to clear. For many businesses and employees this had both a medium and a longer-term effect.

Sources: 'Labour strife disrupts Pacific trade', BBC News Online, 1 October 2002; 'US port dispute hits Asian car firms', BBC News Online, 4 October 2002; 'Bush intervenes in ports row', BBC News Online, 7 October 2002; 'Asia counts cost of US port lockout', BBC News Online, 8 October 2002; 'US industry counts cost of port dispute', BBC News Online, 9 October 2002; 'US ports reopen', BBC News Online, 9 October 2002; 'US dockworkers agree pay deal', BBC News Online, 13 December 2002.

■ What is the macro environment?

This is often described by various mnemonics. For instance:

PEST: politics, economics, society and technology. This is sometimes also presented as STEP.

LE-PEST-C (the LE represents legal and environmental, while the C stands for competitors – thus bringing competitors out of the micro environment into the macro environment).

SPECTACLES (developed by Cartwright 2002, this covers social, political, economic, cultural, technological, aesthetic, customers, legal, environmental and sectoral).

PESTEL/PESTLE.

PESTLE factors

PESTLE is the one adopted for this text for several reasons:

◆ It clearly defines the major external factors that affect organisations both nationally and internationally.

◆ It covers a much wider relevant perspective than a PEST analysis.

◆ It is easy to remember, which is always useful!

◆ The *Oxford English Dictionary* meaning of the word 'pestle' is 'a club-shaped instrument for pounding substances in a mortar (bowl)'. This has some relevance to the effect on business organisations of the PESTLE factors. They can actually grind down a business. Think, for instance, beyond the political factors. If the economic environment is unfavourable, even a company with a good product can face bankruptcy.

Political

This can be subdivided into geopolitical events and national politics.

Geopolitical events

Haven't companies always been powerful?

Geopolitics frames much of what happens within the global community. Geopolitical events can be short-lived or prolonged. Both can and do have an effect on organisations and their ability to market their products and services.

A case in point is the lingering Israel and Palestine conflict. This has seesawed from a form of peace to aggressive hostilities on both sides. Israel is highly dependent on its tourist industry. In 2001 both the Israeli and Palestinian tourism ministers took active steps to promote tourism in their countries. The Israeli Ministry of Tourism aimed to take measures to overcome misconceptions amongst potential and actual travellers (Rosci 2001). These measures included special complimentary 'impression' tours amongst American opinion formers, and deep discounts to tour operators and travel agents. The largest visitor group to Israel is Americans,

with some 48 per cent becoming repeat visitors (Rosci 2001).

However, then followed a combination of events:

◆ the terrorist attack on the World Trade Center

◆ the increasing aggression since the 2000 al-Aqsa intifada or uprising, with Palestinian suicide bombers and the threat of an all-out war from Israel

◆ wider terrorist threats against Americans, Europeans and Australians.

These have drastically reduced the tourist business. Until 2002 no tourist had been killed in the conflict, then a Scottish tourist was a victim of a suicide bus bomber. In 2002 alone some 24 hotels closed in Israel because of the ongoing hostilities. Who knows when they will reopen? In 2003 the intifada resumed, and the then President of Palestine, Yasser Arafat, was unable to control the suicide bombers. In 2004 Arafat, the terrorist turned peacemaker, died, making way for a new leader.

Both Israel and Palestine need their tourist industries, yet while there is conflict it is unlikely, in the short term at least, that there will be the necessary growth and development. This will have a further impact on the economic stability of both countries.

Trading alliances

For centuries there have been trading blocs within which countries form alliances for both trade and military reasons (see Table 2.1). Currently the largest is the European Union, which has 25 Member States and may grow still larger. Such alliances provide for favourable trading status between member nations, but they can be detrimental to non-members who face crippling barriers to entry for their goods.

The World Trade Organization (WTO) has sought to improve the balance between the poor and richer nations through global trade liberalisation, therefore providing a mechanism through which states that do not belong to trading blocs can trade favourably with member states. This is a far from perfect system, though, and has been much

Table 2.1 The main global trading groups

Trading group	Countries
European Union	Member states in 2005: Austria, Belgium, Cyprus, Czech Republic, Denmark, Estonia, Finland, France, Germany, Greece, Hungary, Ireland, Italy, Latvia, Lithuania, Luxembourg, Malta, Poland, Portugal, Slovakia, Slovenia, Spain, Sweden, the Netherlands and the United Kingdom. Turkey, whose membership application has been heavily promoted by the United States and the United Kingdom, engaged in talks with the European Commission during 2004. However it may not be eligible to join until 2007 at the earliest. Bulgaria and Romania may also be eligible to join in 2007. There are also discussions with Croatia. GNP: est. US$6.6 trillion. Population approx. 418 million (2004 figures).
North American Free Trade Area (NAFTA)	United States, Canada and Mexico. GNP: est. US$8.6 trillion (2001). Population approx. 390 million.
Mercosur	Argentina, Brazil and Paraguay. GNP: est. US $1.2 trillion (2001). Population approx. 204 million.
Association of South East Asian Nations (ASEAN Free Trade Area)	Brunei, Cambodia, Indonesia, Laos, Malaysia, Myanmar, the Philippines, Singapore, Thailand and Vietnam. GNP: est. US$632 billion (2001). Population approx. 481 million.
Asia Pacific Economic Co-operation (APEC)	Australia, Brunei, Canada, Chile, China, Hong Kong, Indonesia, Japan, Malaysia, Mexico, New Zealand, Papua New Guinea, the Philippines, Singapore, South Korea, Thailand and the United States.
Central American Common Market	Costa Rica, El Salvador, Guatemala, Honduras, Nicaragua and Panama.
Caribbean Community and Common Market (CARICOM)	Antigua and Barbuda, the Bahamas (not currently a member of the Common Market), Barbados, Belize, Dominica, Grenada, Guyana, Jamaica, Montserrat, St Christopher-Nevis, St Lucia, St Vincent and Grenadines, Suriname and Trinidad-Tobago. The British Virgin Islands and Caicos Islands are Associate Members.
Andean Common Market (ANCOM)	Bolivia, Colombia, Ecuador, Peru and Venezuela.
Economic Community of West Africa (ECOWAS)	Benin, Burkina Faso, Cape Verde, the Gambia, Ghana, Guinea, Guinea-Bissau, the Ivory Coast, Liberia, Mali, Mauritania, Niger, Nigeria, Senegal, Sierra Leone and Togo. Population approx.160 million.
Gulf Co-operation States (GCC)	Bahrain, Kuwait, Oman, Qatar, Saudi Arabia and the United Arab Emirates.
European Free Trade Association (EFTA)	Iceland, Liechtenstein, Norway and Switzerland. It has expanded its relationship with non-European Union States, signing free trade agreements with Turkey (1991), Israel, Poland and Romania (1992), Bulgaria, Hungary, the Czech Republic and Slovakia (1993) and Estonia, Latvia, Lithuania and Slovenia (1995).
Arab Free Trade Zone	In January 2003 Jordan, Egypt, Tunisia and Morocco signed a Free Trade Zone agreement. This is seen as a step towards a Euro-Mediterranean process where EU and Arab countries will create a Free Trade Zone by 2010 that incorporates all 27 countries.

Mini case 2.2

The boycott of US cola drinks

In 2003 a growing boycott of American products in the Middle East provided an impetus for several Islamic-originated cola drinks. The Iranian Zamzam-Cola was introduced as a replacement for US-manufactured soft drinks during the 1979 Iranian revolution. In 2002 the market for Zamzam-Cola, named after the scared spring in Mecca, increased to include Bahrain, Saudi Arabia, Pakistan and some African countries. According to AFP News Agency reports, the growing boycott of US products was in protest at Washington's support for Israel in its dispute with the Palestinians. US product exports to Saudi Arabia declined by more than 40 per cent in the first three months of 2002 alone.

Zamzam-Cola was not the only Muslim-focused cola brand to enter the market. In late 2002 French entrepreneur Tawfik Mathlouthi launched Mecca Cola, and by early 2003 was exporting it to Britain, Germany, Belgium, Italy and Spain. By January 2003 the company had sold over two million 1.5 litre bottles of cola, and reported increasing demand for the product.

In February 2003 a British company – Qibla Cola – entered the market with regular and diet colas. It used the catch line 'liberate your taste'. Qibla is named after the Arabic word for the direction of Mecca. The aim of the company is to market the cola to Muslim communities in major UK cities including London, Birmingham, Manchester, Bradford and Glasgow.

Although switching brands may not have a significant impact on major brands in the short term, the longer-term effect is unknown. For instance, the longer US troops are stationed in Iraq, the potentially greater the impact of boycotts will be on companies that are heavily promoted as 'American'.

Sources: 'Islamic cola benefits from boycott', BBC News Online, 21 May 2002; 'Islamic cola selling well in Saudi', BBC News Online, 21 August 2002. 'Mecca Cola challenges US rival', BBC News Online, 8 January 2003; 'Islamic cola launched in the UK', BBC News Online, 4 February 2003.

Figure 2.2

© Mecca Cola®

A display of 1.5 litre bottles of Mecca Cola with both English and Arabic text.

debated among trade liberalisation pressure groups.

Geopolitical perceptions have a societal influence as well. International concern at the United States's decision to invade Iraq has led to countries and individuals boycotting US products and services. As the mini case exemplifies, when groups of people feel disenfranchised by another group they may seek economic alternatives. Although the individual power to switch brands may not financially damage major brands (in the short run, at least), it does none the less send a clear signal of dissatisfaction. Companies that fail to address increasing dissatisfaction among their customer base risk their long-term health.

Political risk

As Czinkota and Ronkainen (1995) state, there is a degree of political risk within all nations, even those considered the most stable. It should also be borne in mind that the assessment of political risk within a nation can, and does, vary over time.

Mini case 2.3

Political pressure

In February–March 2003 President George W. Bush's administration sought support for tough United Nations resolutions against Iraq. The administration's goal was to win the majority of votes on the Security Council, to place pressure on France and Russia to not use their vetoes. In order to gain the 'onside' vote the Bush administration leveraged political and diplomatic pressure on smaller, often impoverished developing nations. If they voted with the United States and Britain in favour of tough resolutions, substantial aid and debt relief packages would be forthcoming. If not, the Bush administration's memory would 'be long'. In other words there would be no relief packages or trade deals. In fact, where trade was concerned there could be 'hidden' restrictions: non-tariff barriers such as excessive bureaucracy. Such action would directly impact on exports from these countries.

Such an approach to 'diplomacy' creates ethical dilemmas for the small nations: they can either vote against the resolution (if they think that is the right course of action) and face the consequences, or vote for the resolution to obtain the aid and trade packages. The choice was beyond the control of companies in these countries that were attempting to export their products to the wider marketplace. Of course, major countries such as France and Germany which were not in favour of the Bush administration's political posturing could have provided alternative aid and trade agreements to the developing nations.

In the end the United States and the United Kingdom did not table a resolution, deciding that if it were to be rejected (the general view of members of the Security Council), they would take their own action. On 17 March the United States launched a missile attack on Iraq.

Mini case 2.4

War in Iraq

In March 2003 American and British forces invaded Iraq to 'neutralise' the threat of the weapons of mass destruction that the two governments believed Iraq held. Moreover, the British government alleged that these could be deployed in 45 minutes. However, there was confusion over whether these were battlefield weapons (which could not directly threaten the United Kingdom) or long-range weapons. This was a major oversight of government and senior defence officials. Since then it has been proved that there were no weapons of mass destruction, and that Iraq was neither an immediate threat to its neighbours nor a threat to countries such as Britain.

Although the overwhelming force the United States and its allies used meant the war was 'won' and declared over in July 2003, the peace has been much harder to gain. At the time of writing (early 2005), coalition forces (led by the United States and Britain) are still involved in major combat roles. Dissonant Iraqi and external forces are engaged in guerrilla activities that result in the death of both coalition forces and civilians. Car bombs, insurgency activities and kidnapping are almost daily occurrences. This has resulted in more military personnel and civilians being killed than during the actual invasion and occupation of Iraq. No one, it seems, can escape the turmoil and murder that has ensued. United Nation officials and humanitarian relief workers have been among the many casualties of this appalling conflict.

This ongoing conflict has a much wider implication for global society. The disenfranchised and disenchanted among the young and old alike have used, and probably will continue to use, it as their rallying cry against the West and Western interests. The political, economic and societal implications of such activity are significant for the global village. They are not confined to the brutality of terrorism and the murder of civilians: they involve the potential downfall of the Western economic structure. In this scenario everyone gets typecast in the same unjust mould.

However, in reality the vast majority of Muslims who believe in the true teachings of Mohammed are non-violent and want peace to prevail. They want to trade with all nations. Equally, many Westerners want to be at peace with all other nations and to trade.

In January 2005 elections took place across Iraq. Although various groups called for a boycott it is estimated that around 60 per cent of the population participated in the first democratic elections in the country for some 50 years.

Peace in Iraq will arrive. However, it may take several years to rebuild trust in order to gain that peace. Will the rest of the world see an economic decline in the meantime as a result? The sheer scale of the military and rebuilding costs will have an impact, but to what extent? This is but one of many, often baffling, questions that arise from the invasion of Iraq.

Source: P. Reynolds, 'CIA adds to gloom over Iraq', BBC News Online, 7 December 2004.

Table 2.2 Forms of political risk

Form of political risk	Description
Expropriation	The host government takes control of the foreign investor's business. Governments have found this appealing in the past, as it demonstrates nationalism and the transference of wealth to the host country. The host government offers compensation to the foreign company. However, this is usually substantially less than the value of the business. Many governments have moved away from such activity as it discourages foreign direct investment over the longer term, and this investment is likely to be necessary for longer-term economic security.
Confiscation	As with expropriation this is the transference of wealth from the foreign company to the host government. The difference is that the host government does not pay any compensation. Again, governments have become wary of using such harsh tactics as they discourage foreign companies and governments from investing in the country. However, the consequences of confiscation do not always lead to a positive outcome for the host government. This is borne out by a relatively recent example, the land reforms instituted by President Robert Mugabe in Zimbabwe in 2000. All land owned by white farmers (both individuals and groups) was confiscated and handed over to former war veterans. Unfortunately the war veterans had little or no experience of farming. The land fell into disrepair and millions faced starvation.
Domestication	The objective here is for the host government to acquire some control over the foreign investment. This can be achieved through a partial transfer of ownership, some local management responsibility, the purchasing of locally produced components and/or the retention of a proportion of the company's profits within the host country. If, for example, the locally produced components are of poor quality, this can have a detrimental effect on the company's overall quality performance. Equally, if local managers are poorly qualified there can be a breakdown in efficiencies and communication. Some of these problems or issues can be overcome; however there are clearly financial and resource implications.
Revolution, civil wars and civil unrest	Growing political unrest can lead to revolutions and the forced removal of the government of the day. Revolutions can be either peaceful acts of power transference or bloody coups. An example of the former is the fall of the Berlin Wall and the reunification of East and West Germany. A bloody coup occurred in Sierra Leone, which became a politically instable region just after independence in 1961, although it was the 1990s that witnessed the perhaps most extreme violence, descending into genocide. Action by several countries and the United Nations finally brought a decade of civil war to an end in 2002, with UN Peacekeepers disarming thousands of rebels and militia. Now the country must face the struggle of reconstruction. Several African countries have been ravaged by years of bloodshed as a result of warring factions. These countries have witnessed genocide, political and economic instability. It may take generations before peace is restored. However within the time it takes to gain peace many of these countries will have slipped further back economically, negatively affecting both the people and businesses.
Terrorism	Even before the tragic events of 11 September 2001, terrorism was widespread throughout the world. Some terrorist groups focused their attention on political leaders and government institutions and facilities. Others concentrated on various public institutions while also targeting foreign companies, including their personnel. The increase in global terrorism, through radical groups such as al Qaeda and others, will have a profound effect on companies, organisations and ordinary consumers for many years to come.
Strikes	While the ability to strike is viewed in many countries as a legal right and freedom, strikes can, if prolonged, be detrimental to companies not directly involved, for instance component suppliers. Reflect back to the longshoremen mini case (page 21).

Mini case 2.5

Political and financial unrest in Venezuela, 2003

In December 2002 a national strike in Venezuela lead to the virtual collapse of political institutions and the economy. Opposition leaders, right-wing business groups and unions called a strike in an attempt to force President Chavez to call early elections. They accused him of concentrating power and pushing the country into an economic recession.

The general strike paralysed the country for 63 days. Faced with potential bankruptcy, several private businesses, restaurants and stores reopened for business. The strike at the State-owned oil company had the most devastating effect on the country's economy. To support the economy the government suspended all currency exchange in order to prevent a banking crisis. However, the estimated cost of the strike in oil exports alone was placed at US$4 billion. When the strike faltered the government moved to arrest the leaders, and some 12000 workers were sacked, mainly from the State-owned oil company.

During the strike many foreign companies, including Microsoft and Ford, closed their offices and repatriated their staff. In such instable political and economic environments, companies must consider not only the short-term but the long-term consequences of the turmoil.

Sources: 'Firms flee Venezuela's violence', BBC News Online, 22 January 2003; 'Venezuelan strike falters', BBC News Online, 28 January 2003; 'Chavez claims strike victory', BBC News Online, 3 February 2003; 'Fresh Venezuela strike arrests', BBC News Online, 27 February 2003.

Mini case 2.6

Nestlé and Ethiopia

In 1975 the communist military government of Ethiopia confiscated and then nationalised a meat processing company owned by the German Schweiesfurth Group, a subsidiary of Nestlé. No compensation was paid to either Nestlé or its German subsidiary. In 1998 the Ethiopian government sold the company to a local private business for approximately US$8.7 million. Through an Ethiopian lawyer the subsidiary of Nestlé Germany raised the issue of compensation, and initial discussions focused on the figure of US$6 million. As Ethiopia is one of the poorest countries in Africa, this compensation claim led to widespread condemnation by charities such as Oxfam in the United Kingdom, and a media attack on Nestlé.

The World Bank's Multilateral Investment Guarantee Agency brokered talks between Nestlé Germany and the Ethiopian government. On 24 January 2003 representatives of Nestlé and the Ethiopian government signed an agreement reimbursing the company with approximately US$1.5 million. All the proceeds were donated to humanitarian organisations working with the Ethiopian government in providing emergency food aid. Additionally, Nestlé entered into negotiations with the Ethiopian government to explore ways to create longer-term food security and access to water.

This mini case highlights the problems facing companies that have had their assets confiscated by host governments. In the majority of cases this happens in developing or poor nations without the financial and economic power of developed nations. However, it can be argued that companies have a legal right to compensation.

On 23 December 2002 Peter Brabeck, Nestlé SA's CEO, wrote:

> We do think it's important for the long-term welfare of the people of Africa that their governments demonstrate a capacity to comply with international law, but we are not interested in taking money from the country of Ethiopia when it is in such desperate state of human need.
>
> We will devote any money received from this settlement to both public and private efforts to relieve hunger in Ethiopia. This will take the form of both short-term relief aid and longer-term food security.

Sources: 'Nestlé in Ethiopia compensation row', BBC News Online, 18 December 2002; 'Nestlé offers Ethiopia refund deal', BBC News Online, 20 December 2002; 'Nestlé and Ethiopia: a statement by Nestlé CEO Peter Brabeck', Nestlé news release, 23 December 2002; 'Nestlé and Ethiopian government reach settlement', Nestlé news release, 24 January 2003; 'Nestlé and Ethiopia settle dispute', BBC News Online, 24 January 2003.

Mini case 2.7

Diageo and national sensitivities

In December 2002 Diageo, the world's largest alcoholic drinks company, ran a poster campaign on the London Underground's 70-plus stations for its vodka brand Smirnoff Ice. The advertisement showed a half-wrapped Christmas gift with a label that said:

> WARNING. This gift will break down on Christmas morning. Replacement parts available from service centre. Box No 260 Taiwan. Allow 365 working days for delivery.

The advertisement was making fun of Taiwan's past reputation as a producer of poor-quality plastic goods. It has since shed that reputation, and worked hard to build an international reputation for the production of high-quality goods such as laptops, carbon fibre bicycles and microchips.

The Taiwanese Parliament and government did not see the amusing side. Legislator Shen Chih-hwei of the People First Party criticised the advertisements as 'hurting others without benefiting itself', and setting back Taiwan's years of efforts to establish the reputation of its products. In addition to seeking compensation from Diageo, she urged a public boycott of the company's products.

On Friday 10 January 2003 the Taiwanese Parliament voted 115–100 to pass a resolution demanding that the government suspend the sale of all Diageo's drinks in Taiwan for one year, and seek compensation for the damage to Taiwan's reputation. Parliament officials stated that the advertisement portrayed Taiwan as a maker of shoddy goods with poor after-sales service. However, the ruling was non-binding and consumers were left to decide for themselves whether to boycott the company's products or not.

Diageo's brands Johnnie Walker Red and Black Label whiskies are very popular in Taiwan, accounting for approximately 50 per cent of local whisky sales.

Diageo withdrew the advertisement, apologised in both the United Kingdom and Taiwan for the offence that had been caused, and placed advertisements in the local media expressing its deep regret. In London three senior executives of Diageo visited Taiwan's representative in Britain, Tien Hung-mao, to apologise.

This type of ban is generally subject to World Trade Organization (WTO) rulings, but a country can impose it while negotiations take place with the WTO and other relevant organisations. Of course, neither the British nor the Taiwanese government wanted a diplomatic argument. There were no open comments by the British government at the time, however there may have been some behind-the-scenes discussions as part of normal diplomatic routine.

Sources: 'British brewery says it's sorry for advert debacle', *Taipei Times*, 29 December 2002; 'Taiwan stops Johnnie Walker in his tracks', *Sydney Morning Herald*, 12 January 2003; 'Today', BBC Radio 4. 14 and 15 January 2003; Damian Grammatricas, 'Taiwan mulls Diageo ban', BBC News Online, 14 January 2003; 'Johnnie Walker not running out', *Taipei Times*, 13 January 2003; 'MOFA seeks apology over British ad', Central New Agency, 24 December 2002; 'Taiwan slur takes fizz out of drinks', CNN.com, 5 February 2003.

Companies must therefore consider the political risks involved in operating within different country environments. These risks can be divided into subsets which are illustrated in Table 2.2.

National politics

Political influence on a national level

Diplomacy is no longer just the preserve of government diplomats. Organisations too must be aware of the diplomatic sensitivities of nations, and international political issues. Failing to understand such sensitivities can be detrimental to the business in both the short and longer term. In mini case 2.7 , a 'humorous' advertisement from the drinks giant Diageo almost led to the collapse of its market in Taiwan.

Economic

The changes in the economic fortunes of countries and regions affect individuals and companies not only within that region but elsewhere too. We are increasingly living within a globalised economy where everyone is to a greater or lesser extent dependent on everyone else. Economic cycles can to some extent be controlled or managed by the diligent use of economic instruments, but these are imprecise and can have negative as well as

Table 2.3 Business and economic cycles

Event	Description
Depression or slump	A severe and often prolonged downturn in the economy. The depression that followed the Wall Street Crash in America in October 1929 lasted for some four years. At the time of the crash some US $75 billion of US industrial capital was wiped out (Thompson 2000). The Great Depression (as it became known) had a global impact, resulting in millions being made unemployed, severe poverty and countless company failures. Businesses that were once market leaders were bankrupted almost overnight. In 1933 US President Franklin D. Roosevelt launched the 'New Deal', a social and economic reform programme that aided America's recovery.
Recovery	An economy that has been in either recession or depression displays the first signs of growth. There is often a perceived 'feel good' factor associated with recovery, as the population and government look forward to an improved future.
Steady growth	Most governments seek steady and effective economic growth. The economy is growing steadily, manufacturing and service industries are successful and the population is both investing and purchasing. The government and/or central bank monitors growth rates and may take marginal actions such as adjusting interest rates, which assist in either growing the economy or reducing consumer spending.
Boom	The economy is now working at almost full capacity. Overall product and service demands are high, as are wages, while unemployment is low. There is, however, a risk of inflation spiralling out of control as wage demands increase. Moreover, there is a risk of the economy overheating as consumers increase both their spending and debt levels. The government or the central bank may use interest rates to control inflationary activity and consumer spending/debt levels.
Recession	A sharp and prolonged slowdown in the rate of growth of gross domestic product (GDP), associated with falling levels of investment, low manufacturing output, depressed business confidence, rising unemployment and an increasing number of business failures. With increasing unemployment there is a reduction in the level of individual spending power. As a result competition increases, as companies battle to sustain their market share. As has been seen in recent history, all social classes are affected by economic recessions to a greater or lesser extent.
Stagnation	The economy is stationary, neither growing nor receding. The Japanese economy suffered stagnation during the later years of the 20th century. It is only since 2004 that the Japanese economy has shown signs of progressing out of this phase.

Source: adapted from Groucutt *et al.* (2004).

positive outcomes. For example, increases in interest rates to control inflation levels affect both rich and poor. While an interest rate increase may reign in some of the uncontrolled spending of the wealthier in society it will also impact upon the needy and poor.

It is not only economic cycles that affect the fortunes of a nation or region. Severe ecological and environmental disasters can virtually bankrupt nations as they struggle to help their surviving population. The tsunami of December 2004 (see page 40) wrought havoc across vast stretches of Southeast Asia's coastline. Islands such as the Maldives which are highly dependent upon tourism for their economic stability may take years to recover.

Business and economic cycles

Table 2.3 briefly outlines the characteristics of the main types of economic or business cycle. Governments and their central banks endeavour to maintain steady economic growth. However, they cannot be fully in control of a national economy within a globalised economic system, since external factors such as recession, war and natural disasters in other regions have an effect. A major slump in the US economy, for instance, can have repercussions for the economies of many nations. If the population of a major economy is not purchasing goods from overseas, the supplier nation will inevitably be affected, though less so if it has other existing markets, or the opportunity to seek out new markets.

As a result it is important for any company (marketing locally, nationally or internationally) to be aware of changing economic conditions.

Inflation and interest rates

Both governments and central banks monitor inflation rates carefully. Their concern is that inflation will spiral out of control, indicated by increasing price rises and a reduced purchasing power for the national currency. (In other words consumers receive less for the value of their individual currency.) This in turn will have an impact on domestic manufacturing and service industries. Countries that have experienced high levels of inflation typically go on to witness economic recession, with high levels of unemployment.

To control inflation, governments and central banks use interest rate changes to reduce the level of consumer spending. This affects people's mortgage payments, credit card bills and daily expenditure. The aim is to reduce their level of expenditure and borrowing, and so reduce the inflationary pressure on the economy.

Reducing inflation is beneficial to the economy. However, during this period of higher interest rates there is increased pressure on retailers and manufacturers to sell their products. The same number of retailers are vying for the reduced spending power of consumers, so retailers use different pricing techniques to influence purchasing. For instance, in the United Kingdom some furniture retailers make special offers of 'no deposit and interest-free credit for six months'.

Those attempting to regulate inflation through the mechanism of interest rates have to be careful that the economy does not stagnate. If the reduction in consumer spending is too great, retailers and manufacturers will suffer. A stagnant economy can also lead to business bankruptcies and massive unemployment.

Taxation systems

Taxation has both economic and political aspects: its rates and limits are determined by governments, using more general political criteria as well as economic criteria. There are two basic forms of taxation, direct and indirect. *Direct taxation* is taxation on earnings: it is generally taken out of weekly wages and monthly salaries at source, so employees receive their pay net of taxation. *Indirect taxation* is taxation on goods and services, like value-added tax in the European Union. Consumers have a choice whether to spend their income on products or services, or save it, so to this extent they have a choice whether to pay indirect taxes.

In most countries displayed retail prices include indirect taxes, so the amount of tax is not immediately apparent to consumers.

Governments also levy special taxes. For example, in countries such as India and Trinidad special taxes are levied on tourists, usually as a surcharge on hotel accommodation.

Income levels

Marketers need to be aware of consumers' levels of disposable income. This is the amount of money available to consumers after they have paid taxes and key items such as mortgage and utility bills, to purchase other products and services. The level of disposable income is affected by the various factors we discussed earlier in this section (the overall health of the economy, inflation, interest rates and taxation levels). When these factors change, the level of disposable income will also change.

Poverty

There is an assumption in some marketing textbooks that everyone across the world is equal, that we all participate in 'high-level' marketing experiences. This could not be further from the truth. It is estimated that almost 50 per cent of the world's population lives on less than US$2.00 per day (Wolfensohn 1998) and nearly a billion people entered the 21st century unable to read or sign their name (UNICEF 1999). Therefore we have to consider the economic challenges that face individuals and countries across the world.

Various governments and politicians are working to help individuals and countries out of the poverty trap. It is hoped that this can be achieved creating an improved life for millions where they can obtain more than the staples of life.

Societal

Hofstede (1980) defines culture as:

> The collective programming of the mind which distinguishes the members of one human group from another.... Culture, in this sense, includes systems of value; and values are among the building blocks of culture.

Doole and Lowe (1999) refine this for the international marketer, stating that culture is:

> The sum total of learned beliefs, values and customs that serve to direct consumer behaviour in a particular country market.

A global economy presents challenges to managers which they do not confront when their operations are constrained within national borders. They must adapt company operations to different nations' legal, political and economic policies, but they must also deal with varying national cultures – the primary values and practices that characterise particular countries – many of which are very different from their personal backgrounds (Doole and Lowe 1999).

Table 2.4 illustrates the different types of attitude or cultural orientation that people display. However, as Hollensen (2001) states, culture is extremely broad and complex, encompassing virtually every aspect of an individual's life. It is important also to recognise that (whether we like it or not) cultures are not static. Like so many other things, cultures undergo continual change, influenced for example by young people who travel and return with new ideas (perhaps from university overseas) and the development of mass communication.

Attitudes to health

Since the mid-1980s there has been increasing concern about the health of people in Western

Table 2.4 Cultural orientations and behaviours

Cultural orientation or direction	Typical behaviour
Parochialism	Having a very narrow view of the world. Often an inability to recognise differences between people of different cultures.
Ethnocentrism	The belief that one's own cultural values and customs are superior to all others. People who are of an ethnocentric orientation believe that others should fit in with their views of the world and business. For example, the same competitive and product–market strategies are applied to all markets. As a result any cultural differences are ignored. This can be considered as *total standardization*.
Polycentrism	Here the focus is on the local environment, and tends to be culturally sensitive. Generally the country subsidiaries of a multinational are free to formulate objectives and plans to meet local market conditions. This can be considered as *total adaptation*.
Regiocentrism	The synthesis of ethnocentrism and polycentrism, this focuses on regions. It is based on the assumption that there are both similarities and differences across cultures that can be merged into regional trans-national strategies. As many cultures converge, companies may well seek to adopt this strategic orientation.
Geocentrism	A further development of regiocentrism, considered on global scale. Here subsidiaries of a global business see themselves as an integral part of that business.

Mini case 2.8

Obesity

One of the major concerns in the United States, and increasingly in Europe too, is obesity in the public at large, and especially the young. In the United States it is estimated that a staggering 54 million adults can be classified as obese: that is, 15 kg or more over the healthy norm. Data for 2002 indicated that in the United Kingdom 8.5 per cent of six year olds and 15 per cent of 15 year olds were obese, three times as many as ten years earlier. If this trend continued, 40 per cent of the population would be obese within a generation.

A survey by the UK children's charity Barnardo's discovered that peer pressure, taste, money and choice affected what children chose to eat. The research suggested that children accepted junk food as their staple school diet. Tam Baillie, Assistant Director of policy at Barnardo's Scotland, stated, 'If we are really serious about making a difference to the food children eat in schools, we have got to start listening to what they have to say, so that we can understand the meaning of food to them.'

The blame for much of the obesity seen today has been directed at fast-food companies such as McDonald's. In 2003 lawsuits were filed against McDonald's in US courts, accusing it of being directly responsible for obesity, and alleging it 'violated New York State's consumer fraud statutes by deliberately misleading consumers into thinking their products were healthy and nutritious'. The court ruled in favour of McDonald's.

Since the late 1990s there has been an increasing movement towards slimming and healthier eating habits. This has resulted in marked criticism of companies such as McDonald's for not supplying 'healthy food'.

In 2004 over 100 of the UK's leading health and consumer groups urged the government to ban junk food advertisements on the basis that they were fuelling the increasing rates of obesity. However, the government was sceptical about the value of a ban. The UK Food and Drink Federation stated:

> Strict codes of practice already exist.... These state that ads should not encourage children to eat or drink frequently throughout the day, condone excessive consumption, or suggest that confectionery or snacks should replace balanced meals.... There are no quick fixes. Any action needs to be based on sound science, and requires government and all stakeholders to work together with a commitment to achieving real results over the long term.

Also in 2004, a documentary *Super Size Me* was aired in US cinemas, in which journalist Morgan Spurlock eats nothing but McDonald's meals for a month. He not only gains 11 kg, he is advised by his doctors to stop, otherwise he could become seriously ill.

Table 2.5 lists the caloric value and fat content of regular and super-sized options. As you can see, a meal consisting of a super-size Cola with fries and a Big Mac™ contains 1302 calories and 44.1 g of fat.

Table 2.5 Calorie and fat content of McDonald's foods

Food item	Calories	Fat (g)
Large fries	412	18
Super-size fries	486	21.2
Large Cola	226	NA
Super-size Cola	323	NA
Big Mac™	493	22.9

When the movie was released in the UK, McDonald's stated that its premise was 'unrealistic', and launched a series of advertisements promoting its food as part of a balanced diet. It claimed it would take an average customer six years to consume the amount of McDonald's food Spurlock had eaten in 30 days. However in response not only to the movie but to changing attitudes to fast food, it also overhauled its menus, removing the super-size options in favour of lower-fat and lower-calorie options which included salad ranges.

With increasing numbers of news reports on the need for healthy eating, and television programmes dedicated to food, exercise and personal make-overs, people are beginning to realise the need for a combination of improved diets and regular exercise. If this trend continues it will have an impact on fast food retailers. Already companies such as McDonald's have revised their menus and, in the United Kingdom, introduced television advertising that promotes 'healthy options'. However will such retailers have to go further? Will there be organic food on the menu? Will hamburgers be significantly reduced in size and cooked differently? Indeed, will hamburgers be sold at all?

Sources: 'Junk food battle hits US schools', BBC News Online, 30 May 2002; 'Court dismisses McDonald's obesity case', BBC News Online, 22 January 2003; 'Obese children "facing pressure"', BBC News Online, 12 February 2004; 'Minister cold on junk food ad ban', BBC News Online, 3 March 2004; 'McDonald's to scrap "supersizing"', BBC News Online, 4 March 2004; S. Evans, 'McDonald's: the journey to health', BBC News Online, 20 April 2004; 'New menu gives lift to McDonald's', BBC News Online, 22 July 2004; 'McDonald's serves up film blitz', BBC News Online, 20 August 2004; 'Supersize debate on fast food film', BBC News Online, 10 September 2004.

countries. In the mid to late 1980s there was a dramatic increase in the production and sale of exercise videos and keep-fit programmes such as movie star *Jane Fonda's Workout*. By the late 20th century the issue was healthy eating, with the focus on the drawbacks of fast food and 'junk food'. By the beginning of the 21st century there was serious discussion about the potential harm of fast food to the young. Indeed, as is illustrated in the next mini case, health officials in many nations were worried about the type of food young people were consuming. The general view was that continuous consumption of fast food is unhealthy and potentially leads to obesity. This had become a major factor in US society. In order to reduce the risk of obesity and subsequent health conditions, both companies and governments need to take action.

Demographics

As indicated earlier, cultures undergo change. *Demographics* is the study of the characteristics of societies. Table 2.6 lists some of the changing demographic factors facing contemporary society. It is important to look at them not as isolated factors but as an integrated whole. For instance, if it were not for young people taking backpacking vacations and travelling overseas to attend universities, many ideas and concepts would not reach other countries. This is not to say that imported ideas are better than indigenous ones; it is just highlighting one of the many ways in which populations and societies change over time.

Education

As was stated earlier, almost a billion people entered the 21st century unable to read or sign their name (UNICEF 1999). However, educational levels are increasing in most countries, and this has influenced societal change and development. Since the 1990s increasing numbers of young people have gone to other countries for educational purposes.

Table 2.6 Demographic factors

Factor	Description
Role of family	In some Western countries women have become breadwinners while their husbands stay at home to look after the children. Moreover, children have assumed a greater decision-making role within the family. This had led, for instance, to some car manufacturers in Europe devising advertisements that appeal to the whole family. Clearly this is not the case in all countries. In many countries the husband remains the family's main decision maker.
Impact of communication	With improved analogue and the introduction of digital telephone links it is easier, and cheaper, to talk with people over longer distances. Moreover, the introduction of the Internet and e-mail have dramatically increased the ease of communication for both business and pleasure.
Impact of transportation	Until the 1970s air travel was the domain of the rich and famous. Since then the introduction of larger fuel-efficient aircraft, 'packaged' vacations and deregulation have created greater mobility. Initially this was confined to destinations close at hand; however today vacationers seek long-distance sun and enjoyment. With the reduction in airfares this has become increasingly possible. Improved transportation has not only affected vacationers, there have also been greater opportunities for business people to travel longer distances to discuss business opportunities. Equally, cheaper air travel has provided students with an increasing opportunity to study abroad. In many cases once students have graduated they remain in the country of their study to take up employment.
Migration	Migration is not a new phenomenon. In the 1950s, for example, the Australian government provided assisted passage to UK and European residents (mainly Italians and Greeks) for emigration to Australia. This vast country needed to build its working population. Today, through the European Union we see families emigrating across the Member States to improve their opportunities.

This ranges from pre-degree and foundation programmes to doctoral research. Although some who graduate remain in that country, others return home or move to yet other countries. Their career prospects are one factor, though not the only one.

Education is not only linked to attending university. Individuals can be educated in new ways of doing things or new experiences. For instance, the wealth of diverse food products on UK supermarket shelves is in stark contrast to 30 years ago. Today, virtually every food product in the world is available. Consumer tastes have been educated in a variety of ways. In the United Kingdom, for instance, these are some of the factors:

◆ The development of a multicultural society has resulted in the opening up of specialist food stores and restaurants: Afro-Caribbean, Chinese, Indian, Italian, Spanish and many more. In the United Kingdom today there are more Indian restaurants than any other type.

◆ In television cookery programmes, which reach wide audiences, the celebrity chefs use a range of ingredients. Several celebrity chefs have become major influencers in the purchase of food and kitchen items.

◆ There has been an increasing range of cookery books covering both exotic and traditional meals. Cookery books proved to be one of the biggest growth markets in the UK book trade during the late 20th century. Every indication is that this sector will continue to grow.

◆ Numerous magazines over the years have run features on a variety of different foods.

Legal (regulatory)

Legal and regulatory issues are driven by a combination of political and judicial factors. (See mini case 2.10.) The degree of political influence depends on the political system. Even in democratic countries, governments sometimes seek extraordinary legal powers that affect both their citizens and the organisations that employ them. This is particularly so when the government introduces measures to control or limit trade, such as the imposition of sanctions or embargoes.

Mini case 2.9

The cruise industry in US waters: pollution control

The introduction of improved and arguably necessary safety standards within US territorial waters added another dimension to this highly competitive market. Vessels that did not immediately meet the standards were removed from US waters while the necessary updating was undertaken. This is a highly competitive, perhaps overcrowded market, and the withdrawal of vessels affected the ability of various cruise lines to compete successfully. Some companies repositioned the affected ships into other markets. However, it could be argued that the financial burden for others was too great, leading to collapse.

Other legislation and regulation is intended to protect people against dangerous substances. For example, the European Union has introduced a number of regulations controlling the sale and advertising of tobacco products, and is likely to introduce more in future. Briefly they fall into the following categories:

◆ Bans on the sale of tobacco products to individuals below a certain age.

◆ Bans on advertising tobacco products on billboards, racing cars and television.

◆ Requiring messages (both text and images) to be printed on cigarette packs about the potentially harmful effects of smoking. The Canadian government was the first to introduce this, and it has been followed by many other governments worldwide.

Environmental–ecological

These are really interchangeable terms in the context of marketing's external environment. There are four key areas:

◆ the weather

◆ disease

◆ global warming/global dimming

◆ geophysical activities and terrain.

Mini case 2.10

Restrictions on the shipment of wine within the United States in the 21st century

In the United States the 18th Amendment to the Constitution was passed in 1920, creating a ban on the commercial manufacture, transportation and sale of alcohol. Alcohol was banned as a result of three inter-related beliefs:

◆ There was a strong Christian belief that drunkenness breached divine teaching about moderation in all aspects of life. The growing Temperance Movement used its political power to bring about bans in various States prior to the nationwide ban.

◆ There was a growing belief that alcohol was the root cause of the social deprivation and injustice that was ravaging American society.

◆ Finally there was the belief that the imposition of such a ban would break the power of organised crime, which was heavily involved in the drink trade.

Although various powers were introduced to enforce the ban, they did little to halt bootleg production and smuggling across the border from Canada. Moreover, ironically the ban encouraged the formation of major crime syndicates, notably that of Al Capone (1899–1947). This in turn led to the corruption of local police officers and government officials. The production of dangerous unregulated (and untaxed) alcohol made the crime bosses immensely wealthy. However, many who drank contaminated alcohol were not so fortunate: they were killed, blinded or paralysed by it.

By the late 1920s it was clear that prohibition was unenforceable, and in 1933 the 21st Amendment repealed the 18th Amendment, allowing Americans to drink alcohol once more – at least in theory. What the amendment actually did was move the responsibility for control and regulation of the sale of alcohol from the Federal government to individual States. To this day several States permit local communities and municipalities to ban the manufacture, sale and consumption of alcohol.

However, some 70 years after the repeal of prohibition an anomaly remains that affects American wine drinkers. A clause in the 21st Amendment controls the sale of alcohol across State boundaries. There are wineries in 24 States, but they are forbidden to sell their wine directly to customers via mail order or over the Internet if the wine will cross State borders. Out-of-State wine has to be 'imported' and sold through a licensed outlet. For example, the alcohol laws in New York provide for in-State winemakers to ship directly to New York residents. However, out-of-State wineries must first establish a physical presence (such as an office) within the State. This is particularly expensive for small wine producers.

The legislation makes it difficult for small wineries to break into out-of-State markets. Selling direct to customers is more cost-effective than using established distribution channels, but it is this that is banned, and as a result they are unable to compete against the major American and international producers.

The small wineries are challenging the law through the US Supreme Court. If the Supreme Court rules in their favour, it will create an opportunity for them to open up US-wide markets. However, there is strong political pressure on both sides. The question is whether the Supreme Court will rule in favour of the small wineries, and how far it will go in its ruling. Legal challenges to the ruling could follow, so it might be several years before this issue is finally resolved.

Sources: S. Evans, 'Prohibition still hurts America's wine makers', BBC News Online. 8 December 2004; Thompson (2000); K. M. Smith, 'Wineries await Supreme Court decision on alcohol sales,' *Business Gazette*, www.gazette.net, 24 December 2004.

The weather

In recent years there has been much written and debated about the potential threat of global warming, and indeed its current impact. Clearly the weather influences all our lives, affecting choices such as where we vacation and our consumption of ice cream and cold drinks. For instance, in a mild summer the sale of ice creams, cold drinks and suntan lotions will be lower than in an unusually hot summer. In 2004 Coca-Cola issued a profits warning, citing the 'cold and wet weather in northern Europe' as one of the main factors for dragging down earnings (BBC 2004).

The UK Meteorological Office (part of the Ministry of Defence) is now working closely with retailers to understand how weather affects purchasing habits. The British Retail Consortium (BRC) and the Meteorological Office offer 'special packages of weather services for a variety of retailers' (Met Office 2004). John Cormode, chief executive of BRC Trading, stated:

> Our members, from trade associations through mid-tier retailers to large supermarket chains, are aware that the weather has a significant impact on consumer behaviour, which in turn affects what they need to buy, how much and when. But very few retailers have the information at their fingertips to help them understand the specific relationship between the weather and the demand for their products.
>
> (Met Office 2004)

Richard Bennett, the Meteorological Office retail manager, supported the need for retail weather analysis:

> All weather types can impact on a retailer's business. In an increasingly competitive business environment, an understanding of weather and its effects will become more and more crucial to retail supply chain, marketing and general planning decisions, bringing with it improved efficiency and greater profits.
>
> (Met Office 2004)

However, it is not just a case of the weather being too hot, too cold or too wet. Severe weather patterns have a devastating effect on people, their homes and their livelihood. Mini case 2.11 demonstrates how severe weather conditions result in companies having to change schedules to protect their customers. Moreover, it demonstrates the

Mini case 2.11

Storms batter US economy

In February 2003 snowstorms swept across the north-eastern United States, causing havoc in both urban and rural communities. The immediate impact was on retailers. Already suffering from political and economic uncertainties, they had been hoping the President's Holiday on Monday 17 February would afford an opportunity to sell unsold stock. However, the severe weather conditions resulted in many stores being forced to close. Transport was also affected, with rail freight companies running only the most essential services.

For airlines the poor weather only added to the prevalent industry gloom. Their hope of good business over this particular holiday weekend was not to be fulfilled. The appalling weather conditions led to the closure of numerous airports, cancellation of flights and misery for travellers and airlines alike. On 17 February American Airlines cancelled one-quarter of its schedule – 627 flights in all – while United Airlines cancelled some 380 flights. It was several days before airlines were able to resume normal flight schedules.

In August and September 2004 Royal Caribbean International and Celebrity Cruises, among other cruise lines, had to monitor closely the paths of two major hurricanes, Charley and Frances. On 2 September they announced changes to their sailing patterns to avoid Hurricane Frances (a category 4 storm). Two sailings from the ports of Miami and Canaveral were cancelled. Guests booked on both three-night sailings were refunded, and travel agents' commissions were protected. Additionally, three Saturday departures were postponed till the Monday and sailed with modified itineraries. Guest who sailed on these late departures received on-board credit of US$500 per stateroom and a certificate for a 50 per cent discount on future sailings of seven nights or less (excluding holidays) that departed on or before 15 December 2005. Guests who had to cancel received letters of credit for the cruise portion of their sailing. As before, the travel agents' commission was protected.

Clearly companies that are affected by severe weather conditions must protect their customers and staff. They have no control over the weather conditions, but they need to give incentives to lessen the disappointment of delay or cancellation for their customers. Equally they must minimise the impact on supply chain members, in this case travel agents.

Sources: 'Snow storms batter US economy', BBC News Online, 19 February 2003; 'Royal Caribbean International, Celebrity Cruises respond to threat posed by Hurricane Frances', press release, Royal Caribbean Cruises, 1 September 2004; 'Royal Caribbean International and Celebrity Cruises announce modifications to Friday and Saturday Sailings', press release, Royal Caribbean Cruises, 2 September 2004.

economic impact on both companies and national and regional governments.

Disease

Disease is a normal part of our everyday lives, from the common cold to life-threatening and fatal illnesses. Moreover, we see regions and nations devastated by epidemics such as HIV and AIDS. The human and economic consequences can be beyond comprehension.

The spread of disease across borders is far from new. At the end of the First World War in 1918 the movement of troops unleashed a global pandemic of Spanish flu which is believed to have contributed to the deaths of more than 50 million people (BBC 2003). This was at a time when long journeys took days or weeks to complete. Now international journeys take a matter of hours, so the global village is even more prone to the rapid spread of disease. The mini case on the impact of SARS explores both the human and economic cost.

Global warming and global dimming

Since the 1970s there has been much debate whether or not human-made chemicals and carbon emissions have created an imbalance in the world's climate. This has led to speculation that frequent unpredictable and severe weather conditions are a direct result of this atmospheric imbalance (see the mini case on page 40). According to the US Environmental Protection Agency (EPA), since the beginning of the Industrial Revolution (in the 18th century), atmospheric concentrations of carbon dioxide have increased by nearly 30 per cent, methane concentrations have more than doubled, and nitrous oxide concentrations have risen by approximately 15 per cent (EPA 2000). The combination of these 'greenhouse gases' has enhanced the heat-trapping capability of the earth's atmosphere (EPA 2000).

Over the last 50 years of the 20th century there was a significant increase in the release of these gases through the burning of fossil fuels (to produce power to run cars, trucks, homes, businesses and industry), increased agriculture, deforestation, increased use of landfill sites (which release methane), industrial production and mining. According to the EPA, global mean surface temperatures have increased by between 0.5 and 1.0 °F since the late 19th century (EPA 2000). The view in 2000 was that increasing concentrations of greenhouse gases would accelerate the rate of climate change, with global surface temperatures rising by from 1 to 4.5 °F (0.6–2.5 °C) within 50 years. The result would be increased rainfall in some regions (with severe droughts in others), increased rainstorms and rising sea levels (EPA 2000).

However, the situation could be much worse than was originally predicted. Recent research suggests that there is an additional phenomenon, global dimming. It is believed that global dimming is caused by the visible elements of air pollution: soot, ash, sulphur compounds and other particles. This visible air pollution reflects sunlight back into space, preventing it from reaching the earth's surface. Moreover, it is believed that the air pollutants affect the optical properties of clouds, which in turn make them reflect sunlight back into space. There could be several effects of this 'dimming', but the two principal concerns are:

◆ The possible disruption of the pattern of the world's rainfall. It has been suggested that the droughts that ravished sub-Saharan Africa in the 1970s and 1980s were the direct result of global dimming.

◆ That scientists have underestimated the real risk of the greenhouse effect. It is suggested that the warming from the trapped greenhouse gases has been offset by the cooling effect of the dimming process (BBC 2005). In essence one effect has cancelled out the other. However, it is not so simple. Emissions of carbon dioxide are predicted to rise as we continue to burn fossil fuels (for instance in power stations and vehicles). However, particle pollution is slowly being controlled through advanced filtration systems. This means that the cooling effect will reduce, while the warming effect will increase, and at a greater rate than was once thought.

Climatologist Peter Cox illustrates the impact of this relationship between global warming and global dimming:

Mini case 2.12

The impact of SARS

In November 2002 an unknown acute respiratory virus was discovered in Guangdong Province in China. However, it was not until February 2003 that the Chinese Ministry of Health reported that there had been 300 cases (including five deaths). Within a month Hong Kong officials reported cases of the virus among health workers. Within four days of the Hong Kong announcement the World Health Organization (WHO) confirmed that the newly named Severe Acute Respiratory Syndrome (SARS) was now considered a 'worldwide health threat'. By then possible cases had been identified in Canada, Indonesia, the Philippines, Singapore, Thailand, Vietnam, the United States, the United Kingdom, Germany, Spain and Slovenia.

On 2 April the WHO recommended the postponement of non-essential travel to Guangdong Province and Hong Kong. By the end of April the recommendation included Toronto, Canada. The Beijing authorities ordered the closure of all entertainment venues in the capital until the outbreak was brought under control.

By July 2003 the WHO believed the disease had reached its peak. Some 774 people had died and more than 8000 people worldwide had been infected. Although new cases have since been reported, they are not to previous levels. The disease appears to have been contained.

SARS had an impact on the way people behaved. In many countries people shunned the use of public machines such as telephones. There was genuine fear of physical contact, with many people avoiding shaking hands on meeting and exchanging business cards. At Easter masses in Toronto's Roman Catholic churches, for example, the 'sign of peace' – shaking hands with other members of the congregation – was replaced by a bow and a smile. People had a fear of touching even though the medical evidence suggested this kind of physical contact could not spread the disease.

Governments introduced screening systems at airports to detect travellers with particularly high temperatures. In certain regions of the world airlines provided passengers with surgical masks and requested that they wear them (see Figure 2.3). In addition aircraft were disinfected regularly to reduce the risk of the disease spreading.

SARS had an impact on business in several ways:

◆ The world's largest photographic film producer, Eastman Kodak, reduced its profit predictions because of the effect of SARS in Asia. Asian tourism was depressed to the extent that Eastman Kodak's sales in the second quarter of 2003 were cut by almost 50 per cent.

Figure 2.3

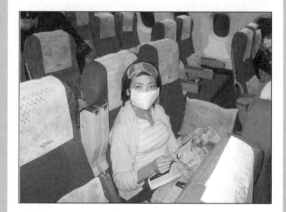

© Catherine Hu. Reproduced with kind permission.

Passengers on this flight from China to Thailand are requested to wear surgical masks as a safety precaution against SARS

◆ In mid-June 2003 the number of scheduled flights worldwide fell by 3 per cent, approximately 2.5 million seats. Compared with June 2002 flight numbers to/from China fell by 45 per cent, flights within China fell by 16 per cent, between Hong Kong and US/Canada by 69 per cent and

If we don't do anything by about 2030 we could have a global warming exceeding two degrees, and at that point it's believed the Greenland ice sheet would start to melt in a way that you wouldn't be able to stop once it started…. Take a long time to melt but ultimately it would lead to a sea level rise of seven or eight metres.

(BBC 2005)

Severe climate change leads to flooding and droughts, as many countries have already witnessed. This impacts on societies, regional economies and

between Hong Kong and Europe by 36 per cent.

◆ In many Asian countries restaurants witnessed a decline in customers. This subsequently affected the Australian fish market. Restaurants in Singapore and Hong Kong are major buyers of Australian fish, but with the outbreak of SARS they stopped buying. The unsold fish on the Australian market led to a dramatic fall in prices, endangering the livelihoods of many fishermen.

◆ The epidemic increased the demand for thermometers, surgical garments and masks. In some countries suppliers were unable to meet the demand, and price rises were common.

◆ With executives not being able to or wanting to fly, there was greater use of the Internet and business television links. (This was also the case after the 9/11 tragedy.)

By mid-2004 the World Tourism Organization stated that the industry was recovering from the slump in 2003 which was mainly attributed to the Iraq war and the global outbreak of SARS. These events had created a 1.2 per cent decline in international travel over the previous year. Although it may not seem a high figure it equals several tens of millions of people.

Although the SARS epidemic appears to have abated, it demonstrates the vulnerability of both individuals and organisations within the global village environment.

Sources: 'Canada's grip on Sars weakens', BBC News Online, 19 April 2003; 'Sars threatens Aussie fish market', BBC News Online, 22 April 2003; Sars: Killer bug, Channel 4 television, aired 28 April 2003; 'Sars boosts thermometer demand', BBC News Online, 29 April 2003; 'How the "global village" faced Sars', BBC News Online, 2 May 2003; 'Sars hit airlines "more than war"', BBC News Online, 13 June 2003; 'Eastman Kodak warns of Sars impact', BBC News Online, 19 June 2003; 'Sars: Global hotspots', BBC News Online, 5 July 2003; 'World tourism recovers from slump', BBC News Online, 25 June 2004; 'Timeline: Sars virus', BBC News Online, 7 July 2004.

potentially the geopolitical balance of power. Food products and other resources that are now readily available may be scarce in the future, leading to starvation and social chaos. If these scenarios become reality, the social organisations and economic networks that support the world will break down (Stipp 2004).

Here lies a dichotomy. On the one hand vast tracts of the world have become consumerist societies fuelled by economic development and marketing. On the other hand, if we continue with this rate of consumerism the world as we know it will change dramatically for the worse. The question is whether consumerist habits and an organisation's need for growth can change to preserve the world for the future. Is society for the here and now, or geared for the future? Indeed, what part can technology play in reducing the risks for the planet's future?

Geophysical

The surface of the earth is a complex structure of tectonic plates which move relative to each other. It is this movement that has created the physical world in which we live. To the world's population these movements are imperceptible, yet to geologists a 2 cm movement is dramatic, and can have catastrophic consequences for local communities. Where the plates are active (that is, moving relative to each other, as at the San Andreas fault line in California, or moving under each other, as on the Pacific rim of South America), there is geophysical activity which can include earthquakes and volcanic activity. Japan, for instance, has three massive plates moving beneath it. That is why there are intermittent tremors on land and near the Japanese coastline. Mindful of this geological fragility, the Japanese authorities regularly practise emergency procedures for use in the event of a major disaster.

Geophysical activity occurs every day somewhere in the world. Society only becomes aware of such activity when it happens on a major scale. The destructive force of geophysical activity, and the reasons we need to understand it, are graphically demonstrated in Mini case 2.13. The devastation wrought by such an event has an impact beyond the sheer physical. It affects lives, livelihoods and the economic stability of nations. In addition, the economic disruption can affect organisations and companies many thousands of km away.

Technology

Technology has driven many aspects of societal development, business and marketing over the

Mini case 2.13

A tsunami devastates Southeast Asia

On the morning of Sunday 26 December 2004 a megathrust earthquake occurred at the interface of the India and Burma tectonic plates. The epicentre was off the Indonesian island of Sumatra. As a result of the megathrust quake, which measured 9 on the Richter Scale,[2] approximately 1200 km of the plate boundary slipped.

It has been estimated that the displacement on the fault plane was about 15 metres, so the sea floor overlying the thrust fault would have been uplifted by several metres. This pushed water upwards, creating a wave that moved at about 500 km per hour in deep water. It dramatically slowed to around 45 km per hour in shallower water, but this shallow water forced hundreds of cubic kilometres of excess water upwards, creating a tsunami (sea surge) wave, which in a matter of minutes devastated stretches of coastlines in 12 countries (Bangladesh, Burma, the Maldives, Malaysia, India, Indonesia, Kenya, the Seychelles, Somalia, Sri Lanka, Tanzania and Thailand). The impact of the dissipating wave was felt as far away as South America.

Indonesia, Sri Lanka, Thailand and the Maldives suffered the worst both economically and in loss of life. It is estimated that over 300 000 people died as a direct result of the tsunami. Many more died afterwards, as a result of disease and injuries.

Many of the most devastated areas were important tourist destinations, including Thailand's Phuket island and the Maldives. According to the World Travel and Tourism Council, tourism provided over 19 million jobs in the affected region (see Tables 2.7 and 2.8). In the Maldives alone 64 per cent of all jobs were dependent on tourism. Continued tourism is vital to the economic development of these areas. Numerous fishing and farming communities were also devastated, as well as other businesses.

The tourist officials and governments of the countries affected encouraged visitors not to cancel their planned vacations. They worked with travel companies to make alternative accommodation arrangements in parts of the countries not affected by the tsunami. It is not only the major hotels that are dependent upon visitor income; so are local stores, restaurants, souvenir shops and taxi drivers. For many of these people tourism provides their own income.

Many of these countries also export goods such as furniture and clothing to European countries, and in some cases raw material suppliers and factories were damaged. One result of the disaster could be a dramatic increase in inflation. Suppliers might demand to be paid earlier, and the cash flow implications of this could be disastrous for small businesses.

Sources: 'Tsunami among world's worst disasters', BBC News Online, 27 December 2004; 'Giant wave damages S. Asia economy', BBC News Online. 28 December 2004; 'Disease could swamp wave zones', BBC News Online, 28 December 2004; 'Asia earthquake toll still rising', BBC News Online, 29 December 2004; 'India issues tsunami alert, people panic', South African Broadcasting Corporation, 30 December 2004; 'Magnitude 9.0 off W coast of northern Sumatra Sunday, December 26, 2004 at 00:58:53 UTC: preliminary earthquake report', US Geological Survey, National Earthquake Information Center, World Data Center for Seismology, Denver.

Table 2.7 Tourist jobs in countries affected by the tsunami

Country	Percentage of tourist jobs	Percentage of GDP
India	5.6	4.9
Indonesia	8.5	10.3
Thailand	8.9	12.2
Maldives	64.0	74.2
Malaysia	12.7	14.7

Table 2.8 Growth in tourism before the tsunami

Country	Percentage growth in tourism, Jan–Aug 2004
Malaysia	70
Indonesia	30
Thailand	28
India	26
Maldives	15
Sri Lanka	7

centuries. The technologies that were developed during the Industrial Revolution in 18th-century Britain fuelled economic expansion and development on a global scale. Since then developments in communication, materials and computing power have revolutionised both manufacturing and service provision.

However, the technological revolutions of the last 100 years have also led to the demise of various industries, products and services. For instance the typewriter has been superseded by the computer. Typewriter manufacturers that did not either ally themselves with computer manufacturers or seek new products and markets were eventually bankrupted.

The introduction of new farming technologies provided the impetus for mass crop production and factory farming. These provided cheaper foods in highly developed nations such as the United States and the United Kingdom. However, the economies of scale created by such large-scale methods put pressure on smaller farms in both developed and developing nations. In many cases, though not all, smaller farms were regenerated through an increasing demand

Mini case 2.14

Studio removes shuttle film trailer

In February 2003, following the Columbia Shuttle disaster when seven astronauts died, Paramount Studios requested cinemas in the United States to stop showing a trailer for a new movie. The science fiction movie *The Core* is about a group of NASA 'terranauts' on a highly dangerous mission. *The Core* sees the NASA crew travel in an experimental craft to the centre of the earth. Paramount reviewed both its advertising and the movie's shuttle scenes to ensure they did not appear insensitive following the Columbia tragedy.

This mini case is a further illustration of how factors beyond the company's control can affect both its product – here, a movie – and its marketing. In this case, while it is expensive to re-edit and shoot new scenes, it is possible to modify the product to fit the new situation. With other products that is not always (relatively) easily achieved.

Source: 'Studio pulls shuttle film trailer', BBC News Online, 5 February 2003.

for produce that is organic and/or not factory or intensely farmed.

Nations and industries have become increasingly reliant on technology. For instance, businesses, organisations and universities are dependent on computer systems. When they fail (which includes being sabotaged by viruses), there is usually significant financial and personal impact. Imagine a network failure at a freight forwarding company. The company's inability to meet its 'marketing promises' to its customers would affect its bottom-line performance, its reputation and that of its customers. There is a whole chain or channel of organisations and individuals that are affected.

Organisations and individuals need to be aware of the development of new technologies and the impact they are likely to have in the future. The combination of scientific and technological research currently being undertaken on the International Space Station (see Figure 2.4) may provide a glimpse into the future. Overall 12 countries led by the American, Russian and European space agencies are engaged in programmes that could

Figure 2.4

Acknowledged source: US National Aeronautics and Space Administration (NASA).

The International Space Station (ISS) is not only an example of how space agencies from different countries can work together for the benefit of humankind, it is also a laboratory that may help solve some of the world's greatest health dilemmas. There are also opportunities for the creation of new materials that could significantly aid how we live and work.

potentially revolutionise many areas of research. These include the development of:

◆ new medicines for use especially in the fight against cancers

◆ high-performance industrial materials (for example, new polymers for the use in computer semiconductors)

◆ low-maintenance robot technology for industrial and commercial purposes.

These products could revolutionise several areas of product development and manufacture, and might allow companies to maintain and sustain competitive advantage over the short and medium terms.

Combinations of events

Of course, we should not view the macro factors in isolation. A variety of factors can converge, increasing the impact on various aspects of marketing a product or service. For example, a country might suffer geopolitical instability which in turn creates economic instability and social unrest. This affects the production and export of raw materials and the population's ability to purchase both indigenous and imported products.

Reversed issues

We also need to consider the 'opposite' impact of negative macro factors. Although macro factors (as we have seen) can and do have a negative impact on organisations, they can have a positive effect as well. Consider, for instance, companies that develop and manufacture rescue craft. These are required at times of distress, on both local and international levels. So while there are negative economic and marketing impacts from disasters, there are also individuals and organisations that benefit in these circumstances.

◼ What is the micro environment?

The micro environment can be described as the environment that is most closely linked to the organisation. Very loosely, it concerns the 'internalities' of the organisation. Some writers have suggested that these are the forces over which the organisation has some 'control'. However, perhaps 'influence' is a better way of describing the level of power the organisation actually possesses.

There must some caution here. While organisations have some control (within legal frameworks) over their employees, and to some extent over suppliers, the level of control over customers is debatable. It is true that organisations can and do influence their customers, but this is not control in the absolute meaning of the word.

Another issue that must also be considered is the cultural 'lens' through which the micro factors are viewed. The vast majority of marketing textbooks are written from a European (mainly British) or American perspective. However, the micro factors from, for instance, a Chinese, Moroccan, South African or Chilean perspective might be very different. In some countries businesses have greater control over their employees, are not so readily affected by shareholder opinions, and are less focused on customer relationship management.

Generally, the constituents of the micro environment should be considered as stakeholders, of both the organisation and the industry sector in which it operates.

◼ Micro factors

Unlike the macro factors, there is no mnemonic to represent the micro factors. Figure 2.5 shows the micro environmental forces that engage within and across the organisation.

The point with micro factors is that they tend to focus on local issues. These could be related to suppliers, employees, the local community, local regulators or local government, or direct customers. However, there must be a word of caution here. With the development of global businesses and the Internet, a customer no longer needs to be 'local' to receive a product or service. For example online book and CD stores can be located anywhere, as long as they have an efficient and effective logistics and distribution system.

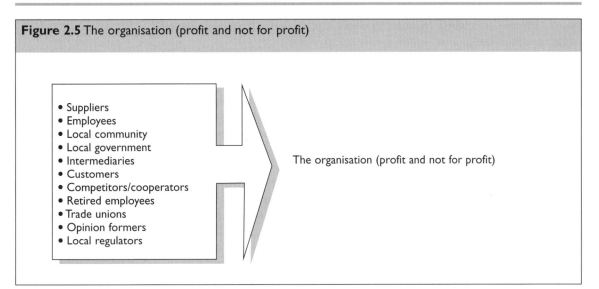

Figure 2.5 The organisation (profit and not for profit)

- Suppliers
- Employees
- Local community
- Local government
- Intermediaries
- Customers
- Competitors/cooperators
- Retired employees
- Trade unions
- Opinion formers
- Local regulators

The organisation (profit and not for profit)

Suppliers

Suppliers are key to any organisation, either profit-seeking or not for profit. Therefore the relationship between the supplier and the organisation is particularly important. As you will see in Chapter 6, organisations have to consider suppliers not only in terms of their individual power (for example, the prices they charge) but also in the value they deliver to the organisation and thus its end customer. In mini case 2.15 we consider a number of potential suppliers to a restaurant. Unless the restaurant has a good working relationship with its suppliers and vice versa, there is a risk that neither the suppliers, the restaurant or its consumers will benefit from the relationship.

The various suppliers to an organisation and how they operate need to be considered in terms not only of the marketing mix (discussed in more detail later in this text) but also of building an effective relationship. It is also important to bear in mind that the same suppliers may well be supplying raw materials or components to competitors. This is often the case in the restaurant industry.

Employees

We discuss in Chapter 13 how individuals and groups of employees are the backbone of any organisation. Although finance is required to set up a busi-

ness and keep it in operation, it is the people within the organisation who drive it forward (or not, as the case may be). If we accept this, we need to consider how employees both develop an organisation and assist in the marketing of its products or services.

Crucial to employees as 'marketers' is their morale. There is a blurring of issues at this

Mini case 2.15

A restaurant and its suppliers

Restaurants typically operate in a highly competitive environment, especially in major cities such as London, Paris, New York, Singapore and Sydney. Many restaurants in the same city use the same suppliers, for example for meat, fish, vegetables and wines and spirits. It is vital therefore that the restaurant builds a relationship with its suppliers to gain the best value produce at a price it can afford. It is also important that the relationship meets the requirements of the restaurant's target clientele: in other words it needs to provide the things they want to eat and drink, at value for money prices.

Of course, part of the value chain is the experience of the chef and the kitchen team, and how they transform the raw ingredients into a gastronomic delight. But the food will only be good if the ingredients are good, which brings us back to the relationship between the restaurant and the supplier.

point. Morale is clearly a management and organisational behaviour issue rather than a purely marketing one. However, to maximise the marketing value of an individual or group, efficient and effective management and organisational behaviour policies need to be in place. In essence the management team need the workforce to be 'on their side'. Unfortunately, business history is littered with numerous examples where management has failed to truly value its employees, sometimes resulting in strikes and unrest. The result is often a loss of market share and competitiveness, and sometimes the failure and closure of the organisation. The clear message is that management must have its employees 'on board' if it is to have any chance of maintaining a competitive stance in today's dynamic environment. (The role of employees links into the value chain (as a competitive instrument) which is discussed in Chapter 6.)

The local community

Organisations have to be aware of the local community that surrounds them. This is for two specific reasons. First, it will include many of their customers. Consider, for instance, how a supermarket interacts with its local community in controlling noise (such as in the timing and frequency of deliveries). Second, the organisation can be expected to support its community, either voluntarily (perhaps donating to a local hospital) or through a statutory agreement (for example, an agreement to improve lighting and security in the area, as a condition of getting planning permission).

Sometimes there is severe pressure on the relationship between the organisation and the local community. Take airports, for example. Consumers like the speed and convenience of air travel, and its growth has meant that airlines look to obtain a greater number of landing and take-off slots at airports. But local residents may have very negative feelings about the noise (especially at night), traffic and disruption that results. There are generally major campaigns and planning battles when major airports such as Manchester and Heathrow seek to expand.

Local government

Local governments both create regulations and build the infrastructure within which the local community (including organisations in the area) operates. For example, in many countries if an organisation wants to extend its buildings it requires permission from local government, even if it owns the land. This is often refused if the extension is contrary to the interests of local people, forcing the organisation to consider alternatives (for example, building elsewhere or reorganising its current buildings) which could be more expensive or inconvenient.

Local government is usually responsible for the road infrastructure, and organisations (such as supermarkets and factories) need to liaise and discuss issues such as access, timings of deliveries, and when road maintenance is undertaken.

As we saw in the mini case on page 35, local legal restrictions can affect a company's competitiveness. Often companies try to obtain the support of opinion formers in an attempt to reverse legislation that they find restrictive.

Intermediaries

Chapters 6 and 12 discuss the important role of intermediaries in the supply chain. These are the organisations and individuals that operate between component suppliers, manufacturers and retailers. There may be several intermediaries in a supply chain (see Chapter 6). It is crucial for the organisation to build a relationship with them in order to ensure the smooth flow of components or finished goods to meet the demands of all those in the supply chain. Any interruption within the supply chain can have a devastating impact, especially on the organisation that deals directly with the end user of the product or service.

Customers

Chapter 13 discusses how customers (sometimes in a wide sense) are fundamental to the existence of any organisation. Generally we think of 'customers' as consumer (you buying the latest CD from a music store) or a business customer (Airbus

Industries buying aircraft engines from Rolls-Royce). However, many organisations have different types of customer (see Table 1.2, page 14), so we need to consider 'customers' in a more 'global' sense.

Without a 'customer' there is no business. Therefore all organisations need to know who their customers are, where they come from and what they require. Much of this is discussed in later chapters of this book. They also need to understand how their customers might be affected by the macro issues considered earlier in this chapter.

Competitors and co-operators

Any organisation working within a competitive environment must be aware of the actions of its rivals (see Chapter 5). Organisations must monitor the actions of their rivals (using methods that are both ethical and legal) in order to be competitive within the marketplace (see Chapter 6). Sometimes organisations that are normally rivals work together for the benefit of themselves and end users. Let us consider two examples, one within the for-profit sector and one within the not-for-profit sector.

Example 1: Bluetooth technology[2]

Various electronics companies have formed a strategic alliance to create a system that will enable unification (or convergence) across different electronic communication systems (Groucutt and Griseri 2004). The aim is to improve the links between different wireless consumer hardware systems.

Example 2: Not-for-profit organisations

Charities are normally in competition with each other, attempting to raise funds from companies, groups and individuals for worthwhile causes. However, at times they work in concert, both in fundraising and in providing assistance on the ground to relieve suffering and deprivation. For example, in parts of Africa where there has been the risk of mass starvation as a result of severe droughts and the after-affects of the tsunami in Southern Asia (see page 40), famine relief charities have worked in close cooperation.

Retired employees

Unfortunately many companies appear to 'forget' retired employees, but retirees can be an asset in a number of ways.

◆ As opinion formers: they can be vocal supporters and ambassadors for the organisation.

◆ They may be customers of the organisation.

◆ Because of their knowledge. Former employees have in-depth knowledge of the workings of the organisation. Although they are retired they might still be called on to help, for example when a technical problem arises and the existing staff cannot solve it. Knowledge is a competitive resource that some organisations lose when staff retire. This often occurs because the organisation does not have effective and efficient knowledge management systems.

It is important to bear in mind that regions such as Europe are witnessing a burgeoning population of retired people who often have significant purchasing power. This could change over next 10–20 years, with retirees facing increasing financial pressures from lower state and company pension payouts and decreased values for investments and private pensions.

Trade unions

The trade union movement developed in Europe and the United States to protect the rights of workers who were being exploited by factory owners and management. Chronic exploitation of employees continues today in some parts of the world, as International Labour Organisation (ILO) research shows. However, in many countries there has developed a close and effective working relationship between trade unions and employer organisations. This has sometimes followed years of argument and unrest; however the unions offer a mechanism for negotiation and arbitration rather than conflict and industrial disputes. As we saw in the mini case of the US longshoremen (page 21), industrial action has a wide negative impact, and it is obviously best avoided.

Opinion formers

Through the use of public relations an organisation will seek to inform (and influence) local opinion formers. These include not only the local media but also influential members of the community. Often opinion forming is viewed only from the organisational perspective: that is, the organisation seeks to influence local opinion in its favour. This is not always the case. Organisations may become involved in local issues because they feel part of the community (for example, an organisation might be the largest employer in the neighbourhood) and want to give back something to it. Local companies often get involved in local charities, or fight to save the future of a local hospital or school.

Opinion forming is a two-way action: the organisation seeks to influence local people, and they also seek to influence it. For example, a local community might try to halt increased goods traffic on its roads or prevent the proposed expansion of a factory or warehouse. In the United Kingdom local communities have sought to influence opinion formers not only locally but nationally: for example, to voice their objection to the proposed expansion of Heathrow and Manchester airports. Their concerns in this case focused on the devaluation of their homes, and the increased noise, atmospheric pollution and road congestion as the result of the expansion.

Local regulators

Here there is an overlap with the macro factors of politics and legal issues, as well as a link to local government. This is especially so when local government is the originator and enforcer of the regulation. However, we must be careful of the world 'local' in this context. In some countries, including the United States, Australia and parts of Europe, legislation and regulations are made at regional, sub-regional and local levels. These should act in concert with each other, but sometimes their aims are contradictory, and this creates difficulties for organisations, including (but not only) in their marketing activities.

It is not only local authorities that make regulations on a local level. In some countries separate organisations have been set up with powers to formulate and impose restrictions on the marketing of products and services. Mini case 2.16 illustrates how local and regional organisations are involved in the regulation of food produce in the United States.

Control of micro factors

The areas within the micro environment can be 'controlled' to a greater or lesser degree by an organisation's management. Often in marketing texts these are considered as the 'controllables'. However they are only controllable to a limited degree, depending on factors such as geographical location, local regulations and political intent.

Thus external factors can influence or determine the micro factors. For example, a company can influence customers to buy a product or service. The element of 'control' is governed by what is acceptable within a particular area or region. For instance, on the one hand there will be consumer protection laws; on the other the organisation will have legal redress in order to obtain payment from customers (both B2C and B2B) if they renege on payment.

■ Analysing the environment

Lynch (2000) suggests that the environmental forces that surround an organisation can be assessed according to two main measures, changeability and predictability. These assessors can help to determine the level of turbulence operating within the environment. If the level of turbulence is particularly high, it will probably be impossible to predict the outcome for the organisation. However, there may be a way to identify key issues that can protect the organisation, especially in the short term. Then more information can be gathered to make decisions to increase its viability over the medium to longer term.

Changeability

This is the 'degree to which the environment is likely to change' (Lynch 2000). It is further subdivided into:

The case of the UglyRipe™ tomato

In 1933 the US Congress established marketing committees which allowed small groups of farmers of fruits, vegetables and nuts to work together to set marketing standards. In 2004 there were 34 boards across the United States with the authority to impose strict quality and packing requirements.

One of these is the Florida Tomato Committee (FTC), established in 1955, which regulates the Florida fresh tomato industry south and east of the Suwannee River, from mid-October to mid-June each year. During the winter growing season the vast majority of America's field-grown tomatoes come from Florida. This is a US$500 million a year industry which exports annually almost 58 million 24 lb packages of tomatoes to other US states.

Typically Florida Round winter tomatoes are round, smooth and picked green. They are then gassed to turn them a pinkish red prior to shipping. Over the years this has become a highly mechanised process.

The FTC sets the standards for grade (shape), size, quality and maturity of round tomatoes that can be exported during the season. (Tomatoes grown west of the river, as well as grape, cherry, Roma and greenhouse tomatoes, are exempt from the rules.) It is this standardisation that has affected the UglyRipe™ tomato.

The UglyRipe™ tomato has derived from the French Marmonde heirloom variety. An heirloom tomato is one where the variety is between 40 and 50 years old, is open pollinated and not a hybrid. A hybrid tomato may lose its rich flavour and colouring after several generations of breeding. The UglyRipe™ tomato has gained a reputation across America for its rich taste, albeit at a premium price. It has become a prize for US gourmet chefs.

During the warmer months UglyRipe™ tomatoes are grown in New Jersey and the southeastern States, and shipped across the United States to supermarkets and restaurants. However, during the winter months they are grown in the Florida region.

The UglyRipe™ is so named because it is misshapen, with a wrinkled appearance – very different from Florida Round tomatoes. This is where the problems begin. To meet the grade 90 per cent of a consignment must meet the FTC shape standard. Producers of UglyRipe™ tomatoes remove approximately 60 per cent of the crop to ensure that shipments meet their own standards, but in order to meet the FTC grading standards, which are not well suited to their product, they would have to remove a further 20 per cent – 80

per cent in all, leaving only 20 per cent to be sold. The additional problem for the UglyRipe™ tomato is that the FTC does not consider taste within its standards classification, so the UglyRipe™ gets no credit for its rich taste.

Reginald Brown, the Manager of Florida's Tomato Committee stated:

> Growers complain that UglyRipes™ could wreck the reputation of Florida tomatoes. To allow misshapen and blemished tomatoes could open the way for a flood of ugly tomatoes to hit the market.... If you allowed the producers of UglyRipe™ to ship any quality of tomato, then how could you justify not allowing any quality of tomato into the marketplace? The first contact you make with any product is visual.. There's a minimal visual quality that needs to be there.

The UglyRipe™ tomato is a registered brand of Procacci Brothers, founded in 1948. Since then it has become the world's largest growers and handlers of fresh tomatoes.

Joseph Procacci, CEO of Procacci Brothers, commented:

> They bred Florida Round tomatoes for shape; we bred an heirloom tomato for taste. The standards are set for shape only. Heirlooms will never be round, nor do consumers care if they are round. So the Florida Tomato Committee is imposing a ridiculous standard that we can only meet by throwing out at least 8 out of 10 very tasty tomatoes. That's wasteful, and the consumer will be the loser.

UglyRipe™ tomatoes can be sold within Florida. However, at the time of writing (January 2005) they cannot be exported outside the State during the winter growing period.

Sources: 'Florida tomato facts', Florida Tomato Committee, www.floridatomatoes.org; 'Focus on flavor: UglyRipe™ tomatoes', Santa Sweets, www.santasweets.com; L. Parker, 'It's a fight in Florida, and it's ugly', *USA Today*, 8 December 2004; J. Kofman, 'Florida keeps ugly tomatoes to itself', *World News Tonight*, ABC Television, 19 December 2004; 'Florida Tomato Committee votes against the "Certificate of Privilege" request for Procacci Brothers' UglyRipe™ heirloom variety tomato: move will deny US consumers the tasty, Florida-grown "back yard" desired this winter', press release, Santa Sweet, 6 January 2005.

◆ Complexity – this can be described as the degree to which an organisation is affected primarily by the macro factors (PESTLE forces).

◆ Novelty – this can be described as the degree to which the 'environment presents the organisation with new situations' (Lynch 2000). It could be argued that SARS was a novel situation. Even though there had been both epidemics and pandemics before (especially in the early 20th century), the onset of SARS was sudden, rapid and terrifying.

Predictability

This is considered to be the 'degree that such changes can be predicted' (Lynch 2000). It can be further subdivided into:

◆ Rate of change – that is, whether the rate of change within the environment can be predicted or not. Consider for a moment how the Internet has changed people's behaviour and business practices. The rate of change was quite dramatic and rapid. Was it predictable? Are the future rates of change of technology predictable?

◆ Visibility of the future – the thought here is that the availability and accuracy of information can help organisations predict the future.

The 'What if?' scenario

With increased complexity and turbulence operating within both the macro and micro environments, organisations are faced with considering potential 'What if?' scenarios. Van der Heijden (2002) suggests that external scenarios (that is, models of the external world) are 'representative of the ranges of possible future developments and outcomes within the external world'. In essence they are external factors that are beyond an organisation's control, but affect its business operations.

Organisations may examine future possibilities internally, or employ 'think tanks' to do so.

The objective is to try to understand what the known and unknown variables might be in the future. However, as we have seen in earlier sections of this chapter, there are many situations that are unpredictable. We can consider scenarios for particular events. However, we cannot predict when those events will occur.

■ Chapter summary

This has been a diverse chapter, examining both the internal and external factors that affect organisations today. Several critical points can be gleaned from these discussions:

1   Both micro and macro factors do not operate in isolation. Often they work in concert (for instance, political unrest and economic turmoil) or at the very least interact or overlap in some capacity.

2   None of these factors are static. Many are often in a state of flux, increasing the dynamics in the local, national, regional and international context.

3   There are major issues, especially in relation to ecology and the natural environment (greenhouse gases, for instance) that could have a profound effect on how societies function in the future. This in turn will affect how organisations and markets operate.

4   A realisation that new materials and technologies are still being created and developed.

5   Organisations need to continually monitor both internal and external factors in order to gauge potential changes within the marketplace. This may, to a greater or lesser degree, be achieved through scenario planning. However, there is no guarantee about its accuracy. Nevertheless organisations need to be proactive in their thinking, otherwise dramatic changes within the external environment, for instance, could lead to a reduced market for their products/services.

Questions for review and reflection

1 Choose a company (it can be in any business field) and two of the macro factors. Then examine how the two chosen macro factors impact/influence the marketing activities of that company within its own domestic environment.

2 Choose a company (it can be in any business field) and two of the macro factors. Then examine how the two chosen macro factors impact/influence the marketing activities of that company within an international context.

3 The micro factors have often been described as 'controllables'. Critically evaluate this belief. What do you think and why?

4 Considering the level of 'turbulence' within the marketing environment, do you think scenario analysis/planning has any value at all?

5 Do you think that companies can 'protect' themselves from the extremes of macro environmental activity? If so, how?

6 Outline the key societal changes that have taken place in your home country over the past 10 to 20 years. Have these changes had an impact or influence on how you live your life?

7 Critically evaluate how the threat of global warming and global dimming could affect business and marketing operations in the future. What do you think are the critical issues that consumers and marketers must consider?

8 Using the Internet and other library resources, evaluate how changes in technology affected the typewriter industry. Do you think other industries can learn lessons from the changes within the typewriter market?

9 There has been a significant increase in the levels of macro environmental turbulence. Such turbulence can be extremely damaging to the development and long-term survival of a company, and indeed an industry. Examine a business sector with which you are familiar, giving recent examples of macro environmental turbulence that have affected that sector. Then critically evaluate the potential long-term impact, and suggest actions that companies in that sector should consider in order to survive.

References

BBC (2003) 'How the "global village" faced Sars', BBC News Online, 2 May.

BBC (2004a) 'Wet weather hits Coca-Cola sales', BBC News Online, 15 September.

BBC (2005) *Global Dimming*, Horizon, BBC 2 television, first broadcast January.

Cartwright, R. (2002) *Mastering the Business Environment*. Basingstoke: Palgrave Macmillan.

Czinkota, M. R. and Ronkainen, I. (1995) *International Marketing*, 4th edn, Fort Worth: Dryden Press.

Doole, I. and Lowe. R. (1999) *International Marketing Strategy: Analysis, development and implementation*, 2nd edn, London: International Thomson Business Press.

Environmental Protection Agency USA (EPA) (2000) *Global Warming*, EPA, www.epa.gov.

Groucutt, J. and Griseri, P. (2004) *Mastering e-Business*, Basingstoke: Palgrave Macmillan.

Hofstede. G. (1980) *Culture's Consequences: International differences in work-related values*, Beverly Hills and London: Sage.

Hollensen. S. (2001) *Global Marketing: A market-responsive approach*, 2nd edn, Harlow: FT/Prentice Hall.

International Labour Organization (ILO) (2004) 'Half the world's workers living below the US$2 a day poverty line: ILO says new policies for promoting productivity growth and decent jobs could improve outlook for working poor', press release, Department of Communications and Public Information, ILO.

Lynch, R. (2000) *Corporate Strategy*, 2nd edn, Harlow: FT Prentice Hall.

Met Office (2004) 'Forewarned is forearmed', press release, Met Office 4 March.

Rosci, F. (2001) 'Down but not out (tourism in Israel)', *Travel Agent*, 16 April.

Stipp, D. (2004) 'Climate collapse: the Pentagon's weather nightmare', *Fortune*, 26 January.

Thompson, P. (2000) *Cassell's Dictionary of Modern American History*, London: Cassell.

UNICEF (1999) *The State of the World's Children*, UNICEF.

Van der Heijden, K. (2002) *Scenarios: The art of strategic conversation*, Chichester: Wiley.

Wolfensohn, J. D. (1998) 'The other crisis', address to annual meeting, 6 October, World Bank, Washington, DC.

PART
2

Tools and
Techniques

Segmentation, Targeting and Positioning

CHAPTER 3

Learning outcomes

After completing this chapter you should be able to:

▶ explain the role of segmentation in B2B and B2C environments

▶ critically evaluate the relevance of segmentation within a contemporary B2C marketplace

▶ critically evaluate the reasons organisations fail to successfully segment their markets

▶ outline how an organisation positions its product or service within the marketplace

▶ explain how and why organisations seek to target a specific audience for their product or service.

Contents

Learning outcomes	53
Introduction	53
What is segmentation?	54
B2B segmentation	55
Segmentation characteristics of B2B markets	57
B2C segmentation	60
Segmenting by geographic location	60
Segmenting by demographics	60
Segmenting by socio-economic status	60
Segmenting by behaviour	60
Segmenting by lifestyle	61
Formulating a segmentation strategy	61
Targeting	61
Positioning	62
Repositioning	63
Perceptual or positioning mapping	63
Chapter summary	64
Questions for review and reflection	65
References	65

Introduction

This chapter examines the relationship between segmentation, targeting and positioning (STP). Prior to the launch of a particular product or service, for instance, an organisation needs an understanding of its market: in other words, who will be buying the product or service. If it has determined who is most likely to buy the product or service, it can then focus our attention on them. This approach can provide the organisation with several interrelated benefits. These include:

◆ A more efficient use of resources. No matter how large and powerful organisations are, they all have limited resources. By judicious STP an organisation maximises its opportunity to use its resources efficiently and effectively.

◆ Adding clarity to marketing planning. STP allows the organisation to develop marketing plans that focus on the requirements of specific customer groups.

◆ Increasing the opportunity to create effective customer relationship management: This area is discussed further in Chapter 8. The issue here is a greater propensity to understand the needs and wants (now and in the future) of the customer base. By targeting the right segment of the population, the organisation has an improved opportunity to learn more from its customers.

◆ Market position in comparison to competitors. Organisations can compare and contrast the positioning of their products or services with that of their current, and potential future, competitors.

◆ Increasing the opportunity to gain and sustain a competitive advantage. By directing resources to customer needs and wants, the organisation has an opportunity to increase its competitive position in the marketplace. Indeed, it may be able to gain and sustain a competitive advantage over its rivals.

The foundation model (the STP schematic) used in this chapter was developed and enhanced by Dibb (1998) and Kotler (2000) amongst others. Figure 3.1 diagrammatically represents the relationship between segmentation, targeting and positioning.

▇ What is segmentation?

Smith (1957) provided an early definition of segmentation:

> Segmentation is based on the observation of evolution in demand and represents a more precise and rational adaptation of the product and the marketing effort to meet customer or user demands.

Everyone is prepared to purchase products and services (depending on their financial status) as long as the products or services meet a particular need or desire. As Wright (2004) suggests, segmentation is thus the ability to 'divide the markets into groups, or clusters, of customers based upon realistic and meaningful criteria so as to offer clear, targeted benefits to every customer'.

Kotler (2000) suggests that market segmentation is:

> the subdividing of a market into homogeneous (or similar) subsets of customers, where any subset may conceivably be selected as a target market to be reached with a distinct marketing mix.

Figure 3.1

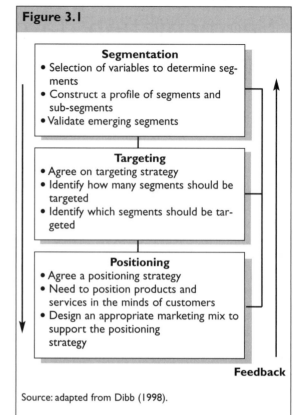

Source: adapted from Dibb (1998).

The STP schematic. This is based upon the work of Dibb (1998) but a feedback loop has been added. While STP is portrayed as top-down model, it is important to consider feedback to the point of origin. Information learnt in positioning a product or service in the mind of the customer could provide valuable insight into the segmenting of particular groups.

It is clear from both Kotler and Wright's definitions that in order to deliver real value to both their customers and the organisation, marketers must seek effective and efficient segmentation. Figure 3.2 illustrates in broad terms how a mass market needs to be subdivided, and that this subdivision can be at many levels. The degree of subdivision will depend on the product or service on offer and the dynamic of the market itself.

In order to gain a better understanding of the segmentation processes it is worth briefly considering the scope and scale of markets. These are outlined in Table 3.1 (page 56). They are broad definitions, but they are important in creating the platform for segmenting markets.

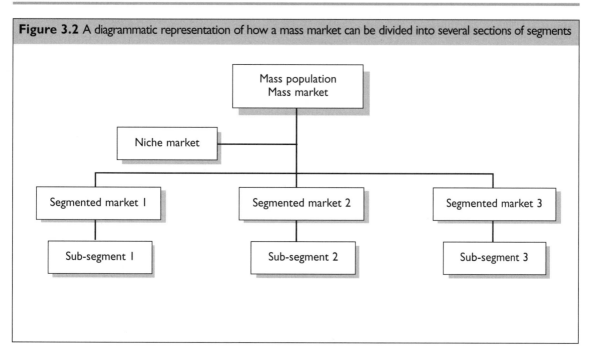

Figure 3.2 A diagrammatic representation of how a mass market can be divided into several sections of segments

The rationale for, and structure of, B2B and B2C segmented markets are different. The methods of segmenting these markets are discussed below.

B2B segmentation

Wright (2004) suggests several reasons that B2B markets require segmenting. These are listed below with additional comments:

◆ To clearly identify disparate customer needs. An organisation operating within B2B markets may have many customers. Thus it is important (in terms of efficiency) to be able to cluster these customers into relevant groups.

◆ To plan strategic and tactical approaches that match each and every customer need. If it knows the composition of the clusters, the organisation can develop the most appropriate tactical plan to meet the needs of customers. At the same time it will be fulfilling the overall corporate strategy.

◆ To develop a portfolio of products and services that match customer needs. By building a relationship with the cluster groups and thus knowing their needs, the organisation can seek to market only relevant products and services.

◆ To focus management and employee attention across every department on customers' needs. This links into Porter's value chain model (Porter 1985), where value can be added at each functional stage from inbound logistics to after-sales service. (See Chapter 6.) Adding value at each stage provides the opportunity to enhance both the perceived and real value of the product or service being marketed.

◆ To build and maintain competitive advantage. In highly dynamic environments organisations normally seek to build and gain a competitive advantage over their rivals in the marketplace. However, once this is gained the organisation will need employee strategies and tactics to defend its position against current and potential challengers.

◆ To provide continuous superior customer service. Many B2B market operations relate to customised projects, for example the design and writing of software packages for specific tasks. In order to provide this kind of front-loaded and back-loaded service the

Table 3.1 The scope and scale of markets

Broad market type	Description
Undifferentiated mass market	The organisation seeks to market a single mass-produced, mass-distributed and mass-promoted item to all buyers. A classic example of this is the launch of the Model T Ford car in 1908. Ford himself referred to it as 'the universal' car (Ford and Crowther 1926), implying that it had to meet mass-market conditions, or in other words appeal to the greater American population without any customisation. However with increasing fragmentation of markets, distribution channels and promotion, the 'one size fits all' approach is difficult to maintain within the majority of markets.
Segments	Kotler (2000) suggests that this 'consists of a large identifiable group within a market with similar wants, purchasing power, geographical location, buying attitudes or buying habits'. Such an approach provides the opportunity to deliver a product or service with the matching marketing mix variables to an appropriate audience.
Niche (single segment specialization)	This can be described as a sub-segment. It is normally a small narrowly defined market where there are only a few suppliers. Niche markets are 'normally' only of interest to small or medium-sized organisations because of the level of returns and overall profitability. However, there are clear examples where strategic business units (SBUs) of much larger organisations have operated in highly profitable niche or specialist markets. Examples of niche markets include specialist publishing (magazines for specific hobbies such as trainspotting), unusual vacation destinations (such as trekking across North African deserts or a polar expedition) and soft-top luxury sports cars such as the UK-built Morgan which are very much aimed at the connoisseur segment of the car-buying market. However not all niche markets are profitable, even if there is only one player in the market.
Multiple segments	An organisation seeks to supply several segments. However it differentiates its products or services to meet the needs of each of the segments. The Hilton® Hotel group illustrates this with a range of separate brands: Hilton® Hotels, Conrad Hotels® (an international luxury brand of hotels and resorts), Doubletree® (an upscale chain of hotels, resorts, suites and clubs), Embassy Suite Hotels® (a pioneer in the all-suite segment of the hotel market in the United States), Hampton Inn and Hampton Inns and Resorts® (accommodation for both business and leisure travellers), Hilton Garden® (mid-priced brand) and Homeward Suites® (an upscale all-suite residential/extended stay hotel chain).
Customised or individual segments or markets	The focus is on one-to-one marketing (also known as micro marketing). This is far from new. For centuries both B2B and B2C customers have been treated as individuals. Consider, for instance, tailored clothing, hairdressing and management consultancy. Increasingly companies have sought mass customisation to achieve economies of scope and scale. The objective here is to produce on a large scale products that meet the individual needs of customers. An excellent example is Dell Computers.
Local customer groups	This is specific to a particular place or location. For instance, the manager of a local supermarket may order in additional qualities of particular products because he or she knows they sell well within that community. Equally, a restaurant might specialise in local delicacies because the owners know this meets the needs of the local community. However, for large supermarket chains there is a risk of diluting their economies of scale and scope by 'localizing'. They will have to balance that against the turnover at the local store.

organisation needs to target specific segments of the B2B software buying market.

◆ To identify new opportunities within existing markets. Only by understanding the needs of the market will an organisation discover, (1) gaps within the existing segment for new products and services, and

(2) how the market needs change over time. Thus the organisation needs to be in a position to exploit possible opportunities.

◆ To identify new opportunities in non-served markets: By breaking markets down into segments or clusters an organisation can clearly see the markets it currently needs to serve. Equally, it might be able to identify possible trends in non-served markets that it could enter at a later stage, perhaps with a new product range. An example is a hotel chain that has been catering for business customers, but sees an opportunity in developing short city breaks (covering Friday to Sunday) for the regional leisure market.

◆ To help bring sales, profit and organisational success. Targeting appropriate segments assists the organisation in controlling costs, developing market potential and long-term profitability.

◆ To prepare all company members for the likelihood of change. Segments do not remain static. As with everything else in business, they are dynamic. Organisations can use the knowledge gained from clusters to analyse how the needs of a segment or market might change over time. Most organisations undergo minor changes, but some are subjected to radical, and at times discordant, change. A historic example is a company that manufactured only typewriters for commercial use. If it had not radically rethought its business and market opportunities when IBM-compatible office computers were introduced, it would have been unlikely to remain in business.

◆ Overall, to make the company more competitive. Again, by building knowledge about the segment and acting on it, an organisation can exploit competitive opportunities.

Segmentation characteristics of B2B markets

The characteristics that define B2B market segmentation can be divided into two broad categories, macro segmentation and micro segmentation.

Macro segmentation

Wright (2004) states that these are 'the factors that distinguish one sector from another, one industry from another and one type of organisation from another'. These could be perceived as the structural factors of the B2B market environment.

The following are the key factors that determine macro segmentation:

Which market(s)?

An organisation needs to determine whether it will operate within the B2B, B2C or both markets, and how, since as we shall see later in this chapter, the B2C market operates differently from the B2B market. If an organisation chooses to operate in both markets, the operations are usually handled by different strategic business units (SBUs). For instance, companies that manufacture household cleaning materials might also have a unit producing a similar product in larger containers for the industrial market.

Business and industrial sectors

In the 1940s the US government introduced a classification system to provide a standardised method of clustering industrial sectors. The principle has been adopted in varying forms by many developed nations. The Standard Industry Codes are valuable to suppliers, since they allow them to develop the right marketing strategy for the most appropriate sector.

Geographic location

Some industries or businesses tend to congregate in specific locations. This might be for several reasons:

◆ They are situated near or at the source of raw materials, for instance coal mines.

◆ The business or industry is dependent on particular natural environmental conditions. This is especially the case in agricultural sectors, such as viticulture. Consider, for instance the weather and soil conditions in the wine-growing regions of South America, France, Italy, Australia, Washington State and California. It is the combination of the weather and soil that provides the conditions for a successful or poor harvest.

◆ It is a centre of knowledge and skill. For instance, Mumbai has a large concentration of advertising agencies and marketing consultancies. On the other hand Bangalore is now the thriving heartland of India's international telemarketing and customer support services operations.

◆ The physical infrastructure supports the clustering of businesses and industries within a particular location.

◆ It is close to particular markets. Some types of SME cluster near major manufacturing hubs. For instance, from the 1930s to the 1970s the UK car industry was situated primarily in the English Midlands. Companies that supplied component parts were also generally situated there.

For profit, not for profit and the public sector

Supplying companies may market their products and services to either all business sectors or a specific sub-sector. These can be categorised under the following headings:

◆ For-profit organisations include micro businesses (usually sole traders), SMEs and public limited companies.

◆ Not-for-profit organisations include registered charities, voluntary organisations, educational centres (in some countries) and friendly societies (also known as mutual assurance societies).

◆ Within a mixed economy the public sector comprises local and national government. Its activities include health, education, defence, the emergency services, waste disposal, social services. The public sector also includes state-owned industries and public corporations such as the British Broadcasting Corporation (BBC).

Increasingly the distinctions between these sectors are becoming blurred, as for-profit and public-sector organisations work in partnership. An example of this is the UK's public–private partnership initiative (PPP), a component of which is the private finance initiative (PFI), where profit-oriented companies invest in public-sector operations such as the London Underground.

Organisational size

Both suppliers and buyers take into account the size of the companies with which they transact business. This is for several reasons including:

◆ The efficient use of resources. This links to Pareto's law that, in essence, states that 80 per cent of the business comes from 20 per cent of the customers (or similar ratios). Thus the company needs to focus upon those customers who are going to deliver significant revenue levels for the company. However, there needs to be a caveat here. There are times when a new customer only buys sporadically and in low volumes. Thus there may be a tendency to de-list this company as a customer simply because it is deemed too expensive to service the account. However there is always a chance that this new company will expand and become a major player in the marketplace. In 'revenge' for being delisted it might place its (now large) orders with the direct competition. Thus careful management of accounts – both large and small – is necessary.

◆ Financial security from both the supplier and buyer perspective. If a company is buying materials or components from a supplier on a regular basis, it need to know its supplier is financially viable. Companies that operate just-in-time (JIT) systems are particularly at risk if a supplier suddenly closes down. Equally a supplier is at risk if a customer fails to pay bills in time or becomes insolvent (see 'Micro segmentation'). However, the size of the company is no guarantee of financial stability. Two prime examples of major financial collapse in recent years have been the US-based Enron and the Italian-based diary giant Parmalat.

Segmentation by products and services provided

The B2B market for products can be further sub-segmented into three categories:

◆ End users, for items such as stationery and other consumables.

◆ Original equipment manufacturers (OEMs) that buy in components for their products. For instance, a computer manufacturer might buy complete chip systems from Intel®, or memory boards from Kingston®.

◆ Distributors, that purchase products to sell on (to end users or OEMs).

Micro segmentation

Wright (2004) states that micro segmentation considers the 'processes involved with the purchasing decision and the behaviour of those involved in making these decisions'. This can be seen on two levels: the behaviour of the organisation, and the behaviour of the individual(s) involved with the supplying company.

Segmenting by organisational buyer behaviour

Several factors can be encapsulated here:

◆ The currency of purchasing. For instance are the buyers current buyers, past buyers or previously non-buyers?

◆ The buying level: light, medium or heavy? Increasingly companies use data warehouses and data mining to produce monthly management reports to identify the level of profitability of each customer.

◆ Buying systems. Some companies operate a centralised rather than a decentralised buying system. For instance, major bookshop chains in the United Kingdom use centralised buying, where the decisions are made at head office rather than by individual store managers.

◆ Single or multiple sources. Some companies buy similar products from various companies. This is for two main reasons. First, they can negotiate competitive rates, and second, if one supplier becomes insolvent the product supply is not interrupted. However, some companies source single suppliers with the aim of building a mutually beneficial relationship. In some cases there is no choice except to have a single supplier, as only one organisation supplies the required product or service.

◆ Payment history: Some buyers settle their accounts with suppliers on the date due. This may not just be a principle of the company but may also be the negotiated basis for a rate reduction. Other companies may take significantly longer to pay. Slow payment is a risk to the cash flow, especially of smaller businesses. Some countries such as Germany have introduced legislation to protect small businesses from larger companies that extend their payment periods.

Segmenting by group and individual buyer behaviour

This can be subdivided into three subsets: the purchasing situation, group buying behaviour and individual buyer behaviour.

◆ **The purchasing decision.** There are many factors involved in the purchasing situation, including the time span from negotiation to the delivery of the product or service. In many cases it is minimal: for instance a company can call a stationery supplier one day and take delivery the next day. However some large-scale projects take years to be completed.

◆ **Group buyer behaviour** concerns the level and number of people involved in the decision-making process. Stationery supplies, for instance, might be controlled by one person, perhaps the senior administrator or facilities manager. In other cases several tiers of management might be involved, especially for large-budget items or projects.

◆ **Individual buyer behaviour:** B2B sales people who see their customers on a regular basis will (or should) have an understanding of their personality and general behaviour. Product or service selling does not only involve knowing a list of features and benefits; it is much more. Groucutt and Telford (1995) emphasise the need to understand relationships:

> Salespeople don't create needs, they exist in the mind of the buyer. The role of the salesperson is to enable the customer to articulate

their needs. That comes through a process of helping customers know what they want – a process whereby the customer talks and the salesperson listens, actively and skilfully.

Thus in a highly competitive B2B environment sales people who build relationships are more likely to 'key in' to the customer's real needs. (Aspects of selling are discussed in Chapter 10.)

■ B2C segmentation

The segmentation of consumer markets is generally very different from that in B2B markets. Segmentation is normally considered under five categories: geographic, demographic, socio-economic, behavioural and lifestyles. It must be stated that while these are considered separately below, they often interrelate and work in concert with each other.

Segmenting by geographic location

We can segment a potential market by considering where customers live and how culture influences them within that location. Consider, for instance, where you live and the culture of that area. What products and services would best suit the people living in your area based upon geography and culture? Consider, for instance, the marketing of food products into the Middle East. There are a range of issues to consider ranging from religious beliefs (what ingredients are acceptable and what are not) to regional tastes and climatic conditions.

Segmenting by demographics

Marketers can analyse and segment the market according to personal characteristics such as gender, age, race and religion, and trends in population movements (such as emigration). These are important characteristics in studying how markets change. For instance, several countries in Europe have ageing populations, where there are more people over 50 than under 18, and the 50-plus group increasingly has a high level of disposable income. Tréguer (2002) argues that:

The over 50s make up an increasingly important sector of the population (often more than

30%) and they possess a purchasing power vastly superior to the under 50 generation (generally in the region of 40% to 45% of the national purchasing power). They increasingly consume everything (their market share of hundreds of consumer, equipment and services markets is often greater than 40%), and yet 95% of marketing and advertising investment continues to be aimed at the under 50s! Less than 5% is devoted to this enormous potential.

(Geographic location and demographics are often merged into *geodemographics*. This combination of information can help to build profiles of groups with similar needs and wants within specific geographical locations. Since the 1970s several companies have developed software models to analyse data on this basis. The two major examples are CACI® with ACORN™ and Experian® with MOSAIC™.)

Segmenting by socio-economic status

This is an analysis of financial status, credit ratings, disposable income, house ownership, family size and occupation. Understanding an individual's financial status enables companies to assign that person to a group, and target the right product or service to match the profile of the group. For instance, a credit card company offering an exclusive Platinum or Black card normally targets a group with income and savings above a certain level, some collateral (as a means of risk reduction) and the propensity to spend using the card. (The card company's revenue is generated from interest and other surcharges.)

Segmenting by behaviour

This focuses on the purchasing habits of individuals that are driven by their individual behaviour. For instance, is the customer loyal to one particular brand? Does he or she buy one type of product or service? Does he or she switch brands, and if so, how often?

A company such as Amazon.com segments its customers on whether they buy only books or CDs, or a combination of both. It can refine the segmenting by considering, for instance, the types of books purchased: perhaps historical romances, contemporary crime thrillers or books on marketing. This knowledge allows Amazon to create a list of recommendations each time a customer logs on to its website.

Segmenting by lifestyle

This is the process of segmenting a market by attempting to understand the way in which individuals (or groups) choose to live their lives. As Groucutt, Leadley and Forsyth (2004) suggest, the factors that determine an individual's lifestyle are often immensely complicated. Moreover, an individual's lifestyle will often change, sometimes in relation to changing socio-economic status and demographic conditions. Returning to the 50+ category illustrated earlier, individuals may have worked hard for most of their lives, and as they reach perhaps early retirement their lifestyle may change. For instance, they may now decide to 'play hard' and spend several months a year travelling. Thus marketers have to account for the fact that individual's lifestyles may go through various metamorphoses through their lives.

■ Formulating a segmentation strategy

Organisations analyse the data gleaned from the various approaches to segmentation, and consider how their products and services match these segments. From this they structure their marketing mix to match the needs of that particular segment or segments. In the mini case study on page 64, the cruise vacation market is briefly analysed.

We discussed earlier (see Table 3.1) how some companies target multiple segments with differentiated brands, using the example of the Hilton® Hotel group and its associated brands. The same situation applies to the cruise vacation market, where the Carnival Corporation has several major brands catering for different segments of the overall market.

Targeting

Whether it operates in the B2B or B2C markets, or both, any organisation has to decide which segment(s) to target. Efficient targeting is fundamental for the following reasons:

◆ The organisation can focus its resources on what it believes will be the most profitable segments. If it operates within several segments, the coverage might spread its resources too thinly, and it might find itself investing resources into marketing to segments that provide a poor return on the investment.

◆ It provides an analysis of the competition. By focusing attention on key segments the organisation can gauge the particular strengths and weaknesses of the opposition against its own. The organisation may discover that there are particular segments that are not particularly well served by the competition. Equally, though it may determine that the competition is particularly strong and protective of its market position within that segment. Thus the organisation will need to consider whether or not it is viable to enter that segment. The organisation may not want to engage in battle with the competitor as this may be damaging and resource depleting in the longer term.

◆ It enables the organisation to consider how it will use the marketing mix to gain entry, grow and sustain position within a segment.

◆ It enables the organisation to find a strategic fit between its marketing strategy and its longer-term objectives. Although the organisation could operate within several segments, it needs to target the segments that fit its overall corporate objectives. For example, a cruise vacation line could possible deploy its ships across several segments. However, if its corporate objectives were to be in the large-scale mass-market themed short-cruise sector in the Caribbean, it would not strategically fit the ultra-luxury Mediterranean segment. It is unlikely be a profitable segmenting of the market for the company, even though the vessels, facilities and crew could physically cater for that market.

◆ It allows the organisation to consider any ethical and legal issues that might affect segments differently. For instance, a company might decide not to target a particular geographic region for fear of offending local cultural traditions. This is particularly the case with foodstuffs that contain ingredients not all religious groups will eat. Equally, a company might choose not to target a country because of its poor enforcement of copyright protection.

◆ It improves communication between the seller and buyer. This provides an opportunity to build a mutually beneficial relationship, especially in the B2B environment.

◆ It allows the organisation to focus its attention on segments it understands. There is always a risk that companies will focus their attention on as many 'relevant' segments as possible. As well as diluting resources (as stated earlier), they risk entering markets where they have only the barest of knowledge. For example, many UK-based universities look to recruit international students to study in the UK, and some look to develop campuses abroad or go into partnership with overseas universities. They have the best chance of success if they build up their knowledge and contacts in a country or region, and focus their marketing efforts there. To target students from regions or countries they do not know well runs the risk of failure which could be damaging not only financially, but reputationally as well.

Positioning

Here the company seeks to position its brand at a particular 'location' within the targeted market segment. Once the product or service is positioned within the market, it will stand alongside its major and minor competitors. The company is then making a clear statement to both customers and competitors about where it believes its product or service is 'located' within that market.

This is particularly important in what Ries and Trout (2001) call the 'battle for the mind'. How and where the product or service is positioned in the minds of customers will generate either success or failure. This is how buyers 'perceive' the value of the product or service being marketed to them. In an overcrowded and cluttered market, product or service positioning is important in order to help it stand out from the crowd.

Different variables help determine a product's or service's (in other words, a brand's) position within the marketplace. These include:

◆ Brand attributes. These are the particular features and benefits of the brand. A buyer expects a brand to deliver the features and benefits that match the brand's reputation. For example, a UK£160,000 Aston Martin sports car will deliver different brand attributes than a UK£10,000 saloon.

◆ Price/quality relationship. A product or service has to be priced at the right level to reflect the quality provided. For instance, a hotel that prices its rooms at UK£400 per night will have to provide the quality expected from a four or five-star hotel and not a two-star one.

◆ Competitor(s) within the segment(s). While competitors will challenge new entrants to the segment, being associated with such competitors can heighten a brand's reputation.

◆ Brand user. The individuals or groups that use the brand (product or service) also assist in positioning it in the mind of other customers. Celebrity promotion can assist in positioning the brand in the mind of those who want to be (or are) like the celebrity. Movie stars, television and sports personalities who have promoted various brands over the years, including Sean Connery (Jim Beam whisky), Laurence Olivier (Olivier cigarettes manufactured by Benson & Hedges) and David Beckham (Brylcreem™ and mobile phones). (See Chapter 10.)

◆ Brand class. This can be defined as the status the brand (product or service) acquires within the marketplace. For instance, an Aston Martin DB5 car is considered an upmarket classic luxury sports car. Equally, the six-star rated Burj Al Arab hotel in Dubai is considered to be one of the most luxurious and stunning hotels in the world.

◆ Positioning across segments. Companies also seek to position their products across related overlapping segments of the market. For instance companies such as Procter & Gamble and Unilever use this strategy in the detergents market. They position different brands within the various market segments. Customers relate to the brand names and not the corporate identities of Procter & Gamble and Unilever. Moreover, both companies tend to have several brands competing within each segment as well as across segments.

Repositioning

Markets are dynamic and turbulent, perhaps more so today than ever before. Therefore companies have to be both proactive and reactive to changing circumstances, and that may include repositioning their brands.

Repositioning may occur for several reasons, including:

◆ Evolution of both the company and the brand. While some companies obtain the 'perfect' position for their brand from day one, for others (perhaps the majority) it is an evolutionary process. The corporate histories of many organisations show repositioning of their brand(s) as the company's image and reputation develop.

◆ Extending the life of the product or service. Chapter 9 examines the product life cycle, the stages a product or service goes through from introduction to decline. A company might reposition in an attempt to rejuvenate an ailing brand. For example, Lucozade was originally introduced as a drink for people recovering from illness. It was repositioned in the market as a high-energy sports drink. This repositioning was supported by effective management of the marketing mix through the creation of new packaging, promotion and variants on the original flavour. This repositioning has been particularly successful.

◆ The wrong segment. A company may have positioned its brand in the wrong segment, perhaps because it underestimated or overestimated the value of the segment. In the latter case, competitors within that segment might exert additional pressure, forcing the repositioning.

◆ Changing societal conditions. Societies as a whole change, and so do individuals within societies. These changes may be the result of new knowledge and socio-economic condi-

tions. Therefore demands for particular products and service levels may also change. For example, overall UK holidaymakers seek today higher quality and service standards from their packaged holidays (Palmer, 2000). Today there are significant differences in the quality of packaged holidays from those of the 1970s. Tour operators have had to reposition themselves within the packaged holiday sector to reflect these changes.

Perceptual or positioning mapping

This is a strategic tool that allows the company to show visually the position of its brand relative to the completion within the marketplace. The mapping exercise can also identify any gaps within the segment that could be exploited, perhaps with a modified product or service.

Figure 3.3 illustrates the positioning of a selection of cruise vacation companies based upon the segments Ultra luxury, Luxury, Premium and Mass market. It has to be remembered that this is a

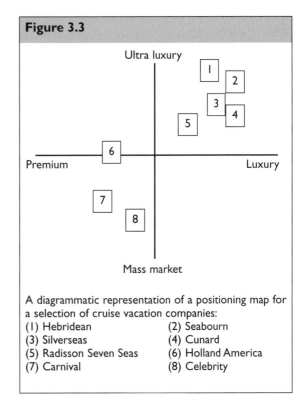

Figure 3.3

A diagrammatic representation of a positioning map for a selection of cruise vacation companies:
(1) Hebridean (2) Seabourn
(3) Silverseas (4) Cunard
(5) Radisson Seven Seas (6) Holland America
(7) Carnival (8) Celebrity

Mini case 3.1

Segmentation, targeting and positioning within the cruise vacation market

The cruise vacation market has become a multi-billion dollar industry with both major and specialist companies operating within highly competitive markets. The companies segment their markets using the criteria discussed in this chapter. From this information they devise a marketing mix to support the positioning of their brand within the market.

The following are key STP factors used in the cruise vacation market:

◆ Geographic – destinations. Some cruise lines specialise in one or two specific destinations. For instance, the Louis Cruise Line offers mini cruises from Cyprus to Egypt, Greece (Rhodes), Lebanon (Beirut), and Syria (Latakia).

◆ Customer profile. Individuals or groups that are targeted include independent travellers, families, singles, wedding parties and honeymooners, gay and lesbian singles and couples. Within all these groups there are a variety of socio-economic levels and lifestyles.

◆ Cruise types. Some cruise lines create particular types of cruise, for instance cruise and stay (a mixture of a cruise and land-based vacation), mini cruises (see the Louis Cruise Line example above) and themed cruises (which vary from the permanent Disney theme on the Disney Cruise Line to specialist cruises that visit locations to study the flora and fauna, antiques or the music of the region). Specialists in the various fields usually accompany such cruises.

◆ Positioning within the market sector (see Figure 3.3). Positions include mass market, premium, luxury, ultra luxury and niche/specialist. For instance, in the niche market sector Poseidon Artic Voyages provides cruises to the Artic Circle on board a nuclear-powered icebreaker.

Figure 3.4

© Hebridean Cruises. Reproduced with kind permission.

Two photographs from Hebridean Cruises illustrating the ultra luxury end of the market sector. These are staterooms on board the *Hebridean Spirit*.

diagrammatic representation of their relative positions within the markets. A company positioning itself within a segment normally does so through a detailed analysis of its brand (and brand values) compared with its immediate competitors.

■ Chapter summary

This chapter has examined the rationale behind and the structure of segmentation, targeting and positioning (STP) of products and services in both a B2B and B2C context.

In order to become and remain competitive within a marketplace, a company must:

◆ separate the market into appropriate segments with a focus upon those that are likely to deliver the best return on investment

◆ target the potential customers within the designated segment(s) who would derive the most benefits from the product or service being marketed

◆ successfully position the product or service in the mind of potential customers by illustrating the benefits they will gain by consuming the product or service

◆ be prepared to reposition their products or services if the market conditions warrant it.

The STP of products and services can only be achieved by the judicious management of the marketing mix. However, the organisation must initially be relatively certain it has chosen the most appropriate segments to enter. The concept of finding the 'perfect' segment might be acceptable in a theoretically oriented debate, but in the real world companies must be aware that their chosen segment may not be the right one. For various reasons, including unpredictable dynamic market changes, the company might realise that the segment(s) is inappropriate for its needs. It then needs to take often-radical actions to protect its brand and indeed its overall business.

The STP model is a viable one, but the whole process of segmenting and targeting markets and positioning brands is far from a perfect science.

■ Questions for review and reflection

1 Critically evaluate the rationale for segmenting a mass consumer market.

2 Working with fellow students, consider how you might segment the following markets within either your home country or the country where you are studying: coffee, chocolate, ready-prepared meals (as purchased in a store or supermarket), toothpaste, take-away meals (as in McDonald's™) and sports shoes (trainers).

3 Working with fellow students, draw a positioning map for your university or college. You will probably need to consider it in relation to national rather than international competition. What factors do you think differentiate your university or college from competitors in the marketplace? Were these differences the reason you personally chose to study there?

4 Reflect back to the societal issues discussed in Chapter 2. Then consider how lifestyles have changed within your home country and how they now influence the segmentation of markets.

5 Using the Internet and other library resources, examine the following issue. There has been much discussion, in various countries, about the ethical implications of segmenting and targeting children under the age of 12 with product marketing. What is your view? Support it with evidence.

References

Dibb, S. (1998) 'Market segmentation: strategies for success', *Marketing Intelligence and Planning* **16**(7), pp. 394–406.

Ford, H. and Crowther, S. (1926) *My Life and Work*, London: Heinemann.

Groucutt, J., Leadley, P. and Forsyth, P. (2004) *Marketing: Essential principles, new realities*, London: Kogan Page.

Groucutt, J. and Telford, A. (1995) *Communicating for Improved Business Performance*, Cheltenham: Thornes.

Kotler, P. (2000) *Marketing Management*, Millennium edn, Harlow: Prentice Hall.

Palmer, A. (2000) *Principles of Marketing*, Oxford: Oxford University Press.

Porter, M. E. (1985) *Competitive Advantage*, New York: Free Press.

Ries, A. and Trout, J. (2001) *Positioning: The battle for the mind*, New York: McGraw-Hill Education.

Smith, W. R. (1957) 'Product differentiation and market segmentation as alternative marketing strategies', *Journal of Marketing* **21**(1), pp. 3–8.

Tréguer, J-P. (2002) *50+ Marketing*, Basingstoke: Palgrave.

Wright, R. (2004) *Business-to-Business Marketing: A step-by-step guide*, Harlow: FT Prentice Hall.

Marketing Research

Contents

Learning outcomes   66
Introduction   66
The role of research in
   marketing   66
Potential benefits   67
Understanding the
   market   67
Forecasting   67
Improving return on
   investment   67
Exploiting new market
   opportunities   68
Reducing the level of
   risk   68
Supporting competitive
   advantage   68
A systematic process for
   marketing research   68
Establishing the need
   for marketing
   research   68
Problem definition   68
Research objective or
   hypothesis   69
Research brief   69
Identifying the relevant
   methodology   69
Questionnaire design   69
Data collection   70
Data analysis   70
Research report   70
Marketing research
   techniques   70
Primary research
   techniques   71
Secondary research
   techniques   73
Does everyone use
   marketing research?   77
Chapter summary   77
Questions for review
   and reflection   77
References   78

Learning outcomes

After completing this chapter you should be able to:

▶ debate the value to an organisation of undertaking marketing research

▶ explain the different marketing research techniques that a company or organisation can employ

▶ examine how marketing research can help an organisation make effective decisions in relation to the marketing of its products and/or services.

Introduction

This chapter examines the role of marketing research within the contemporary business environment. It considers four core areas:

◆ the various techniques that organisations can use with the aim of better understanding the marketplace

◆ how complex environmental forces influence or affect marketing research data

◆ the reasoning behind organisations undertaking marketing research

◆ why some organisations choose not to use marketing research before launching a product or service.

While marketing research is often deemed essential to business, it must be remembered that it is not an exact science. It can only provide an indicator of possible outcomes, and possible reasons for those outcomes. Information gathering is one thing; how it is interpreted and used to make decisions is another. Nevertheless, market research can contribute to a better understanding of how to manage the marketing mix, product/service life cycles, why people buy, and how to improve the product or service offering.

The role of research in marketing

First we should consider a definition of marketing research. One of the most succinct is by Burns and Bush (2000) They describe it as:

Figure 4.1

© Shona Muir. Reproduced with kind permission.

The indoor market in Barcelona, Spain. Why do people buy? Whether it is fruit, vegetables or the latest downloadable music clips, marketers need to understand buyer behaviour and trends. Marketing research helps us to analyse purchasing habits and tastes (both current and potentially those in the future).

> The process of designing, gathering, analysing and reporting of information that may be used to solve a specific marketing problem.

The marketing 'problem' they refer to can be determining anything from the market for a new product, to why an existing product no longer captures the market's imagination. Thus the 'problem' can be diverse in form and structure.

Groucutt, Leadley and Forsyth (2004) suggest that prior to undertaking marketing research organisations need to have:

◆ a reasonable understanding of their targeted segments, and thus an ability to position their product or service

◆ a clear objective as to what the organization is aiming to achieve – both through marketing and corporate objectives.

This gives the organisation a sound basis on which to develop its knowledge of the market, and allows it to be focused.

■ Potential benefits

The effective and efficient use of marketing research can provide organisations with several short and long-term benefits. The outline below is developed from the work of Quee (1999).

Understanding the market

In a hypercompetitive environment[1] (D'Aveni 1995), organisations need to have a clear understanding of the dynamics of the market(s) in which they currently operate. This understanding needs to encompass:

◆ current customers

◆ current competitors

◆ potential customers

◆ potential competitors

◆ the impact of macro environmental forces.

It is only through understanding, or at least attempting to understand, such diverse groups that an organisation can be both proactive and reactive to changing circumstances.

Forecasting

Marketing research provides a systematic approach to the creation of information that will improve forecasting potential. For instance, there is little value in a company producing millions of a particular toy if the market research suggests it will only sell a few thousand. Of course the situation may change, especially if word of mouth (see Chapter 10) builds the profile and it becomes a major success within the marketplace. However, if the initial marketing research indicates a lower market penetration, it would be unwise for the company to produce large volumes. The product will simply be stockpiled in a warehouse, depreciating in value while incurring warehousing costs.

Improving return on investment

Companies should continually seek to improve their bottom-line performance. In other words they need to use their resources both efficiently and effectively. Of course, that does not mean operating 'on the edge', with the absolute minimum of (for instance) human capital. That is a potentially high-risk scenario. However, companies should evaluate ways of improving return on investment. This is particularly the case where substantial funds have been invested in research and development to create the product (or service) in the first instance.

Exploiting new market opportunities

Marketing research is not only about here and now problems. As we have already noted, it can be used for forecasting market demand. Moreover, it can be used to discover potential product and service gaps within the market.

Reducing the level of risk

The development and subsequent introduction of new products and services can present significant financial and business risks to companies. Many companies have introduced new products only to find that they are poorly received in the market-place and no amount of marketing spend will reverse their fortunes. In some cases the company faces bankruptcy as a result.

Marketing research might provide information on whether the product either has a market at all, or needs minor adjustments to meet market needs.

Supporting competitive advantage

As with competitor intelligence (see Chapter 5), knowledge management (in all its forms) provides information on market trends, customer prefer-ences, and competitors and their potential actions. Collectively this information (and its efficient management) can provide the platform for a company to develop a competitive advantage strategy.

■ A systematic process for marketing research

It is generally accepted (based on its definition) that the process of undertaking marketing research is carried out systematically. Several basic steps tend to be completed prior to moving on to the next stage. This is a general overview of the steps in the marketing research process. They are illustrated in Figure 4.2 and explained in detail below.

Establishing the need for marketing research

The organisation first has to determine whether it needs to, or actually can, undertake marketing research. The three key issues here are:

◆ The information that the organisation requires could already be available through sources of secondary research data. For example, commercial research companies produce market reports by sector. Purchasing this data may prove to be cheaper than instigating their own research.

◆ The organisation might not have the time to collect raw data and then process it. Other factors (especially macro factors) might require relatively speedy decision making which precludes the use of marketing research.

◆ It may be too expensive for the company to either originate its own research or purchase research from a commercial market research company. This is especially the case for micro, small and medium-sized enterprises (SMEs).

Problem definition

This relates to the question, 'What are we trying to investigate and why?' Initially you might think this is straightforward. However, it is rarely the case.

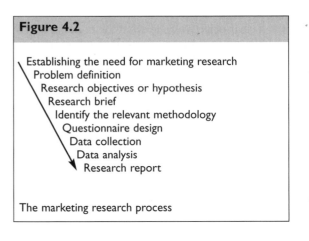

Figure 4.2

Establishing the need for marketing research
Problem definition
Research objectives or hypothesis
Research brief
Identify the relevant methodology
Questionnaire design
Data collection
Data analysis
Research report

The marketing research process

The organisation might have several 'problems' or issues to contend with, and be faced with prioritising them. Again, this could be easier said than done.

The 'problem' needs to be defined clearly so that the researchers can focus on real issues rather than perceived ones. If there is a lack of clarity, the organisation might pursue the wrong course of action. This in turn could lead to loss of market share or poor positioning of a new product within the marketplace. Rectifying such a situation might prove costly.

Research objective or hypothesis

Groucutt *et al.* (2004) suggest that this should be 'developed as a range of scenarios for the marketplace that are plausible, rational and in "reality" quite probable.' It is the hypothesis that in turn defines the type of research technique to be used.

Research brief

This is the brief that is presented to either the internal or external marketing research team. It normally contains:

◆ relevant background information – in essence why this research needs to be undertaken (the problem or research question will be included here)

◆ the objectives of the research – what is to be tested and why

◆ how the testing of the objectives will, or could, assist the organisation's marketing.

From this information the research methodology – using primary data, secondary data or a combination – will be determined. Depending upon the complexity of the issues and/or brief, the marketing research team might conduct exploratory research to clarify the objectives and/or the suitability of the methodology.

Identifying the relevant methodology

The research team needs to determine whether primary research, secondary research or a combination of both will be used. *Primary research* (also known as field research) involves data that is collected and then analysed specifically for the specific project. *Secondary research* (also known as desk research) is the analysis of data that has been collected by other organisations on the subject or topic area. The scope of primary and secondary data is discussed later in this chapter.

Questionnaire design

This relates to primary research where the research team wants to ask specific questions of a defined sample of people. As a student you will be familiar with questionnaires at the end of modules, terms or semesters. These are designed to provide your college or university with an overview of your perceptions and how these relate to your original expectations. However, a questionnaire is not simply a basis for collecting a specific amount of facts. It must be designed in such a way that the information can be collated and then analysed. It is only when the data is analysed that any meaningful information can be determined.

Zikmund (1994) suggests that there are five major areas research teams must analyse in order to develop an effective questionnaire. These are:

◆ What questions should be asked? This leads back to the purpose of the marketing research. In other words, what is the organisation trying to find out? For instance, a college or university module evaluation questionnaire is intended to find out how the module is rated on specific criteria from a student perspective. So for example, it might ask respondents to rate the core textbook on a scale of 1 to 5, with 1 being poor and 5 being outstanding. This gives the module leader an insight into the class's (that is, the sample's) view of the textbook.

◆ How should each question be phrased? Writing questionnaire questions is a complex process for several reasons:

● The question must be phrased in such a way that potential respondents will be able to understand it. Therefore questions tend to be short and succinct, using everyday (non-colloquial) language.

● There must be clarity in the question design to avoid any potential ambiguity. The potential respondent must know what you *actually* mean by asking that question.

● Each question must focus on one issue or topic only. Two or more issues per question will only lead to confusion.

● The question must be phrased so that potential respondents can express their opinion and their opinion only. Questions must not 'lead' the respondent to a particular answer. There is also an ethical issue here. The research must be unbiased, and the research team must approach the project with an objective mindset.

◆ What is the most appropriate sequencing for the questions? Generally questionnaires begin with fairly simple questions (usually to relax the respondent), then gradually build to focus on the specific data to be collected. Some questions incorporate filtering devices. So if a respondent answers, say, question 4 with a 'No', he or she is directed to skip a section of questions that are not relevant to his or her experiences.

◆ How should the questionnaire be presented? Some questionnaires are simplistic in their format, comprising a series of questions with short dichotomous 'Yes' or 'No' type answers. Others are more complex, featuring combinations of question types, for instance, multiple choice (using a scale to rate an experience) and open-ended, where respondents can state their views in their own words. Returning to the earlier example, while the textbook might be scored on a scale of 1 to 5, the next question might be, 'What for you have been the strengths of this module?' Respondents are then provided with a space in which to give a free-form qualitative answer.

◆ How should the questionnaire be tested? It is useful to pre-test questionnaires on a small sample of the target audience. This allows the research team to make any necessary adjustments prior to the rollout of the primary research.

Data collection

This is the bringing together of the data from all sources (primary, secondary or both).

Data analysis

Once the marketing research team are satisfied that they have collected all the necessary data, they can proceed to analyse it. Raw data is of little value. It must be critically evaluated and analysed in order for it to have any meaning. The analysis may range from time-series and regression analysis to testing variance and qualitative explanations of perspectives. Today much of the statistical analysis is undertaken using software packages such as SPSS®.

Research report

The final process element is the production of the research report. It is important that the research team know exactly who will read the report. In the vast majority of cases the readers or decision makers are not marketing researchers. They might have little interest in the minutiae of data gathering and analysis, but will need an overview (usually presented through an executive summary), a presentation of the results (analysis and findings) and a set of justified recommendations (conclusions and recommendations).

The commissioners of the research use the report as the basis on which to make their decision – and as I said earlier, the success or failure of a product or service can rest on that decision, and so on the quality of the marketing research. However, it must be stated that circumstances can and do change, sometimes dramatically, and these changes might make research that was originally valid invalid. Risks like this can only be alluded to in a research document. It is for the decision makers to take into consideration the 'probable situations' when making their final decision.

■ Marketing research techniques

This section gives a brief overview of the different types of primary and secondary research techniques. (Table 4.1 lists the different categories.) The marketing research team needs to determine which technique or combination of techniques is most suitable to use in attempting to answer the research question and meet the objectives. Other limiting factors might need to be taken into consideration, including the time frame available to conduct the research, and the budget.

Primary research techniques

Observation

In this technique an individual's behaviour is observed without the observer communicating with him or her, thus the person is oblivious to the fact that he or she is under observation. Within the term 'observation' there are many sub-categories. These include:

◆ Structured human observation. This is where specific behaviours are observed, for example, how long grocery shoppers spend examining fruit before they decide whether to make a purchase.

◆ Mechanical observation. These can vary from electronic counters that simply log the number of people who enter a store and when they do so. This is useful in planning traffic flows through a store at specific times of the day. Groucutt and Griseri (2004) refer to e-observations, that occur in electronic environments. Organisations can track surfers and regular visitors to their web pages, seeing how they react or behave in that particular web space. This can, for example, identify the most frequently visited pages in a website.

Observation is valuable, for instance, in determining traffic flows or movements of people. This enables organisations to improve the throughput of people in supermarkets, visitor attractions and even metro stations. This is also an useful technique for determining the right height for shelving

Table 4.1 The different research techniques available to marketers

Research technique	Main category	Sub-categories
Primary	Observation	Structured human observation Mechanical observation
	Focus groups	
	In-depth interviews	
	Questionnaires	Personal interview Telephone Mailed or postal e-questionnaire
Secondary	Internal information	Sales history Payment history Inventories Research reports
	External information	Commercial research reports Company directories Competitor information Government reports Industry sources Think tanks

(supermarkets), ticket machines (metros) and purchasing stations (check-out counters). (See also Chapter 13 on people and Chapter 14 on physical evidence.)

There are both legal and ethical issues involved in observation. In some countries it is a legal requirement to inform people that they are being observed, and there also is the issue of privacy. Is observing a group of people shopping for groceries an invasion of their privacy? Some might argue yes, others no. Often it is a fine line that distinguishes an ethical from an unethical act.

Focus groups

The psychologist Ernest Dichter devised the concept of the focus group in the 1930s, and used focus groups to gauge people's reaction to the brand Ivory soap. He developed the concept out of group therapy techniques, which were popular in Europe at the time. A focus group typically contains between six and eight people, who are:

◆ Relevant to the product, service or topic being discussed. For example, for a toy manufacturer's research they might be mothers with children in the three-to-five-year age group.

◆ Potential users of the product or service, or people with a direct link to the topic. For instance, a political party wanting to know what the key issues are for first-time voters could create a focus group of young people who have just reached voting age.

◆ Of a geodemographic composition that is relevant to the product, service or topic of discussion.

An objective moderator usually encourages group members to share their views on a particular topic, for instance the launch of a potential new product. The moderator's role is to keep the group focused on the topic area, without too much digression. Often for the purposes of objectivity the group is not told the name of the manufacturer or supplier of the product or service being discussed.

In-depth interviews

An organisation might decide it needs to conduct in-depth interviews with potential and existing customers. These are usually conducted face to face. An interviewer asks an interviewee a series of questions that might be quantifiable (the interviewee is asked to assigning numerical values to something, for example rating it on a scale of 1 to 5) or qualitative (the interviewee is asked to give his or her personal views in response to open-ended questions).

Questionnaires

A questionnaire consists of a specially designed series of questions focused on a specific topic or a range of topics. The 'range' will be very much determined by the objectives of the research. Questionnaires can be executed in several ways. Often their length determines which is used:

◆ Personal interview questionnaire: a face-to-face interviewer takes the respondent through the questions one by one. These can be conducted in the home, place of work, or a high-traffic environment or thoroughfare such as a metro or railway station.

◆ Telephone questionnaire: an interviewer takes the respondent through the questions over the telephone. This is usually reserved for short questionnaires, especially if participants are phoned at their place of work.

◆ Mailed or postal questionnaire: the questionnaire is mailed to a specific segmented target group, who (it is hoped) complete it unaided and mail it back. This is usually reserved for large questionnaire formats where the organisation is asking a wide range of questions. In the United Kingdom, for instance, there are targeted mail questionnaires that seek to build a picture of the purchasing habits of specific groups of the population. The questions cover topics ranging from the number of credit cards and the frequency of newspaper purchasing, to the type and location of annual vacations. Cash prize draws are usually a feature of such questionnaires, to encourage respondents to spend the time they take to complete.

◆ e-questionnaires: increasingly questionnaires are being used in the electronic environment. There are currently two processes that can be used:

● Emailed questionnaires: the potential

respondents are pre-selected and emailed for their response.

● Web questionnaires: potential respondents self-select a website and choose to complete the questionnaire. There are usually multiple choice or two-choice (yes/no type) answers, and the participants click on their selections. Once the questionnaire is completed the information can be stored automatically ready for computer-generated analysis.

Secondary research techniques

Secondary research is based on material that has already been gathered and analysed. Such information might be available to an organisation internally, externally or a combination of the two.

Internal information

This is the information that exists within the organisation. It can provide valuable data to address the research question and objectives. The range of internal information can include:

◆ Sales history: when individuals or organisa-

tions purchase products or services on either a regular or ad hoc basis they create a sales history. This history will include volumes purchased, incentives/special offers accepted, purchasing time frames (regularity of purchase) and financial value to the business.

◆ Payment history: an analysis of a customer's payment history can show whether or not the customer is creditworthy. In other words, does he or she (or it) pay on time?

◆ Inventories: some products sell on a regular basis, while others are seasonal (for example, overcoats sell in the autumn ready for the winter). Companies need to know (1) which products are selling, (2) which are not, (3) what are the seasonal variations, if applicable, and (4) if there is no seasonal issue, why products are not selling. It is not just the issue of the movement of product out of the warehouse onto the shelves and then into the customer's ownership. The slow or non-existent movement of product has two cost implications for the company: (1) little or no revenue generation, and (2) storage costs.

◆ Research reports: companies or departments within companies often commission a variety of reports. This information can be valuable in understanding market trends, for instance.

Mini case 4.1

Module evaluation questionnaires

Most university colleges, faculties and schools undertake regular evaluation questionnaires. This is in order to establish how students feel about a particular course, module or simply studying at the establishment. The following example was used to gather feedback from first-year, first-term students at a British university. This was done for two reasons:

◆ Provided the recommendations from the current student group had validity (relevance), they could be applied when the course was run for the next student group.

◆ The responses were discussed at staff Quality Assurance meetings, so students who completed this questionnaire could benefit from any changes

made to subsequent modules as a result of the feedback.

One issue with questionnaires like these is that they seem a good idea in theory, but they are of no practical use unless the feedback is acted upon. You may want to consider how they work at your own college or university.

As you can see from the sample questionnaire (overleaf), it is based upon both qualitative and quantitative data gathering. If there were a large student group the quantitative information would be read using optically read data sheets. For example students would mark, in pencil, columns representing A, B, C or D and these would be computer scanned to provide the overall results. This can be achieved in a matter of minutes compared with an individual painstakingly counting up the returns for each value, A, B, C, D or E.

Module I Module Evaluation Questionnaire

Throughout your degree programme at this University you will be asked to complete numerous questionnaires that ask you to evaluate the module you have just undertaken. Whilst this constant evaluation may seem tiresome, it is your opportunity to comment upon the module, and help us to improve it. Please circle, using a pen, A B C D or E for each question to show the alternative that reflects your opinion or view of this module.

PLEASE <u>DO NOT</u> WRITE EITHER YOUR NAME OR STUDENT NUMBER ON THIS QUESTIONNAIRE.

Section I: What is your OVERALL view of this module?

1	It was worthwhile	A B C D E	It was not worthwhile
2	I have learnt a lot about business	A B C D E	I have learnt nothing about business
3	It was well organised	A B C D E	It was not well organised
4	It got me interested in the subject	A B C D E	It did not get me interested in the subject
5	It was intellectually demanding	A B C D E	It was not intellectually demanding
6	Too much material / content	A B C D E	Too little material / content
7	It was enjoyable	A B C D E	It was not enjoyable
8	It was well taught	A B C D E	It was poorly taught

Section 2: What is your evaluation of the LECTURES on this module?

9	They were clearly presented	A B C D E	They were not clearly presented
10	They were interesting	A B C D E	They were dull
11	They were well organised	A B C D E	They were not well organised
12	Helped my understanding	A B C D E	Did not help my understanding

13	How many lectures did you attend? Please tick.	ALL	14	13	12	11	10	9	8	7	6	5	4	3	2	1

Section 3: What is your evaluation of the SEMINARS on this module?

14	They were valuable	A B C D E	They were of little value
15	They were enjoyable	A B C D E	They were not enjoyable
16	They involved discussion	A B C D E	They involved little discussion
17	They were well organised	A B C D E	They were not well organised
18	I was encouraged to participate	A B C D E	I was not encouraged to participate
19	My seminar tutor was approachable	A B C D E	My seminar tutor was not approachable

20	How many seminars did you attend? Please tick.	ALL	14	13	12	11	10	9	8	7	6	5	4	3	2	1

Section 4: What is your evaluation of The Student Workbooks (Main and Supplementary) on this module?		
21	They were well written	A B C D E	They were poorly written
22	They were very useful	A B C D E	They were not very useful
23	There was too much information	A B C D E	There was not enough information
24	They were well presented	A B C D E	They were not well presented

Section 5: What is your evaluation of the handouts you received on this module?		
25	They were well written	A B C D E	They were poorly written
26	They were helpful	A B C D E	They were not helpful
27	There was the right number of handouts	A B C D E	There were not enough handouts

Section 6: How would you evaluate your own PERSONAL contribution to the module?		
28	I prepared for each session	A B C D E	I did not prepare for each session
29	I was always on time for lectures	A B C D E	I was never on time for lectures
30	I always contributed to discussions	A B C D E	I never contributed to discussions
31	I read the business sections of the major news-papers	A B C D E	I never read the business sections of the major newspapers
32	I watched the business news on TV	A B C D E	I never watched the business news on TV
33	I listened to the business news on the radio	A B C D E	I never listened to the business news on the radio
34	I read the relevant sections in the textbook	A B C D E	I never read the relevant sections in the text-book
35	I read other books on the subject areas	A B C D E	I never read other books on the subject areas

Section 7: What is your evaluation of the recommended textbook for this module?		
36	The textbook was very readable	A B C D E	The textbook was not very readable
37	The textbook was very interesting	A B C D E	The textbook was not very interesting
38	I liked the textbook	A B C D E	I disliked the textbook
39	If you disliked the textbook have you any suggestions for a possible replacement? If so, please state below:		

Section 8: What is your evaluation of the COURSEWORK (Assignment and Posters)?		
40	Both involved thinking and understanding	A B C D E	Both required very little thinking and under-standing
41	The assignment topic was interesting	A B C D E	The assignment topic was dull
42	Both the assignment and poster assessed important areas of the module	A B C D E	Both the assignment and poster did not assess important areas of the module
43	Both added much to my understanding of the subject areas	A B C D E	Both added little to my understanding of the subject areas
44	Both related well to the module as a whole	A B C D E	Both related poorly to the module as a whole
45	Both came at the right times within the two terms	A B C D E	Both came at the wrong times within the two terms
46	Working in groups on the posters was enjoy-able	A B C D E	Working in groups on the posters was not enjoyable

/ continued overleaf

Section 9: A few details about yourself

47   Male   M   F   Female
48   I have studied business before   Yes   No   I have never studied business before
49   Ethnic Origin: Please tick the ethnic group to which you feel you belong:

Asian [ ] European [ ] African [ ] Caribbean [ ] Chinese [ ]

Middle Eastern [ ] South American [ ] Canadian [ ] North American [ ]

Other [ ] Please state _____

50   Age (Please indicate your age range) 18–25 [ ] 26–33 [ ] 34–41 [ ]

Section 10: Finally, please will you comment on the following areas:

51: STRENGTHS: What, for you, have been the strengths of this module?

52: WEAKNESSES: What, for you, have been the weaknesses of this module?

53: IMPROVEMENTS: What improvements would you suggest for this module?

54: ADVICE: What advice would you give to next year's students?

Thank you for completing this questionnaire. We take your evaluation and suggestions very seriously.

External information

This is information that the organisation acquires from external sources. In some cases it is free (for instance, information from trade/industry publications) but it is often charged for (for instance, industry and market research reports). The range of external information includes:

◆ Commercial research reports produced by independent research companies. They cover, for instance, B2C and B2B markets, specific countries and societal trends. Many of them can be purchased online and then downloaded.

◆ Company directories which provide information on companies, organisations and the sectors in which they operate. Increasingly, this information is available online by subscription. Previously it was available only in book form, and was prone to becoming dated very quickly. However, online systems provide the opportunity for regular updating.

◆ Competitor information: we explain in Chapter 6 why it is vital for a company to gauge the abilities of current and potential rival companies, especially if it is operating in a highly competitive market. Information such as the annual report and accounts, marketing literature and articles in trade or industry publications can provide an insight into competitor motives.

◆ Government reports: many governments provide reports that cover statistical information (for example, economic data, purchasing trends and census data) and changes in society (for instance, the structure, age ranges and wealth).

◆ Industry sources, generally publications produced by professional and trade bodies that represent particular business sectors and industries. These sources generally provide authoritative information on such areas as market trends, changing legislation, new technologies and government perspectives on the sector or industry.

◆ Think tanks, groups of experts who provide a perspective on emerging trends, societal and commercial issues. Think tanks can be:

  ● commercial organisations, such as the UK-based company Demos

  ● departments within major companies, such as the futures department within UK-based telecommunications company BT

  ● departments within universities which research particular technological or societal issues, for example the impact of nanotechnologies on particular industries and market sectors.

Does everyone use marketing research?

The simple answer is no.

Some companies and organisations do not undertake marketing research because of resource limitations. Some companies and individuals simply reject the notion of marketing research. Chapter 9 outlines the launch of the C5 concept vehicle (page 196), which was not preceded by any marketing research. Its designer Sir Clive Sinclair believed the product would succeed because he would create a market for it (Marks 1989). However sales failed to reach targets, and the financial burden eventually forced his company into bankruptcy.

Whether marketing research would have prevented bankruptcy of the business is of course hard to tell. There are so many factors that can contribute to the collapse of a business. However marketing research might well have raised issues of concern, especially with people's perception of the vehicle on busy congested roads. Sir Clive Sinclair may well have then been able to either modify it or position it for a different market, not one that included a replacement for the car within congested urban areas, especially in a society that has grown increasingly car-oriented.

Both companies and individuals will continue to develop and launch products and services without undertaking any form of marketing research. Statistics suggest that some will be successful, and others will not be so lucky (or astute, depending on your perspective). Consider, for example, how many university courses are created without any investment in discovering whether there is a market for them. Ask your college or university if it undertakes any structured marketing research before launching a new degree programme. You might be surprised at the answer, or indeed lack of one.

Chapter summary

This chapter has briefly examined the rationale for undertaking marketing research and the standard process involved. It has also provided an overview of the different techniques that an organisation can use to gather primary and secondary data. However, it is not just a question of undertaking marketing research for its own sake. There must be a rationale and purpose to justify the investment. In other words the organisation needs:

◆ clear objectives: what is it attempting to discover?

◆ to use the most appropriate techniques to provide a solid and relevant data platform

◆ appropriate analysis techniques to provide the right information in the right format to assist unbiased decision-making.

Not all companies undertake marketing research. Some lack the funds, and others distrust its validity or doubt its relevance to a product or market. Nevertheless, the use of marketing research remains a vital part of marketing operations within most organisations.

Questions for review and reflection

1 You are the managing director of a department store. You are planning to redevelop the store's internal layout and are interested in gaining customer reaction to your plans. You want the layout to be efficient for your business to operate effectively, while at the same time being pleasant for customers. Your organisation values customers' opinions and views, and operates a loyalty scheme to help cement that relationship. What marketing research techniques would you use to gather customers' opinions and views?

2 Critically evaluate the use of secondary data sources in marketing research. What are the potential risks associated with the use of secondary data?

3 With your fellow students debate the potential ethical issues surrounding the use of people observation to gather marketing research information.

4   Evaluate how undertaking marketing research could reduce the level of decision-making risk when it comes to launching a new product or service into a market.

5   Apply the questionnaire development process to produce a questionnaire that could be used in research prior to the introduction of a new snack bar by a confectionery company.

6   Discuss the contribution that marketing research can make to overall marketing decision making.

7   What do you consider to be the possible ethical dilemmas associated with the use of marketing research?

8   Although the objectives might be the same, the execution of international marketing research may differ substantially from domestic marketing research. Critically evaluate the factors that could cause or influence a difference.

9   Critically examine how the Internet, the World Wide Web and e-mail can be used in marketing research.

■ References

Burns, A. and Bush, R. (2000) *Marketing Research*, 2nd edn, New Jersey: Prentice Hall.

D'Aveni, R. A. (1995) *Hypercompetitive Rivalries: Competing in highly dynamic environments*, New York: Free Press.

Groucutt, J. and Griseri, P. (2004) *Mastering e-Business*, Basingstoke: Palgrave Macmillan.

Groucutt, J., Leadley, P. and Forsyth, P. (2004) *Marketing: Essential principles, new realities*, London: Kogan Page.

Marks, A. P. (1989) 'The Sinclair C5: an investigation into its development, launch and subsequent failure', *European Journal of Marketing* **23**(1), pp. 61–71.

Quee, W. T. (1999) *Marketing Research*, Singapore: Butterworth-Heinemann/Marketing Institute of Singapore.

Zikmund, W. G. (1994) *Business Research Methods*, 4th edn, Fort Worth: Dryden Press.

Competitive Intelligence

CHAPTER 5

Contents

Learning outcomes	79
Introduction	79
Defining competitive intelligence:	
what it is and is not	**80**
Marketing research	80
Competitive intelligence (also known as	
business intelligence)	80
Competitor intelligence	80
Economic intelligence	81
Why competitive intelligence analysis	
is important to marketers	**82**
Types of organisational competition	**82**
The need to understand competitor	
actions and intentions	**82**
A competitor intelligence system	**86**
Sources of competitor intelligence	**86**
Sales value and volumes	87
Pricing strategies	87
Product ranges and developments	87
Promotional activities and spend	87
Channel management/logistics	
operations	88
Company and management structures	88
Recorded data	88
Observable data	90
Opportunistic data	90
Analysing competitor intelligence	**90**
Strategic groupings	90
Key competitors	91
Evaluation of the data	91
Potential new competitors	91
Competitor organisations leaving the	
marketplace	91
Legal and ethical implications of	
competitor intelligence	**92**
Regulation	92
SCIP Code of Ethics for competitive	
intelligence professionals	95
Chapter summary	**95**
Questions for review	
and reflection	**95**
References	**96**

Learning outcomes

After completing this chapter you should be able to:

▶ evaluate why companies must seek competitive intelligence (CI) and act on the information gathered

▶ outline the potential sources of competitive intelligence information, and the accuracy of the information gathered

▶ demonstrate an understanding of the dynamics of competition and the global competitive environment

▶ reflect on the relationship between competitive intelligence and other marketing information systems

▶ reflect on the legal and ethical issues associated with competitive intelligence gathering.

■ Introduction

> *Nam et ipsa scientia potestas est.*
> For also knowledge is power.
>   Francis Bacon (1561-1626)
>   English lawyer, philosopher and essayist

Bacon's words above underscore the overall importance of knowledge. Indeed, knowledge management is increasingly seen as a vital part of everyday business life. Over the past 20 years or so there has been increasing use of competitive intelligence gathering in the commercial world. However, as the Prussian military strategist Carl von Clausewitz (1780–1831) wrote, intelligence is often 'unreliable and transient'.[1] Thus the accuracy of intelligence gathered must be verified before it is treated as a sound basis for decision making.

■ Defining competitive intelligence: what it is and is not

Often business writers and academics tend to meld marketing research, competitor intelligence, competitive intelligence and economic intelligence into one. While there are 'some' similarities, as we shall see there are significant and fundamental differences. Thus it is important at this juncture to consider some definitions.

Marketing research

In Chapter 5 marketing research was defined as:

> the process of designing, gathering, analysing and reporting of information that may be used to solve a specific marketing problem.
>
> (Burns and Bush 2000)

While there are links between marketing research (MR) and competitive intelligence (CI) gathering, as we shall see, it is incorrect to say that MR = CI. Their scope and scale are very different.

Competitive intelligence (also known as business intelligence)

McDaniel and Gates (1999) define competitive intelligence as:

> the creation of an intelligence system that helps managers assess their competition and their suppliers in order to become a more efficient and effective competitor.

However, it can be debated that this does not fully reflect the role of competitive intelligence. Sharp (2000) further refines this view when she states that:

> Competitive intelligence targets anything in the business universe that affects the ability to compete.... Intelligence is information that has been analysed and suggests actions, strategies, or decisions. Intelligence reveals critical information or insight and implications beyond data.

There are two key issues here. First, competitive intelligence considers everything within the 'business universe'. If you like, it looks at the macro environment to gain knowledge of the 'big picture'. Reflect back to Chapter 2 and consider some of the macro issues discussed there and how they impact on organisations. Robbins and Coulter (1996) consider competitive intelligence gathering to be part of an organisation's environmental scanning process or activity.

Second, there is Sharp's suggestion that information and actions go way beyond the original data collection. The central issue is how individuals interpret and act on the subsequent information. You may want to reflect back to the brief quote from von Clausewitz (1832) and the need for verification and continual updating.

Lauginie, Mansillon and Dubouin (1994) believe that competitive intelligence is a value added concept, and have subsequently defined it as a competitive strategy. This is a point echoed by Wright and Pickton (1998) when they state:

> Competitive Intelligence is the strategic process of identifying, understanding and using Critical Success Factors.

Critical success factors (CSFs) are based upon the Pareto Principle[1] that it is a few core items that actually drive the long-term viability of the business. In this context Wheelan and Hunger (1992) suggest that the CSFs are the 20 per cent of the total factors that determine 80 per cent of the organisation's or strategic business unit's (SBU's) overall performance, and ultimately success or failure. Wright, Pickton and Callow (2002) suggest that 'using' (in the quote above) involves the active employment of CSFs to direct the competitive intelligence effort. This in turn both informs and drives the development of a competitive strategy.

Competitor intelligence

Sharp (2000) defines competitor intelligence in a more narrow vein, suggesting that it includes 'monitoring and understanding competitors. However, it cannot stand on its own because tracking only the competition is the surest way to develop tunnel vision, and be blindsided by significant marketplace changes.'

Lauginie *et al.* (1994) agree that competitor

intelligence is but one part of competitive intelligence. They add that the focus of competitor intelligence 'tends to be on the problems associated with the daily profitable marketing of a company's products or services'. Here they focus on profit-oriented organisations, but this is equally applicable to not-for-profit organisations.

Economic intelligence

Contrary to what some people may believe, true competitive intelligence gathering does not involve searching through a competitor's rubbish bins in the dead of night. This is generally unethical, in many countries it is illegal, and most often it is a fruitless adventure. It is a plot out of a novel and should be left to fiction writers. However even the most respected of companies can find itself embarrassed by such activities (see mini case 5.3, page 93).

Nor do people have to be trained by shadowy raincoat-clad spymasters from the British Secret Intelligence Service (SIS), the US Central Intelligence Agency (CIA) or France's Direction Générale de la Sécurité Extérieure (DGSE) to be involved in competitive intelligence gathering.

However it would be naïve to think that such activities do not occur. Indeed, the secret services of several countries are actively engaged in economic espionage on behalf of companies. Both Orton (2002) and Cochran (2003) refer to how security services in the United States, France and South Korea have been involved in economic intelligence gathering. In some cases, the government intelligence service has worked in league with companies to gather the data.

Although many competitive intelligence analysts say there is no similarity between competitive intelligence and intelligence gathering by national security services, this it is not the case. The staff of national intelligence services are not all like the fictional spy, James Bond. True, they use electronic surveillance and conduct dangerous covert operations, especially against terrorists. However, there is a large body of national intelligence analysts whose role is not too dissimilar from

---

Mini case 5.1

The Body Shop

In 1976 Anita Roddick, who was then aged 34, and her husband Gordon took out a £4,000 bank loan and borrowed money from a friend to open the first Body Shop in Brighton, England. They specialised in a small range of beauty products using natural ingredients which they packaged and promoted to the increasingly health conscious middle England.

As Jeremy (1998) states, there was:

an increasing concern (post 1950s) for health and beauty. No longer were the models and standards held aloft in Hollywood movies and in television adverts unattainable. In sharp contrast to the 1930s, clean, perfumed bodies, for both men and women, increasingly became the norm.... Anita Roddick drove this new interest in the body (seen previously as self expression or narcissism) forwards, neatly combining concern for health, beauty and the environment.

From this one store in Brighton the Roddicks were able to build a franchised empire that became one of the most respected companies on the London Stock Market. This was a spectacular rise of fortunes, all within in a relatively short period of time. Anita's Roddick's determination to bring animal testing to the forefront of the media agenda also significantly helped to publicise the Body Shop to the consuming public.

The problem for Body Shop's competitors was that they had failed to actively take into consideration changing societal issues – the very issues that the Body Shop had keyed into. Society, especially in the United Kingdom, was looking for beauty products that were natural and where the ingredients had not been tested on animals. In both cases they wanted the statements to be true and clearly stated on the product containers. Although many of the major beauty product manufacturers had either reduced or eradicated the need for animal testing they had failed to alert the public to such changes. Thus when the Body Shop actively promoted products that had not been tested on animals (and that were good for you) the public pounced on the idea. As a result Body Shop franchises began to spring up over the United Kingdom. This added further woes to well-established beauty and cosmetics companies which had failed to effectively analysis the competitive environment in which they were operating.

Source: Jeremy (1998).

competitive intelligence analysts. Both groups conduct painstaking desk research analysing a diverse range of information, and sometimes they even use the same paper sources. However, it is not acceptable for competitive intelligence companies to resort to the more covert operations that are associated with national security organisations. There are more legitimate means of gathering and analysing business information.

■ Why competitive intelligence analysis is important to marketers

Chapter 2 examined the marketplace from both the macro and micro perspectives. It showed how the environments in which organisations operate (and in which we live) are dynamic and complex. They are not static but fluid, constantly changing in relation to each other. In order to survive, let alone be competitive, organisations have to continually scan their environments for both dramatic and subtle changes. Environmental scanning has increasingly become a critical activity within corporate strategic thinking.

As Wright *et al.* (2002) state, 'monitoring, understanding and responding to competitors has long been recognised as a significant marketing activity'. However, they raise the issue that actual analysis of the competitive environment has often been subordinated to other activities. Yet it is the analysis of the 'bigger picture' that can assist in the formulation of effective and efficient marketing strategy. As indicated in Chapter 3, marketers need a firm understanding of corporate strategy in order to make the links between business strategy (at the SBU level) and marketing strategies. In order to achieve this successfully, marketers must constantly scan both the micro and macro environments. The analysis of the information or data gathered can provide a platform from which to either anticipate change or react more effectively to change.

■ Types of organisational competition

Competition exists at a number of levels, and the organisation must be aware of this when considering the types of competitive strategy to follow. The

Mini case 5.2

The political intentions of a government and country

In order to compete internationally, companies need to be aware of both home and host country political environments (see the PESTLE model in Chapter 2, page 22). The business and thus the marketing environment are affected by changes in the political doctrines and structures in countries and regions.

Even in stable democracies, political decisions can pose a significant level of risk to a business. For instance, the fact that the United Kingdom is currently not part of the eurozone places limitations on the ability of many companies to market their products and services across the eurozone. Currency conversion from Sterling to the euro and vice versa has cost implications. British politicians do not all agree whether or not the United Kingdom should join the eurozone. Some political parties are in favour of membership as soon as possible, while others believe that the United Kingdom should preserve its independence from the rest of Europe and retain Sterling as its currency. Companies need to analyse such political thoughts and beliefs and consider how they will affect them over the medium and longer term.

That example is at one end of the scale. At the other extreme are governments or political parties that are in favour of (or indeed carry out) 'hostile' actions against international companies. These range from policies to privatise or confiscate foreign company assets, to a breakdown of civil law and humanity, with a country slowly collapsing into civil war. When this happens

highest is the industry level, followed by the company level and the product or brand level. Not all competitors compete at all levels, so it is important to establish at which level the competition actually exists.

Doyle (1998) identifies four types of competitor. These are outlined in Figure 5.1 (page 84).

■ The need to understand competitor actions and intentions

All too often companies ignore, to their peril, the actions of their current and potential competitors. It is important here to note the inclusion of

many companies seek to exit the engulfing turmoil as soon as possible. If the company had been scanning the political environment of that particular country or region it might well have been aware of the impending disaster, and have had a pre-planned exit strategy.

Between these two points governments and political parties often seek mechanisms to protect indigenous industries, even though this is increasingly against the policies of the World Trade Organization (WTO). Using tariff and non-tariff barriers, countries seek to generate revenues from foreign imports whilst bolstering often inefficient local industries and businesses. The rights and wrongs of such actions are an area of significant debate. However, any company seeking to market its products or services in another country must be aware of current political and governmental activity and possible future intentions.

If they are aware of political intentions in a country or region, organisations can make decisions on a range of issues including:

♦ purchasing raw materials from the country or region

♦ outsourcing manufacturing to particular countries

♦ marketing to that country or region

♦ the appropriate level of foreign direct investment (FDI), if any within the country or region

♦ the overall level of risk or exposure through their involvement with a particular country or region.

potential competitors in the analysis. Companies might observe the actions of current direct competitors. However that might not be where the greatest threat lies. An excellent case in point is Coca-Cola and Pepsi, which were so engaged in combat that they did not appear to see Virgin Cola gaining market share in the Japanese marketplace.

Thus it is vital for companies to understand the actions, and intentions, of their rivals, most especially within highly dynamic markets. Rothschild (1979) suggests seven key questions that companies need to answer in terms of competitor analysis.

1   Who is the competition now and who will be in the future?

2   What are the key competitors' strategies, objectives, and goals?

3   How important is a specific market to the competitors and are they committed enough to invest?

4   What unique strengths do the competitors have?

5   Do they have weaknesses that make them vulnerable?

6   What changes are likely in the competitors' future strategies?

7   What are the implications of the competitors' strategies for the market, the industry and the company?

West (1999) suggests that a typical competitor information profile should cover 12 areas:

1   Ownership and organisational structure.

2   Financial history.

3   Financial resources.

4   Key decision makers and their experience/ track record.

5   Staff resources.

6   Production resources and locations.

7   Product lines (brand extensions) and product portfolios.

8   Patents, licenses and other unique assets.

9   Market and segments served.

10   Distribution channels used.

11   Export activity and country/countries supplied.

12   Sales and marketing activities.

West (1999) also suggests that the depth and quality of information available will vary from one market sector to another, and across borders. However, he contends that data can be obtained on:

♦ Population size, geodemographics.

♦ The structure of distribution and the importance of various channels. (Logistics

Figure 5.1 Competitor types

		Indirect competitor	Direct competitor
Customer	Similar	These offer different products, but to similar customers. A company offering fitted kitchens could be an indirect competitor to the Ford Motor Company, as it is likely to be targeting similar customers who have limited financial resources, so they are likely to buy either a new kitchen or a new car.	A competitor with a similar product that is being offered to similar customers. These are the easiest to identify and should be well known to any organisation in the marketplace.
		Implicit competitor	Product competitor
	Different	Competitors who currently offer different products to different customers. However, that may not always be the case as they seek new market opportunities to develop and grow.	Organisations that offer a similar product but to different customers. These should be monitored closely as they could easily target customers with their product if they believe that they can offer some differential advantage.
		Different	Similar

Source: adapted from Doyle (1998).

operations will also be relevant information to gather.)

♦ Total sales, imports and exports of products.

♦ Imports and exports by origin and destination.

♦ Products available and their specifications.

♦ New product launches.

♦ New contracts and successful bidders for outstanding contracts. (These range from major contracts such as the building of a power plant to a contract to handle the company's advertising.)

♦ Prices/pricing policy.

♦ Advertising expenditure by product, industry sector and supplier.

♦ New market entrants. (It is also useful to consider companies leaving the market and how that will affect the market.)

♦ Staff movements (for example the appointment

of a new marketing director and how that might influence future direction of the company).

♦ Financial performance of suppliers. For example, if a key supplier is struggling to remain solvent, there could be the following reactions:

● The company buys the supplier in order to turn that business around and maintain supplies. This is an example of backward integration.

● The supplier is acquired by another company (which might even be a competitor), and the purchasing company increases prices, which could be detrimental to both companies.

● The supplier collapses and ceases to trade. The company's supply chain is affected, allowing competitors to gain some market advantage through their own continuous supply to the market.

Much of the above and more is covered in the work of Aaker (1995) and Wong and Saunders (1996). This has been brought together in Table 5.1, which examines a process for analysing competitors within the marketplace.

By having a greater understanding of competitors' actions and plans, a company can use a range of business techniques to outperform them. For example, it could improve its competitive performance through the judicious use of the marketing mix variables or value chain processes. However, such analysis should not be considered as merely a 'snapshot' in time. The world, let alone the business world, is complex and dynamic in form, so competitor analysis must be an ongoing dynamic operation, considering how and why competitors behave/react in different ways. It is also important to consider the influence of the wider macro environment and how the various elements affect the competitors and trigger actions.

Table 5.1 Analysing competitors

Stage	Process	Issues
1	Identifying the company's competitors	Here Aaker (1995) asks several relevant questions Who are the competitors? Against which organisations does the company usually compete? Which are the most intense competitors? Who are less intense competitors but still remain a competitive threat? Who make substitute products? (Reflect on the five forces model (Porter 1980): see page 86.) This also links back to the premise that there are four types of organizational competitor (Doyle 1998) – see Figure 5.1.
2	Determining competitors' objectives	Aaker (1995) suggests that knowing the competitors' objectives may assist in predicting how they will move or position themselves within the marketplace. The objectives could be defined in terms of financial performance, technological developments, brand perceptions/image, level of customer satisfaction targeted and future markets to penetrate and sustain. In other words, where is the competitor company now and where does it want to be in the short, medium and longer terms?
3	Identifying competitors' strategies	There is a need to analyse competitors' strategies, both past and present. Simkin (1996) suggests that past strategies need to be analysed as businesses are often predictable in their strategy development and enactment. Thus if a particular tactic or strategy was successful in the past there is a likelihood that the competitor will repeat it. The converse may also be true: if a particular tactic or strategy did not work in the past then the competitor may be reluctant to repeat the exercise. However, it might be an avenue that another competitor could exploit. If it was not successful in the past that does not mean it will not be successful in the future. However, many companies are apt to take the safe trusted route in order to minimise risk.
4	Assessing competitors' strengths and weaknesses	It is vital to identify and then analyse the relative strengths and weaknesses of each competitor or strategic group (Aaker 1995). Equally, a company needs to consider how its own strengths and weaknesses compare and contrast with its competitors. This activity cannot be seen in isolation. As Aaker (1995) states, it should consider what leverage points (the company's strategic weaknesses) competitors could exploit in order to either enter the market, consolidate their position or gain an advantage. Equally, as Aaker indicates, companies need to assess the potential strengths and weaknesses in terms of possible market exit strategies. If exit barriers are high (for example, high costs involved to withdraw from the market and close factories), as Aaker suggests, the competitor may continue to struggle within the market, and thus remain a potential threat. Determining how serious the competitor is in remaining within the market will determine the level of resources need to combat any action from the competitor.

/ continued overleaf

Table 5.1 continued

Stage	Process	Issues
5	Estimating competitors' reaction patterns	As Simkin and Cheng (1997) state, the development of a competitive strategy is not complete without an estimation of competitors' reactions to any moves against them. In the 1960s Xerox enjoyed a virtual monopoly within the photocopier market (Eckles 1990). From its power base it decided to use its market leadership to challenge IBM's leadership in the computer market by introducing a range of main-frame computers. IBM retaliated by launching a photocopier, challenging Xerox on its home ground. However, this was only the beginning of the troubles for Xerox. While it was fighting essentially on two fronts – challenging IBM in the computer market and defending itself against IBM retaliation – Japanese companies saw the possibility of entering the US photocopier market. They entered the market with much improved and less expensive copiers aimed at the SME market. Thus Xerox was fighting on three battlefronts. Eckles (1990) believes that Xerox lost a significant percentage of the copier market to the Japanese companies because it failed to identify, appraise and react to two fundamental changes in its product/market environment: the emergence of new markets, and the emergence of new competitors. Since then Xerox have had to invest in regaining and rebuilding its market position. This example illustrates that: • An attack on a new market can lead to retaliation. • As the two primary competitors battle for position, other newer competitors work their way into the market thus causing potential disruption to the company that initiated the first offensive move. Thus companies must analyse the potential reactions of all competitors within the marketplace, even those that are currently seen as 'lower level' challengers.
6	Selecting competitors to attack and avoid	As stated above, companies need to be aware of the risks of challenging companies, especially if they are market leaders and have the resources to combat a direct attack. Moreover, they need to be aware of other potential players within the market that could acquire market share (as in the case of Virgin Cola mentioned earlier in this chapter) when the two protagonists in the market battle for position in several markets simultaneously.

A competitor intelligence system

Porter (1980) states that for competitor analysis to be effective there needs to an 'organised mechanism' – a competitor intelligence system that will ensure an efficient process of evaluation. Porter (1980) suggested a process for identifying the functions that must be performed prior to actual analysis. Figure 5.2 is an adaptation of Porter's original model. The section that follows outlines some of the background information on companies, and the sources used to obtain such information.

As we saw in Chapter 4, collecting vast amounts of data on an organisation is only the beginning of the exercise. The collated data has to be analysed, effective conclusions reached and strategies drawn from the analysis. Of course, as with anything in business the strategies should not be cast in

concrete and considered final. There needs to be a level of flexibility because of the volatility of the marketplace. As well as companies being proactive in their approach to decision making, they must be prepared to be reactive and change or modify plans as required or demanded by the market.

As Figure 5.2 illustrates, there are a series of stages that companies can utilise in order to gain the necessary material to analyse to provide a structure for the formulisation of a necessary and apt strategy.

Sources of competitor intelligence

Porter (1980) states in his process that the information that forms the basis of the analysis emanates from both field data and published data. Here is a brief overview of some of the data sources that

Figure 5.2 The functions of a competitor intelligence system

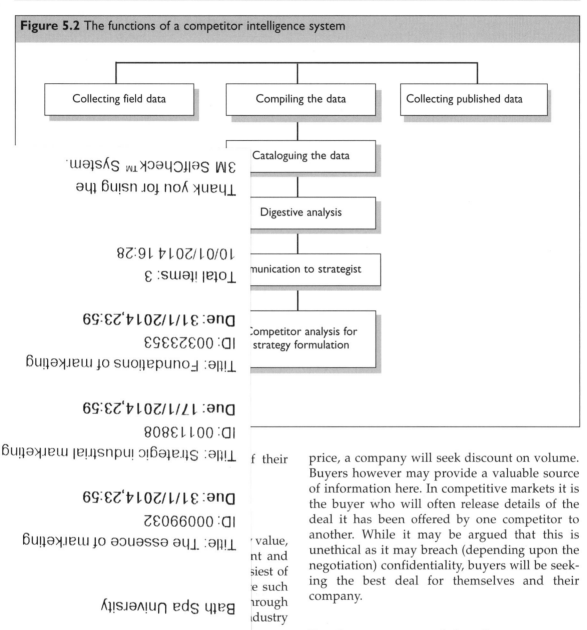

Collecting field data — Compiling the data — Collecting published data

Cataloguing the data

Digestive analysis

Communication to strategist

Competitor analysis for strategy formulation

Whether a company operates within a B2C, B2B environment or indeed both, its pricing structure will normally be a matter of public record. However, what may not be in the public domain is the level of discounting that is available. While a consumer may, normally, pay the stated price, a company will seek discount on volume. Buyers however may provide a valuable source of information here. In competitive markets it is the buyer who will often release details of the deal it has been offered by one competitor to another. While it may be argued that this is unethical as it may breach (depending upon the negotiation) confidentiality, buyers will be seeking the best deal for themselves and their company.

Product ranges and developments

Details of these can often be gleaned from exhibitions and promotional campaigns.

Promotional activities and spend

Details of competitors' promotional activity must be carefully monitored and recorded, and any changes noted. This information can be obtained by collecting copies of the competitors' promotion and calculating the budget from the various media rate cards. Large companies might place all, or various components of, their promotional activity out for pitch. This is usually reported in the media industry press, along with budgets. The media industry press also reports on forthcoming campaign launches and associated budget spends.

Channel management/logistics operations

The way a company distributes its products can help gain it a competitive advantage over its competitors. Buyers are increasingly time-limited as they use Just-in-Time (JIT) management to minimise stock levels and warehousing costs. Therefore they seek efficient and flexible delivery systems. Companies need to understand how their competitors use logistics to meet customer demands. This is equally relevant in the B2C marketplace. In our 24/7 society we can order products online as and when we want, and we look for flexible delivery to match our personal time limitations. One of the reasons for the UK supermarket Tesco's success in online grocery ordering has been its flexible delivery service, which fits customers' requirements. Not all delivery companies have such flexibility, and those without it will lose any competitive edge that they held.

Company and management structures

This includes details of how the organisation is financed and the cost structures. The structure of management and the identification of the key decision makers will allow closer monitoring of the way the organisation operates. This information can often be obtained by analysing annual reports or through press coverage in industry-focused media. For example, companies often announce major staff and structure changes through press releases. Increasingly these can be read on the company's website.

Davidson (1997) identifies three main sources of information: recorded data, observable data and opportunistic data.

Recorded data

This is relatively easily to obtain, and is available in published form either internally or externally. Information can be obtained from a wide variety of sources. These include:

Competitors' annual reports

If the company is listed on a stock market, it has to make available to prospective, as well as current, shareholders copies of its annual report. This provides information on its trading position, as well as its financial position over the previous 12 months. In some countries it is also possible to obtain copies of private companies' reports. In the United Kingdom, for example, all private limited companies must file audited financial statements with Companies House every year. This is a legal requirement. For a small fee, individuals or companies can obtain copies of their competitors' reports directly from Companies House. Additionally, many accounting firms will undertake a full appraisal of a company's financial status, for example its gearing ratio (which relates to its level of borrowing).

Mailing lists

A company executive might join a competitor's mailing list in order to receive copies of the latest promotional literature. This allows the executive to scrutinise the literature at the same time as the competitor's customers. It often provides information of products (features and benefits), pricing and promotional strategies and tactics. The company might be able to react by, for example, offering a product at a lower price than that advertised in the competitor's literature.

Newspapers, trade and professional journals

Timely articles on companies and market sectors can provide valuable information on product successes and failures, as well as potential external opportunities and threats. Often in trade publications CEOs talk at length about their company's activities. If the CEO is somewhat indiscreet with the journalist, he or she might say more than he or she should about his or her objectives and those of the company!

It is also important to consider trade and

industry publications not directly related to the business: for instance publications on packaging, transportation, distribution channels and logistics, and employee development. In these types of publications there might be information on a direct competitor. For instance, a competitor might sign a significant distribution deal with a freight forwarder, and the article or press release appears in freight forwarding trade publications rather the company's industry-specific publications. This is why many companies subscribe to press cutting agencies, often through their public relations departments, requesting cuttings on not only their own press coverage but their competitors as well.

Television and radio

As with publications, information can be gathered from a range of television and radio programmes. For example:

- A news bulletin might reveal that a company is planning to invest within a particular region of the country, stating the level of investment and job provision.

- CNN, Bloomberg and BBC Worldwide broadcast business information on company performance, market share and product launches/developments.

- CEOs and other senior executives are regularly interviewed.

- There is an increasing range of documentaries that feature companies and business sectors. While there is a time lapse between the documentary being made and broadcast, it is possible to glean longer-term intentions or indeed discover inherent weaknesses. Competitors seeking to gain increased market share can exploit such weaknesses.

- Consumer programmes. These tend to be highly current (often live) and thus relevant. They may reveal problems that competitors have in supplying particular products or services, including quality control systems.

Just as with press cutting services, companies can subscribe to television monitoring services that will video record specific programmes.

The Internet

As companies move ever closer to real-time price changes, they need to study competitors' websites on an ongoing basis, A company's website can reveal much about its e-marketing capabilities. Online news databases such as Lexis-Nexis and the Financial Times can provide details on company's financial performance and recent stock and product issues.

Business directories

These also provide vital information. This includes listings of companies and corporations, their executives' names, their subsidiaries, number of employees and product/service range. These are usually updated annually, and are increasingly becoming available over the Internet. Kompass Directories, for example, contain information on over 1.5 million companies in 66 countries, 23 million products and services, and over 400 000 trade and brand names.

Local and regional telephone directories

These can provide information on potential competitors. Most countries have their own version of Yellow Pages that lists companies operating within a defined area. Generally, they are very well cross-referenced, so it is relatively easy to discover which companies operate in a particular market sector. As well as listings under business area, companies also advertise, and their advertisement may reveal product and company details.

Government reports

Governments publish regular reports and updates on statistics, trade and financial information. Much of this is now readily available on government department websites. Such information can help companies determine whether their competitors have access to favourable tax incentives (for example, in regional development areas) or other home-based or host-based trading benefits.

Government research

Governments also publish reports relating to fair trading, trading standards and monopolies and mergers, which often contain significant detail on company activities. In the 1960s the British

Government's Monopolies Commission report on the industrial gas market provided valuable information on the size and segments of the market. At the time the British Oxygen Corporation (BOC) was the market leader, and the report also contained details of BOC's production, distribution, costs and profits. This information was used successfully by Air Products to gain entry into the marketplace (James 1985).

Specialist research companies

Companies such as Mintel and Dun & Bradstreet can provide companies with specialist analysis of markets and the major players within those markets.

Observable data

This data has to be actively sought, and often assembled from a number of different sources. Many companies regularly buy competitors' products to analyse the product itself, its pricing and supportive promotional activities. Retailers often use secret shoppers to discover what special promotions their competitors are offering.

The product analysis may even include the company's engineering and design teams 'breaking down' the product to identify competitive costs, design features, performance characteristics and production methods. This is known as reverse engineering. The Ford Taurus car was a product of reverse engineering, as Ford's engineers examined competitors' cars and incorporated the best features in their own model (Haddigan 1995).

In terms of services, what better way, for example, than for airline executives to fly on a competitor's aircraft rather than their own? By experiencing say a business-class flight on a rival carrier, an executive can gain a better understanding of how his or her company's competitors either maintain their advantage or might leverage advantage.

The removal of older products from the marketplace can also provide useful data on the competitor's perception of the marketplace, and its future marketing strategies.

Opportunistic data

This is much more difficult to collect. Much of this type of data is anecdotal, obtained from suppliers or at trade shows, exhibitions and conferences. However, it might be more gossip than hard factual data. To act on this type of information (without corroborating it) – reflect back to von Clausewitz's quote on the reliability of intelligence at the start of this chapter – would be suicidal for any company. Occasionally customers served by both the company and its competitor prove a rich source of data. Of course a disgruntled customer might exaggerate his or her comments, but this can still furnish the sales team, for instance, with additional information that they can analyse in conjunction with other sources. In such cases the sales team can be a vital source of competitor information.

■ Analysing competitor intelligence

Collecting vast piles of raw data or information is only the starting point. As we mentioned when discussing the competitive intelligence system (Porter 1980), this data has to be analysed, and it is this analysis that contributes to strategy formulation. Cravens (1982) identified six areas that need to be considered as the starting point for the analysis.

Industry structure and characteristics

All industries are structured differently, so it is necessary to define clearly the way the particular industry is structured. The structure needs to be analysed carefully to ensure that no substructures have been overlooked. Details of the characteristics of the industry must also be defined carefully. These will indicate how the industry operates within the structure, and help identify the major players and the type of organisation that might decide to join competition in the future.

Strategic groupings

Within the industry it is also necessary to identify and analyse the strategic groupings of the players. Not all organisations in an industry try to serve the same set of customers, or even provide the same types of benefit to the marketplace. The different groups need to be identified and their strengths and weaknesses analysed. This will provide insight into the opportunities the organisation and its competitors might try to exploit, and threats they must avoid to survive.

Key competitors

The next stage is to identify and describe the key competitors. Not all organisations in an industry will be a company's competitors, therefore it is important that the key ones are clearly identified and analysed. This must include their sales revenue, market share, share price movements (if the company is stock-market listed), details of new products launched into the market, and new senior staff appointments and what values or insights they can bring to the organisation. Much of this information will be known or readily available, but it needs to be collected and formalised. This information establishes not only the company's position in the marketplace, but also that of the key competitors.

Evaluation of the data

Then follows a full evaluation of the data that the company holds or has collected on these key competitors. It is necessary for the organisation to know as much about the workings of the competitors as it does about itself. This needs to go even deeper than a SWOT analysis, as it is necessary to understand how the organisations think and work in practice. From this type of analysis it is possible to anticipate likely future actions by competitors so that the company can be in a position to react to, or indeed pre-empt them.

Potential new competitors

It is also necessary to be able to identify any potential new competitors entering the marketplace, and the likely effect of their entry.

Competitor organisations leaving the marketplace

Likewise the possibility of any competitor organisations leaving the marketplace, and the action the company would need to take to secure their market share. Of course there are costs involved in exiting a market, as there is in entering the marketplace. (Refer to Porter's five forces model: see page 107.)

Johnson and Scholes (2004) list a number of ways of assessing competitors; while this list is not exhaustive, it forms a basic framework from which to assess the strengths and weaknesses of competitors. The assessment is divided into three major areas starting with size and relative market share. This includes the extent of product/service diversity, degree of geographical coverage, number and type of market segments being served and the types of distribution channels being used. An analysis of these areas provides a good indication of the power of the organisation within the marketplace.

Details of the branding philosophy are also required, and these are identified through evaluating the product/service quality, the market position of the organisation providing that product or service (leader, challenger or follower), its technological position (leader, challenger or follower) and its research and development capability. This analysis provides a view of how its customers perceive the organisation in the marketplace, and indicates if there are any gaps in the way it serves its market.

Finally, the cost structure and behaviour of the organisation need to be considered. What is the pattern of ownership? Is the organisation over or under-capitalised? What is its internal culture? Many organisations are paternalistic, while others try to buy staff loyalty through high pay and incentives or benefits. What is the degree of vertical integration? How much control does the organisation have over its suppliers and its channels of distribution? Finally, what is its reputation in the marketplace? Does this reputation give the organisation any differential advantage over its competitors?

By careful analysis of the findings it is possible to compare competitors not only with one company, but also with every other company. This can provide a very useful insight into the way the market operates at the company level.

It is suggested that a SWOT analysis is a very useful tool in establishing competitive position. What is required is identification of the weak points of the competition. A number of factors should be sought when undertaking the weaknesses analysis, and these should include:

◆ Finance analysis: look for low profit margins, poor growth or high-cost operations or distribution.

◆ The markets being served. Is there over-dependence on one market, and more particularly on one customer within that market? Is the competitor only strong in falling sectors of the market, and does its orientation tend to short-term survival rather than long-term growth?

◆ Any indication of industrial relations problems can also indicate weaknesses in the way the organisation operates.

Analysts also need to look for organisations that are predictable, or with products or services that are obsolescent or weak. Companies with high market shares can be as vulnerable as those with low market share. Another sign of weakness is slow-moving bureaucratic structures and fiscal period fixation. Companies that work everything from costs are particularly vulnerable, as they cannot react to market changes quickly enough. Do not forget that the entrepreneur Henry Ford (1863–1947) became famous because he set the price first, to match market conditions, then worried about the cost of producing the product.

It is important to remember that the gathering and analysis of intelligence data is not a one-off exercise. Both current and potential competitors must be monitored on an ongoing basis to maximise the long-term benefits.

■ Legal and ethical implications of competitor intelligence

As stated earlier, competitor intelligence gathering is not about searching through a competitor's rubbish bins in the dead of night. This is unethical, in many countries illegal, and most often a fruitless adventure. However, it would be extremely naïve of us to imagine that such activities do not take place. Companies do engage in industrial espionage, using either their own staff or various private agencies,. Industrial espionage can be described as attempting to discover a competitor's trade secrets by illegal and/or unethical means. This is straightforward spying, and is usually used by companies, and sometimes governments, to gain intellectual or propriety information. (Propriety right is a legal term that refers to, for example, the rights of ownership of a drug trade marked under and protected by a registered trade name.)

The two mini cases that follow are very different in form. In Mini case 5.3, a usually reputable company crossed the line between acceptable and non-acceptable practices. Mini case 5.4 is at the other extreme: it concerns deliberate attempts to steal trade secrets to gain a series of major advantages, politically, technologically, economically and in the marketplace.

Regulation

In February 1999, the US Federal Bureau of Investigation (FBI) and the US Chamber of Commerce announced that US companies were losing a staggering US$2 billion a month because of corporate espionage (NACIC 1999). To counter this loss, governments are increasing turning to their legal systems. In 1996 the US government passed the Economic Espionage Act. The Act makes it a criminal offence for:

> Any person to convert a trade secret to their own benefit, or the benefit of others intending or knowing that it would be injurious to the owner of the trade secrets. The term trade secret refers to all forms and types of financial, business, scientific, technical, engineering or economic information, which includes patterns, plans, compilations, procedures, methods, techniques, codes, processes no matter how the information is stored.
>
> (NCIX 2004a)

The Act covers industrial espionage that occurs within the United States, is a furtherance of an offence conducted within the United States, or where the offender is a US citizen or organisation. The penalties are severe:

> The courts can impose up to a 15 year prison sentence and/or a maximum of US$500,000 fine on an individual, and a US$10 million fine on an organisation who steals or destroys a trade secret of value with intent to benefit a foreign country. Equally, the court can impose up to a 10 year prison sentence and/or a maximum $250,000 fine on an individual and a

Mini case 5.3

Crossing the line in the sand

In 2001 Procter & Gamble (P&G) revealed that it had conducted a corporate espionage programme against several competitors, with specific reference to its major rival Unilever. P&G was particularly interested in gaining information on the competitors' hair care ranges. Unilever's brand ranges Salon Selectives, Finesse, Thermasilk and Helene Curtis were in direct competition with P&G's own brands, which included Pantene, Head & Shoulders and Pert.

In order to obtain the information P&G had hired a competitive intelligence contractor which had, in turn, hired several subcontractors. As the operation expanded, lack of control led to over-zealous analysts breaching both general and company-specific codes of conduct. The analysts acting on behalf of P&G went 'dumpster diving'* at Unilever's US hair care headquarters in Chicago. Over a period of several months it is believed that the analysts obtained over 50 sensitive documents. These apparently revealed significant amounts of data on Unilever's brands, new product developments, proposed selling prices and even margins.

Eventually details of this operation came to the attention of senior executives at P&G, including chairman John Pepper. Shocked by what he heard, Pepper halted the intelligence-gathering operation and launched an immediate investigation. The result was the dismissal of the three managers directly involved in the project. Then in an unprecedented move, in April 2001 Pepper contacted Unilever to reveal what had been happening since 2000.

Pepper's motives in contacting Unilever were probably:

◆ To reveal upfront what had occurred to limit any long-term damage to the reputation of the company. If the story had been 'broken' by the media, P&G would have found it difficult to manage the publicity. Being honest and open and demonstrating that the company had taken action against the instigators placed it in a far better position to deal with the criticism. It was being proactive rather than reactive.

◆ To show that although the company was highly competitive in the marketplace, such activity was against its principles.

◆ To move towards an upfront settlement to prevent Unilever suing P&G. A court battle would most likely have damaged the reputation of the company, and affected its share values. Moreover, if (as was likely) it had lost, P&G might have been forced to pay punitive damages.

In September 2001 executives from P&G and Unilever reached a settlement after several months of negotiation. The terms of the settlement have not been disclosed by either company. However press speculation estimated that P&G paid some US$10 million. John Pepper stated:

We believe the agreement protects both P&G's and Unilever's business interests. I have been personally involved in ensuring that none of the information has been or will be used in any P&G plans. This agreement will have no impact on the effectiveness of our product or marketing plans and will not inhibit fair and rigorous competition in the marketplace. This was an unfortunate incident. The activities were not in keeping with P&G principles and policies. We're convinced we did the right thing by voluntarily and promptly making Unilever aware of this incident, quarantining the information and working with them to protect their interests. We expect this agreement will bring this situation to an end so we can focus fully on serving consumers and building our business.

Sources: A. Serwer, 'P&G comes clean on spying operation', Fortune, 30 August 2001; J. Mclean, 'Unilever threat to P&G on "spying"', London Evening Standard, 31 August 2001; 'Shampoo giant caught spying', BBC Business Online, 31 August 2001; 'P&G and Unilever reach an agreement', P&G press release, 6 September 2001; 'Settlement in shampoo spy case', BBC Business Online, 6 September 2001; 'P&G settles with Unilever', CCN Money, 6 September 2001; A. Serwer, 'P&G's covert operation: an intelligence-gathering campaign against Unilever went way too far', Fortune, 17 September 2001.

* Dumpster diving is also known as waste archaeology. An individual studies the waste collected from rubbish bins in order to find documents or plans of intent. These might include drafts of advertising campaigns, copies of price lists and/or complete drafts of financial and new product development plans.

US$5 million fine on an organisation who knowingly steals or destroys any trade secret with the intent to economically benefit anyone other than the owner; and injure the owner of the trade secret. (NCIX 2004a)

Mini case 5.4

Konkordski

As indicated earlier, governments sometimes work with companies to gain competitive information. Countries such as France and China have been accused in the past of aiding and abetting some of their companies. One of the most infamous incidents was the stealing of the plans for the Anglo-French supersonic airliner Concorde by the KGB, the then Soviet Secret Service. The KGB recruited an aeronautical engineer – code-named 'Ace' – who handed over tens of thousands of pages of technical specifications.

There were three key aims in obtaining this information:

◆ World political prestige. The world was still very much in a Cold War state and the Soviet Union was a major rival to Western industrial, economic and commercial power. It was clear at the time that it could not afford to lose its positioning.

◆ World airline prestige. It was believed at the time that supersonic flight had enormous commercial and financial possibilities. The aircraft manufacturer that built a cost-effective supersonic transport (in terms of purchase price) would gain orders from the leading airlines, and this would give its home country commercial power.

◆ If it could be first into the sky, and thus the market, the Soviet Union hoped to become market leader and take market share from Concorde.

When pictures of the Tupolev TU-144, the plane developed using this stolen information, were first released it was so strikingly similar in appearance to Concorde that it was dubbed Konkordski. It first flew several months before Concorde, and was able to achieve supersonic speeds. However the TU-144 was an ill-fated aircraft. Before it was flown to Paris for the 1973 Paris Airshow, the Tupolev Design Bureau added side fins just behind the cockpit for additional stability. This apparently intrigued the French authorities, who decided to photograph the TU-144 in flight.

There are conflicting reports about what really happened at the Paris Air Show. All airspace above a demonstration flight at an air show is normally kept clear, but it is believed that a French Mirage fighter flew above the TU-144 to take photographs. As the Russian pilot climbed above the cloud he saw the Mirage, and took evasive action. This stalled the engines, and the only way he could restart them was to place the aircraft into a dive and then climb out of the dive once the engines started. It is clear from footage of the incident that the aircraft was coming out of the dive when the tail section broke up, followed by the mid portion. The crash that followed killed the crew, observers on board, and several people in a nearby village who were hit by debris. It is the view of Concorde designers and a former test pilot that Concorde would have survived similar g-forces to those the TU-144 faced, as such stresses on the airframe were built into the original specifications.

The point here is that while the Soviet plane makers had thousands of pages of drawings and notes, they did not have the deeper insight that motivated the British and French designers. Industrial espionage gave them a short-term advantage – being the first supersonic transport – but it did not provide them with a long-term advantage.

After several modifications the TU-144 went into service as a transport aircraft within the then Soviet Union. However, a subsequent crash in 1977 ended the chances of the Soviet Union competing in the commercial supersonic aircraft market, although it clearly had the ability to do so. If such commercial and political pressures had not been exacted on the Tupolev Company, perhaps the history of supersonic flight would have been different. Tupolev might have emerged as an aircraft manufacturer to rival both Boeing and Airbus within the international marketplace. Passenger supersonic aircraft might still been flying today.*

Source: Konkordski, Channel 4 television documentary, 2002.

* Both Air France and British Airways retired their Concorde fleet in 2003.

Bellocchi (2001) believes that the US Act has made significant improvements in protecting the secrets of American corporations. However there are weaknesses in its provisions. Bellocchi believes these shortfalls relate, in part, to the fact that it does not create a mechanism to take action against foreign countries actively engaged in economic intelligence gathering. Indeed the US government's own statistics indicate that 'foreign businessmen, scientists, academics and government officials from more than 90 countries continued targeting sensitive US technologies and corporate trade secrets in both 2002 and 2003' (NCIX 2004b). Bellocchi (2001) claims another problem is that civil suits against foreign companies, and even foreign governments, are not allowed in US courts.

In spite of these problems the US Act appears at least on the surface to be having some impact. Other governments have also sought to protect indigenous industries from such attacks and threats. However, it seems obvious (even if this is a somewhat cynical view) that governments will continue to spy on foreign companies if they believe it is in the best interest of their nation.

Most people involved in gathering intelligence on companies do so without resorting to illegal, and unethical actions. Professionals involved in competitive intelligence gathering abide by codes of ethics. The Society of Competitive Intelligence Professionals (SCIP) Code of Ethics is reproduced in the box.

■ Chapter summary

The gathering of competitor information is vital to the survival and growth of virtually any business. It can be argued that this is now even more true, as companies increasingly operate globally. However, companies gathering such information must be aware of the legal and ethical implications. Some companies, and indeed nations, do undertake illegal industrial espionage to gather covert information. In most cases there is only a short-term return, and the risks associated with such adventures can be overwhelming.

Companies that use ethical and legal avenues can call on a wealth of data resources. However, the key is in analysing and processing the data to provide a basis for individuals and companies to make informed decisions that affect the strategic direction of the business.

It is important to remember that the gathering and analysis of intelligence data is not a one-off exercise. Both current and potential competitors must be monitored on an ongoing basis to maximise the long-term benefits. By monitoring current and potential competitors carefully, a company can protect its market position. Good intelligence is a collection of knowledge that has been verified and analysed, that can be applied to a business scenario to make a viable decision.

■ Questions for review and reflection

1 Outline, in detail and using additional resources, the reasons that competitor intelligence gathering is an important aspect of gaining market share.

2 Outline the types of resource that can be used to gather information on a company.

SCIP Code of Ethics for Competitive Intelligence Professionals

◆ To continually strive to increase the recognition and respect of the profession.

◆ To comply with all applicable laws, domestic and international.

◆ To accurately disclose all relevant information, including one's identity and organisation, prior to all interviews.

◆ To fully respect all requests for confidentially of information.

◆ To avoid conflicts of interest in fulfilling one's duties.

◆ To provide honest and realistic recommendations and conclusions in the execution of one's duties.

◆ To promote this code of ethics within in one's company, with third-party contractors and within the entire profession.

◆ To faithfully adhere to and abide by one's company policies, objectives and guidelines.

© 2004 Society of Competitive Intelligence Professionals.

3   Take an multinational corporation of your choice. Spend a day in a major reference library researching all you can on the organisation. Supplement this with information from the Internet. Then consider what tools and techniques you would require to analyse this information.

4   Take a multinational corporation of your choice and study its website. What sort of information or data does it present that might be of interest to a competitor?

5   We considered the US Economic Espionage Act of 1996. Use the Internet to discover which other countries have, or are considering, similar types of legislation.

■ References

Aaker, D. (1995) *Strategic Marketing Management*, New York: Wiley.

Bellocchi, L. P. (2001) 'Assessing the effectiveness of the Economic Espionage Act of 1996', *International Journal of Intelligence and Counterintelligence* **14**, pp. 366–87.

Burns, A. and Bush, R. (2000) *Marketing Research*, 2nd edn, New Jersey: Prentice Hall.

Clausewitz, C. von. (1832) *On War*, Princeton: Princeton University Press (this edn 1976).

Cochran, E. S. (2003) 'South Korea's intelligence targets U.S. technology', *International Journal of Intelligence and Counterintelligence* **16**, pp. 179–201.

Cravens, D. (1982) *Strategic Marketing*, New York: Irwin.

Davidson, D. (1997) *Even More Offensive Marketing*, London: Penguin.

Doyle, P. (1998) *Marketing Management and Strategy*, 2nd edn, Harlow: Prentice Hall.

Eckles, R. W. (1990) *Business Marketing Management: Marketing of business products and services*, New Jersey: Prentice Hall.

Haddigan, M. (1995) 'Competitor intelligence considered more vital now', *Marketing News* **29**(21) (9 October), pp. 2–5.

James, B. G. (1985) *Business Wargames*, London: Penguin.

Johnson, G. and Scholes, K. (2004) *Exploring Corporate Strategy*, 6th edn, Harlow: Prentice Hall.

Lauginie, J. M., Mansillon, G. and Dubouin, J. (1994) *Action Commerciale Mercatique*, Paris: Foucher.

McDaniel, C. Jr. and Gates, R. (1999) *Contemporary Marketing Research*, 4th edn, Cincinnati: South-Western College Publishing.

Orton, J. D. (2002) 'Cross-national ethical dilemmas in competitive intelligence', *International Journal of Intelligence and Counterintelligence* **15**, pp.440–56.

National Counterintelligence Center USA (NACIC) (1999) *Foreign Economic and Industrial Espionage Remains a Threat in 1999*, Washington, DC: NACIC.

National Counterintelligence Executive USA (NCIX) (2004a) *The Economic Espionage Act of 1996: A brief guide*, Washington, DC: NCIX, www.ncix.gov

NCIX (2004b) *Annual Report to Congress on Foreign Economic Collection and Industrial Espionage*, Washington, DC: NCIX.

Porter, M. E. (1980) *Competitive Strategy: Techniques for analyzing industries and competitors*, New York: Free Press.

Robbins, S. P. and Coulter, M. (1996) *Management*, 5th edn, New Jersey: Prentice Hall.

Sharp, S. (2000) 'Truth or consequences: 10 myths that cripple competitive intelligence', *Competitive Intelligence* **3**(1) (January/February), pp. 37–40.

Simkin, L. (1996) 'Addressing organizational prerequisites in marketing planning programmes', *Journal of Marketing Management* **12**, pp. 375–90.

Simkin, L. and Cheng, A. (1997) 'Understanding competitors' strategies: the practitioner-academic gap', *Marketing Intelligence and Planning* **15**(3), pp. 124–34.

West, C. (1999) 'Marketing research', in M. J. Baker (ed.), *Encyclopedia of Marketing*, London: Thomson Learning, pp. 255–67.

Wheelan, T. L. and Hunger, J. D. (1992) *Strategic Management and Business Policy*, 4th edn, New York: Addison-Wesley.

Wong, V. and Saunders, J. (1996) 'Analysing competitors', in P, Kotler, G. Armstrong, J. Saunders and V. Wong (eds), *Principles of Marketing*, Harlow: Prentice Hall.

Wright, S. and Pickton, D. W. (1998) 'Improved competitive strategy through value-added competitive intelligence', *Proceedings of the 3rd Annual Society of Competitive Intelligence Professionals European Conference, Berlin, November*, pp. 73–83.

Wright, S., Pickton, D. W. and Callow, J. (2002) 'Competitive intelligence in UK firms: a typology', *Marketing Intelligence and Planning* **20**(6), pp. 349–60.

Strategy in Marketing

CHAPTER 6

Learning outcomes

After completing this chapter you should be able to:

▶ discuss the relevance of strategy to marketing

▶ explain the role of the marketing audit in relation to meeting the organisation's overriding objectives

▶ debate how various strategic tools or techniques can assist marketers to meet both marketing and corporate objectives

▶ explain how organisations can gain and defend market share within turbulent markets.

■ Introduction

This chapter examines the relationship between strategy and marketing. It builds upon the knowledge gained in Chapters 2 to 5, and signals some of the issues that will be examined in the later chapters on the marketing mix and branding.

As Grant (2002) suggests, strategy is not a detailed plan or programme of instruction; it is a unifying theme that provides coherence and direction to the actions and decisions of organisations. In order to achieve this aim the marketer must be able to:

◆ analyse both the micro and macro environments using appropriate tools and techniques

◆ continually refine this analysis in relation to changing environmental conditions

◆ continually analyse competitive actions and be able to either pre-empt or react to such actions

Contents

Learning outcomes 97
Introduction 97
What is strategy? 98
Strategy levels 99
Corporate strategy level 99
Business strategy level 99
Functional strategy level 99
The marketing–strategy relationship 99
The marketing audit 100
Environmental audit 100
Marketing strategy audit 101
Marketing organisation audit 101
Marketing systems audit 101
Marketing productivity audit 101
Marketing function analysis 101
Ansoff's portfolio matrix 102
The GE matrix 103
Market attractiveness 103
Business position (also known as business strength) 103
SWOT analysis 104
The five forces model 106
The threat of new entrants 107
The threat of substitution 108
The power of suppliers 108
The power of buyers 109
Industry competitors 110
Competitive advantage: generic strategies 110
Competitive scope 110
Competitive advantage 110
Analysis of generic strategies 111
Focus 112
Stuck in the middle 112
Adding value to the product or service 112
Company infrastructure 112
The human resource management team 112
Technology development 112
Procurement 112
Competitive market positioning strategies 113
Market leader 113
Market challengers 113
Market followers 114
Market nichers 114
Competitive and defensive positions 114
Position defence 114
Pre-emptive defence 114
Counter-offensive defence 115
Mobile defence 115
Strategic withdrawal 115
Frontal attack 116
Flanking attack 117
Guerrilla attack 117
Chapter summary 117
Questions for review and reflection 118
References 118

◆ link marketing to the overall ambitions of the organisation (the corporate strategy), but with a need for flexibility

◆ marshal or group resources and core competences to compete within the market place

◆ marshal the components of the marketing mix to both compete within the market place and achieve the overall objectives of the organisation.

The subject of strategy is a particularly large one, and many books have been written on it. This chapter provides a brief overview of some of the relevant key issues. You are advised to supplement it by reading more widely on this topic. The reference sources mentioned in the chapter provide a good starting point.

■ What is strategy?

Before examining the relationship between strategy and marketing, it is worth briefly considering the meaning of strategy. The word 'strategy' has its basis in military campaigns dating back to the Ancient Greeks. Leaders and their generals devised strategies to conquer nations using appropriate tactics to defeat their enemy. In military terms the concepts have basically remained the same, although the range of weaponry to support the tactics has increased dramatically.

The deployment of strategies and tactics in the military sphere has been around for centuries. However the overt discussion of strategies and tactics within the business world is relatively new. Much of the analysis of the competitive environment and use of strategies and tactics dates from the 1960s. Ideas and concepts have been introduced and refined along the way, and will continue to be so.

Mintzberg *et al.* (2003) describe strategy as:

> The pattern or plan that integrates an organization's major goals, policies and action sequences into a cohesive whole. A well-formulated strategy helps to marshal and allocate an organization's resources into a unique and viable posture based on its relative internal competencies and shortcomings, anticipated changes in the environment, and contingent moves by intelligent opponents.

Being aware of the micro and macro environmental factors is critical in judging the scope and scale or resources necessary to compete within the marketplace. Aligned with this is a key phrase in this definition, 'a well-formulated strategy helps to marshal and allocate resources'. As with a military campaign:

◆ There has to be the appropriate level and type of resources.

◆ They need to be deployed efficiently and effectively to support the organisation's corporate objectives and goals.

◆ There needs to be flexibility to be both proactive and reactive to changing environmental and competitive conditions.

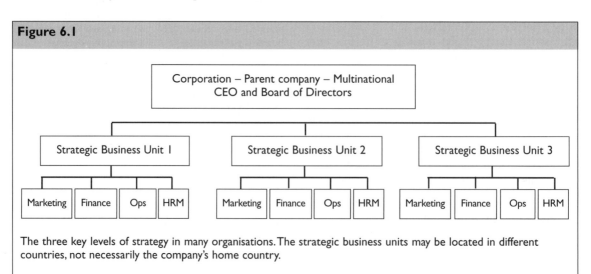

Figure 6.1

Corporation – Parent company – Multinational
CEO and Board of Directors

Strategic Business Unit 1

Strategic Business Unit 2

Strategic Business Unit 3

Marketing | Finance | Ops | HRM

Marketing | Finance | Ops | HRM

Marketing | Finance | Ops | HRM

The three key levels of strategy in many organisations. The strategic business units may be located in different countries, not necessarily the company's home country.

◆ The analyst must continually monitor and analyse micro and macro environments in order to understand and pre-empt market changes.

However, 'strategy' does not occur at just one level within an organisation. It is involved at many levels, as is shown in the next section.

■ Strategy levels

Unless the business is a micro business (with a single owner–operator), strategy will not be carried out at only one level. Strategies are normally conceived and deployed at three levels: the corporate, business and functional levels (see Figure 6.1).

Corporate strategy level

This is the overall strategy that governs the direction of the company. Usually it addresses two fundamental questions: what business are we in? And what business should we be in? These are not one-off questions but ones that should be asked on a regular basis. Only by asking such questions can a company fully understand how the macro environment (see Chapter 2) affects its business objectives. Markets change, and if those changes are not addressed, using appropriate resources, the company might falter, be overtaken by competitors, or discover it is in a shrinking market with no future.

Business strategy level

What are often known as strategic business units (SBUs) can be either divisions or subsidiaries of a much larger organisation, sometimes known as the parent. They usually focus on distinct products or services, and have a defined market segment(s). The business-level strategy usually seeks to address the question, how can the business unit compete successfully within the chosen market segments, achieving competitive advantage? If the business unit is successful at achieving competitive advantage, it might well help the parent to gain and sustain competitive advantage as well. Specific questions within this overarching theme include:

◆ Can new opportunities and new markets be identified?

◆ Can the business unit's strengths and weaknesses be clearly identified?

◆ Can new products and service opportunities be identified that match current and potential customer needs?

◆ Can the business unit deliver the new products and services that match the customer's needs at the price/quality level expected?

◆ Can the business unit counter competitor actions to protect its share within the segment of the market?

◆ Can the business unit exploit external opportunities while countering external threats?

Many of these questions can be answered by the use of such tools as a SWOT analysis (see page 104).

Functional strategy level

These are also known as the operational units of a business although that can be confusing when a company has Operations as one of its functions. It is more appropriate to consider them as the functions of the company, such as finance, human resource management, distribution and operations. Although often considered separately, they must be seen as integrated units working together to achieve both business-level and corporate-level strategies.

At the functional level the key questions are:

◆ What goals have to be achieved at the functional level to ensure strategic success at the business and corporate levels?

◆ What resources are required at the functional level to achieve those goals?

■ The marketing–strategy relationship

Ohmae (1982) suggests that there is strategic triangle that encompasses the organisation's strengths, the competitors' strengths and the customers' needs (see Figure 6.2). While this provides a good starting point for discussion, it is nonetheless a simplistic overview. For instance, the impact of the

Figure 6.2

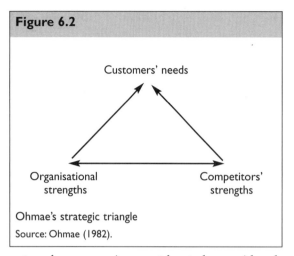

Ohmae's strategic triangle

Source: Ohmae (1982).

external macro environment has to be considered. Equally, weaknesses of the different organisations make them vulnerable to attack. Ohmae himself (1982) suggests that there is the need to move away from 'the realm of the abstract to the realm of the concrete'. Thus, there needs to be wider exploration of how strategy and its tactics operate within the real world.

Taking this theme slightly further, Ohmae's triangle needs to be looked upon as operating in a dynamic (often turbulent) environment. An organisation has to consider not only competitors' positions within the market but also customers' needs and wants. In order for the organisation to compete it needs to consider its strengths. Among these are the resources and competencies (sometimes called capabilities) within the organisation. As Grant (2002) states:

> During the 1990s, the ideas concerning the role of a firm's resources and capabilities as the principal basis for its strategy and the primary source of profitability coalesced into what has become known as the *resource-based view of the firm* [his italics]. Central to this 'resource-based view' is the idea that the form is essentially a pool of resources and capabilities, and that these resources and capabilities are the primary determinants of its strategy.

It is important to note that some authors use the term 'capabilities' whilst others use 'competencies'. Although it can be argued that there are differences in meaning, they are generally taken as interchangeable.

Capabilities or competencies take two forms:

◆ Threshold competencies are the same as those held by the competitors, easy to imitate and necessary to exist within the industry or marketplace.

◆ Core competencies on the other hand are those resources and competencies that are different from competitors', are difficult to imitate and are superior to competitors'.

The combination of threshold and core competencies provides the company with a view of where its strengths lie at a particular point. However, there is the need to continually review these competencies. One of the many areas that must be examined is the organisation's marketing effort, and this can be achieved by carrying out a marketing audit.

■ The marketing audit

Kotler *et al.* (1989) describes this as:

> An independent examination of the entire marketing effort of a company, or some specific marketing activity, covering objectives, programme, implementation and organisation for the purpose of determining what is to be done, appraising what is being done, and recommending what should be done in the future.

However, as Baker (2000) contends, it should also be used to identify future trends, opportunities and threats in both the micro and macro environments. This will then link in to the practical technique of the SWOT analysis (see page 104).

A typical marketing audit consists of the following elements.

Environmental audit

1 Macro environment.

2 Micro environment.

These issues are dynamic and must be reviewed on an ongoing basis (see Chapter 2).

Marketing strategy audit

1 Marketing objectives.

2 Strategy.

The corporate objectives need to be stated clearly and to lead logically into the marketing objectives. Equally, the marketing objectives must be in a clear format to drive marketing planning and perform-ance measurements (for example, benchmarking). The marketing objectives must be appropriate, given the company's positions, resources and competencies.

The marketing strategy must be linked to the objectives and be realistic (achievable) given the level of resources available (now and planned for the future).

Marketing organisation audit

1 Formal structure.

2 Functional efficiency.

3 Interface efficiency.

An organisation can have a brilliant product or service. However, if the marketing team is poorly led and ill-trained, the chances of the product or service becoming a success are limited. Equally, the marketing team needs to interface with other func-tional units, for example, operations and finance. Such interfaces must be effective and efficient to drive not only the marketing effort but the corporate objectives as well.

Marketing systems audit

1 Marketing information systems (MIS).

2 Marketing planning systems.

3 Marketing control systems.

4 New product development systems.

Information is vital, and this emanates from marketing research and competitive intelligence, combined into an MIS. The information must be timely, accurate and actionable. The planning system will utilise MIS data, as well as data from elsewhere, and thus must be well developed and effective. Even within a turbulent environment there has to be some form of control in order to organise and monitor daily, weekly and monthly activities to meet the overall objectives.

Organisations need time to research and test new product ideas (discussed in Chapter 9). There-fore systems need to be in place to generate, screen, organise and test ideas.

Marketing productivity audit

1 Profitability analysis.

2 Cost-effectiveness analysis.

It is important to analyse on a regular basis the profitability of the products or services, segments, markets and distribution channels. Companies also need to examine whether it is profitable to:

◆ enter new markets (and when to enter them)

◆ develop and implement market expansion

◆ withdraw from a segment, a market or an entire industry. If so what are the cost implications of doing so?

As well as looking at profitability, companies need to consider costs. Some companies take a very aggressive stance, seeking to eliminate costs wher-ever possible in the organisation. An example of this approach is Europe's low-cost no-frills airlines. (See Porter's generic strategies, page 110.)

Marketing function analysis

1 Products and services.

2 Price.

3 Promotion.

4 Place.

5 People.

6 Processes.

7 Physical evidence.

8 Psychology.

9 Performance.

10 Packaging.

Each one of these elements has objectives that link into the marketing and hence corporate objectives of the organisation. While these are considered as separate entities for the sake of presentation, in reality a holistic view should be taken. Chapter 8 highlights the origin of the marketing mix, and as the term indicates, they can be 'mixed' together, so an integrated approach should be considered. (This list is adapted and developed from Kotler, Gregor and Rogers (1989).)

■ Ansoff's portfolio matrix

Ansoff (1987) believed there were two related types of strategy that described an organisation's strategic development, portfolio analysis and competitive strategy. Ansoff's matrix is a portfolio analysis that examines the organisation's activities within existing markets and potential markets with current products and new developments. The structure is illustrated in Figure 6.3.

Table 6.1 examines each of the quadrants that comprise the portfolio matrix, giving examples of each activity.

The Ansoff portfolio matrix is particularly good at examining growth strategies. However, it may not be in its best interests for a company to expand. That might sound like a contradiction, but if for example a company is faced with turbulent market conditions, to attempt to maintain its position across several market segments, let alone expand, could be a suicidal strategy in the longer term. The

best strategic option would be for it to retrench and fortify its position.

A retrenchment strategy can take on several forms, and be implemented as either an individual tactic or a combination of tactics. These include:

◆ Divest non-core businesses: this is perhaps the major retrenchment tactic, and usually the one that gains the largest return for the divesting company. Divestment can mean either closure of the business or selling it to another company (ideally not a rival) at an appropriate market value. If the company decides to close a business there will be costs involved. These can include redundancy payments to staff, assistance in finding the staff alternative employment (if this cannot be achieved by redeployment elsewhere in the company), and costs related to the demolition of buildings and sale of land. On the company's balance sheet this expenditure is usually considered as a one-off cost. If a company seeks to close several plants, while this might initially make economic sense, it risks causing harm to itself in public relations terms. The outcome is very much down to how the company handles such closures, which are usually painful for all those involved.

◆ Divestment of products or services: a company may examine its portfolio of products and services and decide to merge the marginally profitable ones and phase out the unprofitable ones. By concentrating on profitable activities it can maximise its investment in terms of the marketing mix. As with the divesting of non-core businesses, the termination of a product or service can result in the closure of a business (SBU) and factories. Therefore the cost implications of such a move need to be considered. Chapter 7 on Branding considers Unilever's Path to Growth strategy in which it divested itself of hundreds of brands in order to concentrate its resources on a core of 400 brands. These core brands form the platform for the company's next phase of growth.

◆ Withdrawal from a market(s): the company may decide to withdraw from a market sector, especially if it is marginally profitable or there are indications it will become unprofitable.

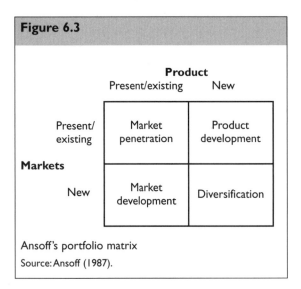

Figure 6.3

Ansoff's portfolio matrix
Source: Ansoff (1987).

Table 6.1 Quadrants in Ansoff's portfolio matrix

Matrix component	Description
Market penetration	The organisation can seek to further penetrate the market by providing customers with the incentive to purchase more product. Such incentives might also bring potential customers over to the organisation from its competitors. They include price competition, special promotions (loyalty card schemes) and/or expanding the usage of the product or service on offer (for example, breakfast cereal as an all-day snack food). However, depending on the competitive forces within the marketplace, such actions may create a highly volatile competitive market with rivals prepared to enter a price war. (See the section on competitive rivalry, page 110.)
Market development	The objective here is to seek out new markets for the company's existing products and services. A company could seek new markets either in its home country or internationally.
Product development	The company seeks the development of a new product (service) to launch within an existing market. Product development can include improvements to existing products as well the development and launch of totally new products into the marketplace.
Diversification	The company seeks to develop new products (or services) to launch within new markets. To achieve this companies may acquire other non-product-related companies in order to move into these new markets. However, not all companies that have diversified have been successful within the diversified area. Often this is because they do not understand the complexities of that particular market. The result is often an expensive withdrawal from that particular market.

Again, there may be costs involved as a result of such a withdrawal.

The GE matrix

General Electric and the management consultants McKinsey developed the GE matrix, or GE business screen, as it is also known. The purpose of the matrix is to classify either strategic business unit activity or major products based on two determinants, market attractiveness and business position.

Figure 6.4 (overleaf) shows the matrix structure. In this 3x3 matrix the options are to invest, protect, harvest or divest. The decisions are based on the level (high, medium or low) of market attractiveness and business position (also known as business strength).

Market attractiveness

Whether a market is attractive or not will depend on numerous factors, some of which may be peculiar to a particular industry. Generally, the factors are briefly considered in Table 6.2 (overleaf).

Business position (also known as business strength)

This concerns the various factors that determine the position of the business in the marketplace. A selection of the key factors are highlighted in Table 6.3 (page 106).

From an analysis of market attractiveness and business position several strategies can emerge. (See Figure 6.4.)

◆ **Invest:** the company seeks to invest resources in the SBU or product/service. The objective is to build and strengthen position over the medium and longer terms.

◆ **Protect:** these SBUs or products/services require protection as they are the cash generators for new products, services or even SBUs. Thus the company must allocate resources and implement actions to protect these in the marketplace.

◆ **Harvest:** there is generally a medium to low business position coinciding with a medium to

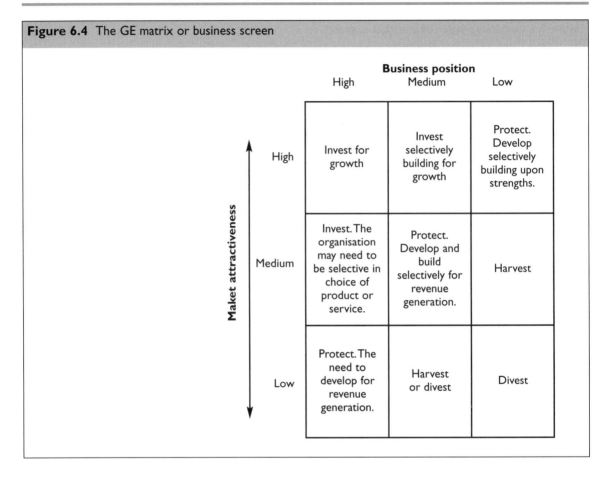

Figure 6.4 The GE matrix or business screen

low level of market attractiveness. The company's objective here is to maximise the revenue stream with the minimum level of investment in resources. There may well come a point where the company will need to consider the following options:

● selling the SBU or product/service to another company

● closing the SBU or terminating the product/service

● finding a way of re-energising the SBU or product/service.

Harvesting can be equated to the declining section of industry and product life cycles. (See Chapter 9 for more on the product life cycle.)

◆ **Divest:** this is the weakest position on the grid, and the company must seek to divest itself of the SBU or product/service. This might mean selling it to another company or closing the SBU and terminating the product or service.

Although the grid is set out in quadrants, that does not restrict movement within its framework. For instance as Stanton, Etzel and Walker (1994) suggest, a company may harvest profits from divesting an SBU or product/service to another company. While there are costs incurred from divesting (even through a sale), the additional resources (including finance) can be invested into SBUs or products/services that require additional protection within the marketplace. Thus a problem within one area can be used as a basis for protecting and developing others.

■ SWOT analysis

The concept of the SWOT analysis derives from the work of Andrews and others at Harvard

Table 6.2 Market attractiveness factors

Factor	Questions and issues
Market share	The focus is on that already held, secured and or potentially gained. This is a performance measure.
Market size	How large is the market? Can it sustain more players? Can the company expand? Or should the organisation consider withdrawal?
Financial performance	An organisation must consider whether or not a market will deliver the level of returns on investment that it expects or needs. With the introduction of a new product or service the initial returns may be poor. However, the organisation has to consider the medium to longer-term prospects of being in that particular market. There are two critical factors though: can it financially sustain poor returns over the short term, and does it have the resource strength to increase its marketability? Organisations may enter markets because they perceive them to be viable but lack the resources to support that entry. The resulting financial performance is often poor.
Barriers to entry	Porter's five forces model (see page 107) considers possible barriers that might prevent a new entrant into the marketplace/industry. At the same time, such barriers protect the incumbents, although it could be argued that new entrants bring a fresh approach to the marketplace/industry that can improve the position of many of the competitors. Competition from new entrants can help revitalise industries.
Strength and power of the competition	This is also reviewed under the five forces model in terms of an industry. Whether it is an analysis of either an SBU and/or product level, the company has to consider the number of competitors currently in the market; their level of power within the marketplace; level of competitors' sustainability; their current and potential future strategies; and potential entrants (a small entrant today could be a major competitive threat in the future).
Technological requirements	As discussed in Chapter 2, technology has had a significant impact on the development of business (and marketing) since the Industrial Revolution of the 18th century. The new technological revolution (based on computer systems) will have an even more dramatic impact. Therefore companies need to consider where their SBUs and products 'sit' in this dynamic and complex technological landscape. As we already know, technology is changing so fast, it is sometimes difficult for companies to identify the best strategic move. In other words companies need to ascertain in which directions(s) the market will go, what is driving it and whether it is sustainable.
Other macro factors	Although technology has been separated out (see above) the remaining PESTLE factors should not be discarded. Chapter 2 examined how the macro factors have had, and continue to have, an impact on business and marketing in particular. The underlying essence of that chapter is that the world is a turbulent place – part created by the human race, part created by the forces of nature. Companies therefore need to examine market attractiveness in relation to these constantly developing forces.

University (Andrews 1986). It analyses two distinct areas, the organisation and the environment in which it operates. (See Figure 6.5.) The organisational analysis focuses on the inherent strengths and weaknesses within the organisation. In contrast the environmental analysis focuses on the external opportunities and threats that exist within the industry or field in which the organisation operates.[1]

In Figure 6.6 the dotted line between 'Internal analysis – micro environment' and 'Industry analysis' is to symbolise the linking of competitors. It is important to realise that there is often a link or overlap between environmental factors.

Once an organisation has established its strengths and weaknesses and opportunities and threats, it can develop the SWOT further through matching and conversion.

In **matching** the organisation links its appropriate strengths with the market opportunities, to exploit opportunities in the marketplace. For instance, there might be a positive change in tariff regulations in a certain region, which leads to a market opportunity, as this makes it cost-effective

---

Table 6.3 Business position factors

Factor	Questions and issues
Brand	An organisation's position is often determined by the power of its brand(s) in the marketplace. The word 'power' covers many attributes from reputation through to value. Branding (discussed in Chapter 7) can convey enormous power in the marketplace.
Marketing mix variables	In later chapters the marketing mix variables are examined. How these variables are presented to the market will create a position for the company in the mind of the buyer. For instance, the quality of a product or service, its price, how it is promoted and how easy it is to obtain illustrate the position or strength of the company offering the product or service. Consider, for example, the business strengths of certain major hotel chains. What is their business position based on?
Management skills and knowledge	An organisation may have a great product. However, if the management is poorly trained, inefficient, and/or just ill equipped for the task there is increased risk of market failure. An effective and efficient management team will not only assist in developing product and service positioning but will also create a viable reputation in the marketplace.

---

to market to that region. If one of the organisation's strengths is flexibility in production, it could immediately increase production to meet the potential demand in this region.

In **conversion** identified weaknesses are either eliminated or transformed into strengths. For example, after an analysis, the organisation might

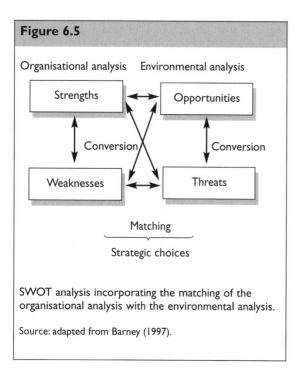

Figure 6.5

Organisational analysis Environmental analysis

Strengths ↔ Opportunities

Conversion   Conversion

Weaknesses ↔ Threats

Matching

Strategic choices

SWOT analysis incorporating the matching of the organisational analysis with the environmental analysis.

Source: adapted from Barney (1997).

discover it is particularly weak at monitoring its marketing budget. Hence the marketing department do not know how much they spend and what they have purchased until the end of the fiscal year. This weakness could be converted into a strength by formulating procedures that provide on-screen tracking of expenditure and the production of monthly management accounts and reports. This can be reinforced by closer working relationships with the finance department.

The organisation might also be able to convert an external threat into an opportunity. For instance, there might be a change in legislation that is a general threat to the industry, such as a new tax. Other companies might have to pass the cost on to their customers, but if the organisation has a extremely efficient production system (one of its strengths) it might be able to absorb the cost (though perhaps only in the short to medium term), keeping its prices stable and possibly gaining it extra market share.

During the process of SWOT analysis, management will also begin to re-evaluate the company's current mission and objectives. If changes are required in the overall direction of the business, this is where those changes are likely to originate.

■ The five forces model

Porter (1980) devised a structural analysis of industries that is commonly known as the five forces

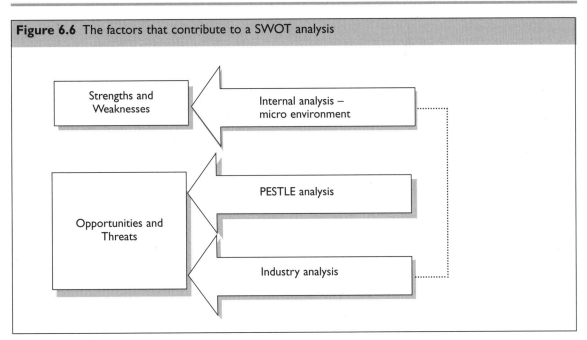

Figure 6.6 The factors that contribute to a SWOT analysis

model (see Figure 6.7). This states that there are five key or distinguishing forces that govern the role of competition in the marketplace.

The threat of new entrants

Porter (1980) suggests that a new entrant into a market creates new capacity with the objective of gaining (and sustaining) market share. To do this it often invests in substantial resourcing. Such an entrant can destabilise the competition, creating a shakeout in the market. However, entry into an industry and/or market depends upon two key factors: the barriers to industry entry, and the reaction from current competitors within the industry (see page 110).

Porter (1980) proposes seven sources of barriers to entry.

◆ **Economies of scale**: where companies are able to drive down unit costs of a product or service as the volume increases. An entrant has two options, either to match or outperform the level of economies of scale, or to start at a level where the economies of scale are less and accept that there will be cost disadvantages that may well be reflected in price disadvantages. Both options may prove to be barriers to entry.

◆ **Product differentiation**: established companies within the industry have had time and opportunity to build customer loyalty through product differences, branding and marketing

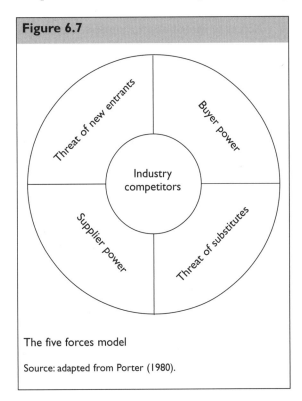

Figure 6.7

The five forces model

Source: adapted from Porter (1980).

communications. A new entrant will have to invest significantly in product differences and marketing communication to establish its brand in the marketplace. This will be resource-intensive with no guarantees that the brand will find a position that generates suitable returns on the investment.

◆ **Capital requirements**: substantial investment may be required to enter and establish a new brand. The venture might be considered highly risky, and the financial risk could deter potential entrants.

◆ **Switching costs**: the costs (often one-off) incurred by existing buyers if they switch from existing suppliers to new entrant suppliers. A change of supplier may mean costs incurred in retraining staff, the installation and testing (proving/qualifying) of the new equipment, acquisition of ancillary materials/equipment and the time (a cost) in building a relationship with the new supplier. Because of these costs, buyers often remain with their established suppliers. This in turn makes it more difficult for new entrants to gain a position in the marketplace.

◆ **Access to distribution channels**: companies that are already well established in the industry will have (or should have) efficient channels of distribution. The new entrant will have to either find a new avenue for distribution (perhaps technological) or persuade existing intermediaries and distributors to take extra supply. In some areas, especially retail, this is particularly difficult. For example, in the consumer detergent market a new entrant would have to persuade supermarket chains to make extra shelf space available in an already highly competitive industry and marketplace. To do this it might need to offer incentives to the channel members, but this would restrict its profitability.

◆ **Cost disadvantages independent of scale**: established entrants may be able to display cost advantages beyond economies of scale which a new entrant cannot readily replicate. These might include technical know-how (secured via patents), direct access to raw materials, an ideal location, government subsidies (includ-

ing protectionist policies) and significant industry or market experience.

◆ **Government policy:** this can range from the regulation of certain industries (for example, the nuclear industry) and protectionist policies for local industry to environmental legislation. Companies faced with such legislation may find it either impossible to enter an industry or very expensive to do so.

The threat of substitution

Products or services that can perform the same or similar functions as the product or services already established within the industry pose a substitution threat. Here Porter (1980) considers how the sugar industry has been confronted with the large-scale commercialisation of high-fructose corn syrup as a sugar substitute. Since then various types of sweetening products have entered the market to challenge sugar.

The power of suppliers

According to Porter (1980) a supplier group can hold significant bargaining power over buyers in some circumstances. For example if:

◆ The supplier group is dominated by a few companies and is more concentrated than the industry it sells to. For example, Groucutt *et al.* (2004) point out there are only a few mainstream tyre manufacturers even though there are hundreds of car manufacturers.

◆ The suppliers are not obliged to contend with other substitute products for sale to the industry. However, substitutes may cover several industries. Sugar has many applications. Equally, so do the variety of sweeteners available.

◆ The industry is not an important industry for the supplier group. If suppliers market to several industries and one of them does not represent a significant proportion of sales, the suppliers can exert more power. In contrast when the industry is an important customer for the suppliers, to maintain their position (including survivability) with those buyers they will be prepared to negotiate favourable rates.

♦ The suppliers' product is an important input into the buyers' businesses. A supplier's power is raised when it is the key provider of a component for the buyer's manufacturing process.

♦ The supplier group's products are differentiated or it has built up switching costs. This creates a difficulty for a buyer to create competition between suppliers for an improved negotiated rate.

♦ The supplier group poses a credible threat of forward integration: that is, an individual or group of suppliers has the power to acquire the buyers of their products, controlling more of the overall supply chain.

The power of buyers

Where buyers are particularly powerful within an industry they have the power to create competition among suppliers. This can lead to the forcing down of prices and demands for higher-quality products and services at the lower prices. This might provide the buyers with short-term gains, but in the longer term there is a risk: if suppliers operate on lower margins they will be particularly susceptible to sudden changes in the marketplace.

Porter (1980) proposes eight conditions where buyers will exercise power.

♦ The buyer group is concentrated or purchases large volumes relative to the sellers' sales. If a buyer acquires products in large volumes from suppliers (especially a single-source supplier) it can exert power. An example is the own-label market in the UK. Their buying power means that large supermarkets can exert pressure on the producers of their own-label products, driving down prices whilst insisting on quality standards.

♦ The product it purchases from the industry represents a significant fraction of the buyer's costs or purchases. If product buying is a major cost, buyers will use their power to find alternative suppliers, if possible, to provide the product at a lower price. Under such

conditions it is worth the buyer's time and money to do so.

♦ It purchases either standard or undifferentiated products. Buyers will use their power to hunt around for alternative (cheaper) supplies. They may also seek to play one supplier off against another.

♦ Customers face few switching costs. If buyers are not locked into a particular suppliers – because of the costs incurred in switching – they can relatively easily move to another supplier.

♦ The company earns low profits. In this case the buyer will seek to further drive down the product price from the supplier. This, of course, can place the supplier at financial risk as its margins are squeezed.

♦ Buyers pose a credible threat to backward integration (also known as vertical integration). Depending upon the size of the buyers they may already have some products manufactured either in-house or by a supplier they have acquired. This posses a threat to other suppliers in that the buyer might decide to increase in-house production of components, for example, and slowly – or even suddenly – close supplier accounts. To limit the impact the supplier is faced with offering the buyer additional product-related benefits and/or financial incentives, or seeking new buyers.

♦ The industry's products are unimportant to the quality of the buyer's products or services. A buyer might be price-sensitive and seek cheaper and lower-quality products (for example, components) if they do not have an impact upon the quality and performance of its finished product. This could give it significant power. However, if the product quality (for example, the component) is important, the buyer will probably be less-price sensitive as it will need to source a quality item that will not fail.

♦ The buyer has full market-industry information. Buyers that have significant knowledge of the market and sellers within the industry have increased bargaining power. They can leverage (through negotiations) this knowledge and power to obtain the best process and product quality from suppliers.

Industry competitors (also known as intensity of rivalry between current competitors)

Porter (1980) suggests that rivalry occurs because competitors either feel the pressure (of competition) or see an opportunity to improve their market or industry position. However, he believes that competitors are mutually dependent, so if one competitor makes a move there is an impact on the others. They may have to retaliate in order to protect their position. (See page 116.)

For example, a company might make a major price reduction, potentially creating price competition in the marketplace. Rivals may retaliate by reducing their prices lower than the initiating company, which would force it to either stay at the initial reduced price (which is now higher than its competitors) or reduce the price even further. A further reduction could damage its profit margins. Other competitors might choose not to reduce their prices, on the basis that their customers buy on quality and/or manufacturing process rather than price alone.

One major hamburger chain in New York dramatically reduced its prices in the belief that it would gain market share from its main competitor. However, its competitor refused to enter into a price war. It believed that its customers were content to pay a higher price because its burgers were flame-grilled rather than fried. The first company had miscalculated, and did not gain the increased market share it had hoped for. Instead it faced a significant shortfall in revenue.

■ Competitive advantage: generic strategies

Porter (1985) suggests that there are three fundamental approaches through which an organisation can achieve sustainable competitive advantage: cost, differentiation and focus. Table 6.4 shows these approaches and their variants. It also links competitive scope with competitive advantage.

First we must ascertain what is meant by the terms competitive scope and competitive advantage.

Competitive scope

This can be defined as the breadth of an organisation's activities. Porter and Millar (1985) suggest it has four key dimensions: segment scope, vertical scope (degree of vertical integration), geographic scope, and industry scope (or the range of related industries in which the organisation operates). These are 'condensed' into broad and narrow categories. Broad refers to companies that can exploit 'interrelationships between the value chains serving different industry segments, geographic areas or related industries' (Porter and Millar 1985). Conversely a narrow scope allows the company to customise the value chain to a particular target segment of the market to achieve lower costs and differentiation.

Competitive advantage

In essence, competitive advantage can be described as any factor that provides an organisation with a market edge over its competitors. For example, a single factor within the marketing mix (such as price) might provide the edge or advantage

Table 6.4 Generic strategies

Competitive scope	Competitive advantage	
	Lower cost	Differentiation
Broad	1 Cost leadership	2 Differentiation
Narrow	3a Cost focus	3a Differentiation focus

Source: Porter (1985).

Mini case 6.1

European low-cost airlines

Since the early 1990s there has been a significant growth in the European low-cost air travel market, which we consider here from the perspective of the five forces model.

Threat of new entrants

With deregulation and the development of new regional airports there are opportunities for new companies to enter the marketplace. However there are significant cost implications in setting up and running an airline business. The risks can be high, as illustrated by various financial casualties over the past ten years. New entrants have to balance the risk against the opportunity to enter the market. Moreover it is an intensely competitive market, and new entrants may not be able to gain the critical mass needed to survive.

Supplier power

There are various suppliers to this industry, including aircraft manufacturers (Airbus and Boeing are the two largest), refuelling facilities and airports.

Buyer power

With the introduction of low-cost fares, discounted fares (from national carriers) and the influx of numerous airlines, buyers (mainly individuals rather than companies) have increased power of choice. Of course, the level of buyer power also depends on the number of airlines flying to the chosen destination. For example, several airlines fly from the London region to Paris, and customers are spoilt for choice, but this is not so for all departure and arrival locations.

Threat of substitutes

There are other modes of travel within Europe – car, coach and train. In some countries the train service is highly efficient, comfortable and cost-effective; in others it is the opposite. Therefore the degree of substitution is highly dependent on the availability and efficiency of the alternative modes of transport.

Industry competitors

This has become a highly competitive market. It could be argued that it is at, or near, saturation point. However, that might not discourage new entrants if they believe they can gain a sustainable competitive advantage through some form of differentiation or focus. (See the discussion on generic strategies opposite.)

necessary to gain a position ahead of the competition. However, it is one thing to gain an advantage, and another to maintain or sustain that advantage. While one factor might create the edge, it might be a combination of factors that provide the sustainability the company needs to stay ahead of the competition.

Analysis of generic strategies

This section briefly examines the three main generic strategies of cost, differentiation and focus, and their variants.

Cost leadership

The company aims to be the lowest-cost producer within the industry. In order to achieve this objective it must seek ways of taking costs out of the business. If it can achieve this it is likely to be an above-average performer within the market as long as it can charge prices at or near the industry average (Porter 1985). The point to remember here is that to be the lowest-cost producer does not necessarily mean that it will sell at have the lowest price. However this is often the case: for example the European no-frills airline Ryanair offers fares at substantial discounts over other airlines flying the same or similar routes, and is also renowned for driving down costs in the business.

Differentiation

In a differentiation strategy the company knows its products or services possess either a single attribute or several attributes that are unique in the minds of buyers. These attributes (which could be either tangible or intangible, or both) significantly differentiate the company from its competitors. This allows it to charge a premium prices for its products or services. For example, a painter or photographer may have styles that clearly distinguish him or her from his or her competitors. If the market values the styles and outcomes, the works are likely to commend high prices either at auction or private sale. On another level, say a food company produces and markets a range of unusual, yet tantalisingly flavoured potato crisps: crisp lovers might choose these products even if they are more expensive than other crisp brands.

Focus

Here the company selects a segment or small group of segments in the market, then customises its strategy to meet the needs of that segment(s). There are two subsets:

◆ cost focus, where the company reduces costs to gain a cost advantage with the targeted segment(s)

◆ differentiation focus, where the company applies a differentiation strategy within the targeted segment.

Stuck in the middle

Porter (1985) suggests that companies must be clear which generic strategy is right for their particular business. If they are not clear, they could end up being, as he calls it, 'somewhere stuck in the middle'. This indecisiveness can have a negative impact on short to longer-term business performance, or even lead to business failure.

■ Adding value to the product or service

Increasingly customers seek more than just the best price from a product or service: they demand quality and forms of added value. Companies seek ways of adding value to their products and services as a means of gaining and sustaining competitive advantage. They have realised that value is not delivered at one precise point, but throughout every element of company operations.

The 'value' can be created by an examination of costs and performance (in all areas – see Chapter 17) in order to discover and then implement improvements that will benefit the customer (and the company). When these activities are grouped together they can be viewed as a value chain running through all aspects of the company, from administration to operations and distribution.

Porter (1985) suggests that for a company to leverage a competitive advantage it must consider itself as part of a larger value chain which encompasses suppliers, distributors and customers. This process is diagrammatically illustrated in the value chain model (Figure 6.8) in which Porter grouped the various activities of a company.

The support activities relate to the infrastructural support that can be provided to the primary activities.

Company infrastructure

This includes the overall structure of the organisation, corporate planning, financial controls, management abilities and the quality control mechanisms.

The human resource management team

This will be responsible for all activities relating to recruitment, training, developing and rewarding people (incentives) throughout the organisation.

Technology development

This encapsulates a multitude of areas and must be considered in the broadest terms. On this basis it includes product design, improving overall processes and the utilisation of resources.

Procurement

This is the acquisition or purchasing of any components or raw materials that are used within the primary activities.

Porter (1985) suggests that the five primary activities represent the activities of physically creating the product or service, then transferring it to the customer with the support of appropriate after-sales service. These primary activities are:

◆ Inbound logistics: receiving, storing and distributing internally inputs (for example, raw materials and packaging).

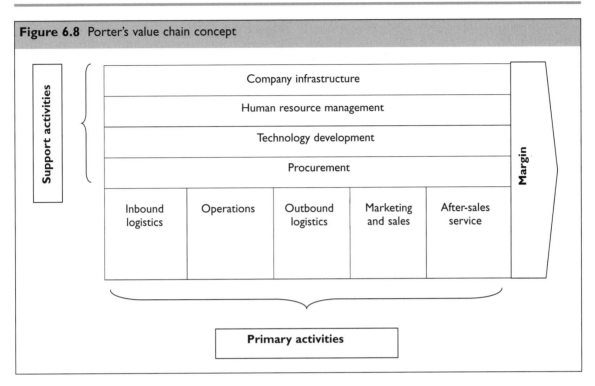

Figure 6.8 Porter's value chain concept

Source: adapted from Porter (1985).

- Operations: the activities that transform the raw materials or other component inputs into a finished product or service. This includes machining, assembly and manufacturing systems.

- Outbound logistics activities relate to the physical collection and distribution of the finished products or services to customers.

- Marketing and sales is the implementation of the marketing mix. This should be integrated to maximise the return on investment to the organisation.

- After-sales service provides the necessary service assistance to support the product or service that is being offered within the market.

After these processes are completed there is the margin: the excess the customer is prepared to pay over the cost of providing resources and value added. It is important to remember that the activities within the value chain affect each other.

■ Competitive market positioning strategies

If organisations operate in a highly competitive world, there will be some companies out in the lead and others following. Kotler (2000) identified four market positions that companies may seek to adopt: leader, challenger, follower and nicher.

Market leaders

This is the position that many (though not all) organisations seek to achieve: in essence to be leaders in one, a selection or all of their market segments. As stated earlier it is one thing to gain leadership (competitive advantage) and quite another to sustain that leadership, especially within volatile markets.

Market challengers

These organisations continually challenge the dominance of the market leader by attempting to win increased market share. They will seek to manipulate their marketing mix, as a tactical weapon, to gain leverage within the market.

Market followers

These companies are satisfied with developing their own profitable market segments or market share. They achieve this through innovation and the use of the marketing mix variables. However, they do not seek to challenge either the market leaders or market challengers, as they consider it too risky. Not only would it require additional resources, the counterattack could be highly damaging. However, if the market leader and challengers become embroiled in a long damaging conflict, followers might be able to sweep up customers who have become disillusioned with both leader and challengers.

Market nichers

These organisations are able to dominate a small market segment or segments. They tend to be small in sector terms, and are unlikely to interest either the market leaders or challengers, so there is an opportunity for them to gain a reputation and be the best within that niche market.

■ Competitive and defensive positions

Organisations (especially market leaders and challengers) need to develop strategies and tactics to gain and sustain market share. This section briefly examines some of the positions that companies may adopt.

Position defence

The market leader introduces a range of innovations to protect its product position within the marketplace (see Figure 6.9).

Pre-emptive defence

Rather than waiting to be attacked, the market leader may either warn of or instigate a pre-

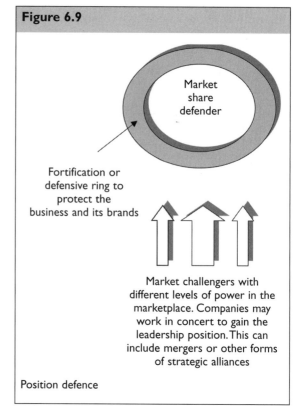

Figure 6.9

Market share defender

Fortification or defensive ring to protect the business and its brands

Market challengers with different levels of power in the marketplace. Companies may work in concert to gain the leadership position. This can include mergers or other forms of strategic alliances

Position defence

emptive strike against a challenger (see Figure 6.10). The company may take the view that 'the best defence is an offensive one'. For instance, a company might launch a major well-resourced

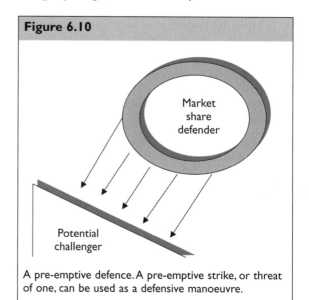

Figure 6.10

Market share defender

Potential challenger

A pre-emptive defence. A pre-emptive strike, or threat of one, can be used as a defensive manoeuvre.

'burst' promotional campaign (which has been kept a closely guarded secret). This campaign will be used not only to reinforce the company's products and services within the market, but also seek to gain market share from the unsuspecting challenger.

Counter-offensive defence

The market share defender often will counter-attack with overwhelming force to dislodge the market challenger's attack (see Figure 6.11). In such cases the market challenger will have little or no choice other than to withdraw. To maintain the attack could severely weaken it, and it in turn could come under attack from another market challenger. This could result in an aggressive takeover bid.

Mobile defence

Market leaders often seek expansion into new territories with the intention of increasing their business opportunities, resources, size and financial strength (see Figure 6.12). When a company has gained strong positions in several markets it may become harder to challenge over so many markets. Instead the challenger may consider attacking the weaker of the leader's markets. However, it risks attack by not only the leader but also other potential challengers within those markets.

Strategic withdrawal

Major organisations often seek to gain competitive advantage (and thus market share) across several territories. This has become apparent with an

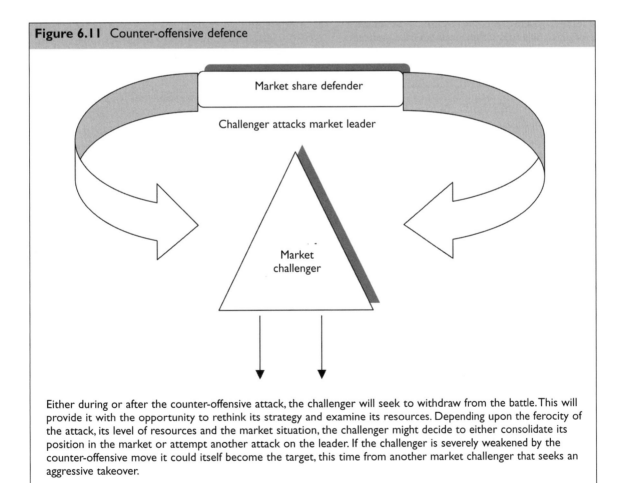

Figure 6.11 Counter-offensive defence

Market share defender

Challenger attacks market leader

Market challenger

Either during or after the counter-offensive attack, the challenger will seek to withdraw from the battle. This will provide it with the opportunity to rethink its strategy and examine its resources. Depending upon the ferocity of the attack, its level of resources and the market situation, the challenger might decide to either consolidate its position in the market or attempt another attack on the leader. If the challenger is severely weakened by the counter-offensive move it could itself become the target, this time from another market challenger that seeks an aggressive takeover.

Figure 6.12

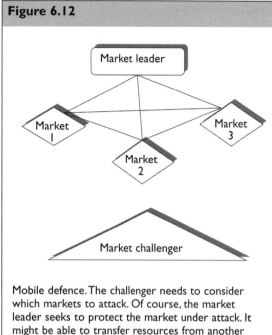

Mobile defence. The challenger needs to consider which markets to attack. Of course, the market leader seeks to protect the market under attack. It might be able to transfer resources from another market (as long as this does not set that market up for attack) to retaliate against the challenger.

increase in globalisation activities. However, there is a risk that the organisation will become involved in too many markets and spread its resources too thinly. This is particularly the case with companies that have grown rapidly and till that point have seemed invincible. However, they create a situation where they could face a massive competitive onslaught from several challengers in different

markets but simultaneously. When an organisation has critically over-extended itself it might need to consider a strategic withdrawal from the market (Figure 6.13). Such a move would protect valuable resources that could be moved to another product/service or market. If it remains within the vulnerable market it might need to use those resources to defend the product or service from an attack by a challenger. If it cannot 'hold' the product or service's position within the market place, the resources will have been wasted.

Frontal attack

In a frontal attack or assault the major challenger builds resources and expertise to directly attack the market leader in its major markets (see Figure 6.14). This requires considerable resources, core competencies and skill to succeed, as it will usually need to be a sustained effort. The challenger also needs to understand the market leader's weaknesses. These may range from the quality of the product, its pricing and distribution to the quality of management

Figure 6.14

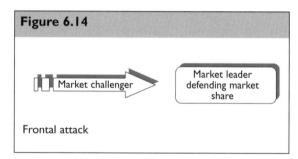

Frontal attack

and after-sales service (elements that can be seen in the value chain and the marketing mix).

Examples include the UK-based supermarket chain Tesco gaining market leadership over Sainsbury during the 1990s. Indeed by 2004 Sainsbury was under attack from both Asda (part of the Wal-Mart group) and Morrisons (which had acquired Safeway in the United Kingdom and now had the market power to challenge companies such as Sainsbury). In aircraft manufacturing Boeing used to dominate the passenger aircraft market. However, by 2004 Airbus had taken leadership in the marketplace by challenging Boeing in the medium, long haul and large capacity aircraft markets.

Figure 6.13

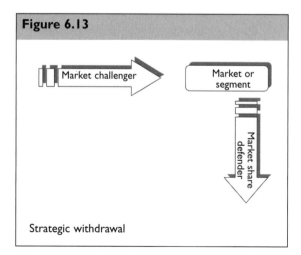

Strategic withdrawal

Flanking attack

Here the challenger seeks to exploit a weakness in the market leader's position. This permits the challenger to go around or flank the market leader and take some market share (see Figure 6.15). During the 1970s and 1980s the US automotive industry failed to realise the growing demand for small, more fuel-efficient vehicles. Several Japanese car manufacturers could see that this was a weakness in the US automotive industry, which they could exploit by marketing their smaller, more environmentally friendly vehicles in the United States. Such a move would also provide a foothold within the US market. This would later lead to their building car plants in the United States to directly feed the American market.

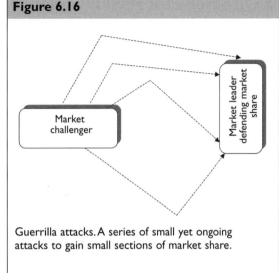

Figure 6.16

Guerrilla attacks. A series of small yet ongoing attacks to gain small sections of market share.

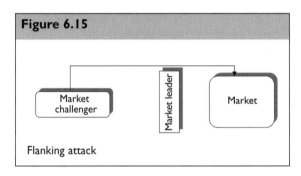

Figure 6.15

Flanking attack

Guerrilla attack

This is a type of competitive attack that is increasingly being used by new entrants into markets, particularly young and vibrant businesses. Guerrilla attacks are a series of small ongoing actions that are designed to (1) frustrate the market defenders, and (2) raise the company's profile in the targeted segments (see Figure 6.16). As the attacks are small – though numerous – it is unlikely that a major market leader or defender will devote the resources to counter-attack on a large scale. There is no guarantee of success and these tactics could make the challenger vulnerable to attack in other sectors of the market.

Guerrilla tactics include use of merchandising, special event marketing, intensive personal selling and linking the brand to an issue, for example, animal rights.

Although these strategies are discussed here as separate actions, in practice they are often combined, especially if a challenger has devoted significant resources to gaining market leadership. The attack might last several years, and challengers and leaders move positions and seek to gain the loyalty of their customers. Either a challenger or defender might change positions or move from one strategy to another. Throughout there needs to be flexibility in order to both react to market conditions and competitive movements and be proactive.

■ Chapter summary

This chapter has briefly examined the relationship between strategy and marketing. It has taken as its starting point the preceding chapters on the micro/macro environment, competitive intelligence gathering and marketing research.

An understanding of strategy is vital to the development and implementation of marketing objectives, leading to the fulfilment of the corporate objectives. When you read the following chapters on the marketing mix you will need to make the link to the strategic objectives of the business. For instance, consider how the marketing mix can be used to strategically place an organisation's brand in the marketplace, in a position that can be sustained competitively over the longer term.

■ Questions for review and reflection

1 What is a strategic marketing audit? What contribution do you think it can make to the formulation of an organisation's marketing policy?

2 What type of defensive marketing strategies could a leading retailer use to protect itself from competitive actions?

3 What strategies do you think a new entrant into a market could use to gain a competitive advantage over incumbents?

4 Use the Internet and other library resources to critically examine how Swatch Watch revolutionised the watch market in Europe. Do you think other companies could learn from its marketing strategies? If so, how?

5 Imagine you are the marketing director of your university or college. What strategies would you consider to attract undergraduate students? Support your view with evidence.

6 Gaining increases in market share is often stated as being the main objective of marketing strategy, yet there are many examples of companies with small market share that are very successful. Debate with your fellow students this apparent contradiction.

■ References

Andrews, K. (1986) *Concept of Corporate Strategy*, New York: McGraw-Hill.

Ansoff, H. I. (1987) *Corporate Strategy*, rev. edn, Harmondsworth: Penguin.

Baker, M. J. (2000) *Marketing Strategy and Management*, 3rd edn, Basingstoke: Macmillan.

Barney, J. B. (1997) *Gaining and Sustaining Competitive Advantage*, Reading, Mass.: Addison-Wesley.

Grant, R. M. (2002) *Contemporary Strategy Analysis: Concepts, techniques, applications*, 4th edn, Oxford: Blackwell.

Kotler, P., Gregor, W. and Rogers, W. (1989) 'The MA comes of age', *Sloan Management Review* **30**(2) (Winter), pp. 49–62.

Mintzberg, H., Lampel, J., Quinn, J. B. and Ghoshal, S. (2003) *The Strategy Process: Concepts, context and cases*, 4th edn, Harlow: Prentice Hall.

Ohmae, K. (1982) *The Mind of the Strategist*, London: McGraw-Hill.

Porter, M. E. (1980) *Competitive Strategy: Techniques for analyzing industries and competitors*, New York: Free Press.

Porter, M. E. (1985) *Competitive Advantage*, New York: Free Press.

Porter, M. E. and Millar, V. E. (1985) 'How information gives you competitive advantage', in M. E. Porter (1998) *On Competition*, Boston, Mass.: Harvard Business School Press.

Stanton, W. J., Etzel, M. J. and Walker, B. J. (1994) *Fundamentals of Marketing*, 4th edn,. New York: McGraw-Hill.

The Branding of Products and Services

Contents

Learning outcomes	119
Introduction	119
What is branding?	**120**
Origins of branding	**120**
Consumer and business	
brands	**122**
Why brand?	**122**
Protection	122
Values	124
Differentiation	124
Segmentation	126
Selection	126
Awareness	127
Recall	127
Recognition	127
Brands that develop a	
cult status	**127**
Extending the brand	**127**
Valuations and equity	131
Promotion	132
Types of branding	**132**
Family brands	133
Individual brands	133
Own-label brands	134
Brand management	**134**
The world's most	
powerful brands	**135**
Rebranding	**137**
Proactive motivations	137
Reactive motivators	139
Brand longevity – do	
brands last forever?	**142**
Reasons for brand	
longevity	143
The disposal or	
termination of brands	**144**
Risks associated with	
brand disposal	149
Chapter summary	**151**
Questions for review	
and reflection	**151**
References	**152**

Learning outcomes

After completing this chapter you should be able to:

▶ outline the different brand structures or architecture that companies use to distinguish their brands from competitors

▶ explain the benefits and risks associated with branding in a global context

▶ debate the reasons companies terminate a brand and the potential risks associated with such actions

▶ evaluate the power of brands in the marketplace

▶ demonstrate an awareness of how customers perceive brands.

▍ Introduction

The branding of products and services has become an integral component of marketing, business and everyday life. Not only do customers closely associate themselves with brands, it is clear that organisations strive to increase and maintain the value of their brands. Brands are the generators of wealth for the organisation.

We are surrounded by brands. You have probably heard of the following brands, for example, even though you might not actually 'consume' them, buy into their 'values' or know who owns them. Nevertheless you will know that they exist:

◆ Airbus Industries

◆ Aston Martin

◆ Boeing

◆ Burger King

◆ Ford Motor Company

◆ Formula 1 Racing

◆ Harley-Davidson

◆ H. J. Heinz

- McDonald's
- Sony
- Toyota
- 20th Century-Fox Entertainment
- University of London
- Werther's Originals.

Brands are not just packaged products, services or icons. How an organisation invests in and positions its brands in the market can have a significant impact on whether (or not) a brand can gain and sustain a competitive advantage. Such investment and positioning also reflects upon the competitive stance held by the organisation. This is even more so in a highly complex and dynamic business environment.

This chapter examines the role of branding in the development and promotion of both products and services. It considers why companies and organisations brand themselves, and how different brand relationships are developed with customers. It also considers the risks associated with branding.

■ What is branding?

In Chapter 1 it was suggested that marketing pervades every aspect of our waking lives. We are literally engulfed by images of products and services. As well as communicating needs and desires, these images also communicate brands, ones we often recognise and trust. It is this awareness, recognition and trust that is fundamental to the successful development and building of brands. Kotler (2000) describes brands as:

A name, term, symbol or design (or combination of them) which is intended to signify the goods or services of one seller or groups of sellers and to differentiate them from those of the competitors.

However this definition is limiting. Dibb *et al.* (1997) suggested that branding is a component of a product's tangible features – the verbal and physical cues that assist the customer in choosing one product over another. However, this is not just applicable to a 'product'. Services also communi-

cate verbal and physical cues. Chapter 14 discusses how physical evidence affects a customer's choice of restaurants and hotels. A five-star hotel providing a range of services transmits a range of verbal and physical cues to potential customers. They are all part of the hotel's brand.

As is emphasised throughout this text, the actions of people, the processes involved, the packaging and the psychology behind the operations all contribute to the branding of a product or service. It is really a combination of these factors that drives branding.

■ Origins of branding

For centuries products were sold unbranded, that is, without any identifiable name or logo attached. Many products such as grain, and later on sweets, were often sold loose from barrels or glass jars. The actual word 'brand' is believed to be derived from the old Norse word 'brandir', which translates as 'to burn'. In other words this can be interpreted as imprinting an idea or symbol onto a product.

While branding is quite rightly associated with the American Wild West, this was not the first time that items were branded. The concept of branding can be traced back to the merchant guilds of 11th century England. These trade or craft guilds became powerful forces within local government. By the 14th century they effectively controlled most of the trade and commerce in Medieval Europe. Branding was important to the craftsmen of the guilds because it directly linked to their reputations. They sought to control the quality and production of the goods they made for market. Indeed, many of the craftsmen realised that quality and availability of the product also affected the pricing of the product. This is as true today as it was 700 years ago.

Farming in Europe tended to be associated with many small or medium-sized farms. Not so in the vast, sprawling American landscape. As the West opened up, there emerged a new breed of farmer – the cattle barons. Increasingly the cattle ranchers faced the problem of identifying their herds from their neighbours', even when vast distances separated two ranches. In order to clearly identify cattle that had either been rustled or wandered onto another ranch, the cattle ranchers introduced the practice of branding their cattle with hot irons. This simple branding technique showed whether the cattle were from the T-bar or Circle O ranches from the branded 'T' or 'O' on the side of the cattle. Thus there could be no mistake who owned the cattle – at least in theory. This did not stop cattle rustlers from stealing the cattle and altering the brand, or the cattle ranch logo on the skin of the cattle, to suit the rustler's own needs. As you will see later in this chapter, such rustling, or brand piracy as it is now known, costs legitimate organisations significant amounts in lost revenue. So the age of the cattle rustler is not dead!

Goldfarb (2001) suggests that one of the first true brands as we know them today was Sunlight Soap. Prior to the launch of Sunlight, soap products were produced by mixing tallow (a hard, usually animal, fat that is melted down) with alkali in large barrels. The solidified material was then cut into large bars that were sliced by the grocer into smaller ones and wrapped in paper for the customer. William Lever, the son of a grocer, realised that consumers were becoming increasingly dissatisfied with the quality, performance, odour (the smell was often quite unpleasant), inconsistency of weight and lack of packaging.

In 1884 Lever registered the name Sunlight Soap, and began developing a revolutionary soap formula that would remain virtually unchanged for years. In 1885 he launched his product, which was a mixture of coconut, cottonseed oil and resin instead of tallow. In addition to the brand name and new formula, Lever produced bars of a uniform size and shape, which were packaged and branded with a logo.

Such was the demand for the new packaged soap that William Lever joined forces with his brother James to create Lever Brothers Limited (later to form part of Unilever). William Lever went on to build the world's largest soap works at Port Sunlight, along with a village for his employees. By the turn of the 20th century Lever Brothers dominated the UK soap industry, selling nearly 40 000 tonnes in the UK alone (Leverfaberge 2004).[1]

Lever's success with Sunlight Soap has been attributed to many factors:

◆ A significant investment in innovative advertising campaigns. As Jeremy (1998) states, 'Lever aimed at drawing the housewife's attention to his soap, using slogans, enamelled-plate signs on railway stations, hoardings [bill-boards], newspaper advertisements, and even the novelette, the melodrama, and doggerel verse [poor or trivial verse]. He went as far as to issue an annual 500-page Sunlight Year Book, combining education and advertisement.' Wilson (1954, cited in Jeremy 1998) stated that in 1885, his first year of trading, Lever spent UK£50 on advertising but by 1905 he had spent UK£2 million. Today that UK£2 million expenditure would equate to a multi-million pound budget – perhaps more than many blue-chip companies actually spend.

◆ Packaging: the wrapping of uniform blocks with packaging that displayed large coloured letters clearly identifying the brand.

◆ Lever's ability to reduce both production and distribution costs while also purchasing low-cost raw materials.

However Goldfarb (2001) argues that its success was more a question of the 'careful management of the Sunlight brand'. This is a point that will be referred to later in this chapter.

While Lever was adopting what were to become brand management strategies and tactics, in the United States Henry Heinz was engaged in similar activities. As Koehn (1999) suggests, Heinz understood the strategic rationale for branding. Koehn (1999) states that Heinz realised consumers had to be 'able to identify a particular product's source, functional attributes, and perceived quality relative to rival goods. Customers also needed to be made to appreciate the intangible aspects of a good – the association and expectations that they attached to it.'

Until Heinz, most customers were unaware of the manufacturers that produced the products they purchased. Heinz went a step further by creating, in 1896, 'Heinz 57 Varieties'. Although the Heinz company was to manufacture many more than 57 varieties, Heinz kept to the number '57'. This was to become one of the most enduring slogans in brand history.

While there were many pioneers, the real impetus for branding came at the turn of the 20th century. The key indicators that led to this development included:

◆ The introduction of mass production techniques. With mass production came the need to visually signify who owned the product, or indeed the patent.

◆ A move towards mass forms of advertising. The development of print media led to an increasing use of advertising as a means of promoting products.

◆ Mobility of people and goods. Through the development of the railways, the car, shipping, and later aircraft there was greater mobility of both people and goods. Products were now shipped more easily across nations and the world. The development of containerisation in the 1950s significantly increased trading opportunities (see Chapter 12).

◆ Increasing national wealth. While this was true during much of the 20th century, it is vital to remember that many countries, especially in Europe and the Far East, suffered deprivation as a result of the agonising conflicts, dictatorships and economic collapse.

This section has very briefly illustrated the origins of branding, but it is not a static story. Branding and how the world perceives it is an ongoing development. As we have seen, while branding is an integral part of all our lives, it is a subject surrounded by much controversy. This issue will be explored further in later sections of this chapter.

■ Consumer and business brands

Initially we can consider brands as two very broad categories, consumer oriented (B2C) and business oriented (B2B). Clearly consumer-oriented brands encompass everything from holidays to washing-up liquids. Equally, business-oriented brands focus on a range of products and services that meet the needs of commercial organisations.

However, it is not that simplistic. Brands can be marketed to both consumers and businesses simultaneously. An example is the London Hilton Hotel in Park Lane. This five-star hotel caters for both business people and tourists (see mini case 7.1). While both groups share a range of facilities, business clients have access to additional business facilities.

Mini case 7.1

London Hilton, Park Lane, London

Located in London's prestigious Park Lane, the London Hilton overlooks Hyde Park and is the flagship hotel of the Hilton Group. The hotel provides a range of services for both business clients and leisure visitors. In addition to the restaurants, room facilities/service and onsite leisure facilities, business clients also have access to the following:

◆ business centre

◆ business phone service

◆ dictaphones

◆ fax

◆ meeting rooms

◆ photocopying service

◆ office rental

◆ secretarial services

◆ video messaging.

Equally, there are dedicated marketing teams to assist business clients and tourists, from booking their stay through to activities and transportation while they are in the United Kingdom.

Source: Hilton Hotel Group.

■ Why brand?

Organisations and companies brand themselves, their products and services for a multitude of reasons. This section considers some of the reasons that branding has become a fundamental component of marketing.

Protection

Branding can be used as a means of obtaining international legal protection for the product or service, and intrinsic features and benefits within the product or service. This protection is enforceable through copyrights, trademarks and patents. For example Microsoft® Word (the program which was used to write this textbook) is a registered trademark of the Microsoft Corporation. Therefore if a company copied Microsoft® Word and attempted to market it under a different name, the Microsoft Corporation would have the legal right to seek damages against that company. In essence the other company would be undertaking theft, or brand piracy.

Branding is fundamental in protecting a company's legal rights. However, brand theft or piracy has become a critical problem for many companies. The International Chamber of Commerce estimates that the annual worldwide sales of counterfeit products are in the order of US$350 million (ICC 2004). The problem for consumers is that reproductions, imitations or fakes often look deceptively authentic. Pavitt (2000) cites the example of Cuban cigars, where only an expert can tell the difference between the real cigar and some counterfeits. A clue is apparently the way the paper is folded at the end of the cigar.

Consumers might buy a product in the belief that it is legitimate only to discover that it is of poor quality, and this will cause them to lose faith in the brand name. Equally, some consumers purchase products they know are fake, but which are cheaper than the originals. For example, fake designer branded watches can be purchased on market stalls in Singapore. They are a fraction of the price of the original, but look the same. However, they often do not weigh the same, keep time as accurately as the originals, nor are they covered by any guarantee. There is no redress if they stop working after a couple of days.

Brand piracy is not limited to direct counterfeiting of products. Companies will also use names and packaging that are similar to the registered name and packaging. This 'passing off' of a product is aimed to confuse customers into thinking they are purchasing a genuine well-known branded product.

In 2000 the Victoria & Albert Museum in London held an exhibition on branding. In one secure room – courtesy of the authentic brand owners – were a collection of products designed to 'pass off' under the brand name and image of legitimate products. These were exhibited alongside the genuine products. While it was possible to distinguish some fake or 'passing-off products' from the genuine articles, it was very difficult in other cases.

Increasingly companies are turning to specialist organisations to help them both protect their brand

Mini case 7.2

The battle against the movie pirates

Although the US film and television business is worth an estimated US$65 billion per year, in 2002 Hollywood studios lost an estimated US$3 billion in revenue to counterfeiting. Many movies appeared on DVD and/or the Internet before their general release in the cinemas. In 2002 the number of pirated videos and DVDs seized worldwide was approximately 60 million, a rise of 161 per cent since 1999. In addition to the breach of copyright, such action can significantly reduce revenue from cinema and legitimate video/DVD sales.

Concerned that piracy could have a similar impact to that which shattered the music business, Hollywood is seeking to protect its brands. The studios are using both international copyright laws and local legislation to protect both their corporate brand identities and the individual movie brands. Production and distribution companies are working with police forces and legal teams in several countries in an attempt to curtail piracy. Production companies have also imposed strict codes for the previewing and distribution of their movies. Surveillance equipment is used to deter would-be pirates from videotaping movies at previews, and the distribution of preview copies is carefully monitored.

Clearly all production and distribution companies must work together to protect their corporate and individual brands. However, some industry insiders suggest that Hollywood and other major production centres are struggling to stop the pirates and protect their brands. If Hollywood does lose the battle, the future of the movie industry as we currently know it will be radically different – that is, if it survives at all.

As you can see from this example, protection of a brand may be core to the survivability not only of that particular brand, but of an entire industry.

Sources: R. Grover and H. Green, 'The digital age presents Hollywood heist', *Business Week*, 21 July 2003; J. Doward, 'Pirates loot the film and music giants' coffers', *Observer*, 8 February 2004.

identities and hunt down those who either counterfeit or pass off products as the genuine brand. There is also pressure on governments to act forcefully against the counterfeiters.

Although brand piracy is the standard term used, this author prefers the stronger term 'brand mugging'. The word 'piracy' can conjure up a romanticised view of theft, but brand theft is far from romantic. It is more akin to 'mugging' in that it is not only the brand owners that are robbed but all the stakeholders of the business (see Chapter 2), including the customers who wittingly or unwittingly buy the counterfeit products.

It may seem from this brief section that brand protection has little value. On the contrary, even though there is counterfeiting, companies must seek legal ways of protecting their brands. It is the only means of assuring that the customer consumes the product at the quality specified by the authentic brand owner.

Values

There needs to be a word of caution before we consider brand values. While there is a link, brand values must not be confused with brand valuation (see page 347). Brand values are the values or intrinsic qualities that the brand communicates to customers. These may include quality, trust and reliability. Therefore a product or service may communicate to its customers a combination of intrinsic values which they can relate to and appreciate.

Chapter 16 on psychology examines how the understanding of emotion is important to our knowledge of consumer behaviour. Barlow and Maul (2000) suggest that high levels of emotional involvement with an organisation, company or brand tend to drive customer loyalty more than specific judgments regarding quality. This author partially agrees with Barlow and Maul's supposition (especially in relation to mini case 7.3). However this cannot be considered as a 'given'. There are cases where the appeal lies in a combination of high emotional appeal and the features and benefits delivered by the product or service. At best it should be considered a continuum – a line along which brands travel depending on the values (real and intrinsic) of a particular product or service.

Barlow and Maul postulate that organisations and companies must be customer focused though the implementation of what they call the five Cs of intimacy (Barlow and Maul 2000). Table 7.1 outlines their 5C framework.

A good example of positive emotional involvement is how the pharmaceutical giant Johnson & Johnson handled a case of product tampering. This is highlighted in mini case 7.3.

Differentiation

Branding helps the company or organisation to differentiate its product and/or service from competitors (see Chapter 6 on strategy). In turn this helps customers to identify the products and/or services that match their individual needs. If the brand is both effectively differentiated and positioned in the market, there is a potential for creating loyalty for that product or service. This might maintain or increase sales for the product or service.

Table 7.1 The five Cs of intimacy

Point of emotional involvement	Description
Communication	Two-way communication that is both proactive and reactive.
Caring	Valuing individuals beyond selling them a particular product and/or service.
Commitment	The company or organisation creating the right emotional environment or climate. Proactive demonstration of commitment to the customer.
Comfort	The establishment of rapport with the customer, being emotionally 'in tune' with that person – empathetic, understanding and concerned.
Conflict resolution	The ability to resolve conflicts in a constructive rather than a destructive manner.

Source: adapted from Barlow and Maul (2000).

Mini case 7.3

Johnson & Johnson and Tylenol®

During the 1960s Tylenol®, an acetaminophen-based analgesic produced by McNeil Pharmaceuticals, a subsidiary of Johnson & Johnson, was introduced to the US market as an over-the-counter (OTC) product. Tylenol® was heavily promoted to doctors, pharmacists and the general public alike as a safe substitute for aspirin, which is known to often irritate the stomach. By the early 1980s it was the leading analgesic on the market, with a 35 per cent share and annual sales of US$400 million (Green 1992).

It appeared that the growth of Tylenol® was assured – until late September 1982, when it was discovered that Tylenol® Extra-Strength capsules had been contaminated with cyanide, leading to seven deaths in the Chicago area. Rigorous checks on the batch numbers followed. It soon became clear that the contamination had occurred not at the point of manufacture but at the point of distribution. Johnson & Johnson removed all Tylenol® products from supermarkets and drug stores across the United States. This cost the company over US$100 million, the retail value of removing 31 million containers.

As reputation risk management expert Peter Sheldon Green (1992) stated,

> The uniqueness of Tylenol®, which enabled it to capture more than a third of the total US painkiller market, was in the marketing of the product. The value of the Tylenol brand was a function of public perception and public perception – not the uniqueness of the product itself.

The Johnson & Johnson strategy

The company's strategy for handling this crisis included:

◆ A focus on the company's credo. In 1935 during the Depression, 'General' Robert Wood Johnson, the son of the founder, stated his belief in a 'new industrial philosophy', defining this as the corporation's responsibility to customers, employees, the community and stockholders. In 1943 this philosophy was formulated as the company's Credo – a series of statements of good conduct. This remains a focal point of the business today. In 1982 it was its ethical stance that drove the company's strategy in dealing with the crisis.

◆ An open public relations policy, the objective being to minimise the potential spread of rumours and disinformation. The board sought clear lines of communication to customers and employees alike. Key board members were interviewed by the media. The CEO, James E. Burke, appeared on networked television shows to answer questions and state the company's position.

◆ Charge-free telephone helplines: in the first 11 days of the crisis more than 136,000 calls were taken. As the number of calls increased, more lines were made available.

◆ Employee information: both current and retired employees were updated on the situation on a regular basis.

◆ Openly working with the US Federal Drugs Administration (FDA): the company supported moves by the FDA for the introduction of tamper-resistant packaging.

The reintroduction of Tylenol®

◆ Although the company was advised by marketing consultants to rebrand Tylenol®, it decided it should be reintroduced into the market under the same brand name. The objective was to reintroduce Tylenol® into the market in tamper-resistant packaging (pre-empting any government legislation).

◆ Within 10 weeks of the original product recall, the capsules were back on the shelves.

◆ By the end of 1982 more than 2000 Johnson & Johnson sales people had made presentations to the medical community. It has been estimated that over a million presentations were made in all.

◆ The company offered coupons to the value of US$2.50 towards the value of the reintroduced Tylenol®. To be placed on the list to receive the coupons, consumers had to call a charge-free number. By the first week of December 1982 over 200 000 calls had been received.

◆ For a relatively short period Tylenol® was withdrawn from the marketplace completely, allowing other brands to capture market share. However, on reintroduction Tylenol® once more became a leading

/ continued overleaf

household brand name. Just over 10 years from this tragic episode the highly competitive US analgesic market was valued at US$2 billion per year. Tylenol® was by far the strongest selling brand, with more than US$1 billion in sales (O'Reilly 1994).

♦   Today Tylenol® is available in a range of line extensions and remains a major brand within the analgesic market.

The general belief is that the successful reintroduction of

Tylenol® would not have been possible had the company failed in its duty of care to act quickly and decisively in the public interest as the news of crisis broke. While this is clearly self-evident, there is another dimension. Johnson & Johnson has, since the 1930s, built a solid trusted reputation. It is a core theme that has become the focus of its communication – caring, committed and nurturing (the comfort of Barlow and Maul's five Cs of intimacy).
Source: Green (1992); B. O'Reilly, 'J&J is on a roll', *Fortune International*, 26 December 1994, pp. 122–8.

However, there are degrees of differentiation. Some products and/or services are very easy to differentiate. For example, a chain of motels can easily be differentiated from a chain of four-star deluxe hotels. Both have a necessary position within the hotel market. However, it becomes increasingly difficult to differentiate one four-star deluxe hotel from another. If both brands have achieved four-star deluxe status, they should be of equally high quality. The differentiation might focus on the size of the hotel (for example, 50 rooms compared with 200 rooms) and the potential for increased personal service. It will depend on the needs and desires of the potential guests. Thus brand differentiation can be determined on both macro and micro scales.

Segmentation

As was stated in Chapter 4, products and services can be segmented into different groups. In that chapter we considered how the cruise industry could be segmented depending on the various companies' market positions. Branding helps to reinforce that positioning. For example, Seabourn, Silverseas and Hebridean have brand images that communicate ultra luxury, and thus can easily be positioned in that market segment (see Figure 7.1).

Selection

This relates to the positioning of the brand in the mind of the consumer. If he or she has an attachment to a brand, the consumer feels comfortable selecting that branded product or service. For instance consider the supermarket environment.

Here shoppers usually recognise brands they have seen in promotions and/or used before. Depending upon how they 'feel' about the brand, they might select it from the supermarket shelves. If there was no branding, all the products would possibly look exactly the same. Shoppers would have no affinity with any of the products, and as a result would buy one at random, which might or might not be inferior to the next on the shelf. They just would not be able to tell.

Figure 7.1

© Hebridean Cruises. Reproduced with kind permission.

The Pan Lounge on board the luxury cruise ship *Hebridean Spirit*.

Awareness

Branding is a mechanism by which companies can create an 'awareness' for the product or service they are marketing. Awareness is where the customer recognises the product or service. This awareness may be 'imprinted' on the mind of the consumer, creating a spontaneous reaction. Equally, awareness can be promoted through, for example, in-store promotions, ambient media or point-of-sale (PoS) materials (see Chapter 10).

Recall

This is very much linked to brand awareness. Brand recall is the extent to which the consumer can recall the name and/or promotional/packaging images associated with a brand. For instance, in marketing research shoppers may be shown images that both depict sections of packaging or a logo from a branded product, and asked to identify the product. Some customers will be able to identity the product immediately from that partial image or logo. Creating logos, names and images that are easy to remember can significantly aid the recall of that brand in the mind of the consumer.

Recognition

Again, recognition links to recall and awareness. This is the extent to which a consumer can recognise a brand from a series of visual or aural clues (reflect back to the opening section on branding). For instance, consumers shopping in a supermarket are literally bombarded by thousands of visual images. Out of that 'wall of imagery' will stand out one or two visual clues that trigger brand recognition and potential purchase. This might be not a conscious act, but very much a subconscious one. Thus the imagery that encompasses a brand must be memorable to aid such recognition.

However, there are negatives to recognition (as with recall and awareness). If the brand has (rightfully or wrongly) gained a negative reputation, recognition will equally result in a negative response from the consumer.

Additionally, it is interesting to note (as we shall see later in this chapter) that not all brands are memorable. It is as if some companies have actively sought to create brand names and images that are easily forgettable. This has often led to a radical rethinking of their brand strategy.

■ Brands that develop a cult status

Both individuals and groups can have an emotional attachment to brands. (This is discussed in more depth in Chapter 16 on psychology.) We are all driven, in one way or another, by emotional responses, and these responses manifest themselves in a variety of ways. For example, consider teenagers (and adults) who collect a particular brand of toy, for instance Barbie™ dolls, or teenagers who become wildly excited when they see their favourite band or singer perform on stage. These are not new phenomena, they have been part of society for decades.

This section focuses on brands as 'cult icons'. These brands are not all packaged goods. For example some bands, actors and football players have achieved an iconic status, being mobbed wherever they venture. However, what actually creates a cult or iconic brand?

Mini cases 7.4 and 7.5 illustrate brands that have achieved a cult status and are emotive for those who are loyal to the brand.

■ Extending the brand (also known as brand elasticity)

Kapferer (1998) states that 'extending the range is a necessary step in the evolution of a brand through time'. This is where additional products are, over time, added to the original brand to serve various markets. The elasticity comes from the view that the brand can be stretched over several products without harming the original branded product.

Kapferer (1998) indicates that there are several approaches to extending the brand – specifically line, range and brand extensions. While it is clearly relevant to the understanding of brands, this nomenclature can be confusing. This is most likely why many marketing texts tend to subsume the three components into 'brand extensions' (see Groucutt *et al.* 2004).

Table 7.2 explains the relevance of the different categories. However, as you can see, some of the 'ingredients' are more subtle than blatant.

Mini case 7.4

Godzilla®

In 1954 the monster Godzilla® (known as Gojira in Japan) came to life on Japanese cinema screens. It is unlikely that anyone at the time thought this first movie would spawn more than 30 movies in a long-running series that would gain cult status, gaining more than 100 million fans in Japan alone. Significantly it has become part of Japanese culture.

In 1954 the low-budget move *Godzilla: King of the Monsters* introduced the dinosaur-like creature to the world. Mutated as a result of the Bikini Atoll tests in the South Pacific, Godzilla goes on the rampage through several movies, fighting foes like King Kong. In the majority of cases Godzilla is represented not by state-of-the arts visual effects but by a man in a green suit. State-of-the-art visual effects were paramount with the 1998 release of a US$120 million Hollywood-made version. This, however, was to prove a box-office failure. Perhaps the streamlining removed the edge that had been so prevalent with the lower-tech Godzilla movies?

What is clear is the emotion that the Japanese hold out for this creature. In 2002 a Godzilla® exhibition opened at Tokyo's Taro Okamoto Museum of Art. It portrayed the monster, not as a trivial character, but as a Japanese cultural phenomenon of the 20th century. Within days of opening over 1000 people per day were visiting the exhibition, such is the iconic value of the Godzilla® brand.

In 2004 the final Japanese-produced *Godzilla* movie was released, ending a 50-year series of 28 movies. *The Final Wars* features ten monsters from previous *Godzilla* movies who go on the rampage in New York, Shanghai, Sydney and Paris.

Although these movies may not have received a universal theatrical release, they have none the less achieved cult status in their home country. Clearly Godzilla® has achieved cult status as a 20th century (and perhaps 21st century) Japanese brand icon.

Sources: 'Godzilla shelved over sub tragedy', BBC News Online, 20 February 2001; 'Japanese flock to "highbrow" Godzilla', BBC News Online, 7 June 2002; 'Final battle looms for Godzilla', BBC News, 3 March 2004; 'Godzilla rises for the final time', BBC News Online, 29 November 2004; 'Godzilla's 50 years of film terror', BBC News Online, 29 November 2004.

Mini case 7.5

Harley-Davidson®

In 2003 Harley-Davidson® celebrated its 100th anniversary as a motorcycle manufacturer. In 1903 the 21-year-old William S. Harley and the 20-year-old Arthur Davidson produced their first Harley-Davison motorcycle – a racer. This was the beginning of a legend that would see the company swing from major success to near failure and closure. Yet through mergers, buyouts and fierce Japanese and European competition the Harley-Davidson® motorcycle has become a brand icon.

The iconic image for Harley-Davidson® is not a recent phenomena. We can perhaps trace back this burgeoning image to the 1940s. When the United States entered the Second World War, the production of domestic motorcycles was suspended in favour of military production. By 1945 Harley-Davidson® had produced some 90 000 bikes for military use. It is interesting that many young Americans experienced their first feel of a Harley® while in military service, an experience they would remember on their return to

Aaker (1991) suggests that effective extension strategies have the following core characteristics:

◆ The original brand has strong positive associations that reinforce consumer expectations. These reduce the level of communication required to establish the extension and help in the differentiation of the brand.

◆ There is already a highly perceived (and real) value associated with the original brand name.

◆ The original brand is well known and thus recognised within its relevant market place.

Kapferer (1998) suggests that brand extensions have become increasingly important strategically. He concludes that companies can employ extensions as a tactic to defend the brand against attack from current and potential competitors. Kapferer (1998) suggests that many companies that have remained in their original market and not considered extensions risk seeing their position eroded.

The Kit Kat mini case is an illustration of a line extension strategy. As you can see, for some 60 years there was no change to the brand. However,

civilian life. This experience created a demand for Harleys® after the war, and one the company immediately geared up to meet.

Equally, magazines and movies enticed an increasingly international audience towards Harley-Davidson® motorcycles. In 1956 a rising young rock star – Elvis Presley – posed on a Harley® for *Enthusiast* magazine. However, it was arguably the image of Marlon Brando as Johnny in the 1953 movie classic *The Wild One* that cemented the relationship between motorcycles and the young. While it was supposedly a social commentary, very loosely based on a true story, the movie became more of a voice for a younger generation who had not yet found their own voice. Although the Brando character was to a large extent an anti-hero, his image became a visual statement for a generation of motorcyclists.

Harley-Davidson® began selling what was to emerge as the classic black leather motorcycle jacket in 1947. This was some six years before Brando made it a fashion accessory. However, merchandising took on a whole new meaning in the early 1980s with the forma-

tion of the Harley Owners Group, affectionately know as HOG®. This soon became the largest factory-sponsored motorcycle club in the world. Harley-Davidson® created the Owners Group in response to riders who wanted ' an organised way to share their passion and show their pride'. By 2003 international membership exceeded 800 000, with 1157 local chapters.

Although Harley-Davidson® actually produces fewer motorcycles per year than its major rivals, it has created an emotional attachment to the motorcycle. It is this emotion or experience that links the rider to the bike. As is stated in Chapter 16 on psychology, emotion and experiences are important influences on our lives and indeed our lifestyles. For Harley-Davidson® riders, the bike is not purely a means of transportation, it is part of who they are, their lifestyle and perhaps their view of life itself. It is this emotional attachment to the Harley® experience that has created a sustainable brand icon.

Source: Harley-Davidson.com.

one can speculate that increasing competition in the 1990s forced Nestlé to rethink its brand strategy for Kit Kat, prompting the various line extensions.

A very good example of a company that has developed numerous brand extensions is the UK-based Virgin group of companies under the control of Sir Richard Branson. The extensions to the Virgin name are listed overleaf.

Table 7.2 Types of extension

Type of extension	Description
Line extensions	This can be described as adding a line of complementary products to the original brand. For example, Unilever's Dove soap brand has been extended to include shampoo, foam bath and shower gels. The Mini case 7.6 on Kit Kat illustrates how Nestlé has extended that brand.
Range extensions	A range of products that carry the original brand's name are associated with the single 'promise' created by that brand and focus on the same area of competence or capability. For example, Heinz is seen as one of the world's leading food producers.
Brand extensions	Kapferer (1998) suggests that this is an attempt to diversify the brand towards different product categories and different target audiences. While there may be an attempt to extend the brand in different product categories, the target audience may actually include the same customers as well as new ones. The reason is that the original brand's customers are still buying into the brand's inherent values. This can be seen in mini case 7.7, which examines how fashion designers have moved into the hotel business.

Source: adapted from Kapferer (1998).

Mini case 7.6

Kit Kat chocolate bar

The Kit Kat brand was originally launched in the United Kingdom in 1935 as Rowntree's Chocolate Crisp. It was rebranded in 1935 as Kit Kat Chocolate Crisp (later becoming known as simply 'Kit Kat'). Although there is much debate regarding the origin of the name 'Kit Kat', it is suggested that it is linked to the literary club of 17th and 18th-century London.[2]

For some 60 years the Kit Kat brand remained a single product. However, as a result of increasing competition within the confectionery market Nestlé introduced various line extensions, some of which were sold for a limited period only.

By the 1990s Kit Kat had become the UK's best-selling confectionery brand with, according to Nestlé, 47 being consumed every second in the United Kingdom alone. In 2000 sales reached some UK£260 million. However sales dipped to UK£116 million in 2003. There are several possible reasons, from the weather to the drive towards healthier life styles.

In 1999 Nestlé introduced Kit Kat Chunky, a single giant finger version of the traditional multi-pack of Kit Kat. Over 200 million Kit Kat Chunky bars were sold in its launch year alone.

In the late 20th century and early 21st century Nestlé launched several additional line extensions, some of which have been more successful than others. These included:

◆ white chocolate

◆ orange flavoured

◆ Kit Kat Cubes (small cubes of Kit Kat rather than in the form of a finger biscuit)

◆ lemon cheesecake Kit Kat, which is sold in Germany and Japan

◆ curry-flavoured Kit Kat for the UK marketplace.

The introduction of these line extensions has been intended to curb falling revenues within a highly competitive marketplace by keeping the brand prominent in the mind of the consumer.
Source: www.nestle.com

Virgin describes itself as the 'third most recognized brand in Britain', claiming that it is now:

becoming the first global brand name of the 21st century. We are involved in planes, trains, finance, soft drinks, music, mobile phones, holidays, cars, wines, publishing, bridal wear – the lot! What ties all these businesses together are the values of our brand and the attitude of our people.

(www.virgin.com)

This is a list of businesses (as of January 2004) that use the Virgin brand name:

Virgin Active	Virgin Atlantic
Virgin Air Cargo	Virgin Balloon Flights
Virgin Bikes	Virgin Blue
Virgin Books	Virgin Brides
Virgin Business Solutions	Virgin Cars
Virgin Cosmetics	Virgin Credit Card
Virgin D3	Virgin Drinks
Virgin Experience	Virgin Express
Virgin Holidays	Virgin Home
Virgin Limobike	Virgin Limousines
Virgin Megastores	Virgin Mobile
Virgin Money	Virgin Pulse
Virgin Radio	Virgin Trains
Virgin Travelstore	Virgin Ware
Virgin Wines	Virgin.com
Virgin.net	Virginstudent.com
Virgin Vacations	

As you can see, there is an extremely wide selection of businesses. In addition there are businesses that do not carry the Virgin branding. These include:

Blue Holidays – innovative package holidays
Limited Edition – exclusive hotels
Necker Island – Branson's own private island in the British Virgin Islands, which can be hired
Pacific Blue – daily airline service between Australia and New Zealand
Radio Free Virgin – digital radio service
Roof Gardens – a venue in Kensington, London which includes the Babylon restaurant
thetrainline – online booking service for UK rail networks
Ulusaba – Branson's private game reserve in South Africa
V2 Music – an independent record label.

Another example of brand extensions as described by Kapferer (1998) can be seen in how major iconic fashion brands have diversified into the travel business. Mini case 7.7 illustrates how some of these fashion brands have extended their valuable brand name into the hotel business.

Another example of brand extension is the French ballpoint pen manufacturer *BIC*. Mini case 7.8 outlines both the successes and the failures of the company as it extended its global brand name.

However, companies need to be aware that there are risks associated with extending their brands. These include:

◆ Attaining a critical point where the value of the original brand is severely diluted because of the number of extensions. It could be argued that the French fashion house brand Pierre Cardin has been over-extended through the sheer volume of licences that have been granted to manufacture products under the brand name. According to Czinkota *et al.* (1998), the label granted 800 licences in 93 countries to create and manufacture a range of items from clothing, luggage and watches to toiletries and pens.

◆ A problem associated with one product within the extended brand range can possibly tarnish the image of the other products: for example, where one product is the subject of a product recall. Customers may be wary of purchasing other products within that brand range for fear there might also be problems with them. This could be an issue of perception rather that actuality. Nevertheless a perceived problem can be as damaging as a real one.

Mini case 7.7

Fashion designers extending their brands

Various haute couture houses have extended their brand into the luxury hotel market. In 2000 the Italian design house Versace entered a joint venture with a German hotel company to open the six-star Palazzo Versace in Queensland, Australia.

In 2001, the Italian fine jeweller Bvlgari entered a joint venture with the Marriott Hotel International to form Bvlgari Hotels & Resorts. In 2003 Bvlgari opened its first five-star hotel in Via Privata Fratelli, Gabbain, Milan's most prestigious shopping and cultural area adjacent to the famous La Scala opera house. The rooms and suites are priced at the top of Milan's high-end hotel market. Such pricing reflects the image and value of the Bvlgari brand.

Other fashion houses that have entered the hotel market include Cerruti, Mulberry and Biba. Although these companies are extending their brands, they are entering a highly competitive luxury hotel marketplace. The possible advantage they have over some of their competitors is that they have a range of branded products they can market to hotel customers, including clothes, travel accessories, bags and cosmetics. Indeed, they have the opportunity to create a lifestyle experience for their customers.

Sources: www.bulgari.com; www.hotelbiba.com; J. Arlidge, 'The rise of the hotel couture', *British Airways High Life*, January 2004, pp. 37–40.

Valuations and equity

Aaker (1991) defines brand equity as:

> a set of assets and liabilities linked to a brand, its name and symbol, that adds to or subtracts from the value provided by a product or service to a firm and/or to that firm's customers.

Aaker (1991) goes onto define the asset categories as brand awareness, brand loyalty, perceived quality and brand associations. Keller (1993) suggests that it is necessary for a company (or organisation) to invest in both brand awareness and brand image in order to create and develop value or equity for the brand. Yet it is really much more than awareness and image, as important as they may be. It goes to the heart of the credibility of the brand, and the trust people have in that brand. We have seen throughout this book that trust is an important 'condition in the mind of the customer', whether it applies to an individual product or service, or an organisation such as a government department.

While image is linked to trust, it really does not go deep enough. The image of a brand might be slightly tarnished, but overall the customer could still be loyal to that brand. However, if the customer loses faith or trust in that brand, it

Mini case 7.8

BIC®

In 1945 Marcel Bich (1919–1994) and his colleague Edouard Buffard bought an empty rectory in a Parisian suburb and developed what was to become a multi-billion-dollar empire. In the 1950s Bich obtained the original patent rights to a ballpoint pen from a Hungarian inventor, journalist and artist Ladislao Biró (1899–1985), who lived in Argentina.

Biro patented the idea in 1938, and fled Germany in 1940 to escape the Nazi regime. He sold his rights to his backer H. G. Martin in 1944, and Martin began marketing the original 'biro' pens in the United Kingdom. They were then introduced in the United States, with a launch in a New York department store. On the first day 10 000 were sold at US$12.50.

It was Bich who had the idea of creating the disposable ballpoint pen, and thus the 'BIC® biro' as we know it today was developed. In 1958 Bich acquired the American-based Waterman pen company, and this provided him with the opportunity to enter the US market. This resulted in sales of over 330 million ballpoints per year into that market.

With such success mounting in the global ballpoint pen market, Bich decided to extend his brand by introducing the disposable lighter. This was to be one of several extensions to the BIC® brand. Initially the disposable lighter was test marketed in Sweden, then a year later he introduced it into the US market. Here it was in competition with the established leader, the Cricket lighter produced by Gillette. Both companies engaged in advertising and pricing battles, with BIC® emerging the winner. In 1984 Gillette sold Cricket lighters to Swedish Match.

Both companies were again to battle for market share, this time with disposable razors. Bich had seen another way of extending the BIC® brand. However, the situation was very different now. This was Gillette's main marketplace, and its reputation and expertise in shaving helped it to outperform BIC® in this particular market. While it has not become market leader within the US market, BIC® shavers have nonetheless gained significant ground in the global marketplace.

While remaining the market leader in ballpoint pens, BIC® has been able to successfully extend its brand across the diverse product ranges of lighters and shavers. By the turn of the 21st century BIC® was selling 4 million BIC® lighters and 11 million BIC® one-piece shavers every day.

As Christensen, Berg and Salter (1980) suggest, BIC® is in the market of selling easy-to-manufacture, low-priced disposable items, and aims to use its significant volume of production to reduce its costs. In 2002 SOCIÉTÉ BIC generated revenues of €1.5 billion (US$ 1.9 billion; UK£1 billion approximately).

Sources: Christensen et al. (1980), Hillman and Gibbs (1998), van Dulken (2000), www.bicworld.com.

---

might well be damaged in the short, medium and indeed the longer terms. As we shall see later in this chapter, brands are damaged by adverse situations, sometimes of the brand's or company's own making. We must remember that brands are vulnerable, and that organisations must be able to recognise that vulnerability for both the sake of the brand and the survivability of the organisation itself.

Brands have a real financial value to a company or organisation. Therefore the company or organisation has to create and develop through its brand managers an environment that will build brand equity over not just the shorter term but the long term as well. The organisation is therefore seeking to create, and most importantly sustain, a competitive advantage.

Promotion

The collective elements of branding (for instance, name, images, ambience and packaging) all contribute to building a communications profile of the product or service. A brand should communicate a set of values and an identity to its audience. These values and identity can be projected across a diverse range of media through an integrated marketing communications campaign. (See Chapter 10.) Although the media may be diverse, the brand message and values should remain the same. This is, it is hoped, will increase brand awareness, recognition and recall.

■ Types of branding

Companies can adopt a range of policies to create a 'brand environment' to encompass their product and/or service. The following list is not exhaustive, and the nomenclature for brand typing varies from textbook to textbook and country to country. Students are advised to read widely on this subject and consider the differences.

Family brands

As the name suggests this is a brand range that adopts the name of the company. This can be done regardless of whether the company is a manufacturer or service provider. Examples include Heinz Foods, Virgin, Cadbury chocolates, Shangri-La Hotels in the Far East and Nestlé Foods.

Individual brands

These are products and services that stand alone, separate from their parent company. They possess a distinct individual identity, and the consumer might not actually know which company owns the brand. Table 7.3 lists some individual brands and their parent companies. As you can see, several international brands are owned by organisations with equally well-known family brands, for example Aston Martin and its parent Ford.

These individual brands will have their own brand strategies to compete within their own marketplace. One of the advantages of individual branding is that a parent company such as Procter & Gamble can have several individual brands competing within the same market segment for a

Table 7.3 Individual brands and their parent companies

Individual brand	Product/service type	Parent	Location of parent company
Ariel	Clothes washing liquid/powder	Procter & Gamble	USA
Asda	UK supermarket chain	Wal-Mart	USA
Aston Martin	Luxury cars	Ford Motor Corporation	USA
Camay	Soap	Procter & Gamble	USA
Conrad Hotels	Luxury hotels	Hilton International & Hilton Hotels Corporation (through a joint venture arrangement)	UK/USA
Cunard	Luxury cruise line	Carnival Corporation	USA
Dove	Soap and shampoo range	Unilever	UK/Netherlands
Durex	Condoms	SSL International plc	UK
Evian	Mineral water	Group DANONE	France
Flash	Kitchen cleaner	Procter & Gamble	USA
HarperCollins	Publishers	News Corporation	USA/Australia
Scandia Hotels	European hotel group	Hilton International	UK
Sheaffer	Premium writing instruments – fountain pens and ballpoints	Société BIC	France
20th Century-Fox	Film and television production and distribution	News Corporation	USA/Australia
Werther's Originals	Caramel and cream candy	Storck	Germany

All brand trademarks and registrations are fully acknowledged.

share of that particular market. Having such brands 'competing' within the same segment can mean that the parent has a greater overall share of that market segment than its competitors, both individually and collectively.

The Carnival Corporation is divided into six brands that cater for different segmented target markets:

Brand name	Segmented target market
Carnival Cruises	Family
Costa	Family
Holland America	Family – luxury
Cunard	Luxury
Seabourn	Niche luxury
Windstar	Niche luxury

Own-label brands

These are brands that are owned and marketed by retailers. They are also known as retailer brands, own brands, dealer brands, private labels, store brands and generics. The major UK supermarkets have, for instance, created a range of own-label brands encompassing everything from chocolate to washing liquids. These compete, normally on price, with the major-label brands such as Heinz, Cadbury's and Kellogg's. The aim of own-label brands is to build loyalty between the customer and the retailer, and to improve store margins.

Supermarkets do not manufacture own-label brands; instead they seek companies that have the experience of manufacturing specific products or ranges of products. For instance the UK-owned company McBride is one of Europe's leading manufacturers and suppliers of own-label household cleaning, personal care and pharmaceutical brands. McBride is a UK£500 million multinational business with 18 factories in seven countries (McBride 2004).

Euromonitor (2004a) reported that in 2002 own-label brands of Over the Counter (OTC) medicines accounted for 6.4 per cent of the global market. The research contends that own-label brands have proved attractive (as a result of their lower price position) in markets where the national economy displays low growth and rising unemployment. Where there are the threat of unemployment and diminishing levels of disposable income, consumers will feel increasingly insecure. This will lead them to purchase lower-priced products, usually own-label brands. In such a competitive market, the major brands may retaliate by lowering their prices to compete on price, or maintain their position. In the latter case they are identifying a quality rather than a price position.

The potential strength of the own-label brands can be seen from an examination of the UK textile washing products market, where the market share of the major players in 2002 was:

Procter & Gamble	40.9%
Unilever	37.5%
Own-label brands	17.0%
Reckitt Benckiser	3.2%
(Euromonitor 2003)	

Euromonitor (2003) suggests that the only threat to the dominance of Procter & Gamble and Unilever came from the development of own-label products. The Euromonitor research indicates that the rise of the own-label brands within this sector, is a result of the increasing sophistication and quality of the retailer brands.

Some companies can manufacture their own branded products as well as own-label products for supermarket chains (see mini case 7.9).

■ Brand management

We have seen that numerous attributes can be assigned to a brand, from advertising to valuation. A brand can also be an individual entity or an integral component of a family of brands. In order for a brand to function effectively and efficiently it needs to be managed, hence the development of brand management.

Brand management can be defined as:

> The strategic organization of the marketing mix to effectively and efficiently build and manage a brand over its life cycle.

We discussed earlier Goldfarb's (2001) suggestion that Lever's success with the introduction of Sunlight Soap was due to his careful management of the brand. Lever focused on a target market, the English working-class housewife of the period. This targeting was carefully linked to the advertising of the brand and, most impor-

Premier Foods and Premier Brands

In 1986 Paul Judge* led a management buy-out (MBO) of the tea and foods businesses of Cadbury Schweppes. As part of the MBO, Premier Brands would continue to manufacture Cadbury chocolate and Cadbury chocolate cakes and drink under licence. Hillsdown Holdings plc later acquired the company. In 1999 Hillsdown Holdings was in turn acquired for UK£822 million by the Dallas-based venture capitalist company Hicks, Muse, Tate & Furst Inc, which owns substantial holdings in diversified business interests.

On acquisition Hillsdown Holdings was divided into two core businesses, Premier Foods and Horizon Biscuits (whose brands include Cadbury biscuits, Wagon Wheels® and Maryland Cookies®).

As of 2004 Premier Foods had a turnover of UK£1 billion. Since the original MBO it has been actively engaged in a series of acquisitions and licensing agreements, including:

1999   Acquired the license to use raconteur Lloyd Grossman's name on a range of cooking sauces.

2002   Acquisition of Nestlé's ambient food businesses for an estimated UK£120 million[3] – Branston (a range of pickles), Crosse & Blackwell (salad dressings), Sarson's (vinegars), Sun Pat (spreads, including peanut butter), Gales (honey) and Rowntree's Jelly.

2003   Acquired from Unilever the UK-based Ambrosia, which produces a variety of desserts, and French and German-based Brown and Polson brands (which supply the catering industry with desserts and cornflour) (see mini case 7.15).

2003   Hicks, Muse, Tate & Furst acquired for UK£642 million the UK-based Weetabix company with the cereal brands Weetabix®, Alpen® and

Ready Brek®. In 2003/2004 Weetabix® was the United Kingdom's number one cereal, and sold in more than 80 countries.

The objective of Hicks, Muse, Tate & Furst is to create a leading UK-based food manufacturer. Premier Foods has developed an expertise in the following areas:

◆   tea

◆   hot chocolate

◆   spreads and desserts

◆   pickles, vinegars and sauces

◆   cooking sauces

◆   convenience foods: canned foods ranging from beans to soups.

◆   retailer (own-label) brands.

It is this last section that is now considered.

Through its SBU Premier Brands, Premier Foods also manufactures own-label brands for many of the UK's major retailers. These cover the areas above, in which the company has developed a strong reputation in the marketplace. In 2004 Premier was the UK's largest manufacturer of own-label canned foods, ranging from beans and spaghetti to vegetables, fruit, soups and meat. It is also a leading producer of own-label teas and beverages for UK supermarkets.

It can be argued that Premier has leveraged its knowledge and expertise, gained through producing its own range of major brands, to penetrate the retailer brand market.

Sources: www.premierbrands.com; 'How the Americans swallowed Weetabix', www.timesonline.co.uk, 23 November 2003.

* Paul Judge left Premier Foods after its acquisition by Hillsdown Holdings plc. He later donated funds to build the Judge Institute of Management at the University of Cambridge.

tantly, the communication of the brand's image to the target audience.

■ The world's most powerful brands

As well as being a powerful weapon in a company's arsenal to gain and sustain competitive advantage, brands have a financial value that companies seek to maximise. Table 7.4 gives the value of the world's ten most powerful brands as of 2004. The UK-based company Interbrand has developed a formula for calculating brand values using several measures, and this table is based on its value estimates. Of course, brand fortunes can change over time, and this table simply gives a snapshot in time.

Table 7.4 The world's top 10 brands

Brand	2003	Value	2002	Value	2001	Value	2000	Value	Country of origin
Coca-Cola	1	70.45	1	69.63	1	68.94	1	83.84	USA
Microsoft	2	65.17	2	64.09	2	65.06	2	70.19	USA
IBM	3	51.77	3	51.18	3	52.75	3	53.18	USA
GE	4	42.34	4	41.31	4	42.39	6	38.12	USA
Intel	5	31.11	5	30.86	6	34.66	4	39.04	USA
Nokia	6	29.44	6	29.97	5	35.03	5	38.52	Finland
Disney	7	28.04	7	29.25	7	32.59	8	33.55	USA
McDonald's	8	24.70	8	26.37	9	25.28	8	27.85	USA
Marlboro	9	22.18	9	24.15	11	22.05	11	22.11	USA
Mercedes	10	21.37	10	21.01	12	21.72	12	21.10	Germany
Value totals		386.57		387.82		400.47		427.50	

Values are given in US$ billion.

Sources: 2003 data: *Business Week* (2003)/Interbrand. 2000–02 data: Interbrand: Copyright Interbrand.

There are several points from this table that you may want to consider in relation to the value and power of these brands.

◆ Coca-Cola has retained its dominance and displayed steady growth over the four-year period.

◆ The top three brands – Coca-Cola, Microsoft and IBM – have held their positions over the four-year period.

◆ Both Disney and Nokia have seen a decrease in their brand values over the four-year period.

◆ There was a sharp decrease in the overall value of the ten brands from 2000 to 2002. However this fall steadied in 2003.

◆ Eight of the top ten global brands are US-owned.

◆ In 2003 the value of the top ten brands was US$386 billion.

An analysis of the world's top 100 brands (as of 2003) shows the following:

◆ US-based companies dominate branding. Table 7.5 shows the breakdown by country of origin of the top 100 brands for 2003

◆ The nearest nations to the United States are the French and the Japanese with seven brands each, but that is clearly significantly below the dominance of the US brands at 62.

Table 7.5 Country origins of top 100 brands

Country	Number of top 100 brands
Bermuda	1
Finland	1
France	7
Germany	6
Italy	2
Japan	7
Netherlands	2
Netherlands/UK	1
South Korea	1
Sweden	2
Switzerland	3
United Kingdom	5
United States	62
	100

◆ Based on *Business Week*/Interbrand statistics for 2003 (*Business Week* 2003), the total value of US brands was US$706 billion. Brands from other nations were collectively valued at US$268 billion. Thus the total value of the top 100 brands for 2003 was US$974 billion. To put this in perspective, Table 7.6 lists the wealth of certain nations (as of 2001). Of course this is not a like-for-like comparison, but a quick comparison with the top 10 brands have significant value or wealth compared with some countries.

Rebranding

In essence rebranding is when a company or organisation decides, perhaps for one of many reasons, to change a significant element of the brand. Contrary to general belief it does not necessarily mean a change in the brand name, although it often does.

The reasons underlying rebranding can be many and varied. Kaikati and Kaikati (2004) have attempted to categorise them into proactive and reactive motivations, and identified seven major factors in each category. Their approach has been adapted to both include and exclude motivational factors. Of course, with any type of listing there need to be caveats, and here there are two. First, these motivators are not necessarily stand-alones within a group. A company may choose to rebrand for several interconnected reasons. Second, the motivators for change can transcend both proactive and reactive groups. What starts as a reactive move could lead to proactive motivators being introduced into the rebranding activity.

Proactive motivations

Consolidation to create an international or globally recognised brand

Kaikati and Kaikati (2004) suggest multinationals may seek to consolidate numerous regional brands into one powerful global brand. Such an approach should maximise the efficiency of design, production, promotion and distribution. For instance, the chocolate bar Snickers was known by different names in various countries: in the United Kingdom for example it was known as Marathon. In the late 1980s the Mars Corporation decided to rebrand it

Table 7.6 The wealth of nations (measured by gross national income)

Country	GNI 2001 (US$ billion)
Albania	4.2
Argentina	260.3
Australia	385.9
Belgium	245.3
Botswana	5.3
Brazil	528.9
Canada	681.6
Chad	1.6
China	1 131.2
Congo	4.2
Czech Republic	54.3
Egypt	99.6
Entrea	0.7
Estonia	5.3
France	1 380.7
Gambia, The	0.4
Germany	1 939.6
Greece	121.0
Haiti	3.9
India	477.4
Italy	1 123.8
Japan	4 523.3
Kenya	10.7
Lithuania	11.7
Malaysia	79.3
Mexico	550.2
Niger	2.0
Pakistan	60.0
Poland	163.6
Russian Federation	253.4
Rwanda	1.9
Singapore	88.8
Spain	588.0
United Kingdom	1 476.8
United States	9 780.8

Source: *World Development Indicators* 2003 (World Bank 2003). GNI (Gross National Income) is the sum of value added by all resident producers plus any product taxes (less subsidiaries) not included in the valuation of output plus net receipts of primary income (compensation of employees and property income) from abroad.

Note: GNI is also known as Gross National Product (GNP) in the terminology of the 1968 United Nations System of National Accounts.

globally as Snickers. This allowed the company to capitalise on economies of scale when marketing this flagship brand.

Corporate diversification

Over time companies and organisations may diversify from their original core business, and their original corporate identity might not adequately represent the business areas in which they now operate. A classic example is British Petroleum (BP). In 1909 the Anglo-Persian Oil Company was formed to exploit the first commercial discovery of oil in the Middle East, in the region then known as southwest Persia. In 1935 Persia was renamed Iran, and the Anglo-Persian Oil Company became the Anglo-Iran Oil Company. Further development of both the oil fields and the business continued. In 1951 the Iran government nationalised the oil fields, precipitating an international crisis. After three years of negotiation the crisis was resolved when a consortium was formed to restart the Iranian oil industry. In the 1954 the Anglo-Iranian Oil Company was renamed the British Petroleum Company, and it held a 40 per cent share of the new consortium.

From then until the 1990s BP diversified into several business sectors as well as continuing as a major oil company. However, it was for the latter that it was chiefly known, and high-profile acquisitions supported that profile or image. During the late 1990s BP shed its British Petroleum image by rebranding itself as BP and introducing a new logo design. BP now wanted to communicate the message that it was more than an oil company. It was no longer an 'oil company', it had become an 'energy company', developing energy sources from oil to solar power.

Development of new markets and market segments

As we explained earlier, in order to remain competitive a brand may need to seek out new markets, or new segments of existing markets. This can sometimes be achieved through extending the reputation of the brand across market sectors, but it might also be necessary to rebrand. This does not necessary mean a name change, instead it can be a 'makeover' of the product and packaging. This is also be associated with re-energising the brand.

Avoiding confusion in the market or potential markets

Confusion might occur for three key reasons:

◆ A company seeks to move into an international market only to discover that there is already a well-established product with a very similar name. The company will rebrand its product in that market to avoid any link with the already established brand.

◆ Equally, the company could face a legal challenge if it entered that market with a brand name similar to the already established one. Depending on the laws in that country, it could be sued for attempting to 'pass off' its product as the established one. This is especially the case if the products have similarities beyond the brand name, such as similar brand promises.

◆ The brand name does not translate well or has a negative meaning in the local language. (See also page 139.)

Appeal to a new target audience

Companies or organisations may rebrand themselves or a product or service range to appeal to a new target audience. British politics in the 1980s and 1990s provides an example. The Conservative Party had been in government since 1979, first under Margaret Thatcher then under John Major. Under Prime Minister Thatcher the party moved to a more right-wing position. In 1990 Thatcher resigned as prime minister, having won three terms in office. John Major succeeded her. During the Thatcher years, as they came to be known, the British Labour Party had been left quietly drifting in the doldrums. It had been tarnished with the 'tax and spend policies' of the 1960s and 1970s. However, it decided to rebrand itself as a more centrist party rather than being known as left wing in varying degrees. In rebranding itself as New Labour the party attempted to cast off some of the socialist trappings it had been renowned for, and embrace many aspects of the market economy. Its view was that this 'Third Way',[4] as it was called, would make it electable as a government. The Conservative Party lost the 1997 election to New Labour, which gained an overwhelming majority in the House of Commons.

However, because of increased pressure on the government from members of its own party as well as the opposition, there was a move to drop the 'new' from the corporate identity. It could be argued that the 'new' was outliving its welcome.

Re-energising the brand

This can also be considered as reinventing the brand, and may be a means of extending the life of the product or brand within a specific or multiple markets. (See also Chapter 9 on products.) An example of successful brand reinvention is the sports drink Lucozade© (see mini case 7.10).

Translation problems

A company might brand a product or service with a brand name and/or set of symbols that are appropriate for it within its regional context. However, difficulties might occur if the company looks to the longer term, and markets that span borders. Brands (as names and identities) do not always transcend location. There are countless examples of brand names and logos that are perfectly innocent in the country of origin, but take on an altogether different meaning in other countries and languages. Creating a 'universal' brand identity is not as easy as it is sometimes suggested in textbooks.

To create brand unity across several markets

Companies can expand from small businesses into multinational corporations. Their growth is often a mixture of acquisition of other companies and organic growth of the original company. As they move into new territories they establish similar brands in different markets. Sometimes this is a clearly planned approach, based on what is seen as the best strategy at the time. However, markets are dynamic, and within an increasingly globalised world there might come a time when it is in the company's best interests strategically to rebrand products in different markets to create a brand unity across several markets. However, as we explained it is not always easy to create a single global identity.

Reactive motivators

To reflect a new status

An organisation might rebrand itself to reflect a change in status. For example, in the 1980s the British government enacted legislation that allowed

---

Mini case 7.10

Lucozade©

In 1927 in the north-east of England an energy drink Gluozade was introduced. In 1929 it was rebranded as Lucozade. In 1938 Beecham acquired the original manufacturing company Eno's Proprietary Ltd. Originally, and subsequently for 50 years, Lucozade was marketed as a 'convalescent drink' for those who were ill. During the 1950s and 1960s Lucozade became Beecham's largest brand.

However with increased market pressures it was repositioned in 1985 as an 'everyday replacement energy drink'. This allowed the company to broaden its market. In 1986 the product line was extended to include orange and lemon variants. In 1989 SmithKline Beckman merged with the Beecham Group to form SmithKline Beecham plc.

The product line was further enhanced in 1990, with the introduction of a new tropical flavoured variant. However, by 1996 it was clear that the brand was in need of a major repositioning. The brand was relaunched with a new-shape 300 ml bottle (later replaced by a 380 ml PET bottle), a new logo and fresh advertising. Further revitalisation of the brand would come in the form of the computer-generated (later live-action) character Lara Croft, the heroine of *Tomb Raiders*. New advertising and a new logo on all packs reinforced its position in the market as an 'iconic energy drink'.

In 2000 GlaxoSmithKline plc was formed through the merger of Glaxo Wellcome and SmithKline Beecham to create one of the world's leading pharmaceutical companies. Lucozade has become one of the world's best-known energy drinks, and comprises three brands: Lucozade Energy, Lucozade Sport and Solstis. Its major markets include the United Kingdom, Ireland, Mexico and Hong Kong. In 2003 a new flavour – Citrus Clear – was introduced to the Lucozade Energy market.

Sources: GlaxoSmithKline plc (www.gsk.com).

---

polytechnics to gain university status, which enabled them to award their own degrees rather than give degrees through the Council for National Academic Awards (CNAA). It can be argued that there was no real difference in the quality of education received in a university and a polytechnic, but there was a perceived difference. Turning all higher education centres into universities removed this perception to some extent. Thus, for example, Oxford Polytechnic became Oxford Brookes University and the City of London Polytechnic became London Guildhall University. London Guildhall was later to merge with the University of North London (formerly the Polytechnic of North London).

A reflection of merger activity

When two or more companies or organisations merge, the new corporate entity will seek a new brand identity to reflect the merger. When the two car giants Chrysler and Daimler merged, the new company rebranded itself as DaimlerChrysler. It was vital for both companies that it was clearly seen as a merger and not as an acquisition by one company of the other. Another approach is to create a completely new brand identity for the merged organisation. That was the approach taken by London Guildhall University and the University of North London: on their merger in 2002 they formed London Metropolitan University.

A reflection of acquisition activity

As a company acquires others it may seek to rebrand the acquired company's corporate identity, products and services. When Nestlé acquired the UK-based confectioner Rowntree Mackintosh it slowly rebranded the corporate identity of Rowntree Mackintosh to that of Nestlé. However, the brand names of products such as Kit Kat remained unchanged.

Demergers (also known as corporate divorces)

A demerger may occur for several reasons:

◆ The company reviews its businesses and decides that one or more business units no longer fit strategically with its longer-term objectives. It might seek to be more focused on its core business(es).

◆ As a strategic defence against a potential hostile takeover bid. The petrochemical company ICI demerged its pharmaceutical business, creating a separate entity – Zeneca – which was listed on the London Stock Market.

◆ While the original merger may have made strategic sense, it might subsequently prove to be an error of judgement.

The demerger activity will see rebranding activity, as both companies or organisations seek to distance themselves from each other. This will especially be the case if the demerger was acrimonious.

Legal compliance

There are two separate issues here. First, a company might enter a market unaware that a product or service with a similar-sounding brand name already exists within that market. The 'resident' brand owners might seek legal redress from the new entrant. As part of the settlement the new entrant will generally either withdraw from the market or rebrand its product. The decision will depend on the costs of exiting the market compared with the costs of rebranding, which can be set against potential revenues from the longer-term development of the market. Second, the company might be forced to rebrand its product or service because of connotations associated with the brand name. This may be the case where the translation of the brand name (if it is not an artificially constructed word) has a different, perhaps obscene, meaning in another language.

Tarnished brand name

A company may decide to rebrand a product or service on the basis that the original brand name has been tarnished. If a brand has been significantly damaged in a market, the company might have only two options: terminate the brand altogether in that market or rebrand it, possibly creating a new lease of life for the product or service. The level of the rebranding activity will depend on the degree of negativity shown towards the brand.

In 1992 the Walt Disney Company opened Euro Disney just outside Paris. Disney's theme parks in the United States and Japan had been a tremendous success, and there were high expectations for Euro Disney. However, various internal and external factors meant the park's performance did not live up to these expectations. To distance it from the negative publicity, it was rebranded as Disneyland Paris. Of course, the rebranding alone would not have provided solutions to Euro Disney's numerous problems. There was significant internal restructuring of the business at the same time, and this rejuvenated the theme park.

Familiarity of previous name

Companies or organisations have sought to rebrand themselves only to discover that the rebranding, for one reason or another, was fatally flawed. Some companies have gone for 'cool, hip, now, trendy' rebranding only to discover – at vast expense – that they have alienated not only their current customer base but the prospective customers they had hoped to attract.

Unpopular rebranding

While this is similar to the last motivator, the difference may not be reflective of the name alone. For example, UK postal services were rebranded as Consignia. Public outcry caused it to revert to being called Royal Mail. (See mini case 7.14.)

When British Airways (BA) decided to dispense with the Union Flag (also know as the Union Jack) on its aircraft tailfins, in favour of a variety of graphic designs, it was unaware of the hostility this would cause. The graphic designs were intended to represent the four corners of the world the airline flew to, promoting an international vision rather than a British one. BA's decision to rebrand was based on sound strategic reasoning. All the recent research pointed to significant growth in the leisure market and flights outside the United Kingdom. It wanted to appeal to both holidaymakers and overseas customers who might choose it over their own national carrier. The new designers were aiming to convey a friendly international approach rather than the perhaps more stuffy 'colonial' identity conveyed by the traditional logo.

However, BA had failed to alert people to the proposed changes and the reasoning behind them (Hilton 2001). Nor was this the only issue. It launched the new look at the time of a cabin crew strike, and was faced with mounting media pressure on two fronts, the crew strike and the new designs. This was also fuelled by the discontent of BA passengers, especially the business and first class passengers who were the real revenue generators for the airline. Then a famous negative photo opportunity landed on BA's desk. At the 2001

Mini case 7.11

Rebranding the British monarchy

In 1840 Queen Victoria (1819–1901) married Prince Albert (1819–1861), the son of Ernst, Duke of Saxe-Coburg and Gotha. Queen Victoria remained a member of the House of Hanover. However, when her eldest son Edward VII (1841–1910) acceded to the throne he took the name Saxe-Coburg. In turn his second son, George V (1865–1936), retained the Saxe-Coburg name. Then the First World War brought Britain into conflict with George V's cousin, the German Emperor and King of Prussia, Kaiser Wilhelm (1859–1941). There was concern among royal advisors that a German name was inappropriate for the British monarch. So the decision was taken to have George V adopt a name that asserted his 'Englishness' while playing down the extent of his German ancestry.

Lord Stamfordham (1849–1931), George V's Private Secretary, considered various options, including Plantagenet, York, England, Lancaster, d'Este and Fitzroy. Some were rejected on the grounds that they might sound slightly comical. One name on the list was Windsor. This derived from Edward III (1312–1377), who was known as Edward of Windsor; and of course there was Windsor Castle which dated from the 11th century and had been the seat of the Royal Family since William the Conqueror. Thus on 17 July 1917 the House and Family name of Windsor was adopted by King George V, and it has been used by his descendants to this day. All German elements associated with the monarchy were revoked, and this led to some other families changing their German-sounding names to more English-sounding ones.

In essence this was a rebranding exercise by Lord Stamfordham at what was believed to be a critical juncture in the war. However, the war had been raging for some three years before the decision was taken.

Conservative Party conference the former Prime Minister Margaret Thatcher (now Lady Thatcher) arrived at the BA stand. She retrieved a handkerchief from her infamous handbag and proceeded to wrap it around the tail fin of a model aircraft with the new design. This image and her words condemning the change circled the world – to everywhere BA flew.

While the rebranding of British Airways had an impact (perceived or real) on the airline, this was later overshadowed by the horrific events of 11 September 2001 and the terrorist attacks in New York and Washington. These deplorable attacks of violence will have a significant effect on the airline industry for years to come.

As can be seen from the various mini cases in this section, rebranding may comprise a 'minor' change in the brand name or a radical rethink of the organisation's position in the marketplace. Just as when a first name for the brand is chosen, serious consideration must be given to how any new name will be received in the marketplace. Rebranding is an expensive operation, and not always successful: in fact some rebrandings have proved a major disaster for the image and reputation of the company concerned.

Chapter 2 examined the external or macro environment within which an organisation operates. Global political dynamics since 11 September 2001 have influenced societal attitudes, especially to international travel. Research indicates that an increasing number of UK citizens are preferring to vacation in the United Kingdom rather than travel overseas (Mintel 2004). This, along with new entrants to the market and easier overseas travel, has forced traditional UK resorts to reinvent themselves. Mini case 7.12 illustrates how external environment and competitive factors led to the rise, decline and possible reinvention of holiday camps.

Brand longevity – do brands last forever?

In a world that is often associated with instant 'disposability' and highly competitive markets, people may be forgiven for thinking that brands are here today, gone tomorrow novelties. That is not the case. Cooper and Kleinschmidt (1991b) conducted research that indicated over 75 per cent of brands had been in the marketplace for more than 40 years. Of course, some of those brands might be at the end of their maturity, and perhaps entering their declining phase. Moreover, in increasingly competitive and turbulent environments, such as the turn of the 21st century, it is hard to determine the impact of such factors on brand longevity. However, the research demonstrates that some brands have a significant life span.

Mini case 7.12

The transformation of UK holiday 'camps' into holiday centres

The uniquely British holiday camp concept was developed by the entrepreneur William Butlin (1899–1980) in the 1930s. During the First World War on a trip to Canada with his parents he visited lakeside holiday centres. He believed something similar could be introduced to the British seaside, and his first holiday camp was opened in 1936 near Skegness, a town on the Lincolnshire coast.

During the Second World War the camp was occupied by the Royal Navy, but it was reopened to the public in 1946 after a refurbishment that included a launderette, tennis courts, swimming pools and a ballroom. However, the 'camp' had the appearance of a military camp, with its communal bathrooms, wire fencing and loudspeaker announcements. Still, after the devastation and sacrifices of the war (food rationing would continue until the 1950s), this experience was viewed by the mass population as a luxury.

While the Butlin's empire grew, so did the competition. Other companies such as Pontins built holiday camps around the UK coastline. However, there were greater challenges unfolding. The postwar UK economy had been transformed, and people increasingly had more disposable income. The introduction of jet aircraft, more airlines and packaged holidays meant that many people were no longer confined to the United Kingdom for their vacation. Overseas travel, especially within Europe, was no longer the privilege of the wealthy. There was also the added benefit of potentially better weather. Countries such as Spain and Greece realised the potential of the tourist trade, and expanded hotels and resorts to entice British holiday makers.

By the 1980s many of the British holiday camps had

Table 7.7 (page 146) shows the longevity of 40 brands. Some have only a regional dimension, while others have gained an international, almost iconic reputation. As you will see, several of the brands, perhaps including brands you personally use or consume, originated before you were born. Many brands may look 'new', but that may only be their packaging and their promotion. In fact they might already have had a significant life span.

closed. However, the late 1990s witnessed a revival of them, for several reasons (Mintel 2004):

◆ Fear of terrorist attacks. The attacks of 9/11 and the invasion of Iraq, together with continuing international unrest, have created a climate of fear. Even though there are numerous low-cost airlines offering cheap travel to European destinations, the fear of terrorism has persuaded some families to remain in the United Kingdom rather than travel overseas.

◆ Segmentation into three types of holiday centre:
   ● Traditional centres (that is, holiday camps in the established style, not 'historical' experiences). Companies in this segment include Butlin's, Pontin's and Warner.
   ● Forest villages: landscaped villages in forest settings that provided a very different experience.
   ● Holiday parks, providing a combination of caravan, chalet and lodge accommodation along with other facilities. In total there were (in 2004) some 3500 such parks in the United Kingdom.

◆ The more traditional 'holiday camps' have been reinvented and rebranded as 'holiday centres'. Significant investment in these holiday centres has transformed them from military-style camps to state-of-the-art accommodation, leisure facilities and exterior landscaping. It is estimated that Butlin's and Pontin's invested about UK£200 million between the mid-1990s and the early 2000s. This rebranding and significant updating created a strategic fit with the expectations of consumers, who are increasingly sophisticated in their choices. It has also allowed the holiday centres to market a higher proportion of premium-priced vacations.

◆ A greater range of options is now available to those who vacation at a holiday centre, for instance in the style and type of accommodation and facilities. This has been driven partly by increased customer sophistication but also by competition, from both leisure centres and parks at overseas destinations, and European companies that have invested in the United Kingdom, bringing with them a new holiday centre experience. For instance, the Dutch company Center Parcs® Europe[5] created in 1968 the first holiday centre amongst forests and landscaped grounds. This provided customers with the opportunity to relax in surroundings of peace and tranquillity.

◆ The UK weather was originally a driver of the exodus abroad (along with the development of packaged holidays, and other factors). Increasingly, though, UK summers are becoming longer, with sustainable higher temperatures. This has led more people to remain in the United Kingdom, even though inexpensive holiday packages for overseas destinations remain available. The holiday centres have also invested in the latest designs and building technologies to provide large enclosed areas. For instance, designer swimming pools can be fully enclosed and enjoyed by the whole family regardless of the weather.

In 2000 some 5.5 million holiday centre vacations were purchased, and this rose to 6 million by 2003. This brought the value of the UK holiday centre market to approximately UK£1 billion.

Reasons for brand longevity

There are no hard and fast rules that ensure a brand will have a long life span. In fact it could be not one action but a combination of actions, over time, that ensure longevity. Companies need to consider both the micro and macro factors that affect both the organisation and its brands over time (refer to Chapter 2).

The company or organisation needs to be strategically focused when considering the growth and development of its brand portfolios. Thus longevity may be attained by a combination of the following factors:

◆ Maximising the brand's positioning in the market place through effective and efficient deployment of marketing communications.

Mini case 7.13

Samaritans

In November 1953 Chad Varah founded the charity The Samaritans (now known as simply Samaritans). In his early years as a minister he buried a 14-year-old girl who had committed suicide when her periods started, because she mistakenly thought they were a sign of sexually transmitted disease. This tragic event affected him, and he wanted to create an organisation where people could share their fears and worries. Initially The Samaritans were run from St Stephen Walbrook church in the City of London with one telephone, but by 2004 there were 203 branches operating 24 hours a day, 80 of which were equipped to reply to e-mails, with 18 300 specially-trained volunteers.

Traditionally people's perception of a person contacting the Samaritans was a suicidal depressive with 'one hand on the phone and both feet dangling out of the window'. In fact Samaritans deal with a much wider range of issues, but cases of suicide are on the increase. Since the 1990s the rate of suicide of young men in the United Kingdom has increased significantly, and it is now the biggest killer of men under the age of 24.

Samaritans' vision:

Is for a society where fewer people die by suicide because people are able to share feelings of emotional distress openly without fear of being judged. Samaritans believes that offering people the opportunity to be listened to in confidence, and accepted without prejudice, can alleviate despair and suicidal feelings. It is the aim of Samaritans to make emotional health a mainstream issue.

The rebranding campaign positioned Samaritans as ' the emotional support charity', and tried to prompt people in the United Kingdom and the Republic of Ireland to reconsider their attitudes towards emotional health issues such as depression and stress. The rebranding (linked to an advertising campaign) placed mental health issues in a context that people could understand.

To quote marketing director David Richards:

We want to encourage a society where people can express their feelings and people are prepared to listen to them.... If people are down, angry, concerned about debt or are in some form of emotional distress, we want people to talk about it. It's all about encouraging good mental health.

Sources: 'Andrew Williams Kicking off the blues', *Metro Focus*, 3 February 2003; 'Samaritans launches campaign to challenge stigma around emotional health', press release, Samaritans, 27 November 2002.

◆ Continual reappraisal of the brand's positioning in comparison with actual and potential competitors.

◆ Product-line extensions could be used to reinforce the brand's overall market positioning and leadership. Consider, for example, the impact the launch of the Kit Kat Chunky bar in 1999 had on the UK confectionery market (See mini case 7.6).

◆ The company could seek new regional or international markets and grow the brand in those markets.

◆ The company could use marketing communications as a means of encouraging an increase in brand usage. For instance, advising customers to use a shampoo twice per week rather than once.

◆ The company could promote the brand to a new target audience. For instance, adults with sensitive skin could use shampoos originally designed for babies.

◆ The brand is highly valued and trusted within the marketplace. Thus the company seeks to reinforce that trust and value within the minds of its target audience.

This is far from an exhaustive list, and the reason for a brand's longevity might be unique to a particular brand and the company or organisation that owns it.

■ The disposal or termination of brands

A company may decide to terminate its association with a brand, and either end its life or

Mini case 7.14

Rebrandings too far

The title for this mini case is a variant on the movie *A Bridge Too Far*. Directed by Richard Attenborough, it depicted the true story of the heroic yet flawed strategy of British and American forces in 1944 to capture a series of bridges over the Rhine in a simultaneous operation. It was only partially successful, and at Arnhem in the Netherlands British forces held out for several days under heavy bombardment, yet were unable to capture the bridge successfully. This was the 'bridge too far' which jeopardised the success of the whole operation.

Some companies have carried out highly criticised rebranding exercises, often leading them to rethink their branding strategies.

In January 2001 Royal Mail in the United Kingdom was rebranded as Consignia, a name based on the word 'consign'. By February 2001, under a deluge of criticism, the newly appointed CEO was considering a further name change. In May 2001 Consignia announced that it would replace the name, and by the end of 2001 it was Royal Mail once more. To take another example, in February 2002 the accountancy firm PricewaterhouseCoopers (PwC) announced that it would 'spin off' its business consultancy business in the wake of issues raised by the Enron scandal. The objective was to protect its accountancy business from any potential 'conflict of interest' if the consultancy business provided the same clients as the accountancy side of the business with advice. In order to remove any perceived 'conflict of interest' PwC decided to de-merge and re-branded its global business consulting and technology unit PwC Consulting. Analysts suggested that the new company would be valued at between US$4 billion and US$6 billion.

Originally PwC Consulting was apparently to be re-branded as PwCC. However, the business was rebranded in mid 2002 as 'Monday'. It is estimated that some US$110 million was invested in developing the new brand identity. Greg Brenneman, CEO of PwC Consulting described the rebranding in February 2002 as a 'real word, concise, recognisable, global and the right fit for a company that works hard to deliver results'.

Unfortunately, the unveiling of the name 'Monday' resulted in derision from the media, competitors and PwC employees alike. One of many PwC employees on

the BBC Online News site wrote:

The re-branding was supposed to produce a globally meaningful identity. Obviously PwC's view of global only extends as far as the western, English speaking world. 'Monday' is global in neither a linguistic, nor cultural sense – apologies to the Middle East, where we would be better off being called Saturday.

A PwC internal communication stated (extracts):

We set out to identify a distinctive memorable name, one that would stand out from the consulting 'crowd'. We want it short, global, a real word (not a contrived made-up moniker), and we believe we've succeeded. Finally, as we mentioned earlier, getting used to our new name and infusing it with new associations and attributes will be a process. It will be up to all of us to make our new name stand out from the crowd; to make it a name we can all be proud of. And you'll know when we've achieved this by the look of recognition and respect you get when you say: 'I work at Monday.'

However, by the end of July of 2002, just a few short months after announcing the rebranding, PricewaterhouseCoopers announced that it was selling PwC Consulting to the world's largest information technology company, IBM. IBM paid approximately US$3.5 billion in cash and stock. PwC Consulting was combined with the Business Innovations Services unit of IBM Global Services, creating a new global unit, IBM Consulting Services. As a result of this acquisition IBM created the world's largest consulting services organisation, with operations in more than 160 countries.

Sources: 'PwC to spin off consultancy', BBC News Online, 3 May 2002; 'Monday name change for PwC', BBC News Online, 10 June 2002; 'What happened next Monday?' BBC News Online, 10 June 2002; 'R.I.P Monday', BBC News Online, 31 July 2002; 'IBM to acquire PwC Consulting', press release, PricewaterhouseCoopers, 30 July 2002; Maggie Shiels, 'Hunt is on for world's worst re-branding', BBC News Online, 13 August 2002; 'IBM, PricewaterhouseCoopers complete sale of PwC Consulting', press release, IBM, 2 October 2002.

dispose of it to another company, for a variety of reasons. These reasons include (separately or collectively):

♦ The brand has been in decline in several markets and as a result is providing diminishing revenues and profits. If this is allowed to

Table 7.7 Brand longevity

Brand	Product or service type	Year of introduction	Country of origin
Adidas	Sports footwear	1920s	Germany
Automobile Association	Car recovery company, insurance and on-the-road repairs.	1905	UK
Barbie	Children's doll	1959	USA
BIC	Ballpoint pens, Biros	1950	France
Blue Nun	White wine	1921	Germany
Body Shop	Cosmetics range and retail outlet	1976	UK
Cadbury's Bournville	Chocolate	1908	UK
Chanel	Perfume and clothing	1921	France
Coca-Cola	Cola drink	1886	USA
Dr Pepper	Carbonated drink	1885	USA
Durex	Condoms	1929	UK
Ford Motor Company	Car manufacturer	1903	USA
Gale's	Honey	1919	UK
Gillette	Safety razors	1903	USA
Godzilla	Movie and cartoon character	1954	Japan
Gucci	Leather accessories, luggage and shoes	1923	Italy
Hard Rock Café	Restaurant chain	1971	UK
Harley-Davidson	Motor bikes	1903	USA
Harvard University	University	1636	USA
Hartley's	Fruit jams	1871	UK
Hello Kitty	Merchandising character	1974	Japan
HP Sauce	Spicy sauce	1903	UK

All brand trademarks and registrations are fully acknowledged.

continue, the brand could slip from minor profitability into a loss maker. If the company cannot sell the brand to another company, it will face costs (for example, plant closure and redundancy payments) to cease production and distribution.

◆ Excessive brand proliferation: this is where there are literally too many similar brands in a particular market. In other words, the market is saturated with brands that demonstrate little or no differentiation in features and benefits. This can, for example, result in too many brands vying for the same shelf space in a supermarket. If they have few or no differential features and benefits, consumers might seek out the cheapest. A company may decide to

remove a brand from such a saturated market, especially if it is yielding low returns on investment (both operational and marketing spend). Indeed, some companies have several individual brands competing in this type of marketplace. The removal of the weakest performer could aid the development of the others in a less saturated market. (That assumes there will be no new entrants to the marketplace; but saturation or near saturation should provide a barrier to entry into the market. See Chapter 6 on strategy.)

◆ Declining markets. If the market itself is in decline, the company may decide to dispose of or terminate the brand before the decline affects revenue streams and profitability.

Brand	Product or service type	Year of introduction	Country of origin
IBM	Computer designers and manufacturers, later becoming the world's largest information technology company	1924	USA
Levi Strauss	Denim and work wear	1853	USA
James Bond	Character in novels written by Ian Fleming and published by Jonathan Cape, London.	1953	UK
Kit Kat	Chocolate	1935	UK
Kleenex	Tissues	1924	UK
Marks & Spencer	Retail	1894	UK
Mercedes-Benz	Car manufacturer	1886	Germany
Nescafé	Coffee	1938	Switzerland
Prada	Leather goods and fabrics	1913	Italy
Qantas	International Airline	1920	Australia
Sarsons	Vinegar	1794	UK
Sony	Electronics	1946	Japan
Starbucks	Coffee shops	1971	USA
Star Wars	Movie series	1977	USA
Sun-Pat	Peanut butter	1960s	UK
Toyota	Car manufacturer	1949	Japan
Typhoo	Tea	1903	UK
Virgin Atlantic	International airline	1984	UK
Wrigley's JuicyFruits and Spearmint	Chewing gums	1893	USA

Note: while the brand name may have remained the same, the owners of that particular brand might have also remained the same or have changed over time. What might have been originally US-owned, for example, could now be French-owned.

Companies need to factor into their analysis the cost of plant closures and redundancy payments. Examples of declining markets over the last 100 years include slide rules (replaced by electronic calculators) and typewriters (replaced by computers). However, there remain some viable international markets for both manual and electronic typewriters.

◆ Companies may decide to focus their attention on their core brands, in order to maximise revenue streams and profits from a small but effective set of brands. This is precisely the action taken by Unilever when it implemented the decision to reduce an 1800-brand portfolio down to 400 core brands. (See mini case 7.15.)

◆ Insufficient promotional budgets. Companies with large brand portfolios that have been created over time may be faced with spreading the budget thinly over the full brand range. In the longer term this may be detrimental to the more powerful brands in the company's arsenal, so it could decide to limit the range of brands in order to allocate marketing spend (usually in the form of promotion) to the strongest performers. Of course, there is a risk to this strategy. A strong performer today might be a weak one tomorrow because of factors beyond the control of the company.

◆ Mounting competition. As we keep emphasising, competition is not static, it is a dynamic, constantly evolving force. Companies that

Mini case 7.15

Unilever and its strategy for growth

Unilever is an Anglo-Dutch company which posted a turnover in 2003 of almost €48billion with net profits of almost €3 billion. The sales of its leading brands grew by 2.5 per cent, and these accounted for 93 per cent of its total business. This growth and development is a key part of a strategy that began in February 2000, when the board of Unilever agreed a five-year strategic plan called Paths to Growth.

The key drivers of value creation in the Paths to Growth strategy were:

◆ significant growth of the leading brands

◆ exit from tail brands in a way that would still create value for the company

◆ delivering earnings per share in a quality way to increase gross margins, with profits partly reinvested in additional support for the leading brands

◆ restructuring the business to create a platform for growth

◆ the need for a critical review of under-performing businesses

◆ the creation of an organisational structure that would enable the execution of the Paths for Growth strategy.

The objective was to accelerate top-line growth and increase brand margins. In order to achieve the objectives within the designed time frame, the board decided to focus the company's attention on fewer but stronger brands to achieve significant brand growth. The overall objective, by the end of 2004, was to achieve annual top-line growth of 5 to 6 per cent and operating margins of more than 16 per cent. Growth would also be achieved through

savings of €1.5 billion by the end of 2004 from restructuring and an additional €1.6 billion (by the end of 2002) from global procurement. (This is a different strategy from the Premier Foods strategy discussed on page 135.)

At the start of 2000 Unilever manufactured and distributed some 1600 brands. One of the objectives of the Paths for Growth strategy was to reduce these to 400 core brands. This linked to, and required, an equally significant restructuring of the business. The principal components of the restructuring plan were as follows.

Overall cost

Estimated at €5.0 billion, mainly spent on restructuring.

Brands

The 400 core brands were expected to deliver over 90 per cent of total sales by the end of 2004 (compared with 75 per cent in 1999), with marketing support increased from 13 per cent to 15 per cent of sales by the end of 2004.

Some Unilever brands have a global presence, while others are more regional in focus, for example the food brands PG Tips (tea) and Marmite (yeast spread) in the United Kingdom, Maille (mustard) in France; Breyers (ice cream), Ragú (sauces) and I Can't Believe it's Not Butter (margarine spread) in the United States, and AdeS (a soya-based drink) in Latin America; and the personal products brands Suave and Vaseline in the United States, Lifebuoy (soap) in India, Robljn in the Netherlands, and Cream Silk in the Philippines.

By 2003 14 brands had a global presence and turnovers in excess of €1 billion, compared with one brand in 1993 with the equivalent turnover in real terms.

Disposals or divestments included DiverseyLever, an institutional and industrial cleaning business, to Johnson Wax Professional (the business was renamed Johnson-Diversey), Mazola (oils) in the United States and Loders Croklaan in Europe.

ignore this 21st century trend will face severe damage to their brand, if not total self-destruction. The competitive environment is in a constant state of flux and thus companies need to consider not only current competitors – local, regionally and internationally – but potential newcomers, because they might become major

threats in the future. Because of competitive threats companies might decide to remove brands from certain markets or dispense with them altogether. This action could be taken on the basis that defending the brand's position in the market would be too costly. If the brand is delivering increasingly small contributions to

Supply chain

The plan involved a restructuring of manufacturing sites, with the closure or disposal of 100 sites at a cost of €2.3 billion.

Simplification

The reduction of overheads and streamlining of the corporate centre had an estimated cost of €2.0 billion.

Under-performing businesses

The reorganisation or divestment of businesses that did not meet the required performance targets. (See above under brands, and the discussion about Premier Foods on page 135.)

Bestfood integration

In 2002 Unilever acquired the American company Bestfoods. The objective was to integrate Bestfoods, which would produce savings of €0.8 billion. This sum was exceeded by the second quarter of 2003. The total cost of the integration exercise was €1.2 billion, mostly associated with the reduction in job numbers (through a combination of redundancy, retirement and resignation) and the sale or closure of about 30 sites.

2004 and beyond

By 2010 Unilever aims to generate over €30 billion of ungeared free cashflow and to increase Return on Capital Invested (ROCI) to at least 17 per cent (compared with 12.5 per cent in 2003). These plans are based upon organic growth rather than acquisition. However, between now and 2010 opportunities might arise that Unilever can exploit to its advantage, including the acquisition of all or part of a competitor company.

Sources: Niall FitzGerald, 'Path to Growth Strategy (Summary)', address to Unilever PLC annual meeting by chairman, 7 May 2003; Unilever (2003) 'Path to Growth Summary and Update (Path to Growth Summary and Progress on Implementation, Second Quarter Half Year, 2003'; Unilever (2003) 'Results: Fourth Quarter and Annual Results', Unilever.

the company's balance sheet as a result of competitive forces, it might be a wise decision to dispose of it and bear the close-down costs (a one-off expenditure in that year's trading accounts), in order to focus attention on other valuable brands and perhaps defend their position in the marketplace.

♦ As a result of acquisitions. A company might acquire another company with a large brand portfolio, when the reason for the acquisition is to add particular brands to the existing portfolio. Brands that do not fit strategically into the purchaser's portfolio will either be sold to other companies (often not direct competitors) or closed altogether (with inherent closure costs). While the acquirer has grown through acquisition, this will mean it has remained focused on its core business and not diversified into unfamiliar territories, choosing to dispose of the unrelated brands instead.

Risks associated with brand disposal

The disposal or termination of brands is not a 'cut and dried' decision: there are many issues and risks. These are some, though not all, of the issues companies face when taking such strategic decisions.

♦ Public outcry. Groucutt *et al.* (2004) suggest that consumers may protest when a company says it is considering terminating a particular brand. In 1999, for example, there was a public outcry in the UK when H.J. Heinz announced that it was thinking of ceasing production of its Salad Cream dressing. The reason was clear – significant competition from an array of other salad dressings and varieties of mayonnaise. Whether or not H.J. Heinz had actually 'planned' the termination of its Salad Cream or not, such was the storm of protest that Heinz Salad Cream remained on supermarket shelves, as it does today (November 2005).

♦ Brand switching. A company may decide to terminate or dispose of a brand in the knowledge that it has other similar competing brands within the market, which it wants to develop and grow within its portfolio. However, it does not mean that when the company axes a particular brand, its customers will automatically switch to another brand in the company's portfolio. Customers might either consciously or subconsciously decide to switch to a competitor brand instead. However, if significant numbers of clients switch to rival

Mini case 7.16

Sunny Delight

Doric Foods, located in Florida, USA, created the citrus fruit drink Sunny Delight in 1964. In 1983 Sundor Brands of Connecticut purchased Doric Foods, and in March 1989 Sundor Brands was acquired by Procter & Gamble (P&G). Since then P&G has attempted to expand the market base for its 'citrus punch'.

In the United States P&G has developed the brand's product line to incorporate Tangy Original Florida Style, Smooth California Style, Smooth California Style with Calcium, Lemonade, Tropical Punch Caribbean Style, Mango Style, Lemon & Lime and Intense Sport.

In 1998 P&G launched Sunny Delight in the United Kingdom, with a UK£10 million promotional campaign. Within a year it had become the third biggest-selling soft drink in the country, behind Coca-Cola and Pepsi, grossing UK£160 million, a growth of a staggering 5 224 per cent. The demand was so great that supermarkets had difficulty keeping viable stock levels, and some ran out of stock.

However, unaware to the consumers dark clouds were looming over the brand. Food nutritionists started complaining that it should not call itself a fruit drink as there was only some 5 per cent fruit content. Also

the UK's Food Commission was begin to consider what was actually contained with this soft drink. According to the Food Commission the marketing campaign had 'attributed' certain 'healthy benefits' to the drink. The Food Commission was concerned as to the justification of these 'attributes'. Subsequent negative publicity alerted consumers and they began to lose faith in the product. Poor advertising only added to the negative reaction from consumers.

By 2001 sales had fallen by over 35 per cent, as Sunny Delight had been hit by the perception that it was less healthy than more natural fruit drink brands.

In March 2002 P&G relaunched the brand as Sunny D, backed by a UK£312 million promotional campaign. It increased the fruit content to 15 per cent and launched four flavours with no added sugar. This added up to a significant makeover of the brand. However, by late 2003 P&G was seeking to sell the brand.

Sources: J. Clayton, 'The rise and fall of Sunny Delight', *The Money Programme*, BBC television, 3 December 2003; 'Delight debut for soft drink', BBC News Online, 15 August 1999; 'Sunny slumps in UK brand chart', BBC News Online, 8 August 2001; 'Sunny makeover to lift sales gloom', BBC News Online, 20 February 2002; Procter & Gamble, www.pg.com.

brands then the removal of the company's brand from the market will have achieved little in the way of developing the other brands within the portfolio.

♦ The potential reduction of the company's revenue streams. If large-scale brand culling takes place, even over a few years, the company runs the risk of incurring reduced revenue and hence (possibly) reduced profitability. This might be a short-term reduction in revenue and profit for which the company can gain the support of its stakeholders. If it has developed an effective disposable and growth strategy, its remaining brands should have the opportunity to become increasingly profitable over the medium and longer term.

♦ Costs of termination. There is always a cost associated with exiting a market and/or terminating a brand. These costs usually (though not always) include severance pay for staff made

redundant, contracting specialists to remove plant and possibly demolish buildings and clear the site, hiring public relations teams to communicate to various stakeholders why production of the brand is ending, and human resource teams to advise staff facing redundancy.

♦ New ownership. There are several issues associated with selling a brand to potential owners, such as:

● The sale price. It has to be set at a level that compensates the company, at least in the short term, for the loss of revenue generated, cost of disposal and potential profit. However the potential purchaser may be reluctant to acquire the brand if it has been starved of promotion over the long term and the current owner is asking a relatively high price. The purchaser must be sure that it will add value to its portfolio.

● There may be risks associated with selling the brand. This may be especially the case if the brand owner has similar products in its portfolio. Sellers must consider whether the acquirer could use the brand to help build a portfolio to challenge its own brands in the marketplace. A company on the acquisition trail might buy brands from several companies in order to build a portfolio that will challenge the position of another company, which could be one of the sellers.

● An acquirer does not have to be an established company. It can be a new business with significant financial resources that is acquiring brands to build a strong portfolio in the marketplace in order challenge existing market leaders. (Here you may want to reflect on Porter's five forces model and potential or real barriers to entry.)

◆ The impact on local communities. There is often a social impact to brand culling, especially if it means plant closure or the transfer of jobs to a new location. The level of social impact depends on factors such as the structure of the local community, the size of the plant being closed, the level of local unemployment, local job prospects and the number of other industries within the area, and the level of fall-out on other businesses that had depended on business from the company. Companies need to factor in these issues when they consider brand culling which will result in plant closure. Apart from the impact on communities, companies might face a public relations backlash that in turn affects consumer confidence and its share price (if it is listed on a stock market).

■ Chapter summary

This chapter has considered how brands are developed and how they can sustain their position in an increasingly competitive marketplace. Brands clearly have an emotional value or appeal to customers, but customers do not always remain loyal to a particular brand.

It is one thing to gain a competitive advantage, but it can be quite another to sustain it. Companies seek to use and develop their brands as a means of sustaining competitive advantage. This drive for sustainability is witnessed through the re-energising of brands and the focus on core brand development.

Purely American or UK brands no longer populate the brand landscape. With the development of globalisation, the Internet and 'freer' trade there are now significantly more brands emerging from Asia and the Far East. These brands display the features and benefits of Western brands, but often at highly competitive prices. Competition within the brand arena is most likely to become significantly more complex in the future.

■ Questions for review and reflection

1 Critically evaluate the risks of having a brand achieve cult status.

2 Compare and contrast the different types of branding that an organisation can adopt. Do you think some companies may have adopted the wrong brand structure? Please cite possible examples and provide evidence for your view.

3 Critically evaluate the rationale for rebranding a product or service. Are there any cases where you think the product should not have been rebranded? If so, state why, with supporting evidence for your belief.

4 Critically evaluate why some brands appear to have a very short life span while others have a much longer one. Are there any lessons that can be learnt from studying brand longevity?

5 'Non-profit organisations can offer considerable value to their customers through an association with their brand.' Critically examine this statement.

6 With fellow students debate a case for and against the branding of a product or service.

7 What is meant by the term 'brand extension'? Consider the positive and negative aspects of a company using a brand extension policy. Provide evidential support for both cases.

8 'If you can build a powerful brand you will have a powerful marketing programme.'

Provide a critical evaluation of branding within marketing.

9   Compare and contrast B2B and B2C branding.

10 Explain why brand valuations and equity are an important asset to an organisation.

■ References

Aaker, D (1991) *Managing Brand Equity*, New York: Free Press.

Barlow, J. and Maul, D. (2000) *Emotional Value*, San Francisco: Berrett-Koehler.

Business Week (2003) 'Best global brands', *Business Week*, European edn, 5 August.

Christensen, C. R., Berg, N. A. and Salter, M. S. (1980) *Policy Formation and Administration: A casebook for senior management problems in business*, 8th edn, Irwin, Ill.: Homewood.

Cooper, R.G. and Kleinschmidt, E. J. (1991b) *New Products: The key factors in success*, Chicago: AMA.

Czinkota, M. R., Ronkainen, I. A., Moffet, M. H. and Moynihan, E. O. (1998) *Global Business*, Fort Worth: Dryden Press.

Dibb, S., Simkin, L., Pride. W. M. and Ferrell. O. C. (1997) *Marketing: Concepts and strategies*, 3rd edn, Boston, Mass.: Houghton Mifflin.

Euromonitor (2003) 'Textile washing products in the UK', *Euromonitor Research*, July.

Euromonitor (2004a) 'Retailing developments: private label trends', in 'Aspects of retailing: global OTC healthcare distribution', *Euromonitor Research*, February.

Goldfarb, A. (2001)' Let there be Sunlight! The rise of Lever Brothers and Sunlight Soap', working paper, Northwestern University.

Hillman, D. and Gibbs, D. (1998) *Century Makers*, London: Weidenfeld & Nicolson.

Hilton, S. (2001) 'Take the wrap', *Guardian* G2, 8 June, pp. 2–3.

ICC (2004) 'Counterfeit products – overview', Counterfeit Intelligence Bureau, ICC Commercial Crime Services, www.icc-ccs.org.

Jeremy, D. J. (1998) *A Business History of Britain, 1900–1990s*, Oxford: Oxford University Press.

Kaikati, J. G. and Kaikati, A. B. (2004) 'Identity crisis: the dos and don'ts of brand rechristening', *Marketing Management*, January/February, pp. 45–9.

Kapferer, J-N. (1998) *Strategic Brand Management: Creating and sustaining brand equity long term*, 2nd edn, London: Kogan Page.

Keller, K. L. (1993) 'Conceptualizing, measuring and managing customer-based brand equity', *Journal of Marketing* 57(1), January, pp. 1–22.

Koehn, N. F. (1999) 'Henry Heinz and brand creation in the late nineteenth century', *Harvard Business School Working Knowledge*, 7 December.

Kotler, P. (2000) *Marketing Management*, Millennium edn, Harlow: Prentice Hall.

Leverfaberge (2004) www.leverfaberge.co.uk/aboutus/history.html

McBride (2004) www.mcbride.co.uk.

Mintel (2004) *Holiday Centres – UK*, Mintel International, January.

Pavitt, J. (2000) *Brand New*, London: V& A Publications.

van Dulken, S. (2000) *Inventing the 20th Century: 100 inventions that shaped the world*, London: British Library.

Virgin (2004) Company details accessed from corporate website, www.virgin.com.

PART
3

The Marketing Mix

The Marketing Mix and Relationship Marketing

Learning outcomes

After completing this chapter you should be able to:

▶ explain the origins of the marketing mix

▶ debate the possible rationale for extensions to the original 4Ps of the marketing mix

▶ explain the development of relationship marketing

▶ debate the merits of the different schools of thought – the marketing mix versus relationship marketing

▶ consider how transaction-oriented and relationship marketing can work in concert with each other.

Contents

Learning outcomes 155
Introduction 155
The marketing mix
 debate 155
The origins of the
 marketing mix 156
Rationale for extending
 the marketing mix 158
Marketing mix network
 or architecture 159
Relationship
 marketing 160
What is a relationship? 160
Chapter summary 164
Questions for review
 and reflection 164
References 164

■ Introduction

This chapter examines the development of two key concepts in marketing, the marketing mix and relationship marketing. It is the view of many authors that the marketing mix is the foundation of the marketing subject. Indeed it is the view of this author that the mix can be extended to include a total of 10 Ps. A rationale is developed for such an extension, that is continued in the chapters that follow. However, not all authors agree with the basic concept of the marketing mix, believing it to be out of place in contemporary society. Their belief is that relationship marketing provides a firm bedrock for the future development of marketing. This rationale will be examined. However, it is not my contention to dismiss relationship marketing in favour of the marketing mix. On the contrary, the reason for placing them together is that it is my belief that they can work in tandem. There is, if you like, a relationship between the two concepts that can help in supporting each other. This rationale is explored within this chapter.

■ The marketing mix debate

First let's consider the development of the marketing mix. Since the 1950s and 1960s the marketing mix model has been widely considered a cornerstone of marketing. However, much debate and controversy surrounds the development and continued use of this framework. In this section two fundamental issues are considered:

◆ the origins of the marketing mix

◆ the rationale for extending the mix from the original 4Ps.

The origins of the marketing mix

Marketing academics and students tend to believe that the marketing mix originated as the 4Ps. However, during the 1940s and 1950s several researchers were debating the link between certain combinations of price and product. In 1948 Culliton (of the Harvard Business School) in his study of manufacturer's marketing costs described the business executive as a:

'decider,' and 'artist' – a 'mixer of ingredients,' who sometimes follows a recipe prepared by others, sometimes prepares his own recipe as he goes along, sometimes adapts a recipe to the ingredients immediately available, and sometimes experiments with or invents ingredients no one else has tried.

(Culliton 1948 and Borden 1964)

We see clearly here the view that business executives mixed elements together in order to effectively market their product.[1] Culliton's phrase appealed directly to Neil H. Borden, also of Harvard Business School, who melded the phrase 'mixer of ingredients' into the 'marketing mix' (Borden 1964). For him it consisted of important elements or ingredients that comprised a marketing programme (Borden 1964). Borden's original 'marketing mix of

Table 8.1 Borden's original marketing mix structure

Element	Description
Product planning	Policies and procedures relating to: • product lines to be offered – qualities and design • markets to sell – to whom, where, when and in what quantity? • new product policy – research and development programmes.
Pricing	Policies and procedures relating to: • the appropriate pricing levels to adopt • specific prices to adopt • pricing policy – one price or varying price or maintaining a constant price • margins to adopt – for the company and the industry.
Branding	Policies and procedures relating to: • selection of trade-marks, patents and copyrights • brand policy – individualised or family brand • sale as a private label or unbranded.
Channels of distribution	Policies and procedures relating to: • channels to use between plant and the end consumer • degree and selectivity among wholesalers and retailers • efforts to gain co-operation of the industry.
Personal selling	Policies and procedures relating to: • the burden to be placed on personal selling and the methods to be employed in manufacturer's organisation, the wholesale segment of the industry and retail segment of the industry.
Advertising	Policies and procedures relating to: • amount to spend – that is, the burden to be placed on advertising • copy platform to adopt – both product and corporate image to be desired • mix of advertising – to the related industry, through the industry, and to consumers.

manufacturers' contained 12 components as outlined in Table 8.1.

Borden did not believe that his list was definitive, and suggested that others might have different perspectives. However, it was E. Jerome McCarthy who in the 1960s developed the mnemonic the '4Ps' which has become the most enduring of the marketing mix frameworks (McCarthy 1965). McCarthy regrouped Borden's 12 elements into:

◆ product

◆ price

◆ promotion

◆ placement (also known as place, for distribution).

As stated earlier this has probably become the most enduring and widely recognised concept in marketing. However what have been its key contributions to marketing? These perhaps can be listed as follows:

◆ It provided a central organised structure or foundation for marketing activity, which managers and company executives could relate to and easily understand, at least in principle.

◆ This structure could be used for any product within any environment. It was not solely linked to marketing activities within the US marketplace.

◆ Each of these elements could in turn be considered as a 'mix; for example product mix, promotion mix, price mix and so on (McCarthy 1965).

Element	Description
Promotions	Policies and procedures relating to: • the burden to place on special selling plans or devices directed at or through the industry • form of these devices for consumer promotions and for industry (B2B) promotions.
Packaging	Policies and procedures relating to: • formulation of packaging and labelling.
Display	Policies and procedures relating to: • the burden to be placed on display to help create and maintain sales • the methods to adopt to secure display within point of sale locations, for example a department store or bookshop.
Servicing	Policies and procedures relating to: • providing the services needed.
Physical handling	Policies and procedures relating to: • warehousing • transportation • inventories.
Fact finding and analysis	Policies and procedures relating to: • securing, analysis, and the use of facts in marketing operations (in essence this was market and marketing research).

Source: adapted from Borden (1964).

Originally McCarthy (1965) defined the marketing mix as:

> A combination of all the factors at a marketing manager's command to satisfy the target market.

With Perreault, he later revised this statement to

> The controllable variables that an organization can co-ordinate to satisfy the target market.
> (McCarthy and Perreault 1987)

McCarthy (1965) makes an interesting linkage here to target market: 'The marketing mix is not a stand-alone model.... The focus has to be on the target market, otherwise the mix cannot succeed'. It was also around this time that Wendell Smith (1956) postulated his work on segmentation, and the two concepts are complementary.

As Baker (1997) contends, it is the manipulation of the elements within the marketing mix that provides a strategic framework for marketing. To some extent this links back to Culliton's vision of the executive as a mixer of ingredients.

Rationale for extending the marketing mix

Yudelson (1999) suggests that there have been six major challenges to McCarthy's 4P framework:

◆ A focus on the customer via the marketing concept or orientation. (However, it can be considered that the customer is the nucleus of all marketing mix decisions.)

◆ The broadening of marketing to include not-for-profit, services, good causes (charities) and even politics. (Thus the need to broaden the marketing mix to embrace services in the widest sense of the term.)

◆ Identification of exchange transactions as the core of marketing. (In one form or another everyone is involved to a greater or lesser degree in an exchange. This may even be a combination of tangible and intangible benefits. For example, making a donation to charity is a transaction. A tangible asset (money) is given to the charity. The giver receives in exchange the intangible asset of feeling good about what he or she has just done.)

◆ The introduction of Total Quality Management (TQM), with the emphasis on customer satisfaction. (The elements of the marketing mix must also perform to standards that satisfy the needs and wants of customers.)

◆ The extension from transaction marketing to relationship marketing. (As will be examined later, there are links between the two concepts.)

◆ Identification of the company or organisation as a member of a complete value chain

---

Table 8.2 McCarthy's 4Ps

Mix variable or component	Description and comments
Product	Traditionally this has been called a 'good'. It has origins in economics (see Chapter 1). It can be considered as a collection of features and benefits that provide customer satisfaction.
Price	This is considered the only element of the mix to be revenue generating, in the pure sense, again a link back to economics. However, price reflects more than the economic cost of producing the product. There is also the value perceived in the mind of the customer.
Promotion	Here the full range of marketing communication activities are considered, including advertising, direct marketing, face-to-face selling, public relations, sales promotions and word of mouth.
Place (placement or distribution)	This covers location, distribution channels and logistics.

(Porter's value chain model is examined in Chapter 6). (While this is true, it can also be argued that the marketing mix supports the principles of the value chain. Consider, for instance, placement in terms of logistics within the value chain.)

As Yudelson (1999) suggests, McCarthy's 4Ps provided a suitable and effective nomenclature for the study and analysis of marketing. However with the greater expansion of marketing beyond a product–sales orientation into services, there was concern that the 4Ps did not relate to services. Magrath (1986) was one of the first (along with Booms and Bitner 1981) to postulate that the 4Ps should be expanded to encompass personnel, physical facilities and process management. (See Table 8.4, page 162, for the Booms and Bitner extended model.)

Since the 1960s there has been no shortage of ideas and suggestions for extending the marketing mix. Table 8.3 (overleaf) provides a list, with proposers, of some 30 possible marketing mix extensions. Of those listed, three have become part of what is now the generic marketing mix (see Table 8.4).

There has been great debate about the validity of some of these suggestions. It is beyond the scope of this textbook to evaluate critically each of the recommendations. However, students interested in pursuing this further are encouraged to seek out the various research papers listed in the bibliography.

As you can see from Table 8.3, there is a diversity of views on how the marketing mix framework can be enlarged. However Rafiq and Ahmed (1995) contend that the proliferation of numerous ad hoc conceptualisations has undermined the concept of the marketing mix, and what is required is a more coherent approach.

As we indicated, there has been concern that the classic 4Ps do not incorporate the characteristics of services, such as inherent intangibility, perishability, heterogeneity (variability), inseparability and ownership. However Table 8.3 shows that the 4Ps can be extended to incorporate factors that bind them to a service orientation. As Rafiq and Ahmed (1995) suggest, the most influential to date of the alternative frameworks has been Booms and Bitner's 7Ps marketing mix (1981). Booms and Bitner extended the 4Ps to

include participants (now referred to in the literature as people), physical evidence (the physicality of the environment) and process (see Table 8.4, page 162).

In their original article Booms and Bitner (1981) intended their additional 3Ps to be limited to service marketing. However, there are academics and writers, for example Levitt, who suggest that 'there are only industries whose service components are greater or lesser than those of other industries. Everybody is in service' (Levitt 1972). Raqif and Ahmed (1995) contended that a marketing mix was needed that cut across the boundaries of goods, services and industrial marketing – a generic marketing mix. Increasingly the Booms and Bitner marketing mix framework has been adopted to meet that need.

My own feeling is that the generic marketing mix of 7Ps is all well and good. However, there are three key fundamentals that need to be added to create a well-rounded and fully integrated marketing mix (see Table 8.5, page 163).

Marketing mix network or architecture

The Marketing Mix can be seen as a network or architecture where all the elements that comprise the mix are interconnected (Figure 8.1). In Chapter 6 it was said that the elements of the marketing mix are presented as separate entities for the purpose of presentation. In reality they should be viewed in a

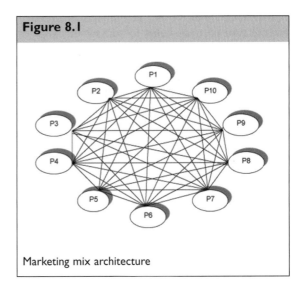

Figure 8.1

Marketing mix architecture

Table 8.3 Possible additions to the marketing mix

Addition	Authors and notes
Packaging	Mason (1958), Nickels and Jolson (1976), Asher (1987), Patty (1997). Mason's article precedes McCarthy's original work on the marketing mix.
Partition (segmenting the market)	Kotler (1991)
People	Booms and Bitner (1981) – their original suggestion was participants – Johnson (1986), Judd (1987), Payne and Ballantyne (1991), Baker (1997)
Penalty	Yudelson (1999)
Perception/perceive	Johnson (1986) and Yudelson (1999)
Performance/perform	Johnson (1986), Harvey, Lusch and Cavarkapa (1996) and Yudelson (1999)
Personalisation	Goldsmith (1999)
Personnel	Magrath (1986)
Physical Evidence	Booms and Bitner (1981) Magrath (1986) – he suggested physical facilities
Plan	Johnson (1986)
Planning	Harvey, Lusch and Cavarkapa (1996)
Politics	Arndt (1979), Harvey, Lusch and Cavarkapa (1996)
Political-based marketing decisions	Wind (1985)
Portfolio of market segments	Wind (1985)
Portfolio of products by segments by distribution outlets	Wind (1985)
Portfolio of countries by mode of entry	Wind (1985)

holistic form. Thus looking at them as a network or architecture perhaps helps to convey this web or interconnected approach.

■ Relationship marketing

What is a relationship?

The *Oxford English Reference Dictionary* provides five definitions (Pearsall and Trumble 1996):

♦ The fact or state of being related.

♦ A connection or association (enjoyed a good working relationship)

♦ An emotional (esp. sexual) association between two people.

♦ A condition or character due to being related.

♦ Kinship.

Since the 1980s there has been a growing body of work on the relationship between suppliers and buyers. Berry (1983) introduced the term 'relationship marketing' within a services marketing context. He viewed it as a strategy to attract, maintain and enhance customer relationships. Grönroos (2000a) defined relationship marketing as:

The process of identifying and establishing, maintaining, enhancing, and when necessary terminating relationships with customers and other stakeholders, at a profit,[2] so that the objectives of all parties involved are met, where this is

Addition	Authors and notes
Position/positioning	Trout (1969), Wind (1985), Brown, (1991), Kotler (1991) and Bixler (1991) have all suggested positioning as a marketing mix variable, although that has been disputed by writers such as Anderson and Taylor (1995)
Power	Kotler (1986)
Predict	Johnson (1986)
Preservation	LeDoux (1991)
Prioritise (specifying markets to target)	Kotler (1991)
Probability	Harvey, Lusch and Cavarkapa (1996)
Probing	Borden and Marshall (1959), Traynor (1985) – probing (to cover market and marketing research – and Johnson (1986). Borden had included 'fact finding and analysis' in his original marketing mix. Kotler (1991).
Program	Wind (1985)
Process/processes	Booms and Bitner (1981), Magrath (1986) – who suggested process management – Payne and Ballantyne (1991) and Yudelson (1999)
Professional	Johnson (1986)
Profit	Wright (2003)
Psychology	Groucutt (2003a)
Publics	Harvey, Lusch and Cavarkapa (1996)
Public relations	Goodrich, Gildea and Cavanaugh (1979), Mindak and Fine(1981), Wind (1985) and Kotler (1986). Wind (1985) called his public relations and public affairs.
Purpose	Johnson (1986)

done by a mutual giving and fulfillment of promises.

Gummesson (2002) defines relationship marketing as 'marketing based on interaction within networks of relationships'. He continues, 'A *network* is a set of relationships which can grow into enormously complex patterns.... In the relationships, the simple dyad as well as the complex networks, the parties enter into active contact with each other. This is called *interaction*' (italics in original).

Rapp and Collins (1990) go further by stating that the goals of relationship marketing are to create and maintain lasting relationships between the organisation and its customers which are mutually rewarding. Håkansson and Snehota (1995) suggest that a 'relationship is a mutually oriented interac-tion between two reciprocally committed parties'. Grönroos (2000b) suggested that in terms of service marketing the' relationship has developed when a customer perceives that a mutual way of thinking exists between the customer and supplier or service provider'.

Blomqvist, Dahl and Haeger (1993) provide an outline of what they see as the key characteristics of relationship marketing:

◆ Every customer is considered an individual person or unit.

◆ Activities of the company or organisation are predominately directed towards existing customers.

◆ It is based upon interactions and dialogues.

Table 8.4 Booms and Bitner's extensions for the marketing mix

Mix component	Comment
People (participants)	This includes customers, employees and suppliers. These are the various 'communities' involved in the marketing relationship. There is also a link here to the micro environment as examined in Chapter 2.
Physical evidence (physicality)	These are the tangible aspects (or physicality) associated with the 'delivery' of the product or service. For example, the physicality of a supermarket includes the layout of the store, the positioning of the checkout counters, the height of the shelving and how products are displayed on those shelves. The physicality of the supermarket influences the buying behaviour of customers. For example, is it a welcoming easy-to-use environment? Equally, the table positions within a restaurant convey something of the ambient environment. The restaurant's management may want to fit as many tables and chairs as possible into the restaurant (to maximise revenue potential). However, too close proximity to other people eating might deter people from going to the restaurant, because they know that their conversations will be overheard.
Process	These are the assembly or flow activities that support the fulfilment of the marketing mix: for example the use of barcodes and bar code scanners, and automated till systems to speed processing at the checkout counter at the supermarket. These processes benefit both customers (efficient service) and the supermarket (increased throughput and stock control updates).

◆ The company or organisation is trying to achieve profitability through the decrease of customer turnover and the strengthening of customer relationships.

However, there remains the issue of what really constitutes a relationship. Zolkiewski (2004) asks, can relationship marketing be applied ubiquitously? In other words, can it be applied to all situations? For that is arguably its *raison d'être*. In Zolkiewski's analysis, 'most writers simply talk about relationships or a move from a transactional [Often stated as the marketing mix approach] to a relational approach'.

Zolkiewski (2004) questions the notion of the relationship. She notes that 'If there is a mutual commitment between the supplier or service provider and the customer then possibly a true marketing relationship can be said to exist. Even so, do both parties believe that they are in a relationship?' She continues:

This is not to deny that relationships are a critical part of many aspects of marketing, but it could be argued that this is only truly apparent in certain contexts. For example, relationships are evident and persistent in many business-to-business contexts , but not all.

Hunt and Morgan (1994) argue that that the process of relationship marketing lies in the development and growth of trust and commitment among partners. They define trust as a 'willingness to rely on an exchange partner in whom one has confidence and commitment … as … an enduring desire to maintain a valued partnership'. They suggest that trust receives positive support from communication and shared values. Relationship commitment is sustained through shared values together with relationship benefits and relationship termination costs (ending the relationship has a cost to be borne by both parties). Morris, Barnes and Lynch (1999) suggest that these variables collectively act positively upon commitment.

Lijander and Roos (2002) investigated the relationship between after-sales service customers and an authorised car dealership. They concluded that there was a continuum, with true relationships at one end and spurious relationships at the other. They define a true customer service relationship as the biased (non-random) behavioural responsive (purchases, word of mouth, information sharing

Table 8.5 Further extensions to the marketing mix

Mix component	Comment
Psychology	Although economics has contributed significantly to the understanding of marketing within a macro environment (see Chapter 2) and pricing (see Chapter 11), psychology significantly underpins so much of contemporary marketing. There is increasingly the need to understand how and why people buy the products and services that they do. Understanding their behaviour helps companies to supply the right product or service at the right time to support buyer behaviour. This is far from new. Consider for instance the work of Strong (1925), Bernays (1920s–1950s), Ditchter (1960) and others which all point to the use and value of psychology in marketing.
Packaging	For many years packaging has been positioned uncomfortably between product and promotion. However, packaging is often so fundamental to the success of a product or service that it cannot really be subsumed into either.
Performance	Performance is often associated with the features and benefits of a product, for example, the performance of an Aston Martin sports car. However, performance is much more than features and benefits. It links, for example, to TQM (one of the suggested challenges to the marketing mix framework – Yudelson 1999), people, processes and economics.

and other positive behaviours), expressed over time by some decision-making unit with respect to one service provider out of a set of such providers, which is a function of psychological (cognitive and effective) processes, including the presence of trust, relationship benefits and the absence of negative bonds, resulting in service–provider commitment. They view a spurious customer relationship as the biased (non-random) behavioural response (purchase), expressed over time, by some decision-making unit, with respect to one or more alternative service providers out of a set of such providers, which is a function of inertia, trust deficit, weak or absent relationship benefits and/or the existence of negative bonds.

Although this was only a small-scale study, it is important to recognise that some customers are engaged in a variety of different types of relationships. Some will be deemed strong while others are weak. However it is very difficult to define the terms 'strong' and 'weak'. They are perhaps dependent on the perception of the individuals involved. As Zolkiewski (2004) suggests, there needs to be 'a move away from the one-size fits all premise'.

Some of the debate surrounding the marketing mix and relationship marketing focuses on the words 'transaction' and 'exchange'. Much has been written about relationship marketing being a paradigm shift from traditional marketing frameworks (that is, the marketing mix).

As Bagozzi (1975) has suggested, marketers have tended to focus on exchange theory being direct transfers of tangible entities between two parties. He argues that marketing exchanges are often indirect, may involve intangible and symbolic aspects, and that more than two parties may participate. Grönroos (2004) states that:

> The relationship marketing perspective is based on the notion that on top of the value of products and/or services that are exchanged, the existence of a relationship between the two parties creates additional value for the customer and also for the supplier or service provider.

Thus it could perhaps be argued that there is a link between the marketing mix and relationship marketing. Figure 8.2 suggests that the customer is in the centre, involved in a relationship marketing interaction. It is only by understanding what the customer requires (the interaction) that elements of the marketing mix can interact (in some form) with the customer. However, it is important to consider the level and depth of the relationship. As we have seen, not all relationships have meaning, so we need to consider where the customer–supplier relationship sits on the continuum. That, however, can only really be judged by the individuals involved in each situation or encounter.

Figure 8.2

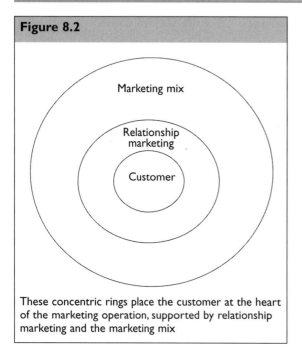

These concentric rings place the customer at the heart of the marketing operation, supported by relationship marketing and the marketing mix

■ Chapter summary

This chapter has examined the development of the marketing mix and relationship marketing. Both concepts have made considered contributions to the development of marketing, both theoretical and practical.

The marketing mix has developed from an original 4P concept to a generic 7Ps that has enhanced the involvement of services. However, it is suggested that there is an opportunity to develop the generic 7P framework further by adding a further 3Ps, psychology, packaging and performance. This is not the first time that additions have been suggested. However, it is believed that these are in keeping with the spirit of the marketing mix and fit the contemporary world.

Much has been written on the development of relationship marketing. However, there has been debate about what actually constitutes a relationship, and whether everyone seeks a relationship with customers or suppliers. Equally, it has been argued that the marketing mix is purely a transactional exchange framework that does not support a relationship approach. It is clear that both frameworks have their flaws, perhaps like any other models or concepts. Nonetheless it is believed that

both frameworks are linked, depending on the nature of the relationship and transactions taking place. It is viewed here that one framework does not replace another. Instead that they can work in collaboration with each other.

■ Questions for review and reflection

1   Briefly outline the development of the marketing mix framework.

2   Critically review the case for and against the continuing use of the marketing mix framework as a key platform for marketing operations. What is your perspective on the marketing mix? Support your view with evidence.

3   The author believes that there is a fundamental synergy between the marketing mix and relationship marketing. Critically evaluate this point of view.

4   Relationship marketing places the customer at the heart of the marketing operation. Do you believe that this is the case in the real world? Support your view with evidence.

5   Working with fellow students, debate the merits and demerits of extending the marketing mix beyond the current 7Ps.

■ References

Anderson, L. M. and Taylor, R. L. (1995) 'McCarthy's 4Ps: timeworn or time-tested?' *Journal of Marketing Theory and Practice*, Summer, pp. 1–9.

Arndt, J. (1979) 'Toward a concept of domesticated markets', *Journal of Marketing* **43** (Fall), pp. 69–75.

Asher, J. (1987) 'Packaging: the interactive fifth "p" of marketing', *Marketing Review*, January, pp. 21–3.

Bagozzi, R. P. (1975) 'Marketing as exchange', *Journal of Marketing* **39** (October), pp. 32–9.

Baker, M. J. (1997) 'People: the fifth P of marketing', in J. Yudelson (1999) 'Adapting McCarthy's four P's for the twenty-first century', *Journal of Marketing Education* **21**(1) (April), pp. 60–7.

Bernays, E. (1923) *Crystallizing Public Opinion*, New York: Boni & Liveright.

Berry, L. L. (1983) 'Relationship marketing', in L. L. Berry, G. L. Shostack and G. Upah (eds), *Emerging Perspectives on Service Marketing*, Chicago: AMA.

Bixler, M. (1991) 'Maintaining your marketing consistency', *Small Business Reports* 16 (January), pp. 27–34.

Blomqvist, R., Dahl, J. and Haeger, T. (1993) *Relationsmarknadsföring: strategi och metod i servicekonkurrens* (Relationship Marketing Strategy and Methods for Service Operations), Gothenburg: IHM Publishing.

Booms, B. H. and Bitner, M. J. (1981) 'Marketing strategies and organization structures for service firms', in J. H. Donnely and W. R. George (eds), *Marketing of Services*, Chicago: AMA.

Borden, N. H. (1964) 'The concept of the marketing mix', *Journal of Advertising Research*, June, pp. 2–7.

Borden, N. H. and Marshall, M. V. (1959) *Advertising Management: Texts and cases*, Illinois: Irwin.

Brown, R. (1991) 'Making the product portfolio a basis for action', *Long Range Planning* 24(1), pp. 102–10.

Culliton, J. W. (1948) *The Management of Marketing Costs*, Division of Research, Graduate School of Business Administration, Harvard University, Cambridge, Mass.

Dichter, E. (1960) *The Strategy of Desire*, New York: Doubleday.

Goldsmith, R. E. (1999) 'The personalized marketplace: beyond the 4Ps', *Marketing Intelligence and Planning* 17(4), pp. 178–85.

Goodrich, J., Gildea, R. L. and Cavanaugh, K. (1979) 'A place for public relations in the marketing mix', *MSU Business Topics* 27 (Autumn), pp. 53–7.

Grönroos, C. (1997) 'From marketing mix to relationship marketing: towards a paradigm shift in marketing', *Management Decision* 35(3/4), pp. 322–40.

Grönroos, C. (2000a) 'Relationship marketing: the Nordic School perspective', in J. N. Sheth and A. Pavatiyar (eds), *Handbook of Relationship Marketing*, London: Sage.

Grönroos, C. (2000b) *Service Management and Marketing: A customer relationship management approach*, 2nd edn, Chichester: Wiley.

Grönroos, C. (2004) 'The relationship marketing process: communication, interaction, dialogue, value', *Journal of Business and Industrial Marketing* 19(2), pp. 99–113.

Groucutt, J. (2003a) 'Extending the marketing mix', Working paper.

Gummesson, E. (2002) *Total Relationship Marketing*, 2nd edn, Oxford: Butterworth-Heinemann.

Håkansson, H. and Snehota, I. (eds) (1995) *Developing Relationships in Business Networks*, London: Routledge.

Harvey, M. G., Lusch, R. F. and Cavarkapa, B. (1996) 'A marketing mix for the 21st century', *Journal of Marketing Theory and Practice* (Fall), pp. 1–15.

Hunt, S. and Morgan, R. (1994) 'The commitment-trust theory or relationship marketing', *Journal of Marketing* 58, pp. 20–38.

Johnson, A. A. (1986) 'Adding more P's to the pod or 12 essential elements of marketing', *Marketing News*, 11 April, p. 2.

Judd, V. C. (1987) 'Differentiate with the 5th P: people', *Industrial Marketing Management* 16, pp. 241–7.

Kotler, P. (1986) 'Megamarketing', *Harvard Business Review* 64 (March–April), pp. 117–24.

Kotler, P (1991) *Marketing Management*, New Jersey: Prentice Hall.

LeDoux, L. (1991) 'Is preservation the fifth 'p' or just another macro environmental factor?', in G. F. McKinnon and G. A. Kelley (eds), *Challenges of a New Decade in Marketing*, Western Marketing Educators Association, pp. 82–6.

Levitt, T. (1972) 'Production line approach to service', *Harvard Business Review* (September–October), pp. 41–52.

Lijander, V. and Roos, I. (2002) 'Customer-relationship levels – from spurious to true relationships', *Journal of Services Marketing* 16(7), pp. 593–614.

Magrath, A. J. (1986) 'When marketing services, 4P's are not enough', *Business Horizons* 29 (May–June), pp. 44–50.

Mason, W. R. (1958) 'A theory of packaging in the marketing mix', *Business Horizons*, Summer, pp. 91–5.

McCarthy, E. J. (1965) *Basic Marketing*, Homewood, Ill: Irwin.

McCarthy, E. J. and Perreault Jr.,W. D. (1987) *Basic Marketing*, 9th edn, Homewood, Ill.: Irwin.

Mindak, W. A. and Fine, S. (1981). 'A fifth 'p': public relations', in J. H. Donnely and W. R. George (eds), *Marketing of Services*, Chicago: AMA.

Morris, D. S., Barnes, B. R. and Lynch, J. E. (1999) 'Relationship marketing needs total quality management', *Total Quality Management* **10**(4/5), July, pp. 659–66.

Nickels, W. G. and Jolson, M. A. (1976) 'Packaging: the fifth 'p' in the marketing mix?', *SAM Advanced Management Journal,* Winter, pp. 13–21.

Patty, T. (1997) 'Mastering the new five P's of marketing', in J. Yudelson (1999) 'Adapting McCarthy's four P's for the twenty-first century', *Journal of Marketing Education* **21**(1) (April), pp. 60–7.

Payne, C. M. A. and Ballantyne, D. (1991) *Relationship Marketing: Bringing quality, customer service and marketing together,* Oxford: Butterworth-Heinemann.

Pearsall, J. and Trumble, B. (eds) (1996) *The Oxford English Reference Dictionary,* 2nd edn, Oxford: Oxford University Press.

Rafiq, M. and Ahmed, P. K. (1995) 'Using the 7Ps as a generic marketing mix: an exploratory survey of UK and European marketing academics', *Marketing Intelligence and Planning* **13**(9), pp. 4–16.

Rapp, S. and Collins, T. (1990) *The Great Marketing Turnaround,* New Jersey: Prentice Hall,

Smith, W. R. (1957) 'Product differentiation and market segmentation as alternative marketing strategies', *Journal of Marketing* **21**(1), pp. 3–8.

Strong, E. K. Jr (1925) *The Psychology of Selling and Advertising,* New York: McGraw-Hill.

Tracy, B. (2004) *Million Dollar Habits,* Irvine, Calif.: Entrepreneur Press.

Traynor, K. (1985) 'Research deserves status as marketing's fifth "p"', *Marketing News* **19** (8 November), pp. 7–12.

Trout, J. (1969) 'Positioning is a game people play in today's me-too marketplace', *Industrial Marketing,* June, pp. 51–55.

Wind, J. (1985) 'The marketing challenge', address given on receipt of the Charles Coolidge Parlin Award, Wharton School Working Paper (excepts appeared in 'Wind sets agenda for marketing to fulfil its potential', *Marketing News,* 16 August, pp. 12, 14).

Yudelson, J. (1999) 'Adapting McCarthy's four P's for the twenty-first century', *Journal of Marketing Education* **21**(1) (April), pp. 60–7.

Zolkiewski, J. (2004) 'Relationships are not ubiquitous in marketing', *European Journal of Marketing* **38**(1/2), pp. 24–9.

Products

Learning outcomes

After completing this chapter you should be able to:

▶ explain how B2C and B2B products are classified

▶ critically evaluate some of the risks associated with developing new products and launching them into the marketplace

▶ explain the process of market diffusion and why it is important in the launching of new products or services

▶ critically evaluate the different stages in the product life cycle.

Contents

Learning outcomes	167
Introduction	167
What is a product and why are they important?	167
Standardisation or adaptation?	168
Reasons for product adaptation – international dimension	168
Technical factors	168
Cultural perspectives	169
Legal or regulatory issues	171
Safety	171
Market classifications	171
Consumer product classifications	171
Industrial and commercial product classifications	176
New product development and service innovations	178
The processes involved in determining NPD	178
Idea generation	179
Idea screening	180
Concept testing	183
Business analysis	183
Product development and testing	184
Market testing	186
Product launch	187
Commercialisation: the diffusion and adoption processes	187
Adoption characteristics	190
New product failure	194
The product life cycle concept	198
Does the product life cycle concept exist in reality?	199
Different shapes and sizes	203
Chapter summary	205
Questions for review and reflection	206
References	206

■ Introduction

This chapter explores the product component of the marketing mix. Three key areas are discussed and evaluated: (1) the development of products and their market classifications, (2) how products are diffused into the marketplace, and (3) the value of the product life cycle.

While products have a logical link with other components of the marketing mix, the topic is also associated with branding, which is covered in detail in Chapter 7.

■ What is a product and why are they important?

It is useful at this stage to consider definitions for what we commonly call a 'product'. The vast majority of us probably take products for granted, since they are a functional part of our everyday life. However, products and the relationship that we have with them are far more complex than we might first imagine. As you read through this chapter it will become apparent that the products and brands that we often take for granted are complex. What we must remember, as Inwood and Hammond (1993) stress, is that a product (including a service) exists to generate value, and this can only be achieved by fulfilling the needs of customers.

Let us start with two definitions. The first is from Kotler (1998), and the second from Dibb *et al.* (1997). In general terms they are similar, but as you will see from Dibb *et al.* they have also stated that a product is 'everything both favourable and unfavourable', and that it is a 'complexity of tangible and intangible attributes'.

Kotler (1998) describes it as:

A product is anything that is offered to a market for attention, acquisition, use or consumption and that might satisfy a want or need. It includes physical objects, services, persons, places, organizations and ideas.

Dibb *et al.* (1997) say:

A product is everything, both favourable and unfavourable, that is received in exchange. It is a complexity of tangible and intangible attributes, including functional, social and psychological utilities or benefits. A product can be ideas, a service, a good or any combination of these three.

So a product can be anything from an idea to a service, a physical good (for example, a mobile phone), or to a combination of these. It is often the combinations that attracts the buyer to make a purchase. For instance, the mobile phone and the after-sales service and care policy are usually a 'package' in the mind of the buyer.

Let us examine some of the attributes described by Kotler (1998) and Dibb *et al.* (1997) in more detail. This will help us gain a clearer understanding of products and their relationship to the buyer. Table 9.1 dissects these attributes.

Standardisation or adaptation?

In 1983 Levitt wrote a seminal article entitled 'The globalization of markets' (reproduced in Levitt 1983). In it he stated:

A powerful force now drives the world towards a single converging commonality, and that force is technology. It has proletarianized communications, transport, and travel, making them easily and cheaply accessible to the world's most isolated places and impoverished multitudes. Suddenly no place and nobody is insulated from the alluring attractions of modernity. Almost

everybody, everywhere wants the things that have all heard about, seen, or experienced via the new technological facilities that drive their wants and wishes. And it drives these increasingly into global commonality, thus homogenizing markets everywhere.

The result is a new commercial reality – the explosive emergence of global markets for globally standardized products, gigantic world-scale markets of previously unimagined magnitudes.

Since the publication of Levitt's articles and books on this topic there has been much heated debate about the truth of this view. Arguments can be put both for and against a standardised view of the world. However, even companies that have become highly globalised such as McDonald's have to adapt to some degree in order to operate within an 'individual' marketplace.

Reasons for product adaptation – international dimension

There can be several reasons that companies have to adapt their products in order to market them internationally. In some cases they need major modification, while in others minor modifications are acceptable. A company needs to analyse whether or not the cost of modification is justified in terms of market entry and sustainability. Some of these reasons will change or adapt over time, so the company will need to continually monitor the need for adaptations (for instance, to meet regulatory changes) and the financial performance of the product. If the demand for adaptation becomes financially unviable, the company may need to consider an exit strategy from that market.

Technical factors

Electrical equipment ranging from computers to televisions and video cassette recorders (VCRs) may have to be adapted to meet different voltage and transmission standards. This is one of the reasons that videos from the United States cannot be played on UK-manufactured VCRs. The colour television standard in the United States is NTSC (National Systems Television Committee), while in

Table 9.1 Product attributes	
Attribute	**Description**
Tangible	This is something that can be touched and/or felt, for example the carton that contains milk or the steering wheel of a new car.
Intangible	This is something that cannot be touched but can be experienced, for example, the pleasure gained from using a product. If the product is a foot spa, an intangible is the relief given to aching feet.
Satisfying wants or needs	This is the degree to which an individual's needs and wants are satisfied by the purchasing of a particular product. For example, if you have a raging headache, the purchase of a branded over-the-counter (OTC) analgesic will relieve the pain. Thus your need for pain relief is satisfied.
Favourable	This can be defined as the features and benefits of the product that the individual considers favourable (or acceptable) to their needs and wants. The degree of 'favourability' will vary from individual to individual and each person's own particular needs.
Unfavourable	There may be product attributes that the individual considers, to varying degrees, unfavourable: for example, the positioning of certain buttons or indicators on a car's dashboard. This might not prevent the individual from purchasing the car, but he or she might find the positioning of the buttons and indicators an irritation (thus an unfavourable attribute).
Exchange	Various exchanges take place. On one level money or goods are exchanged for the product. On another level it is the benefits, features and psychological perceptions of the products that are exchanged when the individual uses or consumes the product. This exchange satisfies (or goes someway to satisfying) the needs and wants of the buyer.
Relationship(s)	This is the relationship(s) that the individual has with the product (or brand). This relationship links to the loyalty the individual displays to the product. For example, you may prefer to buy a certain type of product on a regular basis, such as a high-profile brand of cola drink. Thus there is a 'relationship' between the product and the individual in terms of the individual's loyalty to that brand. However, brand loyalty can be fragile, in that a failure in the product can lead to the individual switching brands, and an individual might be 'loyal' to several competing brands.

parts of Europe, Africa and Australia/New Zealand it is PAL (Phase Alternation by Line), and in France, parts of Africa and Eastern Europe it is SECAM (Sequential And Memory). As you can see the move towards different standards can only be confusing for many consumers.

In theory the advent of digital technologies should overcome these technical problems in the future.

Cultural perspectives

Attitudes and cultural perspectives can vary enormously both within regions and between countries.

In Chapter 2 (page 60) there is a brief discussion of cultural orientations and how people perceive other countries. It is not only other countries that have to be considered. Many people perceive the United States as one homogeneous environment. This is far from reality. It is a vast country comprising not only diverse geographical landscapes but diverse beliefs as well. These beliefs extend beyond a wide political spectrum (liberal to ultra right-wing) to personal attitudes and behaviours.

Alashban et al. (2002) cite how religion can be a focal point of a country's culture. For example, Nike was the goddess of victory in Ancient Greece. While that is not an issue in many countries, in

The Barbie® doll

In 1959 the Barbie® doll was introduced into the United States by the toy manufacturer Mattel. It was the brain-child of Mattel co-founder Ruth Handler, who was inspired by watching her daughter Barbara play with paper dolls. Following market research Handler and her team realised there was a niche for a three-dimensional fashion doll. After several designs, Barbie® was launched to a sceptical toy-buying market at the annual toy fair in New York in 1959.

Although Barbie® was a fashion-conscious doll reflecting all the emerging trends, the American version – tall, slender and blonde-haired – was the only version available. Today, this toy has undergone cultural adaptation and different versions represent 45 different nationalities. The first black and Hispanic Barbie dolls were launched in 1980. In Malaysia, for example, Barbie is known as Kebaya Barbie®, and has long black hair, dark brown eyes and wears traditional Malay clothes (known as sarong kebaya). The Malaysian Barbie® is available in three variations, wearing a white, dark green or pink kebaya.

By 2003 Barbie® was being marketed in more than 150 countries worldwide, and has established itself as the most popular fashion doll ever created. By 2002 it had become a US$2.5 billion per year business, including licensed products under Mattel's Consumer Products Division.

Source: Mattel™ investor relations website.

Saudi Arabia any reference to a god outside a religious context raises disapproval. As a consequence some Saudis may boycott Nike sportswear products.

What these issues and examples suggest is that companies have to be sensitive to a region or country's cultural point of view. Equally, culture does not remain stationary. Like all aspects of life it is in a continuous state of flux or development. This development might or might not be for the good, but nonetheless it has to be understood.

Food

As Doole and Lowe (1999) state, ' food is a particularly difficult area for standardisation, as the preparation and eating of food are often embedded in the history, religion and/or culture of the country'. Fast food companies that have an international presence, such as McDonald's, must vary their menus to take into account religion and local tastes.

Perception of numbers

The intrinsic value placed on numbers is extremely important in certain cultures. In the West we tend to consider the number 13 as unlucky. However, in Japan the number is 4 is considered bad luck, whereas the numbers 3 and 5 are considered lucky. Therefore packaging items in containers of four might not be received favourably in Japan. In many countries the number 7 is considered lucky, but in Ghana, Kenya and Singapore it is considered unlucky.

Perception of colours

Colour can have many meanings, most especially among older generations. In Brazil mourning is represented by the colour purple, in Mexico it is yellow, and it is dark red in Africa's Ivory Coast (Kotler 1998). As a result companies may need to consider the colour of their product and the packaging that accompanies it. (See Chapter 14 on physical evidence.)

Language

Individual languages are complex statements of a country's origins. Even within the country there are misunderstandings when the language is used. Translating a language is often fraught with difficulties and even more misunderstanding. Even

Coca-Cola

As Daniels and Radebaugh (1998) suggest, one strategy a company can adopt for compromising between uniformity and diversity is to standardise as many constituent parts as possible, while changing the end characteristics. An example is Coca-Cola. The company exports its concentrate to bottling plants in numerous countries worldwide. At the bottling plant carbonation, water, colour and sweeteners are added to adapt the drink to local tastes.

English-speaking nations have different words for the same item, as the list below shows:

British version	American version
Chemist/pharmacy	Drug store
Nappies	Diapers
Biscuits	Cookies
Crisps	Potato chips
Footpath	Sidewalk
Taxi	Cab
Lift	Elevator
Solicitor	Lawyer
Long-distance call	Trunk call

We need to consider the meaning of actual words and phrases and their translation. This will impact on brand names and the slogans used to promote brands. A successful brand name in one country could be a household joke or obscenity in another. Table 9.2 gives a few examples that do not travel very well.

■ Legal or regulatory issues

Products may have to be adapted to meet the host country's specific regulatory standards.

Safety

Different countries impose different ranges of safety standards which cover a variety of home-produced and imported components and completed products. The directives regulate such products as cosmetics, pharmaceuticals, textiles (where the main concern is to prevent the use of flammable materials in furniture), toys and fireworks. (You may want to reflect back to the issues raised in Chapter 2.)

■ Market classifications

Products are generally divided into two broad market classifications, consumer and industrial. These can be further divided into a series of sub-categories. In this section we explore the two broad market classifications and their sub-groups.

Consumer product classifications

Products aimed at satisfying personal and family needs and desires can be assembled into particular groups, categories or classifications. These classifications rely heavily on understanding consumer buying behaviour and attitudes (Dibb *et al.* 1997).

Convenience products

These are referred to as basic everyday items or goods. These are purchased frequently and involve little or no pre-planning on behalf of the purchaser. These can be further sub-classified into staple, impulse and emergency purchases.

Here brand awareness becomes particularly important, as manufacturers attempt to position their brand in the mind of the consumer. For such

Table 9.2 Lost in translation: examples of product names that did not travel well

Word	Country	Product	Another meaning
Sweat	Japan	Soft drink	Perspiration in English
Mist Stick	USA	Curling tongs for hair	Excrement in German
Nova	USA-UK	General Motors car range	No'va means 'does not go' in Spanish
Gerber	USA	Brand of baby food	In French gerber means vomiting. Thus Gerber foods are not for sale in France.
Traficante	Italy	Mineral water	In Spanish it means drug dealer
Silver Mist	UK	Model of Rolls-Royce car	Had to be changed in Germany because mist means excrement.

Figure 9.1 Consumer product classifications

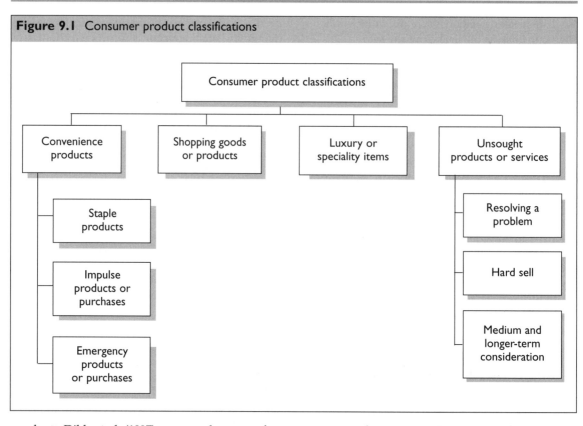

products Dibb *et al.* (1997) suggest that manufacturers expect little promotional effort at the retail end of the chain. Therefore they need to provide it themselves in the form of advertising and sales promotion. Promotion can be through a mixture of advertising and on-pack promotions. Memorable slogans also play a part (often significantly) in reminding consumers of the product's attributes. For example 'They're G-R-Reat!' for Kellogg's Sugar Frosted Flakes. This was first used in the United States in 1951, and is (as of 2005) still used in some markets (Rees 1997).

Staple products or purchases

These are products that are generally consumed on a regular, if not daily, basis. The type and range of products purchased will depend on the geographical location and personal wealth of the buyer. What is a staple product in one country might not be in another, although there will be some similarities. In the United Kingdom, for example, they include bread, tea, coffee, milk, fruits and vegetables and basic over-the-counter (OTC) medicines such as

paracetamol, aspirin or other cold and flu remedies. In other countries the bread might be replaced by rice, and there might be a different selection of fruit and vegetables.

While these staples can be, and are, purchased at regular intervals by most people, it is interesting to consider them at times of economic recession or depression. At such times most consumers will 'normally' resist expensive or luxury purchases, and tend instead, to increase the amount of staple (or basic) food products. Price sensitivity is a critical factor here, especially among consumers who have little disposable income.

Impulse products or purchases

These are product or services purchased 'on the spur of the moment' or immediate following a decision to buy. Products in this category include low-cost confectionery, newspapers and magazines, but are not be limited to these. A customer walking around a bookshop, for instance, may suddenly decide to purchase a book or books because they are on special offer.

In many supermarkets confectionery is displayed near the checkout counters or in newspaper kiosks. As Underhill (1999) states, we must not underestimate the value of impulse buying. It can add value and profitability for both the retailer and the manufacturer. One thing that might be considered is whether impulse buying is affected by downturns and upturns in the economy. Some customers refrain from such purchases in an economic downturn, the aim being to save as much as possible of their income and spending the remainder on staple products. On the other hand, customers might see these as 'treats' to overcome the gloom of recession.

Emergency products or purchases (also known as distress purchasing)

These are goods purchased when the need is urgent, such as an umbrella during a sudden rainstorm or aspirin when suffering from a sudden headache. Stores often anticipate the need for emergency purchases and locate these products near the entrance. In London, for instance, many department stores, convenience stores and even souvenir shops have compact umbrellas conveniently located near the entrance way. You never know when an umbrella might be urgently required with Britain's unpredictable weather!

Traditionally, in the United Kingdom at least, consumers have tended to buy convenience products at retail outlets near to their home. However, with increasingly long working hours and retail outlets, such as supermarkets, opening till late at night, some consumers shop near their offices. Increasingly supermarkets have opened in or near busy office districts.

Linked to convenience products are convenience stores, also known as C-stores. These trade primarily on the appeal of the convenience they offer to local customers. In many countries these tend to be independent outlets (often family-run businesses). They might also be chain stores, such as Londis or Spar in the United Kingdom and the US-based 7-Eleven chain which has expanded its outlets into several countries.[1]

Stanton, Etzel and Walker (1994) suggest that other products may be classed as convenience products, even though they are not purchased on a frequent basis. They suggest Christmas lights and Mother's Day cards. To this we can add products associated with Valentine's Day, birthdays, Easter celebrations and other religious and national festivities (such as the Chinese New Year).

Shopping goods or products

This focuses on durable or semi-durable items that have a relatively long life span. There are several key factors usually associated with shopping goods. For instance:

♦ Shopping goods include such products as clothing, furniture, televisions, video cameras, DVD players, cars, washing machines, dishwashers and refrigerators. These vary significantly in price and durability. There is, for instance, a significant difference between the price of men's shirts and a washing machine.

♦ While some academics have tended to suggest that 'the purchasing of shopping goods tends to be infrequent', that is not always the case. Agreed, it will normally be more infrequent than shopping for the weekly groceries. However some men buy new shirts, for instance, on a reasonably regular basis. Other customers change their cars every year for a new model. The parameters of purchasing may be wider here than first thought.

♦ Shopping goods can be divided into the subsets of homogeneous and heterogeneous.

● Homogeneous goods are products that are similar to each other in terms of performance, features, benefits and pricing. For example, most dishwashers can be considered as homogeneous goods. However, some manufacturers attempt to differentiate their products through design, features and technical performance. Such additional features are usually reflected in a higher price band.

● Heterogeneous goods are non-standard products where features, benefits and image tend to outweigh the price. In this case individuals' personal behavourial factors tend to influence their purchasing decisions. For example, the advent of digital technologies has led some manufacturers to develop highly sophisticated slim-line, wide-screen home entertainment systems. In terms of features, benefits and performance they outweigh standard home television and video/DVD systems. Equally, these systems command an exceptional price.

◆ With shopping goods, the consumer may devote time and effort to gathering a range of comparative information between brands. This information will normally include features, benefits, performance, price, credit facilities, delivery arrangements, guarantees and after-sales service. The time spent on this activity can be significant, especially if it is a high-cost purchase such as a car. Decision makers have to be comfortable in their own mind that they are buying the most appropriate product for them, at the right price and under the right contractual conditions.

◆ Brand awareness can be a critical factor. Companies often engage in high-profile promotional campaigns that assist in creating strong brand awareness in the minds of consumers. Therefore consumers might be influenced to a greater or lesser degree to consider one particular brand over another. A customer might be loyal to one particular brand of car or washing machine, for instance, and tend to buy from that brand range. However, consumers are not always brand loyal. Otherwise, as Dibb *et al.* (1997) pointed out, they would not spend so long in researching the different variables to assist them in their decision making.

◆ The quality of service can be an additional factor in consumers' decision to purchase from a particular store. If the sales people are knowledgeable and supportive, customers may decide to purchase there rather than in another store even if it is more expensive. It is often a question of building rapport or understanding with the customers that leads to the sale. Customers usually do not want to be 'sold to', they want support and advice to help them make the right decision.

◆ The price and quality of after-sales service is an important factor. With the vast majority of products there is at least 12 months of free after-sales service. After that it usually comes at a price, often in the form of an insurance agreement. The scope of such agreements can be a decisive factor in whether a customer purchases the product or not.

Luxury or speciality items and services

As the name suggests these are products or services that possess one or more special or unique qualities or features. Consumers seeking these may devote significant time, and often resources, to obtaining the product or service of their choice. In order to do so they are prepared to pay a premium price. Here are a few examples of luxury items:

◆ In 2003 the multi-millionaire Australian golfer Greg Norman took delivery of a UK£25 million mega-luxury yacht named *Aussie Rules*. The yacht has a cinema, six deluxe cabins for 12 guests, a gym, dining rooms, an observation lounge, swimming pool and spa, and seven boats stored on board. To keep everything in order there are 12 crew members. Of course, the purchase of such a craft is only the beginning – there are running costs of several thousand pounds per day, from insurance and crew salaries to mooring charges and fuel.

◆ Caviar, the roe or eggs of the sturgeon fish, is a luxury food. Although there are many varieties of caviar, the most expensive comes from Russia – most notably the roe of the Caspian Sea sturgeon. Beluga, Sevruga and Osietra (the Russian word for sturgeon) caviar are renowned for their link to luxury and their cost. In 2000 restrictions were placed by the Russian government on the amount of sturgeon that could be caught in the Caspian. This was an attempt to revive depleting stocks. This reduction in availability only sought to increase prices even further. The restrictions also increased illegal fishing of sturgeon, opening up a black market for the delicacy.

◆ *The World* is one of the world's most luxurious ships. It is actually a residence at sea, for she has 106 private apartments, 19 studio apartments and 40 studios. Prices in 2004 ranged from US$2.3 million to US$7.5 million. All apartments have a 50-year lease and potential buyers are vetted for their suitability. At a cost of some US$450 million to construct, *The World* boasts two pools, four restaurants, tennis courts and a golf course. The ambience is much like that of a private yacht, seaside villa or exclusive country club. In 2004 *The World* called on five continents, visiting 136 ports in 54 counties (The World 2004).

◆ Aston Martin is a luxury British car brand that is owned by Ford and was made famous by another British brand, James Bond. Although it has had a turbulent financial past (almost being made bankrupt on several occasions) it is now in the hands of a company that has helped revitalise the brand. In 2002 Aston Martin launched the Volante which retailed for UK£140 000, followed in 2004 with the luxurious DB9 retailing at UK£106 000.

◆ A luxury cruise: there are many cruise companies operating in today's market, but only a few that offer exclusive and luxurious accommodation and itineraries. One is the UK-based Hebridean Cruises, which has two ships, one cruising around Scotland and the other in the Mediterranean and parts of South Asia and the Far East.

Unsought products or services

These are products or services that consumers had not considered purchasing until they were made aware of either a need or a benefit. This category can be divided into three subsets:

Resolving a current or 'near-future' problem

An example of a current problem is the replacement of a window pane, door locks or a complete new door following a burglary. Here the customer requires the skilled services of a glazier, locksmith and/or carpenter. It was not the original intention of the customer to replace the glass, have new locks or a door fitted. The need was driven by actions beyond his or her personal control and to resolve the problem of a broken window and door.

A 'near-future' problem could be the need to renovate a house or repair superficial dents in a vehicle. Although they are not immediately pressing, these problems need to be resolved within a time frame decided by the owner or possibly (for a car) legally determined. On this basis people often 'plan' for future problems.

'Hard sell' techniques

Although these techniques are illegal in several countries, they still exist. A classic example from the United Kingdom is the selling of products by financial service companies. Perhaps unfairly, the majority of sales people in this sector have been tarnished with the actions of the few who opt for the hard sell approach. In some countries the legislation to control hard selling includes cooling-off periods, which give consumers time to consider whether they want to proceed with the agreement or not.

Medium and longer-term considerations

However, we must also consider that unsought products and services can, over the medium and longer term, satisfy customers' needs and wants. Customers do see genuine benefits from purchasing products such as life insurance, pension plans and savings policies. Initially the approach of the sales person (by mail or telephone) might be unsought, but that does not mean the product is automatically undesirable. Of course, the selling of such policies must clearly benefit the customer. Here the sales person has an ethical obligation, and often a legal one too, to ensure that the product is appropriate.

Figure 9.2

© Hebridean Island Cruises. Reproduced with kind permission.

This is the *Hebridean Spirit*, an ultra-luxury cruise ship that has 49 bedrooms

Industrial and commercial product classifications

Commercial and industrial products or materials are generally purchased on the basis of the company's overall goals and objectives (Eckles 1990). Such products or materials can be divided into the subsets shown in Figure 9.3.

Raw materials

These are the basic materials that contribute to a manufacturing or production process. They include natural resources (gold, diamonds, iron ore, tin, coal, crude oil and sand) and agricultural products (cocoa, wheat, soya).

Processed materials

These are materials used directly in production such as various types of chemicals, lubricants, filters, plastics and sheet steel.

Component parts (also known as fabricating parts)

These are identifiable and distinguishable components that form part of the finished product. For example an aircraft manufacturer such as Airbus Industries or Boeing does not produce all the elements that go into the finished aircraft. The vast majority of components are produced by a series of approved suppliers. Either Rolls-Royce or GE, for instance, might manufacture the engines. In turn they will seek approved suppliers to provide essential components for the engines.

There are several key factors to consider here:

◆ The components must meet the quality specified by the assembler/manufacturer of the finished product. It is the assembler's reputation that is often on the line if the finished product fails. A failure of a key component within a jet engine could endanger the safety of the aircraft and its passengers. A disaster will have an immediate impact on the chain of manufacturers involved, as well as the operating airline itself.

◆ Supply chain logistics are often critical in the timely completion of the final product or for necessary repairs later. With a jet engine, components are not just required for the original manufacture, they are also required for normal routine repairs and servicing. Thus suppliers need to be able to provide the required components not just locally but globally. Delays in receiving components can in turn delay the manufacture or servicing of the aircraft, often leading to increasing costs.

Plant and machinery

These are major items of plant, equipment or machinery that are necessary for the production of finished products, from a state-of-the-art computerised printing press for the production of high-

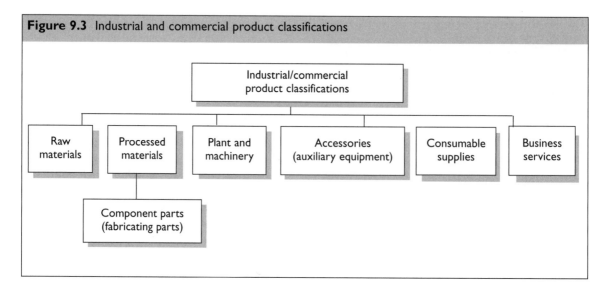

Figure 9.3 Industrial and commercial product classifications

quality pictorial-format books (art or photography books) to computerised car manufacturing lines.

The companies that purchase such equipment will normally consider the following issues:

◆ The long-term financial and operational viability of the plant and equipment. Plant and machinery, for example computerised printing presses, often requires high levels of investment. The company will seek to maximise the return on its capital investment. As technology rapidly develops, previous machinery becomes obsolete in comparison. This may have little immediate impact over the short term, but if competitors invest in the latest technology they might be able to gain an operational cost advantage. Thus the decision to purchase is often linked to the long-term competitive viability of the organisation.

◆ The company's final decision may not be based on the cost of the equipment alone. There are several other factors:

● Payment terms and conditions. The suppliers may offer a range of payment terms, from a discount for full payment in advance to instalments over a specific time period.

● The range of features and benefits currently available. The buyer will also want to consider whether or not the machinery can be 'updated' without the need for purchasing a completely new machine. Increasingly technology allows for 'add-ons' that improve the efficiency of the machine without the need for a totally new purchase. For instance, consider your own computer. You can enhance its performance by installing additional memory chips and new software. While you have to purchase the 'add-ons' this is unlikely to be as expensive as purchasing a brand new computer.

● The cost of operating the equipment in both human resources and material resources (for example, electricity).

● Quality of the after-sales service should there be any operational/functional problems. Many companies provide 24-hour breakdown and servicing coverage, with site attendance within a specific time frame. Some companies offer compensation to their customers if they are unable to reach the site within an agreed time or deliver replacement parts.

Accessories (auxiliary equipment)

This is equipment that does not become part of the finished product, but in one way or another contributes to its successful production and distribution. These items tend to be less expensive than capital purchases, and include office and operational equipment such as computers, software packages and electronic test facilities.

Consumable supplies

These are supplies that facilitate operation and production, but they are not part of the finished product. Within an office environment they include pens, paper, laser and photocopying cartridges. Within an operation and production environment they include gloves, safety glasses, uniforms and hard hats.

Generally, the products are homogeneous and therefore companies may use several suppliers in an attempt to gain competitive pricing and/or delivery times.

Business services

Many companies and organisations use bought-in services to achieve their overall business and corporate objectives. They include legal, financial, accounting, training, catering, market research, printing, advertising, security and management consultancy services. Their cost and relative value to the company or organisation varies enormously depending on the scale of the company. For instance a business partnership might only require a small accountancy firm for a few days per year to conduct an audit and finalise the accounts, costing it perhaps UK£1000. However a corporation with a vast network of subsidiaries or strategic business units (SBUs) will need the services of an accountancy firm on a year-round basis, not just at the time of filing the accounts. The accountancy firm might also provide non-auditing services including due diligence work in respect of acquisitions and disposals, tax compliance and advisory services, and other general consultancy. The fees charged for such services can be very large. For example, in 1999 Unilever paid UK£ 8 million in audit fees and UK£23 million to PricewaterhouseCoopers for non-audit services (Unilever 1999).

Although business services can be very expensive, they are often key to the successful operation of the business, so their importance should not be underestimated.

■ New product development and service innovations

The development of new products or services is often the key to the beginnings of a new organisation, or the continuation of an existing one. Companies normally seek, over time, to develop new products and/or enhance existing ones, so new product development (NPD) must be considered as an ongoing long-term operation. As Drucker (1999) suggests, most innovations usually result 'from a conscious and purposeful search for innovation opportunities which are found only within a few situations'.

A company might engage in NPD for one or more of the following reasons (developed from Inwood and Hammond 1993):

◆ To replace products that are either approaching or have entered the declining phase of their life cycle. This might be as a result of changing technologies: for instance, the launch of inkjet and laser printers saw the decline of much slower, noisier and less efficient dot matrix printers.

◆ The development of enhancements or modifications to increase or rejuvenate the life of the product. In the section on plant and machinery (page 176) we discussed the value of 'add-ons' to existing equipment. In some industries these both enhance the machine's operating efficiency and prolong its overall life expectancy.

◆ The development of products that support the company's longer-term strategic objectives. The objectives may include maintaining a technical-specific competitive advantage over an increasing number of rivals. An example is the enhancements and development associated

with mobile phones since 2000, including picture messaging and video.

◆ The simple adaptation of an existing product or its packaging. (This can be particularly relevant to a product entering an international market. Various factors, ranging from government legislation in the host country through to customer preferences, may determine the level and scope of adaptation.)

◆ An unexpected occurrence which then leads to an unexpected innovation and product. This can also be considered as the 'flash of genius factor!' As we will see later in this chapter, the Post-It Note© that we all take for granted occurred in very much this way.

◆ In response to societal, including demographic, factors. Societies change, and so the needs and wants of society also change. Companies must analyse how societies are changing in order to develop the right products and services. For instance, as we saw in Chapter 2, the demographic structure of Europe is changing, with the 50-plus sector outnumbering the under-20s. As a result companies will consider how to adapt products and services to meet the demands of an increasingly affluent market of those aged 50 or more.

The development of new products is often essential if a company is to survive, let alone grow and prosper within a highly dynamic business environment. Many products become obsolete, as a result of technological developments, aggressive competition, changing societal attitudes and buyer behaviour. Examples include manual typewriters and mechanical cash registers. So in order to survive a company, must be proactive in its analysis of its product range and market demand (present and future).

The processes involved in determining NPD

In this section we consider how a company could approach the implementation of a NPD strategy. The procedure outlined was devised by the international management consultants Booz Allen & Hamilton (Baker 2000). This is currently the most widely used method for the development of a new product.

Generally there are eight stages in NPD, although some authors combine or add stages. We shall examine each stage or phase in some detail.

1   Idea generation.

2   Idea screening.

3   Concept testing.

4   Business analysis.

5   Product development and testing.

6   Market testing.

7.   Product launch.

8   Commercialisation: the diffusion and adoption process.

Idea generation (also known as exploration)

It is obvious that all new products commence with an idea. This idea can be extremely simple or highly complex. Ideas emanate from a variety of sources, and usually require detailed exploration. The sources might include one or more of the following:

◆   Enhancements of an existing product through a refinement or adaptive feature.

◆   External technology, scientific developments or new discoveries. New developments in one technological or scientific field may lead to innovations in another.

◆   Senior management might see a potential opportunity or niche in the marketplace that they believe can be entered relatively quickly and efficiently.

◆   A sales person or the sales team. In their meetings with their customers, members of the sales team may hear suggestions for product improvements and developments. Equally, the sales team themselves may make recommendations for enhanced product

---

Mini case 9.3

Nylon®

In the 1930s organic chemist Wallace Hume Carothers (1896–1937) and his team at the E. I. du Pont De Nemours (now known as Du Pont) laboratory in Wilmington, Delaware were investigating a new area of research: polymers. As a result of their various experiments they discovered a synthetic polyamide, which they called nylon®, and neoprene®, one of the first synthetic rubbers.

Initially E. I. du Pont decided to sell nylon® to the hosiery market for stockings. This was so successful (especially during the Second World War) that stockings became known by the generic name 'nylons'. However this was not the end of the story. Nylon® has since then been used a diverse range of products from parachutes to carpets, clothing, luggage and automotive components.

Mini case 9.4

Bisquick™

In 1930 Carl Smith, a General Mills sales executive, was returning to San Francisco by train. Although he had arrived on the train too late to order dinner, he did receive a plate of oven-hot biscuits. He was so amazed that the cook was able to produce fresh biscuits in such a short time that he went to see the cook in the galley. The cook showed him how he blended lard, flour, baking powder and salt and then stored the mixture in an ice chest (a compartment full of ice to keep food cool). From this batter the cook could make biscuits quickly and to order.

Smith recognised the potential of a pre-mixed baking mix, and took the idea to Charlie Kress, the head chemist of the Sperry Division of General Mills. There were particular challenges in attempting to create such a 'ready mix', one being the right blend of ingredients.

The final product was called Bisquick™. However, General Mills was not the only company considering such a product. Within months of Bisquick's launch there were 96 biscuit mixes on sale in the United States. However, only six brands survived into the following year. Although the recipe has undergone various changes or modifications over the years, Bisquick™ retains a leading market share of the convenience baking mix market in the United States.

Source: General Mills website (www.generalmills.com).

development or the creation of a new product altogether.

◆ Those customers that do not come in direct contact with a sales team might contact a company to suggest improvements they have thought about in using the product on a regular basis. They might also contact a company to complain about the product. While complaints are potentially damaging to a company in public relations terms, they can also provide significant opportunities for product enhancement and development. It is all a question of how the company handles the complaint, and relays the customer's views to the development department. For this to work efficiently there has to be a strong proactive internal communications process. Unfortunately that is not always the case, especially in multinationals, whose size means they might not have an efficient and effective cross-company reporting structure or process.

◆ By watching and analysing the action of competitors, companies may be able to emulate their success, or indeed leapfrog them in terms of product enhancements and development.

◆ Brainstorming sessions, ideally carried out by a mix of people (not just the research and development team) often create a rich variety of ideas and constructive debate. Many of these ideas might not be practical, either at all or at that time, but gems are born out of such creative thinking processes. A brainstorming team needs to take the view that there is 'no such thing as a dumb idea', it just may not be practical at this precise moment in time.

When the television series *Star Trek* started in the 1960s everyone probably marvelled at the crew's 'communicators', which flipped up and were handy pocket sized. Anyone who ventured that such things might be possible by the end of the century was probably laughed at as a mere 'trekkie'. However, consider the similarities with today's mobile phones! In reality we have progressed technologically even further with the 'communicator' than the crew of the *Starship Enterprise*.

◆ New ideas are not just the province of different levels of management. There are numerous examples of employees, at all levels within an organisation, generating ideas that have either saved the company money, or helped it create a new range of products. Some companies, such as 3M, actively encourage all their employees to suggest ideas. This was born out of a management philosophy created by the company's former president, William L. McKnight (chairman of the board 1949–66). He set out a basic rule of management in 1948:

> As our business grows, it becomes increasingly necessary to delegate responsibility and to encourage men and women to exercise their initiative. This requires considerable tolerance. Those men and women to whom we delegate authority and responsibility, if they are good people, are going to do their jobs in their own way.
>
> Mistakes will be made. But if a person is essentially right, the mistakes he or she makes are not as serious in the long run as the mistakes management will make if it undertakes to tell those in authority exactly how they must do their jobs.
>
> Management that is destructively critical when mistakes are made kills initiative. And it's essential that we have many people with initiative if we are to continue to grow.[2]
>
> (3M 2003)

3M believes that anyone, not just the research and development department, has the ability to generate ideas. The company has two rules on ideas generation. The 15 per cent rule encourages every employee (not just technologists) to commit 15 per cent of their time to thinking of new ideas. In essence, employees who generate new ideas become 'product champions'. The 25 per cent rule states that every manager must ensure that at least 25 per cent of his or her portfolio of products is less than five years old (3M 2003).

Idea screening (also known as initial screening process)

The process of developing new products is highly risky and expensive. Ideally a company should

Mini case 9.5

3M and Post-it Notes®

The Post-it Note® that adorns most desks was one of the great research and development accidents of all time. A research chemist, Spencer Silver, was tasked with developing a new glue that would become the strongest on the market. However, Silver's work resulted in a very different type of glue – a glue that would only stick for a very short period of time. He noticed that this glue had particular properties: it could be reused (provided it did not get dirty), and it left no visible marks or residue on the materials to which it had been applied.

For ten years he tried to find an application for this unusual glue without success. Then a colleague, new product engineer, Arthur 'Art' Fry, discovered a solution to Silver's dilemma. Fry was in the choir of his local Presbyterian church, and each Sunday would use scraps of paper to mark the place of the selected hymns in his hymn book. However, as he opened the hymn book his slips of paper often fell out.

He came across Silver asking colleagues if they had a use for a weak adhesive, so he applied the adhesive to a sheet of paper and realised he had his bookmark. However, Fry started using the adhesive beyond the bookmarks in his hymn book. He would write notes on slips of paper and use the adhesive to attach them to reports. He found that colleagues would often write on the slips and return them with the reports. Believing that the adhesive had a longer-term value to the company, Fry began to actively promote it within 3M. His manager Bob Molenda, who helped push the project through the pilot test phase, backed the idea.

As a result, in 1977 3M tested Post-It Notes® in three American cities. The packs were sold, but sales were not encouraging. A final effort was made in the town of Boise in Idaho. Office workers were shown how the note pads worked, and this time given free sample packs. The sales teams returned a week later to discover that 90 per cent of customers wanted to buy packs.

Today, the product has been diversified into some 600 different Post-It® products sold in over 100 countries. There are 62 colours, 25 shapes and eight standard sizes. It is universally recognised and has become an everyday global item.

Sources: Hillman and Gibbs (1998); van Dulken (2000); 3M corporate website (www.3m.com).

undertake a series of screening activities or processes to determine, even at this early stage, whether a proposition is viable or not.

Often companies (especially large multinationals) are quoted in the media saying they invest billions of dollars in research and development. They must clearly seek a return on that investment, over the medium term or more likely the longer term. Some research and development is very much 'future thinking' with little or no immediate practical application. If you like, the 'jigsaw puzzle' that makes up the innovation or development may not be complete: several technologies might have to converge before a product can be mass produced.

A company usually forms a working group or committee to analyse and consider the viability of any new ideas. This might comprise people from various departments – Research and Development, Marketing, Finance, Production and Operations, for instance. Its function is to identify potential winners. As I said earlier, there is no such thing as a 'dumb idea', but companies need to consider what is practical for them over the medium and longer term. This is never an easy task, but the introduction of a systematic approach usually aids the decision-making process.

The company must determine whether the idea strategically fits its corporate objectives, considering resourcing requirements, competitive forces and, most critically, the market demand. As you will see from the questions below, the company must consider a whole range of issues, from production and operations to finance and human resource management. Equally, there will be a range of micro and macro factors that need to be considered.

◆ Does this idea fit with the existing product range? Will the new product affect the viability of an exiting product or a product portfolio? What will be the likely impact on the business of the introduction of this new product?

◆ What is the possible demand for this product? Who will buy it and why? Will the initial purchase be high followed by a rapid decline, or will there be continual growth over a longer time frame? Companies need to consider what the life cycle of the product could be, although it must be remembered that gauging the life of a product is far from an exact science.

- Does the company have the appropriate expertise to develop the idea? If not, can it acquire that expertise, and how long will it take to acquire and assimilate it? What could be the possible negative effects of bringing the expertise into the company – for example, how will the current employees react? (As you can see it is not just a marketing, production and finance issue here, it also very much involves human resource management, and all associated with it.)

- Does the company have the capacity to produce this new product, or will it need to consider building new facilities or outsourcing to suppliers or other specialists? It needs to analyse both the cost and potential time lags.

- Will the company be required to invest in new equipment and other resources in order to manufacture this product?

- What is the likely sales potential of this product? What is the potential size of the market – nationally, regionally, international or globally? What are the possible risks of marketing this product internationally? Is it a standardised product or will it have to be modified for international consumption?

- What are the likely costs involved in the development and production of this new product idea? Will the company need to seek additional funding from external sources, or can it be funded by the current operations budget? If external funding is required, how will it be raised – share market, via banks, venture capitalists or a combination of all three? If the company needs to seek external funding, what will be the cost of such borrowings? And can the company meet these financial demands?

- When will the idea be technically feasible – in the short, medium or longer term?

- Are there any obvious problems that can be foreseen in the development stage of this idea? For instance, are there any regulatory conditions that need to be met? For example, if the product emits background radiation, will it conform to international radiological standards? Or will further research be necessary to find a means of reducing the radiation level?

- What will the potential reaction of the current customers be? Does the idea meet a current market need and trends? Reflect back to the section on ideas generation. There we considered the role of the sales team in developing ideas based on conversations with customers. As the company progresses with new ideas, it can test them out with current and potential future customers. Obviously, companies operating in highly competitive markets will need to consider confidentiality issues. However, discussions with outsiders can be useful in helping companies progress to the development stage.

- Should the product be aimed at a new customer base? What is the potential size of that customer base? Or is it designed for a totally new market? If so, how will that market react, and how will the company contact it?

- What is the possibility of substitution or product obsolescence? If so, are there any measures that can be taken to overcome these, or reduce their potential risk? The company may need to think of how 'add-ons' could possibly enhance the product in the future.

- What is the potential competitor reaction? Could competitors be working on a similar idea? Could they launch a similar product earlier, beating the company to market? If so, what will be the likely impact on the market, and the company?

- Are there any negative/positive environmental considerations? Will the raw materials, the manufacturing process or the finished product harm the environment? Will the processes conform with current and possible future environmental legislation?

- Are there any potential legislative issues to be considered, for example, product safety implications both now and in the future?

- What are the potential advantages and/or disadvantages from the company's perspective?

- To what extent will the proposed product assist in reducing production or marketing costs of other products? In other words, is there a means of achieving economies of scale?

◆ Will the introduction of the new product cannibalise the company's current product range(s)? If so, is it a risk to the business or not? In some cases companies may allow the cannibalisation of existing products in order to build a firm foundation for the new one. However, it can be a very risky strategy. If the life of the new product falls dramatically short of expectations, the company could face serious financial problems.

◆ What will be the impact on current distribution outlets? Will new distribution patterns need to be developed? If so, what are the potential cost and management implications?

◆ What are the estimated time scales from the ideas stage through to prototype and then manufacture? This will need to link into the most appropriate time to launch the product.

◆ Who are the competitors? Are they the company's current competitors, or will new ones enter the market? Consideration must be given to potential international competition, not just local, regional or national competition. With the growth in e-commerce, business is becoming very much a global entity with global competitors, even for SMEs.

These questions are very much inter-related, reliant on cost, and are to some extent future thinking. While it is impossible to predict the future accurately, there are trends that may provide some indication of what could happen in the near future. However, it is advisable to add a word of warning here. As we saw in Chapter 2, the macro environment is volatile to say the least. Companies developing new products or enhancing existing ones must be aware of this volatility. A market might be potentially lucrative one day and dead the next. While global companies may be able to exert certain levels of power, they are usually powerless against severe political and economic turbulence.

Concept testing

As part of the ideas screening process, marketers may have to test the concepts on potential customers. Here the objective is to gain customer reactions to the idea, positive or negative. This can be a valuable exercise, but there are inherent

problems associated with concept testing. These include:

◆ Can the concept be communicated effectively to the potential customers so that they can make realistic judgments? A development team might be able to visualise the final product, indeed the whole production process. However can they accurately translate the idea into a language customers easily and readily understand? It depends on the skill of those communicating with current and potential customers. Often the research and development team will seek the assistance of the marketing team to find the most efficient and effective way of communicating ideas to the customer base. One method that can be employed is the focus group.

◆ Will the reaction to the concept be objective and rational? Will people, for instance, think it is a novel idea and say so, but in reality consider it impractical? This is one of the risks associated with marketing research. Individuals or focus groups might seek to please a questioner, rather than say what they genuinely think. The cultural perspective must also be taken into consideration: some cultures tend to be more vocal and critical than others.

◆ Is the exercise cost-effective in terms of resource expenditure versus the quality of feedback? For some companies extensive feedback research (such as focus groups) is prohibitively expensive. They must be able to see a worthwhile return on their investment.

◆ Companies also need to consider how far individuals are conditioned by 'traditional' views of life. Radical new ideas might be considered bizarre by traditionalists – but convenient and practical for others. The difficulty here is assembling the most appropriate audience to review and comment upon the idea.

Business analysis

Based upon the outcome of the concept testing, management will need to consider the market and financial viability of the potential product. This involves break-even and market analysis, the forecasting of costs, sales and potential profit.

In the case of a radical new product development, some of the forecasts can only be 'educated guesses' based on prior experience. Generally, companies conduct business analyses not only at this stage but throughout all subsequent stages.

At a later stage it may become overwhelmingly clear that the product faces several barriers. For instance:

◆ It will be far too expensive to develop at this time.

◆ It is not technically feasible to develop at this time.

◆ There is no current evidence that a market exists for such a product.

On the basis of such information, a company may decide to shelve, terminated or postpone the project. It might believe that the project could be feasible at another time, depending on technological developments or the development of a new market opportunity.

Product development and testing

This is the stage where a prototype or working model is constructed. This reveals the tangible and intangible attributes of the product.

Mini case 9.6

Viagra®

As Palmer (2000) suggests, while products should be market led, many new products arise by accident. We described in mini case 9.5 how the Post-it Note® came into existence accidentally, yet a market followed.

Researchers at the pharmaceutical giant Pfizer were working on the development of an anti-angina drug when they noticed unexpected side-effects. This led to further tangential development and the anti-impotence drug Viagra® was created. When it was launched in 1998 it was a commercial success. Since then it has been prescribed to 16 million men. According to Pfizer's Viagra® website, nine tablets are dispensed every second.

Sources: Palmer (2000); www.viagra.com.

Products can normally be tested in one of two ways:

◆ The company develops and implements its own tests on the product, this is known as alpha testing. The tests might be of the company's own design, dictated by a regulator, or a mixture of both, depending on the product. Many products have to meet minimum safety standards for example, and these are enshrined in legislation (which changes over time). An example of this is the design and testing of commercial aircraft. Mini case 9.7 briefly examines the development of the Boeing 777. Before the aircraft can enter commercial service in the United States, it must receive Federal Aviation Authority (FAA) certification. Equally before it can fly in UK airspace it must obtain the UK's equivalent certification through the Civil Aviation Authority (CAA). These can be seen as the two main benchmarks for airworthiness. The removal of either one will result in the grounding of not one aircraft but the entire fleet.

◆ Potential customers can also be involved in the testing process. This is known as beta testing. Here the product is tested in order to replicate reality as closely as possible. For example, computer software and hardware manufacturers provide both consumers and business customers with beta test samples of their systems to examine how the products perform under real user conditions. The feedback from beta test sites is important for the development of product refinements and debugging.

While many companies engage in rigorous product testing, others do not. The reasons behind such decisions are many and varied, and some of the key issues are examined below.

◆ The senior management team might have committed the company to launch the product within a restrictive deadline, which means there is time for limited or no testing. It might be that the product actually requires little or no testing, but depending on the product, this could prove to be an error of judgment. A 'rush to market' is not always a successful strategy to win market

Mini case 9.7

The Boeing 777

In June 1994 Boeing's latest aircraft, the twin turbofan wide-body 777 passenger aircraft, took to the skies. The prototype was test flown by the company's chief commercial aircraft test pilot John Cashman and his co-pilot Ken Higgins.

The area where the passengers would normally sit was filled with banks of computer systems to test different aspects of the aircraft's performance, from the hydraulic control systems to individual engine performance. After some four hours of inflight testing Cashman and Higgins landed back Boeing's Everett airfield in Washington State. However, this was only one part of a vast testing programme.

The criticality of such testing was demonstrated with the flying testbed that was created to test the engines under real flight conditions. A 747 was converted so that its existing inboard left engine was replaced by the Pratt & Whitney 4048 engine designed for the 777. On the third test-bed flight in November 1993 the converted 747 sped down the runway at Boeing's Everett test facility. At the point of rotation (the moment when the pilot has committed the aircraft to take-off, the nose is up and the front wheel has left the ground) the 4058 engine surged and two loud bangs could be heard both in the cockpit and on the ground. In addition to the bangs those on the ground saw smoke and flames shoot from the engine. A surge is where airflow turbulence causes air in the back of the engine to move forward, causing a loss of thrust and the engine backfiring, like a misfiring exhaust on a car.

The aircraft is designed to take off on one engine at the point of rotation (when the front wheel leaves the ground and the plane is known as 'committed'). The ability to do this significantly enhances safety, because the risk of crash on take-off is reduced. Thus it increases its marketability to airlines. For any aircraft the two critical points are rotation (speed and engine/flap performance) and touch down (speed/positioning and flap performance), combined of course with weather conditions.

With the engine shut down the plane continued to climb. Such a dramatic incident illustrated the need for both alpha testing and highly trained people to test such prototypes. Maybe such a demonstration enhanced Boeing's reputation for quality and safety whilst increasing the marketability of the 777.

Testing does not stop with the original prototype, however: this is only the beginning. When each new version is developed the prototype version of that aircraft must undergo rigorous testing. In October 1997 the prototype of the Boeing 777-300 took off from Boeing's Paine Field in Everett, Washington State, to begin a seven-month flight test programme. This four-hour flight was the first of some 1400 flight test hours planned for the aircraft. During the test flights, the 777-300 was subjected to extreme hot and cold climates to prove the aircraft's systems' safety and reliability.

In addition to actual proving flights, Boeing has developed special test rigs to 'fatigue' test the aircraft. Fatigue testing provides engineers with key data that help identify the likelihood and causes of premature fatigue damage or wear on the aircraft's structure components. If fatigue damage occurs in the fleet, then it can be addressed effectively through service bulletins and eliminated through subsequent production changes.

Housed in a cage of steel, tubes and wires, a 777 fatigue test aircraft was built to verify the durability of its structure. This is a structurally complete airframe without the systems and interior components. One hundred computer-controlled hydraulic actuators simultaneously applied loads to the airframe to simulate all conditions during typical in-service operations. These tests include pre-and post-flight taxi, pilot manoeuvres, gusts of wind and cabin pressurisation. Within such test rigs, the aircraft receives the treatment it would receive in continual flight. In all the 777 fatigue test plane flew 120 000 flights, which represented an equivalent of 60 years in service, twice the expected service life of the aircraft.

'A commercial airplane represents a huge investment for our airline customers', commented Larry Rydell, chief engineer, 777 Structures. 'It's therefore to be expected that they will be flying them longer in the future. This test shows us what to expect with an eventual aging fleet. We can anticipate maintenance requirements and thereby ensure continued safe, economical operation of the aircraft.'

Sources: 'Boeing 777 fatigue test airplane completes record number of flights,' news release, Boeing, 17 March 1997; 'Boeing 777-300 complete first flight,' news release, Boeing, 16 October 1997; Sabbagh (1996).

share. It can be seen as a short-termist approach.

♦ Only qualitative data, rather than 'hard' quantitative data, might be available. Managers in some companies view qualitative data as 'soft' data. As a result they may be reluctant to halt the project if the qualitative data has signalled a negative response to the product, especially if the project has enthusiastic support from the senior management team. Depending on the culture of the organisation, staff might be reluctant to deliver potentially bad news to senior managers, or might persuade themselves the product will 'work' sufficiently when it is launched. This can be a high-risk strategy. As some companies have found to their cost, a massive advertising budget will not persuade customers to buy an inferior product.

♦ Fear of competitive pressures, can result in a company launching a product without concept (and market) testing. The view in the boardroom might be, what if the competition launches a similar product before we do? Again, this is a high-risk strategy. It might succeed, but if it fails it will not only tarnish the product but affect the company's reputation.

♦ Sometimes companies are prepared to take the risk of 'backing a hunch or a gut feeling'. This is often in the absence of any real demand for the proposed product or service. This approach might work – it has in the past. New markets and market opportunities have been opened up as a result of hunches, but the risks for a company can be enormous. (See mini case 9.8.) If the product fails, the company's survival could be at risk.

Pop music, for instance, is always a risk. A band might spend a year working on a new album, but there can be no guarantee it will be a success. In Chapter 1 complexity theory is discussed. This shows how various dynamics determine what is a hit and what is not, but understanding the dynamics does not by any means guarantee a 'hit'. Even the most successful solo artist and groups, with loyal followings, cannot guarantee that their next single or album will be a massive hit, so the pop music business is high-risk and volatile.

Market testing (also known as test launch)

Before the product is introduced to a wider market segment, it may be market tested. This can be described as a 'sample' launch of the product in a limited area to determine the reaction of customers. Confectionery companies, for example, might launch a new chocolate bar in a limited number of regions, market testing not only the reaction to the bar itself (through the level of purchasing) but also the reaction to its marketing campaign. If the campaign is not found to be successful it can be modified before the national campaign launch. If the chocolate bar proves not to be successful, the company might decide to rethink the formula and/or the packaging. In a drastic move it could scrap the product. Of course, that would be a very expensive alternative.

Market testing can provide several benefits:

♦ It allows product exposure to a natural (rather than a controlled) market, and thus should give a more realistic measure of performance.

♦ It provides the marketing team with an opportunity to test different aspects of the marketing mix. This testing can take place in different locations, allowing marketers to experiment with pricing, packaging and different promotional variations.

♦ The marketing team can observe weaknesses in the product and other components of the marketing mix. This provides them with the opportunity for corrective action prior to the main launch. Testing the mix can lead to more effective use of the mix, and prevent embarrassments such as inappropriate advertising or a product that fails.

♦ Testing can provide additional information for cost, sales and profit forecasts. Prior to market testing companies can estimate sales forecasts (usually based upon similar products and product ranges). However, it is only when market testing takes place that a more realistic idea of sales can be gauged.

♦ Sample launching allows for supplies of the

Mini case 9.8

The movies

The movie industry has for years undertaken test previews to gauge audience reaction to either a movie generally, or specific elements within it. For example, film companies have been known to change the ending of a movie because test audience reaction to the original ending was negative. This does not necessarily make the movie an instant hit, but it can prevent a box-office embarrassment.

A classic example, in more ways than one, is the 1945 movie *The Lost Weekend*, directed by Billy Wilder. It was a particularly outstanding achievement because it showed, with gritty realism, a tense psychological study of an alcoholic novelist. Ray Milland collected an Academy Award for his intense portrayal of a man on the edge of his life. The movie also collected awards for Best Picture, Best Screenplay and Best Director. However, all this success might well not have happened.

When the movie was completed, in their haste to preview it the studio dubbed various tracks from its music library onto the soundtrack. It was 'covered' in an assortment of musical idioms that were totally inappropriate for the intensity of the subject matter. When the movie was test screened in Santa Barbara, California there were howls of laughter from the audience. What had been intended as a dramatic, often morbid and frightening film had been turned into a 'comedy'.

As a result the studio planned to shelve the movie, but producer and co-screenwriter Charles Brackett and composer Miklós Rózsa persuaded them otherwise. Rózsa provided music that understood both the humanity of the main character, and the fear that engulfed him in his moments of intoxication. When the movie was previewed with the new score, the audience reactions were very different. The movie went on to garner both critical and public acclaim.

This is an example of one element having an undeniable impact on the success of the whole product.

Source: Turner (1980).

product to be accumulated over a longer time frame prior to the full market launch. However, there will be warehousing and potential depreciation cost implications.

Product launch

Once the product has successfully completed the concept and market testing stages, it is ready for launching into a wider marketplace, which might be national, multinational or, increasingly, global. Generally, a product can be launched either of two ways:

◆ One launch date: on a given date the product is made available to customers, nationally or internationally. It might be anything from washing powder or a car, to a style of jeans. Such products are usually supported by intensive launch and ongoing promotional campaigns. The important issue for companies is that appropriate quantities of product are available in the distribution outlets prior to launch date. Nothing is more frustrating for consumers than to view a promotional campaign for a new product only to discover that it is not available, and may not be for several days or weeks. This damages not only the product's reputation (often before it has even been tried) but also the manufacturer's reputation.

◆ Roll out: the product is made available in stages, region by region. This can mean geographical area by area within a country, or progressing through several countries. A product might be rolled out through Europe over a period of several months.

Commercialisation: the diffusion and adoption processes

This is the full-scale manufacturing and marketing of the new product. The diffusion and adoption processes focus on how information and experiences of the new product disseminate through the market place.

Often, in textbooks, diffusion follows adoption. However, normally diffusion of the 'idea' precedes adoption. Of course, diffusion can be a reinforcing action (see Figure 9.4). As a product or service is adopted, information about its quality (good or bad) is diffused among the relevant market segment(s). This can reinforce customer behaviour – the decision to buy or reject the product – especially when customers consider repurchasing.

Figure 9.4

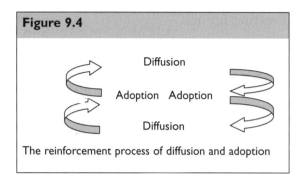

The reinforcement process of diffusion and adoption

Companies and organisations are particularly interested in repeat buyers, because in the long run they are more profitable than one-off purchasers.

The examination of how information is diffused among a population began towards the end of the 19th century and included aspects of sociology, psychology and anthropology. Perhaps one of the most important figures at the turn of the 20th century was the French sociologist, psychologist and criminologist Gabriel Tarde (1843–1904). Although he had no formal training he made several observations about human behaviour. First, he believed that society was entering the age of 'publics': that people can only belong to one crowd at a time, but they can be part of several publics at the same time (Mattelart and Mattelart 1998). Second, he was influenced by the notion of suggestion and suggestibility, which led to his Laws of Imitation (Mattelart and Mattelart 1998). From this analysis he plotted the original S-shaped diffusion curve (Valente and Rogers 1995). (The diffusion

curve looks 'roughly' like an S seen side on – see Figure 9.5.

Further research was undertaken in the 1930s and 1940s by two American rural sociologists from Iowa State University, Bryce Ryan and Neal Gross. In 1928 a new hybrid corn seed was introduced to Greene County, Iowa. It was superior to any other seed that had been used by the local farmers over previous decades, but it was not readily adopted. The reasons behind this reluctance were the essence of Ryan and Gross' research. They studied the attitudes of 255 Greene County farmers. Table 9.3 gives a breakdown of the usage by the 259 farmers.

Ryan and Gross' work renewed interest in Tarde's S-curve. They identified five groups of farmers, and categorised them as:

- innovators
- early adopters
- early majority
- late majority
- laggards.

In his 1960s seminal work Everett Rogers further developed the theories and views on the diffusion of innovations. Rogers (1983) originally defined diffusion as:

The process by which (1) an innovation; (2) is communicated through certain channels [for example direct marketing or advertising]; (3) over time; (4) among members of a social system.

Figure 9.5

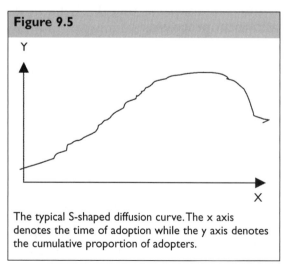

The typical S-shaped diffusion curve. The x axis denotes the time of adoption while the y axis denotes the cumulative proportion of adopters.

Figure 9.6

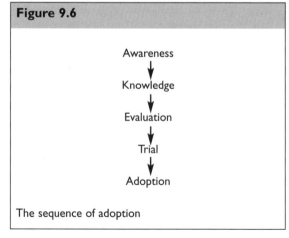

The sequence of adoption

Table 9.3 Level of hybrid corn seed usage over time

Time frame	No. of farmers adopting seed	Type of adoption	Total numbers by type
1928–33	24	Innovators	24
1934	16	Early adopters	37
1935	21		
1936	36	Early majority	143
1937	61		
1938	46		
1939	36	Late majority	36
1940	14	Laggards	17
1941	3		
Non-adopters	2		2

Source: adapted and developed from Malcolm Gladwell, 'The coolhunt', *New Yorker*, 17 March 1997.

Adoption can be viewed as the sequence of events in Figure 9.6.

As Robertson (1984) suggests, while this is a useful approach for high-involvement products, 'this "rational" or "learning" bias may be inappropriate for low involvement products where awareness may be sufficient to encourage trial'. For instance, the consumer might trust a particular brand name and thus readily purchase a new soap or washing-up liquid sold under that brand.

Let us analyse Rogers' original diffusion elements further:

◆ An innovation: this can be an idea, a practice or products that are new, or perceived as new. You may want to reflect back to the descriptions of new product development, which covered both new and revitalised products.

◆ Communication and communication channels: communication is where people participate in both creating and sharing information and ideas. Communication channels are the means or medium by which the information or message is 'transported' from one individual or group to another individual or group. The channels can be mass media (for example, television), interpersonal (face-to-face contact, for example through a sales person) or a combination. While people will seek some scientific research to help them make decisions, many judgments to buy are based on feedback from peers and opinion formers who have adopted the product or service. While this has validity,

some 30 years after it was first suggested Rogers felt that it was 'too linear, too mathematical'. He looked on communication as a 'convergence process in which the participants create and share information with one another in order to reach mutual understanding' (Rogers and Kincaid 1981).

◆ Over time: this can be divided into three subsets. This first relates to the 'innovation–decision' process. This is the mental process through which an individual or group moves from first awareness of the product or service to confirmation of the decision (to buy or not to buy). This is depicted diagrammatically in Figure 9.7 in Rogers' five-stage process.

The second subset refers to the 'relative time' by which the an innovation is adopted by an individual or group. The third subset is the 'rate of adoption' of the innovation into the market or social system. Several variables can affect this overall rate of adoption. They include the type of innovation decisions made (adopt or reject – this may be after some deliberation), the nature of the communication channels diffusing the innovation at various stages in the innovation process, the nature of the social system (for instance, liberal or closed systems) and the level of success of the change agents in diffusing the innovation.

◆ Social system: this can be described as a set of interrelated decision-making units engaged in joint problem solving to achieve a common purpose or solution that has mutual benefits.

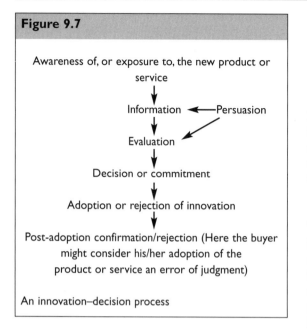

Figure 9.7

Awareness of, or exposure to, the new product or service
↓
Information ←——Persuasion
↓
Evaluation
↓
Decision or commitment
↓
Adoption or rejection of innovation
↓
Post-adoption confirmation/rejection (Here the buyer might consider his/her adoption of the product or service an error of judgment)

An innovation–decision process

particular movie can lead to either the adoption or rejection of the movie. For example, diffusion of vast quantities of positive information on James Cameron's *Titanic* led it to become a box-office smash hit, rather than the most expensive flop ever made, as some had predicted.

Robertson (1984) suggests that diffusion theory is incomplete unless it recognises the proactive nature of marketing and competitive actions. Table 9.4 details the potential impact of marketing activities on the diffusion process.

Adoption characteristics

Rogers (1983) built on the work of Ryan and Gross and devised a broad classification for customers who adopt new products. These are listed below and reflected in Figure 9.8. Rogers apportioned percentages of the population who would adopt a product or service over the course of the lifecycle of the product.

Innovators

As can be seen from Figure 9.8, this is a small group of around 5 per cent of the population. These are

For instance moviegoers consist of a broad spectrum of people of different ages, incomes and life styles. However, the diffusion of information, knowledge and experiences regarding a

Table 9.4 Potential marketing impact on the diffusion process

Diffusion concept	Potential marketing impact
The innovation	Here marketing activity focusing on the product's design and positioning is critical to the consumer's perception of the innovation and its characteristics.
The diffusion process	Marketing activities influence the pattern and speed of diffusion for the total market, and by segments. This is based on marketing mix activities such as pricing and distribution.
The adoption process	Marketing activities can modify the speed and breadth of adoption.
The communication process	Communication strategies and tactics, such as advertising and personal selling, can lead to a purchase without the customer seeking 'objective' independent perspectives.
Opinion formers	Opinion leadership can be important in influencing an individual to either purchase or not purchase a particular product or service. Equally, marketing activity can be deployed in an attempt to counter negativity created by opinion formers.
Adopter categories	Marketing activities can assist in determining who the innovator will be based on market segmentation.

Source: adapted from Robertson (2001).

Figure 9.8 A typical adoption pattern

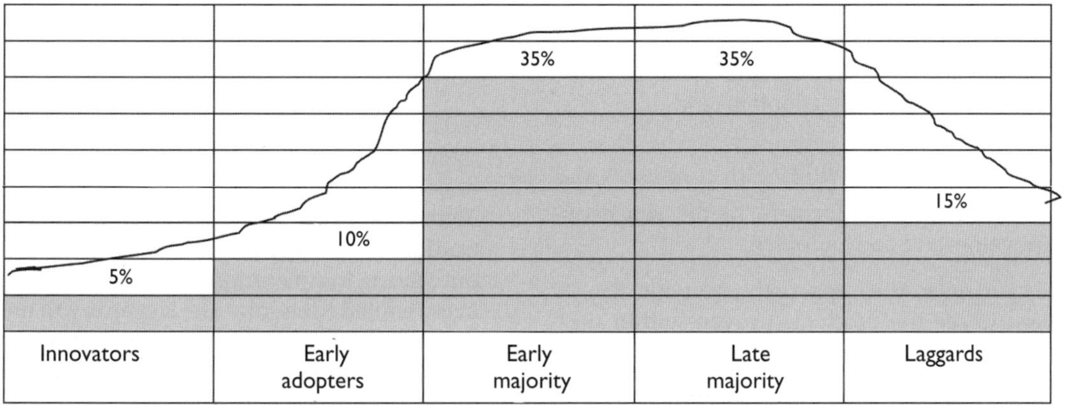

the first customers to purchase the product, and can be perhaps characterised by the word 'venturesome'. In other words they are eager to try new ideas. Innovators are also risk takers as there is generally no guarantee that the product (or the ideas behind the product) will ultimately be successful.

Rogers (1983) suggests that communication networks among innovators are common, although the geographical distance between them may be considerable. Here we can see the use of the mobile phone and the Internet/e-mail as a means of diffusing the relevant information between innovators.

Innovators tend to:

◆ Be younger people.

◆ Have access to financial resources (thus they are able to absorb or recover from the loss incurred by purchasing an 'unprofitable' innovation).

◆ Be reasonably well educated. This may tie in with their ability to understand and apply technical knowledge, for instance in communication via the Internet and adopting 'perceived' technically difficult innovations such as the programmable VCR.

◆ Be confident in their outlook on life and thus able to handle various degrees of uncertainty.

◆ Adopt the product if it is fashionable and thus fits within their current or aspiring lifestyle.

◆ Act as opinion formers (this can be through beta testing – see page 184) for companies to drive the product into a wide marketplace.

Early adopters

This is usually a larger group than innovators, representing some 10 per cent of the population. Early adopters tend to be:

◆ Well educated with high incomes and self-confidence. These are traits that they share with innovators.

◆ More cautious in the level of risk they are prepared to take. This is where they begin to differ from innovators.

◆ Potential change agents as they are respected by society and their peers. They are seen as very strong opinion formers and leaders, and thus can influence other people's views. Often potential adopters will check with early adopters for advice, information and opinions as part of their decision-making process. Therefore companies target them with promotional campaigns to reinforce the features and benefits of the new product or service. Zikmund and D'Amico (1999) suggest that early adopters filter the products accepted by the innovators and popularise them, which in turn leads to acceptance by the majority of buyers in the marketplace.

Early majority

This group accounts for 35 per cent of the population. Early majority adopters tend to:

◆ Be mass market consumers.

◆ Rarely be opinion formers in the sense of innovators and early adopters.

◆ Be cautious in their approach to buying. They want to see the products proven within the market before committing themselves to purchase.

◆ Be a large category and one that cannot be ignored by manufacturers.

Late majority

This group also comprises approximately 35 per cent of the population. Late majority adopters tend to:

◆ Be sceptical and cautious about the product's real long-term value to them. This makes them even more reluctant to purchase the product.

◆ Adoption comes via proof of the product's performance and value, and usually pressure from others to adopt. The latter may be in the form of social and political pressure – for example, adopting unleaded fuels for the family car.

Laggards

This group can also be called Late adopters. They comprise some 15 per cent of the population. Laggards tend to be:

◆ Reluctant to adopt any innovation. They tend to be suspicious of innovation, instead they reflect upon the past. This may be a result of their age, educational background or traditional points of view. Jobber (1998) suggests the innovation needs to be perceived as almost a traditional product before they will consider purchasing it. An example is the mobile phone in the United Kingdom. The laggards will most probably be those that have adopted a 'standard' mobile phone, not one that includes picture messaging and video.

◆ Older, conservative and traditional in their outlook, avoiding risk taking wherever possible.

◆ People with little leverage as opinion formers.

◆ People with often limited financial resources (although this is not always the case). However, those with limited resources tend to be more cautious about investing in innovations just in case the innovation is short-lived and they need to find some form of replacement. They tend to deliberate (often for sometime) before committing themselves to purchase.

Variants on the standard form

Research conducted in the United States by Colby and Parasuraman (2003) suggests that there is a

Table 9.5 Colby and Parasuraman's framework for technology readiness

Technology segment	Technology belief dimension			
	Contributors		Inhibitors	
	Optimism	Innovativeness	Discomfort	Insecurity
Explorers	High	High	Low	Low
Pioneers	High	High	High	High
Sceptics	Low	Low	Low	Low
Paranoids	High	Low	High	High
Laggards	Low	Low	High	High

Source: Colby and Parasuraman (2003).

Table 9.6

Group	Percentage of US population	Description
Explorers	17	This group is the most actively technologically ready, being the first to adopt new technologies. They tend to be affluent, young, generally male and work in technology-related businesses. They are generally advocates of e-related services.
Pioneers	23	While this group is highly motivated to adopt new technologies, a high level of discomfort and insecurity also inhibits them. Their concerns may be generated by, for example, the risk of Internet fraud.
Sceptics	24	This group can be described as the 'doubters', exhibiting few motivations and few inhibitions. They are yet to be convinced about the benefits of embracing the new technologies and related services.
Paranoids	18	While this group may believe in technology's overall benefits, they are constrained by a high level of discomfort and insecurity. These feelings may stem from fear of using the technologies, that it is beyond their abilities to use it, potential Internet fraud and discomfort created by a fear that every transaction may be monitored perhaps by government agencies.
Laggards	18	This group is the least technological ready of the population. They have a low level of motivation and a high level of resistance to embracing new technologies. Laggards can be lower income groups and the elderly (who may see no use for such technologies within their lives, though this is not always the case and this will probably change over time).

This illustrates the percentage of the US population that appears to fit certain adoption categories. However, it should be borne in mind that it is a generalisation. The level of adoption will depend on the product or service and the environment in which it is marketed.

Source: adapted from Colby and Parasuraman (2003).

wide variance in people's technology readiness, that is the embracing and use of new technologies. This is most especially related to e-systems, such as using the Internet and installing intelligent home systems.

Colby and Parasuraman's study indicates that technology readiness is more than a continuum from low to high or adopting early through to adopting late. In essence there are four elements that comprise technological adoption, two contributors and two inhibitors. Their findings also indicate that an individual's beliefs can vary independently over the four elements, with beliefs being a mixture of both positive and negative reactions (Colby and Parasuraman 2003). These are depicted in Table 9.5. The areas shaded in grey are the groups associated with a high degree of technological readiness. The un-shaded areas illustrate

groups that are associated with a low degree of technological readiness.

Colby and Parasuraman (2003) suggest that there is a 'natural cascading of adoption of e-services'. In the early stages the explorers create the demand and become advocates. If effective and efficient marketing supports this, there is an uptake of such technologies as the Internet and resulting e-services by the other groups. In essence there is a filtering of knowledge and information down to these groups, as the benefits of these technologies become known.

Desired and typical diffusion patterns

There is normally a difference between the preferred or desired diffusion pattern and the one that actually occurs. Companies in highly volatile and competitive markets will seek to achieve high-velocity sales within a short time frame. As Shimp (2000) states, companies will specifically aim to achieve the following objectives:

◆ secure initial sales as quickly as possible (a rapid take-off)

◆ achieve cumulative sales in a steep curve (a rapid acceleration)

◆ secure the highest possible sales potential within the targeted market segment (maximum penetration)

◆ maintain sales for as long as efficiently and effectively possible (a long-run franchise).

These objectives are illustrated in Figure 9.9. Line A indicates the preferred route of adoption, while line B indicates the often typical level of adoption over time. Companies seeking a route that coincide with line A will need to clearly focus on efficient and effective marketing communications to achieve their objectives. It is unlikely that this will be a low-cost route. However, in a highly competitive marketplace such as the pharmaceutical and airline industries this may be one of the options to undertake.

A general point on adoption theory

Rogers' model provides a valuable insight into, first, how information is diffused to target groups and individuals, and second, how products are adopted by customers (Rogers 1983). However, a few caveats need to be considered:

◆ Not everyone purchases a product that can be described as an innovation. Therefore individuals or groups that fit this category could be described as non-adopters under any circumstance. As seen in Ryan and Gross's study (Table 9.3), two farmers did not adopt the new hybrid corn seed. There will be many other examples of such non-adoption.

◆ An individual might be classed as an innovator for one product, but decide to be an early adopter for another product. It is feasible for someone who has been an innovator to become a laggard for other future products. This could be an issue of age. For example, people who were innovators in 1950s Britain and bought television sets will have updated their television set since, but when they reached retirement age many will not have invested in the latest digital flat screen surround sound technology. For them a basic colour television set might be sufficient. Therefore the innovators of today may be the laggards of the future.

New product failure

Clearly there are numerous (and often significant) risks associated with the development and launch of a new or modified product. According to some research, the failure rate is extraordinarily high. For instance, Clancy and Shulman (1991) estimated the failure rate of new packaged goods at 80 per cent, and believed that it was similar in financial services. Cooper and Kleinschmidt (1991a) drew similar conclusions, with their research estimating that 75 percent of new products failed at launch.

If this research is to be believed, what are the reasons for such catastrophic failure rates? One very dramatic example of product failure is the Sinclair C5, explored in mini case 9.9 (overleaf).

Potential actions to minimise the risk of failure

While it is impossible to eliminate the risk of failure totally, steps can be taken to help minimise

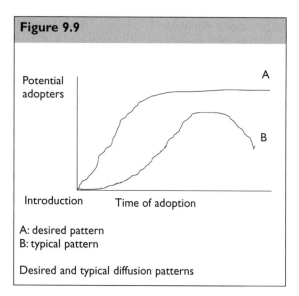

Figure 9.9

Potential adopters

A

B

Introduction   Time of adoption

A: desired pattern
B: typical pattern

Desired and typical diffusion patterns

the level of failure. In this section several characteristics are evaluated in relation to the marketing mix and proposed target markets. Such an analysis may help organisations to minimise NPD risks and ultimately failure.

What is the relative advantage over other products?

As Inwood and Hammond (1993) stress, a product (including services) exists to generate value, and this can only be achieved by fulfilling the needs of customers. Therefore a product that offers consumers *real* benefits over existing products will tend to be adopted more readily than one that does not. An example is a washing powder that includes an advanced stain remover that effectively removes a variety of stains but does not harm the texture of the clothes.

Compatibility with current technologies

Generally, an innovation will have an increased chance of success if it is compatible in some form with current technologies, usage patterns and consumer behaviour. An example is the ability to play both music CDs and DVDs on a computer system using the same drive.

Trialability or testing

This is the opportunity for consumers to test the product before a commitment to buy. If the trial is successful, there is the possibility that they will adopt the product. Such trialability can manifest itself in several forms, for instance:

- The company distributes trial packs, through either in-store promotion or door-to-door drops, for products such as soap and proposed new confectionery brands. This was how Dove soap (a Unilever product) was introduced to the UK market.

- Organised demonstrations, for goods from new kitchen appliances to computer systems. The customer has the opportunity to try the product following the demonstration, and/or ask questions. This hands-on opportunity might be the key that persuades people to purchase the product.

Observed product performance prior to purchase

Adoption is increased when consumers can see how the advantages of the new product relate to their own lives: for example, during the evolution and development of the mobile phone. Consumers could witness the benefits others found in communicating with their friends and family, and this action could persuade non-users to make a purchase.

The levels of product simplicity and complexity

Many consumers who revel in the complexity of products: the more features, add-ons, attachments and gadgets, the happier they are. For them the sheer complexity is value added. However, this is not always the case. Many consumers are reluctant to adopt new products that are complex in either reality or perception. Here too the mobile phone is a good example. Since the mid-1990s it has become increasingly complex, with numerous features from texting to video recording, transmission and display. For many people, these are exciting additions that will be quickly adopted. However, others are looking for a portable phone, not a 'communications toolkit'. The lessons here are perhaps the need for basic versions, and for complex facilities or functions to be relatively simple to operate.

The level of risk involved

In Rogers's analysis, consumers are reluctant to adopt a new innovation if a high degree of risk is perceived (Rogers 1983). This perceived risk can be either individual or collective – monetary, psychological or physically related. With the C5 (mini case 9.9), there was a perceived risk to driving it in heavy traffic in major urban areas. The fear of 'serious injury' discouraged people from buying it in many cases. As stated, the Dutch Government perceived this 'physical' risk to be so high that it banned the product.

Clearly there are risks in everything we do, and we calculate the positives and negatives in order to assist our personal decision making. Certain foods or food ingredients, for example foods high in saturated fats, can contribute to heart conditions. However, people continue to eat them, some in moderation, some not. Here the individual has

The Sinclair C5

The man behind the development of the C5 was Sir Clive Sinclair, a British scientist who had developed the executive pocket calculator in 1972 and the microvision pocket television in 1977. He went on to develop the successful ZX Spectrum personal computer.

During the 1970s various countries became more energy conscious as oil prices soared (controlled by the OPEC cartel) and fuel shortages began to cripple economies. As a result Sinclair believed there was a market for a small personal electric vehicle. In the early 1980s he and his team began working on a prototype vehicle, the aim being to develop a vehicle that would carry one person, replace the moped, be limited to urban areas, have a top speed of about 50 kph (30 mph) and be competitively priced.

By 1981 a basic model had been created, the C1. However it was not until 1983, when Sinclair placed a development contract with Lotus Cars, that the C5 prototype began to take shape. By 1984 an agreement had been reached with Hoover Ltd in Merthyr Tydfil in Wales to manufacture the components that formed the C5. Sinclair envisaged initial sales of 100 000 per year, rising to over 500 000. He planned that the C5 would be sold via mail order, so three distribution centres were arranged, two in southeast England and one in the northwest.

On 10 January 1985 the C5 was launched with a major promotional campaign in London. The initial price was UK£399 plus UK£29 for delivery. Included were an owner's manual, battery charger and accessory catalogue. However, the product failed to capture people's imagination, and both the Consumers' Association and journalists raised serious safety concerns. Although the company maintained that safety had been a priority and various safety groups had been consulted, the Consumers' Association report was damning:

- The height of the C5 was such that the driver's body was directly at car bumper height. This was likely to increase the risk of serious injury in the event of a collision.

- The driver was at a height to inhale exhaust fumes, and be hit by spray from other vehicles, affecting the driver's performance and visibility.

- The C5 was hidden behind other vehicles in heavy traffic, increasing its vulnerability.

- The headlight beam was ineffective.

- The C5 had no reverse gear, so any movement backwards would involve getting out of the vehicle. This would pose a further hazard at night and/or on busy roads.

- The maximum speed of 24 kph (15 mph) could be hazardous considering some urban speeds of 50 kph (30 mph).

- The body of the C5 gave little protection in the event of a collision.

- The basic model was not fitted with any mirrors or indicators.

The collapse of the C5 was swift:

January	The launch of the C5.
February	Unemployed teenagers were hired to drive the C5 around major cities.
March	Production was halted for three weeks for modifications on the gearbox component of vehicles in stock.
April	Production of the C5 was cut by 90 per cent to just 100 vehicles per week.
May	The company admitted stock levels of 6000, twice the level previously disclosed.
June	The Consumers' Association report was published.
July	The Advertising Standards Authority published a report highlighting numerous complaints about statements made in the advertising for the C5.
August	The Comet retail chain cut the price of the C5 to UK£189 including all accessories.
September	Production of the C5 stopped.
October	Receivers were called in to Sinclair Vehicles. Debits were estimated at UK£7.75 million, of which UK£7 million was owed to Sinclair himself. 14 000 C5s had been made and only 4500 had actually been sold. This was a far cry from the original production estimate of 100 000 in the first year.

In ten short months the company had gone from a launch in a hail of publicity to collapse. So what led to such a dramatic failure? Marks (1989) provides many of the answers from his research. These are briefly outlined below.

Ideas generation

The idea was conceived within the company. It was very much a technology-pushed idea rather than one pulled by demand. Although there was no vehicle to compare it with, no market research was undertaken.

Ideas screening

There was only one product. It appears that the only screening was of which concepts were considered better than others. Marks suggests that Sinclair believed that the product would succeed and he could create a market for it.

Concept development and testing

The Sinclair team decided on the core benefit proposition of the product: silent, pollution free, economic and safer than a moped. However they appear to have not sought feedback from potential customers about the original concept of the vehicle – small, one-seated and electric powered. Basically, the concept was not tested with the public, the very people who would buy the product. Marks (1989) suggests that market research would have flagged the potential weaknesses in the concept, and might have prevented the error of launching the product in the first place. Equally, it might have flagged other possibilities for the product, for example, as a 'fun' vehicle that could be driven around leisure complexes where there were no 'traditional' vehicles.

Business analysis

Apart from electric-powered milk vans there was very little historical data on electric vehicles from which sales forecasts could be estimated. It was clear that milk vans would not be a reliable comparator. While production and marketing costs could be determined, estimates of the demand for the product would be very subjective. The Sinclair team perceived their target market to be the number of households that owned a second car, and based their projections on the 2.4 million households that did so according to 1978 UK government statistics. This was a highly risky presumption. The limitations of the C5 could not make it a serious rival to the second car, and for it to be seen as one would have required a major societal change in attitude, which was not likely to occur. The team also considered the C5 to be a rival to mopeds, and targeted '14 year olds, housewives for urban commuting and anyone who wanted to get about'. Once again, the unlikeliness of these groups buying a C5 might have been flagged by market research.

Production, development and testing

Various shapes were developed and tested in order to produce the final model. As Marks states, the vehicle was not extensively tested in heavy traffic before launch. Instead it had been put through its paces on a test track and in a 'crash test simulation'. The Consumers' Association apparently conducted the first tests in 'real' driving conditions.

Test marketing

There was no test marketing, and no feedback from potential customers. Once the C5 was ready it was launched.

Commercialisation

There was a national launch with a high-profile marketing campaign. The product was launched in London in January 1985 – in the middle of winter. The basic product was an open-top vehicle. Waterproofing for the driver came as an extra, at an additional price.

The safety concerns were echoed in numerous newspaper articles. The authorities in the Netherlands – perhaps the most cycle-friendly country in Europe – were so concerned about the C5's safety issues that they banned the vehicle.

Marks suggests that perhaps the launch should have been a rolling campaign. While this might have helped customer awareness, there were inherent flaws in the overall concept of the vehicle. It is unlikely that a rolling launch would have saved this product from failure within the market. There were just too many problems associated with it, both real and perceived.

Was there a market opportunity?

The product had a clear 'identity crisis'. On one hand it was promoted as a serious mode of transport, on the other it was promoted as a 'fun' vehicle. The marketing was contradictory. Market research might have suggested some real market opportunities for such a vehicle, but they were far removed from the congested and dangerous roads of cities such as London. Some people did see opportunities for the C5, using them on golf courses and in other 'safe' environments. These could have been exploited further, but the company was stuck in a groove which led to bankruptcy.

Final points

It is interesting to note that the C5 is now a collectors' item. Second-hand C5s today cost well over UK£1000 to acquire.

In 2003 it was reported that Sir Clive Sinclair was working on a new version of the C5. He described it as 'a new product designed at getting people around town'. By early 2005 there had been no launch of this new version.

Sources: Andrew P. Marks, 'The Sinclair C5: an investigation into its development, launch and subsequent failure', European Journal of Marketing, 23(1), 1989; Tibballs (1999); Jonathan Duffy, 'Move over Segway, I'm planning the C6', BBC News Online, 5 August 2003.

Mini case 9.10

Crest Whitestrips dental kit

Procter and Gamble (P&G) decided to develop and launch a home tooth whitening kit in the United States. No other company had taken this approach before. Crest Whitestrips are clear flexible strips coated with a gel – the enamel ingredient used by dentists – that adhere directly to the teeth.

The product was developed in 1997 and pre-launched in 2000 via the Crest Whitestrips Internet site. Although initial sales provided a few million dollars in revenue, it provided a learning experience for P&G. The company contacted a sample of those who had purchased the product to find out how they had used it and what they liked or didn't like about it. This research helped P&G to shape the brand.

The product was launched in May 2001 to mass-market stores, such as drug stores and supermarkets. For customers who preferred to visit their dentist, a professional version was made available through more than 20 000 dental practices nationwide.

To quote P&G's Global Marketing Officer, James R. Stengel:

When we went national with Whitestrips, we were able to tailor the brand to those who responded in the Internet trial. There were four core groups: teenage girls, brides-to-be, young Hispanics, and gay men. All four of these groups were targets. We launched the brand in the media that went to where the consumer was. As it turns out, Whitestrips was one of the great launches, not just for P&G but for any consumer goods company.

Sources: Kevin T. Higgins, 'P&G reinvents itself', *Marketing Management*, November/December 2002; 'Smile … and get white-hot for summer with Crest Whitestrips', press release, Procter & Gamble, 5 April 2001; 'About Whitestrips', www.whitestrips.com.

inwardly considered the level of risk involved and made a decision to either purchase or not.

■ The product life cycle concept

Fowler and Thomas (1993) describe the product life cycle as a concept that

Is used to predict the strategic needs associated with products as they age within the marketplace. It allows for the development of strategies appropriate to the life cycle stage and anticipate the need for changes in strategy as progression from one stage to the next occurs.

The product life cycle was originally developed in the 1950s (usually attributed to Dean) and popularised by Levitt in the early to mid-1960s.[3] Since then it has become an established framework for the analysis of a company's product portfolio.

Figure 9.10 is a diagrammatic representation of the product life cycle concept. Some authors refer to this as an S-shaped curve, although it could be described as more like a slightly flattened bell shape. The vertical axis represents revenue

generation (through sales) and profit, while the horizontal represents the time frame or life of the product. This could be measured in terms of days, months, years, decades or even centuries. In the latter case you may want to reflect on the life cycle of products such as Coca-Cola or Kellogg's Corn Flakes.

In Figure 9.10 the profit curve is slow to start and continues to the virtual death of the product, although this is not always so. It could be achieved if the company has been able to develop economies of scale.

Opinions vary regarding the number of stages that may occur within a product life cycle (Goncalves and Aguas 1997). Jauch and Glueck (1988) and Reid (1989), for example, presented five stages, whereas Kerin and Peterson (1980), and Cokayne (1991) considered only three stages. Although the vast majority of sources tend to focus on four stages – introduction or development, growth, maturity and decline – this text considers six potential stages. It must be emphasised that these are only potential stages. As is discussed later in this section a product life cycle

Figure 9.10

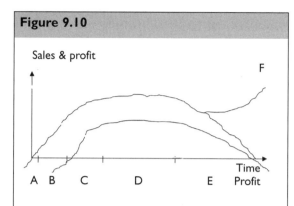

Sales & profit

A B C D E Time / Profit

The stereotypical product life cycle

A This can be a mixture of research and development and marketing planning. A product may undergo changes before introduction to the market that change its market focus. Equally, a product may be terminated or 'killed off' even before introduction into the market. This may be for numerous reasons such as product failure or changes within the macro environment that prevents launch.

B Introduction into the marketplace. Also known as the pioneering stage.

C Growth.

D Maturity within that specific market.

E Decline. This may be either a natural decline or one induced by the company as new products supersede this one. Within the declining stage there has been reference to 'senility'. This can be interpreted as where the product has remained within the market far too long and has become unprofitable. This should only be used as a descriptor for the product life cycle and not the human condition.

F Rejuvenation. This is where the product undergoes some transformation to extend its life cycle.

Mini case 9.11

Rejuvenation of Škoda cars

The Škoda car company of the Czech Republic has had something of a chequered history. It originated in 1905 and by the late 1930s had gained an international reputation for style and craftsmanship. In 1945 the then Czechoslovakia became part of the Soviet Union, and Škoda went from producing stylish sedans and coupes to grey utilitarian vehicles that looked more like square steel containers. Its image and reputation quickly diminished. Škoda cars were not confined to the Soviet Union, they were exported to the West, even at the height of the Cold War. Although relatively cheap to purchase they were unreliable and the brunt of many a joke, especially in the United Kingdom.

In 1989 Czechoslovakia moved towards becoming a nation-state independent of Russia. By 1990 there were moves to start the privatisation of businesses. One company that was placed on the market was Škoda. In 1991 Volkswagen (VW) paid an estimated US$700 million to the Czech government for a controlling interest in Skoda (it acquired the remainder of the shares in 2000).

VW pushed through a programme of rationalisation to improve production processes to match those at other VW plants. Škoda staff were sent to other VW plants to observe production methods and quality control procedures. This was to be the benchmark to which the Škoda plant would have to operate. Between 1991 and 1998 an estimated US$1 billion was invested in capital facilities and equipment. In 2000 an estimated US$500 million was invested in a new engine plant at Škoda's Mlada Boleslav plant. By 2003 a further US$1.7 billion had been invested in technology and new product design and development.

Since its acquisition by VW, the image of Škoda has been radically changed and the product lines dramatically rejuvenated. Škoda has been repositioned within the marketplace and has achieved success both at home and abroad. By 2003 Škoda was one of the best selling car brands in the United Kingdom.

Sources: Peter Fuhrman, 'Memories of development', Forbes, 16 April 1990; 'The people's car', Economist, 3 July 1992, 'My other car's a Bentley', Economist, 19 September 1998; 'VW Group tries to give Skoda image a remake', Automotive News, 22 November 1999; Tom Mudd, 'The last laugh', Industry Week, 18 September 2000; 'Slav Motown', Economist, 1 June 2001; Normandy Maddy, 'Skoda's new face looks in two directions', Advertising Age International, January/February 1997.

might not follow the typical pattern presented in Figure 9.10.

Table 9.7 outlines both the strategic and marketing mix issues that interact with the product life cycle at each stage of its progression. You may want to reflect back upon this table when you read through the other chapters on the marketing mix.

Does the product life cycle concept exist in reality?

There has been much debate over the years whether the product life cycle concept really exists.

Table 9.7 Strategic and marketing mix issues within the different stages of the product life cycle

Stage and subsets	Actions/potential outcomes
Pre-introductory phase	This can be described as the stage where the company completes its research and development and contemplates whether it should launch the product or not. There may be significant investment in R&D with the production of prototypes.
Marketing	The company either internally or externally may undertake extensive market research to see if there is a need and or desire for the potential product. This may include discussing ideas and concepts with known existing customers. The company will have to establish its pricing objectives, taking into account a range of costs and the potential demand forecasts.
Finance	Depending on the product significant financial resources may have already been deployed in the development of the project. Consider, for instance, Airbus Industries decision to develop the A380 passenger aircraft, capable of carrying some 500 passengers. Many years of research and analysis were invested in this project prior to the company's public announcement. If it is a new or start-up company with a revolutionary idea, it will have to secure sufficient finance in order to realise the objectives.
Operations	Depending on the scale of the project there may be significant operational implications in the development of the project: for instance the development and construction of prototype aircraft. Once the product is introduced into the market, and assuming success, the level of operations will need to be scaled upwards.
HRM	People are a key asset in the development of any product or service, from the actual conception of the idea to the construction of prototypes.
R&D	The level of R&D required clearly depends on the type of product being planned. For some products there may be many years of R&D before they can be launched.
Introductory phase (also known as pioneering stage)	Customers' knowledge and awareness are usually limited. Low sales volumes and growth as market becomes familiar with the product's features and benefits.
Customers	Initially few customers. These are likely to be first innovators then early adopters.
Competitors	If this is a totally new product entering a new market sector, competitors will be either very few or non-existent. However, if the company is launching a new product into a market with similar products, the competition could be significant.
Marketing	Activities such as advertising, trialling and special introductory offers are used to increase customer awareness. For a new company and new product the risks are high due to uncertain demand. There may be little or no competition.
Finance	Investment and other expenses will be high relative to revenues. Cash flow will be negative. Established companies may be able to finance new products from existing resources. New companies with new products will seek financing from venture capitalists and banks. This is a potentially high-risk scenario as limited credit may be available.
Operations	A company may need to sub-contract manufacture, especially if specialist work is required. There could be frequent alterations in order to 'perfect' the product. A 'rush to market' before technical problems are resolved could prove damaging for both the company and the product. Later entrants into the market may gain a favourable position and market share because of the better reliability of their product.

HRM	Quality personnel with both the skills and adaptability are necessary. This is true whether it is an established company or a new start-up. Entrepreneurs may have good ideas, but they need the right team to develop and produce the product.
R&D	The company must seek feedback on its product and carry out R&D to eliminate bugs. This is particularly true of computer software packages. Equally, as competitors enter the market, R&D is necessary to create new enhanced versions of the product to help maintain market share and position.
Growth phase	Sales and subsequent revenues grow, often rapidly. Companies need to gain market share before competitors (with better economies of scale) gain position through lower prices. Late entrants may gain position through greatly superior products and services.
Customers	At this stage the typical product is moving into the mass market sector. This is reflected by the increased 'mass' of customers purchasing the product, typically early majority adopters.
Competitors	These will have increased as established companies, as well as perhaps new entrants, see market opportunities.
Marketing	Companies seek out niches and use the marketing mix to build product awareness, and potential customer loyalty.
Finance	Increase in revenues, reduced unit costs. However increase in costs to support growth and counter/defend against competitive attack. Cashflow management important and budget planning for further growth and development.
Operations	Potential expansion of facilities leading to increased costs. Larger production runs increase efficiency (economies of scale). Operations will need to cope with increased demand without compromising quality. Need to balance efficiency costs against promotional activities such as price cuts which could affect profits.
HRM	Increased productivity achieved through more employees, overtime, or a combination of both. Increase in costs. Some employees may not want to work overtime. Also long-term overtime can lead to exhausted employees with an impact on their health, the quality of finished product and deteriorating relationships with management. Potential for strike action.
R&D	Need for continued improvement in production processes to reduce costs and improve the product to successfully differentiate it from competitors' products.
Maturity phase	Product accepted by current and potential buyers. Product may be reaching saturation point within this market. Product differentiation and market dominance important. Profit growth in the early stages of maturity, however it will (though not always) fall in the latter part of the declining stage.
Customers	While the current customer base will continue to purchase there may well be late majority adopters of the product.
Competitors	If it is a financially valuable market sector many competitors will remain active.
Marketing	The company will focus on protecting its market share with the identification of new markets, new segments and/or distribution channels. Companies will seek to increase usage through the current customer base, for example, marketing 'breakfast' cereal as an 'anytime' snack. While some advertising will keep the product in the customer's mind, it is unlikely to gain significant levels of new customers.

/continued overleaf

Table 9.7 continued	
Finance	Companies need to prepare themselves for the eventual decline of the product. As Fowler and Thomas (1993) state, 'care must be taken to insure that sufficient financial support is available to allow the mature product to maintain its market position as long as it remains profitable but to reduce that support as the maturity stage reaches its end making recovery of that investment difficult'.
Operations	Here the company needs to control and minimise costs. This includes inventories and the proper maintenance of facilities (as replacement of equipment is unlikely unless it serves another purpose, for instance a new product).
HRM	This can be an area of significant difficulty, with poor morale and motivation, redundancies and early retirements, and transfers to other parts of the organisation.
R&D	R&D will either have little involvement in this product, focusing its attention on new products, or be seeking ways to improve the product for the current or new markets.
Declining phase	A substantial reduction in demand resulting in decreased revenue and profits. This stage can be very difficult for companies as they can encounter 'variations' in decline. If demand and thus revenues continue to decline the company may decide to terminate the product before a 'natural' death.
Customers	There will now be an overall decline in customers. However, laggards may well be at their adoption stage.
Competitors	With decline in demand competitors will seek to exit the market place in the most cost-efficient manner possible. This may include selling their brand and associated facilities to another company, maybe even to a previous rival.
Marketing	Little marketing activity will take place, the aim being to reduce overall marketing expenditure. Distributors and intermediaries may also seek to reduce the levels of stock they carry.
Finance	Increased costs and reduced revenues eventually lead to losses. A company with a large market share and low production costs might remain in the industry: although profits will fall it can remain in the business for some time. A company with high market share and high costs will encounter losses, but it might decide to remain in a market that others desert in the hope of returning to profitability. A company may seek to terminate the product. It will need to offset this against the costs of exiting the market, such as closing plant and making staff redundant. Alternatively it may seek to sell the product to another company in a different location or region.
Operations	Production is being scaled down, so there will be smaller production runs. Thus there will have to be a balance between managing inventory, the costs incurred through small production runs and the revenue generated. The company could subcontract small runs to other manufacturers (if there are standardised facilities) or devote resources to another product.

In this section some of the key issues for and against the product life cycle are outlined. Like all theories and models, it has its flaws, its supporters and its detractors. Thus it is important to understand the product life cycle within this critical environment.

Table 9.8 (overleaf) summarises some of the possible limitations of, and objections to, the product life cycle concept.

Although there are potential limitations or objections to the concept there remains an over-whelming acceptance of the model, but caution should be exercised: it is not a flawless concept. Urban and Star (1996) suggest that the product life cycle concept has been accepted for three key reasons. First, it is easy to understand as a concept. Second, it is intuitively appealing, and third, that examples have been published for industries where some life cycle patterns have been established. Perhaps as Groucutt *et al.* (2004) suggest, the product life cycle concept should be considered as an aid to determining

HRM	Here there is the possibility of excess personnel. As with the maturity stage companies will seek a reduction in the workforce, which could be achieved through redundancies, early retirements or retaining/relocating workers to other tasks/plants.
R&D	R&D will have a minimal involvement. Its focus will be on the development of new products or improving existing ones (perhaps for other markets or earlier life stages).
Rejuvenation phase (also known as restaging or revitalisation)	This usually takes place during the maturity stage of the life cycle. The company sees an opportunity to extend the life of the product. It might radically overall a range of elements from components, the product itself (perhaps a redesign), or attempt rejuvenation through promotion.
Customers	These will usually be a combination of existing 'loyal' and new customers. The company will need the new customers to prove that rejuvenation of the product was a justified action.
Competitors	Some previous competitors may remain within the market and may decide to rejuvenate their products in a similar way. Equally if the rejuvenated product has moved into another market segment there will be competition from companies already operating in that segment.
Marketing	This may involve 'reinventing the product', positioning it within a previously untapped market or niche (which could be overseas) or a mixture of both. This will require an intense level of promotion, especially if breaking into a new market and battling against established competitors within that market. There needs to be a planned and sustained campaign (using the elements of the marketing mix) to sustain or gain and retain market position.
Finance	The company will need to invest not only in R&D but also in supporting the relaunch and growth of the product.
Operations	Operations will need to gear up (including adding new plant and machinery, where necessary) for both the relaunch and estimated demand for the product.
HRM	While there may still be a reduction of staffing levels (initially) the company must be sure that it has the properly trained workforce to develop and maintain production and sales targets.
R&D	R&D may have attributed in the first place to the rejuvenation of the product. The company may seek to regularly review the product to see if enhancements can continually breathe new life into it. Equally, the introduction of revolutionary new compatible technologies can assist in increasing the life expectancy of the product.

Source: adapted from Fowler and Thomas (1993) and Groucutt et al. (2004).

the position of a product (within its life-span) within a market, but not the sole determinant.

Different shapes and sizes

Although Figure 9.10 shows the archetypical product life cycle curve, this is far from the reality of many product cycles. Kotler (1998) suggests that researchers have identified anything from 6 to 17 different product life cycle patterns. However it is possible that there are significantly more, especially if the focus is placed on specific products rather than generic products or phase (such as short-term or immediate fads). Below are a few examples of varying product life cycles.

Figure 9.11 (overleaf) shows the curve for what is normally referred to as a fad item, although it could equally be a short-lived fashion item. An example is a manufactured pop star or group that has one hit and then disappears from the scene, as

Table 9.8 Limitations of and objections to the product life cycle concept

Author(s)	Limitation or objection	Brief description
Brownlie and Bart (1985)	Clear definition of market	The concept might requires the collection of disparate product segments into one market. This could be misleading where market boundaries cannot be readily and accurately identified. Many products cannot be defined within a generalist life cycle.
	Too general	As a prescriptive tool it is difficult to apply specific strategies. This reflects the problem of knowing when the turning points are within the life cycle. Can that be achieved through market analysis alone?
	Influence of external factors	The issue here is that the concept does not allow for the impact or influence of external environmental forces such as changing economic conditions that might influence short-term buying decisions. These might reflect artificial turning points (or blips) in the life cycle.
	Level of influence over the life cycle	It may not be obvious when, how or if at all that marketing strategies influence the life cycle. It is possible that pioneering companies and those that dominate the market do have influence.
	Length of stages	The length of stages can vary within and across markets. Thus it is difficult to determine the precise length of any stage.
Bennett (1999)	Life span of a new product	Difficult to predict the life span of a new product. It could be quite long or relatively short (see mini case 9.9 on the Sinclair C5)
	Competitors' behaviour	Even with competitor intelligence, it is often difficult to predict the actions of the competition. Their actions may be a primary factor in the longevity of the product irrespective of the product's real or perceived position within the life cycle.
	Marketing input	This is the skill of the marketing department to judge trends and the level of resourcing that they have available.
	Product termination	Death is not inevitable. The decision to terminate a product is a management one. There may be opportunities within the marketplace to repeatedly extend the product's life expectancy.
Groucutt (2003b)	Snapshot in time and location	The life cycle is often viewed as a snapshot in time, and so as static. In reality it is dynamic and fluid. Therefore companies need to view the life cycle as a continually fluctuating entity. This then links back to Bennett's argument that the marketing staff must be highly skilled in understanding the dynamics of the market, from both a predictive and a reactive perspective. Equally it is a 'snapshot' of location. For instance a product may be in decline in one country or region yet in an aggressive growth phase in another country or region.

consumers move on to another group or a completely new music fad.

The curve in Figure 9.12 is feasible for a fashion item within a seasonal collection. A relatively step growth phase is followed by a minimal maturity stage and then a step decline. Prior to decline (or because of it) the price is likely to be drastically reduced to sell off stock, especially as the new season's range will already be in store.

Figure 9.13 shows a possible product life cycle for real Christmas trees, which from the buyer's perspective is clearly a seasonal activity, but one that (currently at least) recurs every year.

Finally, in Figure 9.14 there is the cycle for a

Figure 9.11

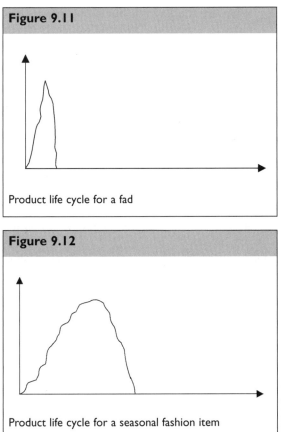

Product life cycle for a fad

Figure 9.12

Product life cycle for a seasonal fashion item

Figure 9.13

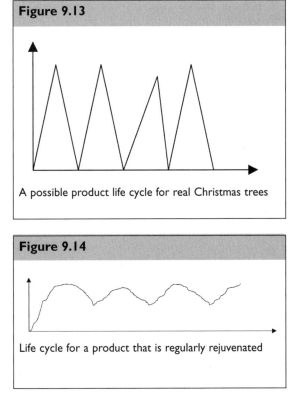

A possible product life cycle for real Christmas trees

Figure 9.14

Life cycle for a product that is regularly rejuvenated

product that transforms itself through various 'mini' lifecycle changes from growth, maturity, decline, then rejuvenation, growth, maturity, decline, rejuvenation and so on. The product may actually enjoy a very long overall lifespan. Examples are classic movies that are originally screened in the cinema, then on television, video, DVD and then again in the cinema as they enjoy a retrospective or indeed an anniversary (perhaps with the launch of a digitally enhanced version). Movies that fit this type of life cycle span include the epics *Gone With the Wind* (1939), *ET: THE EXTRA-TERRESTRIAL* (1982) and *Star Wars* (1977). Will these epics ever disappear, as they still generate revenues for the owners of their rights? Only time will tell.

■ Chapter summary

This chapter has covered a wide range of issues concerning products, their development, and

potential life cycles including adoption and potential destruction. It is vital that you consider the following issues:

◆ How products are developed, including their rationale for development. New products are not always supported by sound market research. Therefore what is the risk assessment?

◆ What products and services are being developed and why. There has to be a clear rationale for the development of products and services.

◆ What markets the products and services are aimed at. Do they constructively meet the needs of these markets?

◆ Not everyone will buy into the company's product or service, therefore the company needs to know why.

◆ If the company operates within a highly dynamic and competitive environment it needs to consider whether it can sustain its position in that market. If not, it may need to consider either terminating the brand or selling it on to another company. Timing is everything in this game.

♦ Overall companies need to understand what makes one product or service more successful than another. It may not just be a case of the financial investment. People play an important part in taking a product or service to market.

♦ What is the expected life stage of the product or service on offer? Can the life stage be extended, and if so, how?

■ Questions for review and reflection

1 The product life cycle is one of the most widely used models in marketing. However, there is significant disagreement among both academics and researchers about its real value. Outline the arguments for and against the product life cycle model. What is your view? Support it with evidence.

2 Can the analysis of product life cycles provide clear indicators for the evaluation of a company's business and marketing strategies and the possible need for change?

3 Research indicates that some 80 per cent of new products launched into the market fail. How can a company reduce the risk of failure when introducing a new product into the market?

4 Briefly outline how B2B and B2C products are classified.

5 Some writers have suggested that products can be 'standardised' so that they can be sold anywhere in the world. Critically evaluate this point of view.

6 'You can market test *ad infinitum* and still fail in the market.' What is your view of this statement and why?

7 Using the Internet and library resources, examine the adoption process in relation to mobile phones in your country.

8 What are the key attributes of a product as noted by Dibb *et al.* (1997) and Kotler (1998)? In your view how do they help marketers gain a clear understanding of the relationship between the product and the buyer?

9 What are the core difference between B2B and B2C products?

10 Why is the S-shaped curve often called the stereotypical product life cycle?

■ References

3M (2003) Information sourced from the 3M website, www.3m.com.

7-Eleven (2003) The history of 7-Eleven, details of its international licensing arrangements and country locations can be found on www.7-eleven.com.

Alashban, A. A., Hayes, L. A., Zinkhan, G. M. and, Balazs, A. L. (2002) 'International brand name standardization/adaptation: antecedents and consequences', *Journal of International Marketing* **10**(3), pp, 22–48.

Baker, M. J. (2000) *Marketing Strategy and Management*, 3rd edn, Basingstoke: Macmillan.

Brownlie, D. T. and Bart, C. K. (1985) *Products and Strategies*, MCB University Press. **11** (1) (cited in M. McDonald (1996) *Strategic Marketing Planning*, 2nd edn, London: Kogan Page.

Clancy, K. and Shulman, R. S. (1991) *The Marketing Revolution: A radical manifesto for dominating the marketplace*, New York: Harper.

Colby, C. L. and Parasuraman. A. (2003) 'Technology still matters: never mind the doomsayers, e-services are alive, well and positioned for growth', *Marketing Management* **12**(4) (July/August), pp. 28–33.

Cooper, R. G. and Kleinschmidt. E. J. (1991a) 'New product processes at leading industrial firms', *Industrial Marketing Management*, May, pp. 137–47.

Cokayne, F. (1991) *Successful Marketing Strategies*, Cambridge: Fitzwilliam.

Daniels, J. D. and Radebaugh, L. H. (1998) *International Business: Environments and Operations*, 8th edn, Reading, Mass.: Addison-Wesley.

Dibb, S., Simkin, L., Pride. W. M. and Ferrell. O. C. (1997) *Marketing: Concepts and strategies*, 3rd edn, Boston, Mass.: Houghton Mifflin.

Doole, I. and Lowe. R. (1999) *International Marketing Strategy: Analysis, development and implementation*, 2nd edn, London: International Thomson Business Press.

Drucker, P. F. (1999) *Innovation and Entrepreneurship: Principles and practice*, Oxford: Butterworth-Heinemann.

Eckles, R. W. (1990) *Business Marketing Management: Marketing of business products and services*, New Jersey: Prentice Hall.

Ford, H. and Crowther, S. (1926) *My Life and Work*, London: William Heinemann.

Fowler, A. R. Jr. and Thomas, J. (1993) 'Functional strategic response to progression through the product life cycle: an accommodation to marketing reality', *American Business Review* (June), pp. 36–44.

Goncalves, V. F. Da. C. and Aguas, P. M. R. (1997) 'The concept of life cycle: an application to the tourist product', *Journal of Travel Research* **36**(2) (Fall), pp. 12–23.

Groucutt, J. (2003a) 'Extending the marketing mix', Working paper.

Groucutt, J. (2003b) 'An analysis of various product lifecycles', unpublished teaching materials.

Groucutt, J. and Griseri, P. (2004) *Mastering e-Business*, Basingstoke: Palgrave Macmillan.

Groucutt, J., Leadley, P. and Forsyth, P. (2004) *Marketing: Essential principles, new realities*, London: Kogan Page.

Higgins, K. T. (2003) 'The rebirth of 7-Eleven', *Marketing Management* **12**(4) (July/August), pp. 18–21.

Hooley, G. J. (1995) 'The lifecycle concept revisited: aid or albatross?', *Journal of Strategic Marketing* **3**(1), pp. 23–39.

Inwood, D. and Hammond, J. (1993) *Product Development: An integrated approach*, London: Kogan Page.

Jauch, L. R. and Glueck, F. W. (1988) *Business Policy and Strategic Management*, 5th edn, New York: McGraw-Hill.

Jobber, D. (1998) *Principles and Practice of Marketing*, 2nd edn, Maidenhead: McGraw-Hill.

Kerin, R. A. and Peterson, R. A. (1980) *Perspectives on Strategic Marketing Management*, Boston: Allyn and Bacon.

Kotler, P. (19   ning, implem   Jersey: Prentice

Levitt, T. (1983) *The Ma*   Free Press.

Mattelart, A. and Mattelart,   *Communication: A short introdu*

Rees, N. (1997) *Dictionary of Slogans,*   Collins.

Reid, R. D. (1989) *Hospitality Marketing Ma*   3rd edn, New York: Van Nostrand Reinhold.

Robertson, T. S. (1984) 'Marketing's potential contrib   tion to consumer behavior research: the case of   diffusion theory', *Advances in Consumer Research* **2**,   pp. 484–9.

Rogers, E. M. (1983) *Diffusion of Innovations*, 3rd edn, New York: Free Press.

Rogers. E. and Kincaid. L. (1981) *Communication Networks: Towards a new paradigm for research*, New York: Free Press.

Shimp, T. A. (2000) *Advertising Promotion: Supplemental aspects of integrated marketing communications*, Fort Worth: Dryden Press.

Stanton, W. J., Etzel, M. J. and Walker, B. J. (1994) *Fundamentals of Marketing*, 4th edn,. New York: McGraw-Hill.

Underhill. P. (1999) *Why We Buy: The science of shopping*, London: Orion Business Books.

Unilever (1999) Annual Report & Accounts.

Urban. G. I. and Star, S. H. (1996) *Advanced Marketing Strategy*, New Jersey: Prentice Hall.

Valente, T. W. and Rogers, E. M. (1995) 'The origins and development of the diffusion of innovations paradigm as an example of scientific growth', *Science Communication*, March, pp. 242–73.

World, The (2004) *The World: Corporate and Media Fact Sheets*, www.aboardtheworld.com.

Zikmund, W. G. and D'Amico, M. (1999) *Marketing*, 6th edn, Mason: South-Western Publishing.

8) *Marketing Management: Analysis, plan-
ntation and control*, 9th edn, New
Hall.

M. (1998) *Theories of
tion*, London: Sage.
ondon: Harper-

keting Imagination*, New York:

agement,

Promotional strategy and tactics	215
Advertising	215
Early development phase	215
Modern development phase	217
Challenge and defence phase	218
Types of advertising	220
Types of advertising media	222
Direct marketing	230
Direct marketing techniques	231
Kiosks	232
Buzz, or word of mouth promotion	232
Product placement	236
Movie tie-ins	236
Merchandising the brand	237
Examples of merchandising	237
Celebrity endorsements	238
Sponsorship	239
Potential benefits of sponsorship	239
Sales promotion	240
Types of sales promotion	240
Sales promotions can be too successful	242
Exhibitions, expos and trade fairs	242
Public relations	242
Scope of public relations	244
Integrated marketing communications	244
The future	246
Chapter summary	246
Questions for review and reflection	246
References	247

n

omes

…his chapter you should be able to:

…ritically evaluate the various communications models

…luate the different types of promotional activities that an organisation could use to market its products or services

▶ discuss the different models used in persuading a consumer to purchase a product or service

▶ evaluate the concept of integrated marketing communications.

■ Introduction

Promotion is an all-encompassing word that describes the tactics used by organisations to raise and sustain the profile of their product or service in the mind of the customer. An organisation's objective is to gain and sustain a competitive advantage in the marketplace. This applies equally to not-for-profit and profit-centred organisations. Charities and other non-governmental organisations need to advance or actively promote their causes in order to generate donations for their important work. As with for-profit organisations, they use promotional tactics to communicate their messages to potential donors.

However, promotion is not only directed at people external to the organisation. Marketing is not only an external activity. Organisations need to consider how they market internally to their employees.

This chapter examines both internal and external marketing in the context of the various promotional tactics organisations use. Psychology (in the background) and the overt use of psychology are important areas in considering how products and services are promoted to individuals and groups. Therefore it is important for you to consider the chapter on psychology and how promotion and psychology interrelate. Moreover, you will see that there are important interrelations with other elements of the marketing mix.

■ Promotional objectives

For a promotion to be effective it must encompass one or more objectives. Rossiter and Percy (1987) identified four key objectives:

◆ **Creating a primary demand or market.** This is particularly relevant where a company is planning to either introduce a new product into an existing market or create a new market. For example, consider the introduction of the first mobile phones. In essence a market had to be created and the focus was on business people working in large cities (which could be networked) who wanted to be at the forefront of communication technology. (You may want to reflect back to Chapter 9 on products and consider the relationship to the diffusion model.)

◆ **Create brand awareness.** Through the various promotional tactics at the disposal of companies, they can inform current and potential customers of the features and benefits of their brands. Whether it is a new or established brand it is vital that companies are able to maintain awareness of it in the minds of customers. This is particularly the case where the market is saturated, there is a high degree of competition and there is a risk of new entrants into the marketplace.

◆ **Enhancing attitudes and influencing intentions.** In developing their promotional campaigns companies seek to create a positive attitude towards their brand(s). By direct statement or inference, the promotion will illustrate how the brand will benefit customers, fulfilling their individual needs and wants. This benefit might be cleaner hygienic floors or the seductive taste of a luscious rich dark chocolate. Each of these benefits psychologically links with a customer's needs and/or desires. If potential customers have been influenced by the promotions they may intend to purchase that brand the next time they seek to fulfil their needs and wants.

◆ **Facilitating purchase.** Clearly developing the market, creating awareness and influencing attitudes are worthless activities if potential customers have difficulty in locating the brand. Just imagine for a moment if after the frantic build-up to the launch of J. K. Rowling's fifth Harry Potter book, *Harry Potter and the Order of the Phoenix* (published in 2003) only a limited number of copies were available in a few hard-to-find bookshops. If this had happened then there would have been much embarrassment for the publishers, distributors and retailers. Equally, there would have been millions of angry Harry Potter fans (and parents!) worldwide. While this might be an extreme scenario, it demonstrates the importance of linking promotion to the ready availability of the product.

The promotional objectives must effectively and efficiently link with the other marketing mix elements. Achieving this generates not only brand awareness but also equity over the term of the brand's life cycle.

■ Communication models

Prior to examining the individual components that comprise promotion, it is important to gain some understanding of the communication processes involved. We are all involved in the communication process. Even before humankind could speak we communicated – through actions – our thoughts and fears. Throughout the centuries individuals have communicated to other individuals and groups through the spoken and written word. Through our study of history, literature and

Figure 10.1

EasyJet uses its planes as a promotional tool

philosophy we have come to appreciate the words of Aristotle, Plato, Lincoln, Dickens, Tolstoy, Descartes and others. Through their speeches and writings they communicated ideals, concepts and often raw emotions. The 20th century brought a proliferation of mass media that would change the nature of communication forever.

Communications has often been seen as a single-step model comprising a sender, the message itself and the receiver of that message (Figure 10.2). While it does work in many situations, this model is far too simplistic to accommodate the realities of life. It does not consider whether or not receivers understand the message communicated to them, an issue that will be discussed later.

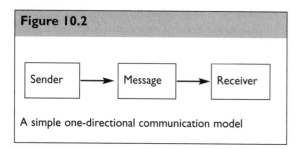

Figure 10.2

A simple one-directional communication model

Lasswell (1927) devised a model that considered:

Who
Says what
In which channel
To whom it may concern
To what effect

The difference between Lasswell's model and the simple communications model in Figure 10.2 is that it considers the channel used and the effect of the message. While this is an useful development, there remained the need for enhancement and an understanding of the environment in which the communication took place. Models on this basis did not originate until the late 1940s.

Shannon[1] (1948) published a theory that encapsulated communications theory. Horgan (1990) stated that Shannon's initial goal was to 'improve the transmission of information over a telegraph or telephone line affected by electrical interference, or noise. The best solution he decided, was not to improve transmission lines but to package information more efficiently.' On this basis Shannon developed a linear model of communications, what is often referred to as a transmission model.

Mattelart and Mattelart (1998) state that this was:

> Based on a chain of constituent elements: the source of information which produces a message, the encoder or transmitter, which transfers the message into signals allowing transmission, the channel, which is the means to send the signals, the decoder or receiver, which reconstructs the message from the signals, and the destination, which is the person or thing that receives the message.

This model is shown in Figure 10.3. What is clear from observing this model is its linearity.

However as Rogers (1994) indicates, the Shannon model is very mathematical in its structure, and still has a linear format. Schramm (1955) adapted the model to include a greater understand-

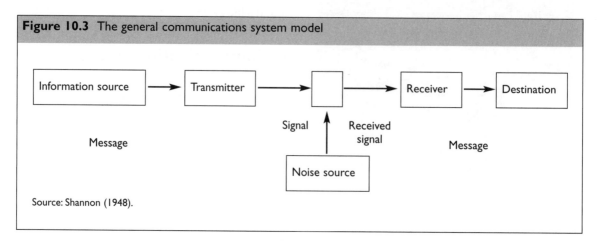

Figure 10.3 The general communications system model

Source: Shannon (1948).

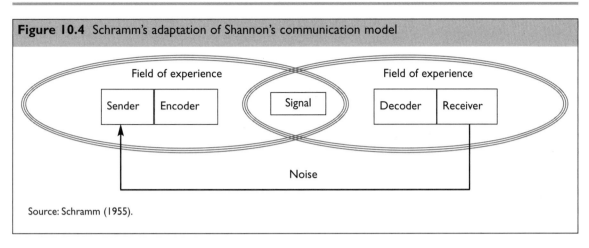

Figure 10.4 Schramm's adaptation of Shannon's communication model

Source: Schramm (1955).

ing of human interaction in the communication process. There was also an increasing debate on the effect of mass communication on society after the Second World War. As we have seen in earlier chapters (and will in later ones), marketers were already studying the psychological aspects of behaviour and communication.

Figure 10.4 shows Schramm's adaptation of Shannon's model. This is the model that you will see in most textbooks on marketing and marketing communications, perhaps with some further minor adaptations. Schramm (1955) believed that communication could not occur unless the field of experience of the sender and receiver overlapped. In the 21st century this aspect of the model might be thought debatable, especially in terms of marketing communications. While similar knowledge or experience of course aids communication, we often communicate to people who have little or no equivalent field of experience. It therefore becomes the art or science of the individual to communicate knowledge to the recipient in a way that can be easily understood and remembered.

Reflect for a moment on the first time you sat in a lecture theatre. What was your field of experience compared with that of the professor presenting a topic to you? Probably very far removed from it. The professor's task was to communicate not only his or her knowledge but also the rudiments of a specific topic within a defined time frame. In many ways marketers have exactly the same task, this time aimed at potential customers who have not previously considered the product or service. They need to find the media channels, a style and a frequency suitable for the target audience.

Although Schramm's model is a further development, it too can be considered limiting. The model tends to assume one-to-one communication as the norm. Although there has been a move in marketing since the 1970s to develop a more one-to-one marketing approach, tactical marketing communication involves several channels. Thus noise, for instance, can affect both single and multiple channels.

Figure 10.5 attempts to illustrate (although one-dimensionally) the following:

◆ More than one communication channel may be used at any one time to communicate to more than one individual. Think about how you would communicate to a mass audience.

◆ How one person decodes the message may be different from how another person decodes it. For example, look at either a television or magazine advertisement. Decide what it means to you, then show it to several friends and ask them the same question. You may find that you do not all 'see' the same thing!

◆ As the communication is to more people, so there is a greater amount of feedback. This feedback will vary in type and intensity. However, the feedback should not be considered as a single loop from the receiver to the sender. On receiving the feedback the sender may need to communicate further with the receiver, so this should be considered more as a double-loop feedback system than as single one-way traffic.

Figure10.5 An expansion of Schramm's communication model

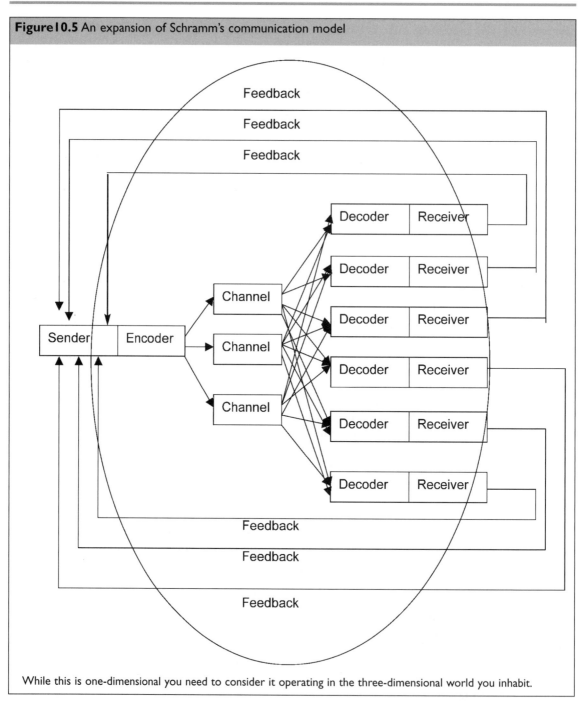

While this is one-dimensional you need to consider it operating in the three-dimensional world you inhabit.

♦ Noise or the potential for noise is all-pervasive across all elements of the communication. This is shown in Figure 10.5 as a wire framework. At any point in the communications process noise can disrupt the communications process itself or the meaning of the message being communicated.

Berlo (1960) devised a communications model that emphasised the relationship between the sender and receiver of the communication. He considered this an important variable in the communications process. Figure 10.6 illustrates a simplified version of Berlo's model.

Feedback and noise

Schramm's model develops two important aspects, feedback and noise (Schramm 1955). To some extent the concept of 'feedback' links to Lasswell's 1927 model and the statement 'to what effect'. Feedback provides an interaction, and can be considered in the following forms:

◆ a discussion, comment and analysis of the issue(s) being communicated

◆ a mechanism for clarification of points and issues – perhaps through focus groups

◆ a critical response to the message, which could be translated, for example, into a boycott of a product or service

◆ a positive response to the message, for example, an increase in purchases.

Noise can be described as the interruptions or distortions that influence the communications process or understanding of a message. Noise can be divided into four subsets: physical, semantic, competitive and channel overload.

Physical noise

As the title suggests, this is anything that 'physically' reduces the effectiveness or efficiency of the message communicated. In other words it is the physical distortion that affects the communication and the resultant understanding of that communication. Imagine for a moment that you are at the end of an aircraft runway. You are on your mobile phone to your favourite person. You are about to tell them how you feel about them, then an A380 flies over your head. If your friend hears anything at all it will be patchy, distorted, noisy and for a large part incomprehensible. In fact, they could mishear words, and this could give them a false impression of how you feel about them. You might say, 'There can never be anyone else,' and they might hear, 'There … else,' which makes them think that there is someone else.

This is an extreme example, but it goes some way to explain that physical distortion affects how we both send and receive messages. Consider another example. You are standing near the edge of a metro platform reading a large poster on the other side of the tracks. You are engrossed in this poster, and half-way through reading the text when a metro train hurtles into the platform and all you see are carriages flashing at speed before your eyes. The message on the poster has disappeared. You might catch it at another station or you might not. In fact you might never see that poster again, or remember the brand name being promoted.

Physical noise is thus anything that physically distracts you from reviewing the promotion, whether it is a poster on the metro, an advertisement in a magazine, a radio commercial, a text message or a television commercial. These physical distractions can range from movements in front of the television set blocking vision to a train hurtling past a poster on a billboard in a railway station.

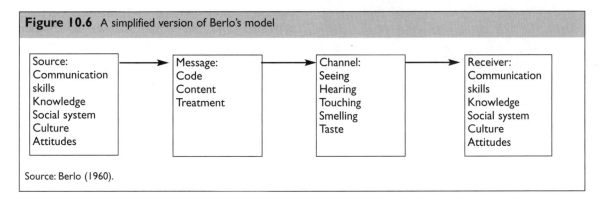

Figure 10.6 A simplified version of Berlo's model

Source: Communication skills Knowledge Social system Culture Attitudes	Message: Code Content Treatment	Channel: Seeing Hearing Touching Smelling Taste	Receiver: Communication skills Knowledge Social system Culture Attitudes

Source: Berlo (1960).

Semantic noise

This relates to the actual meanings of words and phrases, and is often used to discuss 'cultural noise'. Even when the words or phrases are in the native language of the individuals receiving the message, there can be misunderstanding. Consider, for instance, how many times you have misunderstood what has been said to you by relatives. This kind of misunderstanding or 'semantic noise' can happen anywhere. For instance, a company might advertise a product or service using ideas that its home-country staff find funny. However, in another country the humour might not be understood. At best the advertisement would be ignored; at worst it could be considered offensive and the product might be boycotted as a result.

Therefore companies, whether they are advertising in their own country or another, must consider how the language they use will 'play out': that is, how will it be received. These cultural perspectives must be considered closely.

Competitive noise

This aspect of noise is often either overlooked or mixed in with physical noise. Both are

inappropriate, as they assume that competitive noise is a secondary function.

If a company operates in a highly competitive environment, a rival (rightly or wrongly) might attempt to disorientate its customers through spoiler promotional campaigns designed to discredit it. This is a high-risk strategy for the rival company, because its own integrity could be discredited if customers realise it is taking such an approach. This is clearly an ethical issue. However companies do use this approach to 'off-balance' their rivals, and this creates 'noise' in the marketing environment.

Channel overload

Some authors do not consider this as 'noise' in the strictest sense of the word. However, it is clearly something that can lead to the distortion of the communication message, and thus should be included under the category of noise. Imagine you are standing in front of your best friend and he or she is talking to you. Then imagine that 20 other people stand around your friend and simultaneously start talking to you, all saying different things. However, each one is saying something that is relevant to you. You stand there trying desperately to snatch the meaning of each communication from the 21 people in front of you, but you only grasp a morsel of each message. You never see the full picture that the 21 people in front of you are trying to communicate. Thus you stand in a world that is 'cluttered' by communication.

When the only means of communication was the solitary village or town weekly newspaper, there was little in the way of communications clutter. However, consider the communications market now. We are constantly bombarded by 24-hour multi-channel television (satellite, terrestrial and cable), the Internet, newspaper and magazine advertising, various forms of direct marketing, radio and cinema advertising, one-to-one selling, in-store promotions, telemarketing and mobile text messages. It is endless. Thus the communications market is overloaded with various promotional messages. The critical issue for companies in the 21st century is how they can cut through this clutter, this channel overload that creates its own very special presence within the marketplace.

Figure 10.7

© Jonathan Groucutt

Sometimes the simplest of tactics help a company to break through the clutter. Here in a London street a man holds aloft a small billboard to advertise an 'as much as you can eat' buffet lunch.

Promotional strategy and tactics

A company can use various promotional tactics, many of which are listed below. These can be used as either stand-alone or integrated tactics. However, the company needs to carefully consider which are used separately and which are combined. The decision must be based on how best to use the tactic(s) to achieve the overall promotional objectives of the product or service:

◆ advertising

◆ direct marketing

◆ sales promotion

◆ sponsorship

◆ product placement

◆ merchandising

◆ public relations

◆ word of mouth – viral marketing

◆ exhibitions.

Advertising

Advertising is far from new. Cave drawings over 2500 years old illustrate primitive forms of advertising. Commercial advertising was well established in ancient Greece (Fletcher 1999), and burgeoned during the time of the Roman Empire. Just imagine how the 50 000 seats in the Rome's Colosseum were filled with spectators for the gladiatorial events. Posters were placed around Rome and outlying towns announcing the often extravagant events. The gruesome public hangings that took place at Tyburn (now Marble Arch, Oxford Street, London, England) between the 14th and 18th centuries were also heralded by poster campaigns. These hangings were public events, and the lawmakers of the day wanted to show the power of their authority, hence the publicity that surrounded them.[2]

Thus advertising is not a new function of society. However, how it is used and the channels through which it can be used are radically different from those of Ancient Rome and London of the Tyburn period.

Before we consider the different forms of advertising it is appropriate to define advertising. Colley (1961) suggested that the role of advertising could be defined as follows:

> Advertising's job purely and simply is to communicate, to a defined audience, information and a frame-of-mind that stimulate action. Advertising succeeds or fails depending on how well it communicates the desired information and attitudes to the right people at the right time at the right cost.

Perhaps a more succinct version would be:

> A paid for communication vehicle that is intended to inform, influence and/or persuade one or more individuals.

However Colley (1961) raises several interesting points that involve both the potential customer's mindset and the need to target customers via the most appropriate media. These are themes that are discussed throughout this chapter, as they are relevant not only to advertising itself, but to other forms of marketing communications.

It is important to realise that advertising is not for free – it is a commercial transaction between those who want to place the advertisement and the media owners. This links to the channels the advertisers use to most effectively communicate their message to their intended audience. The media owners are providing the communications channels.

Basically, advertising has three overarching functions or objectives: to inform, persuade and sell. Various models have been created to demonstrate a sequential learning pattern that has been called, over time, the Hierarchy of Effects. Barry (1987) suggests that the development of the hierarchy of effects, to date, has encompassed three phases: early development, modern development and the challenge and defence phase. What has to be clear from the outset is that since the turn of the 19th century numerous models and adaptations of these models have proliferated. For the purpose of this text a selection has been made to cover the major developments. This in no way negates the value of the other models, but space limits further examination.

Early development phase

An American salesman, St Elmo Lewis, developed the first of these hierarchy models in 1898, now

Figure 10.8

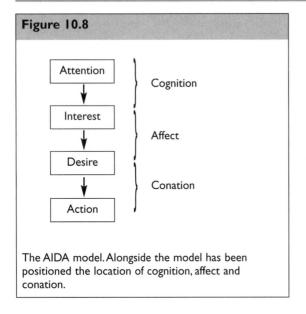

The AIDA model. Alongside the model has been positioned the location of cognition, affect and conation.

commonly known as the AIDA model[3] (see Figure 10.8).

Lewis used this linear process as a means of explaining to sales people how they could improve their sales potential. The sales person had to make the potential customer aware of the product (attention), then raise (interest) by discussing the product's various features and benefits, followed by how these various features and benefits would help the customer (his or her desire), and finally (action) the purchase of the product.

It was not long before revisions to Lewis's model and new models were being conceptualised. Sheldon (1911) added another component to Lewis's model, that of permanent satisfaction to follow action (purchasing). In 1913 the psychologist Walter Dill Scott developed a model (See Figure 10.9)

Figure 10.9

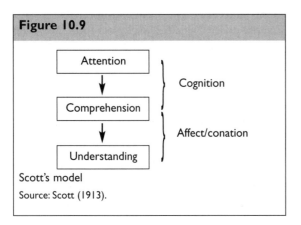

Scott's model
Source: Scott (1913).

which was based on the then current thinking regarding sensory perception and motivation. He applied this model to advertising, and was one of the first to make the link between psychology and advertising. However, while the model leads to understanding it does not necessary result in a purchase.

Strong (1925) postulated a model (Figure 10.10) that has similarities to Lewis's original AIDA model. In Strong's model awareness and interest are combined.

An interesting aspect of Strong's model is the introduction of *satisfaction* as one of the drivers. Perhaps this was the first time that consideration had been given to buyer satisfaction post purchase, in other words buyers' feelings after they have consumed or used the product or service. They might feel positive, negative or even neutral towards the purchase, and how they feel may influence whether or not they purchase and/or recommend the product or service in the future.

Figure 10.10

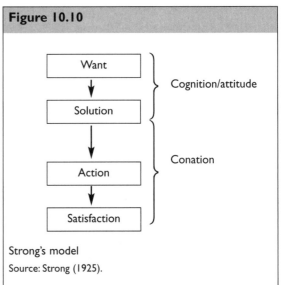

Strong's model
Source: Strong (1925).

Until the 1950s various models were postulated, which mainly relied on the AIDA concept. In summarising this development phase, Barry (1987) contends that:

These early models were descriptive representations based on intuition and logic. There was virtually no empirical analysis of any of them. Some were more psychologically-bounded than others, but it is evident that these models provided the foundation for the discussions of the hierarchy models developed over the next thirty years.

It is interesting to note that the AIDA model remains in use today.

Modern development phase

Lavidge and Steiner (1961) developed from previous models their model for predictive measurements of advertising effectiveness (Table 10.1). They believed much advertising had longer-term effects rather than immediate ones. However, they contended that to gain the potential of the longer-term purchase, there had to be shorter-term actions to build conviction. They developed a model which suggests that consumers move through a series of steps that may not necessarily be equidistant in space and time. The actual purchase depends on the level of need, timing and product/service availability.

It appears that Lavidge and Steiner (1961) were amongst the first to link the hierarchy of effects concept to cognition, affective and conation. They suggested that:

Awareness and knowledge	=	information or ideas (cognition)
Liking and preferences	=	attitudes or feeling (affective)
Conviction and purpose	=	action (conation)

They viewed this more than a semantic issue, suggesting that actions to stimulate a channel are likely to be different from those that provide knowledge. These will also be different from the actions that create a favourable attitude towards the product or service being promoted.

Colley (1961) created a model similar to Lavidge and Steiner's, which has been abbreviated to DAGMAR – Defining Advertising Goals for Measured Advertising Results. Figure 10.11 shows Colley's hierarchy of effects model. Colley was particularly interested in identifying a procedure that would ensure that (Yeshin 1998):

◆ Goals were established and formulated precisely.

◆ The goals could be monitored (benchmarked) and measured.

Table 10.1 Lavidge and Steiner's model

Unawareness	Potential customers are unaware that the product or service exists.
Awareness	The potential customer has become aware of the existence of the product or service.
Knowledge	The potential customer is now informed about the features and benefits the product or service has to offer. Lavidge and Steiner (1961) consider these customers as prospects. It should also be considered here, although not specifically mentioned by Lavidge and Steiner, that prospective customers will seek knowledge not only from the advertising, but potentially from a variety of sources (many of them promotional in form). They will also compare and contrast this product or service with others available on the market to increase their knowledge base.
Liking the product or service	Prospective customers have a favourable attitude to the product or service.
Preference	The product or service has become the preferred choice of prospective customers. It is likely (though not a given fact) that they will have compared its features and benefits of this product or service with those of rivals.
Conviction	Prospective customers are convinced their preferred choice is right. They now have the desire to make the purchase.
Purchase	The final step, the point at which preference and conviction are translated into acquisition.

Source: Lavidge and Steiner (1961).

Figure 10.11

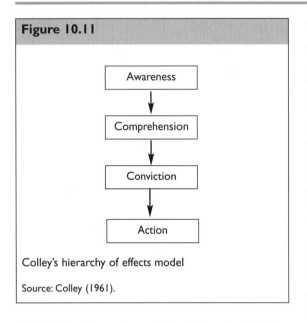

Colley's hierarchy of effects model

Source: Colley (1961).

◆ Precise timescales could be determined for the achievement of the objectives.

◆ The target audience was carefully identified so the right people received the message at the right time and in the right place (channel).

Although Colley's model is often criticised for portraying potential or actual customers as passive, it remains widely used.

Challenge and defence phase

Ray *et al.* (1973) began to challenge how these models were sequenced. Again, as we have seen earlier in this chapter there had been an understandable move towards linearity. As they and others argued, cognition (learning) does not always precede affect (attitude, feeling, emotion) or conation–motivation (behaviour). Taking a different approach, Ray *et al.* (1973) suggested that there were three hierarchy models: the learning, dissonance–attribution and low-involvement hierarchies.

The learning hierarchy

This was considered the learning model. Here the potential consumer proceeds through the cognition–affect–conation stages. This is the traditional model discussed above.

The dissonance-attribution hierarchy

This is considered the reverse of the learning hierarchy model. Here the consumer reacts to the communication, then formulates or develops attitudes and feelings as a result of that reaction or behaviour. The processing of information that supports the original behaviour then follows. For example, you might buy a CD, enjoy listening to it and justify your purchase because you have read rave reviews about it. Thus this is a conation–affect–cognition approach based on the theories of, among others, Festinger (1957). (See also Chapter 16 on psychology.)

Ehrenberg (1974) developed an awareness–trial–reinforcement (ATR) model, which he believed was more in tune with changing patterns of consumer behaviour. Until then models had not considered that most consumers are not brand loyal, preferring instead to switch across brands as it suits them. In 1997 Ehrenberg added a further component to his framework, nudging. Figure 10.12 shows this ATRN model, which is an example of dissonance–attribution.

Ehrenberg's model reflects the following:

◆ Awareness: the potential consumer becomes either initially or further aware, and thus interested in the product or service. Ehrenberg

Figure 10.12

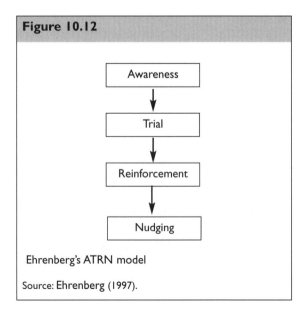

Ehrenberg's ATRN model

Source: Ehrenberg (1997).

suggests that this awareness can be achieved through the use of various promotional tactics.

◆ Trial: the consumer is curious about the product or service and may make an initial purchase to test it. Companies often produce trial-size samples that are either available in-store, distributed through on-pack magazine promotions or delivered house to house.

◆ Reinforcement: marketing communications can reinforce the brand's image and position in the minds of potential consumers.

◆ Nudging: this affects both actual and potential consumers. The objective is to persuade actual consumers to repeat purchase, while encouraging potential consumers to buy for the first time. They in turn may well become repeat buyers over time. Organisations use a variety of communication channels to reinforce the brand's image and values in the mind of the consumer.

Low-involvement hierarchy

This is based upon the early work of Mendelsohn (1962) and later Krugman (1965 and 1966, cited in Barry 1987). Its perspective is that consumers react, and then gain knowledge as a result of that particular behaviour or reaction. As a result of the behaviour and knowledge acquired, they acquire attitudes towards the product or service.

Vaughn (1980, 1986) developed a model based primarily on the low-involvement approach. He suggested four versions:

◆ informative (thinking)

◆ affective (feeler)

◆ habit forming (doer)

◆ self-satisfaction (reactor).

These are shown in Figure 10.13, which to some extent employs the relationship between cognition, affect and conation.

Vaughn (1980) suggests that there are several strategies that can be developed. Quadrant 1 suggests that consumers seek information prior to purchase. The *learn–do–feel* sequence provides an approach where 'functional and salient information

Figure 10.13

Thinking ────────▶ Feeling

	Quadrant 1 **Informative** **(thinker)** High importance Rational decisions Model: learn–feel–do Products: car, new products, furniture	**Quadrant 2** **Affective** **(feeler)** High importance Emotional decisions Model: feel–learn–do Products: fashion, jewellery and motorcycles
High involvement		
Low involvement	**Quadrant 3** **Habit forming** **(doer)** Low importance Rational decisions Model: do–learn–feel Products: food and household	**Quadrant 4** **Self-satisfaction** **(reactor)** Low importance Emotional decisions Model: do–feel–learn Products: drinks and confectionery

Vaughn's model
Source: Vaughn (1980).

is designed to build consumer attitudinal acceptance and subsequent purchase' (Vaughn 1980).

In Quadrant 2 the *feel–learn–do* sequence dominates. Here the strategy relates to consumers' self-esteem, how they 'feel' about a product or service. For example, buyers of Harley-Davidson® motorcycles are not just buying a model of transport, they are buying into an emotional experience.

Quadrant 3 depicts the *do–learn–feel* approach, where the consumer tends to form a convenience buying habit. In other words minimal thought is invested in the decision-making process. This is applicable to the purchase of staple food items. As Vaughan suggests, brand loyalty may also be a function of habit, for instance shopping at the same supermarket or visiting a restaurant on a regular basis. However, within this brand-loyalty mindset, consumers may be loyal to several similar products or service providers. While habits for purchasing particular brands and generic products may form, it must be realised that brands may have a limited life span. Consumers may be introduced to brand replacements through a trialling process (free samples or money-off coupons to entice them to trial purchase the brand).

Quadrant 4 is a *do–feel–learn* approach where consumers are fulfilling their personal tastes through normally short-term satisfaction. Purchases of confectionery, cigarettes and alcohol tend to encapsulate this approach.

As Vaughn (1980) points out, these are not fixed quadrants. That is to say, some products and/or buyer behaviour may overlap quadrants. In an increasing diverse complex world, neither brands nor behaviour are likely to fit comfortably into boxes in all instances.

Barry (2002) suggests that the Hierarchy of Effects concept remains valuable for the following reasons:

◆ It is appealing due to its simplicity, intuitiveness and logic.

◆ It assists in predicting behaviour, no matter how imperfect those predictions appear.

◆ It provides a platform on which advertising strategies should focus (cognition, affect and conation) based on segmentation. It provides a planning, conceptual and training tool.

Hierarchy of effects models have been in existence, in one form or another, for over 100 years. At this stage several points need to be considered:

◆ Several of these models were devised when advertising was the dominant form of promotion. Much of the criticism that surrounds them derives from the fact that the analysis is based on advertising. In some instances it may be advertising that informs and persuades a consumer to take action. However, the sphere of influence is often much wider, encompassing interaction with friends, family, other forms of marketing communication and the rest of the marketing mix. Thus is it important to consider the hierarchy of effects models as not bound by advertising alone, but operating in a wider environmental context.

◆ For ease of description, the models are in a linear form. That suggests two possibilities: first, that there is a linear progression from one position to another, and second, that no external factors influence or intervene in the process. We need to consider these issues in the context of the environments in which these linear models were created. It can be argued that in the late 19th and early 20th centuries researchers and commentators in marketing were at the cutting edge of ideas. It was a time of attempting to understand psychological behaviour, and the introduction of mass production on a scale never before seen. While European countries came to terms with the horror of the First World War and started to rebuild their economies, the United States was prospering – until the Wall Street Crash of 1929. The world has changed significantly and dramatically since those days, and it continues to change, but the concept of linearity has persisted in these models. They still have a value in understanding human behaviour, but they must be considered in the wider context of marketing communications (not just advertising) and in a world governed by complexity, needless to say most of all in human behaviour.

The Hierarchy of Effects models have a value in understanding both marketing within the historic context and processes that customers may undertake to purchase a product or service. However, it is important to consider them in the wider context of marketing communications, the remainder of the marketing mix and the external environment.

Types of advertising

Advertising can be classified into four basic types. Although this is a logical classification, it is important to consider that there are situations where there is an overlap between two or more of these types.

Primary

The objective with primary advertising is to stimulate a demand for a particular product or service (see Figure 10.14). For example, primary advertising is used for the launch of an exhibition, a J. K. Rowling Harry Potter novel or a new James Bond movie. However this form of advertising is not confined to the B2C market: it is equally applicable to the B2B market. Trade organisation as well as suppliers use primary advertising to raise awareness of products and services.

Figure 10.14

© Jonathan Groucutt

An example of primary advertising. A giant poster at the Institut du Monde Arabe in Paris, advertising an art exhibition from 6 May to 17 August 2003.

Selective product or service

Here a manufacturer, for instance, focuses the advertising on a single brand without any reference to its corporate identity. The focus is clearly on the brand and not the brand owner. For example, the various brands owned by Procter & Gamble have their own individual identities. Unless a consumer studied the packaging closely, he or she would not know the brand was owned by or marketed by Procter & Gamble.

Product or service range

Here the focus is on the range of products or services available under one particular brand name. For example, when Unilever advertises its Dove brand,

it might either advertise selective elements of the range, for example, soap, or advertise the full brand range from soap to shampoo. By advertising the whole range Unilever is clearly stating to potential and current customers that there is a Dove product for all their face and body cleansing needs.

Institutional

This is advertising that in some way promotes the corporate identity, image and values of the organisation. For example, in the 1990s BP used television advertising as a channel to promote itself as an energy company rather than (as it originally was) a petroleum company. The advertisement focused not on any one product but on the diverse areas in which the company operated.

Companies and organisations also use advertising as a means of recruiting staff. As well as stating briefly the job requirements, job advertisements usually take the opportunity to emphasise why the organisation is a good one to work for. For example in 2004 the UK Financial Services Authority advertised in *The Sunday Times* newspaper for a director (contract, revenue and information management). The opening section of the advertisement read:

The Financial Services Authority employs 2,300 staff and has a £200m annual budget to tackle a daunting and rapidly changing array of challenges: maintaining market confidence; promote public financial understanding; protecting consumers; and fighting financial crime. It aims to maintain efficient, orderly and clean financial markets and help retail consumers achieve a fair deal. The variety, complex content and wider significance of the issues it deals with equals that of any organisation in Britain. Its launch and early years have been a success. But now it faces a step increase in its regulatory responsibilities, because of the introduction of mortgage and general insurance regulation. Therefore the FSA is reorganizing to realign its strategic priorities, to shift from policy development to policy implementation and to become an easier organization to do business with.

You may want to consider how your college or university advertises for both students and staff (academic and administrative).

Types of advertising media

Simply in terms of advertising, there is an often overwhelming variety of media channels that can be deployed to market a product or service. The following section outlines the key advertising channels. However, it is only an uncritical glimpse of what is currently available. The range of advertising channels will vary from country to country and be affected by the political and legal regime within each country. For instance, government regulations might prevent advertising on television (this is usually the case where the television channel is State owned). You may want to reflect on the advertising environment in your own country.

There may also be restrictions on the type of product/service advertised and the images used to communicate the advertising message. For instance, the advertising (in all its forms) of tobacco products has been banned in several countries.

Print media

As the name suggests this concerns advertisements that appear in newspapers and magazines. The media can be divided into five categories:

Daily newspapers

These can be national or regional, and in broadsheet and/or tabloid format. Generally they have a loyal following, especially if they have a particular political leaning or bias. As a result they are particularly useful for reminder and prestige advertising.

Local and regional newspapers

There are generally two types of local/regional newspaper, those that are free (distributed through either door drops and/or collection at key outlets), and those that are paid for, and sold in (and often delivered by) local newsagents and stores. They contain a mixture of display and classified advertising.

Consumer magazines

Different magazines are published weekly, monthly and quarterly. The subject areas are diverse, ranging from DIY to holidays and women's issues. There are broad classifications such as 'women's magazines', and they can be further segmented by

Figure 10.15

© Jonathan Groucutt

A Parisian news kiosk displaying a wide selection of magazines

their appeal to different ages and socio-economic groups.

Trade and professional magazines

This heading covers two areas: B2B magazines which market products and services to business and industrial customers, and magazines produced by professional organisations or trade bodies as a means of communicating issues with their members. Increasingly these magazines are being placed on web sites (for viewing and/or downloading) rather than published in a conventional print format.

Customer magazines

These are either sold or distributed free to a company's customers. They are produced by the company's marketing department or a specialist contract publishing house. In addition to reinforcing the brand image of the company or organisation, customer magazines provide opportunities for other companies to advertise their products and services. For the publication this creates revenue to cover costs and generate profit. For the advertiser it provides a communications channel to target specific groups.

A company may have different magazines to meet the needs of specific customers. For example, an airline may provide different magazines for economy, business and first-class passengers.

Targeting these groups not only provides a specific link between customers in the groups, it also segments the market for the benefit of advertisers. For instance, Cyprus Airways has *Apollo Executive Review*, which is a quarterly in-flight magazine for its executive club members (business and first-class passengers).

Television, cinema and radio

Television

Overall, this is still regarded as the best medium for achieving large-scale coverage for products and services. As television is a combination of sound and pictures it provides the perfect vehicle to visualise or demonstrate the product or service being marketed, whether that is a car, an airline or a washing detergent.

Advertising is usually sold in 'spots' that range from ten seconds to three minutes. The time and the audience determine the price the advertiser must pay to secure a slot. Prime time television is usually regarded as the period from 19.00 to 21.00 hours (it may vary from country to country). This is the period where the highest fees apply, because of the nature of the programmes being shown and the size of the viewing audience. Television media sales companies operated by the television networks usually offer discounts to buyers who purchase a series of slots in advance, for example every Wednesday evening at 19.20 for one month.

Buying the 'spot' is only one element of the television commercial, the other being its production. Television commercials often look like, and retain the same production values as, mini-movies. Significant investment is often made in the location shooting, the actors, the sets and the music to promote a product or service.

However, not all countries permit television advertising, and in many it is strongly regulated to protect the vulnerable (for example, children) from undue influence and pressures.

Cinema

With its escapist atmosphere and large screen, the cinema can have an enormous impact on its audience. However most people are irregular visitors to the cinema, so a cinema advertisement does not have the regular impact of, say, a television campaign aired at the same time each evening. This medium is useful in supporting press and television campaigns. It can also be used to show advertisements that would not be permitted on televisions stations because of the type of product (for instance, alcoholic drinks), or the way it is advertised (for example, overtly sexual in content).

Radio

State-run radio stations usually do not transmit advertisements. In countries that permit commercial radio stations (for example, the United Kingdom and United States) they have become an excellent outlet for advertising products and services. Companies can choose the radio station that best serves their customer segments. Commercial radio stations cover every type of music and talk (news and current affairs) possible. Thus it is possible to segment audiences by the type of programme and radio station they listen to. It is in the interest of radio stations to conduct audience research so they can use this segmentation to persuade companies to buy advertising slots.

Radio advertising normally costs less than television advertising, so SMEs are able use radio as a means of advertising their products and services.

Figure 10.16

© Jonathan Groucutt

Although outdoor advertising is often considered in terms of posters and electronic billboards there are parts of the world where outdoor advertising is painted onto brick work. This photograph illustrates the meticulous work invested in painting posters for Exide batteries. This is Pune railway station, India.

Figure 10.17

© Jonathan Groucutt

Billboards do not have to be permanent fixtures. During the development/refurbishment of this store in Paris, Gap™ used the protective screens as a billboard to advertise their products and opening date. This is a stunning use of outdoor advertising.

Outdoor billboard advertising

Outdoor advertising is usually strategically located near high-density populations, busy road junctions, walkways, at commuter stations or on vehicles. The objective is to position a poster showing a product or service in a place where it will have high visibility.

Figure 10.18

© Jonathan Groucutt

The Government Assembly building in Paris adorned with photographic images to advertise a major exhibition

Figure 10.19

© Jonathan Groucutt

Outdoor advertising does not have to be on a large scale to be effective. Here is a poster in a Verona street advertising a forthcoming concert by maestro Ennio Morricone. This was one of several posters that appeared in this format in the streets of the old quarter of Verona.

Ambient media (also known as fringe media)

Ambient Media is usually amalgamated with outdoor advertising in many textbooks. However, because of its format and its increasing presence it needs to stand alone as a form of advertising media. As the word ambient suggests, such advertising is positioned 'in the surroundings or in the background'. Table 10.2 lists key forms of ambient media.

Guerrilla ambient media (GAM)[4]

The concept of guerrilla marketing (let alone guerrilla ambient media) stems from the idea of guerrilla warfare. This in turn derives from the Spanish Civil War, where small groups of individuals acting individually took on the might of the regular army. Their action was considered irregular or unusual. This approach has been

Table 10.2 Key forms of ambient media

Medium	Description
Aerial	This includes airships (often referred to as blimps), moving and static balloons, and banner towing. Airships and balloons flying over a location often carrying an array of advertising including illuminated signage across their length. With banner towing, specially equipped light aircraft tow banners across a location advertising, for example, a forthcoming event.
Giveaway postcards	These are normally standard sized postcards that feature an event, product or service. They are often located in racks in hotels, cinemas and restaurants.
Maps	Tourist maps often feature small advertisements for a range of local products and services. These can include details of hotels, restaurants, sightseeing tours, car rentals, museums, art galleries and department stores.
Taxis	This includes both exterior and interior advertising. In London, for example, the famous cabs are often emblazoned with brand logos advertising everything from airlines to newspapers and soft drinks. In some countries, for example, Singapore, taxis have illuminated signs on the roofs of the cabs.
Tickets	Although train, bus and cinema tickets, for example, are used over a relatively short time frame they can incorporate promotional elements. For instance on the reverse of a cinema ticket a soft drink, available from the concession counter, can be advertised. It could be used to publicise a special promotion for a limited period only.
Trolleys	Trolleys at airports, supermarkets and train stations often feature advertising signage. This can range from promoting special in-store offers to credit cards and local hotel and taxis services.
Washrooms	In the United Kingdom especially this is one of the fast-growing forms of ambient media. Everyone has, at some time, the need to use the washroom in the restaurant or shopping mall. The advertising messages can range from health issues (using a condom to reduce the risk of HIV infection and unwanted pregnancy) and warnings about drinking and driving to special offers at local stores.
Other potential sources	These include rubbish bins, lamp posts, petrol pump nozzles, fast-food cartons, carrier bags and even pavements. (See the ethical issue within the section on guerrilla ambient media.)

handed down to various disciplines, including marketing. Here it is considered in the light of using unusual means of ambient media to covey the message.

This can be considered a 'cool' marketing approach for certain groups. However, it must be used carefully for it can sometimes, though certainly not always, pose distinct ethical issues.

Mini case 10.1 provides an example of guerrilla ambient media and how it can have a detrimental effect on society as a whole. It is critically important to remember here that individuals engaged in marketing also have a responsibility to the wider society – not just those individuals who might be vaguely interested in their products or services. It should be apparent that this case describes what is

clearly unethical behaviour on the part of companies, which has significant potential for damaging their brand within the wider consumer group. The CEOs of companies who authorise fly posting would be the first to complain if there was aggressive fly posting in their own neighbourhoods. They do potentially irretrievable harm to their own brand.

As mini case 10.1 shows, the use of fly posting as a form of ambient media can, and does, cause stress among communities. It therefore has to be questioned why companies endorse such unethical and illegal practices, since in the longer term they will only harm the company's reputation. Perhaps some CEOs only look at the short term, rather than the medium and longer terms. If this view is correct,

Mini case 10.1

Fly posting: an unethical approach to ambient marketing

Fly posting can be described as the 'rapid displaying of mini posters within an any unauthorised space to promote a now happening event or service'. The use of fly posting is to circumvent the use of legitimate sites which, of course, incur a cost. However, many of those who use fly posting argue that the use of such a technique is 'in tune with the youth of today'.

By fly posting on the walls of railway tunnels, bridges and buildings legitimate companies avoid the cost of advertising on major poster sites. However, there are clear ethical issues here. Fly posting is unsightly and ugly. In already run-down areas it adds to the degradation. How can an area hope to break out of a downward spiral if it is littered with fly posters? Let us be clear here: many of those that authorise fly posting do not live in the area where it takes place, and would be the first to complain if any fly posting was undertaken in their area. This is a fundamental ethical issue. Why should it be inflicted on any level of society?

In 2004 the local council in Camden, a borough of London, took legal proceedings against two major record companies after receiving over 1000 complaints from local residents regarding fly posting. The council issued antisocial behaviour orders (ASBOs) against the chief executives of both Sony Music (UK) and BMG. According to reports at the time, 'both companies saved more than UK£8 million in advertising costs through fly posting on everything from shop hoardings to pillar boxes in the borough'. Camden Council estimated that cleaning up such fly posting costs the borough's taxpayers some £250 000 each year.

Dame Jane Roberts, Leader of Camden Council, commented:

> Fly posting is a similar sort of behaviour to graffiti, in that it involves the illegal and non-approved use of property, degrading that property and making an area seem uncared for and an unpleasant place to live. Fly posting has a detrimental impact on the value of property and contributes to people's fear of crime and, as a result to actual criminal behaviour, which is why we as a council are seeking to outlaw it.

In June 2004 the CEO of Sony Music (UK) stated that that it 'would not engage in fly posting any more in this country'.

Since Camden Council took this stance, other councils in the United Kingdom have followed in issuing ASBOs against fly posters, no matter whether they are individuals or companies.

Sources: 'Top music chiefs are spared ASBOs', BBC News Online, 1 June 2004; 'Music Chief's anti social orders', BBC News Online, 1 June 2004; 'Jail threat over city fly posting', BBC News Online, 20 June 2004.

then it is a worrying view of the future of many contemporary businesses.

Internet advertising

Yelkur and DaCosta (2001) stated that:

> The Internet represents an extremely efficient medium for assessing, organising and communicating information. As such, the Internet subsumes communication technologies ranging from the written and spoken word to visual images. Internet marketing is one of the newest distribution channels marketers to reach the customer. It is different from traditional channels in that it is also a communication network. Like all communication networks, the Internet is all about establishing and reinforcing connections between people.

This clearly indicates the importance they place on the development of marketing in the Internet environment. As Groucutt and Griseri (2004) intimate in their work, the statistics indicate a rapid growth of the Internet as an advertising medium. There are two critical issues for Internet advertisers. First, do any of the types of advertising irritate the surfer? The key example here is the use of pop-ups. Many Internet service providers (ISPs) have installed software to allow their users to block pop-ups, which are often annoying and offensive. Unfortunately these have, in many cases, been superseded by spam emails which are equally detrimental to the online advertising business. Second, what is the level of conversion from legitimate advertising that appears on the Internet? Associated with this is the psychological perception of Internet advertising. Is it, for instance, seen as legitimate and thus trustworthy, or should all Internet advertising be distrusted because it emanates from potentially 'corrupted' sources?

Clearly some individuals and companies have used the Internet to make a 'fast buck or two' by placing bogus advertisements. While such action cannot be defended, it is far from new. The 'medicine men' alluded to in Chapter 1 are ancestors of the new fraudsters of the 21st century. Whereas in the 18th century they claimed that spring water (if their customers were lucky: it might have been something more harmful) sold from the back of a covered wagon was the elixir of life, today they use the Internet to sell their bogus products and services. It could be argued 'same deceit, different century, different marketing channel'.

While bogus companies use the Internet to market their 'products and services', there are also legitimate organisations, both small and large, using the Internet for honest and lawful purposes. There are several ways that such organisations can advertise on the Internet, and these are briefly discussed in Table 10.3.

As with pop-ups, both individuals and organisations are bombarded by spam, or junk emails. Whether the spam contains legitimate marketing messages or fraudulent ones,[5] they are a serious irritation to both individuals and organisations. According to various sources, spam accounts for over 70 per cent of emails worldwide, with significant costs to businesses (BBC 2004b).[6] Spam affects not only those who receive it but also those organisations that have a legitimate message they want to communicate to their target audience. There is a risk that legitimate companies will be falsely accused alongside the spammers, and this in turn can have a detrimental effect on e-commerce and e-marketing.

Table 10.3 Types of online advertising

Format	Description
Banners	Usually a rectangular graphic that normally appears along either the top or bottom of the page. They can be either static or animated – increasingly the latter as clever animation can increase awareness of the advertisement.
Skyscrapers	Large vertical advertisements that, like banners, can either be static or animated.
Buttons	Usually small oval, circular, square or rectangular objects that often display an image, which might be a company name, logo or brand name. Clicking on this image usually links to either the corporate or brand web site.
Classified	Just as with print media, online provides the facilities for classified advertising. This can cover everything from individuals seeking friendship and romance to education and new business ideas. It could be argued that the classified advertisements we see so often in the print media have leapt online. The difference though is that online classified advertising has the potential, for instance, to enable users to click through to either an individual or company website.
Pop-up advertising	Also known as interstitials, advertising windows that pop up when a new screen is displayed. Usually, when such advertisements are displayed the advertisement can only be closed by the user closing the window. That however will not prevent another pop-up from being displayed. While the pop-up has the advantage of being highly visible, there are several disadvantages. These include: (1) irritation factor: if there is a sequence of pop-ups surfers will just spend their time closing down windows and will possibly be so frustrated that they log off. (2) If a pop-up becomes 'scheduled' within a list of pop-ups then the message is most likely to be missed. The surfer will be too busy closing down the pop-ups. (3) If surfers have been frequently annoyed by pop-ups they are unlikely to trust any company that uses them. (4) With pop-up blockers available, both individuals and companies will use them to prevent this unwanted form of 'junk' advertising.

Shock advertising

Shock advertising (also known as shockvertising) can be broadly described as:

> the inclusion of frightening, visceral, offensive, taboo and emotion-provoking imagery and words to promote a product, service, concept or idea.

It became part of the public's consciousness with Oliviero Toscani's work for the Italian clothing company Benetton. Toscani's advertising focused not on clothes but on images often linked to society or tragic events of the time, including the birth of a newborn baby, the blood-stained clothes of a dead Croatian soldier and the faces of men on Death Row in US penitentiaries. This latter advertising campaign unleashed the greatest controversy, damaging the brand in the United States. This was perhaps an advertising campaign too far for Benetton, and it marked a separation between Toscani and Benetton.

However, shock advertising was used prior to Toscani's startling images. During the First World War, the British government used shock advertising techniques to instil fear into the UK population. Many of the advertisements depicted German soldiers as the personification of evil. Such propaganda advertising techniques have been used by governments ever since to promote and support the reason for war, whether justified or not.

Companies, governments and organisations (including charities) have used shock advertising techniques to promote their messages. For instance, in both the United Kingdom and the United States during the 1980s, there were campaigns against the fur trade and fur coats. In a UK cinema commercial, a model walks along a catwalk and swirls a fur coat around, splattering blood on the affluent audience (Saunders 1999). The aim was to create a powerful advertisement that would be positioned on that fine line between shocking and revolting to get the viewer to address the issue (Saunders 1999).

Shock advertising raises many questions. One that is particularly important is whether or not such advertising is consistent with the brand. It could be argued that some shock advertisements are clearly related or linked to the organisation or brand, where others are not. Some may argue, for instance, that Toscani's advertising for Benetton had no link

Mini case 10.2

Barnardo's

Barnardo's is the UK's largest children's charity, supporting some 100 000 children and their families through more than 300 projects. In 2003 Barnardo's launched an advertising campaign entitled 'There are no silver spoons for children born into poverty'. The aims of the campaign were to:

- Highlight that one in three children in the United Kingdom live in poverty, that these children are disadvantaged from birth, and that children born into poverty are more likely to have a disadvantaged adult life – through ill-health, unemployment, homelessness, crime, drug and alcohol misuse and abusive relationships.
- Highlight Barnardo's role in alleviating child poverty.
- Cut through the misconceptions of child poverty.
- Create support for Barnardo's work.

The campaign featured three advertisements, each depicting an element of poverty – homelessness, alcohol and drug abuse. Each image featured a young baby lying on his or her back, and superimposed were (respectively) a cockroach, a bottle of methylated spirits and a syringe, positioned to create the illusion that they were protruding out of the babies' mouths. These objects metaphorically represented the possible future lives of the babies. The digital composition of the images made them particularly graphic.

Each year the UK Advertising Standards Authority (ASA) receives complaints from the public about advertisements. It is then the responsibility of the ASA Council to decide whether to uphold or reject them. In 2003 the ASA received 475 complaints regarding Barnardo's 'Silver Spoon' campaign. This was the largest number of complaints for a national press campaign in the ASA's history.

There were two areas of objections:

1 'That the advertisements were offensive, shocking and unduly distressing, especially if seen by children'.
2 'That the advertisements were irresponsible and could encourage emulation by children'.

In a news release (12 November 2003) Barnardo's stated:

> [Barnardo's].... made a decision to draw attention to this national disgrace [child poverty]

through the most effective means at its disposal: attention grabbing images placed as adverts in newspapers and subsequent interviews and debate in the media.

As Britain's largest children's charity we do not use powerful images lightly, however we have a duty to act as a voice for the most vulnerable children and young people in this country.

While Barnardo's appreciates that some people find the images shocking we have also received significant support from the public and media alike. Before our advertising campaign child poverty had not captured the public's imagination.

In their adjudication, the ASA stated:

The advertisers said they had intended to draw attention to child poverty and to encourage donations for their work with children living in poverty. They said research had shown 86% of people did not know that one in three children in the UK lived in poverty; they said the UK had the highest rate of child poverty in Europe. The advertisers argued that the advertisements showed the reality of child poverty and its long-term effects and reflected the nature of their work, which was often distressing. They explained that the advertisements that had generated complaints contrasted the opportunities and dreams available to some children with the hardship into which other children were born; they explained that another advertisement in the campaign showed an image of a happy baby with a silver spoon placed gently in its mouth.

The advertisers conceded that not all poor children remained poor as adults or lived troubled lives; they said many poor children, however, were exposed to squalor, homelessness, substance abuse or crime and many of those children would live with similar problems later in their lives. They argued that poor children had fewer opportunities than did more privileged children. The advertisers believed people were shocked by the advertisements but more shocked by discovering the facts about childhood poverty. The advertisers said they had chosen to advertise in national newspapers, because they targeted adults, not children; they believed the advertisements were unlikely to cause serious or widespread offence to adults. They argued that, like road-safety or anti-smoking campaigns, the advertisements caused distress with good reason. They said the babies in the advertisements had been photographed with the permission, and in the presence, of their parents. They said the objects in the babies' mouths were computer-generated, not to scale and did not seem to have been placed there or pushed into the mouths; they believed the scenarios were obviously unreal and argued that the advertisements did not, therefore, show children close to dangerous substances. The advertisers said they had followed the Committee of Advertising Practice Copy Advice team's advice to (a) remove the needle from the syringe in the advertisement, (b) tone down the amniotic fluid in the advertisements and ensure genitals were not visible on the babies. They said they had received positive comments on the advertisements from their project workers, parents of children growing up in poverty and members of the public. They sent five newspaper articles about the campaign and extracts from 16 letters from the public in support of the campaign.

Complaints upheld

The Authority considered that the photographs in the advertisements would be interpreted as stylised illustrations of babies' possible lives. It considered that, because they were unlikely to read national newspapers, children were unlikely to be distressed by the advertisements. The Authority acknowledged the serious message of the advertisements but nevertheless considered that the advertisers had used shocking images to attract attention and that the photographs were likely to cause serious or widespread offence. It told the advertisers not to repeat the advertisements.

Complaints not upheld

The Authority considered that, because they appeared in national newspapers, which targeted adults, not children, and because they featured objects to which children were unlikely to have ready access, the advertisements were unlikely to encourage emulation by children. It considered that, although the babies in the photographs seemed to be in dangerous situations, the advertisements did not condone or encourage unsafe practices; it concluded that the advertisements were not irresponsible.

The advertisements can be viewed on Barnardo's website at www.barnardos.org.uk/resources/students advertising/

Sources: Adjudications: Barnardo's, 10 December 2003', Advertising Standards Association; 'Top ten most complained about ad campaigns 2003', ASA press release, 22 April 2004; 'Advertising campaign in 2003 – Silver Spoon', www.barnardos.org.uk.

whatsoever to the manufacture or marketing of clothes. Others though may argue, perhaps Toscani among them, that the brand is more than clothes – it is about people, societies, life and death – in essence the world around us.

Many charities have used the shock approach in both mainstream advertising and direct marketing to communicate the plight of those suffering, either animals or people. In many cases the images and the tone of the descriptions are shocking, often difficult to accept. However, there are various difficulties for many government and organisations attempting to communicate important messages to society. These difficulties can be summarised as:

◆ Cutting through the clutter of communications messages. As explained earlier, clutter is an element of noise that may prevent an organisation from reaching its target audience with the appropriate message. Clutter can be seen as the volume of messages being communicated at any one time. If many of the messages are similar in format, how does one message stand out from the rest? To achieve this companies and organisations will seek ways of cutting through the clutter, and for some, shock advertising techniques may be effective.

◆ Society becomes numb to issues. If consumers are consistently being bombarded with 'issues' messages they may become indifferent to worthy issues and causes. Shock advertising may bring those issues from the background to the foreground of conversation. However, there is another potential risk in doing so. People, it appears, are becoming increasingly numb to such dramatic images because they are routinely viewing such images on nightly news bulletins.

Mini case 10.2 illustrates how shock advertising can be used to raise the profile of issues in the mind of the public.

■ Direct marketing

There are many definitions of direct marketing. However Tapp (1998) provides one of the more succinct:

Direct marketing focuses on using a database to communicate (and sometimes distribute) directly to customers so as to attract a direct response.

As Groucutt *et al.* (2004) state, direct marketing is often considered as one-to-one marketing. Unfortunately, direct marketing is often seen as purely a process of database marketing. While databases are a fundamental component of direct marketing, it will not succeed as a marketing communications tool unless there is customisation. It is this element of customisation that truly creates the opportunity for one-to-one marketing. The aim is to build a relationship with customers by understanding their preferences so that future offers can be tailored or customised to those preferences.

Grönroos (1990) supports the one-to-one approach when he states:

Marketing is to establish, maintain and enhance relationships with customers and other parties, at a profit,[7] so that the objectives of the parties involved are met. This is achieved by the mutual exchange and fulfilment of promises. This perspective departs from the traditional view of marketing that emphasises only 'exchange' and moves towards the notion of 'exchange in relationships.

Groucutt *et al.* (2004) suggest that direct marketing provides the opportunity for three distinct advantages:

◆ Organisations have the opportunity to track single and/or segmented groups of customers via their database. By tracking customers the organisation can better understand their purchasing/donating behaviour. Thus, the organisation is able to target customers more efficiently and effectively.

◆ It creates an opportunity for 'a dialogue' between the customer and the organisation. In order to better understand the customer the organisation provides the mechanism for feedback. A case in point is the online retailer Amazon. Through its recommendations to customers it can get direct online feedback from customers on whether, for example, a customer already has a book, wants the book when it is available, or is not interested in either the book or the genre it represents. In other cases an organisation could use a range of paper-based or online questionnaires to discover, for example, likes and dislikes, developing interests and changes in personal circumstances such as the birth of a child.

◆ The opportunity to developed enhanced customisation, where products and services can be tailored to meet the needs and desires of the individual. An example is the customisation operations of Dell Computers, where customers can configure the specification of the computer to meet their individual needs.

Direct marketing techniques

There are several techniques that can be employed to direct market a product or service to a customer, whether it is B2B or B2C. This section considers them individually, but it is important to remember that normally they form part of an integrated package.

Door drops (door-to-door distribution)

This is a very basic form of direct marketing where printed information is hand-delivered and placed in individuals' letterboxes. This may form part of a national distribution, for example samples of a new product just launched onto the market. Alternatively, the door drops may be very localised, for example, a promotional leaflet advertising the take-out menu for a nearby Indian restaurant. The point to remember is that door drops are not personalised and thus information is not recorded on a database.

Inserts

Inserts can range from single, folded sheets to mini catalogues that are inserted into newspapers, magazines, bank and credit card statements. While they are very much like a postal form of door drops, there is an opportunity to improve targeting. This can be achieved by selecting the magazines that best match the target audience, for example, for the product and service being promoted.

Door-to-door selling

Although door-to-door selling is practised less than it used to be in many countries, such as the United

Kingdom, it remains a marketing focal point in others. For some people face-to-face contact is more reassuring than buying a product, for example, via direct mail or the Internet.

Direct mail

Here a company mails information direct to a potential consumer or B2B customer. Direct mail can encompass a vast array of products and services, from credit cards to gift catalogues through to requests for disaster relief funds by organisations such as the International Red Cross/Red Crescent and UNICEF.

Telemarketing

While there are many definitions for telemarketing, one of the most effective was proposed by Harridge-March (2002):

An organisation's integrated and strategic use of telecommunications to make effective use of time and resources in order to create and maintain a relationship with its publics.

In this definition Harridge-March is linking telecommunications with resources and writes of building and maintaining relationships with customers. This links back to the Grönroos quote earlier. Telemarketing is not simply a communications channel to promote a product or service, but one that allows the development of a relationship. Like the Internet, it provides an opportunity for two-way communication. This approach can be summarised by considering the operation of outbound and Inbound telemarketing.

◆ In **outbound telemarketing** a representative of the organisation calls either a potential or existing customer to discuss the organisation's product or service range. This also includes organisations following-up potential/actual customer enquiries generated by the completing of pre-paid reply cards or inbound calls.

◆ In **inbound telemarketing** a potential or existing customer initiates the call via a free-phone number. He or she may be responding to a direct response television or radio advertisement or a direct mailer.

There has been a significant growth in telemarketing since the mid-1990s. The US-based Direct Marketing Association estimated that US telemarketing sales grew from US$63.1 billion to over US$100 billion in 2002. At the same time the UK market was worth £3.1 billion and the Australian A$8.8 billion (DMA 2003). Much of this growth has been attributed to the expansion of call centre operations.

Call centres

Since the 1990s telemarketing has been centralised in ever-expanding call centres. A call centre can be defined as:

> A designed physical environment where trained people, using telephone and computer technology, interact with potential and actual customers to provide a combination of inbound and outbound services in real time.

However, telemarketing and call centre operations have faced a barrage of criticism in recent years. These include:

◆ Unwanted or unsolicited calls: the increased number of such calls provoked outrage in the United States, leading in 2004 to 'Do Not Call' legislation. Individuals can register on a central database their wish not to receive unsolicited telemarketing. If a company breaches this legislation it faces heavy penalties. However, to some extent this has shifted the problem overseas, with US-based companies cold-calling individuals in the United Kingdom, for instance, with special offers. While legislation might alleviate the potential problem in one nation, it might only move it to another.

◆ Potential for fraud: fraudsters have seen the potential for using telemarketing to sell products and services that either do not exist or are inferior. This has become a major problem, especially within the United States. According the US Federal Bureau of Investigation (FBI), there was an estimated US$40 billion lost to telemarketing fraudsters in 2002 (FBI 2003).

◆ Offshoring: this is the increasing relocation of call centres overseas. Thus, for example, the UK-based insurance and financial group,

Norwich Union, has call centres in India. For many companies offshoring has become a long-term strategy to reduce costs and improve service. According to Datamonitor (2004) global call centre jobs will expand to almost 5 million by 2007, with 241 000 jobs moving to Mexico and South Africa. However, concerns have been raised about security of information, quality of customer service training and call centre working conditions. These concerns may have reputational impact on the companies who seek offshoring strategies.

■ Kiosks

These can be described as 'interactive touch screens that allow in-store customers to search and retrieve information as well as order products and services'. Kiosks are increasingly being located in busy shopping malls and supermarkets, providing customers with the opportunity to browse catalogues before purchasing goods and services.

■ Buzz, or word of mouth promotion

This is also referred to as viral or contagion marketing, especially in relation to 'spreading the word' on the Internet. However, the use of the terms viral and contagion is equally applicable to non-Internet marketing.

Rosen (2000) refers to buzz as a 'social process' and concludes that it is 'the sum of all comments about a certain product that are exchanged among people at any given time'. He continues, 'Buzz is all the word of mouth about a brand. It's the aggregate of all person-to-person communication about a particular product, service or company at any point in time.'

The final thought here, 'at any point in time', is an important one. Buzz is often, and quite rightly, associated with what is new and cool. However, it can also apply to products, services and companies that are well established in the marketplace. For example, a well-established brand might undergo a transformation or rejuvenation (see the section on the product life cycle, page 198). This revitalised product then becomes the centre of buzz activity, leading a new group of buyers to be added to existing ones.

Mini case 10.3

ipoint: real-time public information system

Devised and developed by Highland Medialinks (HML), ipoint consists of a specially programmed database which can display information on attractions, activities, services, accommodation, restaurants, shopping, business and visitor attractions in the Highlands of Scotland. The information is accessed through simple-to-use touch-screen terminals located in strategic positions to offer maximum access to the public.

Locations

A combination of full-size terminals and smaller desktop units are sited in normally busy locations. It is possible to operate touch-screen systems through ordinary glass windows, so given the right locations, safe access is enabled on a 24-hour basis. ipoint is installed in the following locations: Ballachulish Tourist Information Centre, Dornoch Tourist Information Centre, Thurso Tourist Information Centre, Rothiemurchus Visitor Centre, Made in Scotland, Fairways Leisure, Nevis Range, Inverness Railway Station, Eilean Donan Castle, Highland Wildlife Park, Inverness Floral Hall, the Whisky Shop Dufftown, Loch Ness 2000 Exhibition, Aros Centre and Glenmorangie Distillery. Desktop units are also to be installed in Nevis Sports, RAF Lossiemouth and Glenmore Forestry Commission.

Content updating and presentation

Information on the system is real time and updatable on a daily basis. The terminals operate from an internal hard drive that contains all the current information on the database. Until broadband/wireless access is available to allow a permanent Internet connection, each terminal automatically connects to a remote server to enable the necessary updating and changes to be facilitated. This is generally done at night to allow minimum disruption to the service.

All date-sensitive information is automatically archived throughout. It is possible to place information on location specific terminals thus achieving site or user-specific promotions and information dissemination.

Clients (whose information is given on the system) are able to view monitoring statistics for their entry by logging onto the admin section of the www.ipointhighlands.com website. This section also allows them to update and alter their entry information as often as they wish

Indexed information on the database is programmed to appear in a random manner which allows every entry the opportunity of being in a different position for choice, and not always being presented in a structured order such as alphabetical or order of inclusion.

Languages and the user interface

If desired, the information on the system can be shown in a number of languages. Usually the general user information is translated into the five common European languages, and specific service or activity provider information is only presented in English.

The user interface for the system is uncluttered, highly visual and attractive. It is extremely easy to use and only requires a minimum number of choices to be made before the desired information is reached. The interface does not carry banner advertisements nor does it have a presentation with too many choices, both of which often have a negative effect on users. Information is readily accessible and the system is very simple for first-time users to navigate.

The online statistics provide a level of detail about the effectiveness of the system and overall usage (regarding visitor profiles: who is looking at what entry/piece of information, from which location and how often).

Source: Highland Medialinks.

Rosen (2000) states that:

'65% of customers who bought a Palm organiser told the makers of this device that they had heard about it from another person.

47% of the readers of *Surfing* magazine (USA) say that the biggest influence on their decisions about where to surf and what to purchase come from a friend.

Friends and relatives are the number one source for information about places to visit or about flights, hotels or rental cars, according to the Travel Industry Association (USA). Of the people surveyed, 43% cited friends and family as a source for information.

57% of customers of one car dealership in California learned about the dealership by word of mouth. 'This is not unusual' says Jim Callahan of the Dohring Company, which conducts surveys for about 500 car dealerships (in the USA) every year.

Every year we hear about movies such as *The Blair Witch Project* or *There's Something About Mary* that are driven by word of mouth. 53% of moviegoers rely to some extent on a recommendation from someone they know, according to a study by Maritz Marketing Research. No matter how much money Hollywood pours into advertising, people frequently consult with each other about what movie to see.

70% of Americans rely on the advice of others when selecting a new doctor, according to the same study (above). 63% of women surveyed for *Self* magazine cited 'friends, family or co-worker referral' as one of the factors influencing over-the-counter (OTC) drug purchases.

As you can see from Rosen's research, individuals can place great value on both word of mouth and who communicates the information to them. (You may want to reflect on this when you read Chapter 16. Consider the relationship between psychology and buyer behaviour. As stated in that chapter, trust in other people's judgments, among other variables, is an important factor in helping an individual make a purchasing decision.)

Of course buzz is nothing new. Throughout history there are examples of how buzz has been instigated or used to create awareness – everything from marketing products to launching a revolution. However, it could be argued that with an ever-expanding networked society, the potential for buzz to be a driving force in promoting products or services greatly increases.

However, there needs to be a word of warning. It tends to be assumed that buzz is a positive driver in marketing communications. This is clearly not always the case. As well as telling people how cool

Mini case 10.4

When is a national secret not a national secret? When it is a myth, and on the official website.

The UK Security Service (generally known as MI5) was originally founded in 1909. Its role is to protect UK interests both at home and abroad from foreign intelligence agencies and terrorist groups. Although there were numerous official and 'semi-official' histories, MI5 used to appear cloaked in a veil of secrecy. In 1990s the then Director-General, Stella Rimmington, took a much more enlightened approach and became the public face of MI5. Since then the Service has taken a more open approach in communicating its role. It began by launching a website (which has been continually updated to reflect the changing dynamics of world politics).

As the organisation had for so long been clad in secrecy (for understandable reasons), various myths and misunderstandings abounded. The buzz was that anyone who worked, past or present, for the Service could not reveal anything about it. In reality the official and 'semi-official' histories should have dispelled this particular myth, but this was clearly not the case. The myths, however, have grown in somewhat strange proportions. To quote from the MI5 website:

Our members and former members are prohibited by Section 1 of the Official Secrets Act 1989 from disclosing, without lawful authority, information relating to security or intelligence which came into their possession while in the Service.

It is clearly important that security and intelligence information is protected from unauthorised disclosure, to prevent damage being caused to our sources, operations and methods. But Section 1 is sometimes criticised as prohibiting disclosures even about such unimportant matters as the colour of the Thames House [London Headquarters] carpets (which are blue) and the menu in the staff restaurant. These criticisms are misguided.

Yes, as incredible as it may seem, for years the colour of the carpet was considered a national secret. This is clearly not true, but it does illustrate how buzz can also set up a long-term negative image, producing a set of 'urban myths' about a product, service or organisation. For years the location of MI5's headquarters was also considered a national secret. The joke in the 1970s was that if you asked any London cabbie, he or she would say, 'Oh, you want the old Ministry of Education building in Curzon Street.' Perhaps this is the urban myth that the Service wanted the British public to know anyway?
Source: www.mi5.gov.uk

Mini case 10.5

Eats, Shoots & Leaves

You probably never thought that a book on punctuation could become a best seller! That is exactly what happened to Lynne Truss's book *Eats, Shoots & Leaves*, published in 2003. By June 2004 it had sold almost a million copies in the United Kingdom. It was the publishing phenomenon of 2004, and along the way collected the British Book of the Year Award.

Perhaps like all good books it caught people's imagination. Truss's approach to punctuation is witty and direct. Just consider the following brief quote from the jacket cover:

A panda walked into a cafe. He orders a sandwich, eats it, then draws a gun and fires two shots in the air.

'Why?' asks the confused waiter, as the panda makes towards the exit. The panda produces a badly punctuated wildlife manual and tosses it over his shoulder.

'I'm a panda', he says, at the door. 'Look it up'.

The waiter turns to the relevant entry and, sure enough, finds an explanation.

'Panda. Large black-and-white bear-like mammal, native to China. Eats, shoots and leaves.'

The book, originally published in the United Kingdom by Profile Books, had an initial print run of 5000 copies. Within a month of its launch it was already into its sixth reprint, such was the demand.

Several factors may have led to the success of this book: First, the author's anarchic approach to punctuation made it both relevant and witty. Second, several major booksellers saw its potential, especially for the Christmas market. Third, the media latched onto both the wit and value encompassed in the book. Their glowing reviews spread like wildfire throughout the marketplace. Soon it was topping the best seller lists.

Such was the success of the book that Lynne Truss was commissioned by Penguin Books (USA) to write an American version, which was launched in April 2004. The relatively small British publisher, Profile Books, that had originally commissioned the book went on to republish three previous books by Truss during 2004.

Sources: www.eatsshootsandleaves.com; www.profilebooks.co.uk; 'Grammar book tops bestseller list', BBC News Online, 1 December 2003; 'Grammar book enriches publishers', BBC News Online, 17 February 2004.

a particular product or service is, we are equally prone to tell people how poor a product or service is. One issue here is that not everyone who criticises a product has necessarily tried it. They are simply going on the buzz surrounding them at the time. The risk is that the supposed inferiority of the product or service may become greatly exaggerated in the repeated telling of the story.

When negative buzz circulates, the company needs to be able to consider the following (often interrelated) approaches:

◆ Counteract the buzz by rectifying the negative aspect. A combination of marketing communication tactics may be deployed for this purpose. There needs to be an element of realism here, in that the negativity might be so ingrained that it is difficult or impossible to rectify it. Time will rectify the problem sometimes, but not always.

◆ Counteract the buzz by stating the positive aspects of a product or service, thus to some extent ignoring the negative comments. Politicians, for example, are very good at focusing on what they believe their party has done well for the country rather than any negatives. This is even the case when they are asked direct questions about problems associated with their party's policies. Of course, this is a potentially high-risk scenario as the public become distrustful of the 'spin' placed on the product or service. This could, over time, lead to further negativity.

◆ Counteract the buzz by agreeing that there have been problems with the product or service. This may include accepting the 'untruths' in the short term to build a much more focused and positive image in the future.

The MI5 example illustrates, if perhaps in a slightly ridiculous yet humorous sort of way, that myths can drive negative buzz. Opposite to this is the way in which positive buzz can drive forward and build the reputation of a product. Groucutt *et al.* (2004)

described how word of mouth marketing helped catapult Dava Sobel's book *Longitude*, about the life of 18th century clock maker John Harrison, into the bestseller lists. A similar event happened with Lynne Truss's *Eats, Shoots & Leaves* (see mini case 10.5).

■ Product placement

Product placement refers to a product or service that purposely appears in a television programme or movie. The brand owners invest to have their product or service associated with a particular character, movie or television series. The belief is that such association will help to build brand awareness and cut through the clutter often associated with other forms of marketing communications. However, it can also greatly benefit the movie or

television programme. The brand owners usually invest in campaigns associated with it, which in turn raise and/or maintain the movie's profile.

Mini case 10.6 focuses on the increasing use of product placement marketing in the James Bond movies. Since his first movie outing in 1962, James Bond has become an important global movie character with which brands want to be associated.

■ Movie tie-ins

Another way of linking major brands to potential blockbuster movies is through a product tie-in. For example, the fast food chain Burger King invested an estimated US$45 million in advertising and toys (an estimated 50 million were produced) in their promotion of Disney's®*Toy Story* (1995), and saw a

---

Mini case 10.6

The rise, rise and further rise of product placement in James Bond movies

'Ah 007, so glad you could join us! This is Henderson, your product placement manager. And this time try and bring everything back in one piece!'

'Well, Q, you really do not know how rough it can be out there in the field.'

'Yes 007, we know!'

Since their conception in 1962 the James Bond movies have become the biggest grossing movie series of all time, and this trend is destined to continue. While the actors who play the sophisticated British Secret Intelligence Service agent may come and go, the series has gone from box-office strength to strength. The movies have a long history of product placement. In 1964 James Bond drove a sleek gadget-filled Aston Martin DB5 along Swiss mountain roads in pursuit of Goldfinger in the film of the same name. By 1995 in *Goldeneye* Bond was at the wheels of a BMW Z-3 series.

By the time of *Goldeneye* the power of product placement in a James Bond movie was clear to everyone. The link between the movie and the introduction of BMW's Z-3 was to produce one of the most successful car launches to date. For BMW the use of the Z-3 in the movie proved to be the ideal teaser campaign. The Z-3 was launched some three months after the global release of *Goldeneye*, and was supported by a series of James

Bond-themed television advertisements. The car gained a global recognition, and BMW obtained 12 months worth of orders (Stewart-Allen 1999).

By the time of the next Bond movie – *Tomorrow Never Dies* (1997) – there was reportedly over UK£20 million of product placement (BBC 2001). However, the value to BMW was even more significant. With a range of products from the Z-3 to motorbikes, it is estimated that the return on BMW's investment was over US$100 million (Stewart-Allen 1999)

In *Die Another Day* (2002), Bond returned to driving an Aston Martin (the V12 Vanquish), with its usual array of weapons and gadgets supplied by Q. Bond's villain in the movie drove an equally well-equipped Jaguar. Interestingly, Ford Motor Company owns both the British-made Aston Martin and Jaguar brands.

In all there were 24 major promotional partners in *Die Another Day*, ranging from Aston Martin to Bollinger champagne, Omega and Swatch watches. It was estimated that they would spend some UK£95 million on campaigns associated with the movie worldwide (Bhatia 2002). The actor Pierce Brosnan, who played James Bond in the film, could be seen dressed in a dinner suit adorning posters on Parisian streets wearing an Omega watch. This major watch brand was clearly identifying itself with the cool sophistication of James Bond.

Sources: 'Bond: nobody sells it better', BBC Online, 2001; S. Bhatia, 'Ah, Mr Brand, I've been expecting you', *Observer*, 17 November 2002, p.16; A. L. Stewart-Allen, 'Product placement helps sell brands', *Marketing News*, 15 February 1999.

significant return on its investment (Lukk 1997). During the first week of the *Toy Story* promotion, launched a week prior to the opening of the movie, Burger King doubled the sales of its Kid's Meals over the previous year's figure. It is estimated that Burger King sold 6.4 million Kid's Meals that first week alone (Lukk 1997).

Toy Story was and remains a highly successful movie. However, not all movies are so successful, so choosing the right movie in order to invest in tie-ins remains a high-risk venture. However, if the movie is a box-office hit there can be significant returns on investment.

■ Merchandising the brand

As stated by Groucutt *et al.* (2004), 'virtually every company and organisation is involved, to a greater or lesser extent in merchandising its brand identity. The value of merchandising within this context, should not be underestimated.'

There is often confusion surrounding the word 'merchandise' for it has two meanings:

◆ As a derivative of the word merchant it can and does mean goods or products. In the retail business, for example, the clothes on the racks are referred to as merchandise.

◆ The second definition is a focus on the merchandising of a particular brand, relating it to specific events or organisations.

As you will see in the remainder of this section, the focus here is on the second of the two definitions. Before considering examples it worth considering why organisations invest in merchandising their brand. Table10.4 outlines several potential reasons.

Examples of merchandising

A university

Universities and colleges often market merchandise to their alumni, ranging from pens to teddy bears wearing university shirts or jumpers. In some cases universities have opened their own shops to market merchandise not only to current and past students but to the general public as well. In the United Kingdom Oxford University has a store in the centre of Oxford (also a tourist city) which sells a wide range

of university-related merchandise. As well as university merchandising, departments within a university may develop their own line of merchandising. Mini case 10.7 illustrates how the Business School at Oxford Brookes University developed its own merchandising.

Mini case 10.7

Oxford Brookes University Business School

In 2003 the Business School at Oxford Brookes University launched its own range of merchandising. The objective was to market the Business School's brand to current staff, students and alumni, and in doing so create a scholarship fund. All proceeds from the sale of the merchandise go to the Business Schools' Business Club Alumni Scholarship Fund.

Source:www.brookes.ac.uk/alumni

Figure 10.20

© Oxford Brookes University. Reproduced with kind permission.

Some of the merchandising undertaken by the Business School at Oxford Brookes University

Table 10.4 The rationale for merchandising a brand

Rationale	Description
Brand awareness – visibility	Merchandising takes the brand outside its normal habitat. For example, a child wearing a club football shirt in the street is 'promoting' both the club and possibly a named star player for the team. This increases visibility and thus brand awareness for that club.
Reinforcement and recall	Merchandising can be used to reinforce the brand in the mind of the customer. Some organisations use merchandising as 'giveaways' to current and potential clients: for example, notepads for desks so the organisation's name and contact details are always visible. The objective is that the customer will recall the organisation's expertise from seeing its notepads on the desk, and contact it. Major printing companies, for example, in the United Kingdom have used such merchandising tactics to significant effect.
Identification	Merchandising is a way of associating or identifying with a particular brand or organisation. Graduating students from college or university become members of that institution's alumni. The purchase of alumni merchandising creates a symbolic link between the graduate and the institution.
Extending the brand	There is a case to be made that merchandising is a form of brand extension. Movie companies, for example, sell rights to companies to create and market merchandise using movie brands. The *Star Wars* sagas are an excellent example of how merchandising can increase income generation and promote the movies. This ranged from the introduction of toys through to John Williams' best-selling album, recorded with the London Symphony Orchestra, of the score to the movie. (It went Platinum in the worldwide album charts!)
Revenue generation	There is clear evidence that merchandising can generate significant income for the organisation. One of the most successful companies at merchandising its brand is Manchester United Football Club, which has supporters worldwide. Manchester United originally formed a wholly owned subsidiary, Manchester United Merchandising Ltd, to further develop its global brand name and image. As part of its strategic review, Manchester United signed a deal in 2003 with Nike that was 'designed to generate new value from the Group trademarks by using their [Nike] product development, marketing and distribution reach to supply our existing customers and new customers in Asia'. The partnership arrangement with Nike allowed Manchester United to launch its new 2003/04 shirt in 58 territories simultaneously. The football club believed (at the time of writing, 2004) it would benefit from 'Nike's expertise in developing products and marketing them around the world'. Source: 'Business strategy', Manchester United plc.

A movie

As Table 10.4 shows, the merchandising of a movie brand can enhance its promotion and provide an additional revenue-generating stream.

An airline

Both major international carriers and their low-cost regional equivalents engage in merchandising their brands. In the vast majority of cases the products are available onboard, and some are sold by mail order or via the Internet. British Airways for example has its own retail outlet in London's Regent Street. As well as marketing vacations and travel goods (from luggage to maps), it markets its own merchandise, including postcards of aircrafts, history of the airline and specific aircraft (for example, Concorde), business folders and children's gifts.

■ Celebrity endorsements

The concept of celebrity endorsements of products and services is far from new. Hollywood actors in the 1940s and 1950s endorsed everything from cars to cigarettes (Including former US President the late Ronald Reagan when he was a movie actor). However, what is new is criticism of celebrities for endorsing some products or services. It is most unlikely that any celebrity would today endorse a pack of cigarettes or a fur coat. It could mean the end of his or her career, as he or she would be vilified by the media and boycotted by the public.

One of the most difficult problems facing governments in the West especially is obesity. This is at least in part caused by our fast-food consumer societies, with heavy consumption of foods like hamburgers, French fries and potato crisps. Driven by increasing health care bills, some governments have made moves to seriously restrict the advertising of foods associated with health problems. The difficulty for celebrities endorsing them is the risk of being tarnished by the stigma associated with obesity. On the other hand the product manufacturers have to rethink their manufacturing processes to reduce the content of fat and salt especially. By the end of 2004 companies such as McDonald's™ were actively promoting the need for healthy eating.

■ Sponsorship

This is a specialist form of advertising that can create significant market exposure for the sponsoring organisation. Cornwell and Maignan (1998) describe sponsorship as:

> Sponsorship involves two main activities: (1) an exchange between a sponsor [such as a brand] and a sponsee [such as a sporting event] whereby the latter receives a fee and the former obtains the right to associate itself with the activity sponsored and (2) the marketing of the association by the sponsor. Both activities are necessary if the sponsorship fee is to be a meaningful investment.

Companies and organisations align themselves with an activity with which they want to be associated, such as a series of classical music concerts, a charity or specific cause, or a major sporting event such as the Olympic Games or a sailing regatta (see Figure 10.21).

Potential benefits of sponsorship

◆ The value of the association itself: Organisations involved in sponsoring major arts festivals, for example, can gain significant benefits

Figure 10.21

© Jonathan Groucutt

A telecommunications company sponsored the sailing regatta on Lake Garda, Italy in 2004

(both concrete and in the form of reputation enhancement) through association with the event.

◆ Exposure: depending on the size of the event, the exposure of the organisation and its brands could be on a global scale. Consider the global television exposure of sponsoring a winning Formula 1 racing team.

Of course, this assumes that the events sponsored are a success. Companies have, in the past, sponsored sporting individuals and teams only to see them lose (in a match there can only be one winner), or far worse, be disqualified because of cheating (for instance, taking banned substances).

Mini case 10.8

Orange™ Prize for Fiction

In January 1996 the Orange™ Prize for Fiction was launched in the United Kingdom to specifically honour writing by women. Since its inception, the mobile phone network company Orange™ has actively sponsored the prize, and it has expanded its sponsorship to include the award of a new prize from 2005 – the Orange™ Award for New Writers. This focuses on celebrating emerging female writing talent, and the winner receives UK£10 000 to help her pursue her writing career with greater freedom.

Additionally, Orange™ supports Orange™ Labyrinth, an online site that explores the process of writing a novel, featuring interviews, competitions, reviews and workshops.

Orange was attracted to the Prize for Fiction as much by the educational and lifelong learning initiatives that were planned to run alongside it as by the actual award itself. To quote the company:

> Sponsorship increases awareness of the Orange™brand and values. It adds to the brand personality through the activities supported and endorses the Orange™ philosophy as an investor in the future.

Today, the Orange™ Prize for Fiction is among the United Kingdom's largest annual literary awards.

Sources: www.orange.com, www.orangeprize.co.uk

■ Sales promotion

This is a marketing activity that can be used to:

◆ promote a new product or service

◆ reinvigorate interest in an established product or service

◆ discount a product or service where this is necessary because of overstocking, or to increase off-peak sales, for instance within the vacation market.

As well as introducing a new product or service, a company can use sales promotions to attract new customers to existing products or services, and to maintain a competitive edge.

Types of sales promotion

There are various types of sales promotion that organisations can use. The choice will depend on many factors including the type of product or service on offer. A company may decide to use more than one type of sales promotion.

Free samples

This is the distribution of free samples via door-to-door drops or as on-pack promotions. The objective is that the recipient will try the product, especially as it is free, and consider purchasing it in future.

Money-off coupons

These are vouchers or coupons that allow shoppers a discount (usually time limited) on particular products. They are usually distributed via door-to-door drops, in magazines and newspapers and at retail outlets.

Extra value offers

These are offerings where an extra value is added to the product being promoted. This can take the form of:

◆ More of the product for the same price. For example, a company producing shaving foam might offer 220 ml for the price of 200 ml, so customers receive an extra 20 ml free.

◆ Adding an extra related product to the pack. For example, the Spanish shaving foam Zorrick® was marketed in the United Kingdom with a pack of six twin-bladed disposable razors attached.

Buy one get one free (BOGOF)

Originally this focused on the promotion of one particular product. Therefore if you bought one pack of brand X you received another pack of brand X. This approach was easily emulated, and companies have developed variants on the theme, for example:

◆ three for the price of two – same product

◆ three for the price of two – mix and match

within a product range (for example, vitamin and other supplements manufactured by the same company).

Special offer bins or shelves

These are in-store promotions. The retailer may decide to discount a range of similar products, DVDs for instance, placing them on designated shelves or in special bins. These offers are often used to reduce stock levels of discontinued products.

Bundling

Here ancillary products are bundled with the main product on offer. Bundling is extensively used in the UK computer market, where addi-tional software and hardware are bundled with the computer. Companies usually provide various bundled options so that the customer can choose which bundle of products is best for their needs. (See Chapter 11 on pricing, which discusses the pricing strategy in relation to both bundled and unbundled products and services.)

Privilege points

Various companies now offer 'privilege points' to customers. The most common form is the super-market loyalty card. Such reward schemes are also prevalent in the airline industry (for instance, Air Miles®), the credit card industry (cash-back bonuses or gifts) and retail outlets

---

Mini case 10.9

Hoover® and the free flights offer

In August 1992, Hoover® UK launched a major travel promotion. In essence anyone in the United Kingdom spending £100 on Hoover® products by the end of January 1993 would receive two free round-trip air tickets to selected European destinations. An additional expenditure of £150 resulted in two free round-trip tickets to either New York or Orlando, Florida. Hoover® worked with two travel agencies which intended to obtain low-cost air tickets. Commission would be earned by selling packages (hotels, car rental and insurance) to the customers. For each package sold, Hoover® would receive a percentage of the com-mission, and this was intended to provide a revenue stream that would offset the cost of the promotion. The overall objective was to sell a growing inventory of vac-uum cleaners and washing machines, and turn around a European deficit of some UK£10 million.

Hartley (1998) states that Hoover® executives expected no more than 50 000 responses. Of those, it was estimated that only a few would complete all the steps necessary to take the free trips. However, more than 200 000 customers responded and qualified for the free trips. The demand for Hoover® products was so great that the factory in Scotland, which had been producing vacuum cleaners only three days a week, was forced to operate 24/7.

The demand for the airline tickets caused a major backlog in paperwork. Some customers did not receive their tickets, others were not offered flights on the dates they requested, and some received no reply at all to their correspondence.

The company set up a telephone hot line which processed some 2000 calls per day. The developing crisis was exacerbated by the negative publicity that followed. Additionally, many of those who obtained free flights did not take up the add-on packages, reducing the revenue stream Hoover® had factored into the promotion.

Soon the company was struggling not only to fulfil its promotional promise but also to push back the tide of negative publicity that was engulfing it. It had under-estimated the potential response to the promotion and overestimated the financial returns.

Several senior executives, including the President of Hoover® Europe, were dismissed by Hoover's parent company Maytag. The crisis lasted some six years, and eventually some 220 000 people received free flights. The estimated cost to Hoover® and Maytag was UK£48 million.

One group that did significantly benefit from the promotion was electrical retailers. It is estimated that an additional UK£9 million was added to their profits.

Maytag sold Hoover® Europe to the Italian appli-ance manufacturer Candy SpA, and set up a fund to handle litigation against the company. The factory in Scotland was closed. Overall this was a significant pub-lic relations disaster for both Hoover® and Maytag. It demonstrates the need for accurate cost–benefit analysis when planning a sales promotion campaign.

Sources: Hartley (1998); BBC Television, *Trouble at the Top: Hoover flights fiasco*, broadcast on BBC 2, 12 May 2004.

(one coffee house chain rewards regular customers with a free coffee after 10 visits). All these are designed to increase usage of the product or service.

Sales promotions can be too successful

It is worth briefly noting that sales promotions can be too successful, and thus jeopardise the organisation's reputation. A classic promotion that was 'too successful' was the Hoover® flights promotion considered in mini case 10.9.

■ Exhibitions, expos and trade fairs

Exhibitions, expos and trade fairs are used in both B2C and B2B environments, marketing everything from computer software and cars to various types of machinery, equipment and fashion items. As Table 10.5 illustrates, the exhibition environment can deliver opportunities for companies if they approach exhibitions from a systematic perspective.

Table 10.6 highlights a selection of the key B2B and B2C exhibitions and related festivals used to promote products and services.

■ Public relations

There are many definitions for public relations. Virtually every association that represents public relations practitioners has its own definition. In essence it concerns the relationship between an organisation or individual and its (or his or her) direct and indirect publics. For a greater understanding of public relations it is worth dissecting that definition further.

◆ Organisation: this can be any type including for-profit companies, non-government organisations (NGOs), not-for-profit organisations (such as charities and universities), government departments and units within organisations (such as strategic business units or departments). All these organisations use and need public relations to a greater or lesser extent.

◆ Individual: whilst the majority of definitions focus on organisations it is worth remembering that individuals too use public relations to promote themselves. This is especially true of celebrities and politicians, although ordinary people are sometimes thrust into the limelight of the media.

◆ Publics: each organisation or individual has a

Table 10.5 The value of exhibitions

Indicator	Description
Target audience	It is usually only people interested in the specific products or services on offer who frequent B2B or B2C exhibitions. Thus, exhibitions can focus directly on a specific target audience. Especially in a B2B environment, key buyers or potential buyers can be invited to the exhibition to see the products and services. This is usually accompanied by supportive PR activity such as a reception.
Quality audience	Linked to the point above, usually only individuals or groups who have the resources to purchase the products or services visit exhibitions.
Time spent	If the exhibition stand incorporates some form of interactivity, it is likely that a visitor will spend more time discussing the product or service. For example, this might be a demonstration of the latest software or a presentation on the services available. By being able to increase visitor time on the stand, the company has an increased opportunity to interest the visitor in its products or services.
Launch potential	Exhibitions can be used to launch a new product or service. PR activities to support the launch are usually employed. These include media packs and a reception. As the media will normally spend time at an exhibition, it can be a very good location to launch a product or service, maximizing the number of journalists writing about it. A launch also increases the potential for advance order taking.

Table 10.6 A selection of key B2B and B2C exhibitions worldwide

Location/country	Exhibition-expo-trade fair	Description
Buenos Aires, Argentina	Expo Comm Argentina	B2B Telecommunications exhibition covering a range of products and services from fibre optics to cellular and broadband services.
California, USA	Western Foodservice and Hospitality Expo	Sponsored by the California Restaurant Association. Food and beverage products and food service equipment.
Cannes, France	Cannes International Boat Show	B2B and B2C. Boat builders and importers of sailing and motor boats, ship chandlers, sailing wear and insurance services.
England, UK	Farnborough International Air Show	Aviation and aerospace. Announcements of new aircraft and equipment.
England, UK	Defence Systems and Equipment Exhibition	Defence equipment manufacturers marketing to other companies and government representatives. Thus B2B and B2G.
Germany	Frankfurt International Book Fair	Publishers market rights and permissions for a wide range of book titles.
Kuala Lumpur, Malaysia	International Healthcare Show	Hospital management systems, medical equipment and products, pharmaceuticals and healthcare services.
Paris, France	Visual Communications Europe	B2B exhibition that covers all aspects of visual communication from signs to communication agencies.
Queensland, Australia	Queensland Mining and Engineering Expo	Products and services for the mining mineral processing, power generation, sugar processing and smelting industries.
Spain	Medical Forum Expo	International healthcare systems exhibition.

Figure 10.22

© Shona Muir. Reproduced with kind permission.

The exhibition stand for the Australian-based company Muir Anchoring Systems at the 2004 Monte Carlo Boat Show

set of publics or groups that interact with it (or him or her). These include employees, customers, media, fans, pressure groups and legislators. It is possible to create two subsets of an organisation's publics:

- Direct publics: as the title suggests these are publics that have a direct relationship with the organisation or individual. Depending upon the nature of the relationship they normally include employees, customers, suppliers, competitors and the local community.

- Indirect publics: these are publics that have no immediate direct relationship with the organisation or individual. However they may be influenced, at some point in the future, by its (or his or her) actions. Examples are the proposed introduction of new rules and regulations

Table 10.7 The scope of public relations

Activity	Description
Corporate relations	The relationship between an organisation (at the corporate level) and its publics, who include stakeholders (including shareholders) and the media.
Community relations	The relationship between the organisation and the community within which it operates. A multinational corporation (MNC), for instance, will operate within several, often very different, community environments. Companies may work closely with local communities (including local government representatives) to alleviate problems such as noise from late night deliveries. Equally, companies may become actively involved in local community activities such as fundraising for local schools and hospitals, building a strong link between the organisation and the community. In many parts of the world organisations have become not only the largest employer within a community, but also the centre of that community.
Customer relations	In increasingly competitive markets companies seek to build longer-term relationships with their customers. Customer relations can include the development of loyalty card systems, meet and greet policies in hotels and stores, and how complaints are handled.
Employee relations	This is the relationship between the organisation and its employees, on both a one-to-one and one-to-group basis. Employee relations normally includes communications with retirees who perhaps benefit from the organisation's pension plan. It can be argued that for a for-profit organisation (depending on the nature of the business) retirees can also be viewed as customers. Employee relations is often considered as the core component of internal communications. Research has indicated that good internal communication processes can enhance employee motivation.
Industrial relations	This can be viewed from two perspectives. First is the relationship between different companies operating in the same industrial or commercial sector. While refraining from revealing company secrets, organisations can share information that will have a benefit to the industry as a whole, through special forums and/or through trade/professional bodies. Second, this can be the relationship between the organisation and the various trade unions and professional bodies that represent its employees in negotiations.

by a government department, and how a company or individual handles a crisis management situation.

♦ The relationship: this is the type or nature of the relationship that exists between organisations/individuals and their publics. It includes the reputation and image of the organisation and its brands. For instance, whether an organisation has been ethical in its dealings with its publics will ultimately affect its reputation and performance. An example of a damaged reputation is the US-based energy company ENRON, which collapsed in 2002 amidst corporate scandals.

Scope of public relations

Public relations covers many aspects of communications between organisations or individuals and

their various publics. Table 10.7 outlines the many and varied elements that comprise the all-encompassing term 'public relations'. As you see it is a very broad subject, covering both internal and external communications. Additionally, you will see that several of the elements are interrelated.

■ Integrated marketing communications

Integrated marketing communications (IMC) is the process of creating a uniform message and style that incorporates the different forms of media. Thus the company, organisation or brand communicates to its target audience with a single message using various communications channels.

Schultz, Tannebaum and Lauterborn (1993) encapsulated the relevance of the IMC concept when they stated:

Activity	Description
Government relations	Organisations communicate with government on many different levels. For instance, they may lobby governments to persuade them to either introduce or modify legislation. Equally, government may communicate new initiatives and trade developments directly to the business community: for instance, new levels of financial support available to companies wanting to participate in overseas exhibitions to market their products and services.
Issues management	This is also known as crisis management, and is a major component of public relations. Organisations prepare plans in case a crisis or major issue arises. These can relate to human resources (such as strikes), or to products (faulty goods or contaminated products). Crisis or issues management may be used either as part of an ongoing campaign or to handle a one-off specific crisis. For example, an organisation may have an ongoing crisis that it needs to handle over the longer term, such as a need to counteract consistent attacks by determined campaigners. Various chemical, food and oil companies have for years had to deal with ongoing crisis management issues regarding their operations both at home and abroad. The second major category covers one-off incidents. These range from a major disaster (oil rig fire or plane crash) to mismanagement of the business (for example, the collapse of the energy giant ENRON in the United States).
Investor relations	To some extent this links into corporate relations, as stated above. It focuses on stock market listed companies and how they communicate with their shareholders, and the investment and banking communities in general. It is critical that such companies build a strong relationship with their investor community. Such a relationship becomes 'critical' when companies have to issue profits warning (i.e. profits will not be in line with forecasts and this will impact upon the share price) or the company faces a potential hostile takeover threat. If the investor community (especially large fund holders) are 'onside' with the company, a hostile takeover might be blocked. If they are not 'onside' the investors may vote for the takeover.
Market or supply chain relations	The relationship organisations have with their suppliers and distributors. In an increasingly 24-hour operational environment which is reliant on just-in-time (JIT) movements, organisations have to develop effective relationships through the supply chain.
Media relations	The ongoing communications between an organisation and the relevant media. As with customers, organisations have to build a relationship with the media. Media relations is both a proactive and reactive occurrence.
New product and service launches	Companies and organisations (for example, government departments) use a range of techniques to launch a new product or service into the marketplace. These include product demonstrations, launches at exhibitions (for instance, a new model at an international car show) and service experiences (for instance, the launch of a new train service).
Promotion	The marketing of the individual, organisation, product or service to interested publics. This may be achieved through exhibitions or special events.
Public affairs	Governments, non-government organisations (NGOs) and opinion formers (a component of publics) communicate on issues of public policy and legislation. Again, lobbyists may work behind the scenes to persuade legislators to make amendments to current or proposed legislation.
Publicity	It is often assumed, quite wrongly, that public relations consists solely of publicity. At the turn of the 20th century it could be argued that publicity was the mainstay of public relations. However, public relations is much more today. Publicity can be described as 'the dissemination of planned and executed messages through selected media to further the interests of a person or organisation without payment to the media'. This ties in with media relations as discussed above.

Source: adapted from Groucutt et al. (2004).

In this new era of integrated marketing communications, the communication strategy is the imperative element in the communications process for all departments within the marketing organisation. It forces every aspect of the communications process to reach the consumer in a unified manner, with one personality, one benefit, one selling idea. Every communication tactic that flows from the integrated communications strategy reinforces the reason why the consumer should believe in the product.

As they suggest, for IMC to be successful, organisations need to develop a communications strategy. This following aspects need to be considered:

♦ The strategy needs to link back to the corporate strategy of the organisation. That is what the organisation wants to achieve over the short, medium and longer terms, bearing in mind, of course, that in today's turbulent world long-term planning is usually just 'blue-sky' thinking.

♦ For an integrated strategy to have an opportunity to be successful the different communications channels need to operate in concert with each other. This is often easier said than done. Discussing the various promotional variants in a book chapter is a straightforward exercise. However, these channels of communications are operated by different groups of people, usually operating within different organisations (for instance, PR companies, direct marketing agencies and so on). While they have the same client (the marketing department of the organisation), they remain distinct companies in their own right. Both individuals and organisations often have their own agendas, and while working in concert makes sense, there may be other issues that prevent such an approach. Therefore the onus is on the organisation's marketing department to provide clear direction and control in order to successfully harness the talent within the supplier companies and to overcome any potential rivalries.

♦ Communication, like any marketing planning, needs to be flexible. What might appear to work on paper might not in reality. Even with

the 'best' marketing research to pre-test the communications strategy, promotional activities can, and do fail. Therefore all companies involved in developing the strategy need to be flexible enough to amend it if required.

♦ There must be systems in place to measure and evaluate the level of success of the communications strategy. Linked to the point above, this measurement and evaluation cannot be undertaken only at the final stages of the campaign. Measurement and evaluation must be an ongoing process in order to allow for remedial changes as and when necessary.

■ The future

The future will be determined by the external or macro environment (see Chapter 2). However, contemporary research indicates that the Internet and mobile phone technologies, for example, will play an increasing role in expanding communication channels among the young. However in many countries, especially in Europe, an increasing proportion of the population is aged 50 and over, and many traditional forms of media channel will be of crucial importance.

■ Chapter summary

This chapter has examined the various forms of communication and promotion available to companies and organisations. It has also briefly considered the psychology behind attempts to persuade individuals to buy either products and services. Many of the techniques are over 100 years old, while some are more recent. Nonetheless the principle remains the same: using the right channel of communication at the right time to reach the right target audience in order to fulfil the marketing objectives and then the corporate objectives of the business. This sounds far simpler than it is in reality. The goal, though, is to achieve these aims and objectives.

■ Questions for review and reflection

1 Marketing communications campaigns are normally developed within a competitive and

dynamic environment. Using examples to illustrate your answer, examine the factors that might be considered when planning a promotional campaign.

2   In a contemporary world political parties cannot afford to ignore the role of marketing communications to support their activities. Use examples to explain some of the tactics that political parties may use to communicate their message to a target audience.

3   Sponsorship has experienced significant growth over the past ten years. Using an example of a major sporting event, critically discuss the benefits a company might gain from providing sponsorship.

4   Some companies and organisations have used shock advertising to promote their messages. Critically evaluate the arguments for and against this type of advertising.

5   'Clutter' is often cited as a major barrier to affective communications and promotion. (a) Explain what is meant by the term' clutter'. (b) Using examples, consider what tactics marketers can use to break through the clutter.

6   Critically evaluate the cases for and against the integration of marketing communications.

7   'Noise' within the communications process can dramatically affect how a customer perceives, and thus reacts to, information. Clearly outline what is meant by the term 'noise', then critically evaluate how noise can be reduced.

8   Consider how public relations can be used to promote a fast-moving consumer good. Support your answer with examples.

9   Imagine that you are the marketing director of a retail food store chain in your home country. You are about to launch a new range of own-label foods. Devise a marketing communications plan to launch this new range. State clearly what promotional tactics you would use and why.

10 'In a technologically-driven world the way we communicate with customers makes the role of the individual sales person outdated.' Critically evaluate this statement.

11 You are the marketing director of a major cosmetics company considering the launch of a new sophisticated fragrance for men in the Middle East. Using the Internet and other resources, examine the key issues to consider when developing the promotional campaign. (You may also want to refer to the discussion of societal issues in Chapter 2).

12 Critically examine how direct marketing can be used to develop the lifetime value (LTV) of a customer. Use practical examples to illustrate your answer.

13 'Direct marketing will be the key marketing concept of the 21st century.' With fellow students debate this statement.

14 Briefly outline the potential ethical issues associated with marketing communications.

15 Examine how the Internet can be used to promote a vacation destination.

■ References

Barry, T. E. (1987) 'The development of the Hierarchy of Effects: an historical perspective', *Current Issues and Research in Advertising* **10**(2), pp. 251–95.

BBC (2004b) 'Spam messages on the increase', BBC Online, 25 May.

Berlo, D. K. (1960) *The Process of Communication: An introduction to theory and practice*, New York: Holt, Rinehart and Winston.

Colley, R. H. (1961) *Defining Advertising Goals for Measured Advertising Results*, New York: Association of National Advertisers.

Cornwell, T. B. and Maignan, I. (1998) 'An international review of sponsorship research', *Journal of Advertising* **27**(11) (Spring), pp. 1–27.

Datamonitor (2004) *Global Offshore Call Centre Outsourcing: Who will be the next India?* Datamonitor.

DMA (2003) *DMA Census of the Direct Marketing Industry 2002–2003*, Direct Marketing Association (UK) Ltd, July.

Ehrenberg, A. S. C. (1974) 'Repetive advertising and the consumer', *Journal of Advertising Research* 14 (April), pp. 25–34.

Federal Bureau of Investigation (FBI) (2003)

Telemarketing Victim Call Center Background, Los Angeles FBI Center, www.losangeles.fbi.gov/telemarket.

Festinger, L. (1957) *A Theory of Cognitive Dissonance*, Stanford, Conn.: Stanford University Press.

Fletcher, W. (1999) *Advertising, Advertising*, London: Profile.

Grönroos, C. (1990) *Service Management and Marketing*, New York: Lexington.

Groucutt, J. and Griseri, P. (2004) *Mastering e-Business*, Basingstoke: Palgrave Macmillan.

Groucutt, J., Leadley, P. and Forsyth, P. (2004) *Marketing: Essential principles, new realities*, London: Kogan Page.

Harridge-March, S. (2002) Marketing communications, lecture notes on telemarketing, Oxford Brookes University.

Horgan, J. (1990) 'Claude E. Shannon: unicyclist, juggler, and father of information theory', *IEEE Information Theory Society Newsletter* (June).

Lasswell, H. (1927) *Propaganda Technique in the World War*, New York: Knopf. See also Lasswell, H. (1948) 'The structure and function of communications in society', in L. Bryson (ed.), *The Communication of Ideas*, New York: Harper & Row.

Lavidge, R. J. and Steiner, G. A. (1961) 'A model for predictive measurements of advertising effectiveness', *Journal of Marketing* 25 (October), pp. 59-62.

Lukk, T. (1997) *Movie Marketing: Opening the picture and giving it legs*, Los Angeles: Silman-James Press.

Mattelart, A. and Mattelart, M. (1998) *Theories of Communication: A short introduction*, London: Sage.

Mendelsohn, H. (1962) 'Measuring the process of communication effect', *Public Opinion Quarterly 26* (Fall), pp. 411–16.

Ray, M. L.,Sawyer, A. G., Rothchild, M. L., Heeler, R. M., Strong, E. C. and Reed, J. B. (1973) 'Marketing communications and hierarchy of effects', in P. Clarke (ed.), *New Models for Mass Communication Research*, Beverly Hills: Sage.

Rogers, E. M. (1994) *A History of Communication Study: A biographical approach*, New York: Free Press.

Rosen, E. (2000) *The Anatomy of Buzz: Creating word-of-mouth marketing*, London: HarperCollins Business.

Rossiter, J. R. and Percy, L. (1987) *Advertising and Promotions Management*, New York: McGraw-Hill.

Saunders, D. (1999) *20th Century Advertising*, London: Carlton.

Schramm, W. (1955) 'How communication works', in W. Schramm (ed.), *The Process and Effect of Communication*, Urbana: University of Illinois Press.

Schultz, D. E., Tannebaum, S. I. and Lauterborn, R.F. (1993) *Integrated Marketing Communications*, Lincolnwood: NTC Business Books.

Scott, W. D. (1903) *The Theory of Advertising: A simple exposition of the principles of psychology in their relation to successful advertising*, Boston: Small, Maynard and Co.

Scott, W. D. (1908) *The Psychology of Advertising: A simple exposition of the principles of psychology in their relation to successful advertising*, Boston: Small, Maynard and Co.

Shannon, C. E. (1948) 'A mathematical theory of communication', *Bell System Technical Journal* 27 (July and October), pp. 379–423, 623–656.

Sheldon, A. F. (1911) *The Art of Selling*, Chicago: Sheldon School.

Strong, E. K. Jr (1925) *The Psychology of Selling and Advertising*, New York: McGraw-Hill.

Sunday Times (2004) 'FSA director advertisements', Appointments, Section 7, *Sunday Times,* p. 1.

Tapp, A. (1998) *Principles of Direct Marketing*, Harlow: Financial Times/Prentice Hall.

Vaughn, R. (1980) 'How advertising works: a planning model', *Journal of Advertising Research* 20 (October), pp. 27–33.

Vaughn, R. (1986) 'How advertising works: a planning model revisited', *Journal of Advertising Research* 26 (February/March), pp. 57–66.

Yelkur, R. and Da Costa, M. (2001) 'Differential pricing and segmentation on the Internet: the case of hotels', *Management Decision* 20(4), pp. 252–61.

Yeshin, T. (1998) *Integrated Marketing Communications: The holistic approach*, Oxford: Butterworth-Heinemann.

Price

CHAPTER 11

Contents

Learning outcomes	249
Introduction	249
Pricing objectives	250
Factors that influence price	252
Cost of R&D	252
Cost of production	252
Additionals	252
Economic value	253
Competitive forces	253
Market conditions	253
Geography	254
Pricing tactics	255
Pioneer pricing	255
Price skimming	257
Penetration pricing	257
Price matching	257
Variable pricing	258
Psychological pricing	258
Prestige pricing	258
Odd-even pricing	259
Single/double pricing	259
Promotional pricing	259
Trade-in allowances	260
Discount pricing	261
Buy one get one free	261
Book early discount	261
Special event pricing	262
Direct payment mechanisms	262
Professional services pricing	262
Competitive tendering	262
International pricing	263
Ethical issues	264
Dumping	264
Price fixing – cartels	264
Premium pricing issues	266
Bait and switch	266
Chapter summary	266
Questions for review and reflection	266
References	267

Learning outcomes

After completing this chapter you should be able to:

▶ discuss why price can have the most dramatic and immediate effect on the financial fortunes of an organisation

▶ outline why successful marketing strategies depend upon carefully planned and executed pricing strategies

▶ critically evaluate the different pricing tactics or techniques that companies, organisations and retailers employ

▶ critically examine the potential value of price flexibility at the time of volatility within the marketplace.

■ Introduction

All the following have one thing in common:

◆ a music CD

◆ 10 000 micro chips for a computer manufacturer

◆ a meal at a restaurant

◆ a mega yacht

◆ a nuclear power generating plant

◆ a family car

◆ a bunch of flowers.

They all come with a price tag attached. Agreed, the scale of the price tag will be very different – but it is a price tag nonetheless.

Price is often considered to be the only marketing mix variable that is purely revenue generating. It can be defined as a 'measure of the value exchanged by the buyer for the value of the product or service offered by the seller'. The medium of exchange may be either financial (where money changes hands) or goods. However, like all the variables price cannot be considered as purely independent, but must be related to the rest of the mix. For example, a customer

Figure 11.1

© Jonathan Groucutt

Yachts, super yachts and mega yachts adorning the marina in Monte Carlo. They all come with a very heavy price tag, not just for construction but for maintenance as well.

might become interested in the product through promotion, seek a distribution outlet (place), discuss the product with staff (people), consider the price in relation to his or her perceived needs and the quality of the product (psychology) and use a credit card to pay for the product (process).

It is necessary to consider what constitutes price, the methods of determining what price could be charged, how price affects the other variables and how they in turn affect price.

Various objectives influence pricing decisions:

◆ The need to generate revenues and maximising profits: this is maximising the returns on assets and/or investments.

◆ Maintaining or increasing market share: this involves maintaining (basic option) or increasing (preferred option) customer involvement. This may require different, radical and competitive approaches to pricing. For a company or organisation to have the largest share of the market does not mean it will be the most profitable in the marketplace. Other factors must be taken into consideration, including its financial and operational efficiencies and effectiveness.

◆ Creating a price that is fair and equitable for both the seller and the buyer.

◆ A price that delivers a perceived or real value, or indeed both, to the buyer.

◆ Legal and ethical issues which deter actions that are detrimental to buyers and the competitive environment.

■ Pricing objectives

Buttle (1986) believed an organisation's pricing objectives depend on several key factors. Each one in turn has an impact on the profit line. However, they must not be viewed in isolation as they can have a cumulative effect on pricing.

◆ The cost of producing the product or service. This is the first cost that companies must consider. Initially the costs may be high because of:

● the uniqueness of the product

● limited sales as it is new to market

● market forces – competition

● market opportunities.

You may want to reflect on the issues discussed in Chapter 9 on Products.

◆ The cost of marketing the product or service. This will vary depending on the type of product or service and the competitive environment into which it is launched.

◆ The time frame in which the company requires a return on the investment in the new product or service. Some companies seek a short-term return on their investment, while others take the longer view. This may include developing and expanding markets for sustainable long-term growth.

◆ The profit margin the company wants to achieve. This is the level of revenue generated above the cost of manufacturing and marketing the product or service. It will vary depending on:

● the costs of production

● competitive forces

● the product's or service's position in the marketplace

● its lifecycle position.

◆ Whether the product or service will be marketed as a single purchase, or could become a repeat purchase. For example, a luxury car will be a one-off purchase at least for a couple of years before it is traded in for a newer model. A chocolate bar, on the other hand, could be a regular or repeat impulse purchase on a daily, weekly or monthly basis.

◆ The relationship between the price of the new product and other products in the company's product line. A company that produces and markets several similar products will need to consider the effect of the new product on existing ranges. Pricing the product too low, for example, may cannibalise sales from the company's existing ranges as well as from competitors. While this might in the short term be good for the new product, it will have a financial impact on existing trusted brands. In the longer term this could be damaging to the company, especially if the new product begins to lose ground in the marketplace.

◆ Whether the product or service is new to the market or established. The company may be using a penetrating price policy to create position for the product in the marketplace. If it is an established product the company will need to consider any changes that occur in the marketplace that might affect its pricing position. For example, if several new products enter the market at a lower price, the company might need to consider its position. It might lower the price to match the new entrants, take the price below the competition (reducing margins), or resist changing the price. It could take the latter view if it believes:

● its product is of superior quality

● a change in price will affect customers' perception of the product

● the new entrants will only be able to support the lower pricing position over a short term, and damage to their brand during this period will be minimal

● a combination of these factors.

◆ The level of uniqueness of the product or service compared with the competition. If the company believes its product is superior to the competition (current and potential) it might charge a higher price. Of course, it depends on whether customers also consider the product or service offers superior value for money.

◆ Where the product is located within its life cycle. Price is often affected by life cycle positioning. Higher prices may be charged during the growth stages (depending on the product's uniqueness) whereas lower prices may be charged towards the end of the product's life as a result of competition in the marketplace. The price will depend on many factors, both internal and external to the organisation.

◆ The type of relationship the company wants to establish with its customers: short, medium or longer term? This may reflect the types and level of discount available to a customer.

◆ The type of price comparison the company seeks to establish with its competitors in the mind of its customers.

◆ The extent to which the company seeks to establish a major share of the market. This may be over the short, medium and/or longer term.

◆ The level of inventory for the product. The more stock that is held in warehouses, the greater the cost to the company. If inventory levels are high the company may decide to significantly reduce prices to move stock out of its warehouse and through retail outlets, particularly if a new version of the product is due to be introduced.

Companies must consider these objectives separately and cumulatively. The result will depend very much on the product or service type, its age within the marketplace and the customer profile. The objectives should not be viewed as static. Markets are often in a dynamic flux, thus companies must continually review their objectives in the light of changes within the marketplace.

■ Factors that influence price

There are many factors that influence costs both separately and cumulatively. This section considers some of the key influencing factors.

Cost of research and development (R&D)

Some products or services require very little research and development and thus can be rapidly introduced to market. Others though may require several years of R&D and significant financial support over that time frame. Consider the R&D invested in the Airbus A380 passenger aircraft, or in the software program that was used to write this book. Neither product appeared on the market overnight. Relatively significant levels of resources – financial, technology and people – were invested to develop the prototype prior to commercial production. Therefore companies must seek the means of recouping this investment in the price they charge for the final product.

Clearly such R&D costs cannot be 'normally' included in the initial price to the consumer. If that were the case a word processing package, for example, would cost several thousand euros, which would make it unaffordable to many users. Although R&D costs need to be considered if a product is aimed at the mass market, it still has to be priced at a level prospective buyers can afford. This is a point we return to later in this section.

Cost of production

A major influencer will be cost of production. The price charged must ensure that the cost is recovered, even if this is not achieved immediately. The analysis must include both fixed and variable costs. While the costs of the production process may be fixed to an extent, the cost of raw materials may vary. For instance, a poor cocoa harvest due to exceptionally bad weather conditions will increase the price of cocoa, with the price increase being determined by the level of demand in relation to the level of supply. Chocolate producers would then have to consider either a price rise to compensate for the increased cost of raw materials, or absorbing the cost within their current price (and reducing their margins). A company may be forced to take the latter position if it was operating within a price-sensitive marketplace.

Additionals: local taxes and surcharges

When considering the pricing of a product or service the company must be mindful of any 'additionals'. These are costs added when the bill is finally presented to the customer. They can include:

◆ Local taxes. There might be more than one tax. These range from energy to tourist taxes, and may be imposed by a local government or national legislature.

◆ Service charges. If you are staying in a hotel, for instance, you will most likely be charged for ordering a meal by room service, on top of the cost of the food you order.

◆ Surcharges (such as costs associated with a delivery from your local pizza takeaway).

◆ Value added taxes (these are normally imposed by the regional state and/or national governments).

Although these are often small amounts, they are often hidden and can mount over time.

Figure 11.2

© AIRBUS S.A.S. Photo by exm company/ H. GOUSSÉ.

The prototype of the Airbus A380 in flight. There has been significant investment in R&D to create this advanced aircraft capable of carrying over 500 passengers.

Economic value of the product or service

This can also be considered as the perceived value of a product or service. Just imagine the following scenario:

> You're in the desert. You are thirsty, very thirsty. Your throat is dry and sore from the lack of moisture. The day has been long, hot and the sun continues to beat down upon your body. Perspiration runs, in long thin tiny rivulets, down your face, you can taste the salt as it enters your mouth. The thirst is driving you crazy.

So how much would you pay for a large glass of cooling, refreshing sparkling mineral water?

There are times when products are plentiful and times when they may become scarce, and this is reflected in the price charged. This can happen in developed as well as developing nations.

A product or service may have a uniqueness that is particularly difficult to replicate, and so hold a particularly high economic value. Consider, for instance, any of the following:

◆ a painting by a great artist such as Picasso or Monet

◆ a football or soccer player such as David Beckham

◆ Russian caviar (see page 174).

All of these have an economic value that results in a high price being charged.

Competitive forces

If a company holds a monopolistic position within the market and is not regulated by the government, it is free to charge what it likes. If a company is part of a cartel and the cartel holds control over the market, it too can charge what it likes. However, markets are rarely monopolies or cartels. Companies normally operate in competitive markets, and so need to consider how their products or services compare with their rivals'. A company might be able to differentiate its products or services from its competitors', but this is not always possible. Consider, for example, basic tinned tomatoes on a shelf in a supermarket. With a few exceptions the contents of the tins are essentially the same, although they have different brand names.

A company marketing tinned tomatoes might believe it has a superior brand and thus charge a higher price. However, it will depend on customers' perception of the value they are receiving for the higher price. If customers perceive that they are receiving appropriate value, they will pay the price. However, if the price is substantially different from competitors, customer might not pay it. In order for the company to achieve a higher price there must be a real as opposed to a perceived value. This added value could be in the types of tomatoes used, or the canning process employed to retain the flavour.

In the 1990s there was a price battle over basic tinned tomatoes in UK supermarkets. By the end of this battle tinned tomatoes were selling at 5 pence a tin, significantly reducing margins for the retail outlets. Such a battle could only be short lived.

Companies have to consider:

◆ The dynamics of the competitive environment: new companies will enter the market while existing companies may leave it. Competitors might not only be locally or regionally based. With increasing globalisation and the development of the Internet, competition can be international in context.

◆ Differentiation: in markets where products and services are increasingly being perceived by customers as 'the same', companies need to consider whether they can compete on price alone. If not, then they have to develop a differentiator that allows them to first, stand out within the competitive market – perhaps gaining a competitive advantage; and second, charge a price that reflects the differentiator. However, competitors may be swift to imitate the differentiator in some form. Thus the value-added competitive advantage is lost and price once more becomes what determines purchase.

Market conditions

The marketplace in which companies operate is not static but in a constant dynamic shift or state of movement. The movement is influenced by several factors. These include:

◆ Economic: the economic environment determines the level of disposable income available for purchasing products or services. Generally at times of high employment and sustained economic growth, disposable income will be high. The converse happens when there is a high level of unemployment and an economy in recession or depression. In the latter case, consumers will normally be highly price sensitive.

◆ Societal: as discussed in Chapter 2, societies possess various cultural norms and traditions developed over centuries. However, culture is developed, modified and altered over time. This is partly through the influence of external factors, but also because of generational changes and the desires, needs and wishes of new generations. Demographic changes do not only focus on new generations. Europe, for instance, is witnessing people living longer, and in many cases with a significantly higher level of disposable income than the elderly had in previous generations.

Companies need to monitor market conditions on a regular basis. They must be aware of both gradual, and the possibility of dramatic, changes in the economic and societal components of the market.

Geography

For centuries there has been import and export of various loose and manufactured products, everything from coal to trucks. There are four fundamental factors to consider:

◆ costs of transporting the products

◆ costs associated with product adaptation

◆ government barriers

◆ whether customers in the overseas market will be able to afford the product.

Transportation cost implications

There are various costs incurred when moving products from one location to another, especially if is across national borders and over long distances. In 1936 the International Chamber of Commerce agreed a set of standard trade definitions for use in international sales contracts. These became known as Incoterms, short for International Commercial Terms. Since 1936 these terms have been revised six times, with the latest (at the time of writing) being Incoterms (2000). It is available in 31 languages.

The 13 incoterms[1] cover the obligations between trade buyers and trade sellers and manufacturers in international trade. This includes who is responsible for costs such as shipment and insurance. These costs have to be factored into the price charged by the seller to the buyer throughout the supply chain.

Adaptation costs

Although many products can be classed as standardised, that is, they are usable in the same form across geographical boundaries, others are not. Products may be adapted for various reasons, including legal and technical issues or a combination of these. Any adaptation will incur some cost. Again, it is a question of who will initially incur those costs and whether they will be subsumed into the price of the product to the end customer.

Government barriers

Although the World Trade Organization (WTO) is working towards a reduction in trade barriers, these are still imposed by nations to both protect their indigenous industries and to raise revenues. The barriers can be divided into tariff and non-tariff, and those related to cost are briefly outlined in Table 11.1.

Affordability

A product may be readily affordable within one country but out of the reach of potential customers within another. Companies need to consider a raft of economic conditions (inflation, interest rates and levels of disposable income) to understand whether a product will be affordable or not within another geographic location. Then, as discussed fully later in this chapter, the company has to 'think locally' when developing the most appropriate pricing structure.

Price sensitivity

Customers may be particularly sensitive to either the set price or increases, even if they are marginal.

Table 11.1 Tariff and non-tariff barriers

Tariff barrier	Description
Export tariff	The government of the exporting nation imposes a tariff charge on the products being exported.
Transit tariff	When products are moved by road and rail across borders they may incur a transit tariff. This could be considered as a form of trans-shipment tax. The argument is that if products are moved across a nation to be sold in another nation, the road and rail infrastructure is being utilised and thus there should be a charge levied.
Import tariff	The government of the importing nation imposes a tariff charge on the products being imported into the country. This is often used to protect indigenous companies who may not be able to compete effectively against imported products.
Non-tariff barriers	
Import licences	Generally these apply to products that are restricted in some way, for example, products that contain radiological materials such as scanners. Licences have to be granted prior to shipping and there is an inherent cost to obtaining them.
Administrative procedures	All countries have administrative procedures covering such areas as safety testing and labeling. These are important issues. However, two factors can impinge on companies exporting or importing products. First is the number of procedures to be undertaken and the length of time to complete them. Both administrative procedures and any delays in executing them can impact financially on companies. The question is whether costs are absorbed or recouped through the supply chain and from the end customer.

For example, a 10 per cent price increase on an €30 product would only be €3, but it could prevent some consumers from making a purchase. They will seek an alternative product at a lower price. For them the increase is too high; they are particularly sensitive to it.

In most textbooks, price sensitivity is considered when discussing lower income groups where literally 'every penny counts'. There is a view that it only affects the poor and disaffected. This is an urban myth. Everyone is price sensitive to a greater or lesser extent. Even financially comfortable groups may be particularly sensitive to price changes for several reasons: for example they are considering the relationship between price and the tangible and intangible value of the product or service, or there has been a significant change in the economic environment which is affecting this segment of the market. This was the case in the 1990s when the UK recession was particularly damaging to middle-income groups. Redundancy and falling property values placed severe spending restrictions on households that had been quite affluent during the high-growth phase of the

economy. Even when the economy moved out of recession, many middle-income households remained price sensitive as a result of the impact the recession had had on their lives.

■ Pricing tactics

This section examines the various types of pricing tactics that companies employ. They are listed in Table 11.2. A company may use some or all of these pricing tactics during the life of a product or service, depending on what it is attempting to achieve and the influence of external factors. It is important not to view these tactics in isolation.

Pioneer pricing

As the name suggests the company is exploring or leading the way in terms of pricing for the particular product or service. This tactic may be adopted if the product or service is particularly new to the market and the company is seeking to understand how the market will react. Even though market research may have been conducted, the company

Table 11.2 Pricing tactics

Pricing tactic	Subsets
Pioneer pricing	
Price skimming	
Penetration pricing (predatory pricing)	
Price matching	
Variable pricing (flexible pricing)	
Psychological pricing	Prestige pricing Odd-even pricing Single price/double price
Promotional pricing	Bundling Trade-in allowance Discount pricing Quantity discounts Differential pricing Buy one get one free Book early discounts Special event pricing Direct payment mechanism
Professional service pricing	
Competitive tendering	
International pricing	Standard worldwide pricing Dual pricing mechanism Market pricing

will not know until it launches the product or service in the marketplace whether it is a sustainable price or not.

The company will also need to take into consideration the following issues:

◆ Will the marketplace accept the price?

◆ Is the product or service overpriced or underpriced for the market? Products or services can be underpriced, which may give potential customers the perception that the product or service is a lower quality than expected. Equally, if it is perceived as priced too high, the company will have effectively priced the product or service out of the market. This could also result in a competitor marketing a similar product or service at a lower price and gaining market share. Therefore the follower rather than the pioneer gains the longer-term value.

◆ Will the price set deter competitive pricing actions from companies that market similar products or services?

◆ Can current competitors enter the market with an imitation product or service? If so, what is the time frame to possible launch and what could be the price?

◆ Are there potential new entrants to the market? If so, will they act differently from established competitors?

As you can see, there are overlap issues and potential difficulties in ascertaining the actions of rivals. Although competitor intelligence gathering may help to some extent, it will not provide the complete picture. (See Chapter 5.) The company will have to attempt to calculate the level of risk involved in adopting a pricing tactic.

Price skimming

The objective here is to charge a higher than normal price for a specific time frame. Assuming that the product or service demonstrates volume sales, the difference between the normal price and the higher price can be 'skimmed off'. It thus becomes an additional or marginal 'income' for the company, which may be used to offset some of the initial research and development costs.

A company may choose price skimming during the introductory and early growth stages of the product's life cycle. This is because the product or service may be price inelastic: that is, demand is relatively price insensitive. In other words, relatively high prices can be charged and they will not affect the purchasing decisions of those who want the product or service. This can often be seen in the early adoption phase for a product or service. (Reflect back to Chapter 9 and the adoption process.)

A company is unlikely to be able to maintain a price skimming strategy for a significant length of time. If the product is based on a new technology, once that technology is established and can be imitated there will be new entrants to the marketplace. This was witnessed with the introduction of IBM-compatible computers in the late 1980s and the proliferation of mobile phones.

Penetration pricing (predatory pricing)

The overall objective of penetration pricing is to find a way of accessing a market by cutting through existing pricing structures or strategies. To some extent the associated name (predatory pricing) is a misnomer, for it suggests a form of exploitation and pricing at a significant loss to gain entry. Such an approach could be deemed as short-termism. This is not the point of penetration pricing, because companies are seeking to enter the marketplace and develop a segment or niche for themselves.

Penetration pricing can be used to achieve the following aims:

♦ Entry into an existing market through the introduction and maintenance of very low prices set against the average price for that product or service.

♦ The development of a new low-price segment, often within the existing marketplace.

♦ The acquisition of increased market share over the medium and longer term.

Prices are set deliberately low in order for the company to enter the market, ensure that a high level of sales is achieved, and achieve efficient economies of scale. An example is the introduction of no-frills airlines into the UK aviation market in the mid-1990s. This proved to be a highly competitive market, with other players vying for market share, not just in the United Kingdom but throughout Europe.

Price matching

This is often used in highly competitive markets where competitors are situated in relatively close proximity to each other. So, for instance, two supermarkets may routinely check the prices of

---

Mini case 11.1

ESSO® PriceWatch™ Campaign

In January 1996 the petroleum company ESSO® launched a PriceWatch™ campaign in the United Kingdom. The petrol pump market had become highly competitive. Between 1990 and 1997/8 the share of the supermarket-owned petrol stations had grown from 5 per cent to some 23 per cent. This increased competition with the major oil companies, and the market witnessed a 30 per cent overall reduction in petrol pump prices. This was clearly beneficial to consumers, but for the majors there was a risk of market shrinkage.

The objective of the ESSO® campaign was to continually monitor prices at a range of competitor petrol forecourts within a particular radius of its filling stations. The aim was not to undercut the lowest price charged within the set radius, but to match it. This would demonstrate that ESSO® was competitive in the marketplace without drastically reducing margins and risking the accusation of uncompetitive behaviour by regulatory bodies such as the Office of Fair Trading.

Source: 'Petrol market competitive says OFT', press release no. 23/98, Office of Fair Trading, 18 May 1998.

the leading brands in each outlet to match each other in discounts and associated special offers.

Variable pricing (flexible pricing)

Companies may adopt a variable pricing structure to accommodate changes within a competitive environment, customers' specific requirements, and/or to offer special value-added options. Mini case 11.2 discusses the fare structure for a London to Oxford 24-hour coach service.

Psychological pricing

It could be argued that all pricing relies on a combination of economics and psychology. While pricing may be rooted in economics in terms of supply and demand, it is often from the psychological perspective that we decide to make the purchase. Even when it comes to the relationship between 'value' and 'price' we are making a psychological judgment. The products may be identical, for example, cans of tinned tomatoes at the same price. However, we still might ask ourselves, 'Which one should I buy?'

Although we may argue that psychology permeates all purchasing decisions, there are certain pricing tactics that have particularly strong psychological undercurrents. These are examined in the next section.

Prestige pricing

The word 'prestige' symbolises reputation, glamour, respect, power and influence. These are not

---

Mini case 11.2

London to Oxford coach service

The Oxford Bus Company, a subsidiary of the Go-Ahead Group plc, operates a 24-hour coach service from London to Oxford branded the *oxfordespress*. This is one of three services that operate between the two cities on a 24/7 basis, so there are competitive pressures. The company offers a variety of fares depending upon customers' travel requirements and age group.

Adult fares (as at 2004 in UK£):

UK£9.00	one-way
UK£11.00	day/next day return
UK£13.00	three-month return
UK£47.00	12 trips (12 single journeys valid for 12 months)

Season tickets (unlimited travel on oxfordespress plus free travel on other Oxford Bus Company routes in and around Oxford)

UK£37.00	one week
UK£65.00	two weeks
UK£97.00	three weeks
UK£120.00	four weeks
UK£345.00	13 weeks
UK£670.00	26 weeks
UK£910.00	12 months

Under 16 and over 60 fares

UK£4.50	one-way
UK£5.50	day/next day return
UK£6.50	three-month return

Student and young person's fares

UK£7.00	one-way
UK£8.00	day/next day return
UK£10.00	three-month return
UK£42.00	12 trip (12 single journeys valid for 12 months)

Group fares (up to two adults and three children)

UK£24.00	day/next day return
UK£28.00	three-month return

Night owl fare

UK£7.00	Day/next day return for travel after 3 pm from Oxford.

Additionally, there are special timed offers. Between late December 2003 and the end of January 2004 the 12-month season ticket was available at a special rate of UK£777, a saving of UK£133. During the school Easter vacation, up to two children accompanied by an adult were charged only UK£1.00 each for a day return ticket. This offer was only valid from Saturday 3 April until midnight on Sunday 19 April, 2004.

Such a ticket pricing structure provides customers with flexibility depending on their travelling needs. For the author who lives in London but travels to Oxford every week, the discounted 12-month season ticket provided both perceived and real value.

Source: www.oxfordbus.co.uk

only 'value-driven' phrases but clearly psychological ones as well. Therefore products or services that exemplify such characteristics need to reflect these in the price. Indeed prestige pricing can often be used to create an 'extreme image' of the product or service, which defines it within its prescribed segment of the marketplace. It also significantly differentiates it from other general market segments. Here are a few examples of products and services that demonstrate prestige pricing (see Chapter 7):

◆ Russian or Iranian caviar. In many countries caviar has a prestige value and so carries an associated high price. In the United Kingdom, for instance, a small jar of Beluga Russian caviar may cost several hundred euros.

◆ Luxury sports cars. Whether these are Aston Martins or Ferraris, their prestige value is reflected in their pricing.

◆ Certain types of drinks. For instance fine champagne or Napoleon Cognacs may be priced at €500 or more a bottle.

◆ A five-star hotel.

In all cases the price must reflect (both real and perceived) value in the products or service.

Odd–even pricing

Here the product is priced at an odd number rather than being rounded up to a whole or even number, for example a CD priced at UK£4.99 rather than UK£5.00. While it is obvious it is only one penny cheaper, the perception is that it *is* cheaper. Consumers may focus more on the '4' or even the '99' rather than rounding up the number. This method of psychological pricing may well entice the consumer to buy more products in the price range.

Single price/double pricing

Although this concept predates the retailer Frank Winfield Woolworth (1852–1919), it was he who championed it. When he originally opened his retail venture Woolworths, the stores were known as 'five and dime' stores, reflecting the fact that

products were priced at either five or ten cents. For many years these were the only two prices charged, but as more products were introduced Woolworth began to vary his prices to reflect the variety on offer. However, by this time he had attracted a large customer base on which to build his retail business and empire.

In many towns and cities you will find general retail stores that sell a range of products using the single or double pricing technique. In the United Kingdom, for example, there are retailers which sell products at 50p and/or 99p. While many of the products sold are leading brands, others are less well-known brands or unbranded.

Customers might seek low prices with the knowledge that the quality will be reflected in the price. While there may be a perceived or psychological discount on the items, some products may actually be cheaper in major retail outlets than in 'bargain' stores. This is especially the case with soap products and detergents. Priced at 99p in the discount outlets, they may actually be priced at 85p or 95p in the major supermarkets. The supermarket might be cheaper simply because it has the power to discount further through bulk purchasing from the manufacturer.

Promotional pricing

The objective here is to use a promotional or special price to persuade customers to purchase a particular product or service. The promotional pricing may be ongoing or limited to a particular time frame and/or product range.

Bundling or the all-inclusive concept

Here several products or services are offered as a package at a single price. As Churchill and Peter (1998) suggest, bundling assumes that consumers will appreciate receiving a variety of products or services in one bundle. This is not always the case, as is discussed below.

Vacations, computers, restaurant menus and DVD box sets are four common examples of where companies use bundling techniques.

Thomas Cook (1809–1892) pioneered the concept of the packaged holiday in the 1850s and 1860s, a form that would be developed by his son John Mason Cook. However, this was limited to the middle classes and wealthy of the time who wanted to tour Europe and Egypt, travelling by rail and ship and staying in quality hotels. Packaged vacations as we now know them developed in the late 1960s as air travel increased in popularity and affordability, and countries increased the building of hotel complexes.

Issa and Jayawardena (2003) use the Caribbean as an example of fully inclusive vacations. They state:

> Generally the all-inclusive concept goes much further and covers practically everything a hotel or resort has to offer, including all drinks, taxes, transfers from and to airport to hotel and sports, with tipping being prohibited. A result of such a price package, in most cases, is money being eliminated from the holiday experience and the visitor knowing in advance what their holiday is likely to cost, except for personal expenses, such as telephone calls, laundry, car hire, dining off-property and shopping.

Increasingly some resorts include sporting activities such as golf and scuba diving in their overall package. Such bundling is ideal for families operating on a limited budget. Apart from 'extras' (which can be either purchased or not) a family knows how much its vacation has cost in advance of its departure from home.

Several computer suppliers have opted for price bundling. The bundles usually include the computer, monitor, video/photo camera, printer, scanner, educational software, home software, business software, modem, Internet access and games software. There is usually the option to upgrade to a higher specification package depending on the buyer's requirements. Such bundling may be ideal for a prospective customer who is either purchasing a computer and the peripherals for the first time, or significantly upgrading from an outmoded system. However, someone who wants to upgrade a computer but already has peripherals such as a printer/scanner might consider that bundling is not the right option.

Many restaurants offer two types of menus. An *à la carte* menu allows customers to choose from an array of separate dishes, each carrying an individual price. Alternatively, customers can choose a set menu with a limited variety of dishes, where an overall price is set for a fixed number of courses: for example, a two-course menu (excluding drinks) for UK£12.00 per person or a three-course menu for UK£15.00. Customers therefore know how much the food will cost them. All they then have to do is add the cost of drinks and any service charges or local taxes to the bill.

Fixed price or set menus provide various advantages:

- The restaurant can choose dishes that are relatively easy and inexpensive to prepare.

- The restaurant knows the margin that will be obtained on each set menu consumed.

- Because of the relative ease in preparation, the restaurant may be able to increase the throughput of customers over a lunchtime or evening.

Some restaurants in London's West End offer pre-theatre set menus. Revenue is generated from customers who would like to dine prior to attending the theatre. After a set time, only the *à la carte* menu is available, for customers who want a long leisurely meal with friends and/or family.

Movie or television companies can market DVD products individually or box them together to reflect a particular genre or the entirety of a series. For example:

- The James Bond movies can be purchased as individual DVDs or packaged as a box set.

- Universal Pictures has packaged movies starring Audrey Hepburn as a special DVD collection.

- The BBC has packaged various comedy and drama series into DVD collections. Again, the DVDs can be purchased either separately or as special packages. By bundling them together into a package or collection, the BBC is offering customers the ability to purchase the complete series.

Trade-in allowances

A company may offer a prospective buyer a price reduction for trading in an old item when a new one is purchased. This approach has been used extensively in the car retail business. Car owners trade in their used car for another used car, or a new one. The dealer offers owners a trade-in price for their old car, and this is offset against the price of the new purchase.

Discount pricing

Companies may offer customers discounted pricing when items are either bulk purchased and/or purchased within a particular time frame. The following examples illustrate how discount pricing can operate.

Quantity discounts

The seller offers the buyer a discount based upon the quantity of the product or service purchased. Usually the greater the volume, the greater the discount. Thus there is an incentive for the buyer to carefully consider how much of the product or service will be consumed over a time period. If, for example, the buyer consumes a significant amount of photocopy paper over a 12-month period, there is a financial incentive to negotiate a bulk-buying price. High levels of discounting are usually reserved for the B2B environment.

Differential pricing

This is normally a price reduction for buyers who purchase the product or service out of its normal seasonal pattern. Here are a few examples:

◆ Winter fashions are discounted just prior to the arrival of the spring/summer collections. The discounts are normally higher for women's fashion than men's. This is usually because men's clothes span several winter seasons, and women's fashion does not, particularly in the retail sector known as fast fashion. Here companies need to react quickly to rapidly changing trends. Companies such as the Spanish clothier and retailer Zara have employed logistics normally associated with the automotive industry to rapidly bring new fashions to the stores.

◆ Garden furniture and barbecues may be discounted during the autumn/winter period. Retailers use this type of discounting to move old stock in preparation for the arrival of new lines.

◆ Holiday companies use differential pricing

during peak and off-peak seasons. For example, a vacation in southern Spain will be cheaper in April/May when the weather is milder than in July/August when it is usually hot and dry – ideal for beach and sun lovers. Hotels may charge a premium rate not only during the summer months but also at special times of the year such as Christmas and New Year.

Buy one get one free

This is also known as a BOGOF promotion, and is generally used in the retail sector as a means of promoting own-label brands. Originally it was limited to two identical items such as two bars of soap. Increasingly it has been broadened to include a range of products, but generally they are all own-label brands. Companies that use BOGOF promotions tend to set specific time frames, for example, 'for two weeks only'. This is a further psychological incentive to prospective buyers.

There are several variations on this theme:

◆ Three for the price of two, which as the title suggests is a greater value incentive to the purchaser. The retailer may use this option as a means of reducing a stock inventory.

◆ Lower price item reduced: when two items are bought from a particular range the lower-priced item is discounted. The objective here is to create an incentive for the buyer to try another product within the product range.

◆ Free product with every purchase: this can be used as a co-branding exercise where the company links up with a related product: for example, a toothpaste manufacturer co-brands with one that produces toothbrushes. Although the toothbrush is free it provides the manufacturer with a promotional outlet which may lead to increasing purchases of its product range.

Book early discount

Travel companies use this technique to sell holidays several months beforehand. A holiday booked for July but paid for in January may command a significant discount.

Special event pricing

This is a special price set for a product, product range or service for a limited time frame and event. For example, a supplier or retailer might celebrate an anniversary, and advertise special discounts for the anniversary week or month. These could be based upon, for example:

◆ the length of the anniversary, such as '25 per cent off all products to celebrate our 25 years in business '

◆ the prices for similar products when the retailer first opened.

Direct payment mechanisms

Companies may offer a price reduction to those customers who pay their bills using a direct debit system. For example, in the United Kingdom the utility providers offer discounts to customers who opt for direct debit payments. This allows the utility company to withdraw a set amount directly from the customer's bank account on a specific day, each month or quarter of the year. This reduces potential delays for the utility company receiving payment (subject to there being sufficient funds in the customer's bank or credit card account), and provides an incentive to the customer to adopt a direct payment method.

Professional services pricing

Here individuals and companies such as lawyers, accountants, marketing and strategy consultants, doctors and special advisors charge for their professional services. Such pricing can operate within both B2C and B2B environments. Here are a few examples:

◆ A lawyer acting on behalf of a family who want to purchase a house may offer an all-inclusive price for the conveyancing (the legal transfer of title/ownership of the property). (This is a B2C example.)

◆ Private medical facilities: a doctor or medical centre's charge may be based on a particular time of day or night (for visits), the type of medication and treatment. (This is a B2C example)

◆ A public relations firm might charge its clients a monthly fee plus agreed expenses. This is usually for a set time frame, for instance 12 months, after which time the contract may be re-negotiated. (This is a B2B example.)

◆ An accountant will usually charge a fee based on the time it has taken to prepare an individual or company's accounts for presentation to the Inland Revenue. (These are B2C and B2B examples.)

Competitive tendering

This is also known as competitive bidding or pitching. While most textbooks consider this in a B2B context, it is widely used in a B2C context as well. The purpose of tendering (and associated terms) is an attempt to meet published or known specifications/criteria with a tailor-made proposal or quote that includes the price.

The following are a few examples that explore the tendering process within both a B2C and B2B context:

◆ A family decides it wants to renovate its house. It is unlikely that it will invite only one builder to quote. More likely it will invite several builders to quote or tender for the business. Each tender will include not only the price for the renovation work but also the time frame within which the work will be completed. The family will decide from the tenders (and meeting the builders) the most appropriate for its specific needs. Individuals will again consider the price–value relationship.

◆ Governments are the largest buyers of goods and services, and the vast majority have electorates to report to. They normally use a tendering process to make it clear that the population's wealth is being used both effectively and efficiently. Governments purchase everything from nuclear reactors to stationery supplies and office furniture. Mini case 11.3 outlines one government's product and service requirements.

It is important to remember that contracts are not always awarded to the lowest bidder. The buyer will be seeking reassurance that the proposed

Mini case 11.3

Tendering: Republic of Botswana

The Botswana Government operates a comprehensive tendering and evaluation process for all government department purchases. The requesting government department or ministry issues the requests for tenders. While the tender evaluation is conducted by the requesting department or ministry, the process of tender evaluation is governed by the Central Tender Board, under the auspices of the Ministry of Finance.

In early 2004 the Government of the Republic of Botswana listed, as a matter of routine, products and services required for purchase. The requests for tenders included:

◆ Long-term consultancy for ICT infrastructure services management (operations and networks).

◆ The supply of servers, computers and networking systems for the Ministry of Health.

◆ Supply of television broadcast workshop equipment for the Department of Broadcasting Services – Botswana Television.

◆ The provision of cheque signing, cheque printing machines and network printers for the Department of the Accountant General.

◆ The supply, delivery and installation of a library management system for the Botswana Police College at Otse.

◆ Consultancy to develop a human resource development (HRD) strategy for the Ministry of Trade and Industry.

As you can see from this relatively small selection, both the requirements and those who need the products/services are varied.

Source: Government of Botswana.

supplier can and will actually deliver the products or services by the deadline. However, even when assurance are given, projects do not always go to a planned schedule. With this in mind buyers may build into the agreement financial safeguards or penalties against cost over-runs or delivery delays.

The specifications for the products or services must be clearly identified so that the product delivered fulfils its purpose. However, this is not always the case, as mini case 11.4 clearly illustrates.

International pricing

There are many issues to consider when pricing products and services across international boundaries. As a result companies may adopt a variety of pricing mechanisms for international business. It is important to remember that these mechanisms are not set in stone and thus can be changed depending on the circumstances facing the company.

Mini case 11.4

UK Ministry of Defence and Chinook Helicopters

Chinook helicopters are the workhorse of the US Army and the Royal Air Force (RAF) (among others) for the movement of troops, artillery, fuel and other supplies. They are also used for medical evacuation, search and rescue, disaster relief and fire fighting. In 2004 the RAF had more than 40, making it the largest fleet outside the US Army.

In 1995 the UK government signed a contract with the aircraft manufacturer Boeing for eight Chinook Mark 3 helicopters at a cost of UK£259 million. The aircraft were supposed to be in service in 1998. However, it was found that the radar systems and software – supplied under a separate contract – could not be accommodated in the cockpit. Since their delivery in 2001 the helicopters have been restricted to flying above 152 metres in cloudless skies, with the pilots using landmarks on the ground to navigate.

When the Chinooks were ordered, the Ministry of Defence identified 100 essential requirements for operation. However only 55 were specified in the contract. This is clearly an inadequate position for any combat-ready aircraft.

At the time of writing the cost of fixing the problems was estimated at approximately UK£127 million. Until a solution is found to remedy the navigational software problems, the helicopters are effectively grounded.

Sources: 'Chinook blunder "left RAF short"', BBC News Online, 7 April 2005; P. Adams, 'Chinook helicopters for sale?' BBC News Online, 7 April 2004.

Standard worldwide pricing

This is a pricing tactic that can be used to cover all international markets. It is determined by averaging the unit cost, made up of fixed, variable and export-related costs (including special packaging, insurance, warehousing and tariff charges – refer to Incoterms and other charges as stated earlier). Generally, this has been considered a theoretical model. However, with the development of European Monetary Union (the eurozone countries), it may be possible for companies operating in this zone to create standard pricing for some products.

Dual pricing mechanism

In dual pricing domestic and international prices are differentiated. Two approaches or methods can be used to calculate the international price: the cost-plus method and marginal cost method.

◆ Cost-plus: this is a full allocation of both domestic and international costs, and includes an effective margin. However, there are two key problems with such a method. First, it can make the product too expensive for the intended market. (Reflect back to the earlier analysis on market dynamics.) To overcome this obstacle, companies often build in a degree of flexibility. This usually comes in the form of discounts to meet local market conditions. Second, the company can under price the product or service. In addition to the potential loss of revenues, buyers may perceive the product or service as inferior because of its low price.

◆ Marginal cost: here the company considers the direct costs of producing, marketing and selling the product for export. The fixed costs of plant, equipment, research and development, domestic overheads and domestic marketing costs are not included. As a result, the company can lower prices if it believes it needs to be more competitive (purely on price) within the market.

Market pricing

In such cases, companies price their products and services appropriately for specific individual markets. Such price discrimination involves charging a price each market will accept. The determi-

nants are reflected in the company and its products, the market and external factors. These factors vary to a greater or lesser extent from one country to another. These dynamics are often reflected in the pricing policies of multinational companies.

■ Ethical and illegal pricing issues

Pricing tactics are not without the need for serious ethical consideration. Every one of us makes transactions in order to obtain and consume products and services. In each and every case we are seeking both perceived and real value for the money exchanged. We want to know that we have paid the right price for the product or service. Unfortunately, we are all – individuals and companies alike – susceptible to being cheated by unethical business practices. Here are a few examples of how price can be manipulated to disadvantage both buyers (B2B and B2C) and competitors.

Dumping

Companies may decide to 'dump' their products on the market by pricing them below their marginal cost. This implies that the seller is making a loss on each transaction. This tactic has been used to penetrate difficult or highly competitive markets, and thus increase market share. Once the company has gained market entry and established a position, it can increase prices and/or introduce newer products into that market. While it could be argued that the customer is benefiting in the short term, there are long-term implications. Dumping has been made illegal in many countries, including the European Union, because it is anti-competitive. If a company can gain significant market share by dumping its products, it could reduce the effectiveness of the competitive environment. Some rivals might be forced to seek alternative markets or cease operations. In the longer term this is detrimental to customers because the element of choice is either restricted or removed altogether.

Price fixing – cartel operations

A cartel is where groups of competing companies or countries agree on a set price for a product or

Mini case 11.5

International cartel in vitamin supplements

Between January 1990 and February 1999 several major pharmaceutical companies involved in the production of vitamin supplements operated a global cartel. In 1999 and 2000 both US and European agencies prosecuted the companies for collusion to eliminate fair competition within the marketplace and to overcharge both business and individual customers. EU investigators suggested that the arrangements between the companies were 'part of a strategic plan conceived at the highest levels to control the world market in vitamins by illegal means'.

By the late 1990s the companies F. Hoffman-La Roche and BASF AG held 40 per cent and 20 per cent respectively of the US vitamin market. La Roche's total revenues from vitamin sales were estimated at US$2.5 billion.

In 1999 both companies pleaded guilty in a US court of conspiring to fix, raise and maintain prices and allocate sales volumes of vitamins sold in the United States and elsewhere. Roche agreed to pay US$500 million (at that time the largest criminal fine imposed by the Justice Department), while BASF paid US$225 million in fines. According to the US Department of Justice the inflated prices imposed by the cartel affected products ranging from animal feedstuffs to breakfast cereal. Additionally, five senior executives pleased guilty to participating in the cartel and were sentenced to between three and four months in prison and fined between US$75 000 and US$350 000. However, this was only one of several actions taken by US authorities against international pharmaceutical companies over price fixing.

The following is an extract from the US Department of Justice's Sentencing Statement of F. Hoffman-La Roche. It illustrates the character and dimension of the cartel's organisation and operation.

Throughout the world, on a country and regional level, Roche and other conspirator companies tasked their lower level employees and managers to forward pricing and market share information to higher level management. On a quarterly basis, regional and world marketing managers from the conspirator companies would meet to exchange pricing and sales information in order to have an accurate picture of the overall global demand and price for vitamins. Once a year, the

global marketing directors for each of the conspirator companies, in concert with the various product managers for the companies, would conduct a 'budget' meeting. During this meeting, the overall global sales volume for the vitamins would be determined for the current year, and based on agreed-upon projected growth rates, the global sales volume for the coming year would be determined. Next, each company would be allocated a percentage of this projected global market demand as its 'budget target' for the following year which it would then implement on a regional or country basis. Finally, vitamin pricing would be reviewed and, if price increases were needed to either account for currency discrepancies or to raise profit levels, new pricing would be agreed upon, to include the timing of the price increases and designations of which company would lead the price increase.

It is clear from this extract that the conspiring companies were manipulating the market to their benefit but to the disadvantage of customers and companies not in the cartel.

In 2001 the European Union imposed significant fines against several pharmaceutical companies, including F. Hoffman-La Roche and BASF AG, for operating a series of vitamin cartels. La Roche and BASF were fined US$411 million and US$263 million respectively. Further prosecutions followed from both the Australian and Canadian governments, resulting in further multi-million dollar fines for the companies.

Since these prosecutions the companies have taken significant steps to deter employees from engaging in such anti-competitive activities.

Sources: United States v F. Hoffman-La Roche Ltd, Transcript of Plea of Guilty and Sentencing, US Department of Justice CR-184-R, 20 May 1999; J. Wolf, 'EU probes vitamin cartel', Guardian Online, 22 May 1999; 'Former F. Hoffman-La Roche executive agrees to plead guilty for participating in international vitamin cartel', press release, US Department of Justice, 19 August 1999; 'Four foreign executives of leading European vitamin firms agree to plead guilty to participating in international vitamin cartel', press release, US Department of Justice , 6 April 2000. 'Vitamin cartel fined for price fixing', Guardian Online, 21 November 2001; R. C. Marshall, L. M Marx and M. E. Raiff, Cartel Price Announcements: The vitamins industry, Fuqua School of Business, Duke University, N. Carolina, 2003.

service. The world's leading cartel is the Organization of Petroleum Exporting Countries (OPEC). Formed in 1960, this is a cartel of 13 oil-producing nations which meet regularly to coordinate both the level of production and the price per barrel of crude oil originating from them.

While it could be argued that the formation of OPEC was a justifiable response to the dominance of Western oil producers, contemporary cartel operations cannot provide that justification. Mini case 11.5 illustrates how major pharmaceutical companies were involved in an international cartel operation to fix the market price for vitamin supplements.

Premium pricing issues

This has become of particular concern in the United Kingdom. At the time of writing (2005) several companies are charging people significant prices for product information or the opportunity to win prizes. A company leaves voice messages on recipients' telephones, claiming they have an opportunity to benefit from a major discount on a vacation if they return the call. The recipient is not made aware that the number to call back is a premium rate number, so the call will be expensive. In some cases the discounted vacations do not exist, or are offered under such tight conditions that it is extremely difficult for callers to take advantage of them. Nonetheless they incur significant charges over the length of the call. Under current UK legislation this is a legal practice because the recipient has made the decision to return the call. However, the ethicality of the companies who operate such practices can be questioned.

Bait and switch

According to Hoyer and MacInnis (1997), this is a tactic used to draw a customer into a store by advertising a product at a particularly low price (the 'bait'). Once potential customers are in the store a sales person attempts to persuade them to trade up to a higher-priced product (the 'switch').

Sales staff use several techniques to persuade customers to buy the higher-priced product. For instance, they might claim the advertised product is out of stock, such was the demand for it. Alternatively, the advertised product is 'OK, but not as good as this other product on display'. Of course, the product advertised might not have existed in the first place, or there might be no difference in quality between it and the 'trade-up' product. Clearly, the aim is to get the customer to spend more through the use of deceptive tactics. Such actions may well be illegal as well as unethical.

■ Chapter summary

Price is influenced or determined by several internal and external factors. These range from costs (which are in turn influenced by numerous variables), the competition (local, regional, international and global), general and changing market conditions (influenced by demographics and economics), the product's life cycle position, and people's sensitivity to prices.

Successful marketing strategies depend to a large extent on well-developed pricing strategies. In turn, successful pricing strategies depend on careful ongoing analysis of dynamic market conditions.

The overall influencing factor is the potential buyer. If the customer is not prepared to buy at the set price, the sale is lost. If customers perceives the price as too high they will not make a purchase. Likewise if they perceive the price as too low, they will consider the product or service as inferior and the sale will again be lost. It is therefore very important for companies to ensure that the price set equates with customers' lifestyles and perceptions of value for money. Understanding of the psychology of consumer behaviour is as important in setting prices as is understanding of accounting and financial practice.

■ Questions for review and reflection

1   'Price is the only marketing mix variable that is a revenue generator.' Discuss this statement. Support your views with evidence.

2   Choose a product or service, then explain in detail the factors that may influence its pricing.

3   Critically compare and contrast the advantages and disadvantages of cost-plus and marginal cost pricing. Provide examples of when it is appropriate to use each.

4 Using the Internet and library resources, critically evaluate how a host country's laws can affect a company's pricing policies in that country.

5 Explain how an organisation's pricing strategy can be influenced by both micro and macro environmental factors. (You may want to revisit Chapter 2 before considering this question.)

6 Outline the ethical issues that can be associated with an organisation's pricing policies.

7 Explain why government agencies use a tendering process to purchase products and services.

8 Discuss with fellow students how price affects both you and them in your daily lives. For instance, are you price sensitive?

9 Using the Internet and library resources, explain why a product may be priced differently in two different countries.

10 Under what conditions might a company use price skimming and price penetration strategies?

■ References

Buttle, F. (1986) *Hotel and Food Service Markets*, New York: Holt, Reinhart & Winston.

Churchill, Jr., G. A. and Peter, J. P. (1998) *Marketing: Creating value for customers*, 2nd edn, New York: Irwin McGraw-Hill.

Hoyer, W. D. and MacInnis, D. J. (1997) *Consumer Behavior*, Boston and New York: Houghton Mifflin.

Issa, J. J. and Jayawardena, C. (2003) 'The 'all-inclusive' concept in the Caribbean', *International Journal of Contemporary Hospitality Management* **15**(3), pp. 167–71.

Place and Placement

Contents

Learning outcomes   268
Introduction   268
Defining place   268
Place as a physical
  location   270
Location factors   270
Place as channel
  management   274
A one-stage channel   274
A two-stage channel   275
Three-stage channels   275
Physical distribution   275
Logistics   276
Porter's supply chain
  model   277
Retail outlets   280
Markets   280
Vending (automatic
  retailing)   281
Individual stores   284
Multiples or chain
  stores   284
Online stores   284
Chapter summary   285
Questions for review and
  reflection   285
References   285

Learning outcomes

After completing this chapter you should be able to:

▶ debate the role of 'place' as a concept within the marketing mix

▶ debate the role of 'location' as part of the concept of 'place' within the marketing mix

▶ explain the role of channel management in delivering a product to the end user

▶ examine the different distribution channels that an organisation may choose and the reasons for the choice

▶ compare and contrast B2C and B2B modes of distribution and channel management

▶ debate the future of channel management and distribution in relation to changing external environmental factors.

■ Introduction

Of all the elements of the marketing mix (both new and old), place or placement is perhaps the most unusual. That is, it is 'unusual' in the sense that the word 'placement' does not actually fit as comfortably as perhaps product, price or promotion. It may mean different things to different people, as we shall see later in this chapter. Yet placement (for want of a better word) is key to the success or otherwise of a product or service in the marketplace. This statement is not aimed at denigrating the other elements of the marketing mix; far from it. However, the actual placement of the product or service within a retail outlet, for instance, is crucial to that product becoming a success in the marketplace.

This chapter examines two key aspects of placement, location and distribution channels, for both are integral to the placement of a product or service in the marketplace.

■ Defining place

In numerous marketing textbooks place or placement is associated directly with distribution channels and logistics. That is correct, but there are several authors who believe that placement is far more than distribution, in the traditional sense of the word. Perreault *et al.* (2000) describe place as:

Making goods and services available in the right quantities and locations, and when customers want them. When different target markets have different needs, a number of place variations may be required.

This definition has significance in that one of the authors is E. Jerome McCarthy, who developed the original 4Ps matrix. Within this definition is a consideration for both channel operations and location of the 'retailer'. As the authors state, 'location can spell success or failure for the retailer … the decision about to where to locate a business is therefore very much a marketing strategy decision' (Perreault *et al.* 2000).

There are two points to be taken from this perspective. First, since this book was written, the Internet has developed significantly, not only as a vehicle for ordering products and services but also as a distribution channel (for example, the receipt of electronic flight tickets) as we shall see later. Second, location as a term must encompass far more than purely retail outlets such as department stores and supermarkets. Indeed Bowie and Buttle (2004) separate location from place and consider 'location' as another marketing mix component. They clearly believe that the two issues of location and distribution, while linked, are components of the marketing mix that should be considered separately.

This is an interesting view, and particularly significant when you consider the location, for example, of leisure places such as Disneyland Paris™. The determinant of location is equally applicable to hotels, restaurant and bars. Why are some bars, for instance, highly successful while others close in a matter of weeks? Agreed, there are many factors that can lead to success or failure. However, location does have a significant influence on both success and failure.

There is yet another view of place that should be considered. The research of Inalhan and Finch (2004) examines 'place' within the confines of the environment in which people live and work. They state that 'people are linked through three key psychological processes: attachment, familiarity and identity.' Milligan (1998) defines place attachment as 'the emotional link formed by an individual to a setting that has been given meaning through interaction, comprised of two interwoven components: the interactional past and the interactional potential of the setting'.

Here the 'interactional past' refers to past experiences or memories of the place or location. On the other hand, the 'interactional potential' refers to the expectations of experiences to come. In the case of a vacation, for instance, a family may continually revisit the same location each year because of the stored (and developing) memories they have of that place. Equally, a young couple flying off to an exotic location and staying at a five-star beach resort will have varying levels of expectation. These will include the level of service, the style of food, the views over the sea, the weather, the sea and the beach. Their only 'experience' prior to arrival may have been reading a glossy holiday brochure that includes three or four 'amazing' photographs of the location. Stokols and Shumaker (1981, cited in Inalhan and Finch 2004) suggest that the level of satisfaction gained in relation to their needs and goals will determine their individual judgment of its quality. This, it is contended, will regulate their attachment to the place.

Inalhan and Finch (2004) state that 'place attachment is a pattern of reactions that setting [location] stimulates for a person. These reactions are a product of both cognitive and emotional/symbolic aspects of the bond.' If we accept this perspective,

Figure 12.1

A luxury hotel on the island of Cyprus. This is place as a physical location.

'place' has a strong link to other marketing mix elements such as psychology and physical evidence.

In this context, place clearly relates to the physical world that we inhabit. However, we must also consider 'place' as a location in the virtual world. Increasingly both individuals and organisations conduct their communications and business through cyberspace. This is a trend that is most likely to continue as long as technology provides the tools for such growth. New generations will be more comfortable operating within a virtual environment. However, we already see experiences of 'place' within cyberspace. Individuals already frequent virtual cyber cafés where they can discuss everything from urban myths to what is cool and what is not. Cyber consumers frequent online retailers such as Amazon.com or Tesco.com to purchase everything from books and CDs through to groceries and washing machines. These may become consumers' online favourite places, which they visit regularly. They are all 'places' people visit – the only difference is that they are online.

Companies and organisations also transact business through B2B exchanges (also known as e-marketplaces). These are online portals that function as information brokers and gateways to the purchasing of products services through e-procurement (Groucutt and Griseri 2004).

As you can see from this brief introduction, the term 'place' is far from the straightforward distribution of goods that has often been portrayed.

■ Place as a physical location

Place in terms of location is relevant, whether it is a retail outlet, hotel, leisure park, restaurant or airport. The location of the 'outlet' is often crucial as to its success in the marketplace. There will, of course, be exceptions to the rule, and the importance of location cannot be considered purely as a snapshot in time. Changes in the external environment may make a location unsuitable when once it was ideal. For example, in the late 1950s Beirut in the Lebanon was the travel destination for the rich and famous who wanted to soak up the sun, laze on the golden beaches and experience the hospitality of the local people. In the 1970s all that changed dramatically, as the region was racked by a devastating civil war. Only by the early 21st century was

some normality beginning to be restored. Many other examples can be cited of once-beautiful places that have been devastated by civil wars. Slowly many of them are recovering. However, many of the businesses that once thrived in those locations are no longer viable propositions. Thus location must be viewed as not a static option, but one that needs to be constantly reviewed.

Location factors

This section briefly considers the possible factors that lead to the success or potential failure of a location. The PESTLE model is used, illustrating that it is the macro factors, those beyond the control of the organisation, that will have an influence over success or failure. Organisations need to understand how these factors may affect the location they have identified. However, it is not external factors alone that determine the success of a business. It is also dependent on management expertise, the quality of employees, level of customer service, and last but not least, financial management and accounting practices.

The PESTLE factors should not be viewed in pure isolation. Often they overlap, or one factor influences the development of another. For instance, a government's political mission to invest in high-technology enterprises may result in the introduction of new technologies which in turn have an impact or influence on society, and this helps the economic development of the country. When reflecting on the factors below, consider how they may be interrelated in your own country.

Political

This covers a wide range of issues which can have national, regional and international impacts. Here are a few examples:

◆ The expansion of conurbations and the development of new towns or cities: the government may decide there has to be an extensive building programme to accommodate an increasing population. Major retailers, for instance, will seek to be involved, purchasing or leasing suitable land to provide strategically located outlets. Governments may also actively seek to reduce the level of building on the outskirts of conurbations, in an attempt to preserve the countryside. Instead they may provide incentives to regenerate depressed town-centre locations.

◆ Incentives for new developments: the British government in the 1980s, for instance, provided Japanese companies with financial and infrastructure (new road and rail systems) incentives to locate manufacturing plants in regionally depressed areas of the United Kingdom. The objective was to regenerate the areas through the development of new industries. The same principle was applied to the location of Euro Disney™ (now Disneyland Paris™) near Paris rather than in Spain, which was another possible location. It could be argued that its climate would have made Spain a better choice.

◆ The political situation within a region or country might deteriorate, leading to instability and civil war. Since the 1950s this has happened in several countries in Europe, Africa, the Far East and South America. For companies that have invested in these regions (for instance, hotel chains), political failings have led to the collapse of the local market and closure of the hotels.

◆ At the same time political stability has returned to several nations, for instance Vietnam. This area is now being opened up to tourism, with accompanying hotel developments (often by European and American companies).

◆ However, the spectre of terrorism can strike at any time, and with devastating effect, as was witnessed in Bali in 2002. While Bali might have seemed the ideal location for an escape-from-it all vacation, on that day it became the wrong location. Bali and New York have recovered from such horrific events, but it can be argued that all locations are now prone to such attacks.

Economic

The economic circumstances can be viewed from two perspectives, local and global.

◆ The initial question is whether the local economy can sustain the business, or people will travel from other locations to purchase the products or services on offer. In general, a local supermarket will be dependent on the local economy and local people's level of disposable income. However an out-of-town shopping centre will be dependent on a wider economic base than a local supermarket. Similarly a major hotel in a city will be more reliant on wealthy tourists and the business market.

Local economies are, of course, dependent on political stability. If the country is in political turmoil, the economy will suffer at both national and local levels. The likely outcome is that businesses will collapse, pushing the economy further into recession and potentially depression.

◆ To a greater or lesser extent, economies have converged. Thus the world is linked economically, if not politically. A recession in one region can lead to a recession in another. For example, if the US economy collapses, for whatever reason, there would be severe repercussions in for instance the United Kingdom, which enjoys a significant level of US investment. In essence there would be a domino effect.

Societal

Societal factors should be considered on a local, national, regional and global scale. There is a need to understand geodemographics and how locations may change or adapt as a result of population movements. For example, in the United Kingdom there has been a growing trend for individuals and families to relocate to the country and commute to cities. This is especially the case with London, where several million people travel into the capital each working day. For many the quality of life is better in the country or suburbs than in London itself.[1] Such trends can result in a changing landscape in the outer reaches of a city. Indeed, in England rural communities have been transformed into commuter villages, and this affects the layout and structure of the retail heart of the village. Companies have adapted too: for example the UK retail giant Marks & Spencer has opened several food stores at key London railway stations, providing a service to commuters both arriving for work and leaving for home.

When an organisation is considering a location it must attempt to understand the societal issues that could affect it. This must not be considered purely as a snapshot in time. The quality and value of a location can change over time as a result of societal issues. For instance, a depressed crime-ridden area can be rejuvenated and given a new lease of life. Rejuvenation is far from new: during the 18th and 19th centuries parts of London were depressing slum areas which today contain the homes of the up-and-coming middle classes.

A thriving area can also go into decline. If one company or industry dominates an area, and the company closes or the industry declines, that will have a direct impact on the local community. The United Kingdom saw this with the decline of coal mining and the steel industry. These were the central employers for several areas and entire regions. When the mines and steel works closed there was a direct economic impact on all other businesses in the area. For instance, people who had frequented the local shops and restaurants when they were in work became extremely price sensitive when they lost their jobs. This affected the financial stability of local service providers. For some the result was closure, and either relocation or bankruptcy and further unemployment.

This process led many to leave these areas to seek a new life and employment elsewhere. Migration too has an impact on the local community. However some areas were regenerated through significant government investment and incentives to international companies. This led to the influx of new core employers and secondary business such as suppliers and service providers. As well as regenerating the local communities, this provided the opportunity for people to migrate from other regions, which in turn may be suffering from either high unemployment or full employment with little in the way of job acquisition.

Of course, we must not consider geodemographic changes purely from a micro perspective. The relative ease of global travel, increased freedom of movement[2] and opportunities have led to global movements of people. As ethnic groups mix they begin to share their cultures. London, for instance, has become very much a cosmopolitan city with a wide variety of ethnic groups which have brought richness to the city. To illustrate how societal perspectives may change, for many years the number one take-away food in the United Kingdom was fish and chips. By 2002 it was curry.

Technological

Four technological factors have had a particular impact on location: the car, the passenger jet, the train and new building materials.

◆ The arrival of the car did much to change shopping attitudes and hasten the growth of out-of-town shopping centres or malls. Cars with large boot space allowed American shoppers, for example, to maximise the value of their trips to hypermarkets. Society still has a love affair with the automobile, but today we seek smaller, fuel-efficient and environmentally friendly vehicles. Nonetheless, they remain an essential part of the weekly shopping experience, as is apparent if you look at a UK supermarket carpark on a weekend. This mobility has also led to the development of out-of-town shopping malls.

◆ The introduction of jet-powered aircraft in the 1950s increased the opportunity for overseas travel. The further development of jet passenger aircraft and the introduction of low-cost package holidays, especially in Europe, led to a boom in overseas vacations. The new generation of fuel-efficient passenger aircraft will increase the opportunities for lower-cost travel worldwide. This in turn may lead to the development of new hotels in resorts that have not reached saturation point, such as in parts of Spain.

Figure 12.2

© Jonathan Groucutt

A TGV prepares for departure from Paris's Gare du Nord

◆ While some countries have a poor rail network, others, such as France, can boast of having continually invested in an integrated rail network. This has provided France with significant benefits. French Railways' fast intercity TGVs allow tourists to reach their destinations in a fraction of the time it would take them to drive, and in considerably greater comfort. Thus hoteliers, for instance, throughout France can market their services countrywide and indeed Europe-wide in the knowledge that they can be reached relatively easily.

◆ New types of building materials allow for the low-cost construction of supermarkets and multi-storey shopping malls. These can have a more architectural look rather than the functional box shape of previous hypermarkets and malls, especially in the United States.

Legal

◆ The planning system regulates what can and cannot be modified or built. The level of legal control varies from location to location and country to country. In some countries planning and building regulations are very lax, while in others there is strict control. In the United Kingdom, for instance, there is generally very strict zoning that prevents or limits the scale of building in 'green belt' and rural areas.

◆ The building of out-of-town hypermarkets has probably reached saturation level in the United Kingdom, so the supermarket owners are looking at a combination of alternatives for further expansion:

  ● Renovating town sites, sometimes under a slightly different brand name. For example, Tesco city sites are known as Tesco Metro.

  ● Opening new town sites: for example, Marks & Spencer and its food shops at key London railway stations.

  ● Developing their online capabilities. In this case retailers need a warehouse, but this does not have the same location requirements as a supermarket.

Environmental/ecological

The impact of the natural environment on location is often overlooked in the analysis of marketing. Instead, it is considered a geographical phenomenon. However, the natural environment has a significant influence on marketing as a whole, as we saw in Chapter 2. In terms of location, the phrase 'natural environment' does not only apply to weather conditions: the terrain of the location must also be taken into consideration. For instance, it might seem a wonderful idea to locate a luxurious hotel at the top of a mountain, but apart from the practicalities of access for construction purposes, is the terrain suitable for its construction? Of course, it can be argued that modern building techniques and facilities make this kind of project easier than it once was, but that is only one part of the overall equation. Clearly, the luxurious ski resorts of Europe have conquered the building issue. The quality of the snow and the superb views have helped them attract the right market segment.

Weather also plays important role in where an organisation locates itself, especially in the hospitality business. The impact of global warming will need to be considered by future generations. Will there be dramatic changes in weather conditions, as some writers predict, leading to more storms, more flooding and longer periods of hot weather? Exploring this is beyond the scope of this text, but it is an important issue that requires further investigation not only by scientists in the fields of geography and meteorology but also from the perspective of marketing and its impact on society and business.

Location and place attachment

Earlier in this chapter the concept of place attachment was discussed. Figure 12.3 (overleaf) not only illustrates the link between location and place attachment, but also highlights some of the factors that determine location.

There are several factors that we can extrapolate from Figure 12.3.

Physical features

These include the geographical aspects of the terrain (as discussed above), the infrastructure of the area (roads, rail, ports and so on) and the physical construction of the outlet.

Figure 12.3 Place attachment

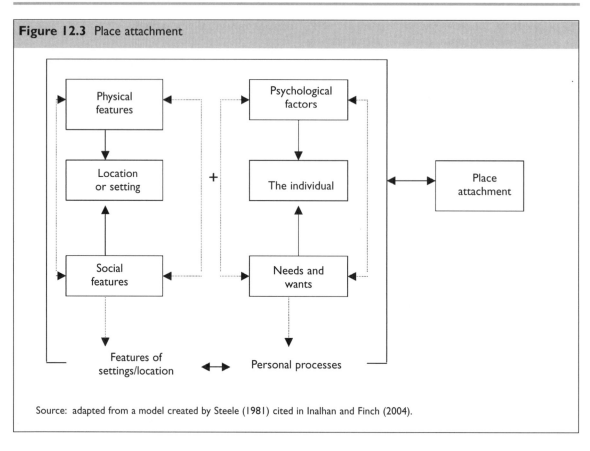

Source: adapted from a model created by Steele (1981) cited in Inalhan and Finch (2004).

Social issues

These include the demographics of the area and market segmentation.

Psychological factors

The location has to be positioned in the minds of customers as being the right place for them to visit. This is relevant whether it is a supermarket or a luxury holiday resort.

Individual needs and wants

The location must fulfil the needs and wants of individuals. For example, a keen golfer is most likely to seek out a holiday resort that has a golf course on-site or nearby. Although an organisation may engage in one-to-one marketing, it will seek similarities among clusters of individuals and position its service to that cluster. So in this brief example, a five-star golfing resort would market the features and benefits of the resort to a particular segment of golfing holidaymakers.

■ Place as channel management

Channel management can be described as the form or channel through which a product or service is distributed to the end user. The number of channels or stages of channel management can vary depending on the number of intermediaries involved between the manufacturer and the buyer. Channel management is an integral component of supply-chain management, especially when it is linked to logistics.

The following briefly outlines the potential channel stages.

A one-stage channel

This is a direct and often straightforward relationship between the producer and the buyer (see Figure 12.4). The buyer could be either an individual or a company, so it is equally applicable in either a B2C or B2B environment.

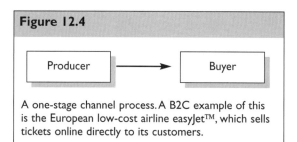

Figure 12.4

Producer → Buyer

A one-stage channel process. A B2C example of this is the European low-cost airline easyJet™, which sells tickets online directly to its customers.

A two-stage channel

Where a two-stage channel is concerned there are several variations which result in the producer selling to an intermediary prior to the product being sold on to the end buyer: see Figures 12.5, 12.6, 12.7 and 12.8.

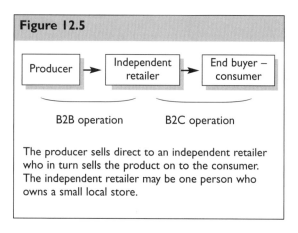

Figure 12.5

Producer → Independent retailer → End buyer – consumer

B2B operation   B2C operation

The producer sells direct to an independent retailer who in turn sells the product on to the consumer. The independent retailer may be one person who owns a small local store.

Three-stage channels

Here the product moves through three channels of distribution before it reaches the end user. The producer is increasingly removed from end users in the physical sense. However, it may seek to build a relationship with them via promotion and marketing communications. An example is a detergent manufacturer that is physically removed from consumers yet seeks to build an emotional bond through television advertising.

■ Physical distribution

A component of the placement process is the physical distribution or movement of the product

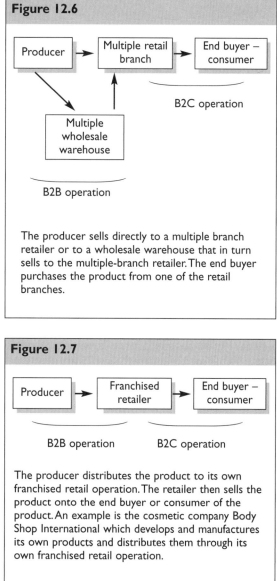

Figure 12.6

Producer → Multiple retail branch → End buyer – consumer

B2C operation

Multiple wholesale warehouse

B2B operation

The producer sells directly to a multiple branch retailer or to a wholesale warehouse that in turn sells to the multiple-branch retailer. The end buyer purchases the product from one of the retail branches.

Figure 12.7

Producer → Franchised retailer → End buyer – consumer

B2B operation   B2C operation

The producer distributes the product to its own franchised retail operation. The retailer then sells the product onto the end buyer or consumer of the product. An example is the cosmetic company Body Shop International which develops and manufactures its own products and distributes them through its own franchised retail operation.

through to the end user. The product may go through several forms of physical distribution before it reaches its final destination. For instance, consider a car manufactured in Japan which is shipped by sea to a port in the United Kingdom, from where it is transported by rail to a central warehouse facility. After checks have been undertaken it is moved by a road transporter to a retail showroom/dealership to be marketed to the end customer. In order for that car to reach the end user it has undergone several physical movements.

Figure 12.8

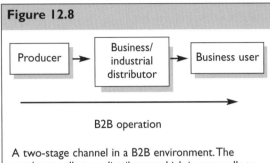

B2B operation

A two-stage channel in a B2B environment. The producer sells to a distributor which in turn sells to a business user. An example is a paper mill that producers photocopy paper. It sells it to a major commercial distributor such as Viking Direct whose customers range from micro-businesses to corporations.

Figure 12.10

© Hapag-Lloyd. Reproduced with kind permission.

Bremen Express at sea with her cargo of containers.

This example focuses on an originally large shipment (perhaps 100 cars) that is gradually broken down to a road transporter carrying approximately six vehicles to a showroom. Several physical movements take place over a large geographical area. Some items are in contrast small and delivered within a localised area: for example, letters delivered by the postal service. Products vary in size, shape and fragility.

The transportation methods used depend on the nature or constituents of the materials or products. Table 12.1 outlines the different types of products and materials that are shipped and the form of shipment.

■ Logistics

Chapman, Soosay and Kandampully (2003) describe logistics as an extension of physical distribution relating to the management of materials and information streams through the various channels to the end user. Contemporary logistics was born out of the massive military campaigns of the Second World War. However, the importance of logistics in moving men, materials (including food supplies) and armaments dates back to the Greek

Figure 12.9

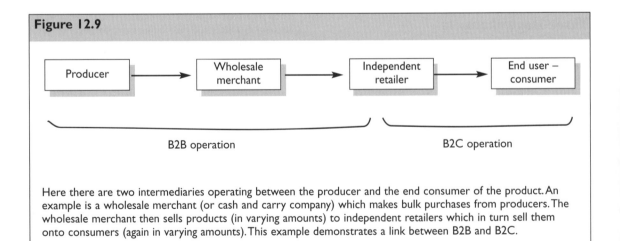

B2B operation   B2C operation

Here there are two intermediaries operating between the producer and the end consumer of the product. An example is a wholesale merchant (or cash and carry company) which makes bulk purchases from producers. The wholesale merchant then sells products (in varying amounts) to independent retailers which in turn sell them onto consumers (again in varying amounts). This example demonstrates a link between B2B and B2C.

Table 12.1 Types of shipment

Material or product	Description
Loose cargoes	These range from coal and ores to liquids such as oil. Specialist containers (including pipelines), vehicles and ships are used to transport such materials. In the case of fish specialised refrigerator containers can be loaded onto cargo aircraft to ensure freshness and quality on long-haul flights. It is the use of such technology that ensures that fresh fish produce is available on supermarket shelves, especially in Europe. Fish caught in the Caribbean one day can be on UK supermarket shelves 24 hours later.
Containerised cargoes	Containerisation has created an efficient inter-modal delivery system. Advantages include: • Several loads can be consolidated into one, creating economies of scale. • Loading and unloading time is dramatically reduced, minimising port costs. • There can be inter-modal movement of products without the containers being opened (which reduces transportation time, costs and the risk of theft or damage).
Hazardous materials	Hazardous materials include everything from corrosive chemicals to oil and nuclear materials. The level of toxicity depends on the material being transported. Clearly a major oil spillage will have a detrimental impact on the immediate environment. It will also have negative impact on the reputation of the oil company concerned, especially if the spillage was caused by negligence. The movement of nuclear material for reprocessing, by road, rail or sea, creates numerous risks including terrorist attack. Both shippers and governments are mindful of the risks.
Valuables	This includes the movement of cash (for banks and stores) as well as diamonds and gold bullion. In many countries private companies transport such valuables in specialist vehicles. To gain, and retain customers, security firms must be able to market their ability to handle and move valuables efficiently, effectively and with the minimum risk of theft.
Vehicles	The type of vehicle moved varies from cars to specialist cranes. A common factor is the need for specialist transporters and trained personnel.
Perishable produce	Perishable products such as food (chilled, frozen and fresh) and flowers must be transported to the marketplace with the minimum of delay in order to maintain their quality. The use of, for example, special containers (for air freighting) and refrigerated vehicles allow such produce to be transported over long distances. Fresh produce was usually only grown in the country of consumption. Thus it had a seasonal limitation. Today fresh produce, for example, strawberries, is available all year round in the United Kingdom. This is due, in the main, to developments in the specialist transportation.
Outsized loads	These are unusual loads that because of their size and shape do not 'fit' any standard criteria. Their movement requires specialist vehicles, ships or aircraft. For example, specialist vehicles are used to move sections of the A380 aircraft to the assembly plant in France.

and Roman Empires. Military planners and strategists achieved this through procurement, maintenance and transportation. The same principles exist today, but on a global business scale.

As Chapman *et al.* (2003) state, 'as organisations globalize to access new markets and achieve higher production and sourcing efficiencies, logistics play an important role in moving materials, products and services through supply chains'. Thus the use of efficient and effective logistics management

becomes a contributor to an organisation's ability to gain a competitive advantage.

Porter's supply chain model

It is important to consider logistics in relation to the overall supply chain from raw material provision through to the end user of the product. Porter (1985) encapsulated supply chain management as a combination of support activities and primary

Figure 12.11

© Jonathan Groucutt

Loose cargoes such as minerals are still moved along waterways. Here sand is moved, on a regular basis, along the River Seine in Paris.

Figure 12.13

© AIRBUS S.A.S. 2004 – e^{x}m company/P. MASCLET

The delicate maneouvring of a section of the Airbus A380 fuselage on a multi-wheeled transporter

activities. As you can see from the primary activities, both inbound and outbound logistics are clearly linked with operations, marketing and service (to the customer).

However, there are not one but several supply chains in the process of delivering a finished product from the manufacturer to a customer or end user. Porter (1985) views this as a value system.

Figure 12.12

© British Nuclear Fuels. Reproduced with kind permission.

A special nuclear flask is loaded aboard a ship for transportation

Figure 12.17 (overleaf) illustrates a possible scenario.

All these supply chains feed into each other in order to deliver the product to end users at the right time (to meet their needs) and in the right place (location). An excellent example of this is the operations behind Airbus SAS. For over 30 years the organisation has been supplied with everything from sheet metal to complete landing gear. Today, more than 1500 companies in over 30 countries supply it with a vast array of

Figure 12.14

© Jonathan Groucutt

A freight yard in Washington State, USA with both open wagons (for carrying minerals) and containers

Figure 12.15

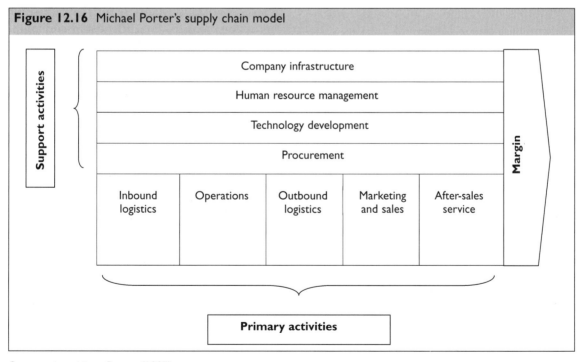

© Civil Aviation Authority of Singapore. Reproduced with kind permission.

Packages in a container are loaded on board a Federal Express cargo plane

products (Airbus 2004). These include the Goodrich Corporation (main landing gear on the A380) and Matsushita Avionics Systems, Sumitomo Precision Products and Jamco Corporation which are providing components, cabin and galley equipment for the A380 (Morris 2004). The suppliers to Airbus for the A380 are from Europe, America (some 50 per cent of content) and Japan (Morris 2004).

Each of the suppliers will have its own supply chain. Just for a moment reflect upon the vast numbers of sub-suppliers and individuals involved in providing Airbus Industries with the tools, facilities, materials and products that enable you to fly in one of their aircraft.

Kandampully (2002) suggests that innovation is a core competency of service organisations, and Chapman *et al.* (2003) believe that there are three requirements for service innovation (based upon Kandampully 2002):technology, knowledge and relationship networks. These are briefly explored in Table 12.2. However, the key for any company is how to exploit these core competencies by linking them to the supply chain to gain (and more importantly sustain) competitive advantage.

Figure 12.16 Michael Porter's supply chain model

Support activities	Company infrastructure					Margin
	Human resource management					
	Technology development					
	Procurement					
	Inbound logistics	Operations	Outbound logistics	Marketing and sales	After-sales service	

Primary activities

Source: adapted from Porter (1985).

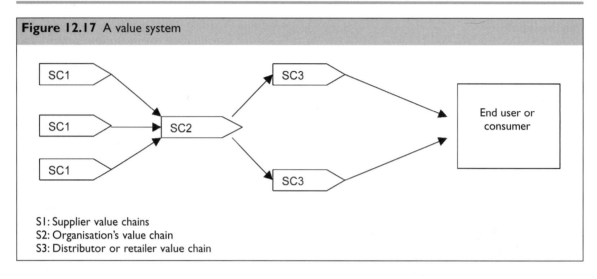

Figure 12.17 A value system

S1: Supplier value chains
S2: Organisation's value chain
S3: Distributor or retailer value chain

■ Retail outlets

There are various forms of retail outlet depending on the location, the nature and form of the transaction undertaken, and size of outlet. This section very briefly outlines the outlets in which goods or products (both branded and unbranded) are sold.

Markets

The structure and regularity of markets varies from location to location. In Morocco, for instance, there are weekly local markets, usually held on a Saturday, where produce from the region is brought for sale or barter. This includes everything from donkeys to vegetables. The marketplace is not only a place for the selling of goods and produce, it is where people meet to exchange their views of the world on a weekly basis, where people actually keep in touch with each other. In many countries it is also the way people conduct business – it is a matter of connection, conversation, friendship and trust. The power of the local market should never be

Table 12.2 Requirements for service innovation

Innovation and logistics	Description
Technology	The focus is on information and communications technologies (ICT), which range from online ordering and monitoring through to vehicle routing and just-in-time (JIT) inventory replenishment.
Knowledge	The management of knowledge is a vital part of any department within any organisation. This is especially so in a world that is being saturated with continuous flows of information. Chapman *et al.* (2003) suggest that knowledge in logistics incorporates ICT which creates a basis for knowledge sharing, and the people who operate within organisations. They believe that for an effective logistics knowledge-management system to operate there has to be an holistic combination of these factors. This would create knowledge networks which provide organisations with the ability to create, share and use knowledge strategically to continually improve operational efficiencies and thus better service customers (Kandampully 2002).
Relationship networks	This suggests that rather than the combative stance that often occurs between suppliers and buyers there needs to be greater 'partnering'. Chapman *et al.* (2003) suggest that when intermediaries act as partners the boundaries between them become fluid. This results in greater integration, information and knowledge flow.

Figure 12.18

© Shona Muir. Reproduced with kind permission

An indoor food market in Barcelona, Spain

Figure 12.19

© Jonathan Groucutt

Traditional wooden market stalls on the left bank of the River Seine in Paris. These stalls sell books, postcards, old magazines (for collectors) and advertising posters.

underestimated, especially where such traditions continue unaffected, in the main, by developments in the rest of the world.

Vending (automatic retailing)

The world's first commercial vending machines were introduced in London in the 1880s and dispensed postcards.[3] However, it was in North America that the vending revolution developed. The value of the global vending market is estimated to be US$ 40 billion, with the major markets concentrated in America, Japan and parts of Europe (CR80 News 2005).

While many common items are vended, the range of products available varies from country to country. This is a very small selection of items that have been, or currently are, dispensed from vending machines:

◆ bait for fishing

◆ beach equipment such as beach balls and toys

◆ business cards and letterheads

◆ cameras (disposable one-use format)

◆ cigarettes

◆ comic books

◆ computer disks (at various universities for students using 24-hour computer facilities)

◆ condoms

◆ confectionery

◆ female hygiene and sanitary protection

◆ hot drinks

◆ hot food

◆ popcorn

◆ soft drinks

◆ tennis balls

◆ travel tickets at metros, bus and railway stations

- video cassettes and DVDs

- washing travel packs containing soap, tooth-brush, toothpaste, a razor and shaving foam. These are found in major railways stations in the United Kingdom, and are increasingly likely to be found in budget or low-cost hotels where clients purchase the room but then must buy sundry items separately that are provided free in more expensive hotels. This is based on the same principle as low-cost airlines.

Vending machines provide various advantages:

- Convenience of location. They can be designed and operated for both interior and exterior use, so products can be dispensed on a 24/7 basis.

- No location staffing requirements. Unlike a standard retail outlet the vending machine does not usually require on-site staffing. The machines are restocked by the operator-owners or leasors.

- On-site branding: they provide branded prod-uct manufacturers with an opportunity to advertise their products on a 24/7 basis.

- Major distribution outlet: for branded confec-tionery, snack and drinks companies, in partic-ular, vending offers a significant distribution channel alongside traditional retail channels.

- Opportunity for higher margins: branded product manufacturers are able to gain higher margins from their own controlled vending outlets. Vending machines are inexpensive in relation to the revenues they can generate, and new machines tend to yield sales in excess of their purchase price within the first year of operation (Euromonitor 2004b). Thus many companies, especially in the United States, have been able to finance market expansion through revenue generation (Euromonitor 2004b).

- New location and market opportunities. Companies have been able to seek out new markets. For instance, in the United Kingdom many offices and factories had their own cater-ing facilities. This was often seen as a cost burden to the organisation, and thus when costs were reviewed these operations were downsized. In many cases a range of vending machines providing hot/cold drinks and snacks replaced the in-house catering facilities. In addition, to reducing catering costs, such actions have also freed up space for other uses.

- Other new locations have included hospitals, universities, schools (see mini case 12.1), rail-way stations and prisons.

- New technological developments in storage, heating and cooling have greatly widened market opportunities. Now a wide range of chilled and ready to cook products are avail-able through vending machines.

- Companies have sought network expansion through both organic growth and acquisitions. For example, the UK-based Compass Group expanded in to the highly developed Japanese market by acquiring, in 2002, a significant share of Seiyo Foods.

- Can drive impulse purchasing. Vending machines that have glass-fronted panels and thus branded products on display, and a greater variety of packaging formats, can drive impulse buying in the 'ready to go' sectors.

Mini case 12.1

Holiday Inn Express®

Holiday Inn Express® is a brand of the InterContinental Hotels Group. The Holiday Inn Express® brand caters for value-oriented cus-tomers. Many of these hotels in the United Kingdom, North and South America have either a separate vending area and/or machines on each floor. These areas may be in addition to a lounge/bar area and a restaurant.

Using the hotel's restaurant or visiting a restau-rant in the neigbourhood may be too expensive for value-driven customers, so vending provides a suit-able alternative. The vending facilities provide a vari-ety of products including hot/cold drinks, hot/cold food, snacks and alcohol. In addition, there are usu-ally facilities that dispense books and toiletries.

Guests do not have to use change to obtain the products. A swipe of their room key immediately transfers the cost of the items to their room bill.

Sources: Mintel (2003), www.ichotels.com

Mini case 12.2

Food and drink vending machines in schools – an ethical issue?

Schools in various countries have introduced vending machines dispensing a range of snacks and soft drinks. However, in recent years there have been growing concerns about obesity in children, most especially (though not exclusively) in North America.

Such is the concern that America's largest school district – Los Angeles Unified School District – banned the sale of soft drinks in all its schools from January 2004. Water, milk and drinks containing at least 50 per cent fruit and no added sweeteners are provided as an alternative. Also of January 2004 Arkansas was the first US State to pass legislation banning vending machines from elementary schools. Other US States have enacted or intend to enact legislation that will limit or prevent the sale of certain products (for instance, carbonated soft drinks) from school vending machines.

In the United Kingdom a survey of 736 parents conducted by FDS International for the *Times Education Supplement* revealed that eight out of ten parents wanted vending machines removed from schools. This followed a survey of 1000 people conducted in October 2003 for *The Guardian* newspaper where the figure was seven out of ten requesting such a ban. However, the UK Department for Education and Skills has stated that it has no plans to ban vending machines from schools, preferring instead for head teachers and school governors to make the decision.

It is estimated that some 95 per cent of secondary schools in the United Kingdom have vending machines,

which can earn the schools significant additional revenues. Estimates have varied from UK£15 000 to UK£50 000 in larger secondary schools. For many schools this becomes a vital revenue source to provide additional facilities, so head teachers and governors are faced with a dilemma.

Various companies, such as Nestlé, have sought to provide alternatives to the normal vending machine range such as mineral water and milk. In the US State of Iowa the Midwest Diary Association™ and Diary Management Inc partnered with Swiss Valley Farms to place vending machines that serve milk, cheese and yoghurt products in several schools as an alternative to other snack foods.

In early 2004 a 1200-student specialist technology college – Queensbury School in Dunstable, Bedfordshire – was the first secondary school in the United Kingdom to remove sugary snacks and soft drink vending machines. They were replaced with new machines that provided additive-free Fruesli bars, organic orange juice and mineral water. Queensbury's head teacher Nigel Hill commented, 'Do you put students' health first or the money you can make selling them chocolate and fizzy drinks?'

Sources: Euromonitor (2004b); National Conference of State Legislature, www.ncsl.org/programms/health/vending.htm; Midwest Diary Association, www.midwestdiary.com; W. Mansell, 'Stop selling junk food to our children', *Times Education Supplement*, 23 April 2004; M. Shaw, 'Coke "too profitable" to lose', *Times Education Supplement*, 3 October 2003; PA News, 'School replaces junk food with healthy snacks', *Times Educational Supplement*, 3 February 2004.

◆ Cashless payments. On page 284 the use of telemetry is linked to cashless payment systems. Increasingly credit card readers and telemetry links have been installed in some vending machines. This has widened the use of vending machines to dispense such items as train and airline tickets. The ability to use credit cards increases the possibility of higher-value goods being dispensed from vending units.

Technical developments in vending

New developments have improved, and continue to improve, both the efficiency and range of products available:

◆ Widening provision and quality. Over the last ten years or so the refrigeration and cooking systems in vending machines have greatly improved. This has enabled companies not only to provide a wider range of products (from coffee to hot snacks and ice creams), but also to improve the overall quality of the products.

◆ Telemetry – remote management. The use of wireless technologies provides companies with several key advantages:

● The monitoring of supply levels: when stocks reach a critical point an employee can be despatched to restock the machine.

This eliminates restockers unnecessarily visiting machines that do not require replenishment, so there is a more efficient use of labour.

- Malfunction analysis and alert: if the machine malfunctions, a central control can be alerted to the fact and the possible cause of the malfunction. A service engineer can be despatched to repair the equipment, knowing in advance the nature of the fault. In the future any software problems will be rectified remotely without the need for an engineer to visit the site. Thus downtime is minimised.

- Cashless payment systems: in many, though not all, cases customers must have either the right monetary change or tokens to use vending machines. This is often the case with ticket machines, for example, in bus stations in London which will only accept (as of 2005) the correct amount of change. In some countries there are facilities that allow customers to use their mobile phones to call a number to release the product from the vending machine. The cost of the item is added to the caller's mobile phone bill (Mintel 2003).

- Location profiling. Companies have used technology to gain a better understanding of the market in which the vending machine is located. The US company Sodexho used geodemographic data on client populations to profile customers and determine potential product offerings (Euromonitor 2004b). Companies have also experimented with the concept of raising and lowering prices (remotely) depending on the levels of demand (Euromonitor 2004b).

Individual stores

These are single store retail outlets which are usually owned by an individual or a family. The term 'individual' implies that the family will necessary remain the owners of one single store, but this is not always so: over time they might purchase other stores in the same area and slowly broaden

their network. Even though the store might expand into a small chain, it is likely to remain an independent retailer, and this offers it the ability to be different from major retailers. An example is a local butcher who prepares meat to individual customers' needs (for instance, de-boning or slicing). This is a personal touch that might not be available in a supermarket. Individual stores often, though not always, provide an example of one-to-one relationships.

Multiples or chain stores

The size of chains (and their individual physical outlets) varies. For instance, a local or regional business might have several outlets but only in one region. On the other hand, the high street retailer Marks & Spencer has outlets throughout the United Kingdom.

Online stores

Traditionally retail outlets were purely 'bricks and mortar'. Today and into the future online stores act as virtual stores. They are unlikely to replace bricks and mortar in the short term, if ever, but they need to be considered as retail outlets. Companies such as Amazon that built their reputation on a limited range of products have significantly expanded their offerings. Likewise food retailers such as Tesco have broadened their range online to include large items (such as televisions and washing machines) that would take up too much store space and thus not be cost-effective in their conventional outlets. By leveraging partnerships and distribution channels, they can deliver larger items to their customers.

As computer technology becomes increasingly sophisticated the virtual store, where consumers can 'walk around' and choose items, will become a reality. While this will not replace an individual's physical movement around a store, and the ability to touch items, it will provide many people with an easy way of shopping.

Perhaps the critical factor is delivery of the products. It is one thing ordering a product online, and very much another for it to be delivered at a suitable time. One of the key factors behind Tesco's success as an online retailer in the

United Kingdom is that it is able to meet customers' delivery expectations, which adds value to its products and services.

■ Chapter summary

This chapter has considered the role of 'place' in the marketing mix. Generally place has come to be associated with distribution. However, it is much more than distribution alone. It covers a vast canvas from actual locations through to channel management, logistics and the physical handling of goods. This is quite a spectrum, and one that continues to be a vital part in the delivery of goods and services to end users, whether they are individuals, companies or governments.

For many goods and services the nature of distribution might not change significantly over the coming years. However, for others radical change is already being undertaken. New technologies have provided many opportunities for companies, for example:

◆ The use of vending machines to dispense a diverse range of products 24/7.

◆ New ways of handling fragile cargoes and shipping them over long distances in shorter time frames.

◆ The use of satellite technology to monitor and plan deliveries.

◆ The use of online distribution. Airline flights, for instance, can be booked online with a reference number acting as the 'ticket'. In this case the intermediary – the travel agent – has been removed from the channel as airline companies such as British Airways and easyJet transact the purchase directly with the customer.

However, it is not just technology alone that has affected the development of distribution and channel management. We have to consider how other external environmental factors such as economics and society have changed. Indeed, we need to consider how they will change in the future, and what therefore will be the impact upon place as a whole. This will vary from the importance of location through to how products and services are delivered to end users.

■ Questions for review and reflection

1 With fellow students debate the role of place as a concept within the marketing mix.

2 'The Internet will replace the physical retail store in the next ten years.' Critically evaluate this statement. What is your opinion? Support your view with evidence.

3 What factors influence place as a physical location? Use examples to support your answer.

4 Using examples explain one-stage, two-stage and three-stage channel management.

5 Critically review how B2C and B2B modes of distribution and channel management vary. Use examples to support your answer.

■ References

Airbus (2004) *Operations: Procurement, Airbus SAS.* www.airbus.com.

Bowie, D. and Buttle, F. (2004) *Hospitality Marketing: An introduction*, Oxford: Elsevier Butterworth-Heinemann.

Chapman, R. L., Soosay, C. and Kandampully, J. (2003) 'Innovation in logistic services and the new business model', *International Journal of Physical Distribution and Logistics Management* **33**(7), pp. 630–50.

CR80 News (2005) 'USA Technologies launches contactless credit card payment systems for vending', 2 June, www.cr80news.com.

Euromonitor (2004b) *Global Vending Corporate Overview – Report*, Euromonitor, May.

Groucutt, J. and Griseri, P. (2004) *Mastering e-Business*, Basingstoke: Palgrave Macmillan.

Inalhan, G. and Finch, E. (2004) 'Place attachment and sense of belonging', *Facilities* **22**(5/6), pp. 120–8.

Kandampully, J. (2002) 'Innovations as the core competency of a service organisation: the role of technology, knowledge and networks', *European Journal of Innovation Management* **5**(1), pp. 18–26.

Milligan, M 1998. 'Interactional past and potential: the social construction of place attachment', *Symbolic Interaction* **21**(1), pp. 1–33.

Mintel (2003) *Vending – UK Report*, Mintel International Group, February.

Morris, J. (2004) 'Aerospace and aviation', special feature, *Business Week* European edition, 26 July–2 August, pp. 46–52.

Perreault, W. D., McCarthy, E. J., Parkinson, S. and

Stewart, K. (2000) *Basic Marketing*, London: McGraw-Hill.

Porter, M. E. (1985) *Competitive Advantage*, New York: Free Press.

Steele, F. (1981) *Sense of Place*, Boston, Mass.: CBI Publishing.

People

Learning outcomes

After completing this chapter you should be able to:

▶ evaluate the role of people (participants) in the marketing environment

▶ debate the complexity of people as decision-making units (DMUs)

▶ appraise the wide-ranging impact of the 'people' element within the marketing mix.

Contents

Learning outcomes	287
Introduction	287
Who is included in 'people'?	288
Right people – right job	290
Building relationships	290
People and not-for-profit organisations	291
What happens when things go wrong?	291
Potential ethical issues	291
Chapter summary	293
Questions for review and reflection	294
References	294

■ Introduction

This chapter considers the role of people in the marketing environment. While some (particularly accountants and finance managers) might argue that finance is the key to the operation of any business, others may well say that people are the real key to success. If it were not for the people element there would be no business in the first place. Kotler (1975) considered people as a 'public', and stated that this was 'a distinct group of people and/or organisations that have an actual or potential interest and/or impact on an organization'.

Harvey, Lusch and Cavarkapa (1996) quote Dawson (1969) who developed a 'human concept of business'. Dawson (1969) suggested that organisations devote their efforts to meeting the needs of people, and he formulated three areas:

◆ **Level 1**: this is internal and relates to the role of the organisation in developing the human resource element. This includes employee training and incentives. However, the level and effectiveness of the training has to be in keeping with the quality of the output required from the employees. Training for the sake of training has proved, countless times, to be a waste of both financial and human resources.

◆ **Level 2**: this is the relationship between the organisation and its customers, competitors, suppliers and distributors. This series of relationships links back to the micro environmental factors discussed in Chapter 2.

◆ **Level 3**: this is the relationship between the organisation and society as a whole. Dawson considered this as the 'market for human fulfilment'. This can be linked to ethical and societal responsibility in the widest sense. For example, both for-profit and not-for-profit organisations invest in improving individual lives. The Royal National Lifeboat Institution is a UK voluntary organisation which, combined with the Coast Guard and air-sea rescue, provides both inshore and offshore rescue cover.

As Kotler (1992) suggests, organisations need to undertake 'wrap-around' marketing, in other words work collaboratively to 'get and retain customers through relationships'.

As we have already seen, a significant amount of marketing relates to transactions. However, transactions cannot take place without the interaction of people, whether they are store assistants or customers. Consider your position as a student, for instance. While your university or college might provide the physical surroundings, it only provides the physicality of the learning space. If it were not for the administrative and academic staff the value of that learning space would not be maximised. It is the people that make the university or college, not the physical assets. It is the people who communicate, who instruct, who teach and support students. Thus any institution cannot exist without the presence of quality academic and administrative staff.

In this chapter we look at the role of people and their interaction with one another. While Booms and Bitner (1981) developed and modified the marketing mix to focus on 'service' elements, including people, Borden (1964) indicated in his work on the marketing mix that people made contributions *'in specific circumstances'* (my italics). Although Booms and Bitner (1981) have not been the only ones to promote 'people' (participants in their original paper) as a marketing mix element (see Chapter 8), they made a very strong claim for their inclusion. Indeed, it could be argued that 'participants' ideally illustrates this marketing mix element, because the focus is on some form of 'interaction'. It is not a static relationship.

Some texts portray 'people' in a stereotypical fashion, but it is important to remember that we are dealing with individuals, not a series of digital codes. This is often a failure of many organisations, a criticism that has been levied at many UK high-street banks. As we shall see in Chapter 16 on psychology, our behaviour is governed by

a variety of stimuli, some pleasant, others not so. Our reactions thus can be highly complex, and it is important that we attempt to understand this complexity and the role of people within the marketing environment.

■ Who is included in 'people'?

At first this may sound like a particularly odd question. Yet often when dealing with the people element of marketing, books and journals tend to refer to two categories, employees and customers. While that is perfectly correct, it is only one part of the whole picture. Indeed some texts only refer to the 'customer services department and the customer', thus making the term 'people' even more restrictive. Clearly 'people' refers to many more individuals that this.

Here we can refer to Porter's (1980) value chain analysis (see page 278) to help us expand the role of 'people'. From Porter's analysis we can see that value can be added to a product and/or service throughout the manufacturing and delivery process. Just as value can be added to a product, so can value be added via people, both as individuals and within groups.

Every day of our waking lives we come into contact with people involved in the marketing of a product or service. We might never meet them on a face-to-face basis, but without them the product or service would not be delivered. For instance, consider the number of individuals who contribute to the creation and development of a movie. The next time you watch either a *Star Wars* or a James Bond movie, stop and watch the end credit list. It is the collective abilities of these people that have placed the images on the cinema or television screen. Without them, the marketing teams that promote the movies and the cinema staff, you would not have had an enjoyable, thrilling couple of hours.

The mini cases in this chapter provide examples of the complexity of the people element within given situations.

Individuals and groups represent the organisations that employ them. In essence they are the ambassadors for that organisation, whether or not they have direct contact with, or access to, customers. Let us consider a selection of diverse examples.

Computer systems operations at a bank

Computer software designers work in the 'back-room' and have no direct interface with the bank's customers. However, how they organise and write the programs that drive, for example, online retail facilities has a direct impact on the bank's customers. For example, bank managers rarely draft individual letters to customers any more. In most Western-oriented banks computer systems produce (and sign) the letters and mass despatch them to customers. If a customer is overdrawn on his or her account, it will often automatically triggering a letter to him or her. Where an individual bank manager may 'personalise' the letter, a computer will produce a standardised letter. The trick is for the computer programmers, working with customer relations staff, to devise letters that add an element of 'tailoring' or 'personalisation'. This provides added value from the customer perspective.

Military personnel

The customers of armed forces are potentially many: their government, the citizens who elect that government, host governments (if they are serving abroad), potential recruits and the innocent civilians that they protect from genocide (this is particularly the case with international peacekeeping forces, often under the control of the United Nations). It may seem ironic, even callous, to discuss this in terms of 'marketing'. However, it is about relationships and the public's perception of the armed services. For example, various military forces around the world (for example the British, French, Scandinavians, Australians and New Zealanders) have built a reputation for calm professionalism (often in the face of extreme adversity), humanitarian relief and peacekeeping. These are very different roles from the combative attitude we see in endless war movies.

Especially in peacekeeping roles, many armed service personnel display immense patience and humanitarian support under very difficult situations. Along the way many of these personnel have gained the respect of aid agencies, governments and ordinary citizens. However, it is a fragile public perception. Any wrongdoing can tarnish the reputation of a whole military force that has been built up over centuries.

Pilots

Passengers board an aircraft in the belief that the pilots, the onboard crew, the ground crew, the airline company and the various air traffic controllers can assure a safe flight. With enhanced onboard security we only hear the voice of the pilots as they welcome us aboard and update us during the flight. We no longer see either the pilot or co-pilot walking through the aircraft during the flight. We place our faith, and indeed our lives, in their ability to deliver us safely to our destination.

As mini case 13.1 shows, people are fundamental to the operations of any organisation. However, the focus must also be having the right people in the right job doing the right thing at the right time.

Should we purely focus on 'people' in the everyday business or university setting? We must broaden out this notion of 'people' to consider all professions and activities. Actors in a movie are people engaged in 'marketing' an idea or an experience to members of the movie-going

Mini case 13.1

Hotels

Whether you consider a major hotel chain such as the Hilton Group or the Shangri-la Group in the Far East, or a small country-style hotel in Southern France, all are dependent on the actions and behaviour of people.

Most of us are familiar with front of house staff. These include the concierge, the hall porters and the restaurant waiting staff. However, there are numerous behind the scenes staff, who do not have a direct interface with the guests. Along with the front of house staff we know that there are cleaners, chefs and other kitchen staff as well as maintenance, marketing and management teams. All these are involved in the smooth running of the hotel. However, they would not be able to undertake their roles if it were not for their suppliers. These range from the providers of fresh fruit and vegetables for the kitchen to the printers responsible for the hotel's letterhead and compliment slips.

All these people are involved in a dynamic chain to provide an efficient and effective service for their customers, whether they are individuals staying on business, couples/families on vacation or delegates using a conference/exhibition facility.

public. Why do young people queue around the block to buy that latest Harry Potter book? It is because the author J. K. Rowling has conjured up in her imagination a storyline that enthrals her millions of readers. Yet, she is not the only person involved in bringing the adventures of young Harry and his friends and foes to a global reading public. Consider the role of the people working for the publishers, printers and distributors. Each and every person involved has contributed to the phenomenal success of these magical books.

An orchestra can 'get into the mind' of a composer and understand the emotions that drive the musical work (Figure 13.1). The conductor (who may also be the composer) can engender their passion and interpretation or nuances of the music. Thus a relationship builds between the composer, orchestra and conductor. It is this combined performance that becomes a 'transaction' with the audience. In return for their attention and interest in the music/orchestra/conductor (in some combination), they receive a

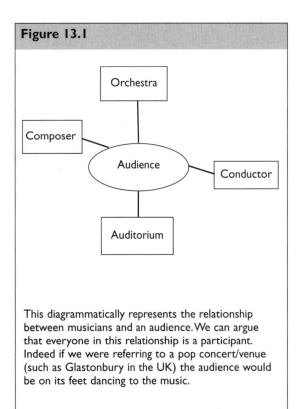

Figure 13.1

This diagrammatically represents the relationship between musicians and an audience. We can argue that everyone in this relationship is a participant. Indeed if we were referring to a pop concert/venue (such as Glastonbury in the UK) the audience would be on its feet dancing to the music.

performance (which might well be memorable). This can be considered as a 'transaction of emotions'.

■ Right people – right job

A company not only needs people in order to function, it needs the right people, and that includes the right suppliers. It is one thing having a brilliant idea for a product, service or new marketing campaign. However, the right people need to be in place to drive the idea forward. Collier (1991) states that participants (customers or staff) are 'the final link in the value added chain of retailing'. He continues by using the international clothing retailer Benetton as an example of developing staff to work effectively with customers:

> Benetton sales people are trained on the job, usually in established stores. They are trained in mix and match colours and outfits. They must be well-groomed and fit the market niche personality for that store, be friendly and polite, and know the procedures of the store.
>
> (Collier 1991)

Following on from Collier's point, the selecting and training of employees to be 'customer-focused' has become an increasingly critical issue in marketing. Almost a decade before Collier, Cowell (1984) emphasised the importance of carefully selecting and training customer contact personnel. However, as stated earlier, customer-contact staff are not the only people bound up in the marketing equation. In essence everyone has, to a greater or lesser extent, an involvement in customer development and satisfaction.

■ Building relationships

As stated in Chapter 3, organisations attempt to develop 'prospects' (potential customers) into loyal customers who act as 'advocates'. However, this relationship building can be a lengthy process, as the various parties involved seek to understand each other and build mutual trust and respect (at least to a degree). Of course people can remain loyal to another individual or

Figure 13.2

© Civil Aviation Authority of Singapore. Reproduced with kind permission.

Information and customer care staff are the public face of the organisation. They support not only the customer but also the organisation that employs them. This can be a pivotal function in any organisation, and can be crucial to the successful marketing of that organisation and the products and/or services it provides. Customer care may be the 'tipping point' in an organisation maintaining an advantage in a dynamic volatile competitive environment.

People and not-for-profit organisations

As we have already seen, for-profit organisations are dependent on people, especially how they interact with customers. However, it could equally be argued (some may say more so) that people are an integral element of not-for-profit organisations. We have already seen how military personnel may be perceived both nationally and internationally. Not-for-profit organisations such as voluntary organisations and charities put an immense reliance on the goodwill of both individuals and groups. Many charities, for instance, are dependent on the support of volunteers to raise funds and organise special events. They are also dependent on the support of individuals and groups to support the charity through donations, financial and/or of facilities and equipment.

What happens when things go wrong?

If we accept that people are at the heart of an organisation, there must be a realisation that there are occasions when relationships fail. This failure may be internal: that is, between the employees, suppliers and management. It can also be external, that is, between the organisation and a customer. These are not mutually exclusive. An internal dispute between employees and management can have a devastating effect on the organisation's relationship with their customers. In mini case 13.2 (overleaf) we examine the impact on British Airways when the relationship between management and its check-in staff broke down, leading to chaos and a public relations nightmare for the company.

Potential ethical issues

Where people are involved ethical issues clearly arise. Dawson (1969: see also page 287) considered his level 3 of the 'human concept of business' to be the relationship between the organisation and the wider society. This can be linked to the wider ethical and social responsibility issues that are increasingly part of our contemporary lives.

As we investigated in other chapters, people use various techniques, such as deceptive pricing

organisation even if they do not have a high degree of respect for it (him or her). This is a perhaps curious factor of human behaviour, yet true. Just consider how many people remain loyal to the organisation they work for even though they do not have the deepest regard for the managing director or chairperson. In such cases other elements link together with the relationship to bind the loyalty.

Mini case 13.2

British Airways

For many years British Airways (BA) used the advertising slogan 'The world's favourite airline'. This memorable tagline, created in 1983 by the Saatchi & Saatchi agency, reinforced the popularity of the airline as an expanding global business flying more people to more destinations than any other airline.

The relationship between an organisation and its customers is paramount. Companies seek to build strong longer-term relationships with their customers. Research indicates that dissatisfied customers will inform more people of their verdict than those who have been satisfied. Thus the pressure is on organisations to create an effective, efficient and long-term relationship with their customers. One key problem is that a major dysfunctional activity can have potentially damaging long-term effects.

In July 2003 British Airways management introduced a new swipe-card system for its check-in staff at London's Heathrow Airport, the world's busiest airport. This was to replace traditional 'clocking-in' systems for the staff. Known as automatic time recording (ATR), the system in itself would make very little difference to the customer service staff, who were already signed in and out by their duty managers.

The real concern covered two key areas. First, neither the staff nor their union were consulted on the introduction of the system. Second, there was concern that this was a new form of monitoring of their activities. There was also apparent concern among staff that this would eventually mean the introduction of an integrated airport resource management system (iARM). The fear was that an integrated system would lead to the restructuring of staff rotas and the introduction of annualised hours and split shift patterns. This could mean staff on duty for two hours, off duty for two hours, then back on duty for two hours. At the time staff knew their rotas three months in advance, and thus could plan their lives around the rota system: for example, booking child care. However, with the introduction of electronic systems staff fears began to focus on being called in at particularly busy times but being sent home if there was a particularly quiet period.

British Airways responded by stating that the airline was planning to move from a paper-based system to an electronic one over a period of five years. It also claimed the introduction of ATR was not linked to the introduction of iARM. The aim, BA contended, was to make the rostering system more productive and accurately record shifts. However, the dispute escalated between management and employees to the point where, on Friday 18 July, the staff took unofficial strike action which lasted for four days. The result was chaos.

The swipe-card system was introduced at one of the busiest periods of the year for both British Airways and Heathrow Airport. This is the period where the British tend to travel abroad on vacation. The impact on BA staff, its customers, Heathrow Airport and British Airways as a company was enormous.

BA staff

One staff member explained:

> The management have been saying we don't care about the passengers and that really hurt a lot of the staff because we do care about them.... The staff have had a really hard time – they've even been spat on and some were shouted at outside the airport when people saw the uniforms.

Customers

It was estimated that up to 100 000 passengers were stranded and some 500 flights cancelled. However, it was not only the four-day strike that was to affect the airline's customers. It took days to clear the backlog of flights and delayed passengers. This led to customers 'camping out' at the airport, and clearly this tested their patience. Many of them claimed they would never fly BA again.

BA and the British Airports Authority (BAA) (which operates Heathrow Airport) erected marquees to take the passenger overflows from the terminal buildings, and provided free food and refreshments.

Heathrow

For BAA the strike led to additional large numbers of people within the terminal complex. Additional resources such as tents (as shelter from the sun and to provide extra catering facilities) had to be provided.

techniques, to deceive others. While some actions can be clearly defined as unethical (and perhaps also illegal), not all actions can be judged so clearly. It may be an issue of degree: for example what is ethical in one country might be considered on the fringe of unethical behaviour in another. It might, after all, be an issue of perception. Mini case 13.3 uses the example of bribery. The giving of a gift in

British Airways

At the end of the strike action BA revealed that the strike had cost the airline in the region of £30–40 million. BA Chief Executive Rod Eddington commented:

> Clearly the disruption at Heathrow two weeks ago was terrible for our customers, terrible for our staff and terrible for our business.... We've got to rebuild our business, our relationship with our customers and restore trust where it broke down with our people.

The underlying issue for BA was its need to restructure itself in the light of depressed economic climates, terrorist threats affecting people's willingness to fly, and increasing competition from low-cost carriers. This resulted in a massive restructuring programme – Future Size and Shape – which in turn led to redundancies and a reduction in both flights and routes. The introduction of the swipe-card system was clearly at the wrong time for all concerned, a view supported by Eddington himself:

> The timing obviously wasn't good. But when you're trying to change as many things as we are having to change at British Airways, we can't always have the flexibility on timing that we would like.

Although there were clearly disgruntled passengers, aviation analysts at the time suggested that the airline's brand was strong enough to survive the disruption and negative publicity. However, they also suggested that British Airways had to build bridges with both its employees and its customers.

Sources: 'BA forces Heathrow changes', BBC News Online, 23 July 2003; 'BA talks break down', BBC News Online, 23 July 2003; 'BA and unions resolve dispute', BBC News Online 30 July 2003; 'Losses batter bruised BA', BBC News Online 31 July 2003; 'BAA unfazed by Heathrow strike', BBC News Online, 11 August 2003; 'BA sees profits halved to £105m', BBC News Online, 10 November 2003; B. Hale, 'Will travellers forgive BA?' BBC News Online, 22 July 2003; M. McGann, 'Tales of travel misery', BBC News Online, 22 July 2003.

one country might be a demonstration of the highest respect for a guest or customer. In another it could be considered a form of bribery, thus unethical.

Chapter summary

In this chapter we have considered the role of people or participants in the marketing mix. People are involved in all aspects of the supply chain, from production to after sales care (See Chapter 12). Often finance is considered the number one priority of an organisation. While finance is critically important to the daily operations of a business, it is equally important to realise that it is people who drive the organisation forward. If it were not for people – both employees and customers – there would be no business at all. That is common sense. The critical issue for many organisations is the recruitment, training and retention of the most appropriate people.

Mini case 13.3

When is a gift a bribe?

It is a fundamental to many cultures to present a customer or visitor with a gift. It can be considered as a token of friendship, of respect. Perhaps it is a precursor to the building of a long-term and valuable relationship or friendship. However the value of the gift might, to some, be out of proportion with the transaction or business relationship. The giving of a high-quality product such as a Mont Blanc™ or Gross™ fountain pen might be considered appropriate (and ethical) by the host, but not by receivers and their colleagues. They might see it as an artificial means of developing customer loyalty.

In such cases cultural sensitivity needs to be considered. To consider behaviour purely in a Westernised framework is insufficient. In many Far Eastern cultures it is considered a natural courtesy to provide a gift: for example, many graduating students consider it a mark of respect to present their tutor(s) with a gift. However, many Western university officials devise complex rules in the understandable fear that such gift-giving could be construed as part of a bribe. While there need to be regulations to protect all parties involved from allegations of this kind, there needs to be an equal measure of cultural sensitivity. Otherwise the graduation ceremony might be a memorable experience for all the wrong reasons.

■ Questions for review and reflection

1   'People are the most important element within the marketing mix.' Critically evaluate this perspective.

2   Using an example, illustrate how people contribute to the development of an organisation.

3   Reflect back to previous chapters and cite where people have had a key role to play in marketing activity.

4   When your lecturers present a class are they involved in a marketing activity?

5   Can people be the link for a company looking to gain and sustain a competitive advantage? Use examples to support your answer.

■ References

Booms, B. H. and Bitner, M. J. (1981) 'Marketing strategies and organization structures for service firms', in J. H. Donnely and W. R. George (eds), *Marketing of Services*, Chicago: AMA.

Borden, N. H. (1964) 'The concept of the marketing mix', *Journal of Advertising Research*, June, pp. 2–7.

Collier, D. A. (1991) 'New marketing mix stresses service', *Journal of Business Strategy*, March/April, pp. 4–5.

Cowell, D. (1984) *The Marketing of Services*, Oxford: Butterworth-Heinemann.

Dawson, L. M. (1969) 'The human concept: new philosophy for business', *Business Horizons*, December, pp. 29–38.

Harvey, M. G., Lusch, R. F. and Cavarkapa, B. (1996) 'A marketing mix for the 21st century', *Journal of Marketing Theory and Practice* (Fall), pp. 1 –15.

Kotler, P. (1975) *Marketing for Non-Profit Organizations*, New Jersey: Prentice Hall.

Kotler, P. (1992) 'Marketing's new paradigm: What's really happening out there', *Planning Review*, pp. 50–2.

Porter, M. E. (1980) *Competitive Strategy: Techniques for analyzing industries and competitors*, New York: Free Press.

Physical Evidence

Learning outcomes

After completing this chapter you should be able to:

▶ evaluate both the positive and negative aspects that can be associated with physical evidence

▶ debate how physical evidence integrates with the other elements of the marketing mix

▶ critically evaluate the role of physical evidence within the contemporary marketing environment.

■ Introduction

In this chapter we discuss the role of physical evidence or 'physicality', and its contribution to the marketing mix. In their original development of the service mix elements, Booms and Bitner (1981) suggested that physical evidence referred to the 'tangible' aspects of delivery. However, we can consider physical evidence in a much wider context. It can be viewed as the 'space, perceived look, feel, ambience and physical presence of an environment'. It does not have to be totally 'physical' in the sense of 'tangible'. The space can exude an ambience, both visual and aural. Churchill and Peters (1998) suggest, for example, that physical surroundings can influence buyer behaviour. They comment:

An attractive display may influence need recognition by stimulating a desire to try something new. A quiet elegant bank lobby may signal that an institution is stable and professional, thereby stimulating the decision to open an account there.

Bateson (1989) argues that the physical environment encompasses more than the location of the operational processes. He states that:

The configuration of room, the décor, the lighting – are all part of the 'tangible clues'. Many of these physical characteristics are seen by the consumer and must therefore be viewed as part of the product.

We only have to consider our own behaviour when we enter an unfamiliar

Contents

Learning outcomes	295
Introduction	295
Physical evidence and psychology	**296**
Exteriors	**296**
The architecture and design of buildings	296
Design of vehicles	297
Landscaping	297
Parking facilities	297
Interiors	**298**
Ease of access	298
Confines of an environment	298
Product access	298
Foyers, entrance areas and public spaces	299
Signage and corporate identity	300
Space	300
Layout and configurations	301
Seating	302
Security and privacy	303
Cleanliness and hygiene standards	303
Ambience and atmospherics	303
Visual factors	**305**
Lighting and illumination	305
Colour	305
Uniforms	306
Stationery	306
Presentation	306
Aural factors	**307**
Music and sounds	310
Air quality	310
Smells and odours	310
Taste	310
Tactile factors	**311**
Temperature	311
Touch	311
Chapter summary	**311**
Questions for review and reflection	**311**
References	**312**

building to know that we have a psychological reaction to that physical space. We also have a reaction when we enter a building with which we are familiar, though this is often very different. Thus it is important for marketers to understand the psychology that lies behind the physical space in which live and work.

Hoffman and Bateson (1997) provide a good summary of the range of physical evidence that consumers can use to evaluate a product and/or service. They contend that:

A firm's physical evidence includes, but is not limited to, facility exterior design elements such as the architecture of the building, the firm's sign, parking, landscaping and the surrounding environment of the firm's location; interior design elements such as size, shape and colours, the firm's entrance and foyer areas, equipment utilised to operate the business, interior signage, layout, air quality and temperature; and other physical evidence that forms customer perceptions, including business cards, stationery, billing statements, reports and the appearance of personnel and the firm's brochures.

Physical evidence and psychology

In Chapter 16 we examine the relationship between psychology (as one of the 10Ps) and marketing. Our ability to relate to physical evidence or physicality is dependent on our senses and our psychological behaviour. As Santrock (2000) states, 'all outside information comes into us through our senses. Without vision, hearing, touch, taste, small and other senses, your brain would be isolated from the world: you would live in dark silence – a tasteless, colourless, feeling less void.' To understand this relationship we need to first consider the meanings of sensation and perception.

Santrock (2000) describes sensation as 'the process of detecting and encoding stimulus energy in the world'. In other words our sensory organs detect physical energy – light, sound and heat – and transform it into a code that can be transmitted to our brains. Perception is described by Santrock (2000) as 'the brain's process of organizing and interpreting sensory information

to give it a meaning'. From this we then use the information as part of a decision-making process.

Although they can be considered separately, the two processes are in reality inseparable. The brain receives information, processes, interprets, analyses and then responds to it. As a result perception and sensation are often described as a unified information-processing system (Santrock 2000; Goldstein 1999).

Our behavioural reactions to the areas covered in the rest of this chapter are dependent on both our sensations and perceptions. Thus it is important that we have a basic understanding of these factors.

Exteriors

The architecture and design of buildings

Buildings can be both inviting and impressive. They can also be repressive (or symbols of repression) and far from inviting. In many ways whether or not we find a building inviting is subjective. A beautiful building to one person is ugly to another. The landscape of London, for instance, is a mixture of the classical (for example, St Paul's Cathedral designed by Sir Christopher Wren) and the modern (for example, the Swiss Re Tower at 30 Mary Axe in the City of London. This unusually shaped 41-storey tower was designed as the Headquarters of Swiss Reinsurance, and is the second tallest building in London).

Marketers have to consider how the design or architecture of a building can affect people's perception of the organisation that occupies it. For instance, grand five-star hotels, whether they are in London, Paris, Delhi, Marrakesh or Kuala Lumpur, tend to have imposing entrances. The buildings may be either classical or contemporary in design, yet their entrances make a statement about the quality and the clientele of the hotel.

Supermarkets, airports and other retail outlets need to be designed to cater for varying amounts of people, and provide comfort and functionality. Although they must be functional, they do not have to be drab and uninviting. Various airports such Singapore Changi International Airport (see Figure 14.3), Kuala Lumpur International Airport and Dubai International Airport are both functional and aesthetically and visually interesting constructions.

Figure 14.1

© Jonathan Groucutt

Designed by Norman Foster and Partners the Swiss Re Tower dominates the London Skyline. Within a matter of a few years this building (affectionately known as the Gherkin) has become one of London's most iconic buildings.

Design of vehicles

Here we mean 'vehicle' in the widest meaning of the word: that is, anything that transports people, materials or products, whether it is a truck, a ship or a plane. At first you may wonder what physical evidence or physicality has to do with the design of a vehicle. However, consider the design of trucks, cruise ships, buses and airplanes. They provide both a physical protective structure and a visual style.

The visual style of a contemporary cruise ship, for example, is very different from those designed and built in the 1950s and 1960s. This has been made possible through the use of computer-aided design systems, new materials that add flexibility and new methods of construction. An example is the Royal Caribbean International cruise ship *Voyager of the Seas*. Launched in 1999, this 138 000 tonne ship is one of the largest and sleekest cruise ships afloat.[1] The state-of-the-art ship boasts the first promenade that runs much of the length of the centre or spine of the ship. The Royal Promenade is the length of two US-style football fields and is four decks high. It comprises a vast selection of shops, restaurants and entertainment facilities. Without the use of new materials and construction technologies this vast promenade would not have been feasible.

Landscaping

It is not only the physical exterior of a building that can influence potential customers, but also the landscaping surrounding it. For example, although the Louvre museum and art gallery in Paris is bounded on all four sides by roads, the central area (enclosed on three sides) contains a spacious open expanse of paving and a parking area. The use of landscaping can enhance hotels and shopping malls, making them welcoming to both guests and visitors.

Parking facilities

There has been a complex relationship between the development of the car and out-of-town super-hypermarkets and shopping malls. This has been especially the case in the United States, where the ready availability of land led to rapid growth, but in other nations too, not only in the West, we have become accustomed to using cars for regular shopping trips. Therefore the need for easy parking has become an integral factor in the design and construction of super-hypermarkets and malls.

'Parking facilities' have gone beyond the location of space near the supermarket or mall. Car and personal security are now key issues, especially though not exclusively where there is 24-hour opening. Individuals and families may be more likely to visit a store where there are secure parking and walkways to and from the shopping area. The security measures might include uniformed

Figure 14.2

Both photos © Jonathan Groucutt

Examples of landscaping at two luxury hotels. In both cases this creates an exclusive haven for guests who seek privacy.

patrols, closed-circuit television systems, clear signage and brightly lit walkways. Security in such areas needs to be overt, not just to prevent potential criminal activity but also to create a perception in the minds of customers of safety and security.

■ Interiors

Ease of access

Here 'ease of access' can have two interrelated interpretations. First, it refers to access in the physical confines of the environment, for instance, a hotel foyer, airport or retail outlet. Second, it refers to ease of access to the products on display in retail outlets. Here the displays are the focal point, yet they are not divorced from the other factors that

govern the physical environment. They must be considered as intertwined.

Confines of an environment

Ease of access in the confines of an environment is something we often take for granted, most especially if we are young, physically fit and able-bodied. Yet not everyone in the world falls into this category, therefore planners and marketers have to consider the following groups:

◆   less-able people – this includes the elderly and the disabled

◆   parent(s) with young children – consider, for example, a mother or father struggling with a young child, pram (buggy) and shopping.

The physical evidence here is portrayed through the installation of ramps to and from buildings, wider isles in supermarkets, special supermarket trolleys that have child seats, and special ramps for passengers on buses and trains. In the United Kingdom, for instance, many buses are fitted with a hydraulic system that allows the bus to 'kneel' at the front to provide easier access.

While many countries have introduced legislation (for instance, those in the European Union) that forces organisations to provide facilities for the less able in society, many other countries have not. Equally, many organisations have been slow to respond in providing facilities for such groups. The irony here is that these are often groups with high spending power.

Product access

Within the second category we can consider two subsets, eye level and accident proof.

Eye level

For this subset let us consider a supermarket. Products are usually displayed in distinct categories: cereals, washing powders/liquids, beverages (tea, coffee, chocolate and other related drinks), tinned soups, and so on. The product ranges tend to be positioned on the shelving units (gondoliers) in specific ways. For instance:

Figure 14.3

© Civil Aviation Authority of Singapore. Reproduced with kind permission.

This image of Singapore's Changi International Airport illustrates the use and dimensions of space, the combination of natural and artificial lighting, ease of access and spacious design style. The architectural design of this airport makes it one of the most welcoming and efficient in the world.

The work of Leed and German (1973) suggests that placing products/brands at eye level tends to increase the sales of those items.[2] This is one of the reasons that major brands tend, though not always, to dominate the middle and upper shelves.

Accident risk

Customers will use avoidance behaviour if they believe that a display is unsafe or insecure in some way.

Foyers, entrance areas and public spaces

The structure and spatial dimensions of foyers, entrance areas and public spaces can influence our behaviour. Entrance areas, for instance, can be thought of as a 'transition zone' between the external world of the street or car park and the internal world of the store itself (Underhill 1999). Therefore, the transition from one zone to another zone needs to be as effortless as possible. For instance, consider a mother or father with children and carrying shopping, trying to push open a door. This can be both difficult and dangerous, especially where small children are involved. However, automatic doors, provide for ease of entry and exit. Creating a much easier 'entry area' can facilitate a greater propensity to shop at the store, especially for families.

Top–middle shelves: the well-known brands, usually produced by companies such as Heinz, Kellogg's, Unilever, Danone and Procter & Gamble.

Middle–lower shelves: these tend to be the store's own-label products.

Lower shelves: these are normally cheaper unbranded products.

However, there are exceptions to this rule. For instance, washing powders are available in a range of package sizes. The larger 2 kg boxes, with their own carrying handles, are usually placed on the lower shelves. This provides:

◆ Ease of access: the customer can simply lift the box by its integrated handle.

◆ Less risk to the customer. If the box was higher there is the risk customers might harm themselves as they struggle to take the box off the shelf. Injuring customers has both legal and public relations implications for the store.

◆ A reduced risk of breakage: a box on a lower-level shelf is less likely to break open (even reinforced ones can split) if it is dropped.

Figure 14.4

© Civil Aviation Authority of Singapore. Reproduced with kind permission.

This bookshop at Singapore's Changi International Airport demonstrates both efficiency in terms of the use of shelf space and ease of access

Foyers, entrance areas and public spaces can convey numerous visual and emotional clues. For instance:

◆ Selective and exclusive: some organisations, such as five-star hotels, want to portray the exclusivity of their brand. This can be achieved through the design of the entrance area (including the driveway and foyer). Whether it is physically imposing or subtle, it can communicate style and elegance and differentiate the hotel from other categories. For instance, the luxurious Burj Al Arab (part of the Jumeirah International hotel group) in Dubai is the world's tallest hotel (as of January 2005), standing at an imposing 321 metres. This billowing sail-shaped structure was constructed on its own island with a causeway linking it to the mainland. The spectacular and elegant structure also houses the world's largest atrium lobby. Its very structure and its construction on a purpose-built island reflect its exclusive brand identity. Equally stores may reflect exclusivity: for instance designer clothing stores in Paris or Monte Carlo, or jewellers in London's fashionable Bond Street.

Figure 14.6

© Civil Aviation Authority of Singapore. Reproduced with kind permission.

Clarity of signage is important to the efficient movement of people, especially where there is a risk of congestion, and in a large complex such as an airport. Here the signage clearly identifies both the departure gates and the other facilities available at the airport.

◆ Open and welcoming: while some stores may reflect exclusivity with their entrance areas (catering for a niche market), others cater for a mass market. This must be reflected in the structure, shape and design of their entrance areas. An example is the expansive glass frontage of department stores, fast-food outlets and supermarkets. Such structures create an openness, inviting the customer to browse and possibly purchase.

Signage and corporate identity

Signage not only has a directional value but also links to the organisation's brand identity. Clear and accurate signage helps customers find the products and services that they require. Such clarity in signage is important in, for example, major department stores and supermarkets. If the signage is confusing and mis-directional, customers are likely to become frustrated and may well leave the store, distancing themselves from the environment.

Space

This can be defined as the space between people, whether they are standing or sitting. As with

Figure 14.5

© Hebridean Island Cruises. Reproduced with kind permission.

One of the lounges on the Hebridean Cruises luxurious cruise ship *Hebridean Spirit*. It clearly demonstrates space, style and quiet luxury.

several of the physical evidence factors, there is a cultural dimension. An invisible circle surrounds us all. Those people we know and love we tend to allow within that circle. Those people we do not know we tend to keep at a distance. The dimension of the circle is at least in part culturally determined: in some cultures people tend to stand close to strangers, in others they stand farther apart.

Of course, there are exceptions to the rule. Crowded public transport systems, whether in London, Tokyo or New York, usually mean strangers are 'crunched' together for their morning and evening journeys. As it is for a short time and unavoidable, people tend to accept this often-unpleasant routine. However, when they have a choice they seek to avoid such closeness to strangers.

Herein lies a problem for restaurateurs as they seek to maximise their revenue. If they place tables close together it makes for the maximum number of 'covers' or seats possible. However a too close proximity of tables can inhibit private conversation, expose diners to the loud intrusive conversation of others, and create overall tension derived from the invasion of individuals' private space. This contributes to a disappointing experience, and the problem can be compounded by other negative factors in the restaurant's environment, such as loud intrusive music, poor-quality food, poor service and a price too high for the service and food quality. Even if customers do not complain (many people will not), they will be reluctant to either use that restaurant again or recommend it to friends.

Using space effectively can be a very real dilemma for organisations. Commercial organisations such as restaurants must maximise their revenues. However, there needs to be a balance in order to generate sufficient repeat business over the longer term.

Layout and configurations

Foxall, Goldsmith and Brown (1998), focusing on the work of Donovan and Rossiter (1982), suggest that customers are likely to remain longer in a larger shopping environment. Of course, this may be because there is more to explore, a wider choice of products and brands, and a greater possibility of finding bargains. While these factors might all be relevant, Foxall *et al.* (1998) also believe the layout or configuration influences customers' perceptions of the store. This point is equally applicable to a hotel, train station or international airport.

As Foxall *et al.* (1998) state, a supermarket layout can be used as a means of 'holding' or keeping the customer in the store environment for longer. For instance, some staple items (milk, bread, alcohol) may be placed at the rear of the supermarket. This means that customers have to walk through the supermarket to reach these items, passing items that they might buy on impulse.

Figure 14.7

© Jonathan Groucutt

The space between tables on a terrace at a luxury five-star hotel. Such spacing allows a couple to have a private conversation without disturbing the guests at an adjacent table. This is not the case at many restaurants, where the objective is to maximise the throughput of dinners. Too-close tables do not always result in customers returning to the restaurant.

With a supermarket environment, for instance, consideration must be given to traffic flow. This can be described as the 'flow and volume of people along an isle or other walkway'. It has several connotations. First, the movement of people in a store needs to be efficient and effective, while allowing them time to browse and purchase. Second, it is vital in emergencies for rescue services to gain quick access, and staff and customers to be able to evacuate the building efficiently.

The analysis of traffic flows is important in determining the width and structure of aisles, for both able and less-able people. Linked to flow and volume is the positioning of check-out counters (and the number available in relation to the size of the store). Once they have decided on their purchases, shoppers do not want to wait to pay. Moreover, the range of check-outs available adds to both the physicality of the store and the efficiency of the buying process (see also Chapter 15 on processes).

Supermarkets tend to provide three types of checkouts:

◆ Express: these are for shoppers who have a small number of items (usually six or fewer) in their baskets. As the name suggests this provides for a rapid or express system of payment, and reduces queueing.

◆ Wide checkouts: these are for shoppers with special needs, for example, those with children's buggies and the less-able in wheelchairs. Additionally, there is room for assistants to help pack groceries and carry them to customers' vehicles.

◆ Standard: the vast majority of the check-out counters for the remainder of the store's shoppers.

Seating

The increasing use of seating provides several potential benefits, although it is dependent on available and easily accessible space. These benefits include:

◆ Encourages browsing: in London, for example, several bookshops including majors such as Borders and Waterstones have incorporated seating on most floors of their buildings. Customers can take books off the shelves and browse through them while relaxing in a comfortable chair. The idea is that when relaxed people will make considered purchasing decisions, and this will increase both overall purchases and the rightness of people's decision which book(s) to purchase. This is not a new phenomenon: evidence suggests some bookstores in both the United States and the United Kingdom in the 1950s and 1960s provided seating.

◆ Comfort for friends and family: this is particularly the case in clothing stores where a customer may be trying on a range of clothes. The provision of seating for accompanying friends and/or family reduces the risk of tension created by boredom. Some fashion stores such as Jaeger in London's Regent Street provide seating, fresh coffee and magazines for accompanying friends and/or family in their women's departments.

◆ Rest area: this is particularly valuable, for example, in the department store, shopping mall and airport environments. Walking around a department store or mall can be tiring, so rest areas are beneficial for customers. If customers know rest areas are available, it may well contribute to their decision to frequent the store or mall.

◆ Food and beverage consumption: outlets that sell food and beverages within a larger complex, for instance an airport or train station, need to provide adequate and comfortable seating. Clearly a difficulty arises when there are delays with a subsequent backlog of passengers. Overcrowding and lack of seating becomes an inevitable consequence.

There are, however, other factors that need to be borne in mind. The seating needs to be:

◆ easy to access: both easy to get to, and not too low to create difficulty in sitting down and standing up, especially for the elderly

◆ clean, with no evidence of marks or spillage

◆ well-maintained – ripped or damaged seating

is a disincentive and projects a poor image of the organisation.

Security and privacy

This is an increasing aspect in all people-focused environments, whether they are supermarkets, shopping malls or hotels. Customers need to feel safe within the shopping environment, for example, or walking to and from their car or public transport. Over the past five years there has been a significant increase in the use of closed-circuit television (CCTV) and uniformed patrols across the world. Originally this was to deter store thefts and muggings.

Since 11 September 2001 much of this heightened security has been terrorist-threat related (See Chapter 2). However, the highly visual profile of security can reassure people, as they perceive this as a deterrent to would-be criminals. As they have a greater feeling of safety, customers may remain within the environment longer, potentially increasing their propensity to purchase.

Cleanliness and hygiene standards

Many countries (for example, Singapore) have strict regulations governing cleanliness and hygiene in public environments. However, not all countries match such rigorous standards. Nonetheless, depending on people's subjectivity, objectivity and environmental conditioning, cleanliness and hygiene standards may well affect their buying decisions.

For example, consider the purchase of food from a small shop or supermarket. Several factors will affect customers' purchasing decisions, from price to size. They will make a visual inspection of both the product (packaging, ingredients, use-by date information) and storage location (condition of the shelves, chill or freezer cabinets). If they have a doubt regarding its freshness and how it has been stored, they may be reluctant to purchase. Two key factors may influence their return to the store:

◆ The condition of both the food and storage areas. Even if they do not make a purchase, the poor condition may dissuade them from returning to that store.

◆ If after making a purchase they become ill through food poisoning, as well as making a complaint (to the store owners and perhaps the local health authority), they are most likely to refrain from using that store. Additionally, they are likely to inform their friends, family and neighbours of their experience. (See the section on word of mouth – viral marketing on page 232.)

Ambience and atmospherics

Kotler (1973) suggests that the ambient dimension includes all the 'background' stimuli within the store environment, which is usually referred to as atmospherics. We should take the word 'store' to mean not just a shop, but any environment where there is an interface between an organisation and a customer. The same factors apply to, for example, restaurants and hotel lobbies.

Mehrabian and Russell (1974) developed an environmental psychological model to provide the basis for understanding the effect of ambient or atmospherics within the retail environment (see Figure 14.8 overleaf). The model aims to show that a person's perceptions of, and behaviour within, an environment result from the emotional states created by that environment. While the authors may relate this specifically to the retail sector, it is applicable to any environment where there is an interaction between the organisation and the customer.

Individuals perceive environmental stimuli in a very personal or unique way. In other words people react differently to the same stimulus. One person may be stimulated by the aroma of freshly brewed coffee and freshly baked croissants and thus be tempted to purchase. On the other hand, another person might not react to the aromas, or might positively dislike them.

If the environment positively stimulates the person, an emotional state is developed. Here three states can be considered:

◆ Pleasure: this can be defined as the degree to which people feel good about the environment in which they are located, which could be a hotel lobby, a department store or a supermarket.

◆ Arousal: this can be defined as to the extent or level that the person feels excited or

Figure 14.8 The relationship between a physical environment and customer behaviour

Environmental stimulus	Emotional response	Customer behaviour
Visual: types of colour and their brightness. The shape or layout of the environment. For example narrow rows may make it difficult (both perceived and real) for shoppers to pass each other. Type of music: for example is it fast or slow? Is it repetitive? Does it convey calm or agitation? Aural (volume and pitch of music). Olfactory (smell and freshness) Tactile (softness and temperature).	Does the stimulus create: • pleasure? • arousal? • dominance? • irritation?	Approach–avoidance Time spent within the environment, such as a store (it may be welcoming or distracting and thus the customer leaves) Willingness to purchase – links to the level of spending Patronage – how often the customer revisits, for example, the store or restaurant

Source: adapted from Mehrabian and Russell (1974).

stimulated. For example, two people may be sitting in a Parisian café involved in joyous animated conversation. While they may have many things to say to each other, the environment in which they are located may be contributing to their excitement. Equally, an exotic location can add to the arousal, for example a moonlit beach.

◆ Dominance: This can be described as the control and power that customers feel or believe they have within the physical surroundings. Donovan and Rossiter (1982) suggest that dominance has a non-significant effect on individual behaviour. However, it could be argued that if individuals feel intimidated by a physical environment, they have no feeling of control and thus will seek to avoid it. Examples of this are seen in various in-town shopping centres constructed in the United Kingdom during the 1970s. With the closure of shops that moved to newer out-of-town malls, the inner town centres fell into disrepair and decay. Although some shops remained open, many customers were reluctant to frequent the centres because they felt insecure, and lacked control. With the

revitalisation of town centres, the introduction of new stores and a safe (controllable) environment, many customers returned.

A behaviour or reaction emanates from the emotional response. This behaviour can be approach–avoidance oriented. Donovan and Rossiter (1982) suggest that, at this stage, individuals will evaluate several stimuli including the environment in which they are situated, attitudes to other environments (that they may have experienced), spending behaviour (or ability to spend and level of possible expenditure) and long-term patronage decisions. Approach–avoidance actions can be described as follows:

◆ Approach: this is a positive effect where individuals explore the environment in which they are located, for instance a supermarket, increasing their propensity to purchase.

◆ Avoidance: this is a negative effect where individuals begin to distance themselves from the environment. This action results in decreased participation and a reduced propensity to purchase.

In the next section several stimuli are considered which affect individuals to a greater or lesser degree in a physical environment such as a supermarket, restaurant or hotel.

■ Visual factors

Lighting and illumination

As Underhill (1999) suggests, lighting and illumination (specific or general) affect all customers, young and old. We can consider lighting under three key headings:

◆ Safety: a safe environment is often conveyed through bright lighting configured to cover the designated area: for example, a hotel or supermarket car park which guests or patrons feel safe using whatever the time of day or night. On a more general note, people need to see where they are walking, thus physical locations need to be well lit to aid movement and prevent injury.

◆ Aiding readability: effective lighting makes it easier to read. Underhill (1999) uses the example of a fast-food restaurant which realised its customer base included an increasing number of over-55s, so it needed to react positively to this changing demographic composition. At that time its menu board was typed and diffi-

cult for many over-55s to read. The retina in the average person over 50 receives about one-quarter as much light as an average 20-year-old receives (Underhill 1999), so the over-50s have increasing difficulty reading boards with small type, especially if the writing is on a dark background and the board is in a relatively poorly lit section of the restaurant. In this example, the restaurant redesigned the board and increased the illumination. Fewer items were listed, but sales increased.

◆ Intimacy: if, for example, a restaurant markets itself as a 'romantic place', the lighting needs to reflect the intimacy of two people dining together. Usually this is achieved by the use of candlelight and more subtle background lighting. Bright lighting would not create the same type of atmosphere.

Colour

Individuals all have their favourite colours. However, we are also influenced by colour on both a cultural and a psychological-emotional basis. Consider, for instance, traffic signals. Most countries have the same sequencing – red for stop and danger, amber or yellow for caution, and green for continue or go. We have all grown up with that sequencing firmly imprinted in our minds. Equally, in generalist terms, the red of fire engines, the white of ambulances and the blue (or black and white) of police vehicles create a mental picture in our minds. Their presence, especially when travelling at speed, with wailing sirens and flashing lights, makes us react immediately, either getting out of the way or stopping to stare. In this case it is a combination of colour, sound and speed that is imprinted into our subconscious. Colour creates an emotional reaction, in one form or another, in all of us.

Hofstede (1980) defined culture as:

the collective programming of the mind which distinguishes the members of one human group from another.... Culture, in this sense, includes systems of value; and values are among the building blocks of culture.

As Hollensen (2001) states, culture is extremely broad and complex, encompassing virtually every aspect of an individual's life. However, we must

Figure 14.9

© Jonathan Groucutt

A luxury five-star hotel bathed in lights at night creates an inviting romantic atmosphere

also recognise that culture is not static. Culture undergoes continual change and reformation, often slowly and imperceptibly. Thus a younger generation may not be influenced by colour in the same way as previous generations. For instance, in the United Kingdom black is the traditional colour to wear at funerals. While a large number of people still observe this cultural colour code, it is by no means universal any more. Some families now ask people to wear brighter colours to funerals, as a way of celebrating people's lives rather than mourning their deaths.

Table 14.1 gives some of the cultural meanings of colour. This is far from an exhaustive analysis. However, it provides a brief indicator of some of the issues that organisations face in an international context.

Uniforms

Uniforms reflect the brand image and identity of an organisation, and often provide a perception in the minds of customers of authority, knowledge, support, security and comfort. Think of the flight and cabin crew of an airline such as Virgin Atlantic or Singapore Airlines. When we fly we place our trust in the knowledge and abilities of both the flight deck crew and the cabin staff to get us to our destination safely and comfortably.

However, this assumes that the uniforms are well designed and in very good condition. Poor-quality designs and staff who look dishevelled in unkempt uniforms do not portray a positive brand image; quite the contrary. One of the many complaints that used to be made against the State-run organisation British Rail in the 1970s and 1980s was the often-dishevelled look of some of its train staff. This conveyed, rightly or wrongly, the impression that the staff did not care about the service they were providing. It only compounded the highly publicised problems of late running trains, ageing rolling stock and expensive tickets.

Stationery

The style of letterheads, compliments slips, business cards and brochures reflects the corporate identity of the organisation. All organisations use stationery to some extent, including micro businesses, government departments and universities.

However, it is one thing to have stationery, and another to define how it should be used. All letters might be written on the same headed paper, for example, but if there is no consistency in the use of fonts and type sizes across the organisation, it will detract from an unified style for the organisation.

Presentation

This covers the visual presentation of the products or goods offered to customers, and ranges from the stacking of tins of baked beans on a display shelf, to the presentation of food on a plate in a restaurant. In some restaurants, for instance, the food is 'sculptured' or layered. This adds another dimension to the overall experience in which the customer participates.

Window displays are used to catch potential customers' attention, so they must be inviting. For example, furniture stores often use set displays showing the furniture not in isolation but accompanied by other products such as bed linen. The aim is to create an image in the mind of potential customers – 'This is how it could look in your own home'. Figure 14.10 shows a delicatessen in Verona, Italy. It very clearly displays what is on offer in this store. Moreover, it conveys a warm, friendly, trusting, welcoming feeling. Figure 14.11 illustrates how strong people images and warm colours sell not only products (suntan lotions) but aspirations as well.

Figure 14.10

© Jonathan Groucutt

A small delicatessen in a side street in the old part of Verona in Italy. The window display just overflows with culinary delights. It is personal, friendly and very welcoming.

Table 14.1 The cultural meaning of colour

Colour	Country	Cultural meaning
Red	China and parts of Africa	Good luck and fortune
	Europe, America and Australia/NZ	Danger – warning/alert
	Parts of Europe	Masculine colour
	Ivory Coast	(Dark red) mourning
	Turkey	Death
Blue	Iran	Immorality
Purple	Brazil	Mourning
	Asian cultures	Symbolises expense
Green	Many Western nations	Organic foods, freshness, environmentally friendly, good health.
	Japan	Considered to be a high-tech colour
	Middle East	Often considered a lucky colour
	Indonesia	A forbidden colour
	Countries with dense jungle areas, for example in South America.	Normally associated with death – fevers that emanate from the jungles and swamp areas
Yellow	In many countries	Feminine
	Mexico	Mourning
	Saudi Arabia	Strength and reliability
Pink	America	Feminine
Black	Most Western nations	Mourning. However, can also reflect style and elegance.
	China	Trust and high quality
White	Japan and other Far Eastern nations	Mourning (especially if a painted face or mask).
	Western nations	A sign of cleanliness and purity. Peace.
Brown	Nicaragua	Disapproval

Sources: Keegan and Green (1997); Smith, Berry and Pulford (1997); Usunier (2000); De Pelsmacher, Geuens and Van den Bergh (2004).

■ Aural factors

Music and sounds

Music evokes very strong opinions and emotions in people. Lovers of classical music, for example, may find Garage or House music too repetitive and aggressive for their tastes. It is known that music and musical sounds have the power to evoke emotions. This was evident from the early days of the cinema. Although we may call it the silent movie era, it was actually not silent. Although the

Figure 14.11

© Jonathan Groucutt

A perfume shop – a dramatic display which uses a
variety of strong warm colours and images to
promote upmarket suntan lotions

technology had not been developed to record
actors' voices, music or sound effects, musical
accompaniment to films was provided in cinemas.
For the most part silent movies were accompanied
by a lone pianist seated below the screen. Using a
mixture of classical repertoire and his or her own
ingenuity, the pianist would conjure up the appropriate music to underscore the emotion on the
screen. Often the success of the movie was literally
in the hands of the pianist, and the emotion he or
she could convey to the audience.

Since the advent of the 'talkies' in the 1920s
music has been used to carry forward the action,
drama and comedy of movies. Music should add
another dimension which cannot be conveyed
through the script, the visual effects, the photography or the skill of the actors. Few directors,
producers and studios have taken the gamble of
releasing a movie without a music score.[3] Film
scores become an integral component of the
movie, and can be linked to both promotion
(merchandising) and performance (the experience the consumer gains from listening to the
score). Soundtrack albums for films such as
Saturday Night Fever, The Bodyguard, Grease and
Titanic have gone on to become blockbuster hits
in their own right.

A classic example of the power of music is Alfred
Hitchcock's 1960 movie thriller *Psycho*. Both the
film and its music score became the forerunners of

the thrillers and musical sounds that chill us today.
(See mini case 14.1.)

For many years there has been debate about the
use of background music in office foyers, stores and
shopping malls. While some customers like it,
others loathe it. For many years it was colloquially
known as 'elevator music'.

The range of background music used today is
far greater than it was from the 1960s to the 1990s,
and now it is sometimes known as 'audio architecture'; but it is nothing new. General George Squier
patented the transmission of background music in
the early 1920s. He found that it soothed his staff
and improved their overall productivity. This was
the birth of the Muzak® Company, and later the
word Muzak® would come to symbolise background music in offices, restaurants and stores.

By the 1950s there had been significant growth
in the use of background music. This was aided by
the development and use of audiotape rather than
phonographic discs or records. The expansion of
shopping malls and supermarkets also heightened
its use.

The Muzak® Company, still perhaps the largest
provider of background music, re-records hit songs
for its clients, but other companies produce compilations of contemporary original artists to be used
as foreground music. As the name suggests, these
tracks are 'upfront' and to be listened to. So, for
example, a café may play jazz or classical music
tracks while its customers sit and reflect over their
double espressos. Foreground music can be considered as an active branding device, reflecting or
helping to define the image of the company using
the music. For instance, the Pret A Manger chain of
sandwich outlets in the United Kingdom tends to
play classical and jazz music, creating a relaxed and
'cool' environment even when the branches are at
their busiest. This helps portray an upmarket feel
that goes hand-in-hand with the chain's image for
freshness, hand-made sandwiches and organic
ingredients.

In the United States in particular some companies sell CDs of their in-house music compilations.
Examples include coffee house Starbucks, fashion
retailer Gap and the book/CD store Borders. Such
sales link the music to the brand, reinforcing its
image. Equally, record companies have found
another distribution channel for their artists,
whether they are established performers or new
talent.

Mini case 14.1

The power of music in Hitchcock's *Psycho*

Director Alfred Hitchcock created several successful movies during the 1950s, featuring such stars as James Stewart, Cary Grant and Grace Kelly. They were inventive melodramas, often graced with elements of comedy. However *Psycho*, based on a novel by Robert Bloch, was very different from his previous work. Indeed Universal Studios were not convinced of the viability of this proposed story of a deserted motel, a crazed murderer with a mother fixation (Norman Bates, chillingly played by Anthony Perkins) and a woman running away from the law after stealing US$40 000 from her boss (Marion Crane, played by Janet Leigh). There were no admirable people in the storyline. Then came the murders, the first of a woman taking a shower and the second of a detective on the staircase. The studio considered it more likely to be a B-movie than to match the calibre of Hitchcock's previous A-list movies.

Hitchcock began shooting his chilling thriller in black and white, with sets constructed on the backlot of Universal Studios. With budget restrictions, he apparently pondered whether or not he could afford to have music composed for the film, and believed that the visuals would in any case carry the action, conveying the fear of the brutal knife attack that became the famous shower murder scene. However, after editing the sequence he realised something was missing. Although the visuals were dramatic, far beyond anything seen on the screen before, they lacked the full impact he wanted. He wanted the audience to be scared!

Hitchcock turned to the composer Bernard Herrmann who had successfully scored several of his previous movies – *The Trouble with Harry* (1955), *The Man Who Knew Too Much* (1956), *The Wrong Man* (1956), *Vertigo* (1958) and *North by Northwest* (1959). Herrmann viewed this black and white movie as a challenge deciding to score it in 'back and white' sound. He chose to score it limiting himself to purely strings. This was a radical departure from the traditional scoring of thriller and horror movies at the time. Without the use of a 'conventional' orchestra he limited the various tonal colours that he could have used. The string section of the orchestra would provide the right tonal colour to emphasize the various emotions (and horrors) that would rain down onto the unexpected audience. Moreover, cinema audiences had come to expect to hear strings during romantic scenes. In contrast to contemporary movies sex had to be 'imagined'. Therefore violins and cellos would be deployed (often in large numbers) to musically

portray the couple making love. However, Herrmann would create fright in the audience by using strings only to illustrate not love but horror.

Although complex in form, the shower murder sequence is stark in its reality – a woman's naked body (although we never see it in its entirety), a porcelain shower tub, a metal drain and shower head, a knife blade and a shadowy menacing figure obscured behind an opaque shower curtain. When the murderer brings down the knife to strike the first blow, the scene changes to a sequence of rapidly edited camera angles accompanied by a chilling music cue.

Herrmann created a 'shrieking effect' by reiterated, dissonant, sharp down-bow strokes and wild glissandos (sliding of the bow across the strings). The combination of the angled shots, fast editing and the music produced a powerful effect. Perhaps what is really interesting is that this combination led the audience to believe they 'saw' the murder, when actually they did not. At no point does the murderer's knife make contact with the victim's skin. It is an impression created in the mind of the viewer.

Psycho is now considered tame compared with more recent thrillers and chillers. However, it remains the blueprint from which these movies developed. It not only projected Hitchcock as the 'Master of Suspense', it also made him wealthy. Arguably it remains a classic because it did not rely on blood and gore.

This low-budget thriller became an instant critical and box-office success. As the film critic Adrian Turner commented:

> Its continuing fascination and power to involve (not to say enslave) its audience is also because *Psycho* is neither a whodunit (Hitchcock was never interested in those): instead, it is an essay on the universality of evil in which the audience plays the most significant role.

This example demonstrates the power of music when combined with dramatic visual images. This is an art form that has continued to be used in movies, television programmes and, of course, commercials.

Sources: G. Burt, *The Art of Film Music*, Boston, Mass.: Northeastern University Press, 1994; S. C. Smith, *A Heart at Fire's Center: The life and music of Bernard Herrmann*, Berkeley, Calif.: University of Los Angeles Press, 2002; A. Turner, '*Psycho*' in *The Movie: The illustrated history of the cinema*, no. 69. London: Orbis Publishing, 1981; J. Groucutt, *A Musical Enigma: The relationship between music and film*, unpublished manuscript.

Decades of research show that music by classical composers such as Mozart and Vivaldi has a soothing and relaxing effect on people. Perhaps this is why companies that have developed subliminal learning systems tend to use music by these two composers (as well as others) as the 'carrier' for the learning text. On the other hand aggressive fast-tempo repetitive music has the opposite effect. It tends to create a more stimulated, excited person.

Retail outlets have used the psychology behind music in an attempt to regulate traffic flows. For instance, if a fast-food outlet is becoming particularly crowded, with the seating full, or virtually full, it might switch to background music with a faster tempo to help increase the rate at which food is consumed. If business is slack, a slower tempo might induce people to stay longer, which is helpful since few people like entering empty take-aways or restaurants.

■ Olfactory factors

This refers to our sense of smell and how we react to both common and not-so-common odours. In many countries we have become sensitive to 'odours' as depicted in the numerous commercials advertising everything from personal body sprays to carpet and rubbish bin fresheners.

Air quality

This is included here to reflect the changing societal view of smoking in public places. People today have several concerns about smoke-filled environments:

◆ Health: there is a growing body of evidence that non-smokers inhaling smoke are at risk of lung and heart disease. Non-smokers also suffer from minor health problems in smoky environments, including nasal irritation and coughing. In premises such as pubs and wine bars, those who worry about, or suffer from, these problems might choose to leave if the atmosphere is smoky.

◆ The odour of tobacco clings to clothes and hair, and smokers might need to spray their clothes with special fresheners or have them dry cleaned to remove the smell.

It is primarily for the first reason that many local and national governments have banned smoking in public places.

Smells and odours

Pleasant smells can portray a sensual quality. Think of how you react to high-quality perfumes and aftershave lotions, such as CHANEL No. 5™, Jean Patou's Joy™ and Christian Dior's Eau Sauvage™. These all convey sensuality, wealth and elegance.

Miller (1991, cited in Hoyer and MacInnes 1997) cites a research finding that pleasant-smelling environments can have a positive effect on shopping behaviour. Consider, for instance, coffee outlets from chains such as Starbucks, Costa and Coffee Republic. Their strong smell of freshly brewed coffee helps sell not only cups of coffee, but loose coffee as well. Similarly, the smell of freshly baked bread permeates many food stores and small shops, so shoppers are aware of it even when they are buying washing powder or baked beans. The smell:

◆ reminds the customer to buy bread, whether freshly-baked or pre-packed

◆ creates a pleasant shopping environment, and helps to mask less attractive smells such as the rather clinical odours from floor cleaners

◆ gives customers the impression that the store provides fresh produce.

Foul-smelling food, in contrast, will drive existing customers out of a shop and prevent others from entering. It creates a barrier (and possibly prevents customers from suffering from food poisoning!). We associate the clinical antiseptic smell of a hospital or doctor's waiting room with a 'protective' environment.

Taste

The senses of smell and taste are closely linked. The relationship between taste and the physicality of the environment can be considered as follows:

◆ Taste experience: this is the experience gained from consuming food or a drink. A positive experience may result in repeat purchases, either there and then or in future. If the experience is negative, the customer might not finish the food or drink, and is unlikely to buy it again (unless there is a dramatic change in circumstances, for instance, new owners of the restaurant.)

♦ In-store promotions: there are numerous types of these (see Chapter 10), but here we are concerned with promoting food products. Both producers and retailers use in-store promotions to encourage people to sample products. The in-store promotion has physicality in its own right, in that there is usually a stand and signage. Staff engage with customers and tempt them to try the product, which might for instance be chocolate, biscuits, pre-cooked or cured meats (such as honey-roast ham, prosciutto and salami), or varieties of cheeses. There is often a special offer (such as a money-off coupon) to make customers even keener to buy the product.

■ Tactile factors

This refers to physical sensations that go beyond the normal touching of a product.

Temperature

Whether it is too hot or too cold can affect buying decisions. Many countries have an infrastructure that can effectively and efficiently handle temperature extremes, whereas other countries are less well equipped to deal with them. Everyone can feel extremes of temperature, but some people handle them better than others. Temperature extremes affect behaviour: for example, heat can create lethargy and reduce people's appetite, although they often increase their liquid intake to compensate for the loss through perspiration.

In extreme temperatures people seek 'comfort zones', which are created using air conditioning or central heating systems, and this can affect a decision to eat in a particular restaurant, visit a cinema or shop at a supermarket.

Touch

Every day we receive stimuli through touching objects, and this too has important psychological and emotional effects on us. Consider, for example, how babies react to their mothers' gentle touch. Think about how you react when you touch objects. What effect does it have on your feelings and behaviour?

Underhill (1999) suggests that the success of many clothing retailers is that 'you can easily touch, stroke, unfold and otherwise examine at close range everything on the selling floor. A lot of sweaters and shirts are sold thanks to the decision to foster an intimate contact between shopper and goods.'

In Chapter 3 we examined levels of buyer involvement (whether customers have high or low involvement in their purchasing decisions). Shopping for clothes usually displays a high level of customer involvement. Customers try on garments, consider how they feel to touch with both their hands and their bodies, and consider how they look in the mirror. They may also seek the views of the store assistant and any friends or family with them. The physical sense of touch thus becomes one of the many determinants in the decision-making process.

■ Chapter summary

This chapter has considered the physical environment or what is often called 'physicality'. Clearly this can influence both the marketing of a product or service and, importantly, buyer behaviour. Marketing is often considered purely in terms of the product or service offered to a potential customer. However, this chapter demonstrates that there are many elements in the physical environment that can and do determine whether or not a product or service is purchased. Therefore marketers have to think beyond the product or service on offer, and seek to create an appropriate purchasing environment.

■ Questions for review and reflection

1 Using the example of a supermarket or a hotel with which you are familiar, critically evaluate both the positive and negative aspects of its physical evidence. If you were to make recommendations to the company, what would they be and why?

2 Clearly 'physical evidence' is not an isolated element in the marketing mix. As stated in Chapter 8, the marketing mix can be viewed as an architecture. Bearing this in mind, use examples to illustrate how physical evidence integrates with other elements of the marketing mix.

3 It is suggested in the text that we are influenced by odours and sounds as part of the physical make-up of our surroundings. Discuss this with your fellow students. Do you agree or disagree? Support your answer with examples.

4 In view of all that has been discussed in this chapter, how do you view your university or college in terms of physical evidence and marketing?

5 What are your favourite colours and why? Do they influence you to make purchases?

■ References

Bateson, J. (1989) *Managing Services Marketing*, New York: Dryden Press.

Booms, B. H. and Bitner, M. J. (1981) 'Marketing strategies and organization structures for service firms', in J. H. Donnely and W. R. George (eds), *Marketing of Services*, Chicago: AMA.

Churchill, Jr., G. A. and Peter, J. P. (1998) *Marketing: Creating value for customers*, 2nd edn, New York: Irwin McGraw-Hill.

Donovan, R. J. and Rossiter, J. R. (1982) 'Store atmosphere: an environmental psychology approach', *Journal of Retailing* 58 (Spring), pp. 34–57.

Foxall, G. R., Goldsmith, R. E., and Brown, S. (1998) *Consumer Psychology for Marketing*, 2nd edn, London: Thomson Learning.

Goldstein, E. B. (1999) *Sensation and Perception*, 5th edn, Pacific Grove: Brooks/Cole.

Hoffman, K. D. and Bateson, J. (1997) *Essential of Service Marketing*, New York: Dryden Press.

Hofstede, G. (1980) *Culture's Consequences: International differences in work-related values*, Beverly Hills and London: Sage.

Hollensen, S. (2001) *Global Marketing: A market-responsive approach*, 2nd edn, Harlow: FT/Prentice Hall.

Hoyer, W. D. and MacInnis, D. J. (1997) *Consumer Behavior*, Boston and New York: Houghton Mifflin.

Kotler, P. (1973) 'Atmospherics as a marketing tool', *Journal of Retailing* 49, pp. 48–61.

Leed, T. W. and German, G. A. (1973) *Food Merchandising: Principles and practices*, New York: Chain Store Age Books (cited in Foxall *et al.* 1998).

Mehrabian, A. and Russell, J. A. (1974) *An Approach to Environmental Psychology*, Boston, Mass.: MIT Press.

Miller, C. (1991) 'Research reveals how marketers can win by a nose', *Marketing News*, 4 February, pp. 1–2.

Santrock, J. W (2000) *Psychology*, 6th edn, Boston, Mass.: McGraw-Hill.

Underhill, P. (1999) *Why We Buy: The science of shopping*, London: Orion Business Books.

Processes

Learning outcomes

After completing this chapter you should be able to:

▶ discuss how processes integrate with other elements of the marketing mix

▶ outline the key forms of processes that are used within contemporary business environments

▶ evaluate both the positive and negative aspects of processes within a contemporary environment

▶ critically evaluate how processes will contribute to the future marketing of products and services.

Contents

Learning outcomes	313
Introduction	313
Types of processes	314
Technological processes	314
Non-technological processes	319
Combination processes	321
The need to adapt and change processes	321
Process standardisation or adaptation	323
Ethical issues	325
Future issues	325
Chapter summary	326
Questions for review and reflection	326
References	326

■ Introduction

Booms and Bitner (1981) in their original research suggested that 'process' was the 'Process of service assembly'. This can be defined as the process involved in providing a service, and thus can be aligned with the service industry. However, 'processes' also have a distinct operational role. It is the contention here that processes have both a service and an operational position in relation to the marketing mix.

To use Booms and Bitner's phrase, the efficiency and effectiveness associated with the 'process of service assembly' will vary depending on the activities involved. Rafiq and Ahmed (1995) use the example of the process of obtaining a meal at a fast-food outlet compared with a restaurant. Although they both serve food, the processes involved are very different. Thus as Rafiq and Ahmed (1995) indicate, the customer must be aware of the factors that govern the process. In this particular example it is the level of understanding of the processes involved in ordering and receiving the two very different types of meal.

This is a straightforward example, and individuals generally know the differences in the ordering processes of the two meal types. However, in other circumstances the processes may not be so clear. Several governments, for instance, have struggled to create a direct taxation self-assessment process that is 'user-friendly'. However, the taxpayer who opts for this system (rather than using an accountant) is often overwhelmed by documentation, paper-based or online. For many it seems a complicated process.

For marketers, whether they work for governments or companies, the objective is to implement processes that are mutually beneficial to the organisation and its customers. This chapter highlights the different forms of processes, citing examples where the process has been beneficial in capturing and retaining customers.

■ Types of processes

Processes are normally divided into two distinct categories: technological and non-technological. However, this gives the impression that there is no relationship between the two categories. This is a falsehood. As you will see in the remainder of this chapter there are direct connections between the two, and they should be considered as integrated rather than separated. On this premise, it is suggested that there is a third core category, combination processes.

These processes also encompass direct and/or indirect actions/responses from the customer or the provider organisation. The 'linkage' between these various relationships can be seen in Figure 15.1.

As can be seen from Figure 15.1, a non-technological process, for instance, can be an operation that has either a direct or indirect action. For example, a student completing the documentation for the submission of a dissertation has a direct action. The student has to complete the process, the documentation having been provided by the university. The student submits the completed documentation to the university office, which in turn processes it. The dissertation is handed to markers who report back to the university office and the grade is added to the student's score sheet. This action is 'indirect' as the student has no input into it. It is a 'behind the scenes' process. The student only experiences the outcome of the indirect action – the final grade. The various examples that follow throughout this chapter provide instances of both direct and indirect actions.

Technological processes

Two subsets can be defined here: manufacturing–production and electronic processes.

Manufacturing–production processes

Customers are generally unlikely to be interested in the processes involved in the creation of mass-produced goods. However, there is an increase in mass customisation or 'tailoring' of products to meet customer needs. This is not new. As the term 'tailoring' suggests, the clothing industry has for centuries been creating bespoke clothes, for example gentlemen's shirts and suits and ladies' dresses. Luxury carmakers such as Aston Martin can 'tailor'

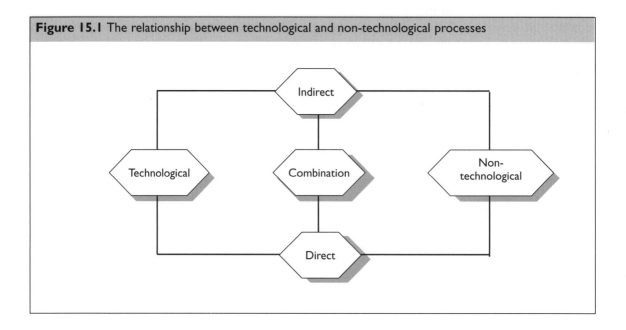

Figure 15.1 The relationship between technological and non-technological processes

their models by adding extras chosen by their clients.

Clearly bespoke tailoring and luxury cars are high-ticket items and beyond the purchasing power of most individuals. However, the development of the Internet and computer-aided logistics systems has enabled a greater degree of mass customisation. An example of this is Dell Computers, where customers can choose, online, a range of options for their 'custom-built' computer. Once the computer has been ordered, the customer can track its progress from manufacturing to delivery. Here customers have a direct involvement through choosing what features and benefits they require for their computer: as a result they are involved in the process.

Of course, while being able to choose the computer's features provides certain distinct advantages, this is not the end of the process stage. Once customers have decided on the features and paid online for the product, they usually seek delivery as soon as possible. This is where the manufacturing and delivery processes must be able to meet the customer's expectation in terms of performance and reliability.

Electronic processes

Normally electronic processes can be categorised into the five groups shown in Figure 15.2, consisting of barcodes, radio frequency identification (RFID), electronic point of sale (EPOS), computerisation, unifying technologies and the Internet.

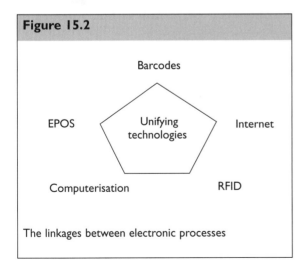

Figure 15.2

Barcodes

EPOS   Unifying technologies   Internet

Computerisation   RFID

The linkages between electronic processes

Computerisation

The development of the computer and accompanying software has revolutionised most lives on the planet. The pioneering work of such notable individuals as Konrad Zuse, Alan Turing, John Vincent Atanasoff with Clifford Berry, John Mauchly, John Eckert and Thomas Flowers laid the groundwork for technological developments that have enhanced people's lives, from providing safer transportation, medical discoveries to the very system that is being used to write, store and rewrite this text. The dramatic revolution in computer technology can be summarised with a simple comparison. There is more computing power in the laptop being used to write this text then there was in the *Eagle* landing craft which allowed the human race to set foot on the moon in 1969!

Barcodes

In the vast majority of countries packaged goods (from groceries to televisions) carry a small label of 13 lines. The combination of these 13 lines with spaces comprises an internationally recognised code representing the manufacturer's identity and product number/details. This information is read by a laser-beam scanner (hand-held or fixed) at the check-out counter, and is relayed to both the check-out till and the store's stock control database. The barcode provides the product description and code for the check-out computer to display and log the price.

The information relayed to the store's stock control database consists of product description, package size, manufacturer and price. This allows retailers to efficiently organise their stock levels. Where land is at a premium, for instance city centres, it is more cost-effective for retailers to maximise their selling area rather than have large stock rooms. As in-store levels of a particular product decline, retailers order further suppliers from their suppliers.

However, it was a long haul of research and development to reach where we are today. In 1929 the Westinghouse Corporation of America introduced the original idea of the barcode, as a means of sorting electricity bills. Unfortunately, the system was not fully developed and thus not fully successful. Between 1932 and 1948 researchers at Harvard Business School and the Drexel Institute of Technology in the United States resolved to develop an

Mini case 15.1

ATMs

In 1967 Barclays Bank in the United Kingdom introduced the world's first automatic teller machine (ATM). This was very different from the ATMs we are now familiar with, which are found in most of the world. As the swipe card had not been fully developed, the first ATMs operated on a paper-based system. Customers received vouchers which could then be exchanged (via the ATM) for £10.00 notes.

In 1972 the UK retail bank Lloyds and the computer giant IBM further developed the ATM concept and installed the first online 'cash-point' machine. This used, for the first time, a plastic card with a magnetic stripe that identified the customer's Lloyds Bank account. The use of the plastic card and a link between the ATM and the bank's central computer system meant that the card did not have to be processed physically, as in Barclays' system. This is basically the same principle that is used today.

By the end of the 1970s the original offline machines, as developed by Barclays, had been replaced by these second-generation online facilities. Work in the United States and Japan extended the self-service banking machine beyond one that simply dispensed cash to the customer. The offering of a range of other services, which we use today, meant that the 'cash dispenser' had truly become an ATM.

The problem for customers though was the limited number of machines available. In the first 16 years of development and operation only 100 000 were installed. However, developments in computing power and the demand (both internal and external to the banks) led to another 100 000 being installed over the following four years. The ATMs we use today are very different from those first introduced in the 1970s. ATMs today feature:

- slim-line design
- full colour screens
- full graphics images
- multiple language capabilities
- increased transaction speeds
- automated balance checks
- ordering facilities for cheque books and statements
- increased security systems – cameras and personal identification numbers (PINs)
- facilities for topping-up pay-as-you go mobile phones.

ATMs have also expanded beyond the lobby of the banks. Today ATMs can be seen in a variety of locations from petrol and gas stations, supermarkets, department stores to student halls of residence in universities.

By the late 1990s the banking industry had invested over US$30 billion in just buying these machines. Significant additional amounts have been invested in installing and operating them. ATMs are available in most countries. In 2003 the Asia–Pacific was the largest market in the world, followed by Europe, North America, then Central and South America. Africa was the only continent where there had been little impact. South Africa had the largest numbers of ATM in Africa, while some African countries had no ATMs. The lack of ATMs highlights the financial plight and poor infrastructure of these countries.

Source: Retail Banking Research Ltd, The Global ATM Market to 2004, www.rbrldn.demon.co.uk/history.htm

effective and efficient barcode system. In 1949 Bernard Silver and Norman Woodland of the Drexel Institute filed a patent application, but the patent was not issued until 1952 (van Dulken 2000).

Various companies sought to turn the idea into an operational reality, but that was not achieved until 1974 when the first fully effective barcode scanner was introduced. On 26 June 1974 a ten-pack of Wrigley's Juicy Fruit Chewing Gum,[1] featuring a barcode, was scanned at the Marsh Supermarket in Troy, Ohio (Hillman and Gibbs 1998). The 'simple' action of scanning this pack of chewing gum

commenced the computerised shopping revolution that most people in most countries now take for granted.

Barcoding is used in both the B2C and B2B environment as it is now a fast and convenient means of tracking items and initiating fast turn-around times. For example, consider the speed of use at the supermarket checkout counter. Barcodes can also speed up shipment and transhipment times by reducing bureaucratic displays in assessing documentation. This is highlighted in mini case 15.2.

Figure 15.3

© Wincor Nixdorf. Reproduced with kind permission.

Wincor Nixdorf's compactBank is a self-service system for self-service areas or mini branches. All the basic branch services are bundled into a self-service system that has a physical footprint of less than two square meters. The components of this system are individual modules that can be configured to meet the needs of the bank facility.

Electronic point of sale (EPOS)

The link between computerisation and barcodes has provided retailers with EPOS facilities. EPOS provides several advantages for customers and organisations. For customers it means:

◆ Faster check-out timing.

Figure 15.4

© Wincor Nixdorf. Reproduced with kind permission.

One of the many ATMs that are available in banks, shopping centres, railway stations and petrol service stations

◆ Increased accuracy of check-though of items over traditional methods. Today the computer

---

Mini case 15.2

Barcodes and export documentation

In order to accelerate the documentation process, importers, exporters and customs officials are using a combination of barcodes and Internet facilities. The move towards digitised documentation will, it is believed, reduce errors and accelerate clearance procedures. The aim is to forward the standardised and codified documentation electronically prior to the arrival of the goods. This Pre-Arrival Review System (PARS) will enable customs officials to determine which goods, on arrival, require close inspections and which can be accepted quickly.

Processes that accelerate shipments through

customs have the potential to reduce costs to exporters, importers and carriers. However, there are two other factors to take into consideration. First, not all countries will readily embrace 'paperless trade documentation'. Therefore shipments will still, in many countries, be subject to closer, and thus potentially slower, inspections. Of course, this will change over time. Second, in the wake of 11 September 2001, customs officials will be working to heightened levels of security and inspection. Thus even shipments with advance 'paperless documentation' may be subjected to necessary security inspection delays.

Source: D. Mandell, 'Digital day dawning', *World Trade* 14(2), February 2001, p. 52.

Figure 15.5

© METRO GROUP AG

A barcode scanner attached to a Personal Shopping Assistant (PSA). See mini case 15.5.

inputs the price of the goods. Previously, the check-out assistant would read the price tag and manually enter the details. This method was prone to error, most especially if the assistant was tired at the end of a long shift.

For staff it means:

◆ As the computer scans and inputs the data, this reduces the error of margin over traditional methods. As stated above, in the manual system, errors could occur because of tiredness after a long shift pattern.

◆ The computer system automatically calculates the change that needs to be handed back to the customer.

For retailers it means:

◆ Faster check-out timings, so the potential for greater throughput of both products and customers.

◆ The potential for the more efficient and effective involvement of staff. While there is a need to train staff on using computerised check-out facilities, they can also be allocated a variety of other functions. These can include customer services (helping shoppers, for instance, to find the right products). This helps create variety in the workplace and provides a valuable service for the retailer's customers.

◆ A real-time analysis of stock levels and thus purchasing timing. This significantly aids the replenishment of stock levels to the benefit of both the customer and retailer.

◆ When linked to a loyalty card system, retailers can build a profile of their customers by analysing the range and type of products purchased. The retailer can use this information to create targeted direct mail opportunities offering customers special limited incentives.

Radio frequency identification (RFID) tags

These are individual wireless miniature computer chips combined with an antenna, which are attached to the product and transport packaging (see Figure 15.6). RFIDs were originally developed at the Los Alamos National Laboratory in the United States for two Federal Government authorities, the Department of Energy for the tracking of vehicles and nuclear materials, and the Department of Agriculture for tracking cattle and the monitoring of their health. Today this technology can be used for overall supply chain management and to provide customers with added process benefits. These benefits include:

Figure 15.6

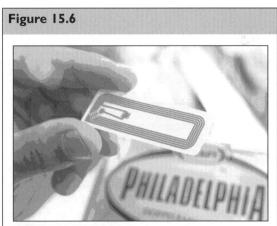

© METRO GROUP AG.

A miniature RFID chip with antenna is attached to the product. This can provide a variety of information including price, use-by date and weight.

◆ The ability to store vast amounts of information: RFID tags have a higher information storage capacity than the current barcode system. Product information such as price, weight, sell-by and use-by dates can be stored. This information is then decoded by an RFID reader which can scan the chip information from a distance of a metre. (A standard current barcode reader needs to be placed close to the product's barcode in order to scan it.)

◆ The ability to optimise the logistics process: packages can be tracked from manufacturer to the point of assembly or sale. RFID tags can also be used to locate components, products or packages (including pallets) in a warehouse, improving delivery times to the assembly line or front of store.

◆ The ability to optimise stock levels: with RFID tags attached to individual products a central computer system is able to monitor stock levels and automatically reorder as required. For manufacturers operating with a just-in-time system this means the risk of component shortfall is greatly reduced. In-store stock levels can also be maintained more efficiently, for example for supermarkets seeking to meet the demands of their customers.

RFID technology is being increasingly used and tested in a variety of industries. For example, Austria and several US states have used such technology for the efficient collection of toll fees on motorways. The RFID tags are integrated into windscreen stickers. As the car approaches the barrier scanners read the tag information.

Mini case 15.5 illustrates some of the practical uses for RFID technology.

Unifying technologies

Technologies have often been developed in isolation to each other, for instance the different television and video standards – NTSC, PAL and SECAM – which have prevailed since the late 1930s. However, the 21st century has witnessed a convergence of technologies. This has been achieved through unifying communications systems such as Bluetooth® technology.[2] The name derives from King Harald 1 'Bluetooth' who unified Denmark, just as Ericsson hopes Bluetooth® will enable the

unification of communications across several different electronic systems (Groucutt and Griseri 2004).

The developments in Bluetooth® technology are driven by promoter companies or members: Agere Systems, Ericsson Technology Licensing AB, IBM Corporation, Intel Corporation, Microsoft Corporation, Motorola Inc., Nokia and Toshiba Corporation (as of July 2005). However, several thousand companies have become associate and adopter companies, able to provide their customers with the benefits and features of this technology.

Internet

The Internet is a valuable tool not just in the process stage but also for the whole of the marketing mix. It has created numerous possibilities for the ordering, tracking, payment and communication associated with buying goods and services, often in real time. Mini case 15.3 briefly illustrates the process involved in establishing an online relationship with a customer. Compare this with mini case 15.4, which outlines how the Internet and other digital communication devices can use processes to 'improve' the quality of an individual's home life.

Non-technological processes

The marketing literature tends to focus on technology as the driver of processes. However, this is clearly not the case. Organisations can instigate

Mini case 15.3

Amazon

The online retailer Amazon is a successful example of order processing and information updating via the Internet. Once customers have established a repeat customer profile, the ordering of books for example via their credit card is further simplified by a reduced number of clicks to verify their order and details.

Once a customer has confirmed an order, Amazon sends an email to him or her, acknowledging the order and giving approximate delivery dates. When the goods are ready for despatch Amazon emails the customer again, and if there is a delay in either obtaining the goods or despatching them Amazon once again advises the customer via email.

Mini case 15.4

The intelligent home

Since the World Fairs of the 1950s, where companies exhibited their views of the future, there has been the dream of a fully automated home. This has proved elusive because of the divergence of technologies and the rivalry between manufacturers, both nationally and globally. Increasingly, though, technologies are becoming convergent through unifying interfaces. Companies such as LG Electronics of South Korea have been developing the concept of the fully integrated intelligent home.

LG Electronics defines the home network as a

> process or system (using different methods or equipment) which provides the ability to enhance one's lifestyle, and make a home more comfortable, safe and efficient. Home Networking can link lighting, entertainment, security, telecommunications, heating and air conditioning into one centrally controlled system.

LG Electronics suggests that the home now becomes an 'active partner' in people's busy lives.

The system is organised through a central microprocessor which receives signals from controlling devices (internal and external sources). The microprocessor then relays messages to the various appliances in the home to modify their operation. The user can interface with the microprocessor (via unifying technologies such as Bluetooth®) through keypads, mobile phones, Internet-linked computers, touch-screens and panic buttons (for security systems).

Within the home Plasma Display Panels (PDPs) in different rooms can relay such information as the security status of the house (which doors and windows are open or locked), provide wake-up calls and display weather and traffic information.

In terms of appliances, the Internet refrigerator is already available. Using scanner technology it can read barcodes of products as they are placed in the refrigerator, and information (such as temperature, use by dates and cooking instructions) can be displayed on the refrigerator's LCD screen. The next step in the development of connectivity will allow the systems to alert the homeowner, via Internet or WAP technology, on what should be consumed that day. Once supplies become low, the computer will be able, via the Internet, to order more groceries from the preferred supplier.

The system provides a range of additional features:

◆ TV screen: By connecting to the DVD player movies can be watched on the TFT-LCD screen.

Figure 15.7

© LG Electronics. Reproduced with kind permission.

The LG Internet Refrigerator

◆ Album: digital photographs can be transferred to the system and used as screen savers or as reminders, for example, of forthcoming birthdays. A memo facility allows for footnotes and dates.

◆ Cooking information: a visual and information display of recipes, classification of food types and the ability to search by ingredients.

◆ Music facility: auto search for FM radio channels and MP3 player with downloadable capabilities.

◆ Memo facilities: voice, picture and text messages can be displayed. Messages can be password protected and checked remotely through, for instance, mobile SMS.

◆ Internet access: the system's virtual keyboard allows the user to access emails and the Internet for shopping and information searches. Handwriting recognition software can replace or augment the virtual keyboard facility.

- Diary facility: this includes scheduling alarms for important dates such as birthdays, storing frequently used telephone numbers and general file management. It can be accessed remotely via a mobile phone SMS.

- System self-management: the system is able to check for problems in real time and inform the user via email. It can also provide information on the nearest service centre.

The retail price of the LG Internet Refrigerator (as of July 2005) ranged from UK£4300 to UK£5700.* In some cases this included delivery.

As of early 2005 the home environment can be modified to operate available 'connected' appliances. Over the next 10 to 15 years there will be greater digital connectivity embedded into newly constructed homes. This will especially be the case in parts of the United States, Europe and the Far East.

The question is whether this enabling digital connectivity will significantly increase the 'convenience' factor. In other words will it enhance people's lives?

* Based on a price comparison of seven online retailers.

Source: LG Electronics, www.lge.com and www.dreamlg.com

Figure 15.8

© METRO GROUP AG.

With intelligent scales the consumer places the product on the scales and the price label is automatically printed out. The customer no longer has to memorise numbers, as the automatic scales will recognise the type of fruit and vegetables being weighed.

processes that are non-technological, yet have significant benefits for their customers.

Direct activities

Usually they are a series of mini-stages that can be relatively quickly completed, benefiting both the customer and seller in terms of resource allocation. Mini case 15.6 gives the example of credit card applications. A sales person in a face-to-face meeting could easily enhance the value of the meeting by completing all relevant documentation for the customer. If the documentation was 'minimal' that would further enhance the processing time. This is relevant whether it is a B2C or B2B transaction.

Indirect activities

These are 'behind the scenes' processes. While the end result may have a direct impact on customers, the process is indirect or hidden. Customers have little or no involvement in the process itself, they only experience the outcome. It could be argued that the customer only 'reacts' to the process if something goes wrong.

Mini case 15.7 considers room cleaning in a hotel, something most people experience, but probably pay little attention to until the process falls below the standard they expect.

Combination processes

As indicated earlier, this is the combination of both technological and non-technological processes. Basically, it can be considered as the relationship or interface between people and technology.

■ The need to adapt and change processes

Changing patterns in customer needs and demands require processes to be evolutionary rather than static. Organisations that can differentiate their processes add value to the products and services they market. As we have seen earlier in this chapter, investment in new technologies can significantly aid in the development of processes that are more efficient and effective for customers.

Mini case 15.5

METRO Group future store initiative

The METRO Group of Germany has joined with various partners in a project to create the potential retailer venture of the future. Based in Rheinberg Germany, the Extra Future Store is an operational supermarket which incorporates a range of intelligent technologies. Many of these are based on the RFID systems discussed earlier in this chapter. Although it is a fully operational store it has provided a unique opportunity to test advanced technologies and innovations.

Personal shopping assistants (PSAs)

Each trolley is fitted with a PSA computer system which can provide the shopper with various benefits. For example:

Figure 15.9

© METRO GROUP AG.

A Personal Shopping Assistant (PSA) attached to the face of a trolley. Customer can recall their previous shopping lists, and self-scan products prior to placing them in the trolley. The scanner is mounted on the left-hand side of the PSA in this picture. Once customers have completed their shopping they alert the check-out via the PSA, and pay on arrival at the check-out. There is no need for them to empty their trolleys, saving time and avoiding long queues.

♦ Customers can insert their personal card into the PSA, which recognises who they are and addresses them by an agreed name. In addition, they may (depending on the store chain) automatically gain bonus points for their shopping. They do not have to wait until their next loyalty card statement.

♦ Customers can be provided with a previous shopping list, very much like a grocery Internet shopper can (usually under the heading 'favourites'), to remind them to make regular purchases.

♦ Special offers can be tailored to the shopper's profile. This happens in many stores now: customers' loyalty card details and the customer's range of purchases are routinely logged by centralised computer systems.

♦ Consumers can call up product information and price by placing the product in front of the onboard scanner.

♦ The PSA can search the store for a particular product. If for any reason the shelf is empty (although it should be automatically restocked under an RFID system), it can trigger restocking.

♦ The PSA can direct particular advertising and promotional campaigns to known consumers, attempting to meet their needs and desires. Point-of-sale information (including videos) can be displayed.

♦ The PSA provides the total price of all the goods selected prior to check-out.

♦ The system speeds up check-outs because the products have already been scanned by the PSA.

♦ Shelf information can also be upgraded, with label correction and updating of prices. RFID tags mean the store team is automatically informed if a product has been removed from the shelves and/or wrongly replaced. In other words the shelves, through the use of embedded technologies, indicate when they have to be replenished.

♦ The combination of RFID tags and PSAs allows consumers to check out their own purchases and pay by cash or credit/debit card. When a customer triggers the 'pay and go' procedure on the PSA the purchase data is transmitted to the check-out. This should greatly reduce the long queuing lines in some supermarkets.

Figure 15.10

© METRO GROUP AG.

A self-check-out system where customers can (if not using a PSA) slide their individual shopping items across the scanner and place them in a bag. They can then pay either by cash or credit/debit card. With the introduction of personal identification numbers (PINs) this can increase safe processing of credit/ debit card information.

Of course customers vary, especially in supermarkets. Some customers are in a hurry (maybe they do not like supermarket shopping) and want to make their transactions as quickly as possible. On the other hand there are customers who want to choose the right brands at the right price. They may take longer to shop and require much more detailed information on the various products and brands on offer. The objective of these new technologies is to serve both groups.

The objective behind the Future Store Initiative is to use various integrated technologies to improve service, create more individuality (similar to the Internet), improve reliability and create greater convenience for the shopper.

Sources: www.future-store.org, www.metrogroup.de, www.siemens.com.

Mini case 15.6

Credit card applications

Completing forms is usually an irritation for most people. Through careful targeting of potential customers several credit card companies have significantly reduced the amount of form filling required. In the 1990s American Express® in the United Kingdom developed a personalised direct mail campaign with a minimalist application form. The personalised introductory letter invited recipients to consider the benefits of owning an Amex® card. To apply, all they had to do was complete three boxes on the attached application form: their signature, the date and their required credit limit (a minimum and maximum was stated). A pre-paid return envelope was enclosed. The rest of the paperwork would be completed by American Express®, including credit reference checks.

The key issue here is that American Express® had carefully selected its target audience prior to the despatch of the application forms. This had allowed them to drastically reduce the number of questions that normally appear on credit card application forms.

Once a credit card company has built a significant profile on a customer (spending and payment habits, for instance), it might seek to upgrade the customer's card. Again, in such cases, the amount of paperwork for the customer is usually limited to a few key questions.

Process standardisation or adaptation

Mühlbacher, Dahringer and Leihs (1999) consider process standardisation as an 'attempt to make the procedures of decision making, implementation and control as similar as possible across all organisational units belonging to the firm or under its control'. Consider, for instance, an international hotel chain such as the Hilton Group. It has a global reputation for the provision of quality hotel accommodation and services. Customers are able to book online for any Hilton hotel, choosing, for instance, the type of room required. This is a standardised procedure.

However, Mühlbacher *et al.* (1999) indicate that it is difficult to standardise marketing processes in an international context, especially if there are divergent cultural and local/national market conditions

Mini case 15.7

Hotel room cleaning

The standard of room cleaning can be a contributory factor in a customer's overall perception of the hotel. The combined factors of housekeeping, catering, maintenance and staff qualities can be, and often are, deciding factors as to whether guests return (become repeat buyers) or recommend to their friends and families (become advocates).

While few guests see the cleaning process in action, they are affected by the quality of the outcomes, for example:

♦   whether the room is actually cleaned or not

♦   new clean towels

♦   the emptying of bins

♦   the replacement of toiletries

♦   the restocked mini-bar

♦   sweeping/vacuuming of floors

♦   dusting of furniture surfaces

♦   how the guest's items are handled – are they placed back where the guest left them or not?

♦   overall cleanliness.

Guests do not want to know the intricacies of the process, but they require a standard of service commensurate with the cost of the room and the hotel's rating. If standards are not maintained, they are likely to complain. How the hotel handles the complaint may be the deciding factor as to whether the guest returns and/or recommends the hotel in the future.

There is a clear link to the value of people, as discussed in Chapter 13.

Mini case 15.8

Airport baggage handling

We normally take for granted, when we hand over our baggage to airline check-in staff, that it will arrive at the destination at the same time as we do. In the vast majority of situations it is there on the right carousel in the baggage reclaim hall of the destination airport. However, consider the sheer numbers of passengers – both arriving and departing – at an international airport at any one time. Some typical annual figures are:

> Dubai International Airport: 13.5 million (2001), expected to be 45 million by 2030.
> Narita International Airport (Tokyo): 24.7 million (2001).
> Haneda Domestic Airport (Tokyo): 57.7 million (2001).
> Melbourne Airport: 3.4 million international passengers.
> Riga International Airport: 633 000 (2002).
> Sharjah International Airport (UAE): 1 million (2002).

London's Heathrow Airport (the busiest airport in the world) processes some 80 million items of luggage each year. To place this in context, Singapore Changi

Figure 15.11

© Civil Aviation Authority of Singapore. Reproduced with kind permission.

The spacious arrivals baggage collection area at Singapore's Changi International Airport

that must be taken into consideration. Processes that are successful in one location might not be in another. To maintain a perceived international quality standard, as expected from customers, is the challenge for many organisations. With increased globalisation many companies work closely with their local offices to implement a local or regionally oriented set of processes rather than an ethnocentric one. This adaptation of company processes not only 'fits' better with the local market conditions

International Airport handles approximately 29 million passengers per year (2002). Its two terminals are capable of handling 20 000 bags per hour for departures and 10 000 bags per hour for arrivals – a total of 30 000 bags per hour being processed (at maximum capacity).

This is achieved by a combination of technological and non-technological processes. Between the check-in staff and the baggage handlers who load and unload the aircraft, there is a computerised system that weighs the luggage and records weight, owner, flight and destination details, and places the baggage in the right place at the right time to be transported to the aircraft for loading.

Of course, when baggage does not arrive at its rightful destination the passenger is severely inconvenienced. The reputation of both the airline and the embarking/disembarking airport are affected.

Sources: British Airports Authority, www.baa.com; Singapore Changi International Airport, www.changi.airport.com.sg; Dubai International Airport, www.dubaiairport.com; Sharjah International Airport, www.shj-airport.gove.ae; Riga International Airport, www.riga-airport.com; Narita and Haneda Airports, Japan, www.narita-airport.or.jp; Melbourne Airport, www.melair.com.au.

Figure 15.12

© Civil Aviation Authority of Singapore. Reproduced with kind permission.

The need for rapid transit systems has been an important component of contemporary airport development. Here a RTS links the main terminal building with the arrival and departure gates. Space is provided for luggage.

but may also improve the relationship between the company and its customers.

■ Ethical issues

The difficulty for many organisations is that simplified processes can have a negative impact. This may sound like a contradiction, but consider the issue of credit cards in the United Kingdom. As mini case 15.6 showed, the application forms can be greatly simplified to include only a few key questions. From both a marketing and customer perspective this is more 'user friendly', but there is an argument that the simplification of application processes encourages individuals to instantly apply for the credit card or loan. Of course, that is the entire purpose of simplifying the procedure, but is there a 'grey' ethical issue here? Making it 'too easy' or 'too encouraging' to apply could lead individuals to live beyond their financial means. While there does not appear to be empirical evidence to suggest that this is the case, it is still a point worth debate.

Another possible ethical issue is the imposition of processes that may conflict within local or regional cultures. It is important that nations keep their cultural identity, maintaining the world's rich diversity. Therefore organisations need to consider how they can adapt their processes to take account of local attitudes. Such actions usually add value to the marketing operation.

■ Future issues

It is worthwhile to briefly consider future developments that may have a significant impact on future processes in the marketing mix. We have already seen in this chapter how barcodes are slowly being replaced by microchip RFID tags.

A key science that underpins these developments is nanotechnology. This, in essence, involves the manipulation of structures at a molecular level, which changes the behaviour of materials. Nanotechnology is fundamental in the development of pervasive technologies (sophisticated devices such as home security and lighting systems that react to human presence) through sensors in the walls and floor. (See mini case 15.4.)

Overall nanotechnologies can be seen as enabling technologies that will help create systems that are smaller, lighter, stronger, more efficient and highly cost-effective to produce. To some extent we are already seeing these developments take shape. Today it is common to see flash memory devices in computers and digital cameras. In the relatively near future a terabit of data (equal to ten hours of superior quality video) will be stored on a device that is no larger than an ordinary postage stamp.

Nanotechnologies will contribute to the miniaturisation of data storage systems with the capacity to store vast libraries, PCs that will contain the power of today's mainframe computer centres, the development of fuel cells that will make our current batteries obsolete, and improved medical procedures and processes. Clearly we are only touching the surface of what may be possible. However, as witnessed with RFID tags, the Internet refrigerator and the intelligent home, technology is already having a significant influence in shaping current and future processes.

■ Chapter summary

This chapter has illustrated the vital link processes make to the remainder of the marketing mix, customer satisfaction and potential to reduce organisational expenditure. Since Booms and Bitner examined 'processes' as a feature of service marketing in the early 1980s much has changed. We have seen the rise of barcoding and ATMs, items that we now take for granted. However, what is perhaps particularly interesting is the dramatic rise in computing power which has enhanced other technologies, enabling companies to develop and offer a vast array of products which provide a service process function. Clearly ATMs furnished this role, but it is now much more linked to the home and shopping environment. This is where the revolution is taking place.

The process of shopping is changing, whether it is in-store or via the Internet. The timescale and eventual extent of the change are perhaps matters of debate. However, discussions of an Internet refrigerator in the late 1990s raised smiles as something out of a science fiction fantasy movie. Now they are a reality. So the development of nanotechnologies may yet yield significant changes in the use of marketing mix processes.

■ Questions for review and reflection

1 Briefly outline the key types of processes that are used within the marketing context.

2 Critically review how processes can be integrated with the other elements that comprise the marketing mix.

3 Debate with fellow students how technology can influence the process element of the marketing mix.

4 Debate with fellow students what you think will be the influence of nanotechnologies on marketing processes over the next five to ten years. You may want to check out ideas via the Internet and a library prior to your debate.

■ References

Booms, B. H. and Bitner, M. J. (1981) 'Marketing strategies and organization structures for service firms', in J. H. Donnely and W. R. George (eds), *Marketing of Services*, Chicago: AMA.

Groucutt, J. and Griseri, P. (2004) *Mastering e-Business*, Basingstoke: Palgrave Macmillan.

Hillman, D. and Gibbs, D. (1998) *Century Makers*, London: Weidenfeld & Nicolson.

Mühlbacher, H., Dahringer, L. and Leihs, H. (1999) *International Marketing: A global perspective*, 2nd edn, London: International Thomson Business Press.

Rafiq, M. and Ahmed, P. K. (1995) 'Using the 7Ps as a generic marketing mix: an exploratory survey of UK and European marketing academics', *Marketing Intelligence and Planning* **13**(9), pp. 4–16.

van Dulken, S. (2000) *Inventing the 20th Century: 100 inventions that shaped the world*, London: British Library.

Psychology

CHAPTER 16

●●●●

Learning outcomes

After completing this chapter you should be able to:

▶ briefly explain the different approaches to psychology and consider how they relate to marketing

▶ debate the relevance of psychology as another component in the marketing mix

▶ examine how psychology can influence buyer behaviour

▶ critically evaluate the different stimuli that can influence our buyer behaviour.

Contents

Learning outcomes 327
Introduction 327
Why psychology? 328
Key approaches in psychology and their relationship to marketing 328
Psychoanalytical aspects 329
Behavioural aspects 331
Humanistic approach 334
The cognitive approach 334
Evolutionary approach 336
Social psychology 336
The relationship between psychology and marketing 337
Categories of buyer behaviour 337
People 337
Culture 339
Lifestyle 339
Financial and economic influences 339
Fear 340
Media 341
Price 342
Necessities 342
Chapter summary 342
Question for review and reflection 342
References 343

■ Introduction

In Chapter 1 you were asked to consider the following questions:

◆ What are your three favourite movies? Why are they your favourite movies? What influenced you to go to see them?

◆ What are your three favourite CDs? Why are they your favourite CDs? What influenced you to go to buy them? If you did not buy them, were they a gift to you?

◆ What is your favourite food? Why is it your favourite food? Did anyone or anything influence you to try this food for the first time?

These may have seemed innocuous questions. However, as indicated in the introduction to Chapter 1, they go to the heart of marketing. This is never more so than when it comes to the discussion of the psychological aspects of marketing. Why we buy certain products or services can be traced back to our inner thoughts, needs, desires and feelings. This was also considered in Chapter 10 on Promotion. There we considered the various hierarchy of effects models, where there is a relationship between the cognitive, affect and conation.

This chapter explores the relationship between psychology and marketing. To some extent it discusses who we are and why we buy particular products and services. Moreover, here psychology is considered as one of the 'P's of a 'revised' marketing mix. While this chapter focuses on psychology it is important to realise that virtually all the chapters in this book link in to the essence of psychology. As suggested in Chapter 1, along with disciplines such as economics, it is one of the cornerstones that comprises what we call marketing.

Succinctly, psychology can be defined as the scientific study of behaviour and mental processes. One of the founders of modern psychology, William James (1842–1910) described psychology (in 1880) as 'the science of mental life … of such things as feelings, desires, cognition (learning/knowledge), reasoning, decisions and the like'. As Santrock (2000) suggests, psychology 'contributes enormously to our knowledge about why people are the way they are, why they think and act the way they do, and how they can cope more effectively with their lives'. Psychology has also been used to motivate our desires to engage in various types of marketing activity.

As psychology and buyer behaviour are so inextricably linked, discussions on buyer behaviours are included in this chapter.

■ Why psychology?

It is interesting to note that very few general marketing textbooks overtly discuss the role of psychology in marketing. Throughout marketing is portrayed as a means of satisfying the wants and desires of a consumer audience. Rarely discussed, though, is the use of marketing strategies and tactics to create those desires, and to some degree even to create needs.

Reflect back to Chapter 10 on promotion. The work of psychologists such as Scott in 1913 and Strong in 1925 illustrates that early in the 20th century there was an attempt to link perception and motivation to acquisition of products and service. Overall the objective of such models as the hierarchy of effects was to link the various stages to cognition (knowledge/learning), affect (attitudes/preferences) and conation (conviction/purpose and resultant action). The contention here is that psychology must be considered a founding 'P' of the marketing mix, for it underpins a considerable amount of marketing activity.

■ Key approaches in psychology and their relationship to marketing

This section of the chapter covers three interrelated areas:

◆   the key approaches in psychology

◆   the main exponents and contributors to those fields of investigation

◆   the relationship between these individual fields of investigation and marketing activity.

The key approaches can be identified as:

◆   psychoanalytical

◆   behavioural

◆   humanistic

◆   cognitive

Figure 16.1

© Jonathan Groucutt

Several hundred people enjoy a summer's evening concert at Kenwood, Hampstead in London. As we examined in Chapter 3, marketers can segment and target a group of people with 'like-minded' interests. However, we are all driven and influenced by different needs, wants and desires. Therefore some in this audience are there to enjoy the music played by a symphony orchestra, others are there because their friends or family wanted to go, while others may be there to enjoy the collective enjoyment of music. There will be a multitude of drivers and reasons, some rational and others perhaps not. However, these are all factors that comprise the 'human condition'.

◆   evolutionary

◆   social psychology.

Psychoanalytical aspects

The psychoanalytical approach emphasizes the unconscious aspects of the mind, conflict between biological instincts and society's demands, and early family experiences (Santrock 2000). The key proponent of the psychoanalytical approach was Sigmund Freud (1856–1939). Freud is considered one of the founders of modern psychology, especially psychoanalysis in relation to a general theory of human personality.

Throughout our lives we process large volumes of information at different levels of awareness. In many cases we are fully aware of this processing, at other times we are not. This is an individual's consciousness – a state that can be defined as an awareness of both internal and external stimuli. The external stimuli derive from activities we participate in during the day, whilst internal stimuli are the awareness of our own sensations (for example, hunger) as well as our thoughts and feelings. It was the American psychologist William James who described the mind as a stream of consciousness. In other words, the mind is a continuous but unstructured flow of changing sensations, images, thoughts and feelings (Santrock 2000). Freud, however, concluded that most of our thoughts were 'unconscious'.[1] That is, they are beyond our conscious awareness. He believed that unconscious thought was a collection of socially unacceptable wishes, feelings and thoughts.

Freud's view was that this unconscious 'self' had to be controlled, either by an individual's conscious thought processes or by external forces. In terms of 'extremes' of human behaviour we can consider this as control of immoral thoughts and actions. For instance, we may become angry with someone but our instinct or conscious thought processes normally prevent us from converting that anger into a physically violent act.

The basis of Freudian theory is the 'self'. This suggests that individuals are driven by the need to fulfil their own particular desires – their wants and needs. Linked to this is the concept of personality, which can be viewed as enduring, distinctive thoughts, emotions and behaviours that characterise how we adapt to the world we inhabit

(Santrock 2000). Freud believed that personality was a structure composed of three elements, the *id*, the *ego* and the *super-ego*. The *id* is an individual's unconscious and thus has no contact with reality. Its focus is on an individual's unacceptable thoughts and feelings. The *ego*, on the other hand, is the element of personality that interacts with reality. It is considered as a facilitator of our higher mental functions, providing for reasoning, problem solving and rational decision making.

While the *id* seeks to satisfy unacceptable desires, our *ego* seeks satisfaction within the boundaries of socially acceptable behaviour. It may push the barriers of what is socially acceptable, but it will not allow us to 'normally' break them. However, like our *id*, our *ego* has no morality function. Freud believed that there must be a moral aspect to our personalities, however. This he described as our *super-ego*, which could also be considered as our 'conscience'. However, like the *id*, our *super-ego* has no interaction with reality. It is there to moderate the feelings and thoughts that emanate from our *id* and seek to satisfy them within a moral framework. Freud likened personality to that of an iceberg. In other words most of our personality exists within the unconscious, and so below our level of awareness, just like the bulk of an iceberg is below the waterline. The *id* is totally submerged, with only a fraction of our *ego* and *super-ego* above that precious waterline.

However, since Freud formulated these elements of personality, several psychologists have challenged his findings. Carl Jung (1875–1961), for instance, believed that Freud undervalued the role of the unconscious mind in our personalities. Jung separated the unconscious into two subsets. First, our *personal unconscious* contains our repressed thoughts and feelings. Second, our *collective unconscious* is an impersonal layer of the unconscious that represents the collective experiences of the past as shared by humanity. This collective unconscious can manifest itself through images and ideas that have rich symbolic meaning, for instance in art, religion and even in our dreams.

After Sigmund Freud died his psychoanalytical work continued through research conducted by his daughter Anna Freud (1895–1982). She believed that changing or modifying the environment around them could influence individuals. This was, as with Sigmund Freud's views, a perspective adopted by his nephew Edward Bernays, as we shall see later in this section.

Alfred Adler (1870–1937) on the other hand believed in individual psychology, where individuals are motivated by purposes and goals, being creators of their own lives. Thus, according to Adler, individuals are able to 'consciously' monitor their own lives, adapting to their surroundings by developing social interests and reducing feelings of inferiority (Santrock 2000).

One of the first to see the value of Freudian psychoanalytical theory in relation to marketing was Freud's own nephew Edward Bernays (1891–1995).[2] Another was Ernest Dichter (1907–1991). Bernays is often credited as creating 'public relations' as a form or component of

marketing. However, he was one of several during the early part of the 20th century who developed a 'public relations orientation' for both government and business.[3] What Bernays arguably did achieve was to mould public relations into a profession that both governments and companies took seriously. He incorporated strategies and tactics to communicate messages and change attitudes. This is where he relied on the work of Sigmund Freud.

Ernest Dichter was, like Freud, an Austrian-born psychologist who believed that consumers needed to verbalise their needs, wants and importantly their desires. To increase his understanding of consumer desires Dichter developed the Focus Group, a means of gathering information and views that is today commonplace in market

---

Mini case 16.1

Introducing women to smoking

Until the 1920s smoking was considered, in America at least, to be a purely masculine activity. Indeed psychologists at the time debated whether or not the cigarette was an extension of male sexuality, power and dominance. Therefore to see a woman smoking in public was normally considered to be socially unacceptable and unfeminine, although many women did smoke in the privacy of their own home. George Washington Hill, the president of the American Tobacco Company, sought to increase sales of the company's cigarettes, especially the Lucky Strike brand (known as Luckies). Bernays was asked to consider ways of opening up the market to women.

Women's rights and the suffragette movement had been growing in popularity. Bernays sought to use this as a means of popularising smoking amongst women. He consulted the American psychologist A.A. Brill, a psychoanalyst and follower of Freud who believed:

> It is perfectly normal for women to smoke cigarettes.... The emancipation of women has suppressed many of their feminine desires. More women now do the same work as men do. Many women bear no children; those who do bear fewer children. Feminine traits are masked. Cigarettes which are equated with men, become torches of freedom.

This gave Bernays an idea. He decided to use New

York's 1929 Easter Parade as the event that would change people's perception of women smoking. He persuaded ten young debutantes to walk down Fifth Avenue with their escorts, carrying hidden Lucky Strike packets, then at a given signal take out a cigarette and light up. He tipped off numerous photographers and journalists with the aim of generating stories that for the first time a group of women had smoked cigarettes openly on the street. This he named 'Torches of Freedom'. In a country that promoted the values of freedom and liberty (though not always supported them) this was seen as a argument that no one could really counter. The Torches of Freedom campaign, though simple in its idea, had a profound effect on the perception of women who smoked. Within days women were seen in streets across America lighting up and smoking cigarettes in public.

Bernays' actions helped to empower women in the eyes of American society, although it can be argued that it has taken several decades since for women in the United States and Europe to obtain any form of real equality. However from an ethical perspective it must be stated that Bernays never revealed to either the debutants or the media that the campaign had been planned by a tobacco company.

Since then numerous commercial enterprises, including tobacco, car and detergent companies, have used psychology to persuade individuals to buy products and indeed change their habits.

Sources: Ewen (1996), Tye (1998).

Mini case 16.2

Dichter and the introduction of the Barbie Doll™

In 1945 Ruth and Elliott Handler formed a company called Mattel Creations (with a partner, Harold Matson, who had left the partnership by 1946). With their expertise in the use of plastics the Handlers developed several toy products. However it was the 1950s that was to have a serious impact on Mattel Creations. This was the time of the post-Second World War baby boom, a significant change in the demographics of both the United States and Europe. By the mid-1950s children's television was witnessing a boom, thanks largely to the work of Walt Disney who realised that it provided huge opportunities for both programming and promotion. The Handlers also realised that television had tremendous potential for their products, and with the help of Walt Disney and ABC Television they used the medium wisely to promote their range of products.

The Handlers had seen a German doll called Lilli, based loosely on a comic strip character. It was aimed at an adult audience, as Lilli was portrayed as 'sexy and immoral', and thus became something of a sexual icon for men. The Handlers believed there was a market for a doll for older children that was different from those for very young children, but clearly Lilli was not the one. They experimented with different forms. However finding the right image would, they knew, be only one part of the battle; they also had to find and convince their target market. It was at this point that they engaged Ernest Ditcher to advise on their marketing plan.

The doll Mattel designed was named Barbie™ after the Handlers' daughter Barbara. Ditcher spent six months researching the project. A key concern was parents' objection to their child playing with in essence a 'grown up' doll with adult-style clothes. Ditcher's research suggested that Barbie™ had to be made 'wholesome and thus innocent as a babe in arms'.

Barbie™ became a role model 'to guide American daughters through puberty into adulthood. Barbie™ is a beautiful single girl, happy and independent. Her life is picture perfect, unspoilt by the demands made on housewives and mothers.'

To support this life style Mattel created and developed an entire life for Barbie™. She was the teenage fashion model, virtuous and glamorous – in essence what every young American girl wanted to be. She not only became an icon (indeed a brand icon), she also became the biggest selling toy product.

Barbie™ has not remained living in a vacuum: she has changed with societal changes and attitudes. She has had a 'relationship' with another doll called Ken (named after the Handlers' son) and they have gone their separate ways. Perhaps this is very reflective of societal changes in Europe and North America.

Although there is competition in the marketplace, Mattel realise that even at 46 (her 'age' in 2005), Barbie™ competing against 'younger' girl dolls has been reflective of changing societal trends.

Source: 'Barbie always a living doll', *American Antiques Journal*, 2003.

---

research (see Chapter 4). Like Bernays, he applied Freudian thinking to business and marketing. Through his Institute of Motivational Research, he was able to investigate ways of motivating consumers to purchase an ever-increasing array of mass-produced products.

Behavioural aspects

Behavioural psychologists tend to see human behaviour as a response to environmental stimuli, while phenomena such as thought, intention and emotion are subjective and minimal in their effect. One of the leading theorists of behavioural psychology was Burrhus. F. Skinner (1904–1990). Skinner was a leading American psychologist whose research concluded that a history of reinforcing

actions determined behaviour. In other words by controlling the rewards (positive reinforcement) and punishments (negative reinforcements) in response to particular behaviours, behaviour could be 'shaped'. This has become known as operant conditioning. Thus behaviour could, according to Skinner's research, be modified or conditioned.

Table 16.1 gives an example of how behaviour can be modified through both positive and negative reinforcement. Positive reinforcement is where the frequency of response increases as a direct result of a rewarding stimulus, in the example, praise from the lecturer for the delivery of course work on time. The opposite of this is negative reinforcement, where the frequency of response increases as a direct result of the removal of an unpleasant stimulus. In Table 16.1 this is the 'removal' of criticism of

Table 16.1 An example of reinforcing behaviour

Reinforcement behaviour		
Positive reinforcement		
Behaviour	Consequence	Future behaviour
Approach 1		
You submit your marketing module assignment at the required time at the undergraduate office.	Your lecturer says well done for meeting the deadline. (This may be either a public or private display of congratulations. Either way we will assume for the point of this exercise that it is affirming and supportive.)	You seek to meet the required deadline for submission with all your assignments.
Negative reinforcement		
Behaviour	Consequence	Future behaviour
Approach 2		
You submit your marketing module assignment at the required time at the undergraduate office.	Your lecturer stops criticising you for the late submission of your coursework. Additionally, you are not penalised with a loss of marks for late submission.	You seek to meet the required deadline for submission with all your assignments.

Source: adapted from Santrock (2000).

you by your lecturer and, of course, the downgrading of the assignment because of its late submission.

Reinforcement can be separated into various subsets, which are outlined in Table 16.2.

Reinforcements can be scheduled or timetabled. Table 16.3 outlines the four components that comprise a schedule of reinforcement.

Of course not all behavioural psychologists agree with Skinner's view of rejecting the level of impact of an individual's thought processes. Albert Bandura (1925–), for instance, proposed a social cognitive theory of human functioning in which behaviour is determined not only by its controlling environmental conditions but also by how thoughts modify the impact of the environment (Santrock 2000). Bandura believed that individuals are self-organising, proactive, self-regulating and self-reflecting, and not only shaped by external environmental forces, as Skinner suggests, or

driven by deeper hidden desires and impulses, as Freud suggests. The theory also suggests that individuals actually regulate their own behaviour and motivations as a result of the positive and negative consequences of their own actions. Individuals seek activities or objectives that provide a degree of satisfaction and self-worth (or self-esteem – see the discussion on Maslow below). Conversely they reject activities or objectives that may undermine their self-worth.

However, as Bandura intimates individuals do not exist in isolation; they tend to work collectively. This links into his more recent work where he considered the power of psychological modelling in shaping human thought, emotions and actions. This includes how individuals and groups are influenced by messages communicated via various media. Consider, for example, how television advertising can be used to persuade a segmented audience to purchase a particular brand of car.

Table 16.2 Types of reinforcement

Type of reinforcement	Description
Primary	Reinforcements that are innately satisfying, in other words an individual does not have to engage in learning to make them satisfying. Examples include the consumption of basic need items such as food and water.
Secondary	Reinforcements that are attained through experience. In other words they are learned or conditioned reinforcers. For example, a credit card company awards bonus points or 'rewards' when the card owner purchases products or services on that particular card. It also acts an incentive to purchase more products and services on that credit card.
Continuous	The response is reinforced every time reinforcement occurs. For example, people continue to visit a particular restaurant, on a regular basis, because of the personal service they receive on each visit. The quality of the service reinforces their behaviour. Added value provided by the restaurant, for example, additional complementary drinks, will help to further reinforce the behaviour.
Partial	A response is reinforced occasionally rather than continuously. An individual entering a weekly lottery is unlikely to win every week, but might win small sums on an occasional basis. This response will usually be sufficient for him or her to carry on buying tickets in the hope of winning something. The person probably still has his or her sights on the 'big' win at some time in the future, even though it might never come his or her way.

Table 16.3 Schedules of reinforcing behaviour

Type of schedule	Description
Fixed ratio	The behaviour is reinforced either after a set number of specific responses or at a fixed time interval. With a credit card, additional bonus points may be awarded if spending exceeds a specific amount within a given time frame, for instance a month. This may encourage the owner to spend more on the card to gain the additional bonus points or the chance to win a prize (for example, a luxury vacation for two and spending money).
Variable ratio	The responses are rewarded on an unpredictable basis. For example a company celebrating its 25th anniversary tells its customers that for the anniversary month only every 30th customer who buys online will receive a special gift. The customers purchasing online will not know whether they are the 30th customer or not, but most likely there will be a steady stream of customers making online purchases in the hope that they will be lucky, especially if it is a high-value prize.
Fixed interval	Behaviour is reinforced after a specific period of time. With a credit card, cardholders may receive additional bonus points six or twelve months after taking out the card, perhaps subject to their having used it regularly and paid the statutory minimum amount by the due date.
Variable interval	The behaviour is reinforced after a variable time period. An example here is an attempt to give up smoking. At times the smoker might abstain from smoking, but at moments he or she might relent and smoke. This could be viewed as peaks and troughs in the act of giving up. The long-term gain may be having given up smoking permanently. Although there are chemical-based supports (nicotine gums and patches) it is after all a matter of personal will that will break the habit.

Humanistic approach

In often sharp contrast to both the psychoanalytical and behavioural approaches there developed the humanistic approach to psychology. This approach places emphasis on individuals' capacity for personal growth, the development of a positive attitude and the freedom to choose their own actions and destiny. This is very much concerned with motivation.

One of the leading architects of this movement was American psychologist Abraham Maslow (1908–1970). You probably have already encountered Maslow's Hierarchy of Needs in organisational studies. The Hierarchy of Needs (see Table 16.4) is equally applicable to the marketing environment. In Maslow's original concept lower-order needs have to be fulfilled or satisfied before higher needs or desires can be satisfied. So, for example, our basic physiological needs (for instance food and water) must be substantiated before we can consider issues of self-esteem and above.

Normally Maslow's Hierarchy of Needs is depicted as a pyramid with self- actualisation at the pinnacle and physiological needs at the base. Here it is presented in tabular form to illustrate both the humanistic and marketing perspectives. It must be understood that as well as moving upwards, an individual can also move downwards. An individual might normally have strong self-esteem, but a series of negative life events could significantly reduce it. Therefore the hierarchy must not been seen as a rigid system, more one of fluidity.

For instance, there might be a downturn in the economy (see Chapter 2). This leads to people being made redundant, which in turn shatters their self-esteem. They in essence 'fall down' the hierarchy and focus upon their basic needs until they can rebuild their lives. This was exemplified in the late 1980s in the United Kingdom with a stock market crash and recession. While it had an impact on all groups in society, it was the middle class who were hit the hardest. Many had purchased large mortgages to acquire homes at vastly inflated prices. When the market collapsed the value of their properties fell dramatically, leaving many with negative equity. With the recession many companies closed, resulting in redundancy, and thus reducing people's ability to continue their mortgage repayments. In such cases people's lifestyles can changes significantly,

and people who had not been particularly price-sensitive in the past become so.

The cognitive approach

'Cognitive' originates from the Latin 'cognitio', meaning to apprehend or to know. The Latin word 'cogito', which has a similar derivation, means 'I think', and is the principle of establishing the existence of individual from their thinking or awareness. The French philosopher René Descartes (1596–1650) expressed this truth in his Cartesian formula, often known as the Cogito argument – 'Cogito, ergo sum' – 'I am thinking, therefore I exist'. Cottingham (1995) suggests that 'the certainty of Cogito is, for Descartes, a curiously temporary affair: 'I can be sure of my existence only for as long as I am thinking.' This philosophy goes to the core of the cognitive approach.

In the cognitive approach an individual's mind acquires, represents and uses knowledge – it is viewed as an active problem-solving system. Thus such an approach will encompass sensation, perception, reasoning, learning, comprehension, memory and problem-solving facilities.

The cognitive approach was influenced by the work of Swiss psychologist Jean Piaget (1896–1980), who conducted research into how children reasoned and their changing perceptions of their external environment. Piaget believed that individuals' learning was based on the progressive structuring of experience – through trial and error – rather than on environmental conditioning as proposed by the behaviourist approach (see mini case 16.3, overleaf).

Here learning can be both experiential and cognitive. Experiential learning can be considered as learning through doing, while cognitive learning can be described as problem-solving learning. An example of cognitive learning is how a family approaches buying a new car. They might consider several factors to help them solve the problem of which model to buy, including price range, how to pay for the new car, type of car (saloon, hatchback, estate), make of car, features and benefits of each make of car being considered, and the future resale value.

Cognitive dissonance

The cognitive approach encompasses sensation, perception, reasoning, learning, comprehension,

Table 16.4 The relationship between Maslow's hierarchy of needs and marketing

Hierarchy of motives – behavioural motivator	Humanistic perspective	Marketing perspective
Self-actualisation	Individuals strive to develop their full potential. Maslow believed that this was the highest form of need and the most difficult to reach.	A university, for instance, could market doctoral programmes as a means of individuals achieving the pivotal point of academic success.
Self-esteem	Belief in one's self, often described as self-worth.	Self-esteem may be exemplified in the goods or services an individual purchases: perhaps a luxury watch costing UK£5000 to demonstrate wealth and the ability to live lavishly. Companies market products and services (such as luxury vacations) by tapping people's need to reinforce their self-esteem, perhaps to indicate that they have 'made it'.
Love and belongingness	Wanting to belong to a particular group and or be involved in the dating process.	This can include the sending of cards, flowers and/or gifts. It can also mean joining a club, group and/or dating agency. All these are marketed to segmented groups.
Safety	The feeling of being secure, for example, in our homes, at our place of work and when we walk down the street.	This ranges from the local police force 'marketing' its presence to the engagement of local security guards (as in some US hotels and neighbourhoods), and the development and marketing of personal protective equipment such as personal protection alarms and biological/radiation protection suits (as witnessed in the United States after the 9/11 attacks and the ensuing fear of a biological/nuclear terrorist attack). A university might market itself on the differential value that it has a very safe campus environment. This would appeal to students who are away from home for the first time, as well as their parents.
Physiological	Basic needs for survival within the environment in which the individual lives.	This includes the availability of produce from the local market or supermarket.

Direction of fulfilment or satisfaction

memory and problem-solving facilities; but this suggests that such activities operate as a constant. When we buy products or services we often have to balance the positive and negative aspects of them against others.

Festinger (1957) developed the idea of cognitive dissonance (see Chapter 10). Think back to the family attempting to decide on a new car. Dissonance may occur as an element of post-purchase behaviour. The family buying the car, for instance, might reflect on the positive features of the alternative models they did not buy, and the negative aspects of the car they actually chose. It is these 'differences' between the two alternatives that cause the dissonance.

The cognitive approach and marketing shampoo

A company may decide to launch a new range of shampoo. It is aware it is entering a highly competitive marketplace, and that customers may be 'loyal' to a particular brand. A customer might also not want to invest in a large bottle of the new shampoo just in case he or she uses it once and does not like it.

The company could introduce trial-size sachets. These might form part of a door-drop promotion, be attached to the cover of a magazine, and/or be made available free in stores. This form of promotion allows potential customers to trial the product prior to deciding whether or not to purchase, for instance a 500 ml bottle. If the company decides on product line extensions, sachets can be attached to the bottle of the already established shampoo so that customers can trial the new product.

Williams (1992) suggests that the degree of dissonance will depend on several factors:

◆ The level of significance an individual places on the purchasing decision: the greater the significance, the greater the degree of dissonance. Therefore the dissonance may be relatively high for items such as a luxury cruise vacation or a diamond engagement ring.

◆ The more attractive the attributes of the rejected alternative compared to the chosen one, the greater the degree of dissonance.

◆ The greater the negative attributes of the chosen one compared with the alternatives, the greater the degree of dissonance.

◆ The greater the range of alternatives available to the buyer, the greater the degree of dissonance. As the number of positive alternatives increases, so does the number of positive characteristics that will have to be rejected.

Evolutionary approach

As the word 'evolutionary' suggests, this approach emphasizes adaptation, reproduction and the 'survival of the fittest' in explaining individual and group behaviour. Pinker (1997) suggests that the mind operates in an evolutionary format, learning, developing and adapting from experience in order to survive. Of course, so the argument develops, organisms that do not evolve or develop fail to survive.

We could argue here that experience, memory and learning can be the basis of such an evolutionary approach. We gain experiences over time, and these can be viewed as a series of mini learning events, although not all such events will be small. These events might be small and repetitious such as buying a coffee on the way to college or university first thing in the morning. Perhaps you find the coffee is of increasingly poor quality and taste, or it even begins to make you feel ill. Therefore you seek, through this experience, to adapt to the changing conditions and either find another outlet or stop buying coffee on the way to college.

Another example in relation to evolutionary psychology and marketing is eating healthy food and keeping fit. People who eat healthy food and keep fit look and feel better. This will in turn persuade them to continue with the healthy eating. This has further reinforcing effects in terms of friendships, meeting people and shopping for clothes that complement their healthy look. As this continues and evolves, the health regime becomes a key component of their lifestyle. Therefore we adapt to the circumstances and changing environment.

Social psychology

Social psychology focuses on an individual's social thinking, influence and relationships. This is born out of the need to understand the combination of culture, ethnicity and gender. Social psychology or the socio-cultural approach emphasizes that culture, ethnicity and gender are essential to understanding behaviour, thought and emotion (Santrock 2000). The components can thus be described as:

◆ Culture – Mühlbacher *et al.* (1999) define culture as 'the standards of belief, perceptions, evaluation and behaviour shared by the members of a social group'. In their definition they also refer to Hofstede (1994), who defines culture as the 'collective programming of minds' which distinguishes one group from another.

◆ Ethnicity – this originates from the Greek word 'ethnos', which means nation, and focuses on a social group that shares a common nation, traditions, heritage, characteristics, religion (though not always – there may be multiple religions), race and language (though dialects will vary within nations).

◆ Gender – Grimshaw (1999) describes gender as:

> a social construction of male/female identity which is distinguished from sex, the biologically based distinction between men and women. Gender is an integral part of the process of social classification and organisation. It is both a set of ideas (a away of thinking about relations, of influencing behaviour, a set of symbols) and a principle of social organisation (allocation to roles and division of labour).

It is useful to explore here the term 'role' in relation to gender. Raban and Torrance (1999) describe 'role' as the 'bundling of formal and predictable attributes associated with a particular social position, as distinct from the individual characteristics of the individual who occupies that position'. In terms of gender it has often been associated with the man going to work and the woman staying at home to care for the family. These have, in many countries, become stereotypical roles which are often exploited by society as a whole.

Out of these develop our individual reaction to social thinking, influence and relationships.

■ The relationship between psychology and marketing

The above has provided a brief outline of the main approaches to psychology and some of the key contributors to those approaches. Already you have perhaps begun to see some of the possible links to marketing. The remainder of this chapter is devoted to some of the drivers that underpin why we buy products and services. This is not an exhaustive commentary. However, as you reflect back over the previous chapters you should be able to see how psychology has an influence (often a significant one) in how products and services are marketed to us. Moreover, you should also see how we react to those influences through our purchasing behaviour.

■ Categories of buyer behaviour

In order to develop an understanding of buyer behaviour it is worth attempting to categorise the drivers for that behaviour. However, there needs to be a word of warning here. It is very easy to fall into the trap of thinking that an individual is influenced by one category and one category only. That is not the case. As we have seen earlier in this chapter, the human mind is an extremely complex system, which is still not fully understood, and might never be. Therefore it is rational to say that an individual may be influenced by some or all of the factors. Indeed there may be factors that might influence buyer behaviour that have not, for one reason or another, been included by researchers.

People

We are influenced to a greater or lesser extent by the people we consider part of our lives. We may know them either directly or indirectly. Those we know directly include friends, family, teachers, neighbours and co-workers. Those we know indirectly are usually people we admire, aspire to be or call our heroes, be they football players, pop stars or actors. Both direct and indirect contacts can have an enormous influence upon our lives.

Let us unpack this section by subdividing it into three subsets:

◆ immediate family

◆ relatives

◆ friends.

However, while they are examined as individual subsets there is most likely to be some form of cross-influence. Equally, other factors such as culture will have an influence.

Immediate family

When considering the influence of the family you will need to examine it from various cultural standpoints. For instance, the cultural history of the family, where they live now and how contemporary culture influences the family as a whole and its different members.

For instance, if we look at the dynamics of family life in the United Kingdom since the 1960s there have been significant changes. The stereotypical view of a nuclear family where the husband is employed and the wife stays at home to look after the house and family has generally faded. This equally applies to the husband making all the decisions for the family.

Women have become career oriented and independent. Households are not stereotypically comprised of a husband, wife and two children. There is a greater number of childless couples living together, as opposed to being married. Many families only have one child. Decisions are increasingly made collectively, so even children may have an influence, or at least a contribution to make to a significant purchase. In the UK in 2002 one car company aired television advertisements where it was the young girl who was the influencer in the purchase of a new car.

Family experiences, both positive and negative, can subsequently influence our behaviour. Companies often reflect back on people's childhood experience to market to them a similar product as they become adults. For instance, consider the warming bowl of soup you may have been given by your parents after being out in the cold, perhaps playing a sport. The bowl of soup not only helped to warm you up but there were probably several psychological actions underpinning the experience. These range from basic environmental comforts such as warmth and safety through to love and affection from your parents (reflect back on Maslow's hierarchy of needs).

Manufacturers of soup and similar types of food have used such childhood experiences to promote their products. The objective is for viewers to reflects back to their childhood and the importance of a bowl of soup in their lives. When they then go shopping they might buy soup because it reflects security and affection as well as nourishment. However, they may not necessarily buy the brand they saw in the television advertisement, preferring perhaps an own-label brand if they are price-sensitive.

Mini case 16.4 again makes a psychological connection to childhood and the relationship between a grandfather and his grandson.

Relatives

As Groucutt, Leadley and Forsyth (2004) stated:

> The level of influence may depend upon the 'closeness' of the family in emotional terms, and their ethnicity. Families, for example, of Indian or West Indian origin tend to be more closely-knit. Here various members of the family be they grandparents, uncles, aunts, cousins and so on can have an impact upon the decisions of others.

Again, while in some cultures there may be both a physical and emotional closeness, this will not be the same in all cases.

The development of, for instance, mass transportation and widening job opportunities has seen

---

Mini case 16.4

Werther's Originals

In 1903 the Wertherian Candy company (later to be renamed August Storck) was established in Werther, Germany. Originally the company produced a mixed caramel and cream candy without giving it a brand name. As brands were developed Storck chose a product line to be named Werther's Echte (original). In 1998 this was rebranded as Werther's Original to provide a universal appeal.

The advertising storyline for the brand focuses on the relationship between a grandfather and his grandson. In many ways the grandfather can be described as 'everyone's favourite grandfather'. He is the image we would all like our grandfathers to be, whether ours actually fits this mould or not. In the series of advertisements the grandfather explains the tradition of eating Werther's original from one generation to another. Once again there is a sense of tradition, of security, of love and affection. The candy becomes the link over the generations.

As of 2005 Werther's Originals is one of the leading caramel and cream candies in the world. It is sold in over 80 countries and is Storck's most successful brand worldwide.

Source: www.storck.com.

families fragment as individuals move away from the family home. Relatives may maintain some influence over distance (especially with the use of email) – but this is likely to diminish across generations.

Friends

Friends can be a significant influence on our behaviour especially in two key ways:

◆ We trust our real friends to give us their honest opinion, as we would them. This trust element may remain with us for the rest of our lives. Chapter 10 on promotion cited the work of Rosen (2000) in relation to the power of word of mouth, or buzz. Rosen states that '47% of readers of *Surfing Magazine* (USA) say that the biggest influence on their decision about where to surf and what to purchase comes from a friend'.

◆ The need for friendship. This may lead us to want to be one of the 'group' and thus buy into how the group operates, for example, through the fashion clothes that the group wears. However there is a risk of group think. Santrock (2000) describes this as 'involving impaired decision making and avoidance of realistic appraisal to maintain group harmony'. An example is where the group wear a particular fashion brand, and to be a member of that group you have to purchase that fashion brand. That might be financially advantageous for the fashion brand, but it raises some ethical issues, particularly where young children are concerned. A primary school in England in the late 1990s banned major brands of trainers because children who did not wear a particular brand were 'excluded' by other children. Such 'exclusion' placed enormous pressure on the children and their parents.

Culture

Culture is often described as the norms, attitudes and beliefs of a particular nation or group. The essence of culture varies throughout the world. It is diverse and in many ways ever-changing and adapting to external influences and pressures (both positive and negative). Depending upon who we

are and where we live, this may have a greater or lesser influence upon our lives. Some cultures have a very strong influence, whereas others are much weaker. This relative strength or influence can range from the types of foods that are consumed to the style of gifts purchased for family members.

Lifestyle

Lifestyles can be both real and aspirational. We may, as individuals, be content with our lifestyles, and purchase products and services that fit our particular lifestyle. Equally we may be aspirational, seeking a lifestyle that reflects how we really want to live. At this point you may want to reflect back to Maslow's Hierarchy of Needs, especially the issues of self-actualisation.

Financial and economic influences

Clearly our personal financial circumstances dictate or influence our buyer behaviour, to a greater or lesser degree. Consider the following scenarios.

◆ Example 1: people who are unemployed and living on state benefits may be aspirational in outlook. However, they have to live within

Figure 16.2

© Jonathan Groucutt

People purchase products and services that fulfil their particular lifestyle. In this photograph some people have relatively small boats compared with others in the marina. They may be content with their lifestyle, or they might aspire to one day owning a luxury yacht like the one in the background.

their financial constraints at that particular point in time, and this will make them particularly price sensitive. Thus they seek to maximise the benefits of their purchases with what little money they have. In the majority of cases their disposable funds will be used to purchase essential items, such as food. When they become fully employed again, with a regular salary, their buying habits may adapt to their increased weekly income. They may not be as price sensitive as before, and should be able to purchase a wider range of products, not just basic necessities.

◆ Example 2: in example 1 individuals living on state benefits focused their limited financial resources on the basic necessities, but that is not always the case. People might try to balance the basic necessities with what they describe as 'personal luxuries', ranging from a bar of chocolate to alcohol to gambling. The latter might be not just a 'personal luxury' but a vain hope that a significant win on a racehorse or the lottery will provide riches and thus create a better life. (It should be noted here that the vast majority of the world's population in countries where gambling is legal dreams of winning a lottery fortune, for instance.)

◆ Example 3: entrepreneurs who have turned an idea into a product that dominates the market usually reap the rewards of their success, both emotionally and financially. An individual who has achieved such success will have financial stability, and thus purchasing power. However, normally financial limits still apply. Even multimillionaires have faced bankruptcy as a result of living (or spending) beyond their financial limits.

Having access to financial resources does not mean that an individual will use those resources fully. There has been a tendency, in the West at least, for those with significant financial resources to use that wealth to display their social standing, for example living in large houses. This is not always the case. Some will be ostentatious, others not.[4]

The changing economic fortunes or a region or country must also be considered here. Chapter 2 reviewed the macro factors through the PESTLE model, where economics acts as an externality that influences both individuals and organisations.

Consider, for instance, the impact on individual buyer behaviour when a country moves through the economic cycle from growth to recession. In the 1990s in the United Kingdom, all socio-economic groups were affected by the recession that took place. Individuals and families that used the value of their homes as collateral for increased borrowings (loans and credit cards) often saw the value of their properties decline significantly relative to their borrowings. With increasing insecurity within the job market, this led many to face the potential risk of personal bankruptcy. The experience of this recessionary period led many to be price-sensitive and to control their individual spending limits. This was particularly noticeable with the UK's middle classes. Their behaviour was influenced, it could be argued, by the fear of losing everything they had worked to achieve. This would have a detrimental impact on their individual self-esteem.

What is interesting to note, however, is the possible change in behaviour as the UK economy experienced strong growth, aligned with low inflation and interest rates. Since 2001 there has been a significant increase in personal debt, alongside increasing property values. By 2005 the level of personal debt in the UK was calculated in trillions of euros!

Fear

This can be viewed on two levels: as a result of macro events (such as the threat of terrorist attacks) and micro events – for instance, safety from crime.

Macro level

During the 1950s a climate of fear developed as a result of the Cold War, a period when the West and the Soviet Union viewed each other with immense suspicion. This led to the build-up of nuclear arsenals, a legacy that remains with us today. The Cold War lasted until the 1980s, when relationships improved and there was an active move to reduce the arsenals, although they remain substantial. During this period there were degrees of fear over whether the world would be plunged into a devastating nuclear conflagration.

The peaceful revolution that swept through Eastern Europe in the 1990s significantly reduced the fear of a nuclear war between the superpowers. However, the aftermath of the Twin Towers attack in New York on 11 September 2001 has once more created a climate of fear. Various reports from the US administration on the threat of biological, chemical and nuclear attacks from terrorists resulted in a rush by ordinary American citizens to purchase a range of products and services, from stocking up on canned foods to purchasing biological protection suits.

Micro level

The micro level can be sub-divided into three areas:

- local crime
- safety online
- future financial security.

Local crime

The fear of crime (real and perceived) at the local level can have a profound effect on individuals, families and communities. To reduce this fear individuals and groups purchase a range of products and services to protect themselves and their property. These range (depending on the country they live in and their economic status) from alarm systems and paper shredders to handguns and personal protection teams.

In the United Kingdom concerns over personal identity theft have led to a significant rise in the number of paper shredders bought in the consumer market. Previously shredders were the domain of the B2B environment, but the rise of identity crime created a new consumer market for low-cost shredders.

Safety online

Partially linked to the threat of identity theft, there is the risk from hackers even on personal computers. Internet service providers (ISPs) have built in safety features to protect users from hackers and potentially offensive sites (through parental controls). Online banks and organisations that provide online payments incorporate additional levels of security (encryption) against hackers. However, as hackers increase their skill, ISP and online organisations have to improve their expert security systems. This appears, at the moment, to be an ongoing battle. Media coverage of high-profile incidents, such as attacks on bank accounts,

have increased not only consumer awareness but their fears as well.

Future financial security

We perhaps all dream of a long life and financial security into our old age, although worries of financial security may not become paramount in a person's mind until they reach their 30s. However, increasingly in highly developed nations there is concern about future financial security. There is a view that unless individuals invest at a much younger age, they will not have savings or pensions that will deliver a comfortable standard of living in their retirement years. This has been a particular debate in the United Kingdom, and both insurance companies and the government have been encouraging younger people to invest in their future early. The approach has often been based on the fear of little income in the future, when they actually retire.

Media

The media has a tremendous influence on our lives, for it is from the media that we gain daily information on events in and beyond our own country. Global reporting may influence our beliefs in terms of the macro factors (see Chapter 2). Equally it can influence our buying habits. Chapter 10 on promotions described how various techniques can influence our buyer behaviour, ranging from advertising through to point of sale and public relations.

It is key here to understand that promotion or marketing communications can use psychology to influence our decision making (as we have already seen with the work of Edward Bernays). However, in order to avoid such issues as cognitive dissonance the media messages must not be used to exaggerate the positive features of the product or service. Clearly, if the media message persuades customers to purchase a product and it does not live up to the claims made, customers will judge it negatively. This in turn may lead to no further purchases and possibly a complaint. In addition, disgruntled customers may use word of mouth and viral communication (via Internet user groups and chat rooms) to vent their dislike of the product or service.

Price

Psychology permeates several pricing decisions, such as prestige pricing, odd–even pricing, single/double pricing and even sale items (see Chapter 11, and Figure 16.3). Even when it comes to the relationship between 'value' and 'price' we are making a psychological judgment. For example, a person who pays €250 000 for a sports car is not only seeking quality and performance from the car, but also seeking a psychological value for him or herself and in the eyes of others.

Necessities

Maslow's hierarchy (see page 334) drew attention to our physiological needs. We can translate these into the basic necessities people must have in order to live. For most people this covers items such as basic foods and shelter. However, we can argue that for millionaires the basics are very different from the basics for those living at subsistence level. Therefore we have to interpret 'necessities' in relation to the society and people's position within it (for want of a better phrase).

Figure 16.3

© Jonathan Groucutt

A sale at a London men's clothing store. There are significant reductions prominently displayed. However the buyer will still be making a psychological judgment in relation to 'value' and 'price'. The objective is to make the right decision and avoid cognitive dissonance.

■ Chapter summary

This chapter has introduced the idea of psychology as another 'P' in the marketing mix, because psychological behaviour underpins a significant proportion of buyer behaviour and thus marketing. Psychology is a major discipline in its own right, and only a snapshot can be given in a general marketing text. However, it is clear that psychology has and continues to be a major contribution not only to marketing in itself, but also to how we, as individuals, make our daily decisions. On this basis consider how psychology influences not only your buyer behaviour but everything else that is discussed with this text, from branding and pricing through to the shape of packaging.

■ Questions for review and reflection

1   Maslow's theory suggests several levels of need. Outline his hierarchy and suggest how the different levels apply to buying a family car.

2   Using the Internet and library resources, critically evaluate how and why culture can be core to an individual's decision to purchase a product or service.

3   Bernays was able to change attitudes to women smoking in public through his 'Women and Smoking' campaign. Can you (a) think of a campaign that used similar techniques to persuade the public to change their attitude to certain products or services, and (b) think of a product that could benefit from such a campaign? Justify your choice.

4   Reflect on two or three purchases you have made over the past month – perhaps clothing, CDs, games or a DVD. Consider the degree of cognitive dissonance. Was it significant, marginal or nonexistent? If there was significant cognitive dissonance, could you have prevented it? If so, what preventive action could you have taken?

5   Do you think psychology is used to promote any of the following brands? If so how?

Ford Motor Company

Haagen-Dazs ice cream

Cunard cruise line.

6 At the beginning of this chapter you were presented with three questions that also appeared at the start of Chapter 1. Explore these questions and consider how psychological influences may have affected your decision making. You may also want to consider if there was any cognitive dissonance post purchase.

■ References

Cottingham, J. (1995) 'Rene Descartes' in T. Honderich (ed.), *The Oxford Companion to Philosophy*, Oxford: Oxford University Press.

Festinger, L. (1957) *A Theory of Cognitive Dissonance*, Stanford, Conn.: Stanford University Press.

Grimshaw, A. (1999) 'Gender', in A. Bullock and S. Trombley (eds), *The New Fontana Dictionary of Modern Thought*, London: HarperCollins.

Groucutt, J., Leadley, P. and Forsyth, P. (2004) *Marketing: Essential principles, new realities*, London: Kogan Page.

Hofstede, G. (1994) 'The business of international business is culture', *International Business Review* **3**(1), pp. 1–14.

Mühlbacher, H., Dahringer, L. and Leihs, H. (1999) *International Marketing: A global perspective*, 2nd edn, London: International Thomson Business Press.

Pinker, S (1997) *How The Mind Works*, New York: Norton.

Raban, J. and Torrance, J. (1999) 'Roles and role theory', in A. Bullock and S. Trombley (eds), *The New Fontana Fontana Dictionary of Modern Thought*, London: HarperCollins.

Rosen, E. (2000) *The Anatomy of Buzz: Creating word-of-mouth marketing*, London: HarperCollins Business.

Santrock, J. W (2000) *Psychology*, 6th edn, Boston, Mass.: McGraw-Hill.

Williams, K. C. (1992) *Behavioural Aspects of Marketing*, Oxford: Butterworth-Heinemann.

Performance

17

CHAPTER

Contents

Learning outcomes   344
Introduction   344
What is performance?   344
Measured
  performance   346
Product or service
  performance   346
Brand performance   346
Revenue performance
  and sales
  performance   347
Market share   348
Distribution and
  logistics   349
Marketing plans   349
Experiential
  performance   349
Quadrant 1: passive
  participation–
  entertainment–
  absorption   350
Quadrant 2: active
  participation–
  educational–
  absorption   350
Quadrant 3: active
  participation–
  escapist–immersion   351
Quadrant 4: passive
  participation–esthetic
  (aesthetic)–immersion 343
Experience is a dynamic
  function   354
Future issues   354
Chapter summary   355
Questions for review
  and reflection   355
References   356

Learning outcomes

After completing this chapter you should be able to:

▶ debate the reasons for including performance within the marketing mix framework

▶ explain the different types of performance measures that can be used to gauge the success or failure of a marketing activity

▶ examine the methodology behind brand equity and brand values.

■ Introduction

This chapter examines the role of 'performance' both in marketing as a whole and as an integral component of the marketing mix. In Chapter 8 the development of the marketing mix was considered. Research indicates that the role of 'performance' has previously been considered in relation to the development of the marketing mix. Yudelson (1999), for instance, suggested that 'product' be redefined as 'performance'. He believes that this redefinition:

> Conveys the sense of benefit to the customer. The 'performance' of the tangible product or the proffered service is what generates the benefit to the customer. Alternate forms of 'performance' create product lines. Branding, as a value-adding part of the product, 'performs' by reducing search time or by guaranteeing expectations. 'Performance' over time is thus the basis for an enduring relationship and trust.

While it is not suggested in this text that product should be redefined as performance, Yudelson (1999) provides an insight into other areas that could be categorised under performance: the performance of the product/service itself, and the brand. While these are considered in this chapter, additional indicators are also examined.

■ What is performance?

The *Oxford English Reference Dictionary* (Pearsall and Trumble, 1996) provides various definitions of the word 'performance':

The act or process of performing or carrying out.

The execution or fulfilment (of a duty etc.)

A staging or production (of a drama, piece of music etc).

A person's achievement under test conditions.

The capabilities of a machine.

A fuss or a scene; a public exhibition.

Of high capability.

In finance the return on an investment.

There are many other definitions or perspectives. As the definitions indicate, the word 'performance' has many connotations. These range from how well an orchestra played at a concert to what grade you achieved in your last assignment. They are both performances requiring skills, knowledge and an outcome. In both cases the 'performance' creates a 'reaction'. This reaction can be both qualitative and quantitative. In the case of the orchestral performance, the audience's reaction will be qualitative to the performance. On the other hand a musicologist reading the score during the performance may be more analytical or quantitative in his or her approach. Both have a value. A professor marking your assignment will consider your overall performance both qualitatively and quantitatively. Did you, for instance, use the appropriate data sets and analyse them effectively? Did you express your own opinion in the work and substantiate your views?

As you can see from these brief examples, we are all involved in creating 'performance' in one form or another. Moreover, this chapter shows that a performance can also be an 'experience'. For instance, your time as a student is an 'experience' – hopefully an enjoyable and rewarding one. You along with your tutors are involved to varying degrees in performances. They perform to convey to you ideas and concepts. You perform in terms of your work, presentation and examinations. The quality of the performances may or may not vary. Just as with a business, the quality of the performance will be affected by both internal and external forces. Organisations (including companies or governments) survive, develop or die on the basis of their performance – what they have achieved (or not, as may be the case).

From the definitions performance can be considered as two interconnected arenas, measured and experiences (see Figure 17.1). Measured, as we shall discuss later, relates to the quantifiable part of the performance. Reflecting back on the example of you, the student, your performance in an examination is measured by the mark or grade awarded. Experiences, on the other hand, are more qualified.

However, that does not mean that there cannot be some form of measurement linked to the experience. For instance, you may visit the cinema and watch the movie *Spider-Man 2*™, becoming totally enthralled by the visual effects and the dramatic roller-coaster rides. Being in a darkened cinema watching this movie is an escapist experience. You have watched a performance created by numerous people both in front of and behind the camera, including the marketing team who promoted the movie to a mass audience. Although this is an 'experience' you could quantify it by rating it alongside the first *Spider-Man*™ movie. You might choose to rate the overall experiences with a straight comparison between movies one and two. Alternatively, you could compare and contrast the various elements that come together to make a movie – acting, script, sets, music, special effects and so forth. Each could then be rated to provide an overall score for each movie. This would, to some degree, measure your experience of the performance of the two movies.

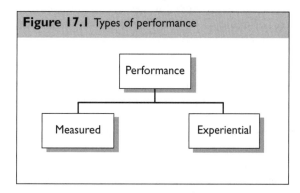

Figure 17.1 Types of performance

The remainder of this chapter is divided into two major sections: measured performances and experiential performances. The division is necessary for the purposes of explanation. However, as illustrated above, they should not be considered in isolation. Thus when you reflect upon these issues consider the possible linkages between the two.

■ Measured performance

Often one of the criticisms levelled at marketing is that it is not measurable; rather, that it is a drain on resources, being a cost, rather than a profit centre. This is a negative approach to marketing as both a subject and a practice. Marketing, as with accounting, can and should be a measurable entity. The performance of the marketing investment should be measured. Only by analysing performance can a marketer really know whether or not there will be a realistic return on investment and the level of market share.

This performance measurement should not be confined to the final outcome (see the section on marketing plans, page 349). Then it may be too late to react to the changing dynamics. It is therefore proposed that measured performance covers the following areas:

◆ Individual areas of the marketing mix, for instance, an analysis of the performance of the marketing communications campaign: perhaps using recall factors and the opinions of focus groups.

◆ Brand values/equity: brands contribute both an asset value and a revenue generation potential to the business. These are usually the largest generators of wealth for a business.

◆ Cumulative effect: in essence the outcome of bringing all the elements together. Success or failure is usually reflected through the statistics in the organisation's annual report.

Contemporary business operates in a hyper-competitive global environment. Whether the organisation operates solely or in concert with others (via strategic alliances) the environment remains hyper-competitive. On this basis organisations must 'perform' if they are to survive. As the marketing contribution to this success is crucial, its performance must be measurable. It is on this basis that performance is considered an integral element of the marketing mix.

Product or service performance

Here there is a link between operations and marketing. Marketing may demand a specific level of performance, but one that cannot be met by operations. The 'gap' between the two may be the result of levels of expectations and/or resource capabilities/competences in the organisation.

Brand performance

The value apportioned to brands is discussed in Chapter 7. In this section the link between brand values and marketing performance of brands is examined.

As Keller (2003) states, the marketing advantages of strong brands can be summarised as:

◆ improved perceptions of product performance

◆ greater opportunity for loyalty

◆ less vulnerability to competitive marketing actions

◆ less vulnerability to marketing crises

◆ larger margins

◆ more inelastic consumer response to price increases

◆ more elastic consumer response to price decreases

◆ greater trade cooperation and support

◆ increased marketing communications effectiveness

◆ possible licensing opportunities (reflect back to Chapter 7 on branding and consider the various examples discussed)

◆ additional brand extension opportunities.

Research conducted at Otago University suggests that brand strength is linked to three main practices (*NZ Marketing Magazine*, 2002):

◆ investment in marketing communications

◆ improving the quality of service

◆ encouraging good communications between customers and employees.

While these are key factors, they are not the only factors that drive brand development and equity. The wider issues discussed in Chapter 7 have to be considered. Although strong brands have the propensity to create a marketing advantage, they are still 'governed' by decisions made by customers. Customers' decision to purchase may be rational or irrational. Whichever it is, their behaviour will be affected by the 'emotions' they associate with the brand. Haigh (2003) suggests that brand equity is a 'measure of the emotional reservoir which shows how far the demand curve has moved and what the future cash flows will be. Brand valuation is a snapshot of those future cash flows.'

As discussed in Chapter 7, individuals build their own relationships with brands; they associate themselves with particular names and logos. Brands provide reassurance, aspiration and self-expression (Haigh 2003). As Haigh (2003) suggests, 'strong brands with high 'brand equity' possess the ability to persuade people to make economic decisions based on emotional rather than rational criteria. They consequently have a profound economic impact and economic value.'

As Leiser (2003) notes, the lifetime value of repeat customers (the loyalty factor) ties directly in to the financial performance of the business. Consider, for instance, the loyalty that buyers have to Procter & Gamble, Unilever and Virgin's products. The lifetime value of each customer delivers (cumulatively) significant value to the balance sheet, together with gaining and maintaining share in the marketplace.

The US-based customer loyalty research consultancy Brand Keys (www.brandkeys.com) has, since the 1980s, been analysing the value of customer loyalty to companies (refer to Chapter 7). Their research indicates that:

- It costs seven to ten times more to recruit a new customer than to keep an existing one.

- An increase in customer loyalty of only 5 per cent can lift lifetime profits per customer by as much as 95 per cent.

- An increase in loyalty of 2 per cent is, in some sectors, equivalent to a 10 per cent cost reduction.

From this research it is clear that brand loyalty can be a significant performance indicator. The number of times individuals purchase a particular product or services indicates how they rate its performance. For instance, cities like Paris or Prague have a range of hotels to suit different tastes and price preferences. However, regular visitors to those cities may choose to stay at the same hotel. This could be for several reasons including location (see Chapter 12) and how they rate the quality drivers of that particular hotel. In other words they consider the performance of the hotel overall, including the efficiency of the staff, the quality of the food and whether all the facilities work efficiently.

There must be a methodology to measure brand values. Knowles (2003) suggests that performance measurements of brand equity can be analysed by integrating brand health measures from the BrandAsset® Valuator[1] (BAV) database maintained by the global marketing and communications agency Young & Rubicam with measures of financial performance from global consultants Stern Stewart's Economic Value Added (EVA®) database.[2] The research company BrandEconomics has developed a model using BAV and EVA data. Some 400 observations of monobrands[3] were made across several industry sectors between 1993 and 2000. Their analysis 'demonstrates that financial factors explain around 55 per cent of the market value of companies, brand explains around 25 per cent and other factors (especially industry context and economic cycle) explain much of the remaining 20 per cent[1](Knowles 2003).

Revenue performance and sales performance

All organisations, whether for-profit or not-for-profit, seek to generate revenue that provides both stability and growth potential. In order to maximise revenue performance all functions of an organisation should work in tandem. That is the 'ideal' theory; however it is not always the case in practice, which is one (though not the only) reason many companies do not survive in a hostile market environment.

A contributor to revenue performance is sales. Sales tends to be a numbers-driven operation where outcomes are measured against predetermined targets. While this is a 'measurable' performance it is often plagued with difficulties. These 'difficulties' can include:

◆ The potential associated risks of targets being set 12 months in advance. It assumes accurate forecasting of the future.

◆ The set targets do not take into consideration changing environmental conditions. These include changing weather conditions (a poor summer in the United Kingdom can significantly reduce the sales of ice creams in that market), regional conflict (such as the US-led invasion of Iraq in 2003), increased/decreased competition in the marketplace and changing customer tastes.

◆ The targets may be 'unrealistic' even assuming market growth. Thus the preconditions on which the targets are set could be flawed.

◆ The facilities, including support staff, are inadequate or inappropriate. Without such facilities it may be difficult to meet the required targets.

◆ Poorly recruited and trained sales staff. This issue links back to Chapter 13 on people, where the recruitment and effective training of employees was considered critical to building an operational relationship with customers. Without knowledge and interpersonal skills, it is difficult for a sales person to develop the long-term relationship with a customer that creates the lifetime customer values organisations seek.

◆ The creation of short-term outcomes. Some sales people with often unrealistic targets to meet have opted for short-term solutions. These have sometimes resulted in unethical practices, such as the mis-selling of, for instance, insurance policies and pensions. Although there is a short-term measurable outcome (revenue generation), the longer-term costs will probably outweigh any short-term gain. This was the case in the late 1990s for several UK-based insurance houses that were prosecuted over regulatory breaches associated with the mis-selling of pensions. Similar problems have occurred in the United States and continental Europe.

Some organisations have attempted to overcome these potential difficulties by implementing policies that take account of environmental considerations. For instance:

◆ Regular comparisons between forecast target and actual outcomes, taking into account any variations in the marketplace.

◆ Resource allocation that can support the forecasts.

◆ Appropriate initial and ongoing training of sales people. This is more than understanding of the product or service's features and benefits. Effective training encompasses interpersonal skills in order to fully appreciate the needs of the customer.

◆ Some organisations do not pay bonuses based on an individual's sales targets. Instead they examine the overall performance of the department and the organisation. If these larger holistic targets are met, department-wide/company-wide bonuses are paid. While it can be argued that this is not a totally fair system (some people may work harder than others), it reduces the risk of unethical activities such as mis-selling.

However, we must not consider sales in isolation. This is only one component of the promotional or communication mix within an organisation. Within an integrated marketing communication strategy, for instance, sales will be reinforced by other promotional activities and vice versa. This inter-relationship subsequently reinforces the brand's identity in the marketplace.

Market share

Company performance is often measured by its share of the market. This is often reflected in the annual report and accounts. The ability to penetrate a market and increase market share is clearly important if a company is to grow its major brands and sub-brands.

As Chapter 6 explained, it is one thing to gain a competitive advantage and another to maintain or sustain it. The same is perfectly true with market share – gaining is only one element of the performance. The company has to be able to use the marketing mix and other techniques to sustain and further develop its share of the market.

Distribution and logistics

As discussed in Chapter 12, it has become increasingly important for companies to use hyper-efficient channels to deliver products or services to end users. In highly competitive markets it may be the efficiency of distribution that gains a company a competitive advantage over its rivals. Thus companies throughout the supply chain must consider the question, how efficient is their distribution network?

Distribution and logistical performance must be benchmarked not only against industry standards[4] but also against customer requirements (and expectations). This is particularly demanding when customers (for example in the automotive industry) operate a just-in-time (JIT) supply operation. Such companies cannot afford to have disruption to their supply chain and JIT systems. Otherwise that could mean operational downtime, with the production line lying idle, costs mounting and falls in revenue. Mini case 2.1 gave a good example of a labour dispute that led to this type of disruption.

Buyers often judge a company on the performance of the distribution/logistics company it uses, especially if they could purchase the product from another supplier that guarantees delivery to meet their needs. One of the dichotomies of the Internet is that potential buyers can make a purchase 24/7, but may be faced with only a very limited delivery window. For instance, a major delivery company in the United Kingdom only delivers on Monday to Friday from 8 am to 6 pm. That has no value to a product buyer who works and thus is faced with three choices: (1) collect the product from the depot him or herself; (b) ask a neighbour to accept delivery, that is, if any of his or her neighbours are not employed or (c) take the day off, possibly with the loss of pay (depending upon the type of employment) to receive delivery of the product. Such inflexibility by the delivery company is unlikely to win any customer loyalty for suppliers. With an increase in online providers and customers buying online, delivery companies that remain locked into the Monday to Friday (8 am to 6 pm) mindset are unlikely to survive.

Marketing plans

The vast majority of organisations create marketing plans in one form or another, usually for each fiscal year. Some organisations plan further ahead in order to forecast longer-term revenue streams and costs. The marketing plan usually consists of an analysis of the marketing mix variables in terms of projected needs, budget requirements and revenue generation. Such a plan must fit strategically with the overall corporate ambitions.

However, a marketing plan is not a static entity. As explained earlier, both internal and external forces can dramatically alter an organisation's plans. Thus it is not a question of measuring the performance of the marketing plan only at fiscal year end: it is vital to measure it as the year progresses. By gauging movements in both the micro and macro environment an organisation can make any required changes. These changes may be driven by a combination of proactivity and reactivity, depending on the nature and suddenness of the environmental changes. Thus some organisations measure performance against the plan on a weekly basis, while others do so on a monthly basis. Of course, there are organisations that only measure performance on a quarterly and bi-annual basis. This, however, reduces their ability to counter threats and exploit opportunities within the marketplace.

■ Experiential performance

Pine and Gilmore (1999) suggest that organisations 'stage an experience whenever they *engage* [their italics] customers, connecting with them in a personal, memorable way'. This engagement is not only in the form of the customer service relationship but is likely to include the wider physical environment. An example is a theme park where visitors spend time engaged in a series of mini experiences, from rides through to merchandise shopping and eating. These mini experiences combine to provide the visitor with an overall experience. If the theme park has been successful, visitors will leave feeling they have had a positive and memorable experience, one they will remember and may repeat later. They may also become an ambassador for the theme park, promoting it though viral marketing.

However, there is more than one experiential dimension. Pine and Gilmore (1999) suggest that individuals can experience several 'realms of experience'. These are shown in Figure 17.2.

Figure 17.2 Pine and Gilmore's experience realms

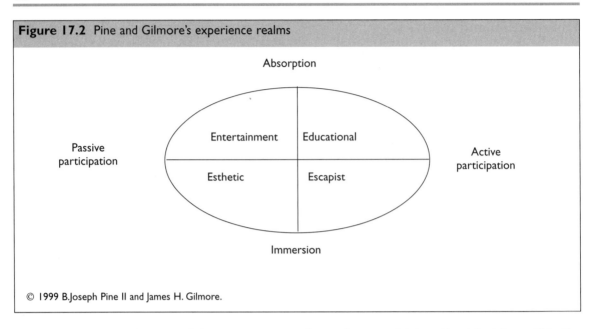

© 1999 B.Joseph Pine II and James H. Gilmore.

Quadrant 1: passive participation–entertainment–absorption

Here there is little active involvement with the entertainment experience. For example, most people passively watch television. However, they may, to a lesser or greater extent, be absorbed in the sounds and images coming from the television. They could move from being passive to active through the use of interactive television systems, thus their position would shift into another experience realm.

Another example is a patron sitting in London's Barbican concert hall watching the London Symphony Orchestra perform a classical work. He or she is passively absorbing the experience through the sights and sounds of the performance. Listeners may or may not be influenced by those sitting around them. They may be fully absorbed by the experience of watching and listening to the performance.

Quadrant 2: active participation–educational–absorption

The educational experience can be viewed from several standpoints: for example, from the perspective of an undergraduate at a university, a child visiting a museum with interactive elements, and

increasing use of interactive television within the learning environment.

The undergraduate experience

The global university sector has become a highly competitive marketplace. Thus universities seek to provide an overall student experience that includes not only what happens in the lecture theatre but also the quality of accommodation, computer/library facilities, social/sporting activities and catering. For instance, the teaching environment has undergone a quiet revolution in many countries. In many universities today it consists of a mixture of traditional lectures, group/individual workshops, seminar activities and independent study. The move is towards greater interaction in seminar activities, so students are no longer passive listeners. They must be actively engaged in preparation and then participation in the workshop environment.

In many universities students complete an evaluation form after the completion of each module, so the performance of the teaching staff and the module itself is measured, as of course are the student's knowledge and abilities through course work and examination assessments. The student's degree is the outcome measure of the student's performance during his or her time at university.

Moreover, many universities conduct exit surveys to measure the overall student experience. This can be a valuable assessment highlighting various strengths and weaknesses. The university (like any organisation) can enhance its strengths while seeking to remedy the perceived and actual weaknesses highlighted by such surveys. In turn the performance strengths can be used to market the university. (You may want to consider the overall performance of your current college or university.)

A child visiting a museum

Traditionally the vast majority of museums were emblazoned with signage stating 'Look, but do not touch!' The signage was for clear and understandable reasons – many of the exhibits were fragile and potentially dangerous. Modern technologies have permitted museums to create hands-on experiences where children and adults can be fully engaged in activities. Mini case 17.1 describes one of many interactive exhibitions at London's Science Museum.

Interactive television

Although interactive television is often associated with shopping channels and the self-programming of television evenings, it also has educational value. Children can use hand controls, for example, to key in possible answers to onscreen questions. This provides them with an instant response. Moreover, it can lead them into another programme package that provides higher-level learning capabilities.

Interactivity also allows for viewers to comment on issues being discussed in live broadcasts. An example is the BBC's current affairs programme *Question Time*. Members of a studio audience put topical questions to an invited panel, usually comprising politicians, business leaders, writers and academicians. The studio audience comment on the panel's answers, and viewers can also comment if they have a digital television system. They can also text messages to the studio.

The BBC has used such interactive capabilities on a wide range of one-off programmes which have covered everything from the war in Iraq to general knowledge skills of the UK population. It is clear that interactive television has not only entertainment potential but also the means of enhancing people's knowledge and skills base. However, for it to have any real value there will need to be active participation, and organisations will need to seek to market the engaged performance element of the overall experience.

Mini case 17.1

Science of Sport exhibition

In 2004 the Science Museum in London opened its Science of Sport exhibition, supported by SPORTENGLAND and UKsport. The exhibition explains how science contributes to sportsmen and women achieving high performances such as Olympic gold medals. The state-of-the-art exhibits provide interactive displays and simulated experiences. For example, visitors can dribble a football against the clock, climb an indoor rock face, test the accuracy of their tennis shots, or compete against friends in a quick track sprint, then watch the action replay. The interactive displays provide visitors with the ability to learn more about their level of fitness by checking their pulse rate, measuring their height and weight and testing their reaction times.

The combination of hands-on exhibits and information throughout the exhibition was designed to help both children and adults understand such issues as the effects of exercise on the body, the role of nutrition in sporting activities and how to analyse individual performance data.

The exhibition is also supported by a website which includes video clips and additional educational information for teachers, parents and students.

Source: Science Museum, London
(www.sciencemuseum.org.uk).

Quadrant 3: active participation–escapist–immersion

Pine and Gilmore (1999) suggest that this is the point where the customer seeks immersion in totally participative escapist activity. We can consider this in the here and now and the future possibilities.

The movies

We can argue that movies fit into this category. Consider, for example, a darkened cinema with the latest state-of-the-art Surround sound™ system and a movie that totally engages you and everyone else in the audience. There are several performances being rolled into one in this experience. First, there is the performance of the cinema itself in providing the atmosphere, the comfort and the projection/sound quality. Second, there is the combined artistry of the film makers: the director, scriptwriter, composer, actors, designers, visual effects teams and so on. Their collective work is after all what is seen and heard in the cinema. Finally, there is the audience who immerse themselves in the emotion and drama of the movie set out before them.

An example of this collective participation is Steven Spielberg's 1982 movie *E.T.: THE EXTRA-TERRESTRIAL*. Respected movie critic and writer Derek Elley (Elley 1993) called Spielberg's movie about a stranded alien, E.T., who is protected by three children until he can return home, 'captivating, endearingly optimistic and magical at times'. Audiences became engrossed in the story of this lovable lost alien. In one sequence the search is on for E.T., who is found by the children in a watery ditch and near to death. By this point in the storyline audiences have come to love E.T., this magical alien, and they too are in tears at the discovery of the dying E.T.

In a later sequence the three children rescue E.T. from the Federal authorities and seek to take him back to the landing site ready for his journey home. They are joined on their bikes by countless other children in the neighbourhood to help thwart the authorities who are now in hot pursuit. ET is seated in the basket on the front of the lead child, Elliot's bicycle. As they approach a police roadblock Spielberg builds the tension by having a police office raise his shotgun towards the children and ET. The tension is underscored by John Williams's music. At that point the audience does not know what is going to happen. Will a police officer actually shoot a child to stop the alien escape? That is the premise. However, ET closes his eyes and suddenly (with the assistance of John William's transforming uplifting score) he and Elliot have taken off and are flying above their pursuers. At this moment audiences tend to cheer, at one with Elliot and ET. Spielberg and his team have engineered a situation where the audiences became actively engaged in the performance. The movie's combination of charm and drama has made it one of the largest-grossing box-office hits of all time. Yet it would not been such a success if it had not been for Spielberg and his very talented

team being able to totally immerse the audience in a performance of drama and emotion.

Extreme sports

Until the 1990s it could be argued that extreme sports such as long-distance car rallying and motor racing were the domains of the wealthy. Today though there are numerous opportunities to actively participate in extreme sports such as bungee jumping, riding the rapids and parachuting. Whatever the duration, the participant is actively immersed in the experience.

Extreme vacations

These can be described as vacations beyond those normally experienced by the vast majority of families, and include trekking across deserts, mountains and icescapes. Consider for instance trekking across a desert landscape for ten days living in a tent attached to a Land Rover vehicle. Increasingly individuals and families seek the thrill of being part of wild and stunning landscapes. The performance is in the experience, and how well the trek is organised and supported.

From extreme to relaxing rides

Ever since the first roller-coaster rides in 19th century Paris, the leisure industry and thrill-ride designers have been seeking to develop more thrilling and dramatic rides. Coasters and thrill rides now utilise computer design systems and the latest in construction materials and technologies to create mind-blowing experiences. For instance, Ride Trade, a division of the Liechtenstein-based Intamin Company, developed the Giant Drop, where participants are hoisted to the top of a tower, reaching speeds of up to 5 metres per second, then wait to plummet in a freefall down to earth. The moments of anticipation both prior to and during the ride (the wait at the top of the tower) add to the overall performance, creating a real thrill-seeking experience.

Of course not all escapist rides need be extreme in pushing people to their limits of endurance. Rides can provide thrills because of their location. For example the British Airways London Eye, located near the Houses of Parliament, provides a stunning panoramic view of the historic and contemporary London skyline (see Figures 17.3 and 17.4).

Future escapism

In the opening sections of Paul Verhoeven's futuristic movie *Total Recall* (1990), based on a short story by Philip K. Dick, a construction worker Douglas Quaid (Arnold Schwarzenegger) sees a commercial about a virtual vacation. The advertisement announces, 'Have you always wanted to climb the mountains of Mars – but now you're over the hill? Then come to Rekall [sic] Incorporated where you can buy the memory of your ideal vacation – cheaper, safer and better than the real thing.' Of course, Quaid's virtual experience (being a secret agent on Mars) is transformed into a non-stop

Figure 17.4

© Jonathan Groucutt

A pod on the British Airways London Eye which towers over the River Thames near the Houses of Parliament

Figure 17.3

© Jonathan Groucutt

The British Airways London Eye. In the immediate background is St Stephen's clock tower (which houses the clock Big Ben), part of the Houses of Parliament. You can see how the London Eye towers over this historic landmark.

action thriller before he meets his alter ego Hauser when the plot or plots are revealed.

Of course this is fantasy, or is it? Clearly the storyline of the movie *Total Recall* is fantasy, but the premise behind it – virtual reality – is not. For several years research has been conducted in creating virtual reality experiences. Already there are games that can be played using virtual reality systems. There are also experiments in creating virtual reality supermarkets as an extension of online shopping. By wearing a special headset you enter and 'walk around' the supermarket and choose your items off-shelf, as you would do in a 'bricks and mortar' store.

While virtual reality systems have potential use in retail and games environments, their development stems from improving military capabilities, for example developing battle and flight simulators for training. From such technologies will be developed commercial systems that will enhance the virtual experience. Therefore the virtual vacation remains within the realms of the possible.

Quadrant 4: passive participation–esthetic (aesthetic)–immersion

The esthetic (aesthetic) is concerned with the appreciation of or sensitivity to beauty. Here individuals immerse themselves in an environment simply because they want to be there. They are 'soaking up' or appreciating the beauty of the surroundings that envelop them. Examples include standing at the base of a gigantic waterfall, watching the sunset over a desert or the views from a mountaintop hotel. These are all experiences that potentially immerse the individual in an esthetic environment. The same images are often used by travel companies to illustrate the experience that customers will enjoy when they book a vacation. This can be considered an element of the performance that is part of the experience of a vacation.

Figures 17.5 and 17.6 are images that might invite people to visit these locations should they be displayed in a travel brochure or on a travel website.

Experience is a dynamic function

If we accept the premise that experience is a dynamic function, we must view the experience realms model not as a static two-dimensional image but as a sphere divided into four sections or wedges, displaying three-dimensional characteristics. Such an approach gives fluidity to the concept. We all engage with an experience at different levels within a quadrant. Thus we can then plot where an individual is involved in the experience as a point on a curved surface.

We must also take the view that individuals can change their experience realm during the experience, and move from one quadrant to another. For

Figure 17.6

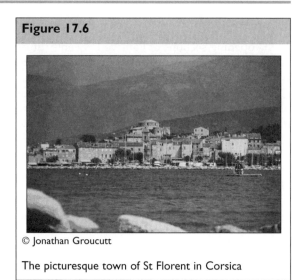

© Jonathan Groucutt

The picturesque town of St Florent in Corsica

example, consider the BBC Proms concerts held at London's Royal Albert Hall annually during July, August and September. During this period numerous classical works are performed by some of the world's greatest symphony orchestras, conductors, instrumentalists and singers. For many of the performances the concertgoers (known as promenaders) fit into the passive participation–entertainment–absorption category. However, during the last night of the season the audience are encouraged to actively participate by singing, cheering and becoming involved in the music. Thus there is a transformation from passive participation to the active participation side of the model during the evening's performance. By the end of the evening the promenaders are immersed in the atmosphere of the occasion. This process of conversion illustrates that we can move in and out of performance states, that the environment can change to allow an increase in our level of active participation (or not, as the case may be).

■ Future issues

As we have done throughout this chapter, we can look at performance in the future from the two standpoints of measured and experiential.

The difficulty with many forms of performance measurement is that they are historical in context. While historical data can be used to plot or suggest future trends, the result can be far from accurate.

Figure 17.5

© Jonathan Groucutt

The stunning snow-capped Atlas Mountains in Morocco

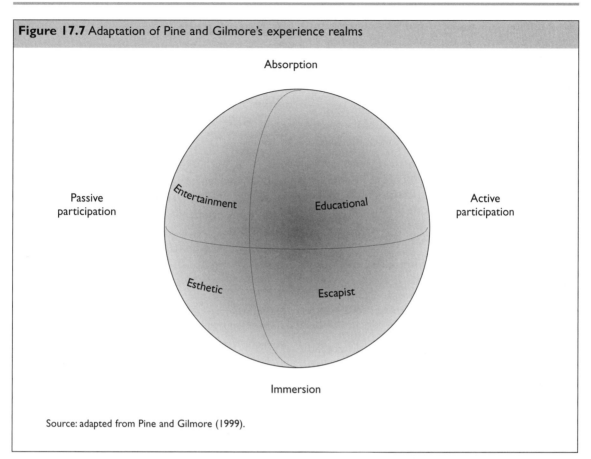

Figure 17.7 Adaptation of Pine and Gilmore's experience realms

Absorption

Passive participation

Entertainment

Educational

Active participation

Esthetic

Escapist

Immersion

Source: adapted from Pine and Gilmore (1999).

The increased complexity in the current global environment (for instance, hyper-competition and terrorism) makes it increasingly difficult to forecast performance based on past results. We have to accept that complexity will affect how we measure performance in the future.

We shall also have to research further into experiential performances and devise or expand models that explain a consumer's relationship with performance.

Chapter summary

This chapter has examined an additional marketing mix element, performance. It was concluded that there are two broad areas of 'performance', measured and experiential, although these are not mutually exclusive. Measured performance allows the marketer to benchmark and quantify results against industry standards and organisational

forecasts, while experiential illustrates the degree to which – using Pine and Gilmore's model – individuals engage in an 'experience' as part of the overall performance created by the organisations involved, such as a thrill ride at a theme park.

Taking these various elements together we can see how performance integrates with and supports other elements of the marketing mix.

Questions for review and reflection

1   Using the Internet and library resources, compare and contrast the market share of key pharmaceutical brands. For instance, you may discover that certain over the counter (OTC) brands of painkillers have different market shares in different countries or regions. Why do you think that this might be the case? From the evidence you find, do you think there is

anything companies can do to increase the market share of a particular brand? This is an issue you may want to debate with a fellow student.

2 Do you think that from a strategic marketing perspective, the measured performance indicators can be linked? If so how would you do it? You may want to discuss this with fellow students.

3 Critically evaluate Pine and Gilmore's model of experience realms. You may want to undertake this exercise by asking a random sample of your colleagues how they relate (or not) to the four quadrants in the model.

4 In terms of the performance indicators (Quadrant 2: active participation) of Pine and Gilmore's model, consider the overall performance of your current college or university.

5 Take your next CD or music download purchase and consider the 'performance'. How would you describe the experience, and how would you consider it in terms of 'marketing'?

6 If you have recently been, or are planning to go, on an experience-ride at a theme park, what words would you use to describe the experience? Do they have marketing connotations, both positive and negative?

7 Critically evaluate the rationale for including performance as an additional 'P' in the marketing mix framework.

■ References

Elley, D. (1993) *Variety Movie Guide 1994*, London: Hamlyn.

Haigh, D. (2003) 'An introduction to brand equity: how to understand and appreciate brand value and the economic impact of brand investment', *Interactive Marketing* **5**(1) (July/September), pp. 21–32.

Keller, K. L. (2003) 'Understanding brands, branding and brand equity', *Interactive Marketing* **5**(1) (July/September), pp. 7–20.

Knowles, J. (2003) 'Value-based brand measurement and management', *Interactive Marketing* **5**(1), pp. 40–50.

Leiser, M. (2003) 'Strategic brand value: advancing use of brand equity to grow your brand and business', *Interactive Marketing* **5**(1) (July/September), pp. 33–9.

NZ Marketing (2002) 'Performance measures', *NZ Marketing* **21**(8) (September), p. 2.

Pearsall, J. and Trumble, B. (eds) (1996) *The Oxford English Reference Dictionary*, 2nd edn, Oxford: Oxford University Press.

Pine, B. J. II, and Gilmore, J. H. (1999) *The Experience Economy: Work is theatre and every business a stage*, Boston: Harvard Business School Press.

Yudelson, J. (1999) 'Adapting McCarthy's four P's for the twenty-first century', *Journal of Marketing Education* **21**(1) (April), pp. 60–7.

Packages and Packaging

CHAPTER 18

Learning outcomes

After completing this chapter you should be able to:

▶ discuss the different types of packaging that are relevant to marketing

▶ critically evaluate the relationship between packaging and the other components of the marketing mix

▶ explain the various attributes that comprise packaging.

Contents

Learning outcomes	357
Introduction	357
What is packaging?	358
Combination or bundling	358
Product or brand packaging	358
Physical packaging	359
Attributes of physical packaging	359
Chapter summary	364
Questions for review and reflection	365
References	365

■ Introduction

The word 'package', like 'place' (Chapter 12), is not as clear-cut in its meaning, in marketing terms, as say the word 'promotion'. Packages and packaging can have several relevant meanings. This chapter explores the various meanings of the words package and packaging in a marketing context.

As Hine (1995) suggests, packaging has become an important part of our everyday lives. From both the consumer and business perspectives packaging is integral to our existence. You just have to look in your kitchen or bathroom to see the extent to which packaging invades our everyday lives. However, 'packaging' can as easily refer to the agglomeration, combining or bundling of several items into one form. An example is the package vacation (see also Chapters 10 and 11).

Packaging has usually been associated with the marketing mix in one of three ways:

◆ as an element of the product

◆ as an element of promotion

◆ as something that straddles both marketing mix components.

This has been, by and large, an unsatisfactory outcome. Packaging in its many forms contains sufficient diversity to be considered as a marketing mix component in its own right. That is the *raison d'être* of this chapter.

This chapter briefly explores the background to packaging and the various attributes that contribute to its form. As you will note, packaging is more than a protective device for a product.

■ What is packaging?

In any dictionary you will find various meanings for the words 'package' and 'packaging'. The same is applicable to marketing, and this has already been indicated in Chapters 10 and 11 with the concept of bundling.

The package or packaging can be considered under the following categories.

Combination or bundling

This is the bringing together of several items to create one package. It is common in the media industries, where programme makers talk of the 'package' being transmitted. For example, a company may supply a news broadcaster with a video news release (VNR) which includes video footage of new facilities and technologies. The news broadcaster might add to this an interview or a report to camera. The material from the company is then combined with the news broadcaster's material to form a news item or package for transmission. While the material supplied by the company will have a company public relations angle, the news broadcaster's material may take a more objective stance, raising questions or issues for future debate.

Similarly, in the hospitality and tourism industries the word 'package' has long been synonymous with specific types of vacations or tours. In a vacation package several related and complementary offerings or elements are combined into one. The packaged vacation may include airfare, transfers between the destination airport and hotel, hotel accommodation (this could be on a bed and breakfast, half-board or full-board basis), the services of a tour guide and entrance to specific attractions. The combination will vary depending on customer requirements, the vacation location and tour operator. However, packaged vacations provide customers with several benefits including increased convenience (arranging and buying), greater economy (competitive pricing as a bundle) and budget awareness (the majority of the cost is known and paid for in advance of the vacation).

A company may also seek to repackage existing material. This is often undertaken in order to market the repackaged product to a new or existing audience. In the latter case it may be because there are enhancements to the original product or packaging, and/or it was not easily available at the time of its original launch.

Here are a couple of examples:

◆ Compilation CDs which feature selections from various previously released CDs. In addition to possible enhanced sound quality, the repackaged CD will usually feature new cover artwork and liner notes. In July 2004 Decca Classics (part of the Decca Music Group) released the two-CD compilation *John Williams and the Boston Pops – Encore!* The CDs feature John Williams (the multi-award-winning composer of the music for the *Star Wars* and Harry Potter movies) with one of America's major orchestras. This compilation is derived from many recordings that were produced for the Philips label (part of the Decca Music Group). However, the repackaging provides another market opportunity, especially in the American marketplace.

◆ DVD reissues of movies previously released on VHS video. Increasingly major movies (past and present) are being released on DVD. The digital domain allows for more material to be presented on the disk. Hence, as well as the movie, there are usually trailers, interviews with the director, cast and crew, and background to the development of the movie itself. This repackaging with additional material provides an enhanced experience for viewers, especially if they are movie buffs.

Product or brand packaging

Lee and Lye (2003) state that product packaging is 'the science, art and technology of protecting products for the purpose of containment, protection, transportation/storage and information display'. While packaging is often described in terms of the physical protection of a product from the external environment, it is much more than that. It also expresses the visual, tactile, emotional and functional (convenience) values of a product or brand.

■ Physical packaging

What we know as physical packaging can be categorised into three inter-related subsets:

◆ Primary packaging: the packaging that 'surrounds' the product itself and is intrinsically linked with it, for example the case that protects the inner workings of the watch on your wrist, or the case that protects the inner workings of the computer used to write this textbook.

◆ Secondary packaging: the packaging that protects the product in transit and storage. An example is the packaging of washing powder. In the watch example, the watch will be stored and sold in a presentation box. Once the watch is purchased the owner might either throw away the box or keep it for storing the watch when he or she is not wearing it.

◆ Tertiary packaging: this is packaging that protects often large quantities, of primary and secondary packaged items in transit. For instance, boxes of washing powder may be carried in a freight container from the point of manufacture to a supermarket's distribution depot. This container, loaded onto a vehicle,

train or ship, protects the boxes from external elements that might damage the packaging and/or the contents.

In our daily lives it is the primary and secondary packaging that we tend to come into contact with. Again, you just need to view the contents of your home to see that physical packaging is very much part of our everyday lives.

Attributes of physical packaging

Packaging, however, is no longer designed just to protect the product: it has become a highly sophisticated marketing tool. In this section the various attributes that can be associated with physical packaging are examined. Companies can use these to differentiate their products from their competitors'. Consider, for instance, the shelves of detergents at a major supermarket. Each manufacturer is, in essence, selling the same outcome – cleaner, fresher clothes. While it is not the only reason to purchase, packaging does contribute to the decision-making process to buy.

The motivational psychologist Ernest Dichter stated that the product must literally reach out and 'tap the shopper on the shoulder' (Nickels and Jolson 1976). Nickels and Jolson also state that packaging needs to 'catch the consumer's eye, hold their attention and initiate an interaction between the product and the consumer'. In Chapter 10 Schramm's communications process was examined (Schramm 1955). A feature of the process is noise, of which a subset can be described as clutter, that is, a high intensity of competing messages that are vying for the consumer's attention. Therefore packaging plays an integral role in placing the product within the reach of the consumer.

Figure 18.2 (overleaf, based on the work of Lee and Lye 2003) shows the main attributes of physical packaging. They are briefly discussed below. These attributes work not in isolation but in concert with each other to present the customer with an holistic offering.

Protection and preservation

Most definitions of physical packaging emphasize, first, its protective nature, being a barrier against external environmental factors. These factors include excessive temperature changes,

Figure 18.1

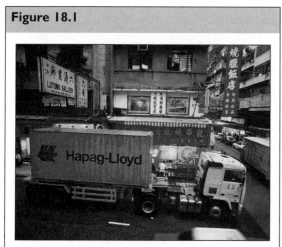

© Hapag-Lloyd. Reproduced with kind permission.

A container is an example of tertiary packaging as it contains numerous packages in a safe protective environment

Figure 18.2 The main attributes of physical packaging

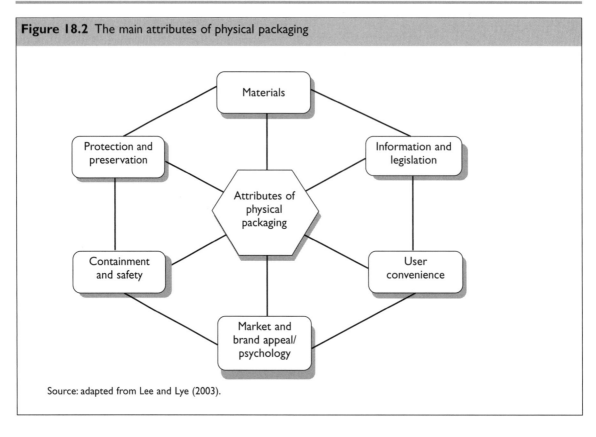

Source: adapted from Lee and Lye (2003).

cross-contaminants, liquids (such as water), corrosive materials, and disturbances while in transit (for example, poor roads or turbulence during air transportation).

Physical packaging also preserves the longevity of the contents. For example, food and beverage canning techniques and materials means that produce will normally stay fresher longer.

Containment and safety

Physical packaging contains the product, whether it is washing powder, sardines or tomato soup. The packaging may be constructed of any number of different material types from plastics to aluminium and glass.

While containment of the product prevents spillage under normal circumstances, increasingly packaging has had to feature additional safety devices. Following the Tylenol™ incidents in the United States in the 1980s (see Chapter 7), companies, especially in pharmaceuticals, sought to devise tamper-resistant containers. These provide two core safety benefits: they prevent a consumer

terrorist adding poison (which is what happened with Tylenol™), and they prevent children from opening the package and playing with or ingesting the contents.

Today tamper-resistant or safety closures are used on a wide range of products from medicines to kitchen and bathroom cleaners. Such safety devices are also applicable in a B2B environment, especially where corrosive materials are stored and used.

Market, brand and emotional appeal

Physical packaging aids in the creation of an emotional appeal for the product. A product that is simply packaged (for instance, an own-label brand) can convey several emotional responses in the consumer. These can include:

◆ Simple packaging, thus it is an easy-to-use uncomplicated product.

◆ Simple packaging, thus it has simple (pure) ingredients. One soap manufacturer has

Figure 18.3

©Tetra Pak. Reproduced with kind permission.

SlimCap opening – Tetra Brik Aseptic 1500S package.
An example of an easy-to-use pour device

prestigious quality of Cartier™ or with an individual who would purchase such a distinctive pen. Thus packaging often reflects the inner values of the purchaser.

Consider, for instance, the image and value statements of chocolate. Depending on the brand, its ingredients and price, chocolate ranges from an everyday 'convenience' bar to those individually wrapped in gold foil and displayed in a stylish box at the luxury end of the market. Both have their value within their respective markets.

Sandwiches in plastic containers also allow the consumer to make a judgement about value for money. The transparency provides the sandwich retailer with a promotional opportunity – the amount of filling in the sandwich can reinforce the value-for-money concept. The sandwiches can also be made to look mouthwatering, thus 'persuading' the consumer to purchase. However if the sandwiches are poorly presented, consumers might not purchase them.

As we can see, the design of the packaging contributes significantly to our perception of the product we are purchasing. Product design can be described as encompassing three areas:

◆ It is an inherent feature of any product no matter what its price range. It is not just about making something practical or 'nice' to look at, it is a marketing variable and thus can be used to enhance the marketing effectiveness of a particular product. Chapter 14 considered how colour is important in providing the right physical evidence to convey emotion. Exactly the same is true in packaging. Colour, in most countries, conveys important psychological meanings for many people. Hence, for instance, the use of green to convey that a product is 'natural', safe or environmentally friendly. Colour can also be used to get the product to stand out from similar products on crowded supermarket shelves.

◆ Design is used to convey product quality, which includes such qualities as durability. Customers will consider the relationship between design, quality and price. The value for money may be either real or perceived; either way design makes a valuable contribution to the customer's decision to purchase.

adopted this approach to convey the purity of its products.

◆ Simple packaging, thus low cost. The view is, 'I am paying for the product and not elaborate packaging.' This is especially true where companies promote 'no frills' grocery and beauty products.

Expensive-looking packaging (for instance, jewellery boxes) also needs to convey the value of the product contained within. To provide an extreme example, it would be incongruent for a UK£200 Cartier™ pen to be packaged in a brown-paper bag. It clearly would not fit with either the

This is often reflected, as indicated above, in the no-frills variety of products.

◆ It may link directly to fashion and current life styles. The sleek and often unusual designs of Swatch™ watches from Switzerland are an example. These have been linked to both fashion and the creation of fashion statements.

Integral to the overall design of the packaging will be the use of textures, typology and illustrations. In addition to inviting us to look at the product they also aid our purchasing memory. It is more than purely remembering the brand name, for instance. Consider the classic-shaped Coca-Cola® bottle. This has become a design icon and is recognisable anywhere in the world. You could remove the contents, the label, the top and it would still be recognised as Coca-Cola®, such is the memory impact. This is perhaps true even if you do not drink Coca-Cola®. Of course, not all products have packaging that has developed such iconic value. However, it is important to understand that the visual (design) component of packaging has a psychological imperative that needs to be explored. It is this psychological link that could make or break a product as it is launched into the marketplace.

User convenience

The consumer seeks convenience of use. Here are a few examples:

◆ Easy to open ring-pull tops on beverage cans.

◆ The drinking spouts found on the top of plastic bottles that allows easy drinking of the contents, and prevents spillage.

◆ Reclosable plastic or cardboard pour devices often found on milk and fruit juice cartons.

◆ Polystyrene cartons to carry fast-food products such as hamburgers.

◆ Squeezable pouches for single-serve food products. These are used for pet foods as well as soft drinks and fruit juices.

◆ Microwaveable containers or films: These allow for convenience foods to be quickly and easily prepared.

Figure 18.4

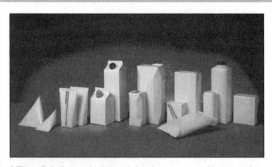

©Tetra Pak. Reproduced with kind permission. Photographer: Stellan Stebe.

Tetra Pak packages, from left: Tetra Classic, Tetra Wedge, Tetra Rex, Tetra Prisma, Tetra Brik, Tetra Fino, Tetra Top, Tetra Recart. These are easy to open and pour examples of packaging for liquids and powders.

◆ Refill packs: for example, concentrated fabric conditioners can be stored in smaller refill pouches. This reduces the wastage of producing plastic containers, the refill pouch may be recyclable, and it is less bulky, so easier for consumers to carry in their shopping.

◆ Plastic measuring cups enclosed in washing powder packets: These help consumers measure the right amount of powder for a particular type of wash. The packaging design provides clear pictorial instructions on the right quantities to be used.

◆ Pump-action dispensers, for example the introduction of liquid soaps (used for years in industry) in the consumer market. The promotion of these focused on eliminating the wet congealing soap stains around sinks. Additionally, there is ease of use. Other products available in pump-action dispensers include toothpaste, shower gels, shampoos and conditioners.

◆ Availability of different sizes: the combination of technology and specific demands has led to products being packaged in different sizes. For example, washing powders are often made available in 1.1 kg (15 wash), 3.3 kg (45 wash) and 5.5 kg (75 wash) sizes. Products such as toothpaste are available in a range of sizes to cater for vacation as well as home use.

◆ Easy storage and carrying of the product: for example, there has been a move away from the use of glass to PET (polyethylene terephthalate) jars for food products. These jars are safe, non-breakable and can incorporate moulded side grips for easily handling. Another example is the large packs of washing powder that incorporate sturdy plastic carrying handles.

Information and legislation

Customers require on-packaging information in order for them to make an informed decision to purchase the product or not. Legislators (especially in the European Union) also seek clear and specific on-package information to ensure that customers are well informed. This is normally seen as part of a government's manifesto for consumer protection.

◆ Features: information conveys the product's features. These can range from natural ingredients (no artificial colourings or additives in food, for instance) through to special enzymes in washing powders and the ability to microwave certain foods.

◆ Benefits: these are the benefits derived from the features of the product. For instance, a re-seal tab that allows ground coffee to remain fresh in its original foil packaging, and the container that you can place directly into the microwave to obtain a fast-ready cooked meal.

◆ Contents or ingredients: this may be important to the customer for a variety of reasons. For instance, the purchaser might:

● have an allergy, for example to nuts

● want to avoid artificial additives and colourings (for instance E numbers[1]) in the belief that they may inflict long-term harm

● seek high levels of a particular ingredient (for example, 100 per cent fruit rather than concentrates or sugar in a fruit-based drink)

● want organically grown ingredients and/ or want to avoid genetically modified ingredients

● want to know whether the ingredients have been tested on animals

● wants the packaging to be environmentally friendly and thus biodegradable.

◆ Country of origin or manufacture: customers may be interested in knowing the country of origin or manufacture for several reasons:

● they know that the best produce (for instance, fruit) comes from that region

● they want to support the farmers in that region, for instance the coffee growers allied to a fair trade scheme in a particular country

● the quality of manufacture for a particular product is of a particular high standard

● they want to avoid poor manufacturing standards

● the country's human rights record might influence their purchase.

◆ Suitability: who the product is suitable for will concern groups such as vegetarians-vegans, children (within certain age ranges) and the elderly depending on the product and its ingredients or attributes. For example, some toys are not suitable for children under five because small working parts might break off, and the child might pick them up and inadvertently swallow them, risking choking.

◆ Use by date: the packaging of food products, in many countries, now carries use by dates. This is the latest date the product should be used before it is considered unfit for human consumption. In some cases this date can be extended if the product is frozen on the day of purchase.

◆ Storage instructions: various products have to be stored under certain environmental conditions. For example, food may need to be frozen or chilled after purchase and used within a certain timeframe (see point above). Other examples include household cleaners such as bleach where the container must be stored upright to prevent the risk of spillage and thus staining, and out of the reach of children.

◆ Opening instructions: some packaging is easy to open while others may have an element of difficulty for a particular reason. As stated earlier, some products (for example, medicines) have to be packaged in tamper-proof containers. In such cases the lid may only be opened if it is pushed down and unscrewed. In other cases the opening instructions include a warning to open the product away from the face or using gloves. This is particularly the case with certain garden chemicals or bleaches that can burn the skin on contact.

◆ Usage instructions: how to use or apply the product, whether it is shampoo, medicines or suntan cream. These need to be accurate, especially for medicines. In many cases additional information is provided in leaflet form (within the pack) to supplement the on-package information.

◆ Disposal instructions. These often cover three distinct areas.

● Any remaining ingredients or product. For example, medicines need to be disposed of safely to prevent them being ingested by children or animals.

● Where the packaging can be recycled (particularly for glass, certain plastics and aluminium cans).

● Where the product and packaging are intrinsically linked such as in an aerosol can. In such cases because of the flammability of the product they must be disposed of safely, and not for instance, thrown onto a fire where they will explode.

◆ Quantity: an accurate statement of the weight or the number of items in a packet.

◆ Nutritional information: for food and health products most governments require accurate labelling of their nutritional values.

◆ Quality statement: most companies now add quality statements to their products.

◆ Customer service information: many companies now include on the packaging a dedicated telephone or email address, in case the purchaser has a product query. This is seen as

good customer relationship management in that the company can gain an understanding of customer issues. The knowledge gained can then be translated into product and packaging development.

◆ Potential hazards: for instance most beauty products (skin cleansers and shampoos, for example) state,: 'Avoid contact with eyes. If the product gets into your eyes rinse immediately with water'. The warnings will vary depending on the risks involved.

◆ Ecological issues: companies have increasingly moved towards green labelling, stating, for example, whether the product is environmentally friendly, dolphin friendly and contains recyclable materials.

Materials

The importance of materials cannot be underestimated in the development of packaging, especially in relation to convenience foods. In 1812, for instance, both Nicolas Appert and Bryan Donkin worked, separately, on the development of the tin canning process. As a result we can now purchase everything from meat and fish to fruits in cans which ensure they are preserved, and remain fresh, for a significant amount of time. Such packaging clearly protects and preserves the contents. Equally, it is part of the convenience and emotional appeal of the product.

Since the introduction of the tin can, there has been a myriad of packaging developments, especially in plastics and plastic films. The introduction of such packaging has had an impact on society. For instance, new types of packaging not only preserve the contents of food, for example, but allow it to be microwaved in its packaging. This is especially the case with industrial catering.

As Groucutt *et al.* (2004) suggest, you may want to reflect on how packaging materials have both influenced societal behaviours and created new market opportunities.

■ Chapter summary

This chapter has sought to illustrate how packaging is an integral component of the marketing mix. While it has a direct relationship to product and promotion, for instance, there are sufficient elements in its composition for it to be considered as another component in the overall mix.

Packaging, as we have seen, displays certain characteristics beyond that of a physical 'envelope' that protects its contents. Various materials and ideas can be packaged, products can be repackaged, and indeed physical packaging displays various attributes beyond that of protection.

While we may or may not pay conscious attention to packaging, it has become an essential part of our everyday lives. Virtually every item we handle in our homes, college or office has been packaged in one form or another. Thus marketers must consider how the packaged item, whether it is a CD or a box of ice cream, interests or tempts us to purchase it over all the others on the shelf. While packaging alone may not be the final trigger for the decision to purchase, it will have been one of them.

■ Questions for review and reflection

1 Using the Internet, library and other resources, briefly explain how packaging has developed over the past 100 years. Then consider how this changing in packaging may have influenced the marketing of products.

2 Although packaging is a tangible asset (in other words we can touch and feel it), sometimes companies refer to packaging as having intangible assets or values. What do you think these could be? Why do you think that they may be important to both the marketers and the product itself?

3 Go to your kitchen cupboard. Briefly outline the basic attributes that the packaging of the goods in it conveys to you. Would you have consciously considered any of these attributes if you had not been directed to do so?

4 Select an example of a piece of packaging that you think is both innovative and useful. Then explain to a group of fellow students why you have chosen it. Do they agree with you? Ask them to justify their views. What, if anything, would they do differently and why?

5 Packaging companies today emphasize that containers are much easier to open and use. Do you agree with this statement? You may want to use the Internet and library resources to investigate this question further.

References

Groucutt, J., Leadley, P. and Forsyth, P. (2004) *Marketing: Essential principles, new realities*, London: Kogan Page.

Hine, T. (1997) *The Total Package: The secret history and hidden meanings of boxes, bottles, cans and other persuasive containers*, Boston and New York: Back Bay Books, Little, Brown.

Lee, S. G. and Lye, S. W. (2003) 'Design for manual packaging', *International Journal of Physical Distribution and Logistics Management* 33(2), pp. 163–89.

Nickels, W. G. and Jolson, M. A. (1976) 'Packaging: the fifth 'p' in the marketing mix?', *SAM Advanced Management Journal*, Winter, pp. 13–21.

Schramm, W. (1955) 'How communication works', in W. Schramm (ed.), *The Process and Effect of Communication*, Urbana: University of Illinois Press.

Notes

Chapter 1

1 This normally relates to a person who is believed to have special healing powers. Equally it could be argued that marketers are 'witch doctors' in that they are supposed to keep evil spirits at bay. In other words, the competition in the marketplace.

2 Paracelsus, originally Philippus Aureolus Theophrastus Bombastus von Hohenheim (1493–1541), was a Swiss-born alchemist and physician who travelled Europe and the Middle East. He is renowned for establishing the use of chemistry in medicine. He was also the first to argue that a small dose of what makes people ill can also cure them – the premise of the vaccine.

Chapter 2

1 The Richter Scale is named after US seismologist Charles F. Richter (1900–1985). He devised it with fellow geophysicist Beno Gutenberg (1889–1960), to measure earthquake magnitude on a scale of 1–10.

2 Bluetooth is named after Harald I Gormsson (c910–985) who was the first King of Denmark to unify all the (often warring) factions and provinces of the country under a single crown. Through his conversion to Christianity, he was able to strengthen the unity and central administration of the country. King Harald's nickname was 'bluetooth'. This, so legend suggests, referred to the discolouration of his teeth because of his love for (and overindulgence in) blueberries and blackberries.

Chapter 4

1 D'Aveni (1995) states that hypercompetition results 'from the dynamics of strategic maneuvering among global and innovative combatants'. He continues by stating that:

> it is a condition of rapidly escalating competition based on price–quality positioning, competition to create new know-how and establish first-mover advantage, competition to protect or invade established product or geographic markets, and competition based on deep pockets and the creation of even deeper pocketed alliances. In hypercompetition the frequency, boldness and aggressiveness of dynamic movement by the players accelerates to create a condition of constant disequilibrium and change…. In other words, environments escalate toward higher and higher levels of uncertainty, dynamism, heterogeneity of the players and hostility.

Chapter 5

1 Originally published in 1832, Clausewitz's *On War* became perhaps the most significant attempt in Western history to understand war, both from the perspective of its internal dynamics and as an instrument of policy. There have been attempts to link the work of von Clausewitz to business strategy. Another major military strategist was Sun Tzu who over 300 years ago also wrote a text on warfare. This too has been used as the basis of books analysing both business strategy and warfare.

2 The economist and sociologist Vilfredo Pareto (1848–1923) postulated the 80/20 rule as a means of understanding income distribution; that is, 80 per cent of a nation's income will benefit 20 per cent of the population. Since he formulated this ratio, Pareto's law or principle has been extended to cover numerous business functions and activities. For instance, 80 per cent of business revenue is typically generated by 20 per cent of the organisation's customers.

Chapter 6

1 It is a common error to think that the opportunities and threats are issues that exist within the organisation rather than external factors.

Chapter 7

1 In 1925, following the death of William Lever (then Lord Leverhulme), Lever Brothers Limited merged with the Dutch Margarine Union. This merger was later to form Unilever. In 2001 the Lever Brothers brand was merged with Elida Fabergé to form the Lever Fabergé brand. Sunlight Soap is no longer sold in the United Kingdom, but it is currently (2005) available in India, Sri Lanka and Australia.

2 The Kit Kat Club was founded in the late 17th century

by prominent Whigs (a liberal-oriented political party) and literary figures of the time. According to the English poet Alexander Pope (1688–1744), other writers such as the Irish essayist Sir Richard Steele (1672–1729), the English poet Joseph Addison (1672–1719) and the English dramatist Sir John Vanbrugh (1664–1726) were members.

3 Ambient foods are food products that are not cooked by the purchaser. They range from general confectionery to food dressings and spreads.

4 This can be viewed as a middle way or position between the left wing often associated with socialism and the right wing often linked with parts of the Conservative party. Others might view this as a liberal approach as espoused by the British Liberal Democratic Party.

5 In 1989 the UK brewery and leisure company Scottish & Newcastle acquired Center Parcs Europe, but it disposed of it in 2001. It was acquired by the private equity firm MidOcean Partners. In 2003 MidOcean sold Center Parcs UK to a group of fund managers for around UK£300 million. In turn the fund managers floated the company on the London Stock Market.

Chapter 8

1 It must be remembered that the emphasis at the time was on manufacturing and selling products. Services industries did exist (including advertising and marketing in the B2B arena), but for the vast majority of people, especially in the growing consumerist United States, it was very much a production and sales orientation.

2 Although we generally think of the word 'profit' in financial terms it does not have to be so. It could be looked on as benefit derived, and that could be emotional (intangible) as well as money in the bank (tangible).

Chapter 9

1 The concept of the convenience store was created in 1927. The Southland Ice Company in Dallas, Texas sold blocks of ice for the preservation of food, then an employee began selling milk, bread and eggs on Sundays and evenings when the normal grocery stores had closed. This new business soon became popular, and the Southland Ice Company created convenience outlets which it named Tote'm stores (The name was based upon the American colloquial expression tote, to carry or convey, especially a heavy load.) In 1946 the name was changed to 7-Eleven to reflect the stores' new opening hours – 7 am to 11 pm,

seven days per week. The company remained a leader in the convenience store field until the late 1980s when it faced a financial crisis. Ito-Yokado Co. Ltd, the parent of the licensee 7-Eleven Japan, acquired the majority of the 7-Eleven stock in 1991, preventing a possible bankruptcy. By 2003 7-Eleven was the world's largest operator, franchiser and licenser of convenience stores, with more than 24 000 stores worldwide, primarily in North America and the Far East. Total sales in 2002 were US$33 billion (Higgins 2003, 7-Eleven 2003).

2 At the time of writing (2005) the underlying principles created by McKnight had generated over 50 000 innovations. 3M has become a diversified technology company with operations in more than 60 countries and serving customers in some 200 countries. Global sales (2002) were US$16 billion.

3 The introduction of the product life cycle is generally attributed to J. Dean (1950). Levitt is cited in Hooley (1995) as popularising the concept: see Levitt (1965).

Chapter 10

1 This is sometimes presented as the Shannon and Weaver model, since Warren Weaver and Claude Shannon wrote a book entitled *The Mathematical Theory of Communication* (1949), which included Shannon's original work with some amendments. This book refers instead to Shannon's original article (1948).

2 Depending on a person's status in society there might have been one last chance of a reprieve from the gallows. If an aristocrat stood before the crowd and made an impassioned speech, a public apology in effect, denouncing his (or her) own crimes and those of others (perhaps implicating others in the process), he or she might be spared the hangman's noose. Many chose death rather than make such a plea on the basis that there was honour in death. Public hangings were stopped because the government believed there was a risk of rioting, as increasingly the crowds began to rage against the injustices handed down from the courts and government on individuals (both rich and poor) who were considered by the masses to be innocent of the crimes laid before them. A plaque now marks the spot where the Tyburn gallows once stood.

3 The AIDA model is often attributed to the Stanford University psychologist Edward K. Strong. It was Strong who publicised it, in *The Psychology of Selling and Advertising* (1925).

4 I am totally against both fly posting and graffiti. Both are detrimental to society as a whole. I argue that such guerrilla types of ambient media should be made illegal. Clearly, the problem for some countries is the level

of enforcement powers. That is clearly the role of the judiciary. However, the use of fly posting brings marketing as a whole into disrepute.

5   There are spam messages that suggest that an individual can gain a BA or BSc degree in 30 days. This is clearly a falsehood and those who 'buy' such degrees are being enticed into purchasing a useless piece of paper.

6   In 2003 these costs were estimated as US$10 billion for US businesses and £3.2 billion for UK companies and organisations (BBC 2004). The sheer quantity of spam messages fills inboxes, which need to be cleared, and this slows down even the most powerful systems.

7   Although Grönroos uses the term 'profit' the issue should not be confined purely to for-profit organisations. Not-for-profit organisations (including charities) aim to generate revenues and surpluses. Equally, they aim to build a relationship with their donating and supporting customer base in order to both generate further revenues and fulfil their commitment to society.

Chapter 11

1   Readers are directed to the International Chamber of Commerce (ICC) website www.iccwbo.org/incoterms where full descriptions of the 13 Incoterms can be read. Various official publications can be purchased from the site including Jan Ramberg's *ICC Guide to Incoterms 2000*, which shows how Incoterms can be implemented in an international trading environment.

Chapter 12

1   As well as the perceived quality of life, there is the issue of the cost of accommodation, both rental and for purchase. It is significantly more expensive living in London and the surrounding area than in many other parts of Southeast England.

2   During the late 1990s many countries began to relax entry requirements to allow for greater freedom of movement. This was especially so within the European Union. There was also a greater opportunity for students to study in various countries, such as the United Kingdom. Since the events of 11 September 2001 governments have understandably tightened security and entry requirements. Although there may be the reimposition of exacting entry restrictions, the trend in global migration appears to be continuing.

3   The Greek mathematician and engineer Hero of Alexandria (1st century) developed the first vending machine. He devised a machine that on the payment of a token would dispense holy water in Egyptian temples.

Chapter 14

1   The *Voyager of the Seas* was the largest cruise ship ever built until the launch of the Cunard Line's *Queen Mary 2* in late 2003. Her maiden voyage was undertaken in January 2004. Cunard Line is an operating unit of the Miami-based Carnival Corporation.

2   While this may be a factor, it may not be the only contributory reason for purchasing. Other factors such as colour and shape of packaging, for instance, need to be taken into consideration.

3   There have been only a few major movies that have not featured a music score, most notably the boardroom political drama *Executive Suite* (1954) and two Cold War nuclear thrillers, *Fail Safe* (1964) and *The War Game* (1966).

Chapter 15

1   This pack of chewing gum was not consumed. Instead it was taken to the Smithsonian Institution's National Museum of American History (www.si.edu) where it is on display.

2   See Chapter 2 note 2.

Chapter 16

1   Here Freud considers 'unconscious' as a state of mind, rather than the unconsciousness that would result from, for example, a blow to the head or being in a coma.

2   Bernays lived to the grand age of 103 and was still giving company executives advice almost until his death.

3   In the 1920s the UK General Post Office (GPO), which was responsible for both telephone and postal services, actively used PR techniques (mainly film) to promote its services to a wider general public. It can be argued that the difference between the GPO's approach and Bernays was that the GPO was directly 'informative' whereas Bernays attempted to base his work on psychological principles.

4   An example of an entrepreneur who became a millionaire but decided on a relatively simple life was the English-born Percy Shaw (1890–1976), the inventor of the reflective road studs which he called and patented as Cat's eyes®. Shaw came from a working-class background and was one of 14 brothers, sisters, half-brothers and half-sisters. Although he left school at 13 he later went on to study at evening classes. He had an enquiring mind that led to several inventions and ideas. Even after his success Shaw continued to live a simple life in the house he had grown up in, in Hali-

fax, Yorkshire, which was now next to the factory he had started to manufacture Cat's eyes®. It is reported that he disliked travelling and that his house was furnished in a simple style. His only luxury was a Rolls-Royce.

Chapter 17

1   The BVA database contains data gathered over a ten-year period on 20 000 brands across 40 countries.

2   The EVA database is a financial performance measure which indicates the economic measure of an organisation.

3   BrandEconomics® defines Monobrands as those companies whose principal revenues (those in excess of 80 per cent) are derived from products or services sold under the company's primary brand. According to Knowles (2003), Coca-Cola® is designated a Monobrand while Pepsi®is not. As of August 2003 the Pepsi-Cola® brands numbered over 30. Knowles (2003) states that while the 'use of this set of Monobrands enabled the overall company financial results to be related definitely to the health of the core brand, it could be argued that all the brands in the Pepsi®stable make, to a greater or lesser degree, a contribution to the health of the Pepsi® brand.

4   Industry standards must be viewed in the wider context of an industry in one country. Companies now operate on a regional, international and global basis. Thus companies need to consider what would be deemed efficient and effective in a wider global context.

Chapter 18

1   This is a specific code number that is designated for food additives under EU legislation. There are currently some 200 additives registered as E-numbers in the European Union (2005). The 'E' represents the word European. While E-numbers are acceptable within the European Community some are not accepted in other countries, namely the United States where the Food and Drugs Administration (FDA) believe that some additives with E-numbers may present a health risk.

Glossary of Marketing Terms

Adding value An organisation through, for example, cost reduction or performance enhancements, adds value (in the mind of the customer) to the product or service. When several such activities are grouped together they can be viewed as a value chain.

Adaptation A product is adapted for a particular market. For example, some cola drinks and chocolates have increased levels of sweetener added to meet consumer tastes in certain markets.

Adoption The level by which customers adopt or use the product or service over the course of the life cycle of the product. Adopters can be grouped as innovators, early adopters, early majority, late majority and laggards.

Advertising A paid-for communications vehicle that is intended to inform, influence and/or persuade one or more individuals to buy into a product, service or idea. It can be used by for-profit and not-for-profit organisations.

Advertising media The range of advertising media channels available will vary from country to country. These cover print media, television, radio, cinema, outdoor (billboard), ambient and the Internet.

AIDA model Developed by St Elmo Lewis, this is a hierarchy of effects model. The acronym stands for Attention, Interest, Desire and Action.

Ambient media Also known as fringe media, this is advertising that is positioned in the surroundings or background. Includes aerial (aircraft towing banners), give-away postcards, and advertising on maps and tickets.

B2B marketing An abbreviation of business-to-business marketing operations.

B2C marketing An abbreviation of business-to-consumer marketing operations.

Brands Kotler (2000) defines a brand as a 'name, term, symbol or design (or combination of them) which is intended to signify the goods or services of one seller or groups of sellers and to differentiate them from those of the competitors'.

Brand awareness The level of customer recognition of a branded product or service.

Brand disposal An organisation decides to sell or dispose of a brand to another company. This may

be for several reasons including strategic withdrawal from declining markets and focusing resources on core profitable brands.

Brand elasticity The level to which a brand can be stretched over several products without harming the original branded product.

Brand equity Aaker (1991) defines this as 'a set of assets and liabilities linked to a brand, its name and symbol, that adds to or subtracts from the value provided by a product or service to a firm and/or to that firm's customers'.

Brand extensions Additional products or services are, over time, added to the original brand to serve various markets. Linked to this is *brand elasticity*.

Brand longevity The age span of a brand. For example, many everyday brands have been in existence for over 40 years.

Brand management The strategic organisation of the marketing mix to effectively and efficiently build and manage a brand over its life cycle.

Brand recall The extent to which a customer can recall the name and/or promotional/packaging images associated with the brand.

Brand recognition This links to *brand awareness* and *brand recall*. It is the extent to which the customer can recognise the brand from a series of visual or aural clues.

Brand termination A company decides to prematurely end the life of a brand. This may be for several reasons, for instance declining markets and/or customer resistance to the brand.

Brand values The intrinsic qualities that the brand communicates to potential and current customers.

Branding The tangible features – the verbal and physical cues – that assist the customer in choosing one product or service over another.

Bundling Several products or services are combined in a single package at a single price. Alternatively products can be unbundled and sold separately and individually priced.

Business level strategy This links to strategic business units (SBUs) where the focus is normally on products and/or services within defined market segment(s).

Business services *B2B* services that a company can buy in to achieve its overall corporate objectives.

These include legal, financial, accounting and management consultancy services.

Buzz Also referred to as viral, contagion and word-of-mouth marketing. A social process where person-to-person communication highlights both positive and negative aspects of a brand.

Cartel A price fixing operation where a group of companies or countries agree on a set price for a product or service. This is often deemed unethical and within some countries, illegal too.

Celebrity endorsement A promotional activity where a personality usually movie or music star endorses a product or service.

Channel overload We are constantly bombarded by communications messages via, for example, 24-hour multi-channel television, the Internet, newspapers and magazine advertising, various forms of direct marketing and in-store promotions. This can lead to overload and clutter, reducing the opportunity for the communication message to be fully understood.

Communication models Models that explain the communication process from sender to receiver.

Competitive advantage An organisation gains a market edge or advantage over its competitors. While an organisation may be able to gain an advantage, the critical issue is whether it can sustain that advantage over the longer term or not. An advantage may be gained through cost leadership, where the organisation becomes the lowest-cost producer within the industry. Alternatively, it may gain and sustain an advantage by differentiating its products and services from its competitors.

Competitive noise In highly competitive environments companies may use spoiler promotional tactics to disorientate their rival's customers.

Competitive scope The breadth of an organisation's activities. In some instances an organisation may be able to 'collectively' exploit these activities to gain a competitive advantages. Alternatively it may be able to customise activities for a particular target segment.

Competitor intelligence Also known as business intelligence, the gathering and analysis of information relating to an organisation's competitors. Organisations must operate to clear ethical and legal guidelines.

Convenience products Basic everyday products which can be subdivided into staple, impulse and emergency purchases.

Corporate strategy The overall strategy that governs the direction of an organisation. It usually addresses two questions: 'What business are we in?' and 'What business should we be in?'

Cost plus pricing A dual pricing mechanism that accounts for the full allocation of both domestic and international costs plus a suitable margin.

Counter-offensive defence A strategic position where a market share defender will counter-attack the challenger with overwhelming resources to dislodge it. The challenger may have no option but to withdraw in order to protect its existing market share.

DAGMAR Colley's 1961 work on Defining Advertising Goals for Measured Advertising Results. An hierarchy of effects model: awareness, comprehension, conviction and action.

Demographics The use of population data (gender, age, race, religion and emigration trends) to understand market segments. *Geodemographics* considers population data in relation to geographical locations.

Diffusion Rogers (1983) defines this as 'the process by which (1) an innovation; (2) is communicated through certain channels [for example, direct marketing or advertising]; (3) over time and (4) among members of a social system'.

Direct marketing Tapp (1998) describes this as a focus on 'using a database to communicate (and sometimes distribute) directly to customers so as to attract a direct response'. Techniques include door drops, inserts, direct mail, telemarketing and door-to-door selling (personal selling).

Discount pricing Companies may offer customers special discounts when items are bulk purchased and/or purchased within a particular time frame.

Dumping An action where companies sell their products within the marketplace at below marginal cost. This tactic has been used to penetrate difficult or highly competitive markets. Many consider this an unethical pricing tactic while some governments state that it is anti-competitive and thus illegal.

Ehrenberg's ATRN model A hierarchy of effects model – Awareness, Trial, Reinforcement and Nudging.

Emergency purchases Also known as distress purchasing. Products or services that are purchased when the need is urgent, such as an umbrella during a sudden rainstorm.

Family brands The brand range adopts the name of the parent company, for example, Cadbury's chocolate.

Five forces model Developed by Michael Porter of Harvard Business School, this analyses an organisation at an industry level. It comprises five components: the threat of substitution, the power of suppliers, the power of buyers, the threat of new entrants (into the marketplace) and the level of rivalry between competitors.

Flanking attack A market challenger seeks to exploit a weakness in the market leader's position. This action permits the market challenger to move around or flank the market leader and gain market share.

Focus group A marketing research technique where a group normally of six to eight people, who match the product or service's target audience, are asked to respond to questions relating to an unspecified product or service.

Frontal attack Normally where a market challenger builds a combination of resources and expertise to directly attack the market leader in its major markets and territories.

Functional strategy The operational level of an organisation, which can include HRM and finance as well as marketing. This is where the marketing strategy is determined.

GE matrix An analysis of either strategic business unit (SBU) or product activity based upon market attractiveness and business position (business strength). Developed by General Electric and the management consultants McKinsey.

Generic marketing mix Also known as the 7Ps – Product, Price, Place, Promotion, People, Physical Evidence and Process.

Guerrilla attack A series of small competitive attacks that are designed to frustrate the market defender, and raise the guerrilla attacker's profile within the target segments. Guerrilla tactics include the use of merchandising, special events marketing, intensive personal selling and linking the brand to a specific high-profile issue, for example, animal rights.

Heterogeneous products Non-standard products where features, benefits and image tend to outweigh the price.

Hierarchy of effects models Models that demonstrate a sequential learning pattern from awareness through to reinforcement of the brand's image in the mind of the customer.

Homogeneous products Products that are similar to each other in terms of performance, features, benefits and pricing.

Impulse purchases Products that are purchased on the spur of the moment without little or no prior purchasing analysis. They can include low-cost confectionery, newspapers and magazines.

In-depth interviews A marketing research technique where an individual is asked, in a face-to-face situation, a series of questions relating to specific products and services.

Individual brands Branded products or services that stand alone, separate from their parent company. They provide a distinct individual identity, and the customer may not actually know which company owns the brand. For example, the sports car brand Aston Martin (which is owned by the Ford Motor Company).

Industrial and commercial products *B2B* products that can be subdivided into raw materials, processed materials, plant and machinery, accessories and consumable supplies.

Integrated marketing communications The process of creating a uniform message and style so that an organisation communicates to its target audience with a single message using various communication channels.

Internal factors Also known as micro factors, these are environmental factors that are normally internal to an organisation. They can include the relationship with suppliers, the local community and customers.

Internet media Advertising on Internet sites, classified as banners, skyscrapers, buttons, classified and pop-ups (interstitials).

Kiosks Interactive touch screens that allow in-store customers to search and retrieve information as well as order products and services.

Lavidge and Steiner's model A hierarchy of effects model – predictive measurements of advertising effectiveness: unawareness, awareness, knowledge, liking the product or service, preference, conviction, conviction and purchase. This was amongst the first to link the hierarchy of effects concept to cognition, affect and conation.

Lifestyle analysis Used in segmentation, targeting and positioning as a means of understanding how individuals and groups choose to live their lives.

Logistics The management of materials and information streams through the various distribution channels to the end user.

Luxury items Products or services that possess one or more special or unique qualities or features. For example, sports cars and five-star hotels.

Macro factors External factors that impact upon an organisation. The mnemonic PESTLE is usually used to delineate these factors.

Marginal costing A dual pricing mechanism where the company considers the direct costs of producing, marketing and selling the product for export. The fixed costs of plant, equipment, research and development and domestic overheads are not included.

Market challengers Organisations that challenge the dominance of the market leader for increased market share.

Market followers Organisations that are satisfied with developing their own profitable market segments and seek not to attack either the *market leaders* or *market challengers*.

Market leader An organisation that is the leader in one, or a selection of all of its markets.

Market niche A small, often specialised, segment or market.

Market nicher An organisation that focuses on a particular niche (or niches) within the marketplace.

Market pricing A tactic where companies price their products and services appropriately for specific individual markets. Such price discrimination involves charging a price each particular (usually overseas) market will accept.

Marketing The American Marketing Association (2004) defines marketing as 'an organizational function and set of processes for creating, communicating and delivering value to customers and for managing customer relationships in a way that benefits both the organization and the stakeholder'.

Marketing audit The examination of the entire marketing effort of an organisation from planning to implementation, including the structure and operation of the marketing department.

Marketing department An organisational department comprising staff engaged in a range of marketing and related activities. Depending upon the size of the organisation this will range from administrative support to marketing planning and marketing research. A marketing director who may or may not be a member of the organisation's executive management board usually controls the operations of a marketing department.

Marketing environment The environment in which marketing activity takes place, which covers both internal (micro) and external (macro) factors.

Marketing mix A combination of tactics that are used to market a product or service. Originally comprised 4Ps: Product, Price, Place and Promo-

tion. A further 3Ps were added in the 1980s Physical Evidence, Process and People (participants). Also known as the *generic marketing mix*. A further 3Ps, Psychology, Performance and Packaging are now suggested.

Marketing research Burns and Bush (2000) define this as 'the process of designing, gathering, analysing and reporting of information that may be used to solve a specific marketing problem'.

Marketing strategy The strategy that will determine the marketing function within an organisation. This feeds into the SBU and overall corporate strategy.

Merchandise Products that are introduced to support (promote) a particular brand. For example, toys based on *Star Wars* movie characters.

Micro factors Environmental factors that are normally internal to an organisation. These can include the relationship with suppliers, the local community and customers.

Mobile defence A strategic position where the market leader expands into new territories with the intention of increasing its business opportunities, resources, size and financial strength. When the organisation expands by such means it becomes harder to challenge across so many markets.

New product development Organisations often seek, over time, to either develop and launch new products or enhance existing ones.

Noise The interruption or distortions that influence the communications process or understanding of a message. There are four subsets: physical, semantic, competitive and channel overload.

Observation A marketing research technique where an individual's buying behaviour is observed without his or her knowledge.

Own-label brands Brands that are owned and marketed by retailers such as supermarkets. They are also known as retailer brands, own brands, dealer brands, private brands and store brands. Such brands are produced by independent manufacturers for the retailer.

Packaging An additional marketing mix variable that includes both tangible and intangible attributes of a product or service. These attributes include containment materials, bundling and emotional appeal.

Penetration pricing Also known as predatory pricing, this is a tactic for accessing a market by cutting through existing pricing structures. Prices are often set deliberately low in order for the company to enter the market, ensuring a high level of sales.

People Also known as participants, this is one of the generic marketing mix variables. People are a core element in the operation of an enterprise, whether it is for profit or not for profit.

Performance An additional marketing mix variable that analyses measured (such as the level of sales and subsequent revenue generation) and experiential (activity participation) actions.

PESTLE A mnemonic that describes the external (macro) environment – Politics, Economic, Societal, Technological, Legal and Ecological/Environmental. There are a range of alternatives such as PEST.

Physical evidence Also known as physicality, this the space, perceived look, feel, ambience (visual and aural) and physical presence (tangibility or tangible clues) of an environment, such as a hotel.

Physical noise Anything that physically reduces the effectiveness or efficiency of a message being communicated between the sender and receiver.

Pioneer pricing A pricing tactic adopted if a product or service is particularly new to the market and the company is seeking to understand how the market will react.

Place This can be the confines of the environment in which a person lives and work. It can also be the placement (or distribution) of a product or service through channels to the target market segment.

Portfolio analysis Also known as Ansoff's matrix, this examines an organisation's activities within existing and potential markets with current and potential new product/service developments.

Position defence A strategic position where the market leader introduces a range of innovations to protect its position within the marketplace.

Positioning The 'location' of a product or service alongside key competitors and in the mind of the consumer. Positioning can depend on several factors including price/quality relationships.

Positioning map Also known as a perceptual map. The visual representation of a brand, within a specific marketplace, showing its position relative to close and distant competitors.

Pre-emptive defence A strategic position where the market leader launches an attack against a market challenger. For example, the market leader may launch a major promotional campaign aimed at protecting its position and destabilising the challenger.

Prestige pricing This symbolises reputation, glamour, respect, power and influence. These are not only value-driven phrases but clearly psychological

ones as well. Products or services that exemplify such characteristics need to reflect these in the price.

Price The measure of the value exchanged by the buyer for the value of the product or service offered by the seller. It is often considered the only marketing mix variable that is purely revenue generating.

Price matching A tactic often used in highly competitive markets where competitors are situated in relatively close proximity to each other. The competitors check each other's prices and then match each other in discounts and associated special offers.

Price sensitivity The point at which an individual will be sensitive to a set price or an increase in price, even though it may only be a marginal increase.

Price skimming A pricing tactic where a higher than normal price is charged for a product or service for a particular time frame. Assuming that the product or service demonstrates volume sales, the difference between the normal price and the higher price can be 'skimmed off'.

Primary research Also known as field research, the collection and analysis of original data for the purpose of addressing a specific research question or project.

Print media Advertising that appears in newspapers and magazines divided into five categories: daily newspapers, local/regional newspapers, consumer magazines, trade/professional magazines and customer magazines.

Processes A marketing mix variable that highlights direct or indirect actions from the customer or the provider organisation to the benefit of the end user. Processes can be technological and non-technological in form. Applying for a credit card is a process-driven action.

Product Dibb *et al.* (1997) suggest that a product 'is everything, both favourable and unfavourable, that is received in exchange. It is a complexity of tangible and intangible attributes, including functional, social and psychological utilities and benefits.'

Product adaptation Organisations may need to adapt their products in order to market them internationally. The adaptation may be for technical, cultural and/or legal reasons.

Product life cycle The life stages of a product or service, normally depicted as an S-shaped curve and encompassing introduction, growth, maturity, decline and death. There can also be rejuvenation of the product or service. Some product life cycles are relatively short (for example; fashion items).

Product placement A form of promotion where a product or service is purposely placed (used) within a movie or television series. Product placement is often used to cut through the advertising clutter in the marketplace.

Professional service pricing This tactic is used by individuals and companies such as lawyers, accountants and management consultants who charge various rates for their services.

Promotional mix The combination of tactics used to raise and sustain the profile of a product or service in the mind of the customer. Tactics include advertising, merchandising, public relations and sale promotion.

Promotional pricing A tactic where a special price is used to persuade customers to purchase a particular product or service. The promotional price may be limited to a particular time frame, for example 'special offer – for one day only'.

Psychological pricing A tactic that explores the relationship between 'value and price' in the mind of the customer.

Psychology An additional marketing mix variable that studies the behaviour and mental processes (cognition, reasoning, desires and feelings, for instance) of customers. This knowledge leads to a better understanding of why customers choose certain products and services over others, in other words why we buy and how we can be influenced to buy.

Public relations A promotional activity that focuses on the relationship and communication between an organisation and its various publics.

Questionnaire A marketing research technique where an individual is presented with a series of questions that focus on a specific topic or a range of topics. Questionnaires can be conducted face to face, over the telephone or via email.

Rebranding An organisation decides to change a significant element of the brand, often its name. Rebranding may be used to create, for instance, an internationally or globally recognised brand. However, such rebranding may not always be successful.

Rejuvenation of a brand When a brand is in the declining stage of its life cycle a company may seek to re-energise it. This may be achieved by, for example, repositioning it to a new target market segment(s) or repackaging it.

Relationship marketing 'The process of identifying and establishing, maintaining, enhancing, and when necessary terminating relationships with customers and other stakeholders, at a profit, so the objectives of all parties involved are met, when this is done by mutual giving and fulfilment of promises' (Grönroos 2000a).

Repositioning Brands may be repositioned over time to exploit new market opportunities. Can be used to rejuvenate brands.

Sales promotion Promotional activities that are normally used to introduce a new product/service, reinvigorate a current product/service or reduce stock levels. They include free samples, money-off coupons, extra value offers and bundling of products.

Schramm's model A communications model developed by Walter Schramm (1955) that depicts sender – receiver – feedback and noise. This was an adaptation of *Shannon's model*.

Scott's model A hierarchy of effects model – Attention, Comprehension and Understanding – developed by psychologist Walter Dill Scott.

Secondary research Research that is based on material that has already been gathered and analysed internally and/or externally. Secondary research can comprise previous research reports and/or government statistics such as a census.

Segmentation The subdivision of a market into similar subsets of customers that can be targeted with a specific marketing offer. *B2B* segmentation can occur by type of product/service or business sectors. *B2C* segmentation can occur by demographics, socio-economic status, behaviour and lifestyle.

Semantic noise The language or cultural noise that can negatively impact upon the communications process.

Shannon's model Also known as Shannon and Weaver's model, a communications system that depicts a linear process from information source to destination. Adapted by Schramm (1955).

Shock advertising Also known as shockvertising, this can be broadly described as the inclusion of frightening, visceral, offensive, taboo and emotion-provoking imagery and words to promote a product, service, concept or idea.

Shopping goods Durable or semi-durable products that have a relatively long life span. They include clothing, furniture, televisions, DVD players and washing machines.

Sponsorship Cornwall and Maignan (1998) describe this as '(1) an exchange between a sponsor [such as a brand] and a sponsee [such as a sporting event] whereby the latter receives a fee and the former obtains the right to associate itself with the activity sponsored and (2) the marketing of the association by the sponsor. Both activities are necessary if the sponsorship fee is to be a meaningful investment.'

Standard worldwide pricing A tactic used to cover all international markets. It is determined by averaging the unit cost, made up of fixed, variable and export related costs. Generally considered a theoretical model.

Staple products Products that are generally consumed on a regular, if not daily, basis. Staples may include (depending upon geographical location) bread, tea, coffee, rice, milk and vegetables.

Strategic withdrawal An organisation decides to withdraw from a particular market. Withdrawal may be for several reasons, for example, increasing competition demanding significant resources to maintain position within that particular market, or attempting to maintain too many brands within the organisation's portfolio.

Strong's model A hierarchy of effects model – want, solution, action and satisfaction – developed by Edward Strong in 1925.

Supply chain The process of delivering the raw materials to and finished product from the manufacturer to the customer and end user. Depending upon the complexity of the end product there will be several supply chains involved.

SWOT analysis An analysis/comparison of the organisation's Strengths and Weaknesses (Internal) with the environmental analysis of Opportunities and Threats (external) prevalent within the industry. A *PESTLE* analysis can be undertaken to provide potential industry Opportunities and Threats.

Targeting The process of focusing marketing resources (*marketing mix*) to a segmented audience.

Unsought products or services Items that consumers had not considered purchasing until they are made aware of either a need or a benefit. There are three subsets: resolving a current or 'near-future' problem, 'hard sell' techniques and medium/longer-term considerations.

Value chain When activities (such as cost and performance) are grouped together they can be viewed as a value chain running throughout all aspects of the company from administration through to operations and distribution. The objective is to examine costs and performance to implement improvements that will benefit the customer.

Variable pricing Also known as flexible pricing, this is where a company varies prices to accommodate changes within the competitive marketplace and customer needs.

Vaughn's low involvement model A hierarchy of effects model that is divided into four quadrants: (1) Informative (thinker), (2) Affective (feeler), (3) Habit forming (doer) and (4) Self-satisfaction (reactor).

Bibliography

3M (2003) Information sourced from the 3M website, www.3m.com.

7-Eleven (2003) The history of 7-Eleven, details of its international licensing arrangements and country locations can be found on www.7-eleven.com.

Aaker, D (1991) *Managing Brand Equity*, New York: Free Press.

Aaker, D. (1995) *Strategic Marketing Management*, New York: Wiley.

Airbus (2004) *Operations: Procurement, Airbus SAS.* www.airbus.com.

Alashban, A. A., Hayes, L. A., Zinkhan, G. M. and, Balazs, A. L. (2002) 'International brand name standardization/adaptation: antecedents and consequences', *Journal of International Marketing* **10**(3), pp. 22–48.

American Marketing Association (AMA) (1948) 'Report of the definitions committee', *Journal of Marketing* **13** (October), p. 202.

AMA (1960) *Marketing Definitions: A glossary of marketing terms*, Chicago: AMA.

Anderson, L. M. and Taylor, R. L. (1995) 'McCarthy's 4Ps: timeworn or time-tested?' *Journal of Marketing Theory and Practice*, **3**(3) (Summer), pp. 1–9.

Andrews, K. (1986) *Concept of Corporate Strategy*, New York: McGraw-Hill.

Ansoff, H. I. (1987) *Corporate Strategy*, rev. edn, Harmondsworth: Penguin.

Arndt, J. (1979) 'Toward a concept of domesticated markets', *Journal of Marketing* **43** (Fall), pp. 69–75.

Asher, J. (1987) 'Packaging: the interactive fifth "p" of marketing', *Marketing Review*, January, pp. 21–3.

Bagozzi, R. P. (1975) 'Marketing as exchange', *Journal of Marketing* **39** (October), pp. 32–9.

Baker, M. J. (1997) 'People: the fifth P of marketing', in J. Yudelson (1999), 'Adapting McCarthy's four P's for the twenty-first century', *Journal of Marketing Education* **21**(1) (April), pp. 60–7.

Baker, M. J. (2000) *Marketing Strategy and Management*, 3rd edn, Basingstoke: Macmillan.

Barlow, J. and Maul, D. (2000) *Emotional Value*, San Francisco: Berrett-Koehler.

Barney, J. B. (1997) *Gaining and Sustaining Competitive Advantage*, Reading, Mass.: Addison-Wesley.

Barry, T. E. (1987) 'The development of the Hierarchy of Effects: an historical perspective', *Current Issues and Research in Advertising* **10**(2), pp. 251–95.

Bateson, J. (1989) *Managing Services Marketing*, New York: Dryden Press.

BBC (2003) 'How the "global village" faced Sars', BBC News Online, 2 May.

BBC (2004a) 'Wet weather hits Coca-Cola sales', BBC News Online, 15 September.

BBC (2004b) 'Spam messages on the increase', BBC Online, 25 May.

BBC (2005) *Global Dimming*, Horizon, BBC 2 television, first broadcast January.

Bellocchi, L. P. (2001) 'Assessing the effectiveness of the Economic Espionage Act of 1996', *International Journal of Intelligence and Counterintelligence* **14**, pp. 366–87.

Berlo, D. K. (1960) *The Process of Communication: An Introduction to theory and practice*, New York: Holt, Rinehart and Winston.

Bernays, E. (1923) *Crystallizing Public Opinion*, New York: Boni & Liveright.

Berry, L. L. (1983) 'Relationship marketing', in L.L.Berry, G. L. Shostack and G. Upah (eds), *Emerging Perspectives on Service Marketing*, Chicago: AMA.

Bixler, M. (1991) 'Maintaining your marketing consistency', *Small Business Reports* **16** (January), pp. 27–34.

Blomqvist, R., Dahl, J. and Haeger, T. (1993) *Relationsmarknadsföring: strategi och metod i servicekonkurrens* (Relationship Marketing Strategy and Methods for Service Operations), Gothenburg: IHM Publishing.

Booms, B. H. and Bitner, M. J. (1981) 'Marketing strategies and organization structures for service firms', in J. H. Donnely and W. R. George (eds), *Marketing of Services*, Chicago: AMA.

Borden, N. H. (1964) 'The concept of the marketing mix', *Journal of Advertising Research*, June, pp. 2–7.

Borden, N. H. and Marshall, M. V. (1959) *Advertising Management: Texts and cases*, Illinois: Irwin.

Bowie, D. and Buttle, F. (2004) *Hospitality Marketing: An introduction*, Oxford: Elsevier Butterworth-Heinemann.

Brown, R. (1991) 'Making the product portfolio a basis for action', *Long Range Planning* **24**(1), pp. 102–10.

Brownlie, D. T. and Bart, C. K. (1985) *Products and Strategies*, MCB University Press. **11** (1), cited in M. McDonald (1996) *Strategic Marketing Planning*, 2nd edn, London: Kogan Page.

Burns, A. and Bush, R. (2000) *Marketing Research*, 2nd edn, New Jersey: Prentice Hall.

Business Week (2003) 'Best global brands', *Business Week*, European edn, 5 August.

Buttle, F. (1986) *Hotel and Food Service Markets*, New York: Holt, Reinhart & Winston.

Cartwright, R. (2002) *Mastering the Business Environment*, Basingstoke: Palgrave Macmillan.

Chapman, R. L., Soosay, C. and Kandampully, J. (2003) 'Innovation in logistic services and the new business model', *International Journal of Physical Distribution and Logistics Management* **33**(7), pp. 630–50.

Christensen, C. R., Berg, N. A. and Salter, M. S. (1980) *Policy Formation and Administration: A casebook for senior management problems in business*, 8th edn, Illinois: Irwin.

Churchill, Jr., G. A. and Peter, J. P. (1998) *Marketing: Creating value for customers*, 2nd edn, New York: Irwin McGraw-Hill.

Clancy, K. and Shulman, R. S. (1991) *The Marketing Revolution: A radical manifesto for dominating the marketplace*, New York: Harper.

Clausewitz, C. von. (1832) *On War*, Princeton: Princeton University Press (this edn 1976).

Cochran, E. S. (2003) 'South Korea's intelligence targets U.S. technology', *International Journal of Intelligence and Counterintelligence* **16**, pp. 179–201.

Cokayne, F. (1991) *Successful Marketing Strategies*, Cambridge: Fitzwillam.

Colby, C. L. and Parasuraman. A. (2003) 'Technology still matters: never mind the doomsayers, e-services are alive, well and positioned for growth', *Marketing Management* **12**(4) (July/August), pp. 28–33.

Colley, R. H. (1961) *Defining Advertising Goals for Measured Advertising Results*, New York: Association of National Advertisers.

Collier, D. A. (1991) 'New marketing mix stresses service', *Journal of Business Strategy*, March/April, pp. 4–5.

Cooke, E. F., Rayburn, J. M. and Abercrombie, C. L. (1992) 'The history of marketing thought as reflected in the definitions of marketing', *Journal of Marketing – Theory and Practice*, Fall, pp. 10–20.

Cooper, R. G. and Kleinschmidt. E. J. (1991a) 'New product processes at leading industrial firms', *Industrial Marketing Management* **20**(2) (May), pp. 137–47.

Cooper, R. G. and Kleinschmidt, E. J. (1991b) *New Products: The key factors in success*, Chicago: AMA.

Cornwell, T. B. and Maignan, I. (1998) 'An international review of sponsorship research', *Journal of Advertising* **27**(1) (Spring), pp. 1–27.

Cottingham, J. (1995) 'Rene Descartes', in T. Honderich (ed.), *The Oxford Companion to Philosophy*, Oxford: Oxford University Press.

Cottrell, S. (2003) *The Study Skills Handbook*, 2nd edn, Basingstoke: Palgrave Macmillan.

Cowell, D. (1984) *The Marketing of Services*, Oxford: Butterworth-Heinemann.

Cravens, D. (1982) *Strategic Marketing*, New York: Irwin.

CR80 News (2005) 'USA Technologies launches contactless credit card payment systems for vending', 2 June, www.cr80news.com.

Culliton, J. W. (1948) *The Management of Marketing Costs*, Division of Research, Graduate School of Business Administration, Harvard University, Cambridge, Mass.

Cunningham, W. H. and Cunningham, I. (1981) *Marketing: A managerial approach*, Illinois: Irwin.

Czinkota, M. R. and Ronkainen, I. (1995) *International Marketing*, 4th Edn, Fort Worth: Dryden Press.

Czinkota, M. R., Ronkainen, I. A., Moffet, M. H. and Moynihan, E. O. (1998) *Global Business*, Fort Worth: Dryden Press.

D'Aveni, R. A. (1995) *Hypercompetitive Rivalries: Competing in highly dynamic environments*, New York: Free Press.

Daniels, J. D. and Radebaugh, L. H. (1998) *International Business: Environments and Operations*, 8th edn, Reading, Mass.: Addison-Wesley.

Datamonitor (2004) *Global Offshore Call Centre Outsourcing: Who will be the next India?* Datamonitor.

Davidson, D. (1997) *Even More Offensive Marketing*, London: Penguin.

Dawson, L. M. (1969) 'The human concept: new philosophy for business', *Business Horizons*, December, pp. 29–38.

De Pelsmacher, P., Geuens, M. and Van den Bergh, J. (2004) *Marketing Communications: A European perspective*, 2nd edn, Harlow: Financial Times (FT) Prentice Hall.

Dean, J. (1950) 'Pricing policies for new products', *Harvard Business Review* **28**, pp. 45–53.

Dibb, S. (1998) 'Market segmentation: strategies for success', *Marketing Intelligence and Planning* **16**(7), pp. 394–406.

Dibb, S., Simkin, L., Pride. W. M. and Ferrell. O. C. (1997) *Marketing: Concepts and strategies*, 3rd edn, Boston, Mass.: Houghton Mifflin.

Dichter, E. (1960) *The Strategy of Desire*, New York: Doubleday.

DMA (2003) *DMA Census of the Direct Marketing Industry 2002–2003*, Direct Marketing Association (UK) Ltd, July.

Donovan, R. J. and Rossiter, J. R. (1982) 'Store atmosphere: an environmental psychology approach', *Journal of Retailing* **58** (Spring), pp. 34–57.

Doole, I. and Lowe, R. (1999) *International Marketing Strategy: Analysis, development and implementation*, 2nd edn, London: International Thomson Business Press.

Doyle, P. (1998) *Marketing Management and Strategy*, 2nd edn, Harlow: Prentice Hall.

Drucker, P. F. (1999) *Innovation and Entrepreneurship: Principles and practice*, Oxford: Butterworth-Heinemann.

Eckles, R. W. (1990) *Business Marketing Management: Marketing of business products and services*, New Jersey: Prentice Hall.

Ehrenberg, A. S. C. (1974) 'Repetive advertising and the consumer', *Journal of Advertising Research* **14** (April), pp. 25–34.

Eldridge, C. E. (1970) *Marketing for Profit*, London: Macmillan.

Elley, D. (1993) *Variety Movie Guide 1994*, London: Hamlyn.

Environmental Protection Agency USA (EPA) (2000) *Global Warming*, EPA, www.epa.gov.

Euromonitor (2003) 'Textile washing products in the UK', *Euromonitor Research*, July.

Euromonitor (2004a) 'Retailing developments: private label trends', in 'Aspects of retailing: global OTC healthcare distribution', *Euromonitor Research*, February.

Euromonitor (2004b) *Global Vending Corporate Overview – Report*, Euromonitor, May.

Ewen, S. (1996) *PR! A social history of spin*, New York: Basic Books.

Federal Bureau of Investigation (FBI) (2003) *Telemarketing Victim Call Center Background*, Los Angeles FBI Center, www.losangeles.fbi.gov/telemarket.

Festinger, L. (1957) *A Theory of Cognitive Dissonance*, Stanford, Conn.: Stanford University Press.

Fletcher, W. (1999) *Advertising, Advertising*, London: Profile.

Ford, H. and Crowther, S. (1926) *My Life and Work*, London: Heinemann.

Fowler, A. R. Jr and Thomas, J. (1993) 'Functional strategic response to progression through the product life cycle: an accommodation to marketing reality', *American Business Review*, June, pp. 36–44.

Foxall, G. R., Goldsmith, R. E., and Brown, S. (1998) *Consumer Psychology for Marketing*, 2nd edn, London: Thomson Learning.

Glaser, E. (1941) 'An experiment in the development of critical thinking', New York: Teachers' College, Columbia University, cited in S. Cottrell (2003) *The Study Skills Handbook*, 2nd edn, Basingstoke: Palgrave Macmillan.

Goldfarb, A. (2001)' Let there be Sunlight! The rise of Lever Brothers and Sunlight Soap', working paper, Northwestern University.

Goldsmith, R. E. (1999) 'The personalized marketplace: beyond the 4Ps', *Marketing Intelligence and Planning* **17**(4), pp. 178–85.

Goldstein, E. B. (1999) *Sensation and Perception*, 5th edn, Pacific Grove: Brooks/Cole.

Goncalves, V. F. Da. C. and Aguas, P. M. R. (1997) 'The concept of life cycle: an application to the tourist product', *Journal of Travel Research* **36**(2) (Fall), pp. 12–23.

Goodrich, J., Gildea, R. L. and Cavanaugh, K. (1979) 'A place for public relations in the marketing mix', *MSU Business Topics* **27** (Autumn), pp. 53–7.

Grant, R. M. (2002) *Contemporary Strategy Analysis: Concepts, techniques, applications*, 4th edn, Oxford: Blackwell.

Green, P. S. (1992) *Reputation Risk Management*, London: FT/Pitman.

Grimshaw, A. (1999) 'Gender', in A. Bullock and S. Trombley (eds), *The New Fontana Dictionary of Modern Thought*, London: HarperCollins.

Grönross, C. (1990) *Service Management and Marketing*, New York: Lexington.

Grönroos, C. (1997) 'From marketing mix to relationship marketing: towards a paradigm shift in

382   BIBLIOGRAPHY

marketing', *Management Decision* **35**(3/4), pp. 322–40.

Grönroos, C. (2000a) 'Relationship marketing: the Nordic School perspective', in J. N. Sheth and A. Pavatiyar (eds), *Handbook of Relationship Marketing*, London: Sage.

Grönroos, C. (2000b) *Service Management and Marketing: A customer relationship management approach*, 2nd edn, Chichester: Wiley.

Grönroos, C. (2004) 'The relationship marketing process: communication, interaction, dialogue, value', *Journal of Business and Industrial Marketing* **19**(2), pp. 99–113.

Groucutt, J. (2003a) 'Extending the marketing mix', working paper.

Groucutt, J. (2003b) 'An analysis of various product lifecycles', working paper.

Groucutt, J. and Griseri, P. (2004) *Mastering e-Business*, Basingstoke: Palgrave Macmillan.

Groucutt, J., Leadley, P. and Forsyth, P. (2004) *Marketing: Essential principles, new realities*, London: Kogan Page.

Groucutt, J. and Telford, A. (1995) *Communicating for Improved Business Performance*, Cheltenham: Thornes.

Gummesson, E. (2002) *Total Relationship Marketing*, 2nd edn, Oxford: Butterworth-Heinemann.

Haddigan, M. (1995) 'Competitor intelligence considered more vital now', *Marketing News* **29**(21) (9 October), pp. 2–5.

Haigh, D. (2003) 'An introduction to brand equity: how to understand and appreciate brand value and the economic impact of brand investment', *Interactive Marketing* **5**(1) (July/September), pp. 21–32.

Håkansson, H. and Snehota, I. (eds) (1995) *Developing Relationships in Business Networks*, London: Routledge.

Harridge-March, S. (2002) Marketing communications, lecture notes on telemarketing, Oxford Brookes University.

Hartley, R. F. (1998) *Marketing Mistakes and Successes*, 7th edn, New York: Wiley.

Harvey, M. G., Lusch, R. F. and Cavarkapa, B. (1996) 'A marketing mix for the 21st century', *Journal of Marketing Theory and Practice* **4** (4) (Fall), pp. 1–15.

Higgins, K. T. (2003) 'The rebirth of 7-Eleven', *Marketing Management* **12**(4) (July/August), pp. 18–21.

Hillman, D. and Gibbs, D. (1998) *Century Makers*, London: Weidenfeld & Nicolson.

Hilton, S. (2001) 'Take the wrap', *Guardian* G2, 8 June, pp. 2–3.

Hine, T. (1997) *The Total Package: The secret history and hidden meanings of boxes, bottles, cans and other persuasive containers*, Boston and New York: Back Bay Books, Little, Brown.

Hoffman, K. D. and Bateson, J. (1997) *Essentials of Service Marketing*, New York: Dryden Press.

Hofstede, G. (1980) *Culture's Consequences: International differences in work-related values*, Beverly Hills and London: Sage.

Hofstede, G. (1994) 'The business of international business is culture', *International Business Review* **3**(1), pp. 1–14.

Hollensen, S. (2001) *Global Marketing: A market-responsive approach*, 2nd edn, Harlow: FT/Prentice Hall.

Hooley, G. J. (1995) 'The lifecycle concept revisited: aid or albatross?', *Journal of Strategic Marketing* **3**(1), pp. 23–39.

Horgan, J. (1990) 'Claude E. Shannon: unicyclist, juggler, and father of information theory', *IEEE Information Theory Society Newsletter* (June).

Hoyer, W. D. and MacInnis, D. J. (1997) *Consumer Behavior*, Boston and New York: Houghton Mifflin.

Hughes, D. G. (1978) *Marketing Management: A planning approach*, Reading, Mass.: Addison-Wesley.

Hunt, S. and Morgan, R. (1994) 'The commitment-trust theory or relationship marketing', *Journal of Marketing* **58**, pp. 20–38.

ICC (2004) 'Counterfeit products – overview', Counterfeit Intelligence Bureau, ICC Commercial Crime Services, www.icc-ccs.org

Inalhan, G. and Finch, E. (2004) 'Place attachment and sense of belonging', *Facilities* **22**(5/6), pp. 120–8.

International Labor Organization (ILO) (2004) 'Half the world's workers living below the US$2 a day poverty line: ILO says new policies for promoting productivity growth and decent jobs could improve outlook for working poor', press release, Department of Communications and Public Information, ILO.

Inwood, D. and Hammond, J. (1993) *Product Development: An integrated approach*, London: Kogan Page.

Issa, J. J. and Jayawardena, C. (2003) 'The 'all-inclusive' concept in the Caribbean', *International Journal of Contemporary Hospitality Management* **15**(3), pp. 167–71.

James, B. G. (1985) *Business Wargames*, London: Penguin.

Jauch, L. R. and Glueck, F. W. (1988) *Business Policy and Strategic Management*, 5th edn, New York: McGraw-Hill.

Jeremy, D. J. (1998) *A Business History of Britain, 1900–1990s*, Oxford: Oxford University Press.

Jobber, D. (1998) *Principles and Practice of Marketing*, 2nd edn, Maidenhead: McGraw-Hill.

Johnson, A. A. (1986) 'Adding more P's to the pod or 12 essential elements of marketing', *Marketing News*, 11 April, p. 2.

Johnson, G. and Scholes, K. (2004) *Exploring Corporate Strategy*, 6th edn, Harlow: Prentice Hall.

Judd, V. C. (1987) 'Differentiate with the 5th P: people', *Industrial Marketing Management* **16**, pp. 241–7.

Kaikati, J. G. and Kaikati, A. B. (2004) 'Identity crisis: the dos and don'ts of brand rechristening', *Marketing Management*, January/February, pp. 45–9.

Kandampully, J. (2002) 'Innovations as the core competency of a service organisation: the role of technology, knowledge and networks', *European Journal of Innovation Management* **5**(1), pp. 18–26.

Kapferer, J-N. (1998) *Strategic Brand Management: Creating and sustaining brand equity long term*, 2nd edn, London: Kogan Page.

Keefe, L. M. (2004) 'What is the meaning of "marketing"?' *Marketing News*, 15 September, pp. 17–18.

Keegan, W. J. and Green, M. C. (1997) *Principles of Global Marketing*, New Jersey: Prentice Hall.

Keller, K. L. (1993) 'Conceptualizing, measuring and managing customer-based brand equity', *Journal of Marketing* **57**(1), January, pp. 1–22.

Keller, K. L. (2003) 'Understanding brands, branding and brand equity', *Interactive Marketing* **5**(1) (July/September), pp. 7–20.

Kerin, R. A. and Peterson, R. A. (1980) *Perspectives on Strategic Marketing Management*, Boston: Allyn and Bacon.

Koehn, N. F. (1999) 'Henry Heinz and brand creation in the late nineteenth century', *Harvard Business School Working Knowledge*, 7 December.

Knowles, J. (2003) 'Value-based brand measurement and management', *Interactive Marketing* **5**(1), pp. 40–50.

Kotler, P. (1973) 'Atmospherics as a marketing tool', *Journal of Retailing* **49**, pp. 48–61.

Kotler, P. (1975) *Marketing for Non-Profit Organizations*, New Jersey: Prentice Hall.

Kotler, P. (1986) 'Megamarketing', *Harvard Business Review* **64** (March–April), pp. 117–24.

Kotler, P (1991) *Marketing Management*, New Jersey: Prentice Hall.

Kotler, P. (1992) 'Marketing's new paradigm: What's really happening out there', *Planning Review* pp. 50–2.

Kotler, P. (1998) *Marketing Management: Analysis, planning, implementation and control*, 9th edn, New Jersey: Prentice Hall.

Kotler, P. (2000) *Marketing Management*, Millennium edn, Harlow: Prentice Hall.

Kotler, P., Gregor, W. and Rogers, W. (1989) 'The MA comes of age', *Sloan Management Review* **30**(2) (Winter), pp. 49–62.

Lasswell, H. (1927) *Propaganda Technique in the World War*, New York: Knopf. See also Lasswell, H. (1948) 'The structure and function of communications in society', in L. Bryson (ed.), *The Communication of Ideas*, New York: Harper & Row.

Lauginie, J. M., Mansillon, G. and Dubouin, J. (1994) *Action Commerciale Mercatique*, Paris: Foucher.

Lavidge, R. J. and Steiner, G. A. (1961) 'A model for predictive measurements of advertising effectiveness', *Journal of Marketing* **25** (October), pp. 59–62.

LeDoux, L. (1991) 'Is preservation the fifth 'p' or just another macro environmental factor?', in G. F. McKinnon and G. A. Kelley (eds), *Challenges of a New Decade in Marketing*, Western Marketing Educators' Association, pp. 82–6.

Lee, S. G. and Lye, S. W. (2003) 'Design for manual packaging', *International Journal of Physical Distribution and Logistics Management* **33**(2), pp. 163–89.

Leed, T. W. and German, G. A. (1973) *Food Merchandising: Principles and practices*, New York: Chain Store Age Books (cited in Foxall *et al.* 1998).

Lehmann, D. R. (2002) 'What's on marketers' minds?', *Marketing Management* **11**(6) (November/December), pp. 16–20.

Leiser, M. (2003) 'Strategic brand value: advancing use of brand equity to grow your brand and business', *Interactive Marketing* **5**(1) (July/September), pp. 33–9.

Leverfaberge (2004) www.leverfaberge.co.uk/aboutus/history.html

Levitt, T. (1965) 'Exploit the product life cycle', *Harvard Business Review* **43** (November–December), pp. 81–94.

Levitt, T. (1972) 'Production line approach to service',

Harvard Business Review (September–October), pp. 41–52.

Levitt, T. (1983) *The Marketing Imagination*, New York: Free Press.

Lewis, St. Elmo E. (1915) *Getting the Most Out of Business*, New York: Ronald Press.

Lijander, V. and Roos, I. (2002) 'Customer-relationship levels – from spurious to true relationships', *Journal of Services Marketing* 16(7), pp. 593–614.

Lukk, T. (1997) *Movie Marketing: Opening the picture and giving it legs*, Los Angeles: Silman-James Press.

Lynch, R. (2000) *Corporate Strategy*, 2nd edn, Harlow: FT Prentice Hall.

Magrath, A. J. (1986) 'When marketing services, 4P's are not enough', *Business Horizons* 29 (May–June), pp. 44–50.

Marks, A. P. (1989) 'The Sinclair C5: an investigation into its development, launch and subsequent failure', *European Journal of Marketing* 23(1), pp. 61–71.

Mason, W. R. (1958) 'A theory of packaging in the marketing mix', *Business Horizons*, Summer, pp. 91–5.

Mattelart, A. and Mattelart, M. (1998) *Theories of Communication: A short introduction*, London: Sage.

Mazur, P. (1947) 'Does distribution cost enough?', *Fortune* 36 (November), p. 138.

McBride (2004) www.mcbride.co.uk.

McCarthy, E. J . (1965) *Basic Marketing*, Homewood, Ill: Irwin.

McCarthy, E. J. and Perreault Jr.,W. D. (1987) *Basic Marketing*, 9th edn, Homewood, Ill: Irwin.

McDaniel, C. Jr. and Gates, R. (1999) *Contemporary Marketing Research*, 4th edn, Cincinnati: South-Western College Publishing.

McDonald, M. (2002) *Marketing Plans: How to prepare them; how to use them*, Oxford: Butterworth-Heinemann.

McDonald, M. (2003) 'Marketing died in the last decade', *Interactive Marketing* 5(2) (October/ December), pp. 144–59.

McNair, M. P., Brown, M. P., Leighton, D. S. R. and England, W. B. (1957) *Problems in Marketing*, 2nd edn, New York: McGraw-Hill.

Mehrabian, A. and Russell, J. A. (1974) *An Approach to Environmental Psychology*, Boston, Mass.: MIT Press.

Mendelsohn, H. (1962) 'Measuring the process of communication effect', *Public Opinion Quarterly* 26 (Fall), pp. 411–16.

Mercer, D. (1997) *New Marketing Practice: Rules for success in a changing world*, London: Penguin.

Metrological Office (2004) 'Forewarned is fore-armed', press release, Met Office (UK), 4 March.

Miller, C. (1991) 'Research reveals how marketers can win by a nose', *Marketing News*, 4 February, pp. 1–2.

Mindak, W. A. and Fine, S. (1981). 'A fifth 'p': public relations', in J. H. Donnely and W. R. George (eds), *Marketing of Services*, Chicago: AMA.

Mintel (2003) *Vending – UK Report*, Mintel International Group, February.

Mintel (2004) *Holiday Centres – UK*, Mintel International, January.

Mintzberg, H., Lampel, J., Quinn, J. B. and Ghoshal, S. (2003) *The Strategy Process: Concepts, context and cases*, 4th edn, Harlow: Prentice Hall.

Morris, D. S., Barnes, B. R. and Lynch, J. E. (1999) 'Relationship marketing needs total quality management', *Total Quality Management* 10(4/5), July, pp. 659–66.

Morris, J. (2004) 'Aerospace and aviation', special feature, *Business Week* European edition, 26 July–2 August, pp. 46–52.

Mühlbacher, H., Dahringer, L. and Leihs, H. (1999) *International Marketing: A global perspective*, 2nd edn, London: International Thomson Business Press.

National Counterintelligence Center USA (NACIC) (1999) *Foreign Economic and Industrial Espionage Remains a Threat in 1999*, Washington, DC: NACIC.

National Counterintelligence Executive USA (NCIX) (2004a) *The Economic Espionage Act of 1996: A brief guide*, Washington, DC: NCIX, www.ncix.gov

National Counterintelligence Center (NCIX) (2004b) *Annual Report to Congress on Foreign Economic Collection and Industrial Espionage*, Washington, DC: NCIX.

Nickels, W. G. and Jolson, M. A. (1976) 'Packaging: the fifth 'p' in the marketing mix?', *SAM Advanced Management Journal*, Winter, pp. 13–21.

NZ Marketing (2002) 'Performance measures', *NZ Marketing* 21(8) (September), p. 2.

Ohmae, K. (1982) *The Mind of the Strategist*, London: McGraw-Hill.

Orton, J. D. (2002) 'Cross-national ethical dilemmas in competitive intelligence', *International Journal of Intelligence and Counterintelligence* 15, pp.440–56.

Oxenfeldt, A. R. (1966) *Executive Action in Marketing*, Belmont: Wadsworth.

Palmer, A. (2000) *Principles of Marketing*, Oxford: Oxford University Press.

Patty, T. (1997) 'Mastering the new five P's of marketing', in J. Yudelson (1999) 'Adapting McCarthy's four P's for the twenty-first century', *Journal of Marketing Education* **21**(1) (April), pp. 60–7.

Pavitt, J. (2000) *Brand New*, London: V& A Publications.

Payne, C. M. A. and Ballantyne, D. (1991) *Relationship Marketing: Bringing quality, customer service and marketing together*, Oxford: Butterworth-Heinemann.

Pearsall, J. and Trumble, B. (eds) (1996) *The Oxford English Reference Dictionary*, 2nd edn, Oxford: Oxford University Press.

Perreault, W. D., McCarthy, E. J., Parkinson, S. and Stewart, K. (2000) *Basic Marketing*, London: McGraw-Hill.

Peters, T. (2003) *Re-imagine!* London: Dorling Kindersley.

Pine, B. J. II, and Gilmore, J. H. (1999) *The Experience Economy: Work is theatre and every business a stage*, Boston: Harvard Business School Press.

Pinker, S (1997) *How The Mind Works*, New York: Norton.

Porter, M. E. (1980) *Competitive Strategy: Techniques for analyzing industries and competitors*, New York: Free Press.

Porter, M. E. (1985) *Competitive Advantage*, New York: Free Press.

Porter, M. E. and Millar, V. E. (1985) 'How information gives you competitive advantage', in M. E. Porter (1998) *On Competition*, Boston, Mass.: Harvard Business School Press.

Pyle, J. F. (1931) *Marketing Principles*, New York: McGraw-Hill.

Quee, W. T. (1999) *Marketing Research*, Singapore: Butterworth-Heinemann/Marketing Institute of Singapore.

Raban, J. and Torrance, J. (1999) 'Roles and role theory', in A. Bullock and S. Trombley (eds), *The New Fontana Dictionary of Modern Thought*, London: HarperCollins.

Rafiq, M. and Ahmed, P. K. (1995) 'Using the 7Ps as a generic marketing mix: an exploratory survey of UK and European marketing academics', *Marketing Intelligence and Planning* **13**(9), pp. 4–16.

Ramberg, J. (2000) *ICC Guide to Incoterms 2000*, ICC publication 620, International Chamber of Commerce, www.iccwbo.org/incoterm

Rapp, S. and Collins, T. (1990) *The Great Marketing Turnaround*, New Jersey: Prentice Hall,

Ray, M. L.,Sawyer, A. G., Rothchild, M. L., Heeler, R. M., Strong, E. C. and Reed, J. B. (1973) 'Marketing communications and hierarchy of effects', in P. Clarke (ed.), *New Models for Mass Communication Research*, Beverly Hills: Sage.

Rees, N. (1997) *Dictionary of Slogans*, London: HarperCollins.

Reid, R. D. (1989) *Hospitality Marketing Management*, 3rd edn, New York: Van Nostrand Reinhold.

Ries, A. and Trout, J. (2001) *Positioning: The battle for the mind*, New York: McGraw-Hill Education.

Robbins, S. P. and Coulter, M. (1996) *Management*, 5th edn, New Jersey: Prentice Hall.

Robertson, T. S. (1984) 'Marketing's potential contribution to consumer behavior research: the case of diffusion theory', *Advances in Consumer Research* **2**, pp. 484–9.

Rogers, E. M. (1983) *Diffusion of Innovations*, 3rd edn, New York: Free Press.

Rogers, E. and Kincaid, L. (1981) *Communication Networks: Towards a new paradigm for research*, New York: Free Press.

Rogers, E. M. (1994) *A History of Communication Study: A biographical approach*, New York: Free Press.

Rosci, F. (2001) 'Down but not out (tourism in Israel)', *Travel Agent*, 16 April.

Rosen, E. (2000) *The Anatomy of Buzz: Creating word-of-mouth marketing*, London: HarperCollins Business.

Rossiter, J. R. and Percy, L. (1987) *Advertising and Promotions Management*, New York: McGraw-Hill.

Rothschild, W. (1979) 'Competitor analysis: the missing link in strategy', *Management Review*, July.

Sabbagh, K. (1996) *21st Century Jet: The making of the Boeing 777*, London: Pan.

Santrock, J. W (2000) *Psychology*, 6th edn, Boston, Mass.: McGraw-Hill.

Saunders, D. (1999) *20th Century Advertising*, London: Carlton.

Schramm, W. (1955) 'How communication works', in W. Schramm (ed.), *The Process and Effect of Communication*, Urbana: University of Illinois Press.

Schultz, D. E., Tannebaum, S. I. and Lauterborn, R. F. (1993) *Integrated Marketing Communications*, Lincolnwood: NTC Business Books.

Scott, W. D. (1903) *The Theory of Advertising: A simple exposition of the principles of psychology in their relation to successful advertising*, Boston: Small, Maynard and Co.

Scott, W. D. (1908) *The Psychology of Advertising: A simple exposition of the principles of psychology in their relation to successful advertising*, Boston: Small, Maynard and Co.

Shannon, C. E. (1948) 'A mathematical theory of communication', *Bell System Technical Journal* 27 (July and October), pp. 379–423, 623–656.

Sharp, S. (2000) 'Truth or consequences: 10 myths that cripple competitive intelligence', *Competitive Intelligence* 3(1) (January/February), pp. 37–40.

Sheldon, A. F. (1911) *The Art of Selling*, Chicago: Sheldon School.

Shimp, T. A. (2000) *Advertising Promotion: Supplemental aspects of integrated marketing communications*, Fort Worth: Dryden Press.

Simkin, L. (1996) 'Addressing organizational prerequisites in marketing planning programmes', *Journal of Marketing Management* 12, pp. 375–90.

Simkin, L. and Cheng, A. (1997) 'Understanding competitors' strategies: the practitioner-academic gap', *Marketing Intelligence and Planning* 15(3), pp. 124–34.

Smith, P., Berry, C. and Pulford, A. (1997) *Strategic Marketing Communications*, London: Kogan Page.

Smith, W. R. (1957) 'Product differentiation and market segmentation as alternative marketing strategies', *Journal of Marketing* 21(1), pp. 3–8.

Stanton, W. J., Etzel, M. J. and Walker, B. J. (1994) *Fundamentals of Marketing*, 4th edn,. New York: McGraw-Hill.

Star, S. H., Davis, N. J., Lovelock, C. H. and Shapiro, B. P. (1977) *Problems in Marketing*, New York: McGraw-Hill.

Steele, F. (1981) *Sense of Place*, Boston, Mass.: CBI Publishing.

Stipp, D. (2004) 'Climate collapse: the Pentagon's weather nightmare', *Fortune*, 26 January.

Strong, E. K. Jr (1925) *The Psychology of Selling and Advertising*, New York: McGraw-Hill.

Sunday Times (2004) 'FSA director advertisements', Appointments, Section 7, *Sunday Times*, p. 1.

Tapp, A. (1998) *Principles of Direct Marketing*, Harlow: Financial Times/Prentice Hall.

Thompson, P. (2000) *Cassell's Dictionary of Modern American History*, London: Cassell.

Tibballs, G. (1999) *Business Blunders*, London: Robinson.

Tracy, B. (2004) *Million Dollar Habits*, Irvine, Calif.: Entrepreneur Press.

Traynor, K. (1985) 'Research deserves status as marketing's fifth "p"', *Marketing News* 19 (8 November), pp. 7–12.

Tréguer, J-P. (2002) *50+ Marketing*, Basingstoke: Palgrave.

Trout, J. (1969) 'Positioning is a game people play in today's me-too marketplace', *Industrial Marketing*, June, pp. 51–55.

Turner, A. (1980) '*The Lost Weekend*', in *The Movie: The illustrated history of the cinema*, London: Orbis.

Tye, L. (1998) *The Father of Spin: Edward L. Bernays and the birth of public relations*, New York: Holt.

Underhill, P. (1999) *Why We Buy: The science of shopping*, London: Orion Business Books.

UNICEF (1999) *The State of the World's Children*, UNICEF.

Unilever (1999) Annual Report & Accounts.

Urban, G. I. and Star, S. H. (1996) *Advanced Marketing Strategy*, New Jersey: Prentice Hall.

Usunier, J-L. (2000) *Marketing Across Cultures*, 3rd edn, Harlow: FT Prentice Hall.

Valente, T. W. and Rogers, E. M. (1995) 'The origins and development of the diffusion of innovations paradigm as an example of scientific growth', *Science Communication*, March, pp. 242–73.

Van der Heijden, K. (2002) *Scenarios: The art of strategic conversation*, Chichester: Wiley.

van Dulken, S. (2000) *Inventing the 20th Century: 100 inventions that shaped the world*, London: British Library.

Vaughn, R. (1980) 'How advertising works: a planning model', *Journal of Advertising Research* 20 (October), pp. 27–33.

Vaughn, R. (1986) 'How advertising works: a planning model revisited', *Journal of Advertising Research* 26 (February/March), pp. 57–66.

Virgin (2004) Company details accessed from corporate website, www.virgin.com

Weaver, W. and Shannon, C. (1949) *The Mathematical Theory of Communication*, Urbana: University of Illinois Press.

West, C. (1999) 'Marketing research', in M. J. Baker (ed.), *Encyclopedia of Marketing*, London: Thomson Learning, pp. 255–67.

Wheelan, T. L. and Hunger, J. D. (1992) *Strategic Management and Business Policy*, 4th edn, New York: Addison-Wesley.

Williams, K. C. (1992) *Behavioural Aspects of Marketing*, Oxford: Butterworth-Heinemann.

Wind, J. (1985) 'The marketing challenge', address given on receipt of the Charles Coolidge Parlin Award, Wharton School Working Paper (excepts appeared in 'Wind sets agenda for marketing to fulfil its potential', *Marketing News*, 16 August, pp. 12, 14).

Wolfensohn, J. D. (1998) 'The other crisis', address to annual meeting, 6 October, World Bank, Washington, DC.

Wong, V. and Saunders, J. (1996) 'Analysing competitors', in P. Kotler, G. Armstrong, J. Saunders and V. Wong (eds), *Principles of Marketing*, Harlow: Prentice Hall.

World, The (2004) *The World: Corporate and Media Fact Sheets*, www.aboardtheworld.com.

Wren, D. A. (1979) *The Evolution of Management Thought*, 2nd edn, New York: Ronald Press.

Wright, R. (2004) *Business-to-Business Marketing: A step-by-step guide*, Harlow: FT Prentice Hall.

Wright, S. and Pickton, D. W. (1998) 'Improved competitive strategy through value-added competitive intelligence', *Proceedings of the 3rd Annual Society of Competitive Intelligence Professionals European Conference, Berlin, November*, pp. 73–83.

Wright, S., Pickton, D. W. and Callow, J. (2002) 'Competitive intelligence in UK firms: a typology', *Marketing Intelligence and Planning* **20**(6), pp. 349–60.

Yelkur, R. and Da Costa, M. (2001) 'Differential pricing and segmentation on the Internet: the case of hotels', *Management Decision* **20**(4), pp. 252–61.

Yeshin, T. (1998) *Integrated Marketing Communications: The holistic approach*, Oxford: Butterworth-Heinemann.

Yudelson, J. (1999) 'Adapting McCarthy's four P's for the twenty-first century', *Journal of Marketing Education* **21**(1) (April), pp. 60–7.

Zikmund, W. G. (1994) *Business Research Methods*, 4th edn, Fort Worth: Dryden Press.

Zikmund, W. G. and D'Amico, M. (1999) *Marketing*, 6th edn, Mason: South-Western Publishing.

Zolkiewski, J. (2004) 'Relationships are not ubiquitous in marketing', *European Journal of Marketing* **38**(1/2), pp. 24–9.

Index

3M, 180, 181, 368
3Ps, xxiii
4Ps, 157–9
5Cs, 124
7-Eleven, 173, 368
7Ps, xxiii, xxiv, 159
10Ps, xxiii

A

Aaker, D., 131
Abercrombie, C. L., 5, 6, 7, 8
adaptation costs, 254
adding value, 112–13
    firm infrastructure, 112
    HR, 112
    procurement , 112
    technology development, 112
Adler, A., 330
adoption characteristics/groups, 188–94, 371
advertising, 28, 215–30, 368–9, 371, 377
    Advertising Standards Authority, 228–9
    AIDA model, 216, 368, 371
    ambient media, 224–6, 368–9, 371
    billboards, 224
    Colley's hierarchy of effects model, 217–18
    direct marketing, 230–2
    dissonance–attribution hierarchy, 218–19
    early development, 215, 217
    Ehrenberg's ATRN model, 218–19
    fly posting, 226
    hierarchy of effects models, 215–20, 373, 377
    institutional, 221
    Internet, 226–7
    Lavidge and Steiner's model, 217
    learning hierarchy, 218
    media, 222–30, 371

    misleading, 6
    offending people, 28, 228–9
    primary advertising, 220–1
    print media, 222–3
    product or service range, 221
    Scott's model, 216
    selective product or service, 221
    shock advertising, 228–30, 376
    Strong's model, 216
    television, cinema and radio, 223
    of tobacco, 34
    types of, 220–2
    Vaughn's model, 219–20
affordability, 254
after-sales service, 113
AIDA model, 216, 368, 371
AIDS, 37
Airbus, 116, 252
aircraft, 16, 94, 116, 184–5, 209
air travel, 21, 33, 38–9, 111, 272, 296
    airport baggage handling, 324–5
    airport noise/disruption, 44, 46
    cheap airlines, 33, 111
    and SARS, 38–9
alchemy, 10
alcohol
    advertising of, 28
    restrictions on sale, 35
Amazon.com, 60–1, 270, 284, 319
American Airlines, 36
American Express, 323
American Marketing Association, 5, 6, 8
Andean Common Market (ANCOM), 23
Ansoff, H. I., 102, 375
approaches to marketing
    consumer, 6
    economics, 5–6

    societal, 6–7
Arab Free Trade Zone, 23
Arafat, Yasser, 22
architecture and design of buildings, 296–7
Asda, 116
Asiana Airlines, 21
Asia Pacific Economic Co-Operation (APEC), 23
Association of South East Asian Nations (ASEAN), 23
Aston Martin, 133, 175, 236
Attenborough, Richard, 145
audit
    accounting, 177
    marketing, 100–2, 374
aural factors, 307–10
automatic teller machines (ATMs), 316–17

B

B2B *see* business to business (B2B) marketing
B2C *see* business to consumer (B2C) marketing
Bacon, Francis, 79
bait and switch, 264
Bandura, A., 332
banking, 316–17
barcodes, 317
Barbie Doll, 127, 170, 331
Barcelona, 67, 281
Barclays Bank, 316
barcodes, 315–16
Barnardo's, 228–9
Barlow, J., 124
Bateson, J., 295, 296
BBC, 89, 351
Benetton, 15, 228–30
Bernays, E., 330, 369
beta testing, 184
BIC, 131,132
Bisquick, 179
Bitner, M. J., xxiii, xxv
Blomqvist, R., 161
Bloomberg, 89

Bluetooth technology, 45, 319, 367
BMW, 236
Body Shop, The, 81
Boeing
    Airbus, 116
    777, 184–5
BOGOF, 240–1, 261
Bond, James, 81, 220, 236, 260, 288
Booms, B. H., xxiii, xxv
Borden, N. H., xxiii, 156–7, 288
Borders, 308
Botswana, Republic of, 263
boycotts, 15, 24
brainstorming, 180
brand names
    tarnished, 140
    translation problems, 139
    unpopular, 141
branding, 119–52, 371
    acquisition activity, 140
    avoiding confusion, 138
    awareness, 127
    creating brand unity, 139
    definition of, 120
    demergers, 140
    equity, 17, 131–2, 371
    legal compliance, 140
    market development, 138
    new target audience, 138
    origins, 120–2
    promotion, 132
    rebranding, 137–42, 376
    reasons for, 122–7
    rebranding of organisations,
        139
    segmentation, 126
brands, 106, 371
    attributes, 62
    awareness, 127, ,209, 217,
        371
    consolidation, 137–8
    consumer and business, 122
    corporate diversification,
        138
    counterfeit, 123
    cult, 127
    differentiation, 124–6, 253
    disposal, 149–51, 371
    elasticity, 371
    extension, 127–31, 371
    family, 133, 372
    favourite, 3, 327
    individual, 133, 371, 373

luxury, 62, 174–5, 259, 373
management, 17, 134–5 (see
    also branding)
monobrands, 370
own-label, 134, 374
packaging, 358, 360–3 (see
    also packaging)
performance, 346–7
powerful, 135–7
protection, 122–4
recall, 127, 371
recognition, 126–7, 371
re-energising/rejuvenation,
    139, 376
repositioning, 376
selection, 126
switching, 15
types of, 132–4
valuation, 131
values, 124, 346–7, 371
Branson, Sir Richard, 129
bribery, 293
Bridge Too Far, A, 145
British Airways, 141–2, 238, 292–3
British Monarchy, rebranding of,
    141
British Oxygen Corporation
    (BOC), 90
British Petroleum, 138
British Retail Consortium (BRC),
    35–6
bundling, 241, 259–60, 371
Burj Al Arab hotel, 300
Burns, A., 66–7, 80
Bush, G. W., 21, 24, 25
Bush, R., 66–7, 80
business to business (B2B)
    marketing, 14, 55, 57, 122, 275,
        276, 371–2, 373
        market characteristics, 57–9
        micro segmentation, 59–60
        segmentation, 55–60
business to consumer (B2C)
    marketing, 14, 47, 60–4, 122,
        275
business to employees marketing,
    14
business to government
    marketing, 14
business intelligence see
    competitive intelligence
business to non-governmental
    organisations marketing, 14

Butlin's Holiday Camps, 142–3
Buttle, F., 250–1
buyers see customers
buying systems, 59
buzz, 232–6, 372
Bvlgari 131

C
Cadbury chocolates, 133, 134
Cadbury Schweppes, 135
call centres, 232
Callow, J., 82
Canada, 38
Caribbean Community and
    Common Market (CARICOM),
    23
Carnival Corporation, 134
cartels, 264–5, 372
Cat's eyes, 369–70
Celebrity Cruises, 36
celebrity endorsements , 62, 239,
    372
Center Parcs, 143, 368
Central American Common
    Market, 23
change agents, 190
change management, 57, 82
    rate of change, 48
channel management, 83, 88, 108,
    274–5
chaos theory, 20
Chapman, R. L., 276, 277
charities, 7, 8, 9, 46
Chavez, H., 27
children, 298
China, 13
    SARS in, 38–9
China Airlines, 21
Chinook Helicopters, 263
cinema, 223
    see also movies
Clausewitz, C. von., 79, 79, 367
CNN, 89
Coca-Cola, 35, 83, 136, 170, 198,
    362, 370
Coffee Republic, 311
cola drinks, 24, 35, 83, 136, 170,
    198, 362, 370
Colby, C. L., 192–3
Colley, R. H., 215, 217–18
Collier, D. A., 290
colour, 304, 305–6
    perception of, 170

Columbia Shuttle disaster, 41
communications, 17, 144, 189,
    190, 372
    buyer–supplier dialogue,
        9–10, 62, 230–1
    electronic, 33
    integrated marketing (IMC),
        244–6, 373
    models, 209–13, 368, 372,
        376
    strategy, 246
    see also advertising, media,
        promotion
community, local, 44, 56
competencies, 100
competitive advantage, 54, 55, 68,
    110–12, 372
    cost leadership, 111
    differentiation, 111–12
    focus, 112
    indecisiveness, 112
    scope, 110, 372
competitive forces, 252
competitive intelligence, 79–96,
    372
    analysis of, 90–2
    channel management see
        channel management
    company and management
        structures, 88
    competition, level of, 82
    competition, actions and
        intentions of, 82–5
    competitor analysis, 85
    competitor intelligence
        system, 86
    competitor types, 84
    competitor's annual reports,
        89
    data, 90–1
    definition, 80–1
    economic intelligence, 81–2
    government reports, 89
    importance of, 82
    Internet, 89
    legal and ethical
        implications of, 92–5
    mailing lists, 89
    newspapers, journals and
        directories, 89
    pricing strategy, 87
    product range, 87
    promotional activities, 87–8

    recorded data, 88–90
    sales value and volume, 87
    sources of, 86–90
competitive positions, 54, 114–17,
    372–5
competitive tendering, 262
competitors, 45, 105, 147–8, 200
    analysis of see competitive
        intelligence
    assessment methods, 91–2
    generic strategies, 110–12
    and hypercompetition, 67,
        367
    key, 91
    potential new, 91, 107–8
    rivalry between, 110
    types of, 84
components, 176
computing, 13, 15, 41, 289, 315
    failure of systems, 41
    future developments, 13
    manufacturers, 59
    see also technological
        processes
Concorde, 94
confiscation of goods, 26
Conservative Party, 138, 141
Consignia, 141, 145
consumers see customers
consumerism, problems of, 39
Cook, T., 259–60
Cooke, E. F., 5, 6, 7, 8
co-operators, 45
Core, The, 41
Cornwell, T. B., 239
Corsica, 16
cost
    disadvantages, 108
    focus, 112
    leadership, 111
    of marketing, 10–11, 147
    of market entry, 108
    of product development,
        182
    switching, 108, 109
    see also pricing
cost centre, marketing as, xxv
Costa, 311
Cottrell, S., xxii
Council for National Academic
    Awards (CNAA), 139
coupons, money off, 240
Cox, P., 37–8

Cranfield University, 11
credit card applications, 60, 323
Crest Whitestrips dental kit, 198
critical success factors (CSFs), 80
Croft, Lara, 139
cruises, 34, 36, 61, 64, 126, 134,
    369
Culliton, J. W., 156
culture, 62, 169–71, 339
    changes in, 31
    definition, 30–1
    and meaning of colour, 307
    orientations and behaviours,
        31
Cunningham, I., 7
Cunningham, W. H., 7
customers, 44–5, 163–4
    analysis see segmentation
    behaviour, 59–60, 304,
        337–42
    business see business to
        business marketing
    loyalty, 290
    needs of, 6–7, 9, 55, 100, 274,
        321, 335
    power, 109–10
    relationship marketing see
        relationship marketing
    service, 55–6
    types of, 45
customisation, 56, 231
Cyprus airways, 223

D
DaCosta, M., 226
DAGMAR, 217, 372
Dahl, J., 161
Dahringer, L., 336
DaimlerChrysler, 140
data
    analysis, 70
    collection, 70
    mining, 59
    observable, 90
    opportunistic, 90
    sources, 88–90
    warehouses, 59
    see also competitive
        intelligence, marketing
        research
database marketing, 230, 370
Davidson, D., 88
Dawson, L. M., 287–8, 291

defensive positions, 114–17, 372
deliveries of goods, 15
    see also logistics
demergers, 140
demographics, 33, 60, 372
    geodemographics, 83
depression, economic, 29
Descartes, R., 334
developing world, 13, 25
Diageo, 28
Dibb, S., 54, 168, 171, 172
Dichter, E., 72, 330–1, 351
diplomacy, 26–8
direct marketing, 230–2, 372
disasters, natural, 15, 28–9, 36, 40, 45
disease, 36–7, 38–9
Disney Organization, 10, 64, 136, 140, 237
    Euro Disney, 14, 140–1, 269
distribution, 59, 108, 183, 275–6, 349
    see also channel
            management, logistics
diversification, 103, 138
divestment, 102
domestication (political risk), 26
Doole, I., 31, 170
Doyle, P., 82, 84
Dubouin, J., 80, 81
dumping, 264, 372
Dun & Bradstreet, 90

E
e-business, 17
    see also Internet
e-mail, 33, 72–3, 369
E.T. THE EXTRA TERRESTIAL, 205, 352
Eastman Kodak, 38
Eats, Shoots & Leaves, 235
ecological issues, 39
    disease, 36–7
    geophysical, 39
    global warming, 15, 34–9
    pollution control, 34
    weather, 34–9
Economic Communityof West
    Africa (ECOWAS), 23
economic issues, 28–30, 254, 271
    business cycles, 29
    income levels, 30, 60, 254, 339–40 (*see also* socio-economic factors)

inflation and interest rates, 30
instability, 42
intelligence, 81–2
poverty, 30
taxation systems, 30
economic value, 253
economics approach to marketing, 5–6
educational issues, 33–4
Ehrenberg, A. S. C., 218–19, 372
electronic processes
    ATMs, 316
    barcodes, 315–17
    computerisation *see*
        computing
    EPOS, 317–18
    RFID tags, 318–19
    see also technological
        processes
Eldridge, C. E., 7
employees, 43–4, 84
    exploitation of, 45
    retired, 45
    training of, 348
    see also people
environment, marketing, 19–49, 100, 374
    audit, 100–1
    changeability of, 46–8
    macro environment, 21–42, 98, 105, 374
    micro environment, 42–6, 98, 373, 374
    predictability of, 48
environment, physical, 15, 34–40, 273, 364
    threats within, 15
environmental audit, 100–1
EPOS, 317–18
escapism, 351–3
espionage, industrial, 92–5
ESSO Price Watch campaign, 257
ethical issues, xxiii–xxiv, 61–2, 92–3, 264–5, 291–3, 325
    code of ethics, 95
Ethiopia and Nestlé, 27
ethnocentrism, 31
Etzel, M. J., 104
Euromonitor, 134
European Free Trade Area (EFTA), 23

European Union, 22, 23, 30, 33, 34, 265
exhibitions, expos and trade fairs, 14, 242
experience realms, 349–50, 355
expropriation, 26
extreme activities, 352

F
facilities management, 13
family, role of, 33
Fantasia, 10–11
fashion industry, 131
Federal Bureau of Investigation (FBI), 92
feedback loop, 54
Ferrell, O. C., 168, 171, 172
Finch, E., 269
five forces model 106–7, 373
fly posting, 226
focus
    cost, 112
    differentiation, 112
    groups, 71, 72, 373
Ford cars, 56, 133
Fonda, J., 31
food, 34, 135, 277, 313, 368
    additives, 370
    cultural aspects, 60, 170
    diversity available, 33–4
    junk, 31–2
    legislation regarding, 47
    tomatoes, 47
    see also individual food
        companies/brands by
        name
for-profit organisations, 58
forecasting, 67
    see also future trends
foreign direct investment (FDI), 83
Forsyth, P., 230, 338
Fowler Jr., A. R., 198
France, 14
franchising, 81
Freud, A., 329–30
Freud, S., 329–30, 332, 369
future trends, 13-16, 48, 318–26, 354–5

G
Gap, The, 308
General Electric, 103–4
    GE matrix, 103–4, 373

geocentrism, 31
geography, 57–8, 254
    and business location, 57–8
    impact on price, 254
    and segmentation, 60
    geophysical events, 39, 40
geopolitical events, 20, 22, 42
Germany, 26
Ghoshal, S., 98
Gilmore, J. H., 349, 351
Glaser, E., xxii
GlaxoSmithKline, 139
global dimming, 15, 34–9
global warming, 15, 34–9
global businesses, 31
globalisation, xxiii, 13, 17, 20, 42,
    168, 271
    of conflicts, 20
Godzilla, 128
Goldfarb, A., 121, 134
Gone With The Wind, 205
government
    action over SARS, 38–9
    activity in marketing, 14–15,
        245
    barriers, 254
    confiscation of property, 27
    incentives, 14, 271
    information, 89–90
    local, 44
    policy, industrial, 108
    systems, 313
Grant, R. M., 97–8, 100
Grimshaw, A., 337
Grönroos, C., 160, 163, 230, 369
Groucutt, J., 59–60, 230, 338
Guardian, The 283
guerrilla marketing, 224–6
Gulf Co-Operation States, 23

H
Haeger, T., 161
Haigh, D., 347
Hammond, J., 178, 195
hard selling, 175
Harley-Davidson, 128–9
Harridge-March, S., 231
*Harry Potter and the Order of the
    Phoenix*, 209
health and safety, 36–7, 38–9, 42,
    360
    attitudes to, 31–2
Hebridean Cruises, 175

Heinz Foods, 133, 134, 149, 299
Hero of Alexandria, 369
Herrmann, B., 308
Hilton Hotels, 56, 122, 323
Hitchcock, A., 308, 309
HIV, 37
Hoffman, K. D., 296, 336
Hofstede, G., 30, 31, 305
holiday camps, 142–3
Hoover, 196, 241
hotels, 56, 57, 122, 269, 289, 300,
    301, 305, 323
    room cleaning, 324
Hughes, D. G., 7
human resource management, 13
hygiene, 303

I
IBM, 57, 86
ICI, 140
Inalhan, G., 269
income levels, consumer, 30, 60,
    254, 339–40
    see also socio-economic
        factors
Incoterms, 254
India, 5, 13, 30, 58
industrial action, 21, 27, 44, 45
industry structure and
    characteristics, 90
inflation, 30
ipoint, 233
industrial espionage, 92–4
information
    market, of buyers, 109–10
    external, 71, 76–7
    internal, 71, 73, 280
    main sources, 88–90
    systems, 101
    see also competitive
        intelligence, marketing
        research
innovators, 190–1
integrated marketing
    communications (IMC), 244–6
intelligent home, the, 320–1
interactive television, 351
interest rates, 30
intermediaries *see* supply chain
International Chamber of
    Commerce, 123, 254, 369
International Labour
    Organisation, 45

International Space Station, 41
Internet, 13, 33, 39, 42, 72–3, 319,
    373
    advertising on, 227
    future developments, 13–14
    online stores, 284–5
interviews as research technique,
    72
Inwood, D., 178, 195
ipoint, 233
Iraq war, 24, 25, 348
Israel–Palestine conflict, 22
Issa, J. J.. 260
issues management, 245
Italy, 5

J
James, W., 328
Japan, 29
Jayawardena, C., 260
Johnson & Johnson, 125–6
Jung, C., 329
just-in-time systems, 58, 88

K
Kandampully, J., 276, 277
Keefe, L. M., 8
Keller, K. L., 346
Kellogg's, 134, 172, 198, 299
KGB, 94
Kincaid, L., 189
kiosks, 232, 373
Kit Kat
    chocolate bar, 128, 130, 140,
        144
    club, 367–8
Koehn, N. F., 121
Kompass directories, 89
Konkordski , 94
Kotler, P., 7, 8, 54, 100, 120, 168,
    170, 203, 288

L
Lampel, J., 98
Lasswell, H., 210
Laughinie, J. M., 80, 81
Lauterborn, R. F., 244
Lavidge, R. J., 217, 373
LE-PEST-C, 21
Leadley, P., 230, 338
legislation and regulations, 46,
    171, 273
    compliance with, 140

consumer, 6, 34, 46
   hostile, 82–3
   levels of, 46
   information on packaging,
      363–4
   safety, 182
   trade, 35, 47, 255, 317
Leihs, H., 336
Leiser, M., 347
Lever Brothers, 121, 367
Levitt, T., 168, 368
Lewis, E. St. Elmo, xxv, 215–16
LG Electronics, 320–1
life cycle of products, 142–3,
   198–205, 251, 368, 375
lifestyle, consumer, 61
   see also socio-economic
      factors
Lloyds Bank, 316
lobbying, 14–15, 20
local
   community issues, 44, 46
   government, 44
   regulators, 46
logistics, 42, 83–4, 88, 112–13, 176,
   276–9, 319, 349, 373
Londis, 173
London Eye, 353
London Metropolitan University,
   140
London Stock Market, 140
longshoremen dispute, 20, 21
Lost Weekend, The, 187
low cost airlines, 111
Lowe, R., 31, 170
loyalty, brand, 15, 290
Lucozade, 63, 139
luxury brands see brands, luxury
Lynch, R., 46, 47

M
macro environment, 21–42
macro segmentation, 57–9
   see also segmentation
Maignan, I., 239
Major, J., 138
management, marketing, 106
Mansillon, G., 80, 81
market
   analysis see segmentation
   attractiveness, 103
market classifications
   consumer products, 171–5

industrial and commercial
      products, 176–8
market
   conditions, 253–4
   decline, 146–7
   development, 103, 138
   function analysis, 101–2
   mass, 56
market positioning strategies,
   113–14, 372–4
   challengers, 112–13, 374
   followers, 114, 374
   leaders, 112, 374
   nichers, 114, 374
market
   pricing, 264
   share, 348
   size, 105
marketers
   as alchemists, 10–11
   groups engaged, 12–13
marketing
   audit, 100–2, 374
   campaigns, cost of, 10
   as cost centre, xxv
   current and future trends,
      12–16
   definitions, 5–10, 374
   direct, 230–2
   ethics and social responsibil-
      ity see ethical issues
   groups involved in, 12, 14
   history of, 4
   and other subject areas, xxiii
   as organisational function,
      8, 11–12
   plans, 349
   relationship to psychology,
      328–42
   as science or art, 11
   strategy see strategy
   team, 12
   as university subject, xxiii, 5
marketing mix, 155–64, 373, 374
   3Ps, xxiii
   4Ps, xxiii, 157–9
   7Ps, xxiii, 159
   10Ps, xxiii
   architecture, 159
   debate about, 154, 160
   extension of, xxii, xxv, 158–9
   origins, 156–8
   packaging, 357–65

TQM, 158
   see also individual elements
      by name
marketing research, 66–77, 374,
   375, 376
   brief, 69
   competitive advantage, 68
   data collection and analysis,
      70
   establishing need for, 68
   exploiting new market
      opportunities, 68
   external information, 76–7
   focus groups, 72, 373
   forecasting, 67 (see also
      future trends)
   identifying methodology, 69
   internal information, 73
   key trends, 17
   objective or hypothesis, 69
   observation technique, 71–2
   potential benefits, 67–8
   problem definition, 68
   production of final report, 70
   questionnaires, 69–70, 72–3,
      376
   reducing risk, 68
   return on investment, 67–8
   role of, 66–67
   systematic process, 68–70
   techniques, primary and
      secondary, 70–7, 375, 376
   understanding the market,
      67
   widespread use of, 77
   see also competitive intelli-
      gence
Marketing Science Institute (MSI),
   13
markets
   new, 57
   street/retail, 5, 67, 280–1
Marks & Spencer, 271, 284
Mars Corporation, 137
Maslow, A., 334
   hierarchy of needs, 334–5
materials
   high-performance industrial,
      42
Mattel, 170, 331
Mathlouthi, T., 24
Mattelart, A., 210
Mattelart, M., 210

Maul, D., 124
Mazur, P., 7
McBride, 134
McCarthy, E. J., xxiii, 157–9, 269
McDonald, M., 10, 11
McDonald's, 32, 168, 170
measurement, 15
    of performance, 17
Mecca Cola, 24
media, the, 34, 88–9, 341, 375
    for advertising, 222–7, 371
    ambient, 224–5, 371
    as opinion former, 46
    relations, 245
    see also advertising
Mercer, D., 8,9
merchandising, 237–8, 374
Mercosur, 23
mergers, 140
messages, marketing, 4–5
    directed to computers, 13
    see also advertising,
        communications, public
        relations
metrics, marketing, 17
METRO Group future store
    initiative, 322–3
Mickey Mouse, 10–11
micro environment, 42–6, 98, 373,
    374
micro segmentation, 59–60
    see also segmentation
Microsoft, 122–3, 136
migration, 33, 369
Miller, V. E., 110
Milligan, M. 269
mind, battle for the, 62
Mintel, 90, 142
Mintzberg, H., 98,
Met Office, 35,36
Morrisons, 116
movies, 358, 369
    and Columbia Shuttle
        disaster, 41
    escapism, 345, 351–2
    piracy, 123
    product placement, 236
    test previews, 187
    tie-ins, 236–7
Mugabe, R., 26
Mulbacher, H., 336
multiculturalism, 34

music and sounds, 304, 307–10,
    358
Muslim brands, 24
Muzak Company, 308

N
nationalisation, 27
nations
    identity marketed, 14
    symbols of, 4
    wealth of, 137
Nestlé, 15, 27, 133, 135, 140
New Labour Party, 138
new product development
    adoption characteristics,
        187–90
    business analysis, 183–4
    concept testing, 183
    commercialisation, 187–90
    idea generation, 179–80
    idea screening, 180–3
    life cycle concept, 198–204
    market testing, 186–7
    minimising risk of failure,
        194–8
    product failure, 195–8
    product launch, 187
    processes, 178–9
    product testing, 186
niche markets, 55, 56, 114
    see also segmentation
Nike, 170
noise
    airport noise/disruption,
        44, 46
    control of supermarket, 44
    as communications concept,
        213–14, 372, 374, 375, 376
non-governmental organisations,
    14, 15
Norman, Greg, 174
norms, societal, 254
North American Free Trade Area
    (NAFTA), 23
not-for-profit organisations, xxiii,
    7, 45, 58, 158
    non-technological processes,
        321
Nylon, 178

O
obesity, 32

objectives, organisational, 61, 102,
    178
objectivity in book, xxii
observation as research technique,
    71–2
Ohmae, K., 99, 100
oil industry, 27
olfactory factors, 310–11
operations function, 13
opinion formers, 45, 46
Orange, 240
    Prize for Fiction, 240
organisational function of
    marketing, 11–12
organisations
    acquisition activity, 140
    environmental forces, 46–8
    functions other than
        marketing, 13, 99, 200–3
    marketing as function of,
        11–13
    merger activity, 140
    rebranding of, 139
    size, 58, 99
    structure, 88, 98, 101
Organization of Petroleum
    Exporting Countries (OPEC),
    266
original equipment manufacturers
    (OEMs), 59
origins of marketing, 4–5
Oxford Brookes University, 140,
    237
Oxford Bus Company, 258

P
packages
    convenience, 362–3
    containment and safety, 360
    information and legislation,
        363–4
    market appeal, 360–1
    materials, 364
    protection and preservation,
        359–60
packaging, 163, 357–65, 369, 374
    attributes, 359
    brand packaging, 359
    definition of, 358
    in marketing mix, xxv, 157,
        160, 163
    physical, 359–64
    product, 358

Palestine, 22
Paracelsus, 10, 367
Parasuraman, A., 192–3
Pareto's Law, 58, 80, 367
Paris, 4, 281
Parkinson, S., 269
parochialism, 31
participants *see* people
payments, problems with, 46, 59
people, 162, 287–94, 375
    building relationships, 291
    computer software
        designers, 289
    ethical issues, 293
    hotel staff, 289
    in marketing, 288
    as marketing mix element,
        xxv
    in not-for-profit
        organisations, 291
    military personnel, 289
    pilots, 289–290
    psychology of, 337–9
    relationships breakdown,
        291–3
    at British Airways, 292–3
    right people in the right job,
        290
Pepsi, 83, 370
perceptual mapping, 63–4
Percy, L., 209
performance, 163, 344–56, 375
    brand, 346–7
    definition, 344–5
    distribution and logistics,
        349
    as a dynamic function, 354
    experiential, 349–54
    future issues, 354–5
    in marketing mix, xxv, 160,
        163
    marketing plans, 349
    market share, 348
    measurement, 17, 346–9
    product or service, 346
    revenue, 347–8
    sales, 347–8
Perreault Jr., W. D., 158, 269
personal shopping assistants,
    322–3
personnel *see* employees, people
PEST, 21
PESTLE, 22, 48, 82, 270, 375

physical evidence, 162, 295–312,
    375
    air quality, 310
    ambience , 303–5
    architecture and design of
        buildings, 296–297
    aural factors, 307–10
    cleanliness and hygiene, 303
    colour, 305–6
    ease of access, 298
    environmental confines, 298
    exteriors, 296–8
    foyers, entrances, public
        spaces, 299–300
    interiors, 298–305
    landscaping, 297
    layout, 301–2
    lighting, 305
    in marketing mix, xxv
    music and sounds, 307–10
    olfactory factors, 310–11
    parking facilities, 297
    presentation, 306
    product access, 298–9
    seating, 302–3
    security and privacy, 302
    signage, 300
    smells and odours, 310
    space, 300–1
    stationery, 306
    tactile factors, 311
    taste, 310–11
    temperature, 311
    touch, 311
    uniforms, 306
    vehicle design, 296
    visual factors, 305–6
Piaget, J., 334
Pickton, D., 80, 82
Pine, B. J. H., 349, 351
piracy (of brands), 123
place/placement, 268–85, 375, 376
    channel management *see*
        channel management
    definition of, 268–70
    distribution, 275–6, 349
    economic, 271
    environmental, 273
    legal, 273
    logistics, 276–7
    physical location factors,
        270–4
    political, 270–1

Porter's supply chain model,
    277–9
    societal, 271–2
    technological, 272–3
    retail outlets, 280–5
placement, product, 236
political factors, 22–8, 82–3, 158,
    270–1, 368
    doctrines and structures of
        government, 82–3
    legal, 34
    pressure, 25
    risk, 26, 271
pollution, control of, 34
polycentrism, 31
Pontin's Holiday Camps, 142–3
Porter, M. E., 55, 86, 87, 90, 91,
    106–10, 112–13, 277, 373
    five forces model, 106–7
    supply chain model, 277–9
portfolio matrix, 102–3, 375
positioning, market, 62–3, 375
    see also segmentation
Post It Notes, 178, 181
Premier Foods, 135
premium pricing, 264
Pret A Manger, 308
price, 249–67, 342
    ethical and legal issues, 264,
        266
    factors influencing, 252–5
    fixing, 264–5
    matching, 375
    objectives, 251
    and psychology, 342
    and quality, 62
    sensitivity, 254–5, 375
PriceWaterhouseCoopers (PwC),
    145, 178
pricing factors, 252–5
pricing tactics, 84, 87, 255–64, 372,
    375, 376, 377
    book early discount, 261
    BOGOF, 240–1, 261
    bundling, 259–260
    competitive tendering, 262
    differential discounts, 261
    direct payment mechanisms,
        262
    discount pricing, 261
    dual pricing mechanisms, 264
    ethical and legal *see* ethical
        issues

flexible, 258
international, 263–4
marginal costing, 374
market, 264
odd–even, 259
penetration, 257, 374–5
pioneer, 255–6, 375
prestige, 258–9, 375
price matching, 257–8
price skimming, 257
promotional, 259–60
psychological, 258
quantity discounts, 261
single price/double price,
    259
special event, 262
standard worldwide, 264,
    377
see also competitive
    positions, strategy
Pride, W. M., 168, 171, 172
privacy issues, 72
private finance initiative, 58
privilege points, 241–2
prizes, offers of, 266
processes, 162, 313–26, 375
    adapting and changing,
        321–5
    combination, 321
    ethical issues, 325
    future issues, 325–6
    as part of marketing mix,
        xxv
    standardisation or
        adaptation, 323–5
    types of, 314–21
    non-technological, 319–21
    technological, 314–19
Procter & Gamble, 92, 133, 150,
    221, 229, 347
procurement, 112–13
production, cost of, 252
productivity, marketing, 101
products, 167–206, 375
    access, 298–9
    accessories, 177
    adaptation, 168–71, 371, 375
    attributes, 169
    business analysis, 183–4
    business services, 177
    commercialisation, 187–90
    concept testing, 183
    consumable supplies, 177

consumer product
    classifications, 171–6
convenience products,
    171–3, 372
cultural perspectives,
    169–71
definition, 167–8
differentiation, 107–8,
    111–12
emergency, 173, 372
food, 170 (see also food)
heterogeneous, 373
homogeneous, 373
idea generation, 179–80
idea screening, 180–3
impulse purchases, 172–3,
    373
industrial and commercial
    classifications, 176–8
language differences, 170
legal issues, 171
life cycle concept, 142–3,
    198–205, 251, 368, 375
luxury goods, 174–5
market testing, 186
perception of colours, 170
perception of numbers, 170
plant and machinery, 176–7
ranges, 87
shopping goods, 173–4, 376
staple products, 172, 377
substitution, 108, 149–50,
    182
technical factors, 168
unsought, 175, 377
products, new, 17, 84, 102, 251
    development, 178–98, 374
    diffusion, 187–94, 372
    failure, 194–8
    launch, 187, 245
professional services pricing, 262
profit, 57
    margin, 250, 347–8, 368
promotion, 87–8, 132, 157, 208–47,
    376
    celebrity endorsements, 239
    exhibitions, expos and trade
        fairs, 242
    future of, 246
    integrated marketing
        communications, 244–6
    kiosks, 232
    merchandising the brand

237–238
movie tie-ins 236–237
objectives 208
product placement 236, 376
sales promotion, 240–2
sponsorship, 239
strategy and tactics, 215 (see
    also strategy)
word of mouth, 232–6
see also advertising, direct
    marketing, public
    relations
protectionism, 15
Psycho, 308–9
psychology, 163, 188, 269, 274,
    327–43
    behavioural aspects, 331–3
    categories of buyer
        behaviour 337, 342
    cognitive approach, 334–6
    evolutionary approach, 336
    fear, 340–1
    financial and economic
        influences, 339–40
    humanistic approach, 334
    key approaches, 328–37
    lifestyle, 339
    in marketing mix, xxv, 161, 163
    media, 341
    necessities, 342
    people, 337–9
    price, 258, 342, 376
    and physical evidence, 296
    psychoanalytical aspects,
        329–31
    relationship with marketing,
        337
    social psychology, 336–337
public–private partnerships, 58
public relations, 46, 242–4, 369,
    376
public sector, 58
    see also government
publicity, 245
purchasing decision, 59
Pyle, J. F., 7

Q
quality
    and price, 62
    of products, 6, 15
Quee, W. T., 67
Question Time (BBC), 351

questionnaires, marketing
    research, 69–70, 72–3, 376
        student module evaluation,
            73–6
Quibla Cola, 24
Quinn, J. B., 98

R
R&D, 41–2, 178–81, 200–3
    cost of, 252
        see also products, new
Raban, J., 337
radio, 223
Rayburn, J. M., 5, 6, 7, 8
rebranding, 137–42, 376
recessions, 29, 255
regioncentrism, 31
regulations *see* legislation and
    regulations
reinforcing actions, 331–3
relationship marketing, 13, 17,
    53–4, 160–3, 288, 290–3, 376
relationship networks, 280
rescue operations, 42
research and development *see*
    R&D
research, marketing *see* marketing
    research
restaurants, 9, 34, 39, 43, 260, 313
    suppliers to, 43
retail outlets, 16, 280–5, 306, 308,
    317–18, 368
        future store initiative, 322–3
        Holiday Inn Express, 282
        individual stores, 284
        markets, 280–281
        multiple or chain stores, 284
        online stores, 284–285
        in schools, 283
        supermarket layout, 301–2
        technical developments,
            283–4, 317–18
        vending *see* vending
        window displays, 16
retired people, 45
return on investment, 67–8, 250,
    345
RFID tags, 318–19
risk management, 68, 82, 194–8
    political, 24, 26, 271
    product, 6
risk taking, 191
robots, 42

Roddick, A., 81
Roddick, G., 81
Rogers, E., 188–91, 195
Roosevelt, F. D., 29
Rosen, E., 232–4, 339
Rossiter, J. R., 209
Rothschild, W. , 83
Rowling, J. K., 209, 220
Royal Caribbean International, 36
Royal Mail, 141, 145

S
Sainsbury, 116
Safeway, 116
sales promotion, 240–2
    see also promotion
Samaritans, The, 144
Santrock, J. W., 296, 328, 330, 336,
    338
SARS, 37, 38–9, 48
scale, economies of, 107
scenario planning, 48
Schramm, W. 376
Science of Sport Exhibition, 351
Schultz, D. E., 244
Scott, W. D., 216, 376
security issues, 303
    security services, 81
segmentation, 54–64, 126, 373, 376
    B2B, 55–60
    B2C, 60–1
    behaviour, 60
    characteristics, 57
    demographics, 60
    geographic location, 60
    lifestyle, 61
    macro segmentation, 57–9
    micro segmentation, 59–60
    perceptual mapping, 63–4
    positioning, 62–3
    products, 58–9
    repositioning, 63
    services, 58–9
    socio-economic behaviour,
        60–1
    strategy formulation, 61–4
    targeting, 61–2
services, 56
    business, 177–8, 371–2, 376
    to customers, 55–6
    packaging of, xxv
    sector, 8
shampoo, 336

Shangri-La Hotels, 133
Sharp, S., 80
Shaw, P., 369–70
Shell, 15
shipbuilding industry, 20
shops *see* retail outlets
Sierra Leone, 26
Simpkin, L., 168, 171, 172
Singapore Changi International
    Airport, 296, 299, 324–5
Skinner, B. F., 331–2
Skoda cars, 199
Smith, W. R., 57
Sinclair C5, 77, 194–7
societal approach to marketing, 8
societal issues, 30–4, 254, 271–2
    demographics *see*
        demographics
    education, 33–4
    health, attitudes to, 31–2
    social psychology, 336–7
    social unrest, 42 (*see also*
        political factors)
    technology, 42 (*see also*
        techological processes)
Society of Competitive
    Intelligence Professionals, 95
socio-economic factors, 60, 190–2,
    369
        see also demographics,
            economic issues
Soosay, C., 276, 277
Spar, 173
special offers, 30
SPECTACLES, 21
Spielberg, S., 352
sponsorship, 239, 376–7
Spurlock, M., 32
stakeholders, 8, 15
Stanton, W. J., 104
Starbucks, 308, 311
Star Trek, 180
Star Wars, 288
stationery, 306
Steiner, G. A., 217, 373
Stewart, A., 269
stores *see* retail outlets
strategic business units (SBUs),
    56, 57, 98, 99, 371
strategic industry groupings,
    90–1
strategy, 13, 97–117, 371, 373–4, 377
    adding value *see* value

adding
  Ansoff's portfolio matrix,
    102–3
  business, 99
  business strength, 103–4
  buyer power, 109–10
  competitive advantage,
    110–12
  competitive positions, 54,
    114–17, 372–5
  competitive scope, 110
  of competitors, 85, 86, 110
  corporate, 99, 372
  cost leadership, 111
  defensive positions, 117
  definition, 98–9
  differentiation, 111–12
  five forces model, 106–7
  functional, 99
  GE matrix, 103–4
  market attractiveness 103
  market function analysis
    101–2
  market positioning 113–14
  marketing audit 100–2
  new entrant threat, 107–8
  relationship with marketing,
    99–100
  substitution threat, 108
  supplier power, 108–9
  SWOT analysis, 104–6, 367,
    377
Strong, E. K. Jr., xxv, 216, 368, 377
students as audience for book,
  xxii
Sunlight Soap, 121, 367
Sunny Delight, 150
supermarket layout, 301–2
Supersize Me, 32
suppliers, 43, 84
  financial performance, 84
  multiple sources, 59
  power, 108–9
supply chain, 44, 377
  model, 277–9
Swiss Re tower, 297
SWOT analysis, 104–6, 367, 377
symbols, national, 4
systems approach, 7

T
tactile factors, 311
Taiwan, 28

Tannebaum, S. I., 244
Tapp, A., 230
Tarde, G., 188
targeting, consumer, 61–62, 377
targets, sales, 348
taxes and surcharges, 30, 252, 255
  direct and indirect, 30
technological processes, 272–3,
  280, 314–19
  electronic, 315–19 (see also
    electronic processes)
  impact of changes, 39–42,
    112, 282–4, 321–5
  Internet, 319
  manufacturing-production,
    314–15
  nanotechnology, 325–6
  national differences, 168–9
  see also computing
telemarketing, 231–2
television, 34, 89, 168–9, 223
  interactive, 351
Telford, A., 59–60
terrorism, 20, 22, 25, 81
Tesco, 116
  Tesco.com, 270, 284
Tetra Pak, 361–2
Thatcher, M., 138, 141
think tanks, 48, 71, 76
Thomas, J., 198
time element, 9
  for new product adoption,
    189
Times Educational Supplement, 283
tobacco, xxiii, 34, 330
tomatoes, 47
Tomb Raider, 139
Torrance, J., 337
Toscani, O., 228–30
Total Quality Management
  (TQM), 158
Total Recall, 353
tourism, 33, 56, 63
  and terrorism, 22
  and natural disasters, 28–9,
    39, 40
  in Southeast Asia, 40
  taxes on, 30
  see also cruises
Toy Story, 236–7
trade, international, 27, 82–4, 254,
  317
  barriers to, 15, 34

into the United States, 21
trade-in allowances, 260–1
trade unions, 45
  longshoremen, 21
trading alliances, 22–4
transactions, 9
transportation, 33, 275–9
  costs, 254
  types of shipment, 277
  see also distribution,
    logistics
travel, 358
  impact of consumer, 33
  see also cruises
Treguer, J-P., 60
trials, product, 195
Truss, L., 235
tsunami in SE Asia, 28–9, 40, 45
Tupolev aircraft, 94
Tylenol, 125–6, 360
typewriter, superseded, 41, 57

U
Ugly Ripe tomato, 47
UNICEF, 15
Unilever, 92, 102, 135, 147, 148–9,
  178, 221, 299, 347
  path to growth, 102, 148–9
United Airlines, 36
United Kingdom
  car industry, 58
  political activities, 25
  shipbuilding industry, 20
  Ministry of Defence, 263
  National Security Service
    (MI5), 234–5
United Nations, 15, 25, 26
United States
  Chamber of Commerce, 92
  Economic Espionage Act, 92
  Environmental Protection
    Agency, 37
  Great Depression, 29
  levels of regulation, 46
  longshoremen's dispute, 21
  political issues, 25
  territorial waters, 34
  wine shipments, 35
  weather, 36
universities
  course evaluation, 73–6
  marketing research by, 77
  as a market place, 350–1

University of North London, 140

V
value adding, 80, 112–13, 371
value chain, 43, 55, 377
Vaughn, R., 219–20, 377
Van der Heijden, K., 48
Varah, Chad, 144
vehicle design, 296
vending, 281–3, 369
Venezuela, 27
vertical integration, 109
Viagra, 184
Victoria & Albert Museum, 123
Virgin, 83, 129–30, 133, 347
virtual reality, 353
vitamin supplements (cartel), 265
Volkswagen, 199
Voyager of the Seas, 297

W
Walker, B. J., 104
Wal-Mart, 116
Wall Street Crash, 29
Warner Holiday Camps, 143
weather, the, 20, 34–9
    and wine growing, 57–8
Werther's Originals, 338
West, C., 83–4
Western philosophical approach, xxi, 42
Wilder, Billy, 187
withdrawal from markets, 102–3, 115–16
Woolworth, F. W., 259
World, The, 174–5
World Bank, 27
World Health Organization, 38
World Trade Center disaster, 22, 39

World Trade Organization (WTO), 22, 28, 83, 254
Wright, R., 54, 55–7, 59
Wright, S., 80, 82

X
Xerox, 86

Y
Yelkur, R., 226

Z
Zamzam Cola, 24
Zeneca, 140
Zikmund, W. G., 69–70
Zimbabwe, 26
Zolkiewski, J., 162